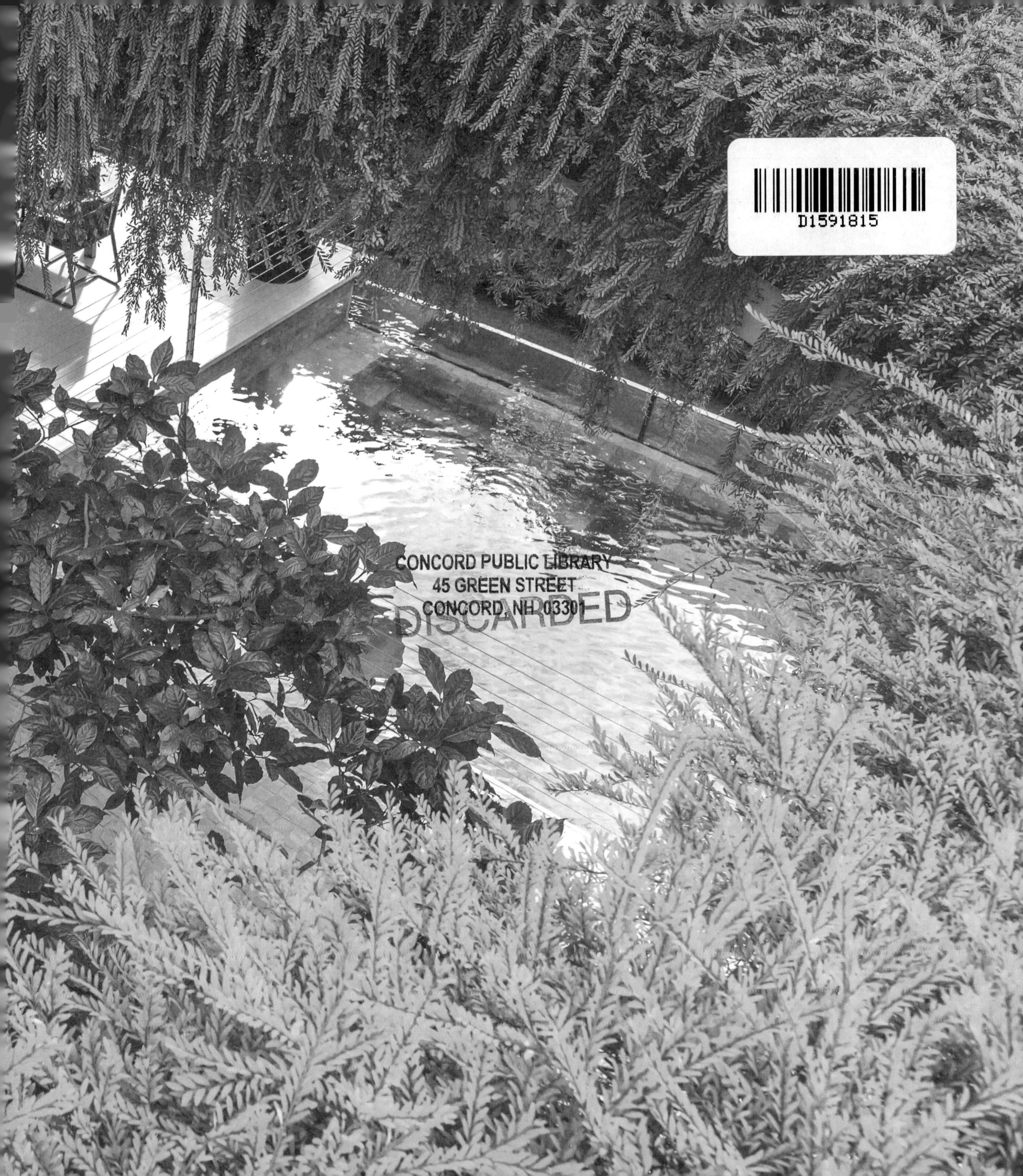

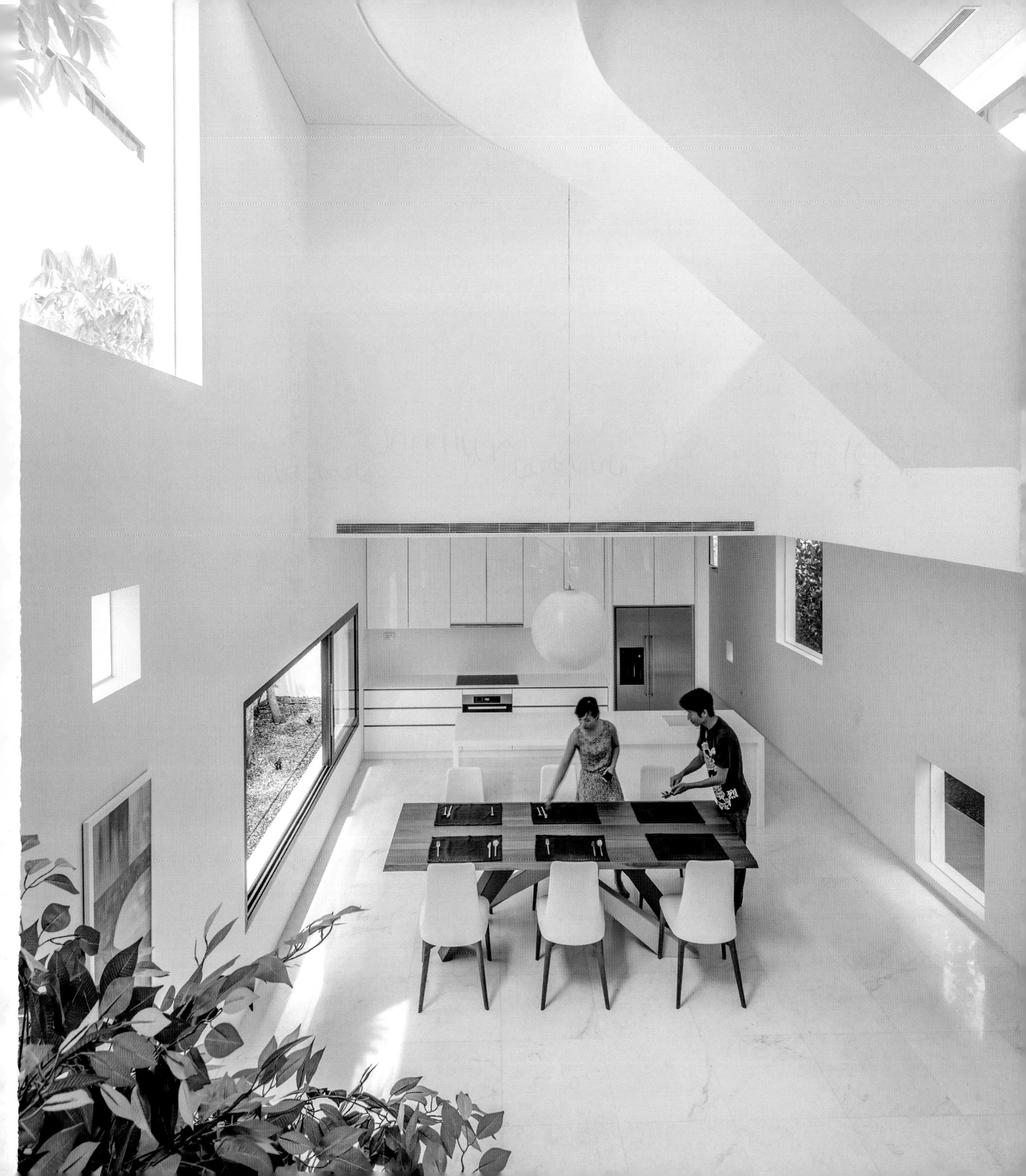

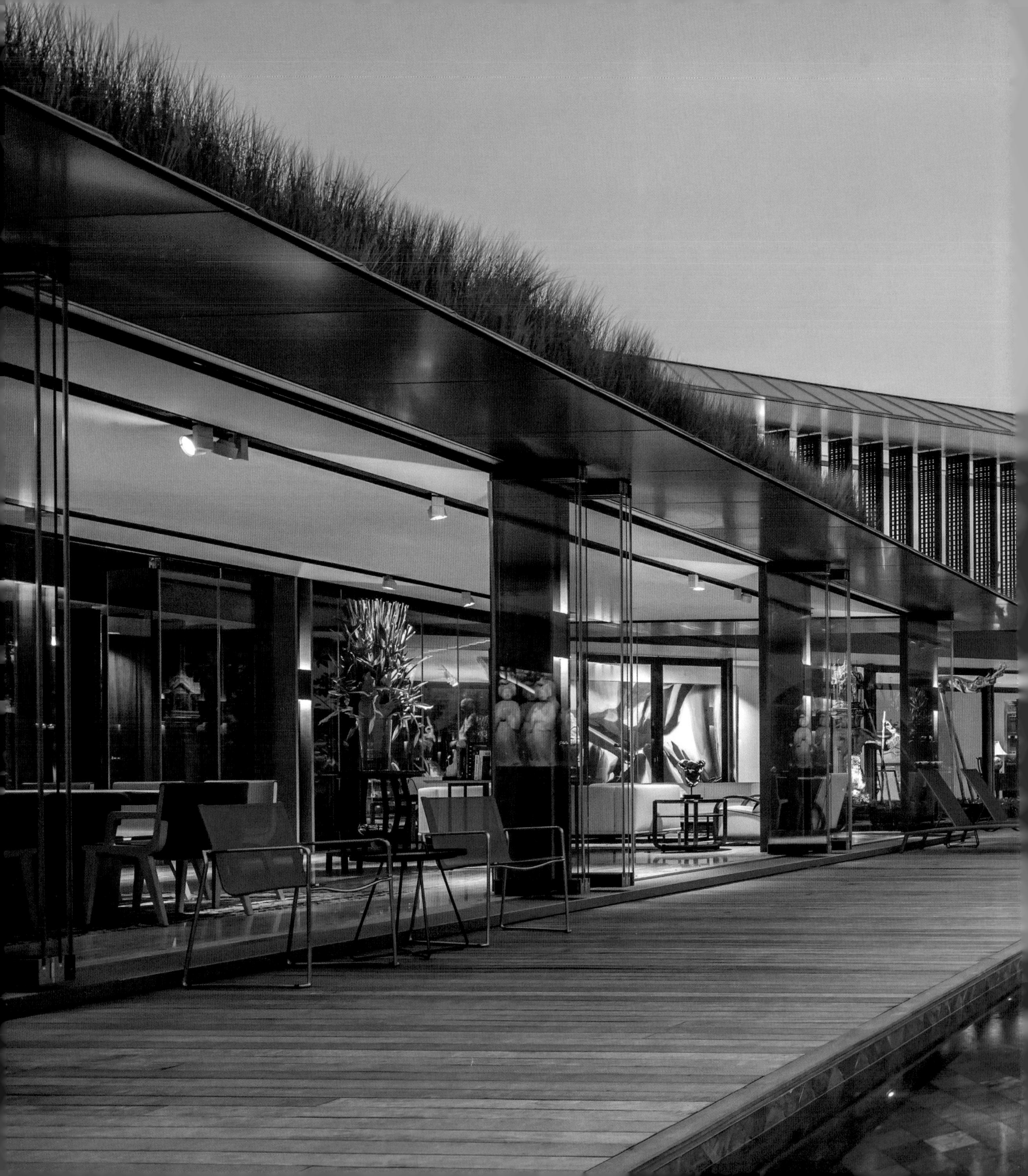

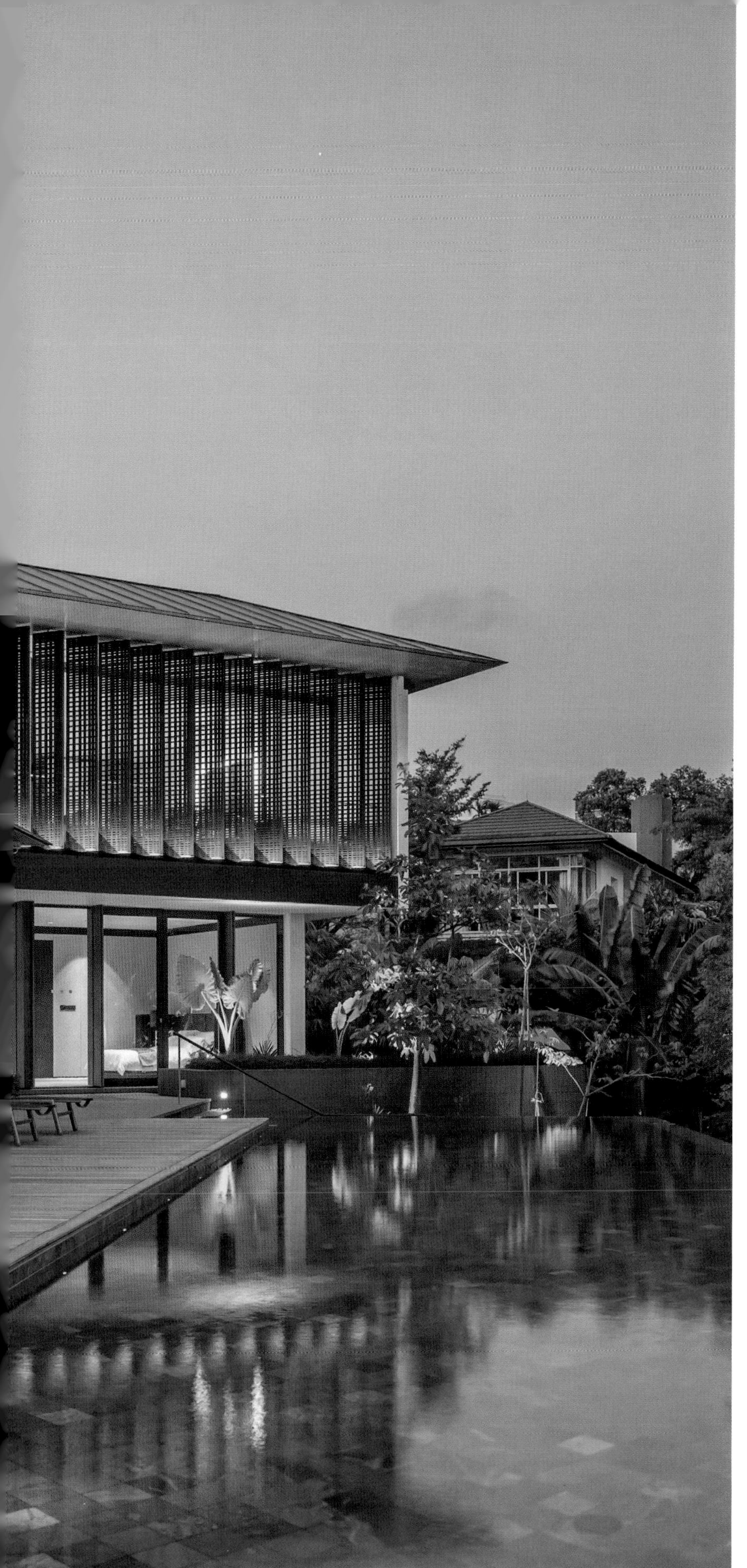

sustainable luxury

THE NEW SINGAPORE HOUSE SOLUTIONS FOR A LIVABLE FUTURE

PAUL McGILLICK

Photography by MASANO KAWANA

TUTTLE Publishing

Tokyo | Rutland, Vermont | Singapore

CONTENTS

INTRODUCTION SUSTAINABLE LUXURY: IS IT A CONTRADICTION IN TERMS? 06

TANGLIN HILL HOUSE (ECO:ID ARCHITECTS) 18
NEIL ROAD SHOPHOUSE (EXPERIENCE DESIGN STUDIO, ONG&ONG) 26
MANDAI COURTYARD HOUSE (ATELIER M+A) 34
NAMLY DRIVE HOUSE (CHANG ARCHITECTS) 40
OLIV APARTMENTS (W ARCHITECTS) 48
ANDREW ROAD HOUSE (A D LAB) 54
HOLLAND GROVE HOUSE (A D LAB) 62
SEMBAWANG LONG HOUSES (FORMWERKZ) 70
TREE HOUSE (FORMWERKZ) 78
THE CORAL HOUSE (GUZ ARCHITECTS) 86
WATER LILY HOUSE (GUZ ARCHITECTS) 98
BELMONT ROAD HOUSE (CSYA) 104
CHATSWORTH PARK HOUSE (ECO:ID ARCHITECTS) 112
THOMSON HEIGHTS HOUSE (AAMER ARCHITECTS) 120
JALAN MAT JAMBOL HOUSE (ZARCH COLLABORATIVES) 128
INTERLOCKING HOUSE (LATO DESIGN) 136
TRAVERTINE DREAM HOUSE (WALLFLOWER ARCHITECTURE + DESIGN) 142
BARNSTORM HOUSE 150
DAKOTA APARTMENT (JONATHAN POH) 156
BAMBOO CURTAIN HOUSE (ECO:ID ARCHITECTS) 162
SUNSET PLACE HOUSE (IP:LI ARCHITECTS) 170
WATTEN RESIDENCES (IP:LI ARCHITECTS) 178
THE GREEN COLLECTION (RT+Q ARCHITECTS) 184
VERANDAH HOUSE (RT+Q ARCHITECTS) 192
THE CRANES (EXPERIENCE DESIGN STUDIO, ONG&ONG) 200
CAIRNHILL ROAD SHOPHOUSE (RICHARDHO ARCHITECTS) 210

THE ARCHITECTS AND DESIGNERS 218
BIBLIOGRAPHY 223
ACKNOWLEDGEMENTS 224

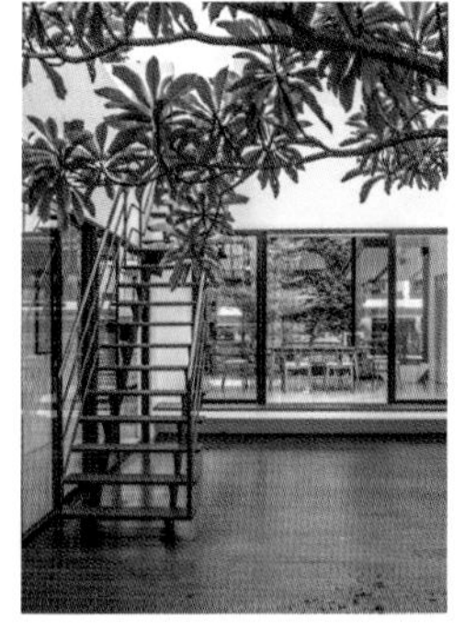

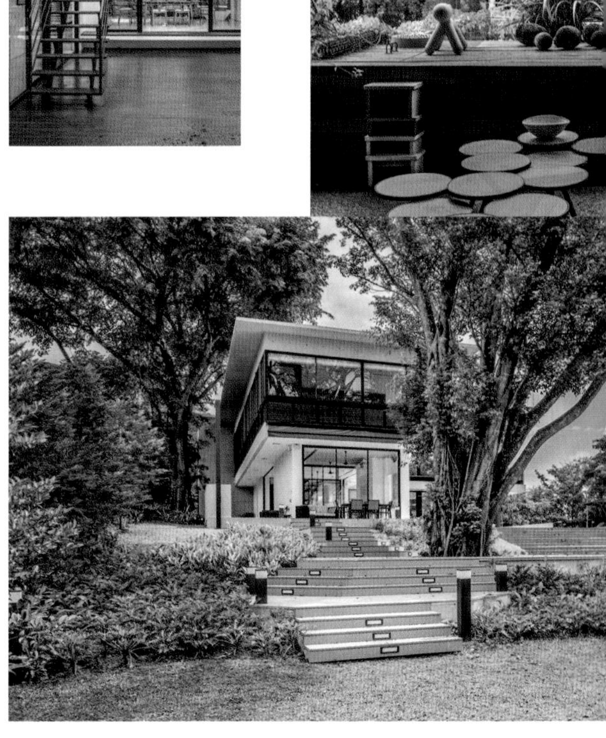

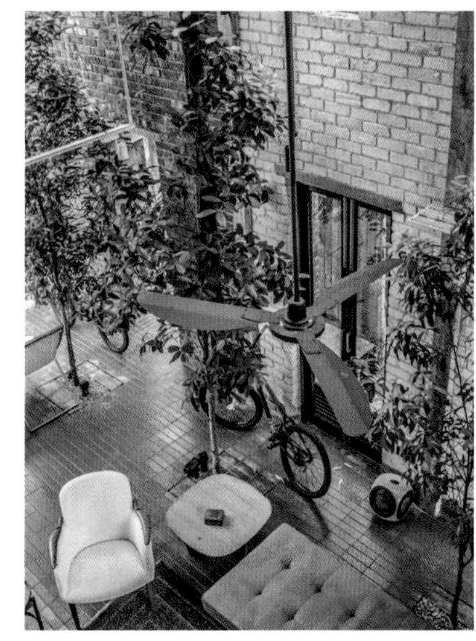

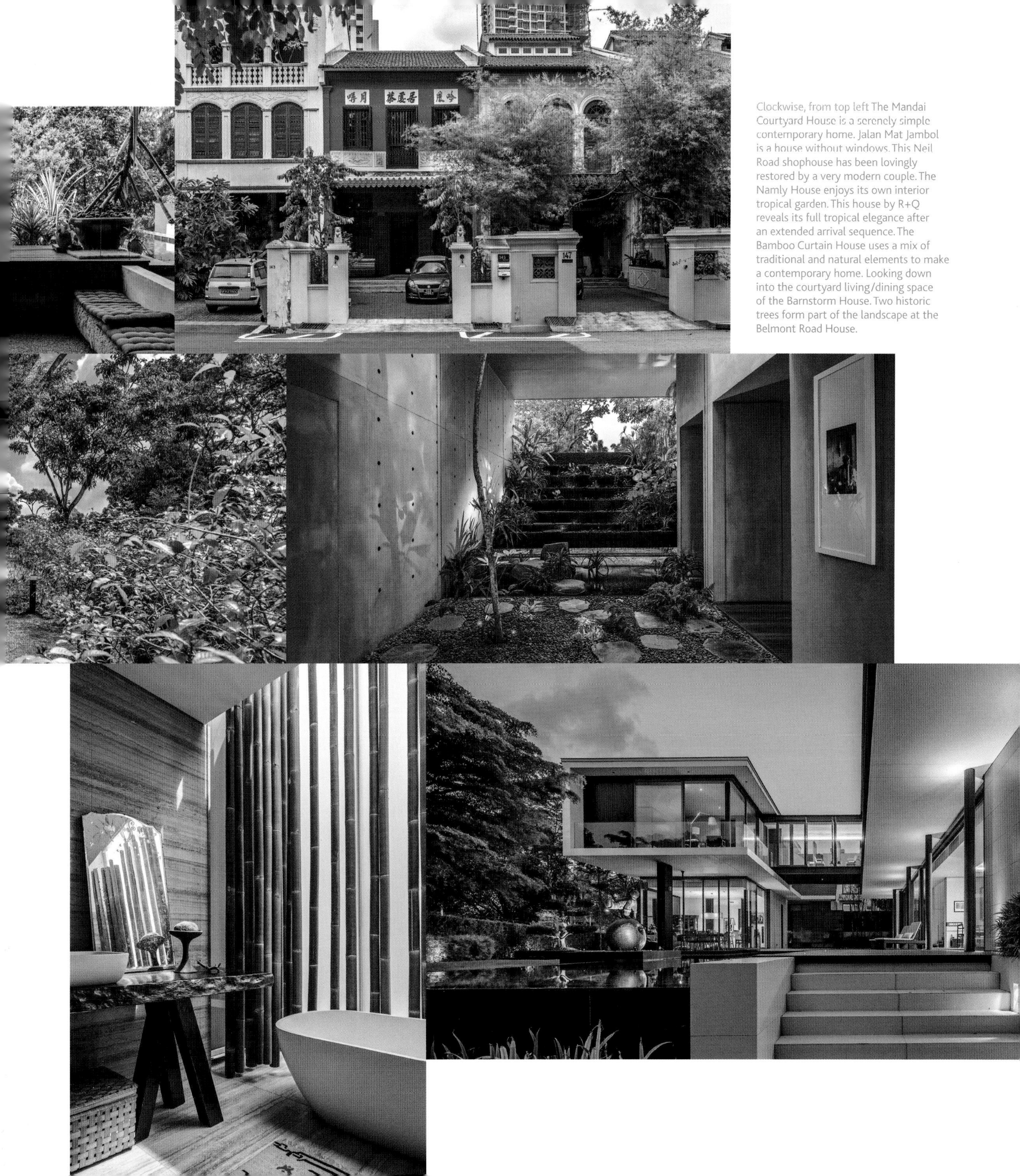

Clockwise, from top left The Mandai Courtyard House is a serenely simple contemporary home. Jalan Mat Jambol is a house without windows. This Neil Road shophouse has been lovingly restored by a very modern couple. The Namly House enjoys its own interior tropical garden. This house by R+Q reveals its full tropical elegance after an extended arrival sequence. The Bamboo Curtain House uses a mix of traditional and natural elements to make a contemporary home. Looking down into the courtyard living/dining space of the Barnstorm House. Two historic trees form part of the landscape at the Belmont Road House.

The true splendour of the Andrew Road House by A D Lab (page 54) lies below ground level where there is a lush, cool water garden court.

SUSTAINABLE LUXURY: IS IT A CONTRADICTION IN TERMS?

This book presents some of the very best and most luxurious new homes in Singapore. Each of them, in one way or another, represents a response to the challenges of creating luxurious yet sustainable homes in one of the world's most expensive cities—and in a sweltering tropical climate!

You may assume that luxury is inherently self-indulgent and, therefore, non-sustainable. But is it? The architects of these homes, together with their clients, demonstrate that this is emphatically not the case. This book reveals the many innovative solutions they found in doing so, illustrating in the process how Singapore has become an incubator of innovative residential design.

Crucially, each home achieves its own special kind of luxury through the creativity and imagination of its designers working in close collaboration with their clients. As architect Mark Wee, puts it, 'Designing a house for a client is, for them, a highly emotional thing ... it is not just money invested, it is meant to be a setting for them to live for a long time.' In fact, with most of the homes in this book, the marriage of luxury and sustainability has been achieved not by spending huge sums of money but by the application of some simple, imaginative and well thought out strategies.

Most of these homes are free-standing landed properties. In the tiny island state of Singapore, this means, by definition, that a lot of money is spent to acquire the land even before the design process begins. Money, though, is forever the elephant in the architectural room. Despite the many lessons learned from traditional architecture about how to live in a tropical climate, money has always provided the resource—as everywhere else in the world—that has enabled architecture to experiment, explore and innovate. Over time, the lessons learned from these 'luxurious' projects are applied across the board, including to medium- and low-cost housing.

Rather than viewing luxury and sustainability as being mutually exclusive, it may actually be that true innovation is driven by the desire for luxury, especially given that luxury and comfort mean such different things to different people. Let me give just one example of how a current trend in Singapore is bringing together the issues of luxury, sustainability, innovative design and financial capacity. This is the way in which architects are currently experimenting with multi-generational houses. They are responding to the desire to maintain the extended family, to the high cost of real estate (that encourages adult children to remain at home longer) and to changing social mores which result in people, especially the younger generation, seeking greater independence and privacy. In other words, how do we reconcile privacy and community within the contemporary family home? The result is some very beautiful houses, but houses that are also highly sustainable—socially, culturally, economically and environmentally.

Sustainability: The Big Picture

'Sustainability' has become a somewhat rubbery term, so let us put things into perspective. There is a lot more to sustainability than simply throwing out the air-conditioner. Showing me over his Travertine Dream House (page 142), architect Robin Tan Chai Chong made himself very clear: 'We don't buy into the trendy new way of describing green architecture. We look at it in a holistic manner.... What are our limitations in Singapore? We don't produce anything. We import everything. The task of architecture is to balance consumption.'

In this case, the client had worked his way up through a series of modest dwellings to this, his dream house. He wanted all marble finishes. Tan suggested travertine, just as beautiful but less expensive and less ostentatious. The client agreed and went off to Italy to source the travertine himself at a fraction of the cost. 'That', says Tan, 'saved resources. Saving money is a kind of sustainability.'

The back story to this house is reflected in different ways in all the other homes in this book. Yes, there is money to play with and, yes, these homes are luxurious. But each home is luxurious in a way that is right for the people living

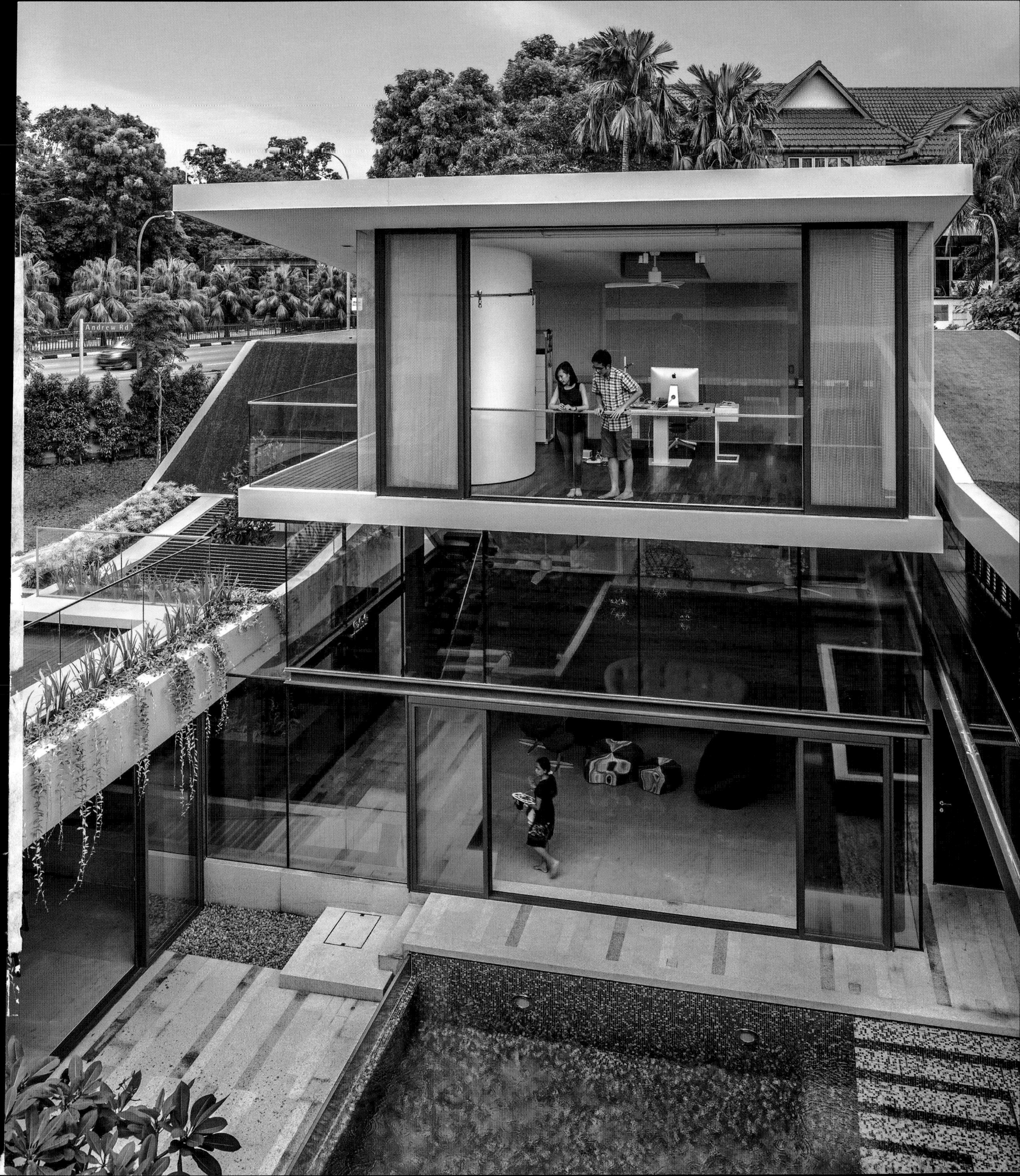
Andrew Rd

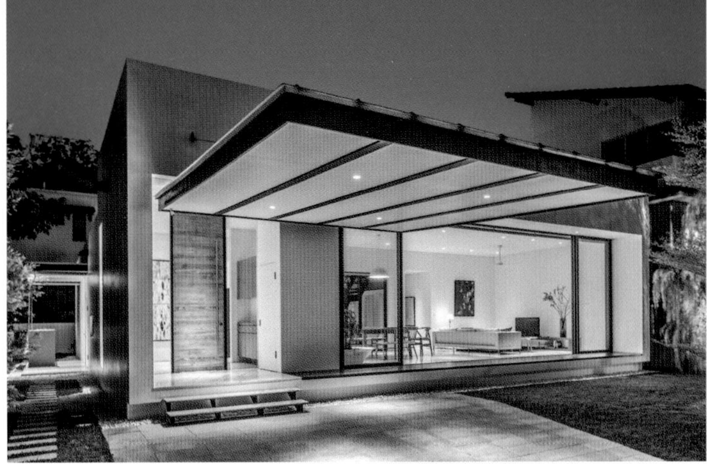

Left The Mandai Courtyard House (page 34), with its modestly scaled living/dining space and *engawa* deck, is the epitome of the 'good neighbour'.

Opposite The idea behind the Barnstorm House (page 150) is the image of a large-scale barn made from traditional materials and tailored for outdoor tropical living.

in it, and each represents a thoughtful and innovative approach to the challenge of sustainability.

Just as important is the way the architects and their clients have viewed environmental sustainability as part of a bigger picture. The result is that residential architecture in Singapore is setting new benchmarks, not just in the tropics but throughout the world.

In my previous book, *The Sustainable Asian House* (2013), the word 'sustainable' was used in the broadest sense, and a number of readers commented that they appreciated the fact that I was not just looking at sustainability in a narrow environmental sense. In this book, I want to be clear from the outset how I define the term since it is often used too loosely and ends up being applied to things that are not even remotely sustainable.

The term 'greenwashing' is sometimes used to describe this sleight of hand, applied to design which only pretends to be environmentally responsible. Nonetheless, one can argue that a mixture of legislation and good intentions has resulted in an architectural agenda that is now broadly, and genuinely, sustainable. As Robin Tan also points out: 'Architects have always been environmentally sensitive, socially sensitive... but we look at it in a holistic way. There needs to be a holistic view of sustainability.'

Today, sustainability looks less like a single aspect of design, for example, using specifically sustainable materials, and more like a systemic challenge that involves looking at how all the elements fit together as a whole. It may not be simply a case of using particular materials to conserve energy or reduce carbon emissions but more about examining the big picture. It is not so much the particular materials that are used but what is done with them!

There is much more to sustainability than the materials used and whether a house uses too much air-conditioning. It involves the entire *habitus* of the society, the aggregate of all the things that enable a community to sustain itself physically, socially and culturally over the longer term. It is what makes the community unique and encompasses the physical environment (including climate), the language, the cultural heritage and the memories of people, without which there would be no culture, language or competence in the performance of everyday tasks.

It is this broader context that frames this book. Sustainability consultants Leyla Acaroglu and Liam Fennessy have commented that 'Sustainability is the equity of social, economic and environmental resources.'[1] In other words, a sensible balance of these three core factors creates an ecology in which all the participating elements influence one another and work together to achieve a common end. As Acaroglu says elsewhere: 'When you step back from the hype, sustainability is really about understanding and working with systems.'[2]

When I talk about sustainable living in the Singapore context, I am referring to a broad range of environmental, social, cultural and economic issues that are currently shaping this vibrant island nation as it approaches the fiftieth anniversary of its founding as a nation state, and specifically the way in which its residential architecture is responding to these issues. As architect Mark Wee says, 'Singapore may still be less than fifty years old but there is a fair degree of nostalgia... the task of the architect in Singapore is to create new spaces that can add to the soul of the city.'

Architecture is not produced in a vacuum. It responds to the programmatic requirements of its clients, to the specifics of location and to regulatory constraints, which in turn reflect established societal goals and values. This makes up what the great anthropologist of the South Pacific, Bronisław Malinowski, referred to as the *immediate context*, the actual situation we find ourselves in. Beyond that, however, is what he terms the *wider context*, or the broadly cultural context which shapes our responses. Meaning, he said, was function in context, what we are doing at any given moment within the broader context.

While it may not be always apparent amongst the swirl of professional obligations, shopping lists, domestic chores and getting the kids to school on time, meaning is what drives our lives. Take meaning out of someone's life and the result is alienation: psychological breakdown, anti-social behaviour and aimlessness. Our lives become unsustainable.

The primary factor in sustaining ourselves is the home; in other words, a house (or shelter) imbued with meaning. The home services Abraham Maslow's famous hierarchy of needs: physiological, safety, love and belonging, esteem and self-actualization. These needs have to be met if we are to sustain ourselves physically, personally and spiritually.

While we exist as individuals, we are also members of successively larger human clusters, from one-on-one relationships, families and social groups to entire nations. We cannot separate ourselves from the larger picture. Therefore,

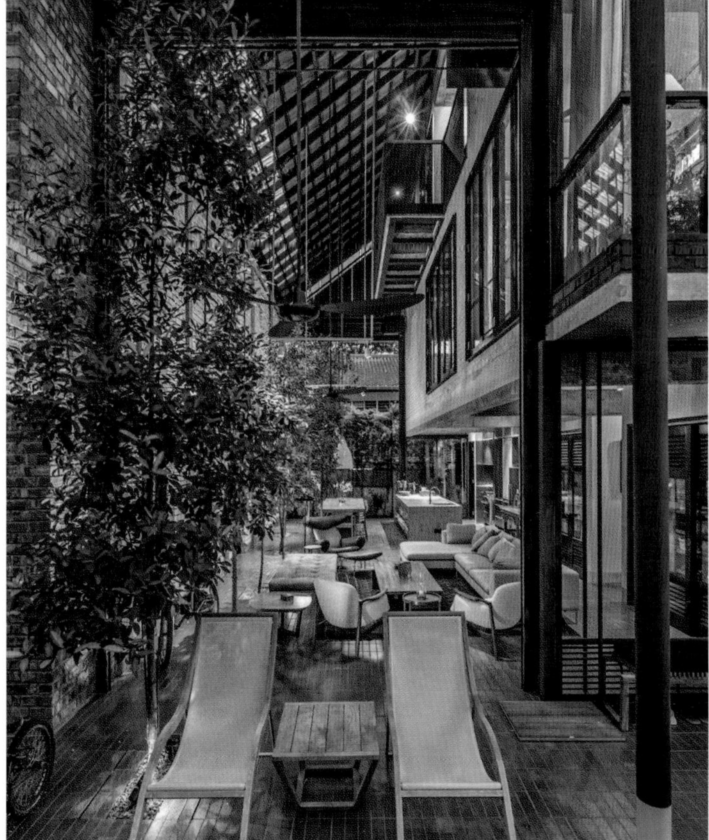

sustainability is about how we share this planet with everyone and everything else over the long term. Every dwelling has its own responsibility to contribute to the long-term sustainability of the planet so that this and subsequent generations of human beings can live effective and fulfilling lives.

This book explores how the contemporary Singaporean home sustains its occupants physiologically while also contributing to the wider agenda, looking at a number of approaches to emotional, familial and cultural sustainability.

This is the immediate context. The wider context is Singapore itself. The island state can be viewed as an ongoing experiment in sustainability. Since deciding to go it alone in 1965, the key driver has been how to sustain itself economically given that its only resource is its people. This has required constant adaptation, largely in response to global economic change. However, other issues have emerged over time, in particular the question of how the island state sustains its people across all those other needs—housing them and providing for their non-material needs in order to sustain a stable and socially healthy community.

Sustainable Luxury looks at how recent changes have impacted on and been reflected in residential architecture: economic changes, the emergence of new professional categories and new kinds of clients with new kinds of expectations and lifestyles, the impact of housing affordability, and new approaches to traditional multi-generational living and changing family patterns (smaller families, singles and childless couples). Added to this is a growing sense of the nation's own history and how it connects with the history and cultures of its neighbours and with a long tradition of coping with a tropical climate.

Sustainability: The Singapore Context

After a period of gradual evolution towards full self-government, the Federation of Malaysia was inaugurated on 9 July 1963, incorporating Malaya, Singapore, Sabah, Sarawak and Brunei. The life of this new country was, however, short-lived and Singapore separated from the Federation to become the independent Republic of Singapore on 9 August 1965.

Driving this separation was the issue of ethnic inequality. Article 153 of the Malaysian Constitution legislated affirmative action in favour of the ethnic Malays. Singapore's Prime Minister, Lee Kuan Yew, argued this was intolerably discriminatory towards other ethnic groups and reluctantly concluded that there was no alternative but for the countries to go their separate ways.

This non-negotiable principle has been crucial to the development of Singapore. It was, of course, a moral issue. But we need to remember that for Confucians the moral and the ethical are inseparable.[3] As a result, there is always a powerful pragmatic corollary at work, namely, that what is right is also what ultimately benefits us.

What was 'right' was the principle of an inclusive multi-culturalism—a genuine pluralism—and an acceptance of the benefits of cultural diversity. Inclusiveness and diversity bring many benefits, including an openness to new ideas and an awareness of different ways of doing things and alternative ways of seeing things and resolving problems. In turn, this leads to a resilient and innovative economy and to a society with the texture that makes it worth living in. In other words, social equity or 'equal opportunity in a safe and healthy environment'. Social equity has long been regarded as an aspect of sustainable development, which itself comprises three key elements: economic, political and cultural sustainability. While social equity may be seen as morally desirable, even to be a universal human right, the notable thing about Singapore is that from the beginning it was seen as a driver of prosperity.

Singapore regards social equity as a matrix of collective and individual responsibility rather than some kind of right. The Singaporean government is nothing if not pragmatic. Individuals are encouraged to take responsibility for their own lives rather than look to the state. Hence, they are required to contribute to a 'provident fund' to ensure their own health care and retirement income. On the other hand, through the Housing Development Board (HDB), established in 1960, the government undertakes to provide affordable housing for all citizens. Flats constructed by the HDB are priced according to affordability rather than construction costs or resale pricing. Accordingly, the risks associated with development—rising land prices, construction and labour costs—are borne by the HDB, representing a substantial subsidy. Likewise, the government invests heavily in high quality universal education, with a strong emphasis on producing an adaptable workforce geared to innovation.

Such measures, along with a progressive taxation system, have seen per capita income grow more than ten times since independence. Even allowing for growing income inequality and falling housing affordability, the achievement has been significant, making the country the most affluent in the region.

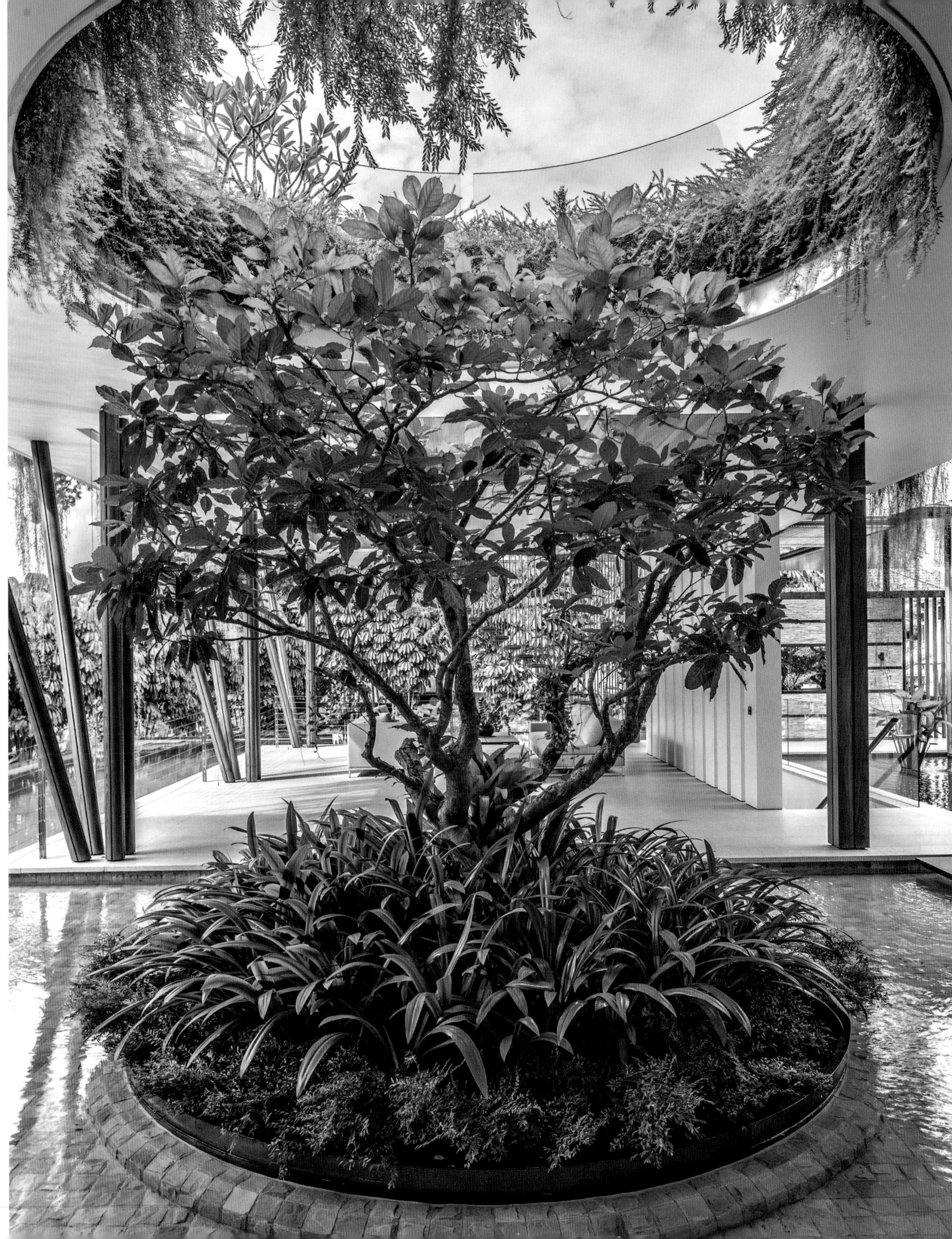

Left Architect Guz Wilkinson is known for his gorgeously luxuriant houses, such as The Coral House (page 86), which merge seamlessly with verdant tropical gardens and water features.

Right Formwerkz typically brings nature into the home, often with mature trees providing indoor greenery, such as in the Tree House (page 78).

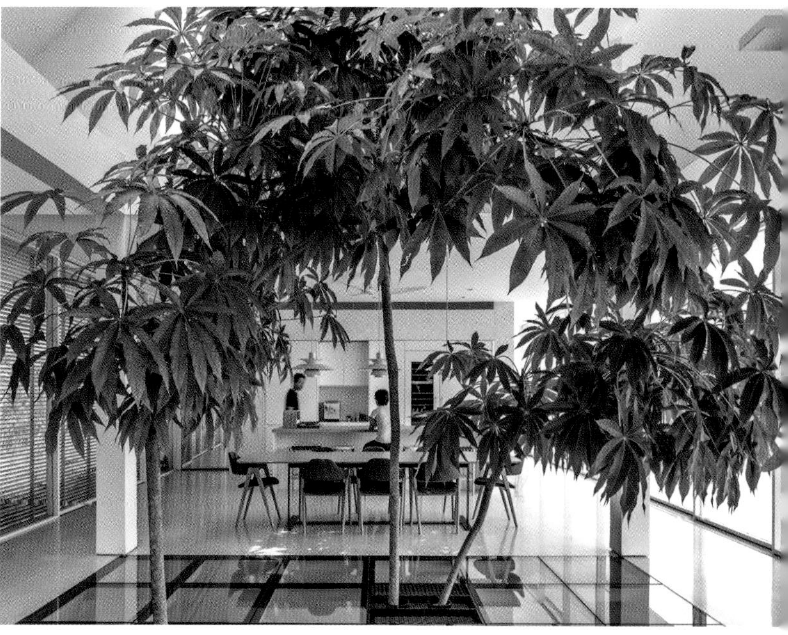

Even more significant is the fact that Singapore is also highly adaptive, which is another way of saying it has sustained itself very successfully during an era of rapid change in the global economy. The global economy is arguably more important to Singapore than any other country because Singapore, apart from its strategic location and deep water port, has no natural resources. It follows that social equity is more than simply a lofty ideal. For Singapore, it is a necessity because social equity means optimal participation by everyone in the economy and in social affairs. Without genuine social equity, Singapore would be unsustainable.

Singapore is an island of 714.3 square kilometres. Its current population is 5.3 million, which means a spread of 13,700 people per square kilometre. The population is projected to reach 6 million by 2020 and 6.9 million by 2030. This prompted a controversial White Paper, released in 2013, significantly titled *A Sustainable Population for a Dynamic Singapore*.

Growing public disquiet about population growth, which has contributed to a housing affordability and availability crisis, has resulted in new restrictions on expatriate workers. These currently make up 44 per cent of the workforce and the previous ratio of one expatriate worker for every four native Singaporeans has been replaced by a ratio of 1 : 8. This has contributed to a labour crisis, especially in the construction sector where the shortage of labour is now becoming a major impediment to development. Like other affluent societies, service industries have become dependent on expatriate labour to do the jobs local people are no longer prepared to do.

In response to an overheated property market, the government has introduced a number of dampening measures, including restrictions on mortgages. At the same time, the HDB has increased its construction of public housing apartments, from 58,731 under construction in 2011 to 72,737 under construction in 2012. Notwithstanding this increase, there was actually a fall in completed flats, contributing to long waiting times and leading to overcrowding as extended families squeeze into apartments of inadequate size.

Nor is population growth an 'urban myth'. It is very real and is widely regarded as contributing to recent problems as seemingly unrelated as more frequent train breakdowns and urban flooding.

Alongside housing affordability, the cost of living overall is becoming a major concern in Singapore. It is now the eighth most expensive city in the world and the third most expensive in Asia. Again, this can be seen as partly an imported problem. As one architect remarked to me while researching this book, 'Singapore is the new Monaco—a place to park money.' It is certainly a tax haven with a low tax rate on personal income among a number of factors—such as other tax measures, Singapore's location, the fact that it is almost entirely corruption-free, the availability of a skilled workforce and advanced infrastructure—attracting large amounts of foreign money. It is estimated that one in every six Singaporean households have at least $1 million in disposable income. Despite growing disparities in income, real economic growth continues.

Because it is so exposed to shifts in the global economy, Singapore has also experienced demographic changes related to economic change and the emergence of new professional groups. Its highly diversified economy is a result of deliberate government policy to ensure that Singapore remains sustainable. It is now, for example, the fourth most important financial centre in the world, the fourth largest foreign exchange trading centre in the world and the world's largest logistics hub. With new professional groups, an ever increasing level of education and the emphasis on maximum connectivity with the rest of the world, Singapore's lifestyle is becoming increasingly diverse. This diversity, along with the economic issues discussed above, is having a fascinating impact on the residential architecture of Singapore.

Almost paradoxically given the seeming 'internationalization' of Singapore, it has an emerging identity that many once felt it would never achieve. After a period of frantic and indiscriminate demolition and reconstruction, Singapore rediscovered its built heritage and, with it, a cultural heritage. Consequently, precincts such as Tiong Bahru, Joo Chiat, Chinatown, even the raffish Geylang, which managed to maintain their cultural continuity, have become sites for

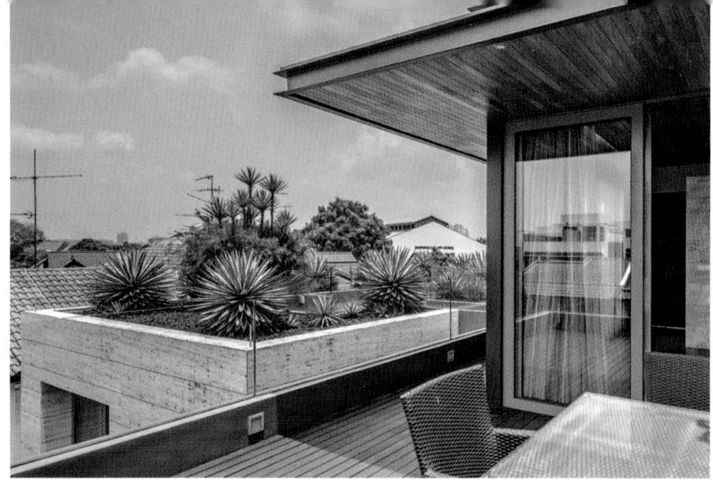

The Travertine Dream House (page 142) has a rooftop garden, which cools the master bedroom below it.

the kind of cultural memory that is essential to a nation's identity. As Singapore approaches its fiftieth birthday, there is a growing sense of the island state's uniqueness. Even the much satirized 'Singlish' is a marker of this. Singapore English consists of more than quaint inflections like 'la'. It has its own emergent lexicon and phonology, making it a distinct form of English. Mixed in with the other indigenous languages, supported by the government's four official languages policy, this makes Singapore unique linguistically.

From Tropicality to Sustainability

A language does not stay the same. It is constantly evolving. Words come to mean different things over time without necessarily losing their history, and words can mean different things in different parts of the world because different places have different histories. English, for example, is not a single language but a whole variety of languages which may look the same on the surface but which vary considerably lexically and phonologically.

I have already mentioned how Singapore English is a distinct variety that is gradually becoming even more distinct. I also suggested that this is a pointer to Singapore's emerging identity. Far from being an 'instant city' or just a giant shopping mall, Singapore has a unique character that goes back much further than 1965.

Pursuing the linguistic model for the moment, let us imagine the contemporary Southeast Asian home as an intersection of past and present, a combination of Malinowski's immediate and wider context.

In her pioneering study of traditional housing in Southeast Asia, *The Living House: An Anthropology of Architecture in South-East Asia* (1990; 2009), Roxana Waterson comments that 'Architecture involves not just the provision of shelter from the elements, but the creation of a social and symbolic space—a space which both mirrors and moulds the worldview of its creators and inhabitants.'[4]

Here we have the intersection of two functions that make the home sustainable. On the one hand, the home is a shelter and a refuge from the world, a place where we eat, sleep and raise our families, where we sustain ourselves as physical entities. On the other hand, the home is a repository of all our values and beliefs, accumulated over generations, and so sustains us emotionally and spiritually.

Waterson's book not only describes the physical forms of traditional housing in tropical Southeast Asia but also demonstrates the important role it has played socially and symbolically. Two points are worth highlighting. First, unlike Western houses where walls were important both as enclosures and as supports for the roof, the vast majority of traditional tropical houses consisted largely of a platform supported by piles and a dominant roof, with only token walls made from perishable natural materials like palm fronds.

Secondly, the house, typically occupied by a number of related families, combined habitation and ritual. Indeed, ritual often predominated, meaning that there was less of a need for separate places or buildings for worship or public functions.

Is it casting too long a bow to suggest that these original characteristics of the Southeast Asian home linger on in the homes of today as they increasingly aspire to respond to their place in a tropical climate and as part of a tradition of tropical living?

Take, for example, the strong connection between the inside and the outside, with terraces extending out from the interior spaces. Especially notable in this respect is the growing enthusiasm for open bathrooms, which is partly a sensual indulgence involving the pleasure of bathing in outdoor tropical luxury but partly a pragmatic anti-mould strategy for airing the wet areas of the house. There are numerous examples in this book, but no better example of deliberately revisiting vernacular tradition than Randy Chan Keng Chong's 'windowless' house, the Jalan Mat Jambol House (page 128), which is almost completely open and effectively raised off the ground as though on piles.

Today, however, the 'sustainable Singapore house' has moved on from the 1990s explorations in 'contemporary vernacular'[5] and the quest to reconcile modernist principles with cultural history and a tropical climate. While these preoccupations remain, they have taken on more sophistication. Today, it is more accurate to speak of place-making, that is to say, a mix of geographic, cultural and temporal place. Moreover, sustainability is seen as a broader and more complex imperative involving not just passive strategies for cooling (cross-ventilation, breezeways, shading, use of greenery and water, etc.) but other things, such as recycling (of materials, and of entire buildings to avoid demolition and rebuilding), minimizing waste and incorporating flexibility for future reconfiguration.

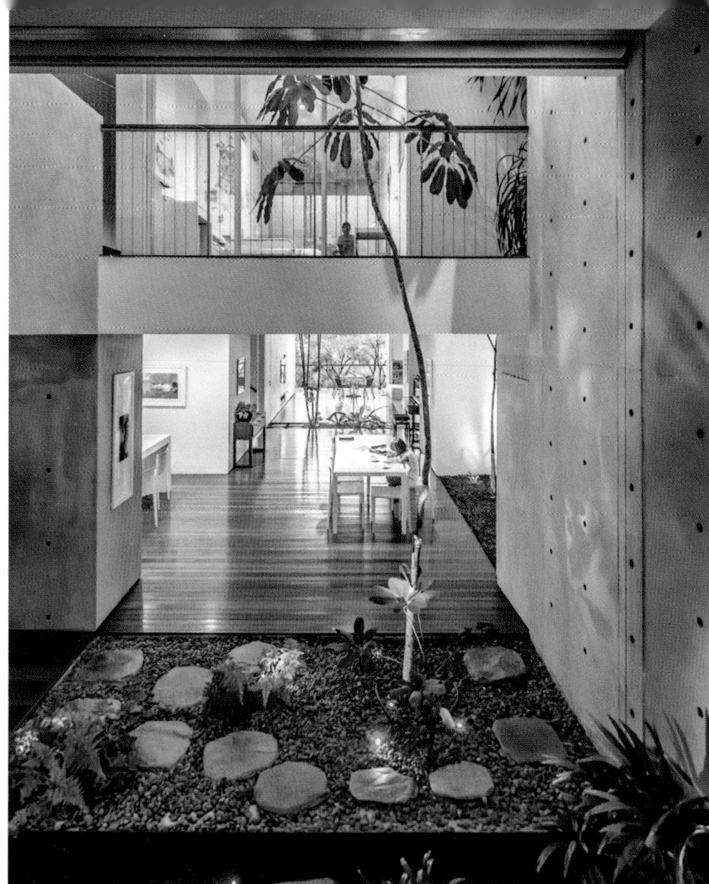

The award-winning Namly Drive House (page 40) has a water garden in the living room, which draws and cools air through the entire house.

Sustainability: A Broader Agenda

Singapore is not unique in fretting about whether it has an identity or not. But, like other countries that also fret, it is probably just a case of not having noticed up until now that it has had an identity all along. I began by reviewing the circumstances of Singapore's birth and by noting the importance of cultural diversity and inclusiveness—surely at the heart of the Singaporean identity—along with its position as a key *entrepôt*. It has always been a melting pot and it is even more so today with such a large percentage of its population made up of expatriates and permanent residents. This demographic diversity is increasingly reflected in greater urban diversity and lifestyles.

There is also the ongoing issue of space or, rather, the lack of it. The government has responded to this with the vision of Singapore as a garden state where the public realm is effectively also the private realm, thus compensating for the lack of private space. This merging of the public and the private is one thing that gives Singapore its distinctiveness.

Nonetheless, there will always be a need to separate the private from the public domains. The traditional Asian emphasis on family and the collective is increasingly required to accommodate a new individuality, a demand for more private space. The ongoing issue is how to be together and yet separate, played out both in the domestic context and in the wider urban context. Domestically, it is reflected in the planning of the home and in the various strategies for dividing and linking space—gardens, courtyards and promenades. In the wider community, it is a case of developing a sustainable urbanism where Singapore, as an intensely urban society, can nonetheless service the non-material needs of its citizens.

The homes in this book have been chosen to illustrate the various ways in which residential architecture is responding to all these issues. A particularly interesting example is the way in which high-density and high-rise living is increasingly seen as an opportunity rather than a drawback. In high-rise apartment buildings, this is signalled by emphasizing and enhancing the panoramic views and by vertical connection with nature—green walls and green terraces—to generate a sense of being connected with nature even when living many storeys up in the air. Inside, there are initiatives (currently being driven by the HDB) to rethink the planning of apartments to more effectively accommodate the multi-generational family.

This also reflects a new sensitivity to the needs of clients, an acknowledgement of the need to make multi-residential living sustainable in the social, familial and personal sense. While the HDB is encouraging new apartment configurations to accommodate the extended family in public housing, at the other end of the property spectrum developers are building open-plan apartments—'semi-white plans'—to allow occupiers to customize their personal space. As with the idea of vertical landscapes, the aim is to replicate the feeling of living in a landed house with all the individuality that implies and a shift away from the standardization of traditional apartment design.

Waterson points out that 'Inhabited spaces are never neutral; they are all cultural constructions of one kind or another.'[6] In other words, they embody meaning. But an ongoing issue is the tension between architects and their clients as to who decides the 'meaning'. There is always a tendency for architects to 'over-design' in order to control the 'meanings' embodied in the home. The problem with this is that the meanings are the architects' meanings, not those of the people who will be living in the home. This is not a sustainable way to go about things. Happily, the houses in this book exemplify a trend towards a sustainable collaboration between architect and client.

It may seem an obvious thing to do, to design a house that is right for the occupants, but actually houses are very often designed to reflect only what the *architect* thinks is important. However, there is now a marked trend in Singapore to highly customize residential design. It is, as architect Alan Tay says (see the Sembawang Long Houses, page 70, and the Tree House, page 78),

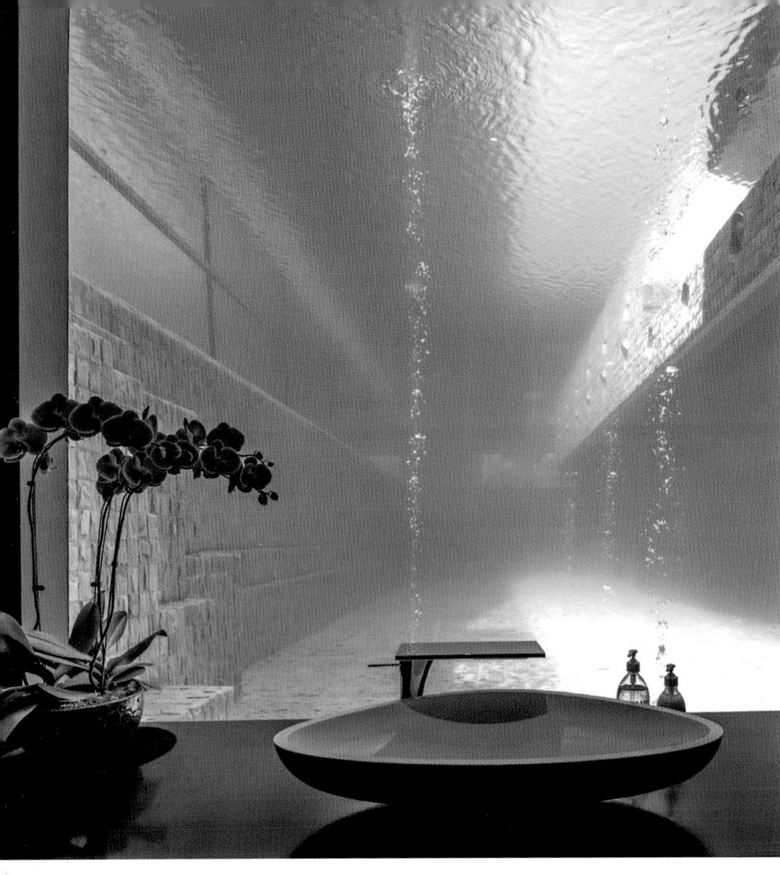

Left This is a powder room in the basement of The Coral House (page 86) that no one wants to leave because of its view of the sunken swimming pool).

Opposite The Oliv Apartments (page 48) create a vertical landscape, the green common spaces providing natural cooling to the apartments.

a matter of asking 'how the client would use the house' and this can involve a lot more than the basic programme, with its number of bedrooms, etc. Occupiers have an annoying habit of filling and decorating a house with their favourite things, which can often result in a contradiction between the way the house has been designed and the way it is used. An obvious way to avoid this mismatch is to work closely with the client from the beginning.

Clients now often insist on being part of a collaborative process. This book has many examples of clients being actively involved. With the remarkable shophouse conversion by Mark Wee in Neil Road (page 26), the client had a clear vision of a sustainable marriage of heritage and the contemporary and made it clear, saying 'I didn't want a house, I wanted a home.' In Chang Yong Ter's award-winning Namly Drive House (page 40), the client wanted 'two homes in one house'. The client at Guz Wilkinson's The Coral House (page 86) comments, 'I was born in Singapore. This is the tropics. And I don't like being cooped up in an air-conditioned room. When we were looking for an architect, we were very mindful that we wanted someone who would blend with our taste and style, not someone because he has a name.' At The Cranes in Joo Chiat (page 200), the client, whose day job is in shipping and whose boutique developments are almost a hobby, worked closely with the architect to devise a multi-residential model that catered for a new demographic of professionals, but nourished by the rich, local urban heritage.

Indeed, there are architectural practices, such as eco:id, who only work on residential projects that are truly collaborative and where there is a natural empathy between architect and client.

This is not just a matter of clients briefing their chosen architects. This is a whole new paradigm for the client–architect relationship, which involves an ongoing conversation between the two that is intense and highly personal. Sustainability—environmental, personal and cultural—is a key driver for all parties and it is an approach which is drawing attention from all over the world.

Sustaining a Changing Singapore

Sustainability is not an option for Singapore, it is an imperative. In environmental terms, this means conserving water, looking for ways of moderating dependence on air-conditioning, attempting to restrict the use of private motor vehicles and making the best use of the available land. This, in turn, has implications for the social sustainability of the country. Land shortage and the cost of land—as one architect, Chu Lik Ren, said to me, 'Space is a universal constraint'—imply high-density, high-rise and smarter ways of using space. If the use of private motor vehicles is to be discouraged by ownership restrictions and financial imposts, then an affordable, convenient and efficient public transport system has to be provided. Moreover, such a system has to be attractive and comfortable if it is to compensate for the lack of a private car. In the same way, to maintain social harmony the emotional well-being of the community needs to be ensured by providing communal amenities to compensate for the constraints of apartment living.

Economically, the country needs to be infinitely adaptive, constantly sensitive to shifts in the global economy and alert to new opportunities. Hence, the government has placed great emphasis on education, aiming for a highly skilled, flexible and innovative workforce, significantly aiming to make Singapore the design hub of Asia and a centre of creativity.

The key to sustaining an adaptive economy is diversity and inclusiveness, and with more than one-third of the workforce of non-Singaporean origin, not to mention its natural ethnic mix, Singapore is nothing if not diverse. The challenge will be to address certain contradictions, notably the perceived need for a stable consensus (which tends not to entertain deviant ideas) as against the need for a plurality of competing ideas and values if the country is to remain genuinely adaptive and innovative. This points to what some people believe is a fourth dimension to sustainability—political sustainability.

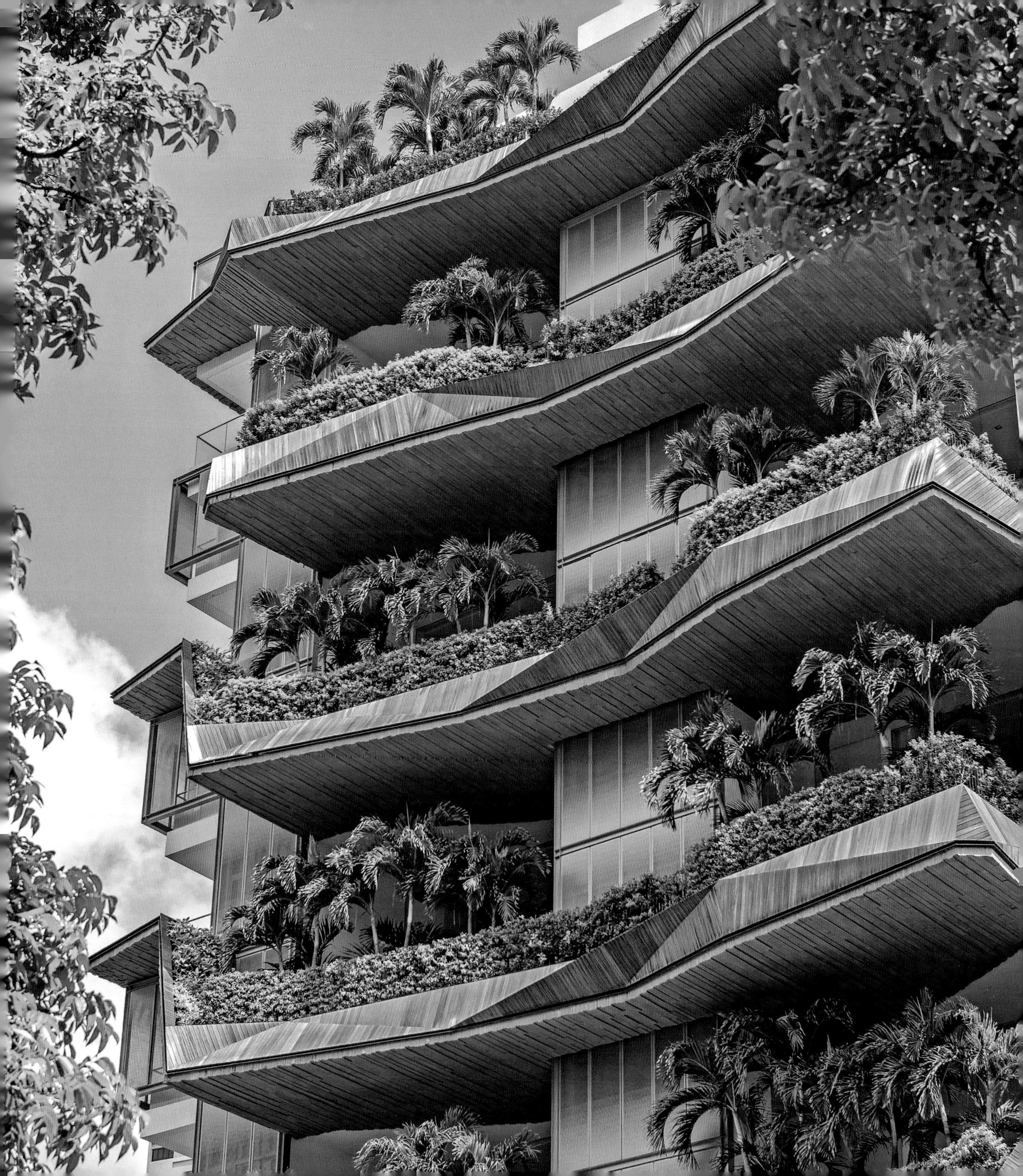

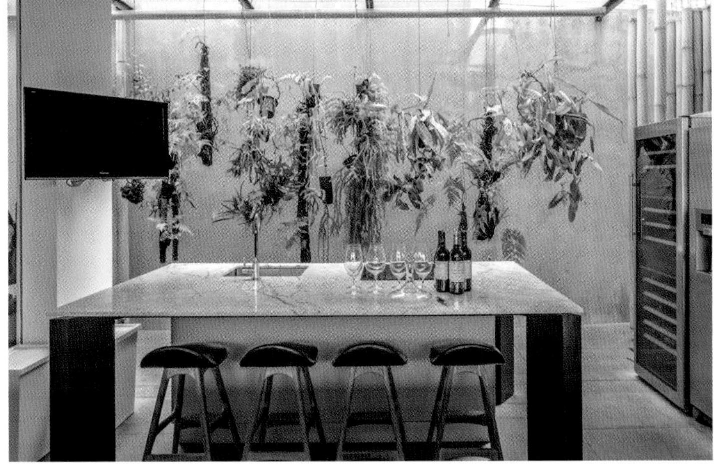

The Bamboo Curtain House (page 162) opens up to the outside, as seen in the kitchen with its courtyard and greenery.

New Homes for a New Society

The more things change, the more they stay the same. Despite the encroachment of a 'global culture' and its inherent stress on freedom, individuality and independence, in Singapore the family remains the foundation of society, and accommodating the extended family is a major preoccupation. Designing for the extended family, however, must now take into account changing cultural circumstances

As in other countries, escalating property values in Singapore make it increasingly difficult for younger generations to buy their own home. One solution has been to turn to the mass market, in particular the resale HDB apartment market where (as we see in the Dakota Apartment, page 156) there is a growing appreciation of the potential to renovate for a more up-to-date lifestyle, allied to an emerging sentimental attraction to a housing type once looked down upon. Another emerging solution is to buy into places like Johor Bahru and Sembawang in Malaysia, where land is more affordable, and to commute to the city.

Younger people living at home longer have provided a boost to the sustainability of the extended family and pleased the parents. But it comes with a rider because changing mores now require greater degrees of privacy and independence. The result has been a new form of multi-generational house, one which distinguishes far more clearly than before between the respective private domains. Adult children's quarters now tend to be far more self-contained, often with their own entrances, allowing the children to come and go as they please without disturbing the rest of the household.

At the same time, greater flexibility is being designed into multi-generational houses, which is about designing for the next generation and for the future generally. On the one hand, the aim is to build in the ability to reconfigure the house as parents and grandparents age and as children grow up, and so allow for changing needs. Parallel to this is a preoccupation with resale value, leading to an avoidance of prescriptive design and enabling the house to remain attractive to future owners who might have different needs and values.

It may seem odd that decentralization should be a driver on such a small island. But as part of the strategy to spread density, relieve the pressure on both private and public transport and generally prevent Singapore from becoming an environmental pressure cooker, the government is constantly developing new and self-sufficient towns that complement a growing suburbanization. One result has been a more focused idea of urban living, especially among the younger generation.

Again, this is impacting the direction of residential design, with people wanting to be part of the action and yet still having their own private refuge. For one market sector, conservation houses or other existing houses remain desirable, partly because of their proximity to urban attractions and partly because of their potential for interior redevelopment while retaining the aura of history and culture. For a less affluent part of the market, the resale HDB market is increasingly attractive, especially if it is in or near fashionable and well-located precincts.

We also need to consider the new kinds of clients who are emerging and whose residential requirements are different from an earlier generation. These include single people, couples without children or with only one or two children. There is also the expatriate market, not all of whom earn huge salaries but who have their own preferences. The Cranes (page 200) is one example of a possible new direction in catering to this sector of the market, while the Watten Residences (page 178) and The Green Collection (page 184) are two other distinctive terrace housing models that provide many of the amenities of a landed house but with cost offsets.

Models like these also represent new propositions for a sustainable balance between privacy and community. In Singapore, as elsewhere in tropical Southeast Asia, the relationship of privacy to community remains the single most important theme. If anything, the issue of balancing the two is even more important now than it ever was with the diversification of lifestyles reflecting the growth of cities and the continual development of a new world economic order.

Traditionally, of course, the issue has been how to attain a degree of privacy in a strongly communalist society. But the issue is now more nuanced. This more complex view of how privacy and community should coexist is well put by Tan Ji Ken, who worked with Mark Wee on The Cranes. In a note on the project he writes, 'Privacy is an under-estimated catalyst for community. It creates security and a sense of having something of one's own to fuel the courage and respite needed for productive and meaningful communal engagement. All the best community platforms have privacy settings.'

Another feature of Guz Wilkinson's work is the tropical garden, which cools the house. Here in The Coral House (page 86), the garden is elevated off the ground.

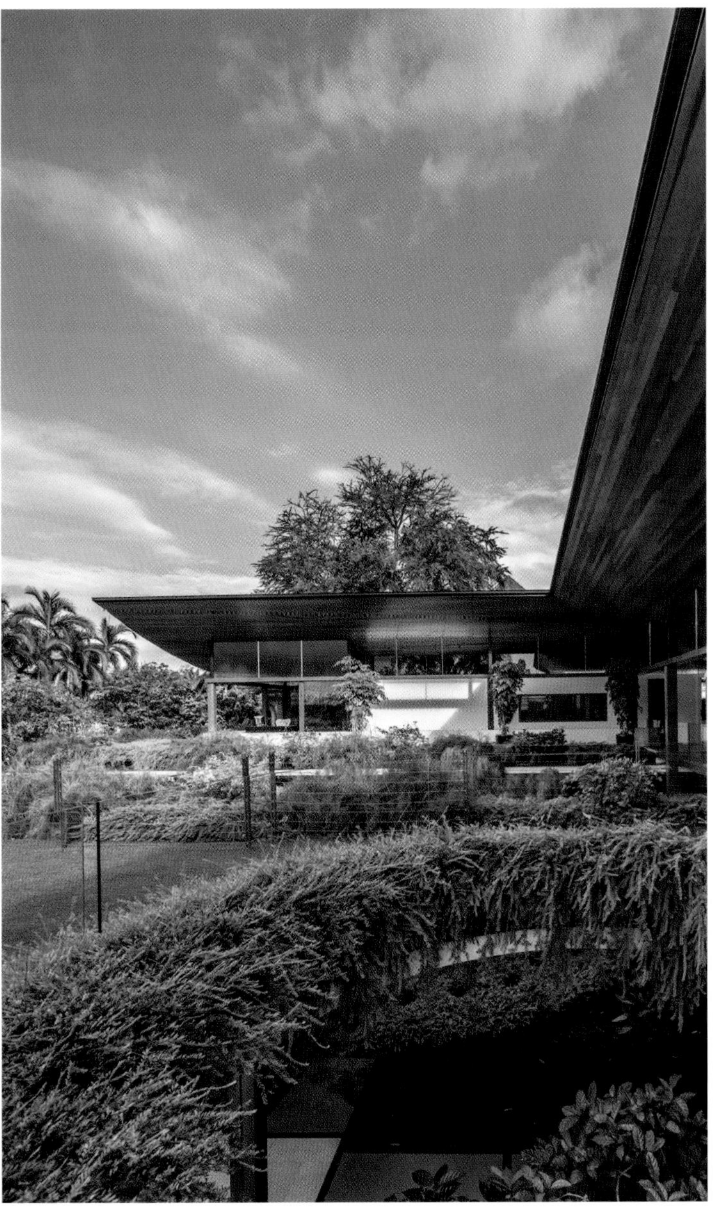

For our lives to be sustainable, we need both privacy and community for a sense of belonging. At the very least, being part of a community helps us to shape our values and to define who we are. Historically, however, the emphasis has been on how we as individuals or as families can achieve a reasonable degree of privacy and refuge from the larger world without losing the benefits of belonging to the collective. The benefits are contingent on each of us bringing something to the table.

Arguably, we live in a world which is becoming more communal, more *connected*. With digital technology, it can seem as though there is no private space left and that we are all living in one gigantic public space. This begs the question: how meaningful is this connectedness, how genuinely engaged are we? Tan Ji's point is important—productive and meaningful engagement in communal life is only possible when we approach it with the secure sense of self, which is generated in the private domain. In other words, it is a two-way street; we need both as privacy and community feed one another.

The opportunity to be together and yet separate is the big theme in tropical Southeast Asian residential design. For Singapore, it is especially crucial and key to the country's sustainable future.

In this book, I offer a selection of projects ranging from free-standing houses to terrace houses and multi-residential projects to high-rise multi-residentials. Each is an example of one or more of the three key components of sustainability: environmental, social and economic. At the same time, the houses reflect a variety of changes taking place in modern Singapore.

My argument has been that sustainability is the key to Singapore's future. In that sense, the high-quality luxury homes gathered together in this book illustrate how residential design is both contributing to and reflecting that sustainable agenda.

1 Leyla Acaroglu and Liam Fennessy, 'Rapid Adjustments Required: How Australian Design Might Contend with a Carbon Constrained Economy', paper presented to the agideas International Research Conference, 22 May 2012.

2 'Material Matters', *Indesign No. 56*, March/May 2014, p. 193.

3 More than 74 per cent of the Singaporean population is ethnically Chinese, of whom over 34 per cent claim to be Buddhist, 10 per cent Taoist and 16 per cent Christian. However, Confucianism acts as a unifying ethical force, best exemplified by a powerful governmental ideology of social responsibility and inclusiveness that places social values above individual preferences.

4 Roxana Waterson, *The Living House: An Anthropology of Architecture in South-East Asia*, Singapore: Tuttle reprint, 2009; first published Singapore: Oxford University Press, 1990, p. xv.

5 The term was originally used in William Lim and Tan Hock Beng's pioneering study, *Contemporary Vernacular: Evoking Tradition in Asian Architecture*, Singapore: Select Books, 1998.

6 Waterson, *The Living House*, p. xvi.

TANGLIN HILL HOUSE
ECO:ID ARCHITECTS

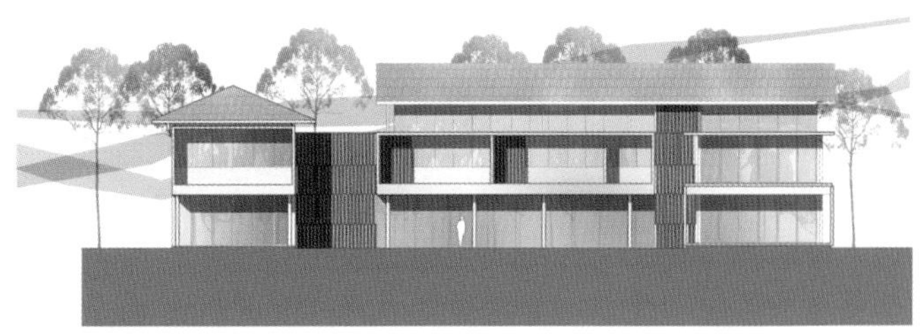

'Our brief to Boon was a very simple one: Give us a space that we can grow old in and where our friends can come visit in their shorts and flip-flops without ever feeling out of place. But, at the same time, a place where the artist, if he were to visit our house, will not feel that we have disrespected his work.'—OWNER

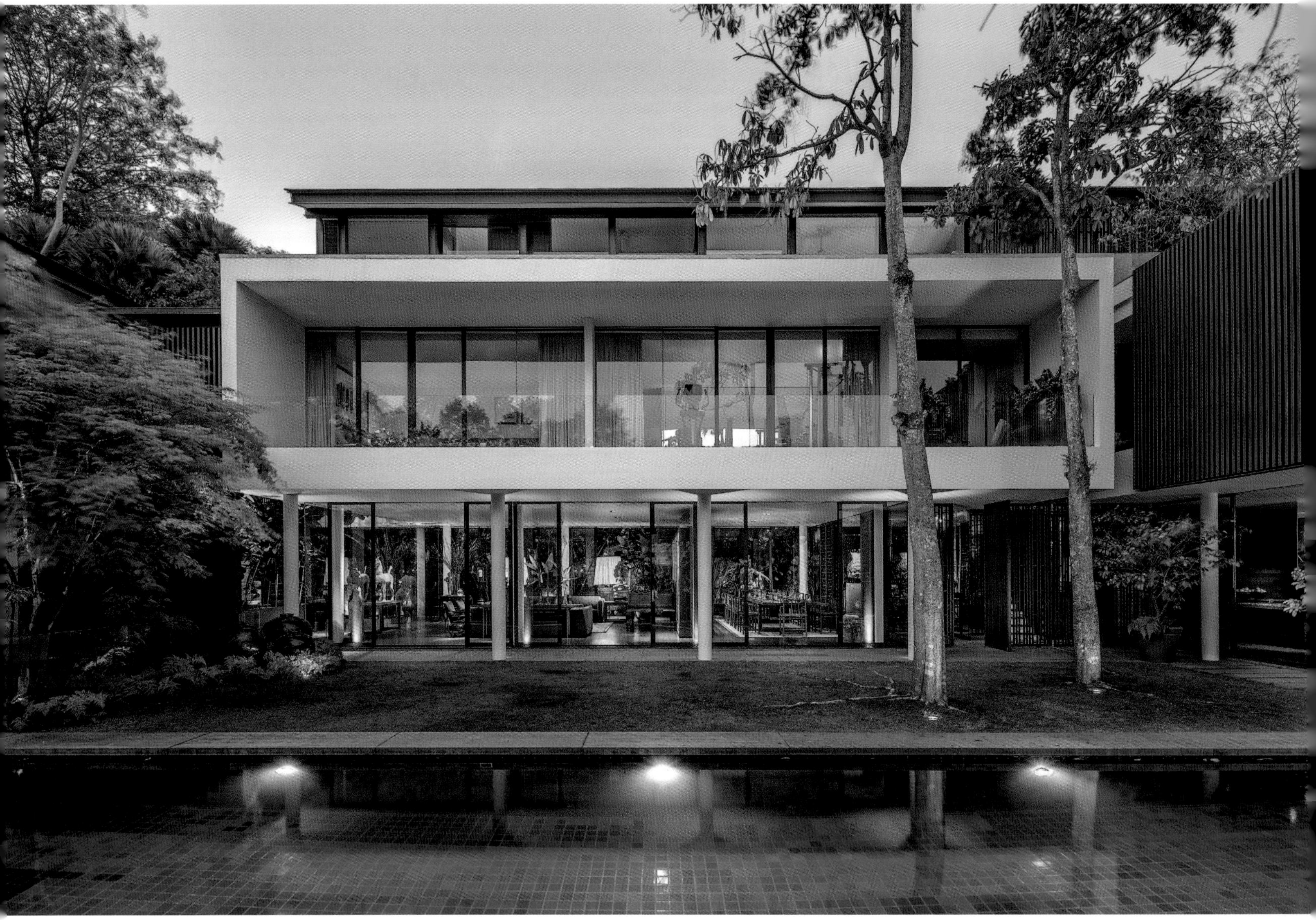

Left Long section.

Below left From across the pool, the house seems to dissolve into the landscape.

Right A screened deck blocks the master bedroom at one end of the pool.

Below Entry to the house is at the top of a steep hill and gives no suggestion of what lies beyond.

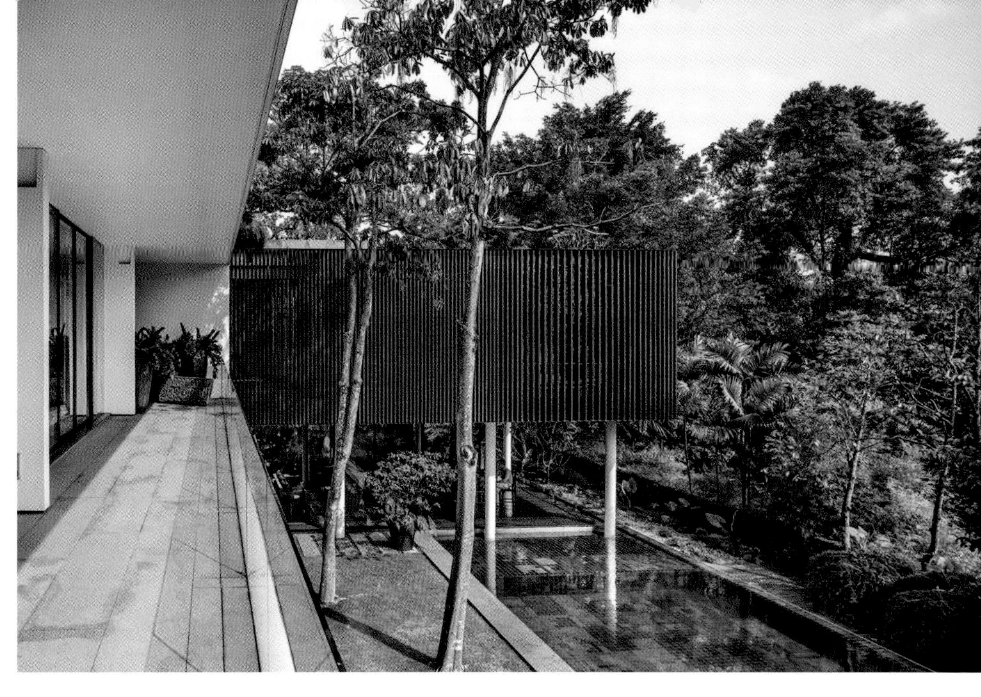

Well known for its high quality hospitality design, eco:id Architects restricts its residential work to clients for whom it feels a close affinity. It reminds me of the novel *Elective Affinities* by the great German author Johann Wolfgang von Goethe, which takes its name from the theory of chemical affinities whereby certain compounds only interact with each other under specific circumstances. In the case of architect Sim Boon Yang and his client, there were a number of affinities between them, the strongest being art. Both collect art, but art of a certain kind, art which is 'neither ostentatious nor superfluous', in the words of the client, art predominantly from Asia and art with a delicate balance between the aesthetic and the functional.

The client, a boutique developer of high-end houses, and eco:id had worked together before on a number of projects, to the extent that he and his wife now enjoy a friendship with Sim and his wife. The affinities which sustain this friendship go beyond art to include a love of gardens, of a connection between inside and outside and of a relaxed and informal lifestyle.

The garden is the heart of this house. It is not clear whether the well-established and relaxed tropical garden embraces the house or whether the house embraces the garden. The U-shaped building—actually a cluster of three connected pavilions—wraps around the garden, with the long swimming pool forming an edge to the garden and a row of mature trees screening the property wall. At night, adroitly placed lighting creates reflections of the trees in the water and, looking down from the upper levels of the house, the garden seems to dissolve into one grand and darkly luminous space.

In order to entertain friends in a completely informal way and in the knowledge that people tend to congregate around the kitchen, a large open kitchen and family room are situated with direct access to the garden and pool. Hence, this 'heart of the house' becomes not just a generous public gathering place but also a destination.

Like any good destination, this one also has an arrival sequence, with glimpses along the way of what is to come. The first of the three pavilions on the street side is self-contained, with a living room and study on the ground floor and the master bedroom and bathroom on the second storey. Entry to the house is down a path past the study and through a courtyard and down the outside flank of the grand living and dining space, giving the visitor initial views through to the garden. It is also an introduction to the clients' extraordinary art collection, which is not so much displayed as blended into the spaces it inhabits. This journey of arrival now doglegs around the dining space before bringing the visitor to the kitchen and the informal public domain.

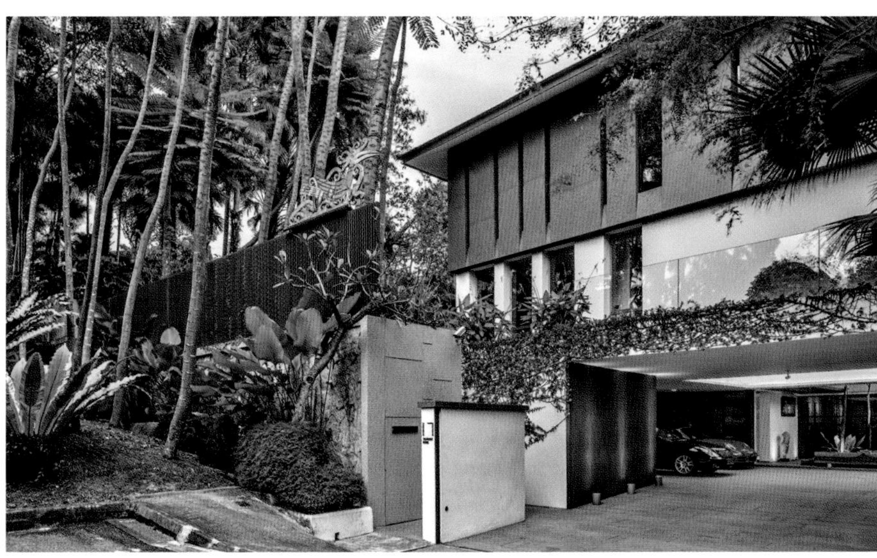

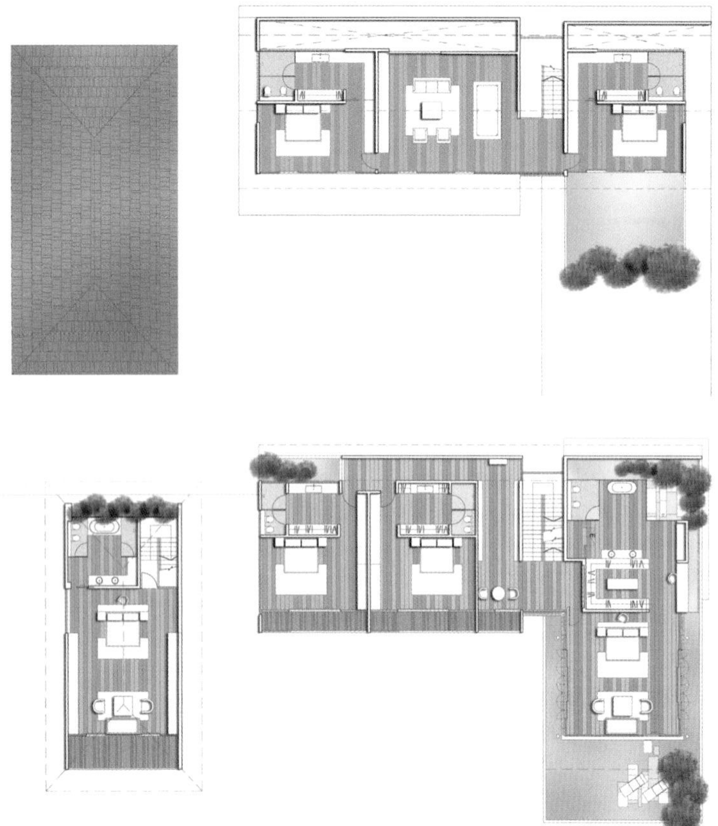

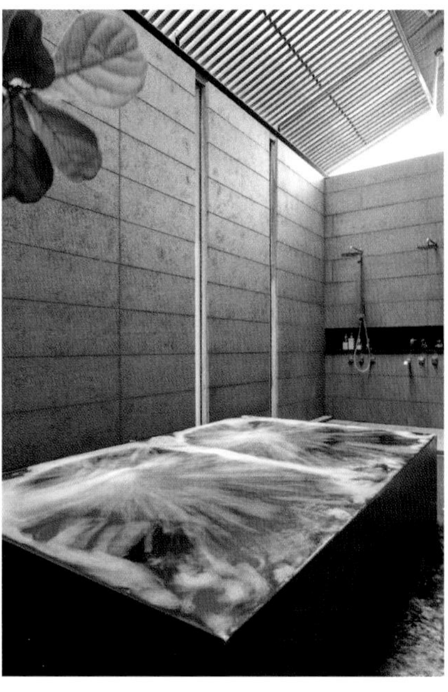

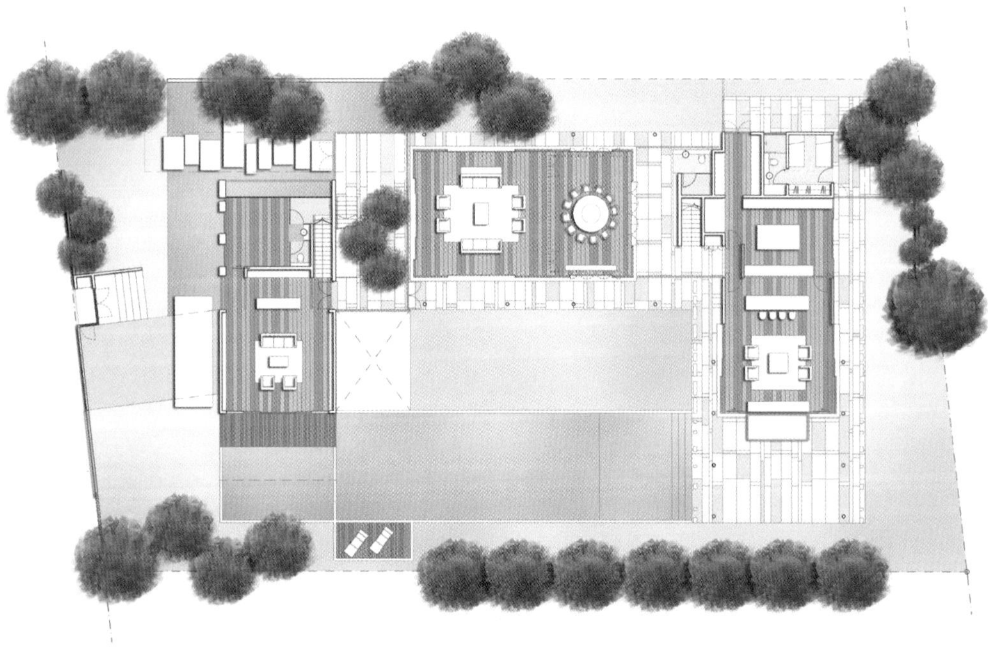

Public and private areas are clearly separated, with the bedrooms all upstairs on the second storey and attic levels. To sustain the connection with nature and also provide a private area of respite, the master bedroom is surrounded by a pond with aquatic plants. 'This space,' says the client, 'has now become a huge bird bath and we wake up every morning to the chirping of many birds—and, periodically, to the rummaging of a resident stork!'

The private domain continues on the attic level, with a family room and two bedrooms, one of which extends to an open roof terrace where the family can relax over a drink and enjoy dramatic views.

The client and architect worked closely together on the design of the house, although the main idea was established right at the very beginning. 'Both Boon and I,' says the client, 'took one look at the site and we both knew intuitively what should be done on it.' Key to the design was the art collection because, just as the garden is totally integrated with the house, so the art collection is also fully integrated into the house. An important aspect was the understanding that the house needed to be

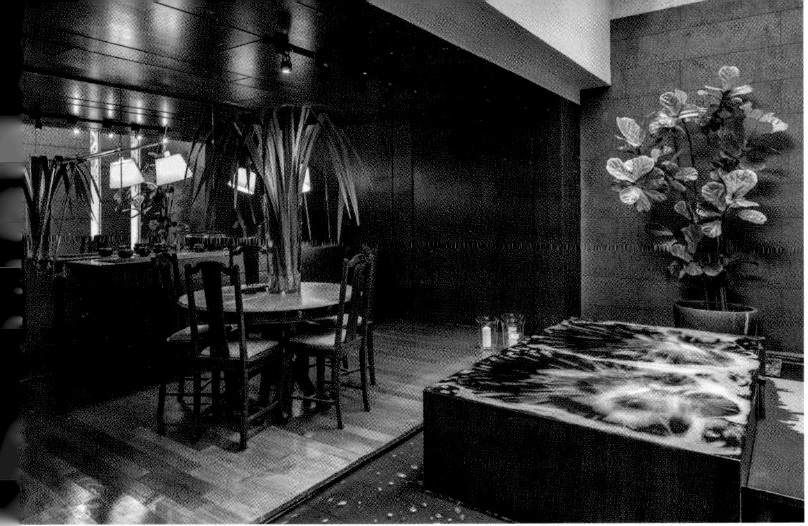

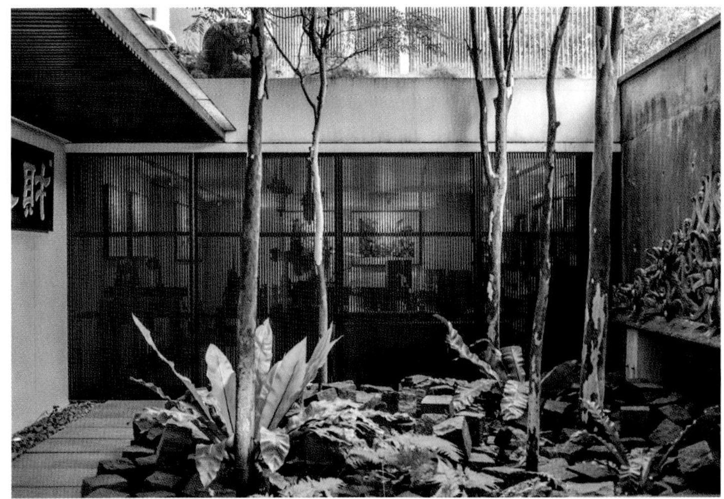

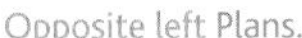

Opposite left Plans.

Opposite right The wet areas continue the theme of living in a natural tropical paradise.

Above The breakfast pavilion is fully transparent and connected to the garden.

Right An enclosed courtyard supports the theme of a house wrapped around the garden.

Below The deck off the breakfast pavilion seems to float over the pool.

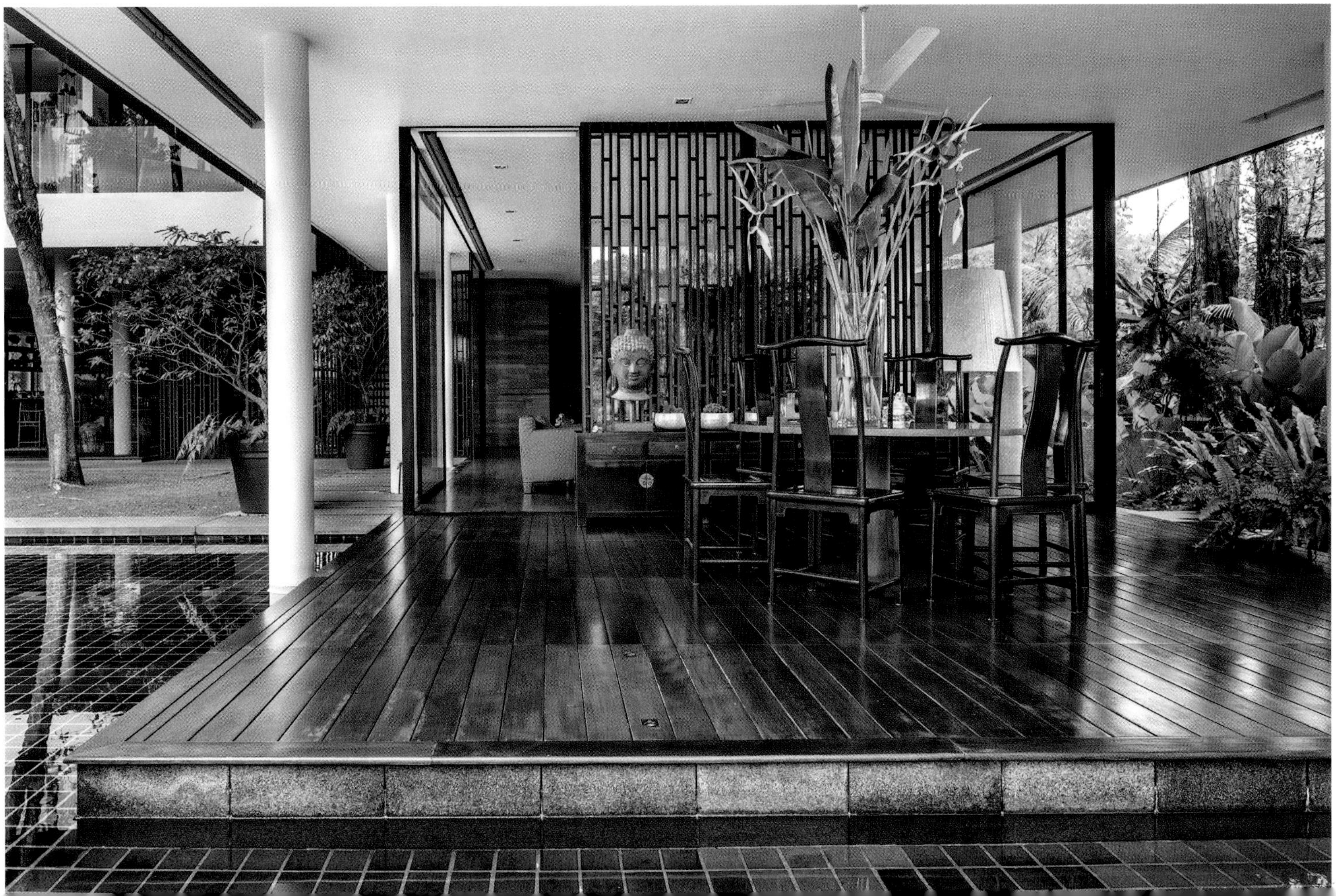

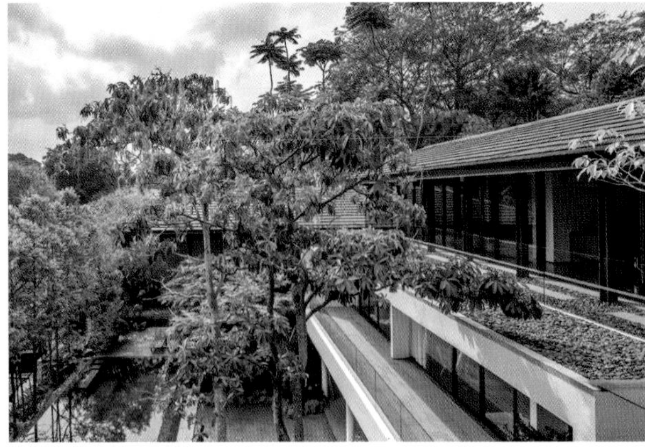

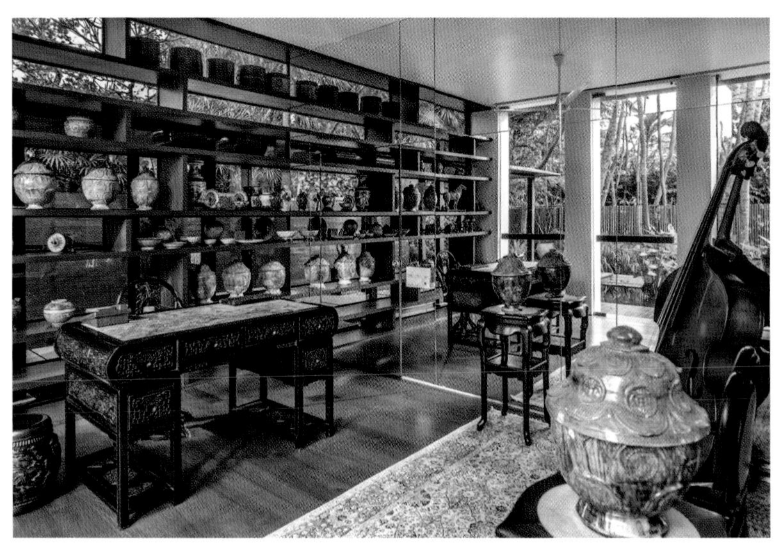

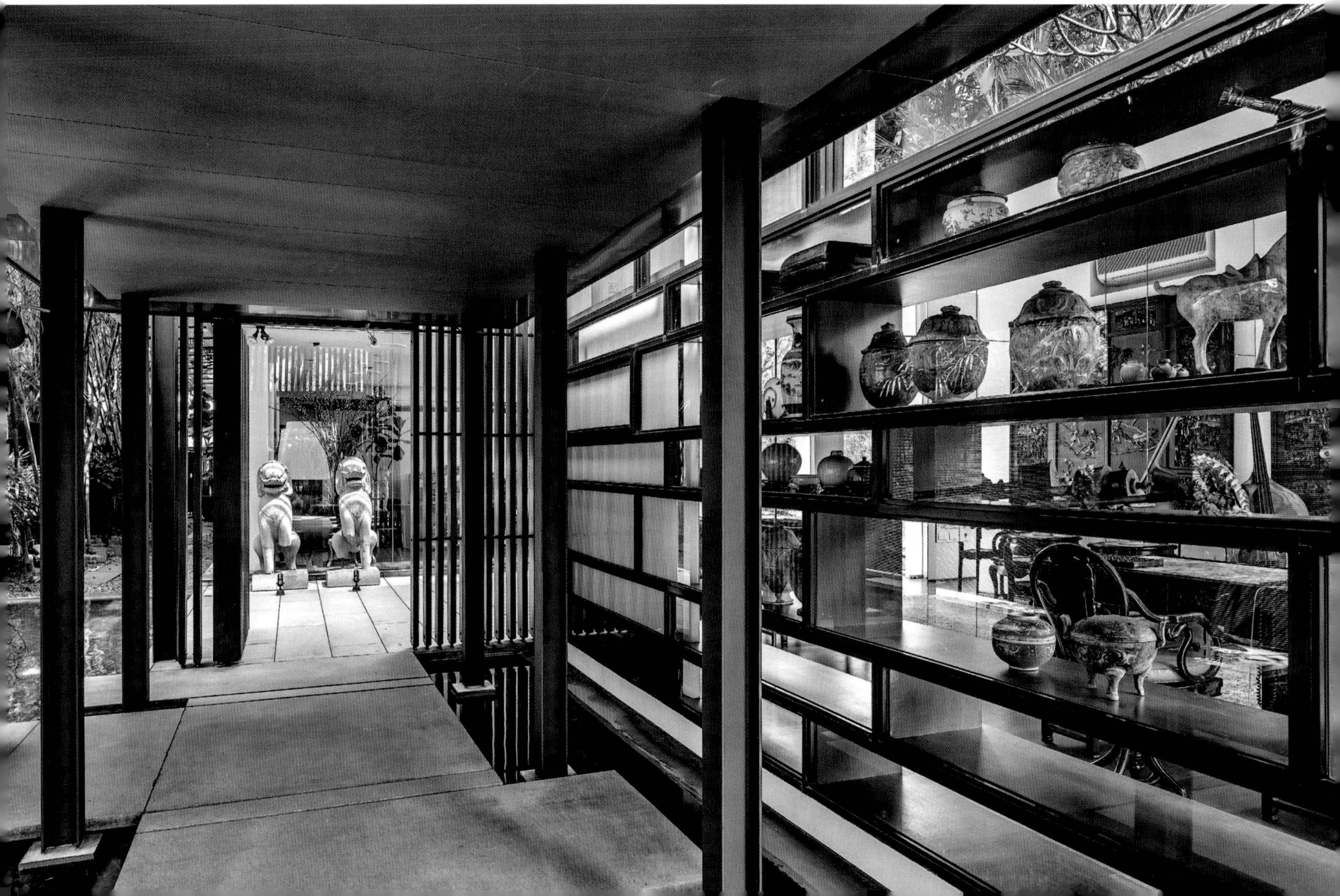

Far left Looking back towards the front of the house and the private domain.

Left The main living and dining space also act as a gallery for the client's extraordinary collection of cultural artefacts.

Below left The arrival sequence provides glimpses of the cultural cornucopia inside.

Right Light is suffused throughout the house, enhancing the exquisite joinery, timber flooring and art works.

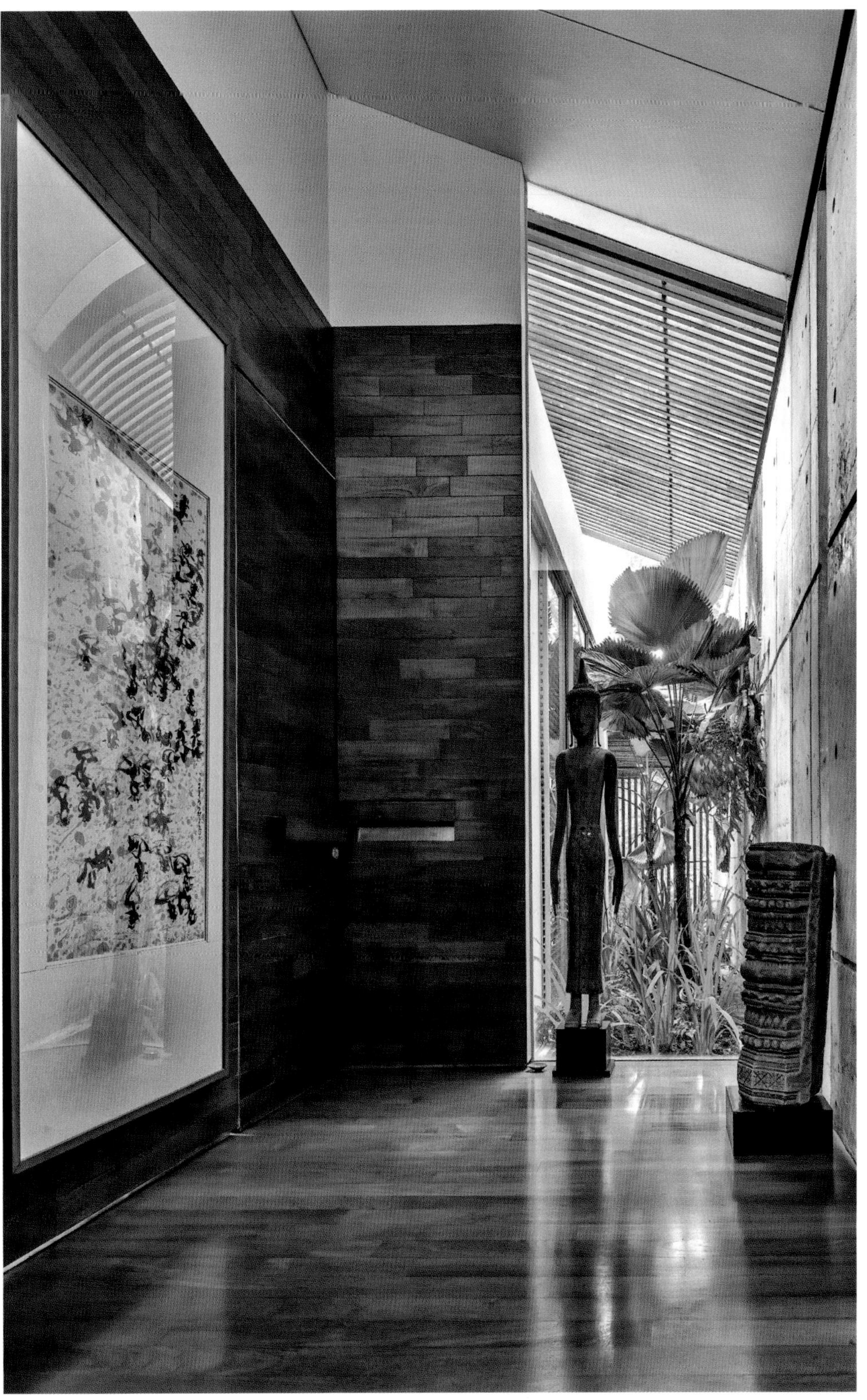

home not just to an existing collection but one that would continue to grow. The solution to this—a similar solution to that in Boon Sim Yang's own home (see the Bamboo Curtain House, page 162)—was to provide a 'blank canvas', in other words, a transparent context in which the art remained autonomous and not in competition with the house.

As with so many other homes in this book, the passive cooling and ventilation strategies were never in question given the seamless connection between the inside of the house and its lush garden and the variety of breezeways, courtyards and open linking spaces. What makes it especially fascinating from a sustainable point of view is the way it supports a way of life based on the enrichment of nature, friendship and art. 'My wife and I honestly believe that the house has a life of its own,' says the client. 'Once we started on the design process together with Boon, we were led to what the house is today—a refuge for my family and friends.'

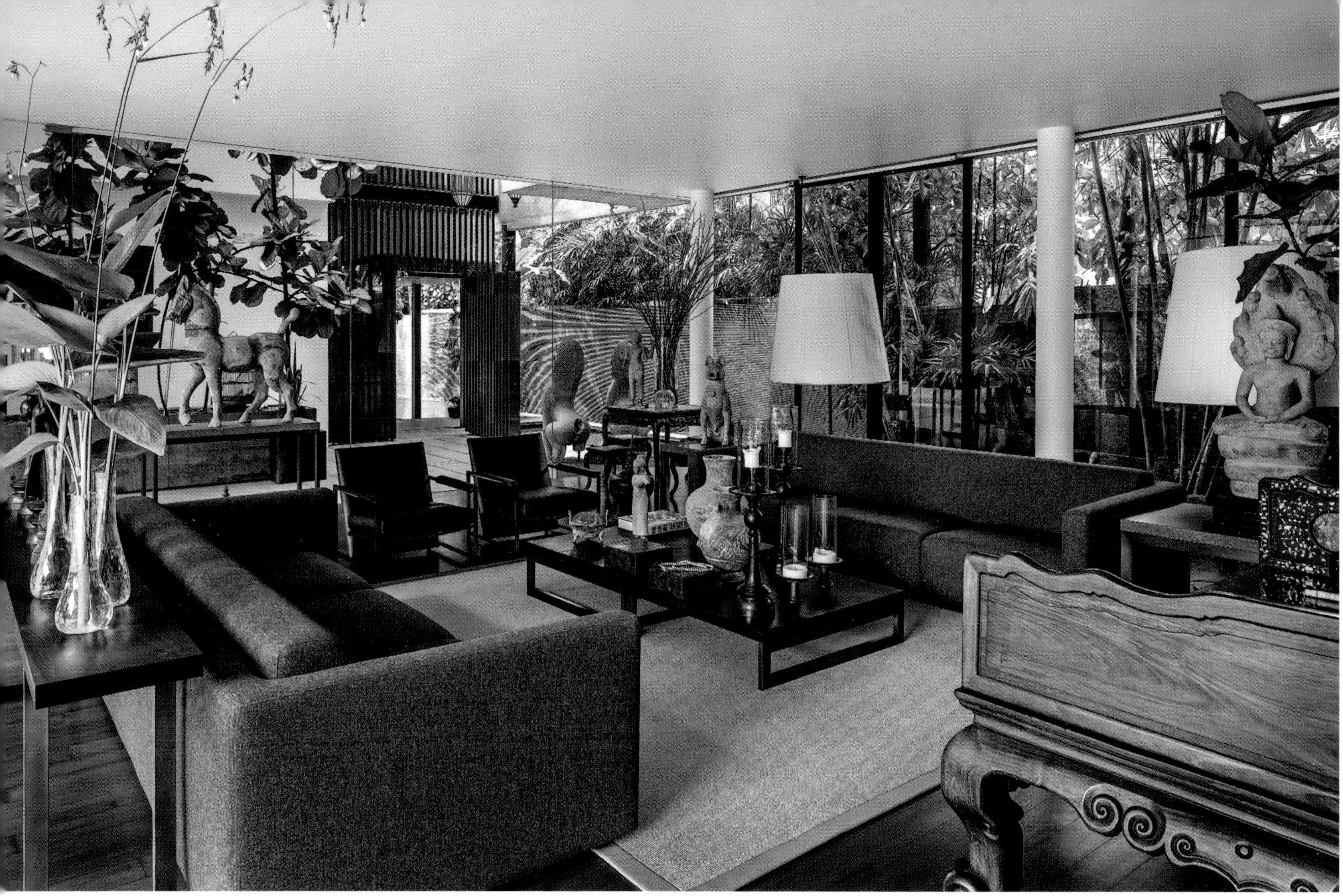

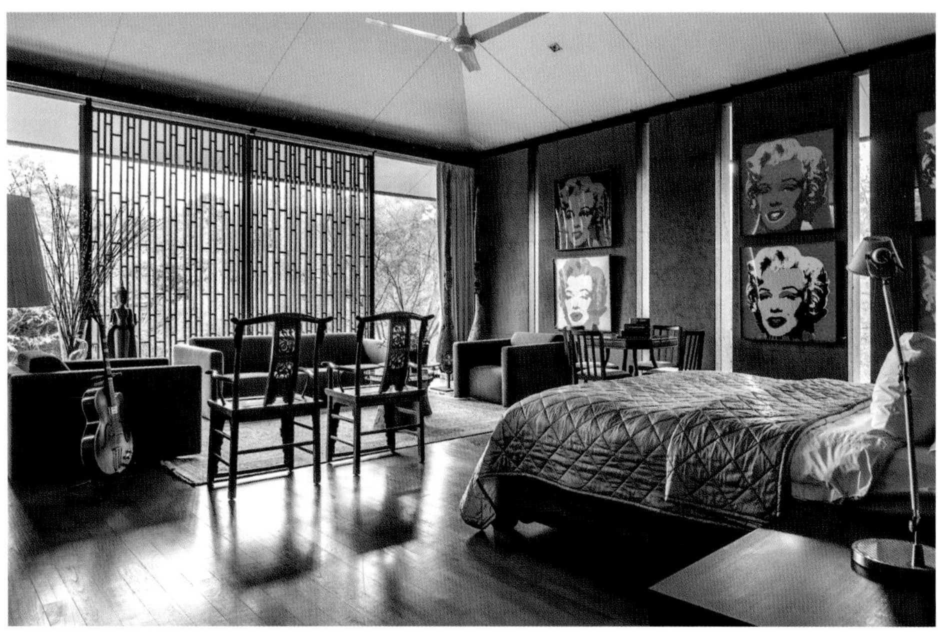

Above Light in the main living room is filtered through the surrounding greenery outside.

Left A bedroom along the connecting wing.

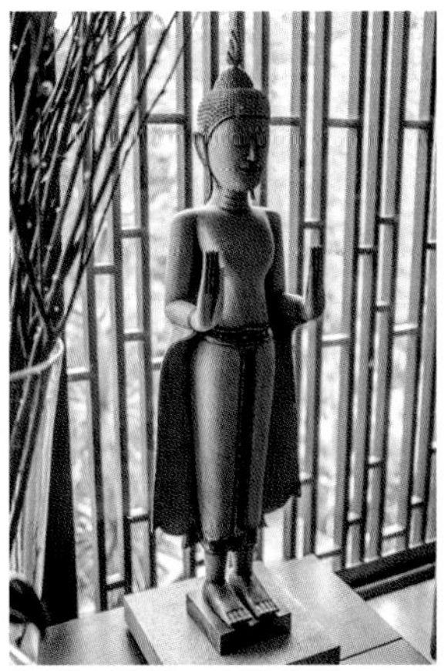

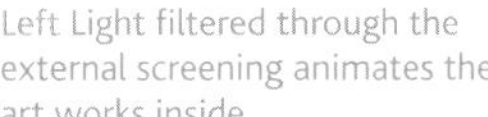

Left Light filtered through the external screening animates the art works inside.

Right The connecting wing is essentially a white frame, with the glazed façade recessed well back for sun protection.

Below At night, concealed lighting brings a magical quality to the garden heart of the house.

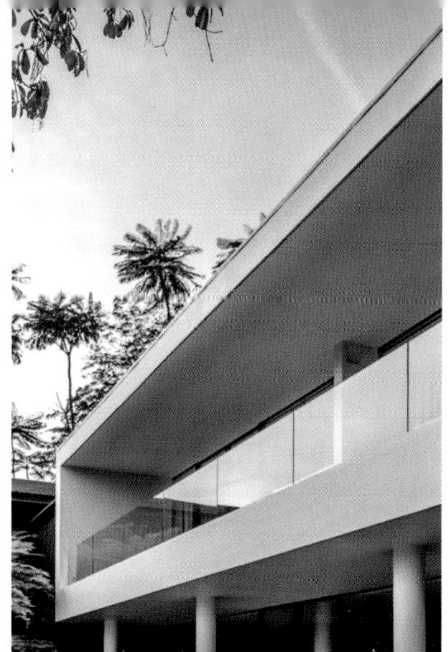

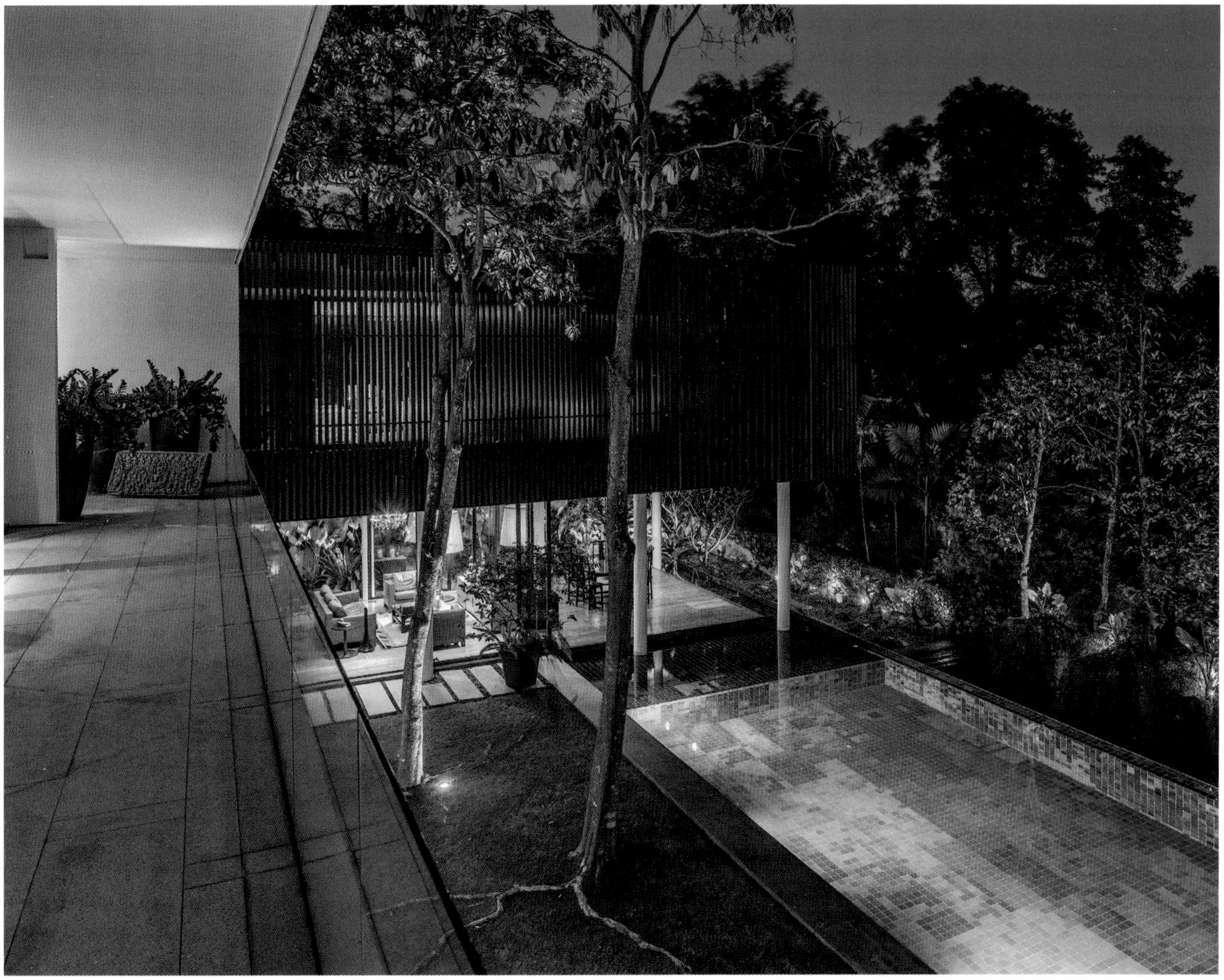

NEIL ROAD SHOPHOUSE
EXPERIENCE DESIGN STUDIO, ONG&ONG

'The brief was for a place she was truly comfortable with. The question was: How could we create a place where she could feel she had lived forever?'—MARK WEE, ARCHITECT

Below Looking from the entry through the original house, past the two courtyards to the new addition.

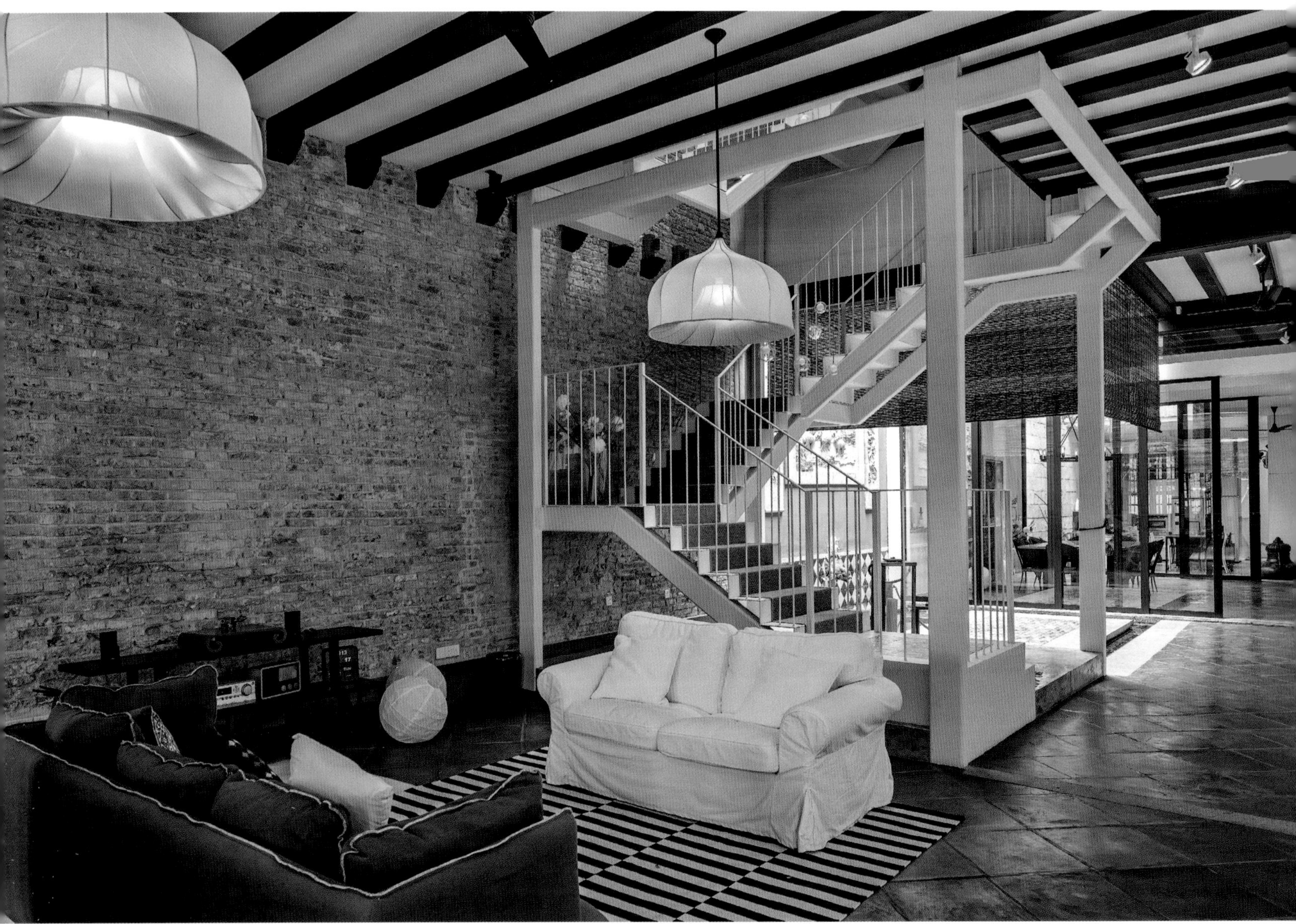

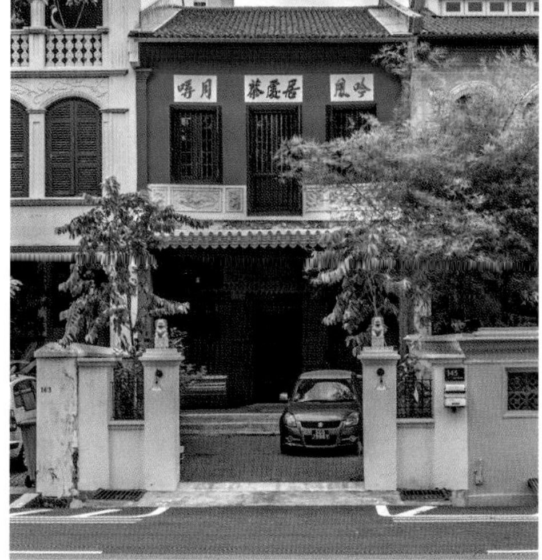

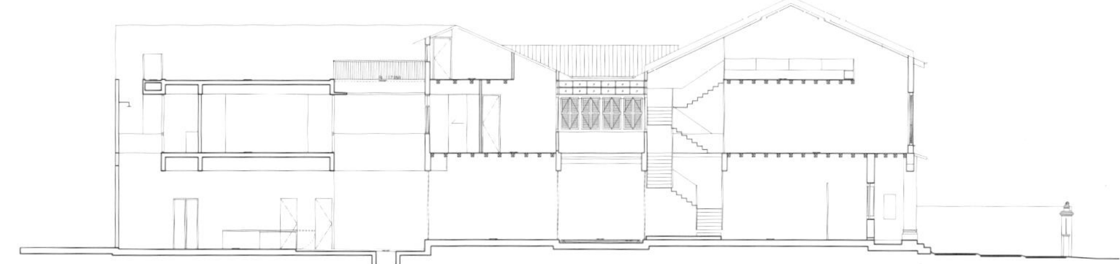

This is a house that addresses sustainability from several perspectives: personal, cultural and environmental. It is one of a strip of conservation shophouses which, in terms of their heritage value, are in the top category because of the historical value of their façade ornamentation. Shophouses in Singapore display a variety of influences (British, Dutch, etc.). This one is undeniably Chinese, dating possibly from the 1860s, and was originally the home and business premises of Straits Chinese (Peranakan) merchants. In fact, another house in this strip (the Baba House at No. 157) was donated to the National University of Singapore who have restored it and now manage it as a museum open to the public.

It has, of course, become highly fashionable among both locals and expatriates in Singapore to try and get hold of shophouses and refurbish them internally (the exterior can only be restored) as contemporary homes. What makes them so attractive? Part of the appeal is that they offer urban living but with a high degree of privacy. At the same time, they offer character along with the opportunity to modernize them without compromising that character. They also cater to that very human need to feel part of some kind of cultural continuity. Finally, because of their organization around an internal lightwell, they provide a natural source of light, fresh air and cooling.

This house had been in the family for over twenty years and the daughter felt a very special attachment to it. When she returned to Singapore to live, she wanted to use it as a home for herself and her family. 'I told Mark,' she says, 'that I didn't want a house, I wanted a home.' The restoration and additions that followed were therefore very much to do with home-making and place-making. The project for Mark Wee and his client was to have the house tell its story through sensitive restoration, including interior features whose restoration was not mandatory, while including all the amenities of a contemporary home.

Part of the strategy was to reveal the historical layering and, at the same time, add to it by using recycled elements as loose furniture, for example,

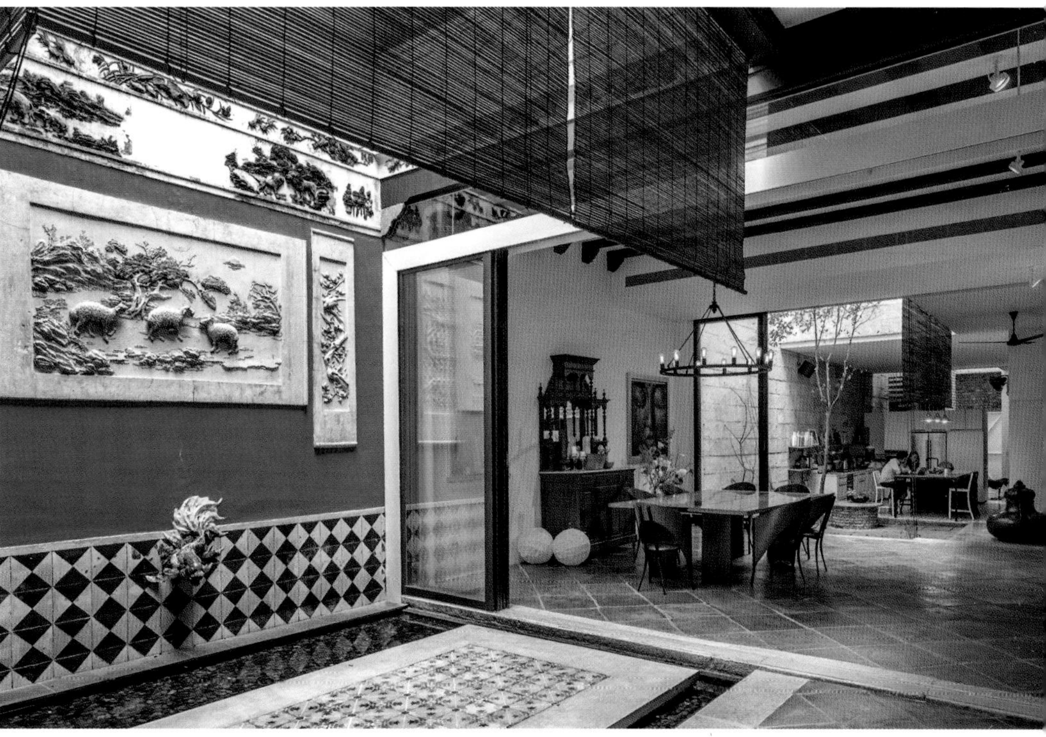

Top left The street façade has been completely restored, including the original brilliant blue colouring.

Top Long section.

Above Beyond the original courtyard is a traditional dining room and a new contemporary kitchen.

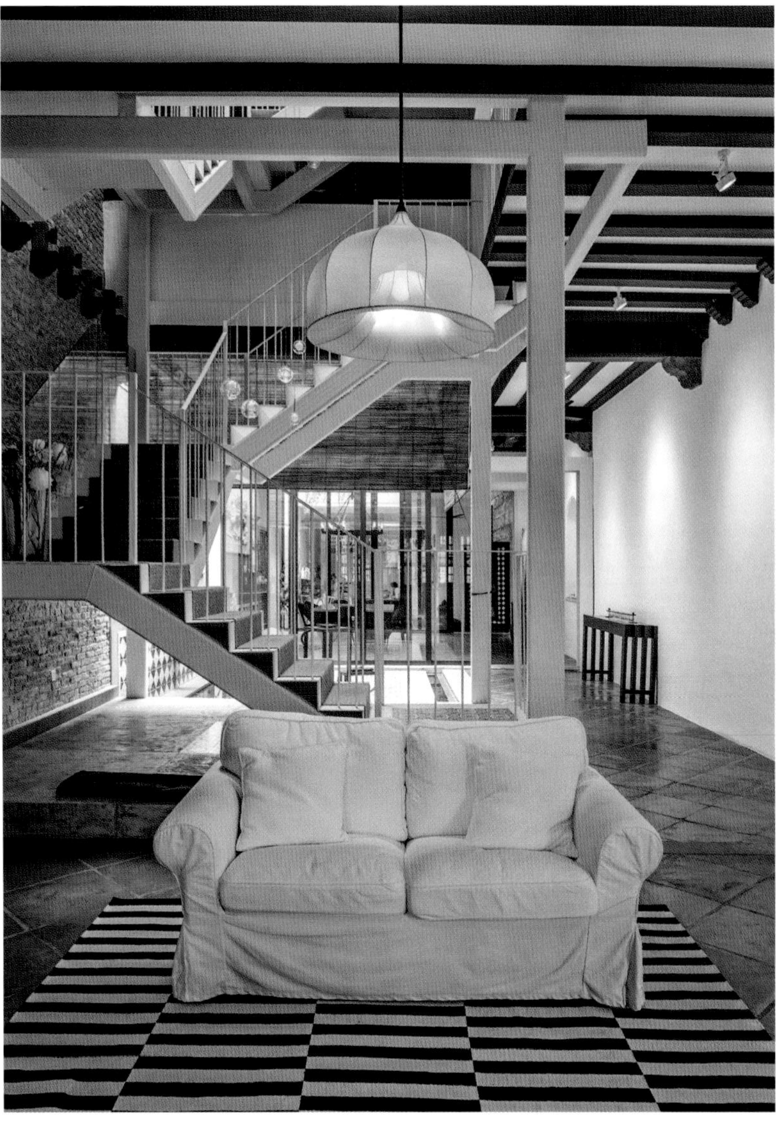

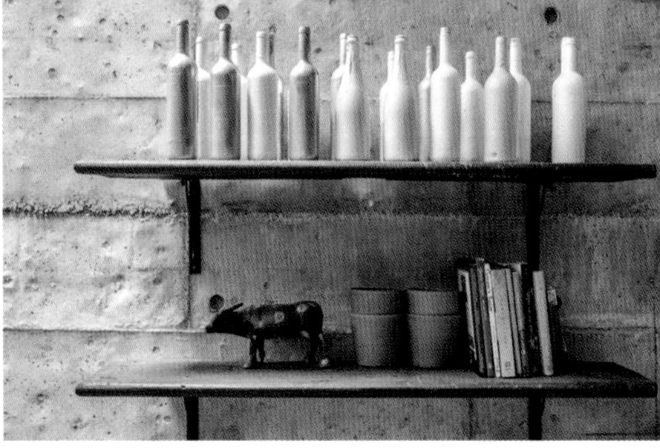

Left Looking from the sitting area near the entry, the new seems to evolve seamlessly out of the old.

Below left Typical of many recycling elements throughout the house are the display shelves made from former stair treads.

Right A new steel stairway connects the ground and upper floors of the original house.

the use of original stair treads as book shelves, and by new structural work which, in its form and materials, complemented the existing house.

This process begins at the street front of the house where, apart from ongoing restoration of the façade ornamentation, the side wall has been stripped back to reveal the old patina. Inside, the traditional screen at the entry to the shophouse has been retained, and in keeping with tradition two mirrors stand guard on either side of the door to trap evil spirits. The plaster has been stripped back to expose the original wire-cut bricks, and the frescoes and remarkable relief sculptures that form part of the original water feature in the lightwell/courtyard have been restored. Upstairs, the original operable timber shutter windows have been retained and restored, as has the original teak flooring.

This is all part of an agenda for cultural sustainability. Key to this is the idea of giving the house a voice and allowing it to tell its story. This story is historical, but it is also a living story that is embodied in the way the house itself is a journey. Wee and his client have now embellished that story with additions that not only add to the functionality of the house but also serve an environmental agenda. Having questioned his client about her childhood memories and about where she spends most of her time, the idea emerged of creating a second enclosed courtyard using the open courtyard land at the rear, which would connect

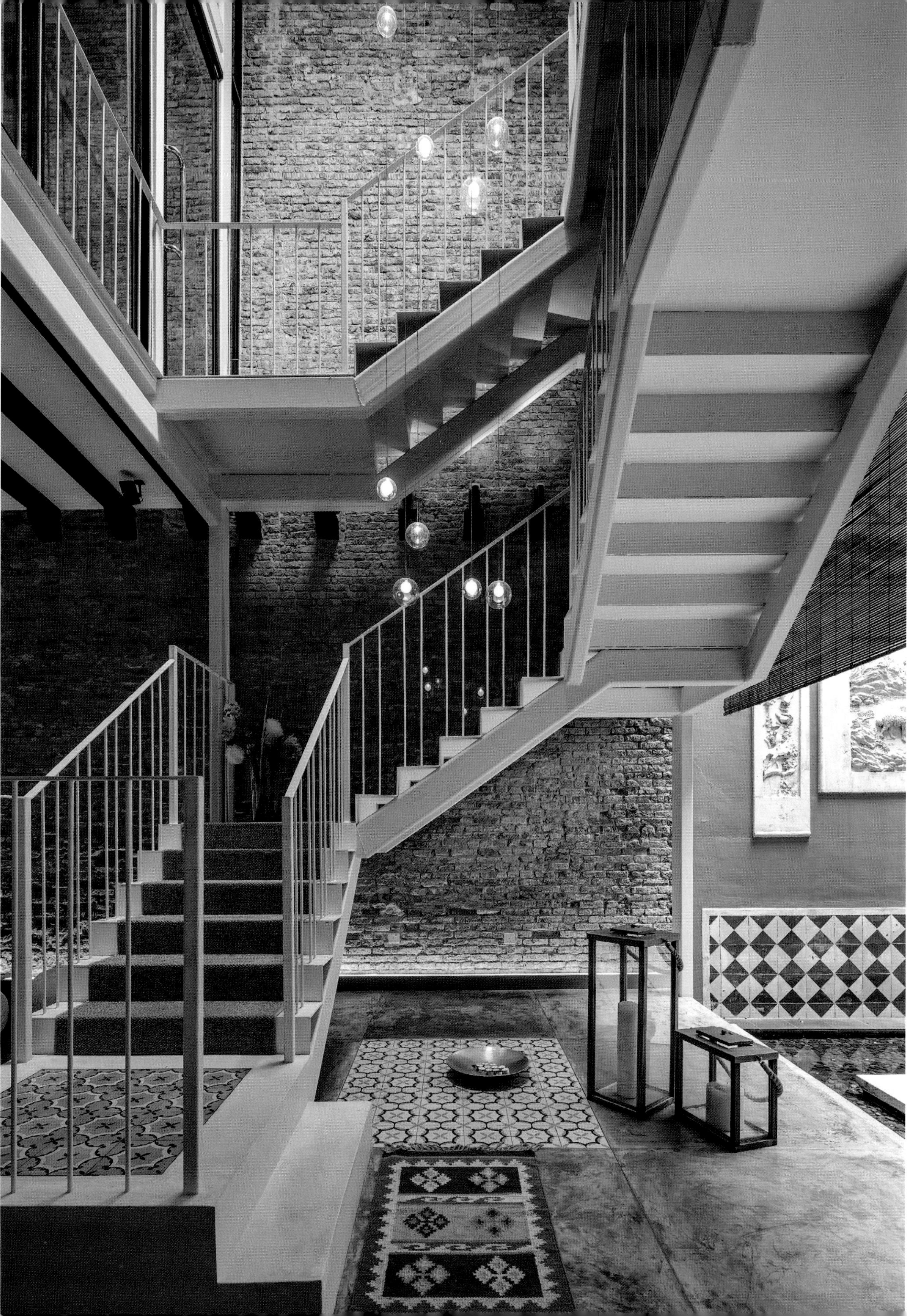

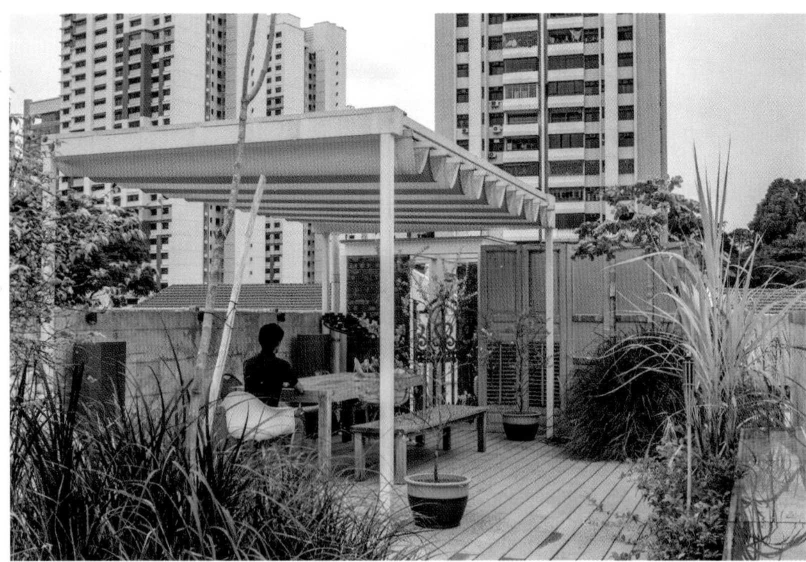

Left The roof garden terrace.

Below The new kitchen looking back across the new second courtyard.

Opposite above left The new master bathroom, partly open to the outside.

Opposite above right The new kitchen with the home office above.

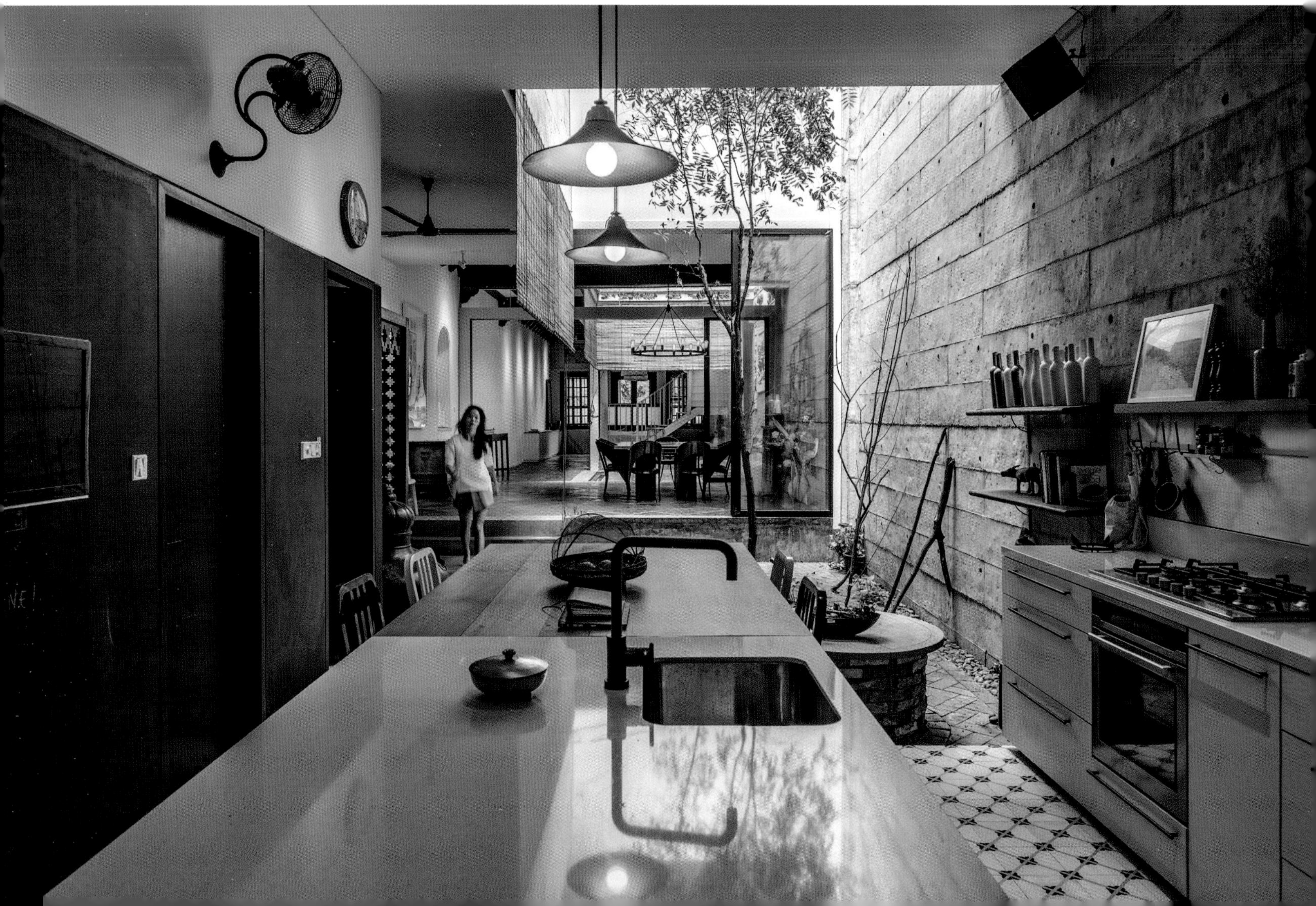

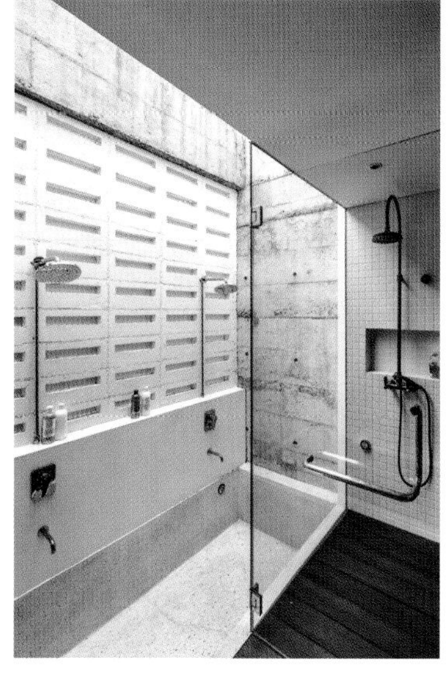

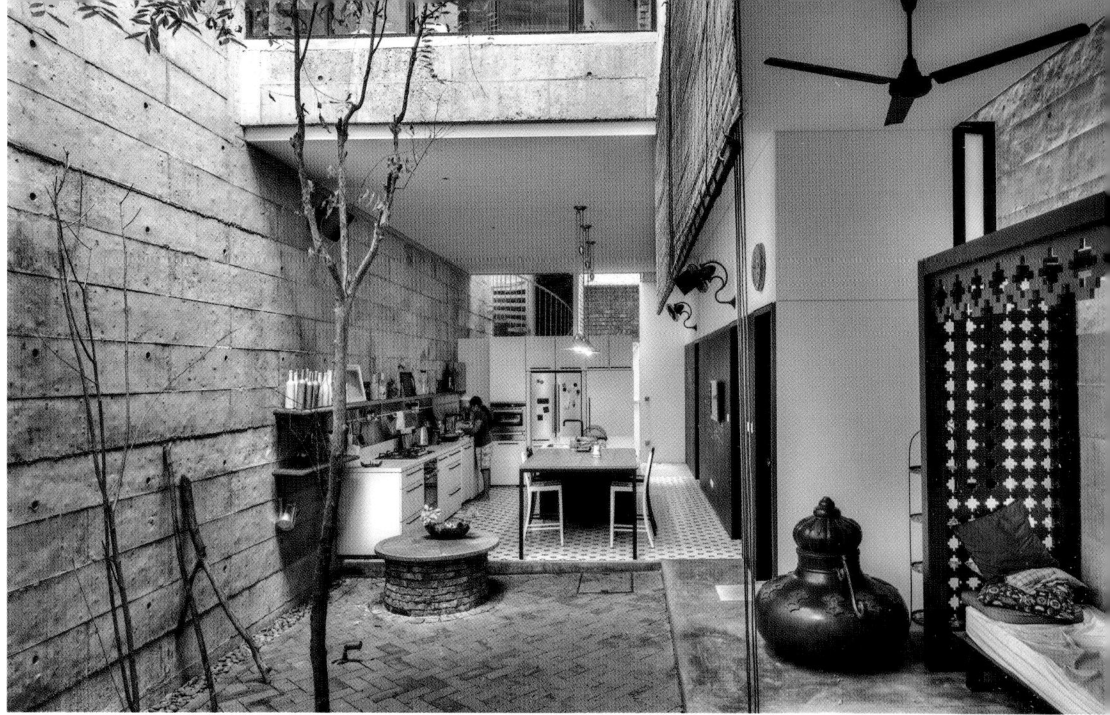

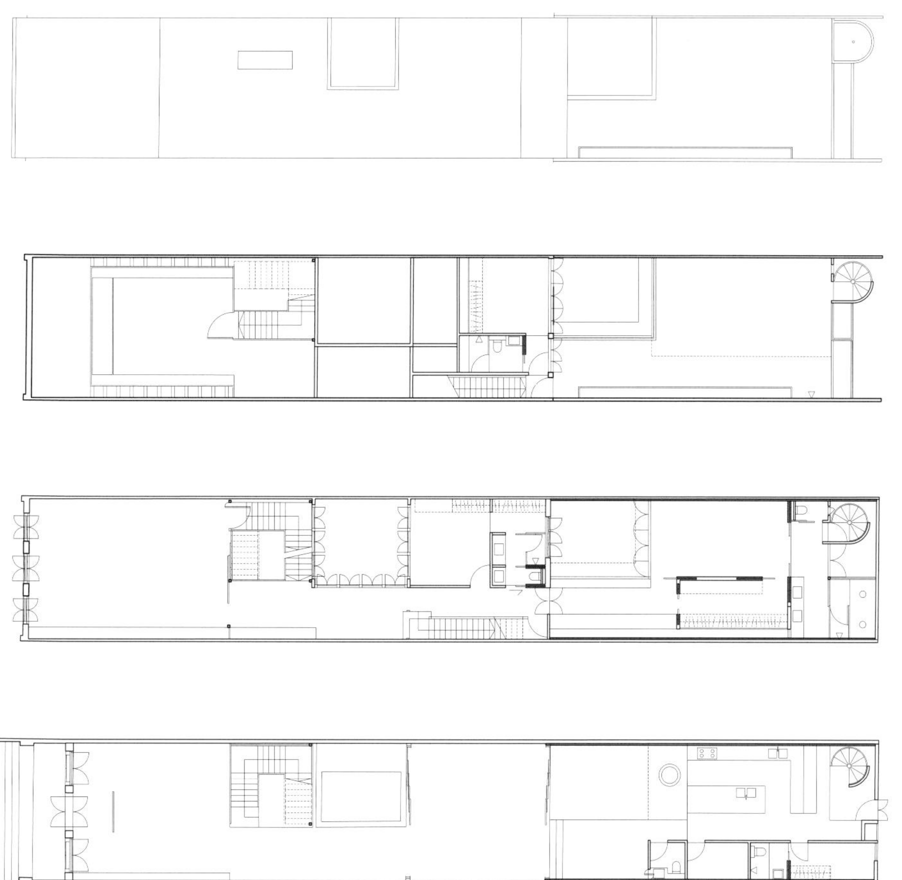

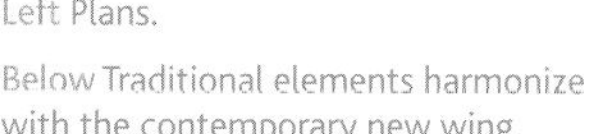

Left Plans.

Below Traditional elements harmonize with the contemporary new wing.

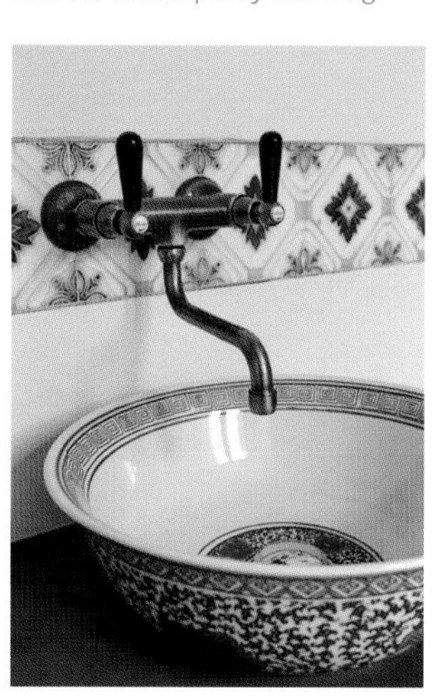

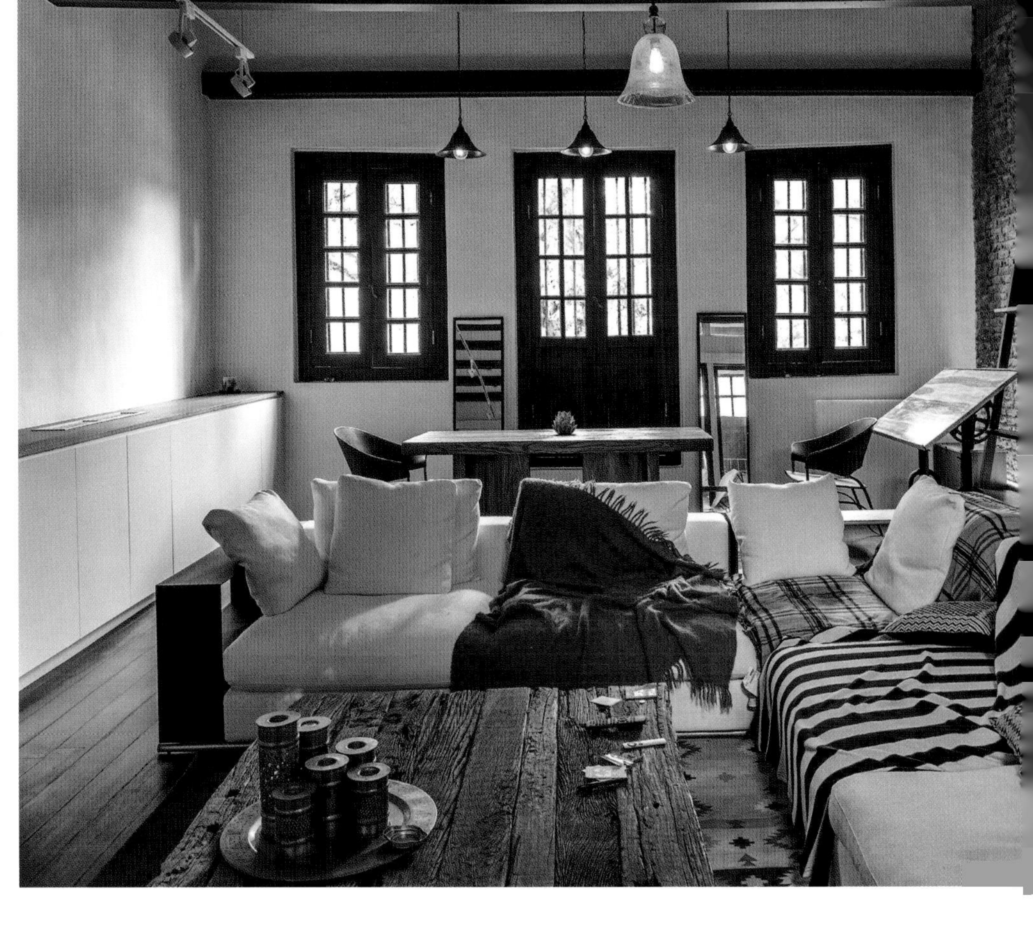

seamlessly with a new kitchen/dining space. The kitchen is now the hub of the house and forms the base of an addition that includes a home office, the master bedroom, a roof garden and an attic above, all linked by a supplementary staircase (there is a new steel stairway linking levels in the original front part of the house).

The new courtyard draws in further light and air, minimizing the need for air-conditioning. It also sets up layers of transparency through the house by adding to a network of transition spaces. In fact, at nearly every point in the house it is possible to see the rest of the house, creating constant visual stimulation and a sense of how the house comes together as a family of spaces.

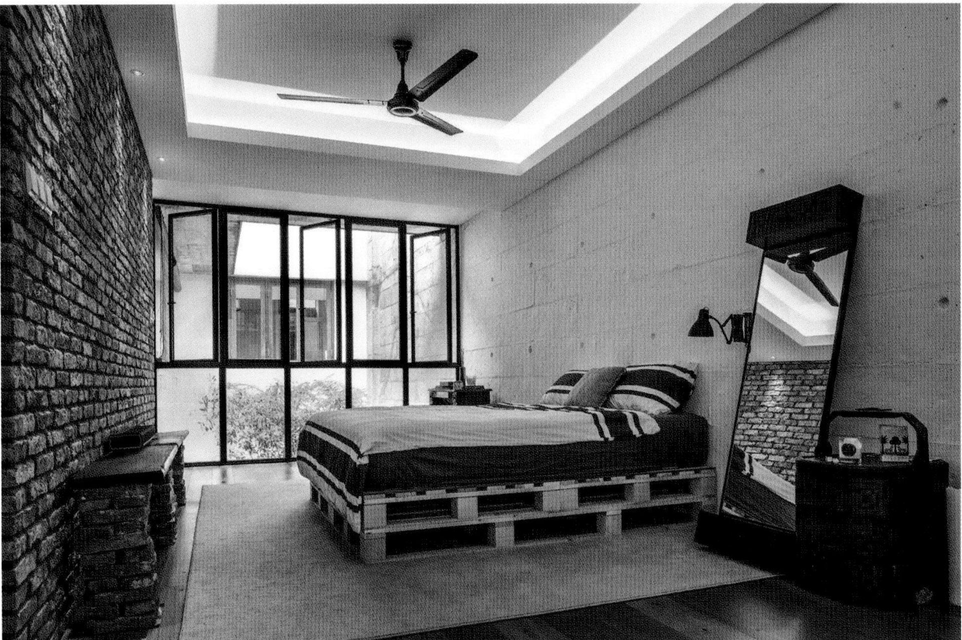

More light is drawn into the house by a skylight down the side wall. This draws light into every level, including the walk-in wardrobe of the master bedroom, also notable for its wall of recycled bricks and the inside–outside shower in the en suite.

The house now has clearly demarcated functional areas. The original part includes an entry lobby on the first level, a library and TV room on the second level and the husband's study at the top. The ground floor is now one extended communal space, culminating in the kitchen, with private areas in the upper levels of the addition.

This house exemplifies a programme of what might be called holistic sustainability. It is environmentally responsive in both its passive climate control and in its preference for recycling. But it also sustains a sense of identity by nourishing personal and cultural continuity without compromising the fact that it is a contemporary home.

Below Upstairs, a corridor links the old and new wings. The stairs lead to the guest bedroom in the attic.

Bottom The original courtyard is surrounded on the second level by restored timber shutters.

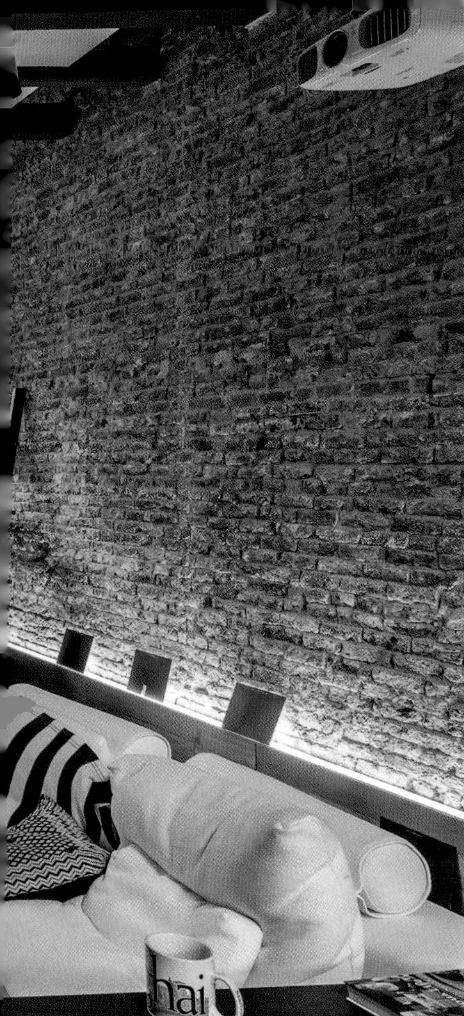

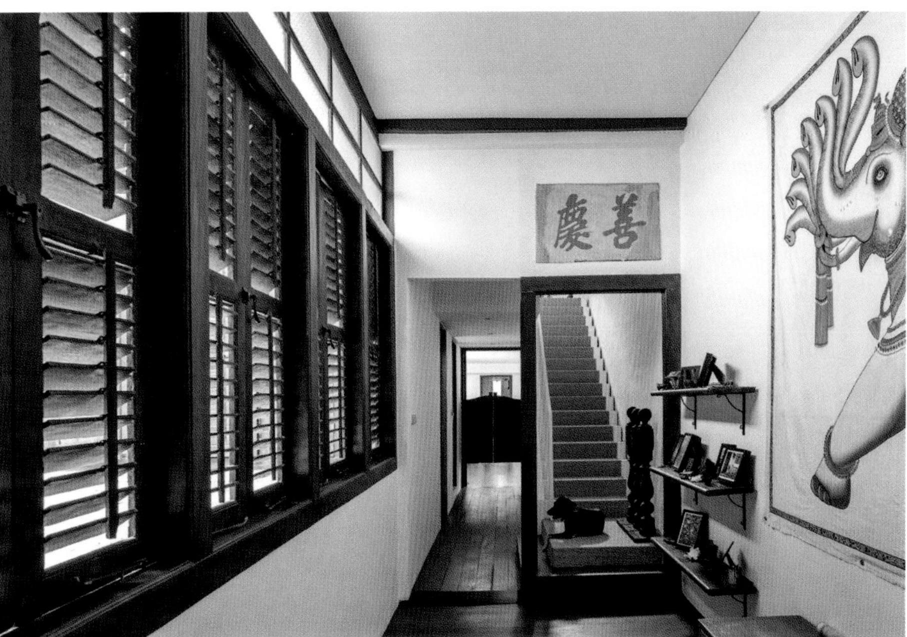

Above The entertainment room upstairs in the original house has a brick feature wall and restored fenestration.

Left The master bedroom upstairs in the addition combines the contemporary with antique and recycled elements.

Below Restored original brickwork contrasts with modern materials.

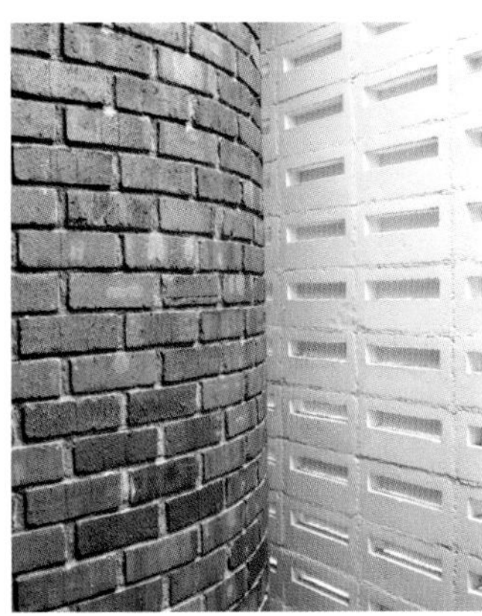

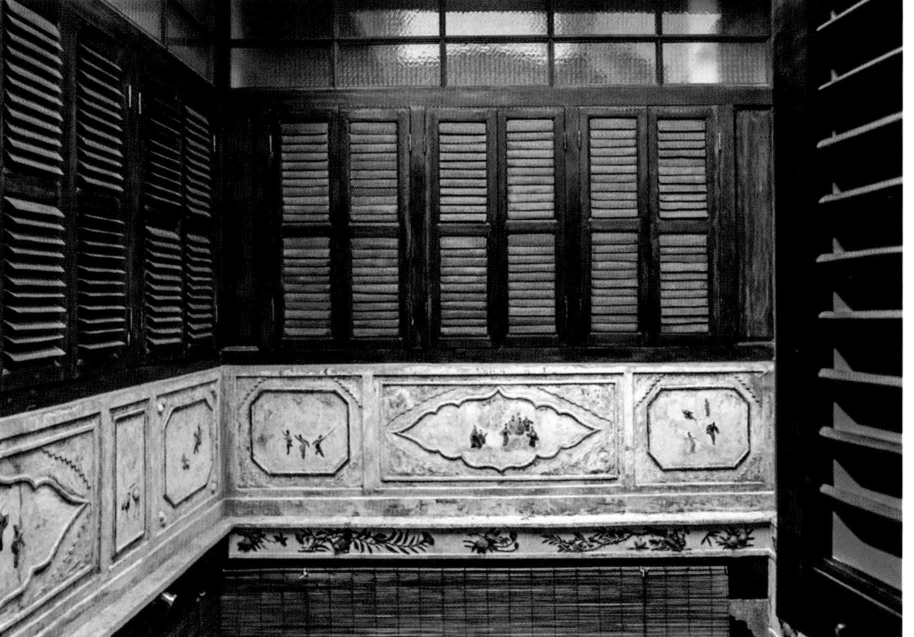

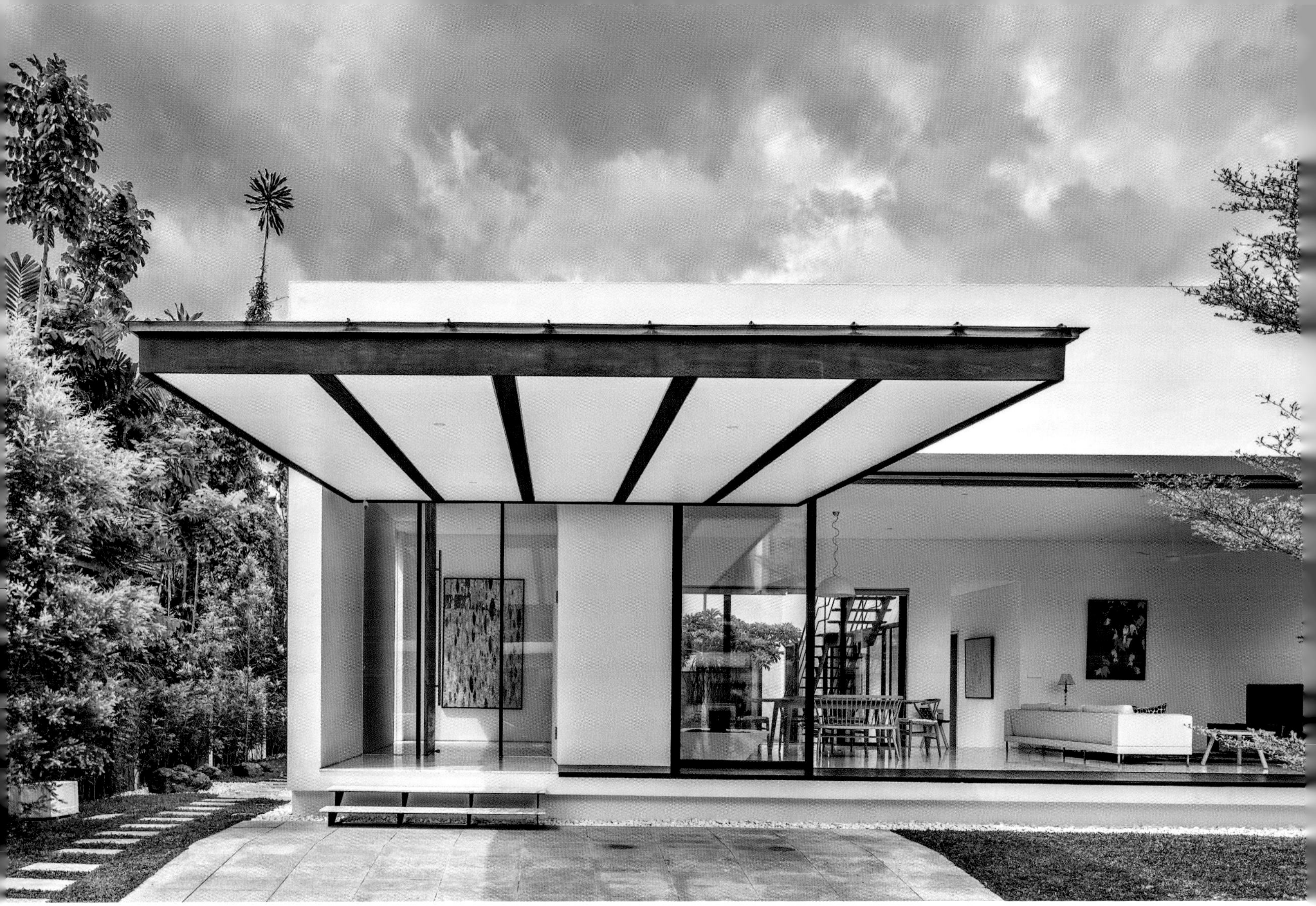

MANDAI COURTYARD HOUSE
ATELIER M+A

'The idea of an outdoor space inside the house came from the Chinese shophouse. This brings light and air into the building, although typically they are closed-up buildings and hence very dark except around the courtyard. But this idea was suited to the climate of Singapore.'—MASAKI HARIMOTO, ARCHITECT

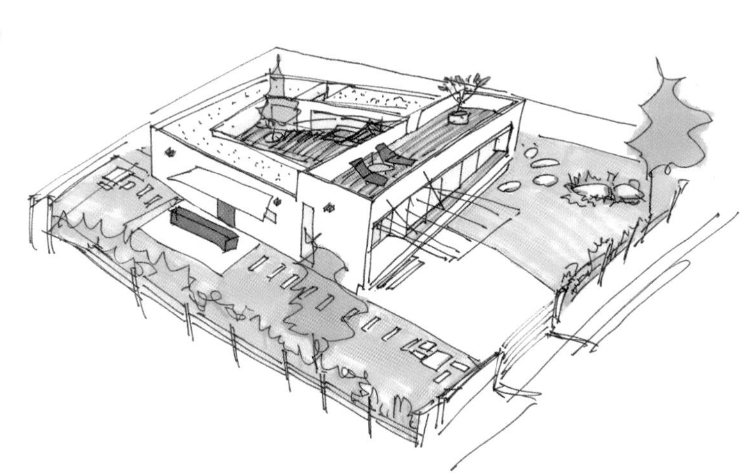

Left The street façade has a massive overhang protecting the entry.

Below left Perspective of the house and its context.

Right A flight of stairs in the courtyard leads to the rooftop entertainment area.

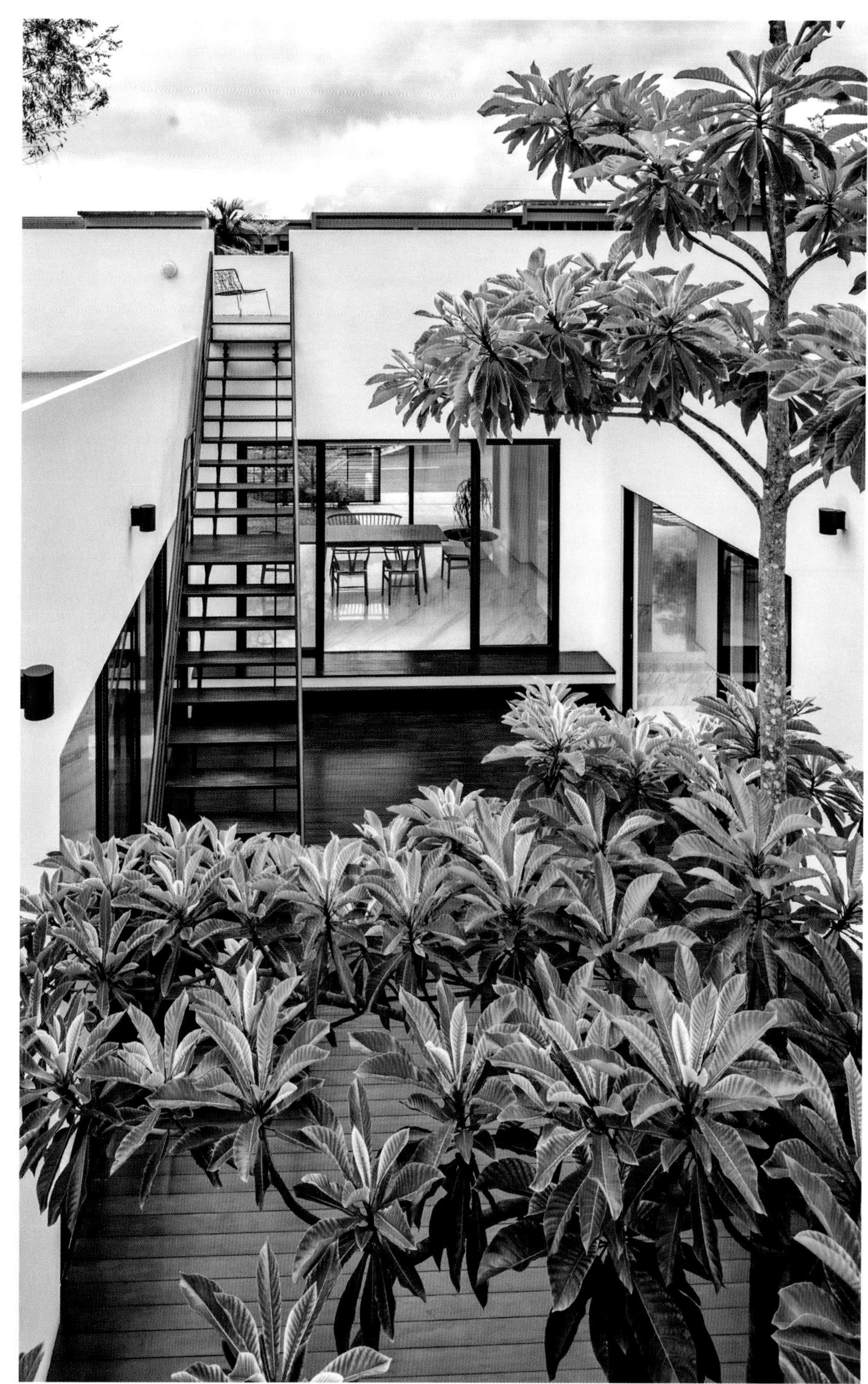

The area around the Upper Seletar reservoir is leafy, with a sense of tranquillity that contrasts with the rest of bustling Singapore. In a place where land is scarce and expensive, it is perhaps not surprising that most Singaporeans who can afford a landed house want to maximize the buildable area. Atelier M+A's client was unusual. A single lady, she did not want a large, two-storey house. Instead, she wanted a single-level house where she could stay in touch with nature while enjoying adequate security and feel connected with the neighbourhood. Her other requirements were ample and free-flowing spaces for entertaining and a minimal need for air-conditioning; only the bedrooms and walk-in wardrobes have it.

All white with black window frames, the house subtly references the colonial black-and-white houses of Singapore. Set on a slight rise, the house is, in the architect's words, 'doughnut-shaped', with its rooms organized around a five-metre-wide central courtyard adorned by a single tree. A second, smaller (one-metre-wide) courtyard leads off the master bedroom and airs the en suite bathroom. The organization of the house enables every room to open on to the central courtyard through sliding glass doors, creating a single, flowing space. Peripheral doorways and windows can be locked to secure the house. From the timber deck of the central courtyard, a staircase leads up to an entertainment deck above the living/dining space.

The white minimalist aesthetic of the house is complemented by the warmth of timber. The exterior timber, including the huge 3.2-metre-high ceremonial entry door, is the sustainable, long-life Accoya whose grain contrasts well with the white rendered walls. Accoya is also used for the timber grilles on the bedroom windows which, with mosquito netting, can be left open for air flow.

Architect Masaki Harimoto makes up one half of Atelier M+A. The other half is Ng Ai Hwa from Malaysia. He comes from Japan and an understated Japanese aesthetic informs the whole house, from the 'Japanese' rocks found on site and positioned strategically down the side gardens to the beautiful interior detailing using shadow grooves where walls meet ceilings and joinery. This aesthetic also informs the arrival sequence, where a 5 x 5-metre canopy shelters the entry, not touching the walls but apparently floating (suspended by two wire struts) without solid boundary walls (just cables and plantings), its soffit feathered by fine timber strips.

Right A view through the living/dining pavilion to the interior courtyard.

Below right The transparency of the house is highlighted at night.

Below The raised timber deck or *engawa* outside the living/dining space.

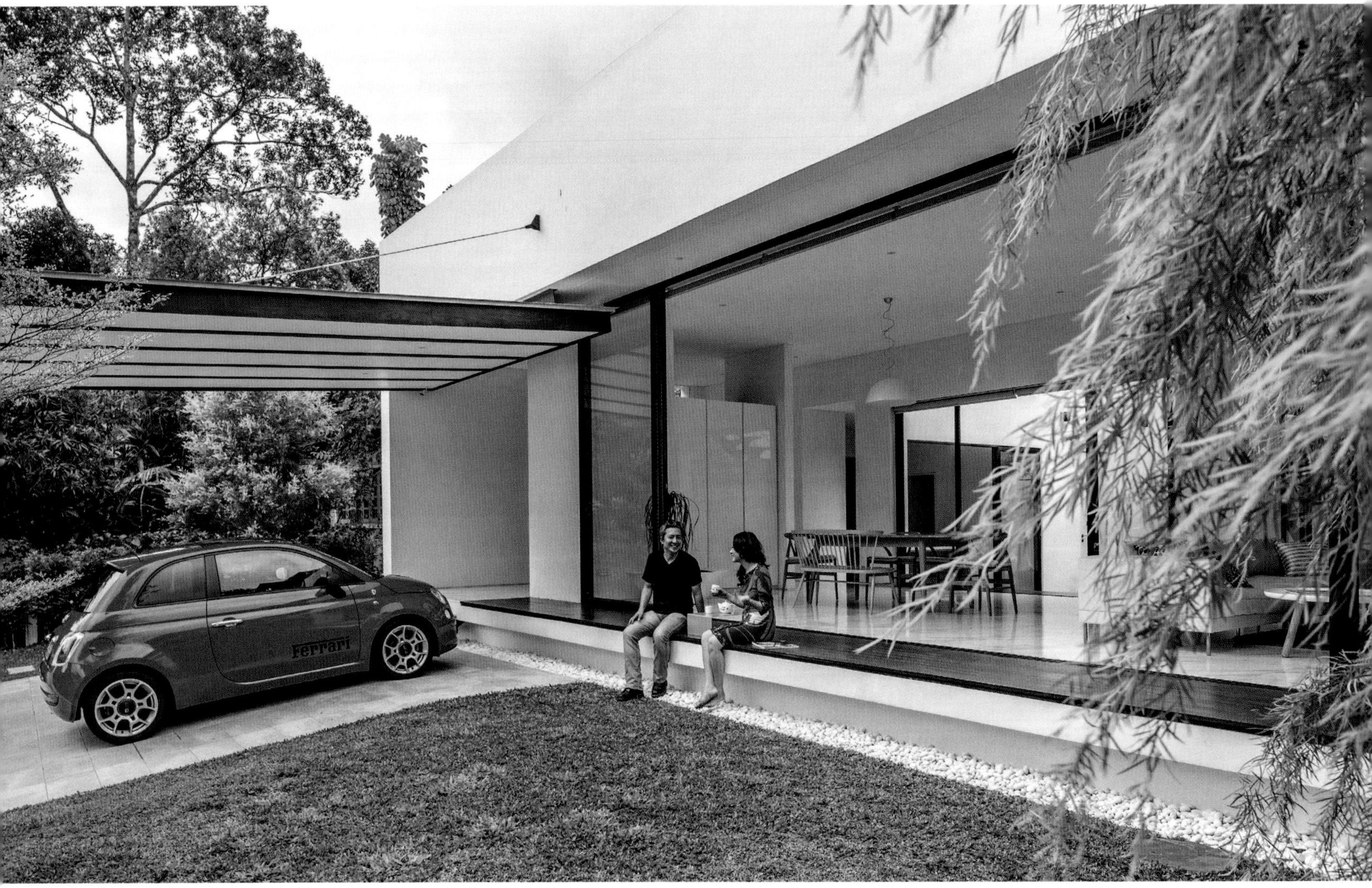

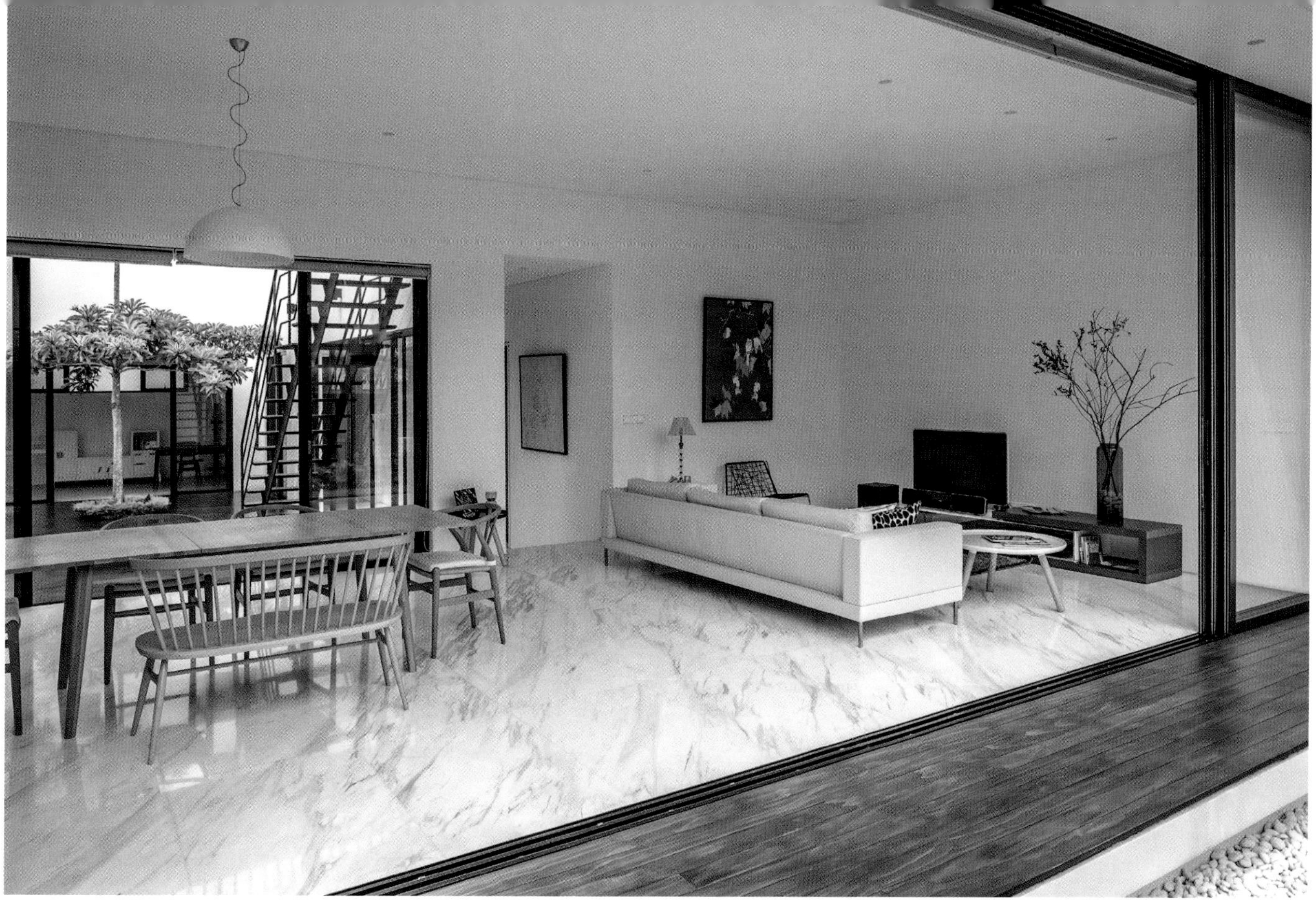

The front of the house consists of the living/dining space, fully glazed to allow total transparency and a spatial continuum from inside to out. This space sits like a glass pavilion, slightly raised above street level. Outside, a floating timber deck runs from wall to wall. This acts as a transitional space between inside and outside, much like the traditional Japanese *engawa*. But it is equally reminiscent of the raised outdoor sitting place found throughout Asia where—as happens at this house—people commune together in an informal way while looking out over the neighbourhood.

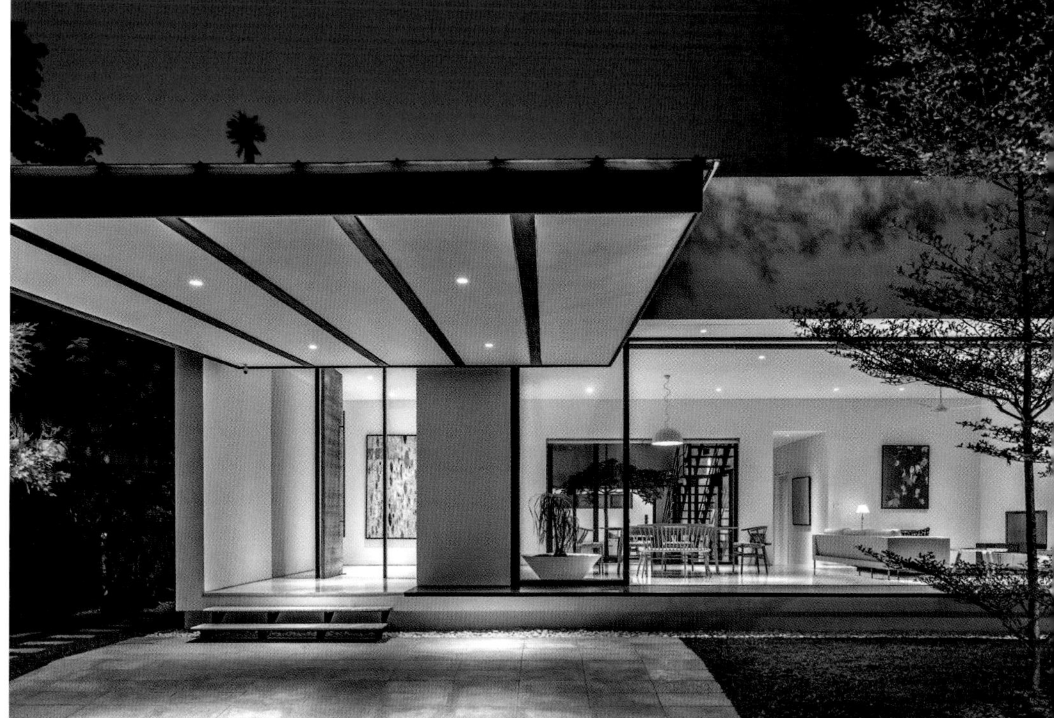

This is a house of contrasts and complementarities. Its modernist credentials are unapologetic, even down to the De Stijl-like colour accents in the laundry and wet kitchen area. Yet, there is a warmth to the way the black steel and dark timber of the decks, stairs and grilles relates to the white render. Likewise, there is a reassuring modesty to the scale of this house, which not only makes it feel very habitable but also makes it a 'good neighbour' in that it does not impose itself on the street but

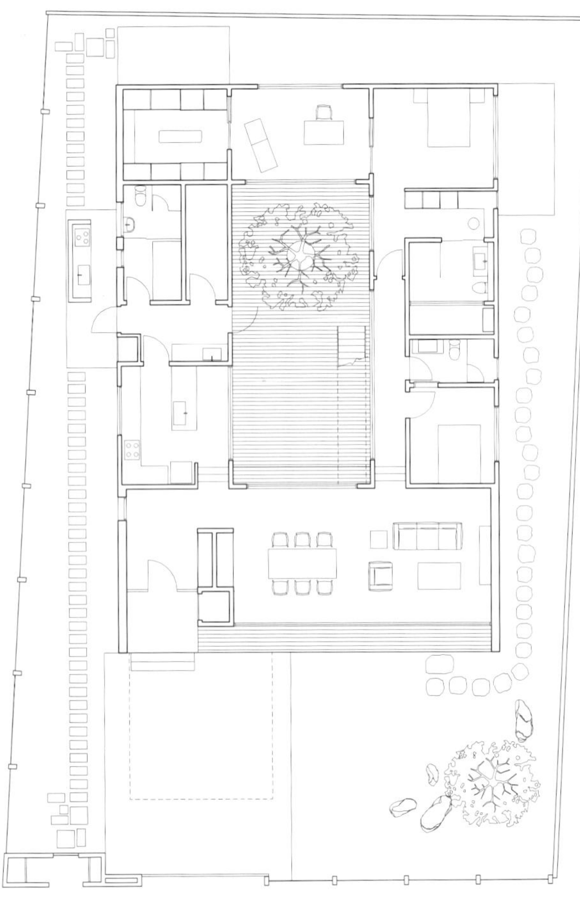

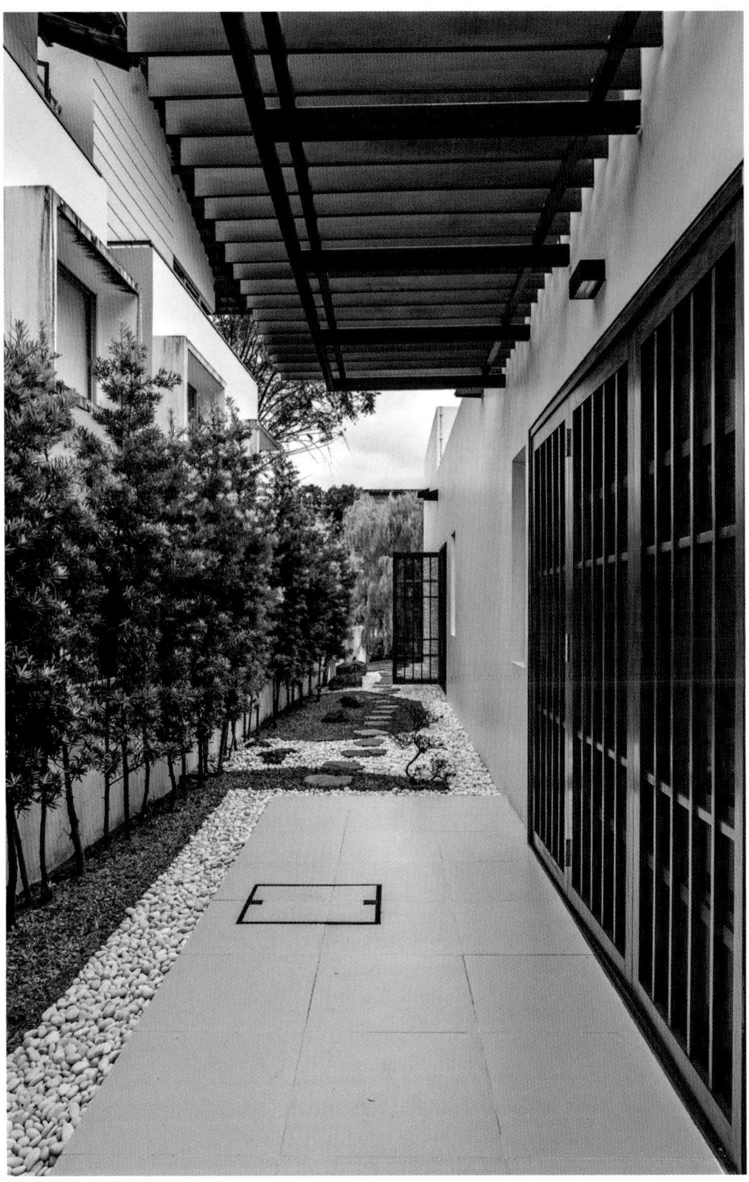

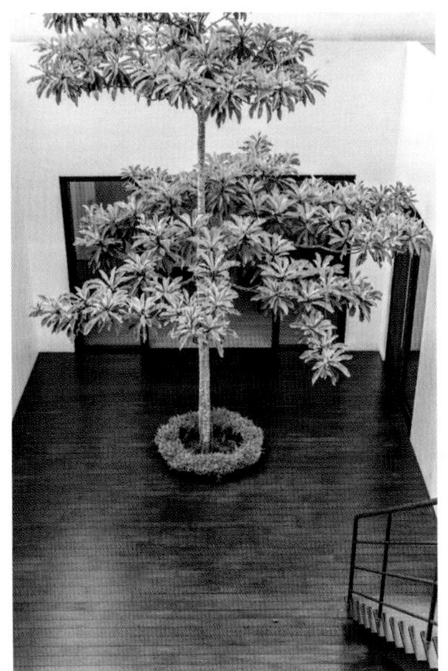

Above left Plan.

Above An extended courtyard runs along the bedroom wing, which is accessed through the timber screen doors.

Left The single tree in the central courtyard brings greenery to the interior but also emphasizes the simplicity of the house.

Opposite above The internal courtyard looking from the living/dining pavilion.

Opposite below The internal courtyard, with stairs to the roof terrace and a view through to the guest bedroom.

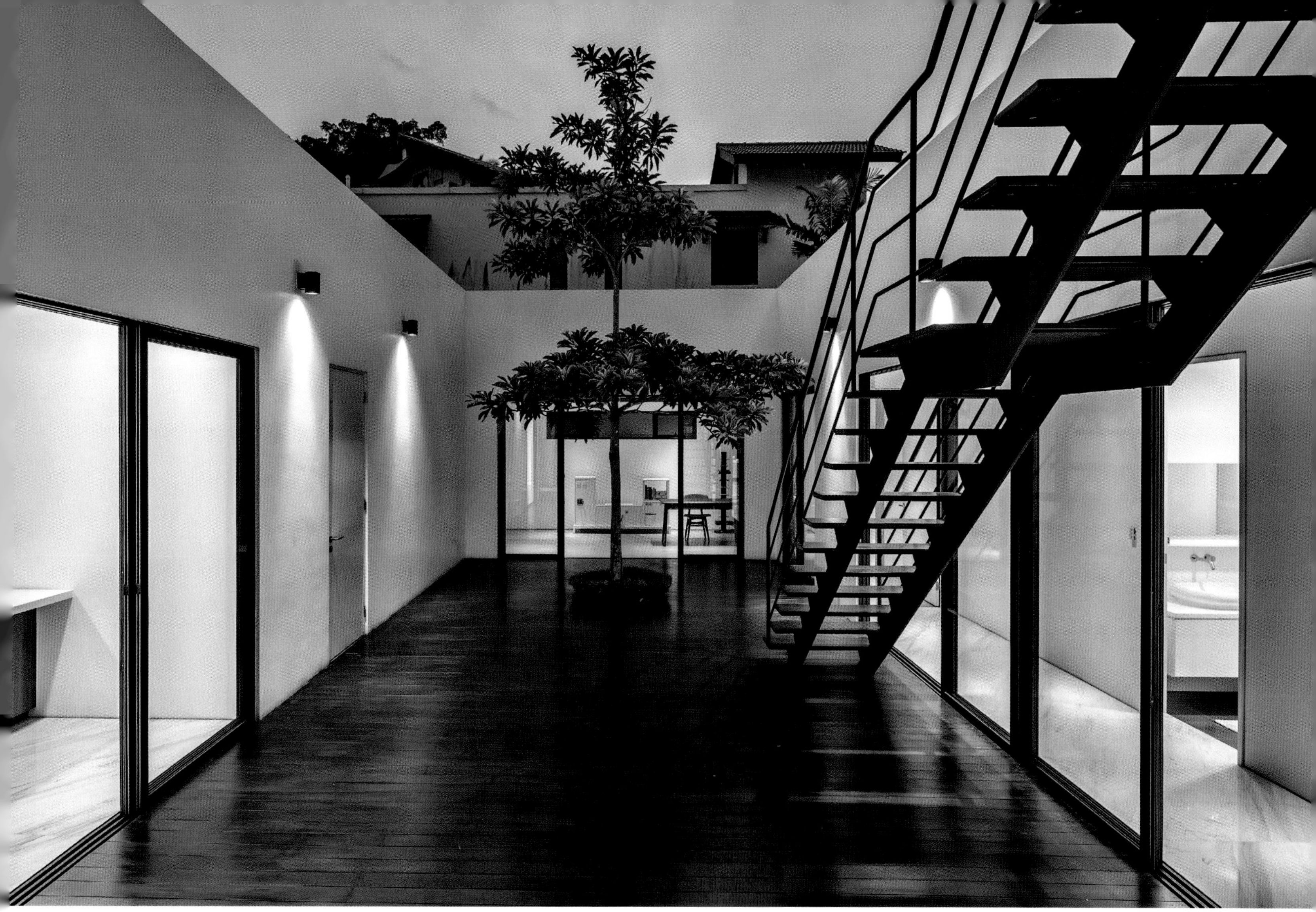

blends in with the environment. Despite its bold modernity, the house relates well to its context. The fact that it is different animates the street, as does its transparency. Far from turning its back on the street, the house engages with it.

How is this a sustainable house? It is clearly sustainable in the way it cross-ventilates, passively cools itself and draws light into its shallow volume; artificial lighting is never required during the day. But it is also socially sustainable in the way it engages with its immediate neighbours through a sympathetic scale and through its transparency and its *engawa*, which facilitate an easy and neighbourly communality.

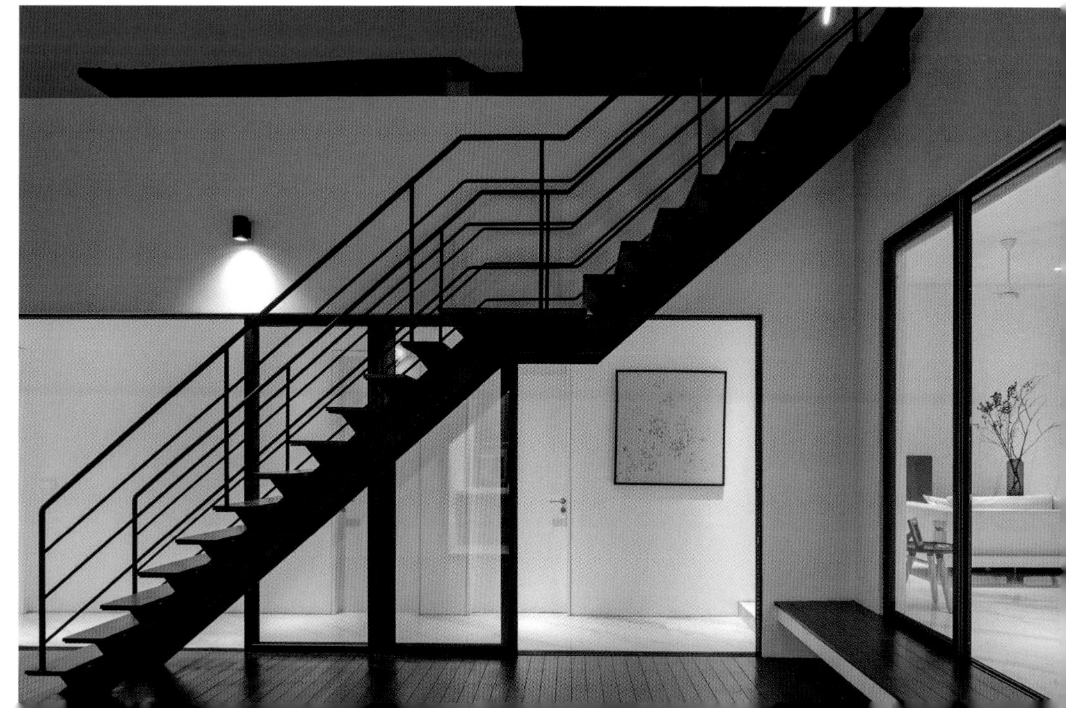

NAMLY DRIVE HOUSE
CHANG ARCHITECTS

'He wanted two homes in one house. He wanted privacy but also ways for interaction. That was quite a challenge for me.'
—CHANG YONG TER, ARCHITECT

This house won the 2013 World Architecture Festival Award for Best Villa and a Design Award at the 2013 Singapore Institute of Architects awards. It is easy to see why. It is an endlessly fascinating house with a spatial richness that belies the relatively small plot size. It is also a deliciously beautiful house, full of nooks and crannies, which mixes intimacy with sensational views.

The house is a highly imaginative response to the challenge of multi-generational housing where the problem is invariably how to be 'separate but together'. At the same time, it is a wonderful

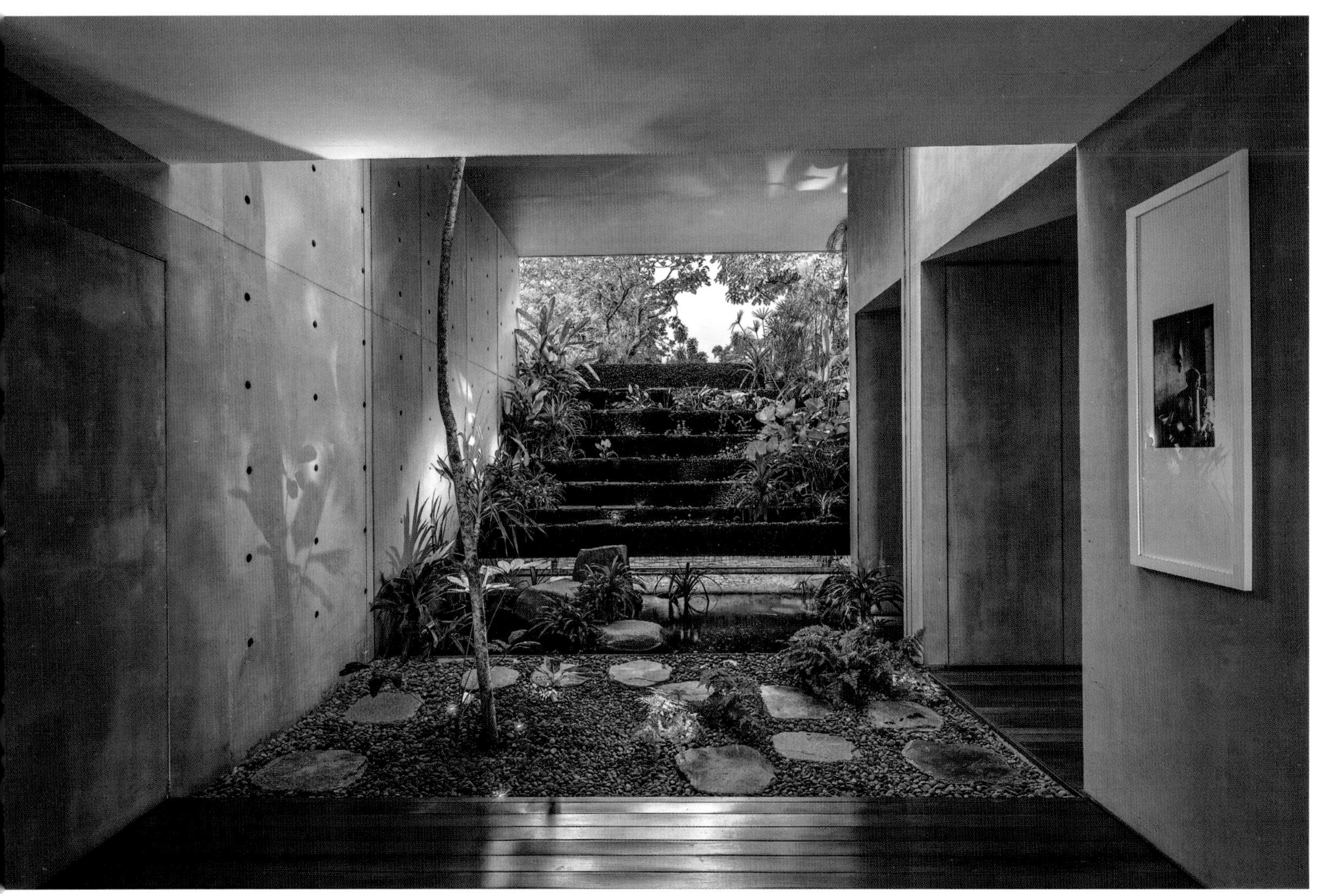

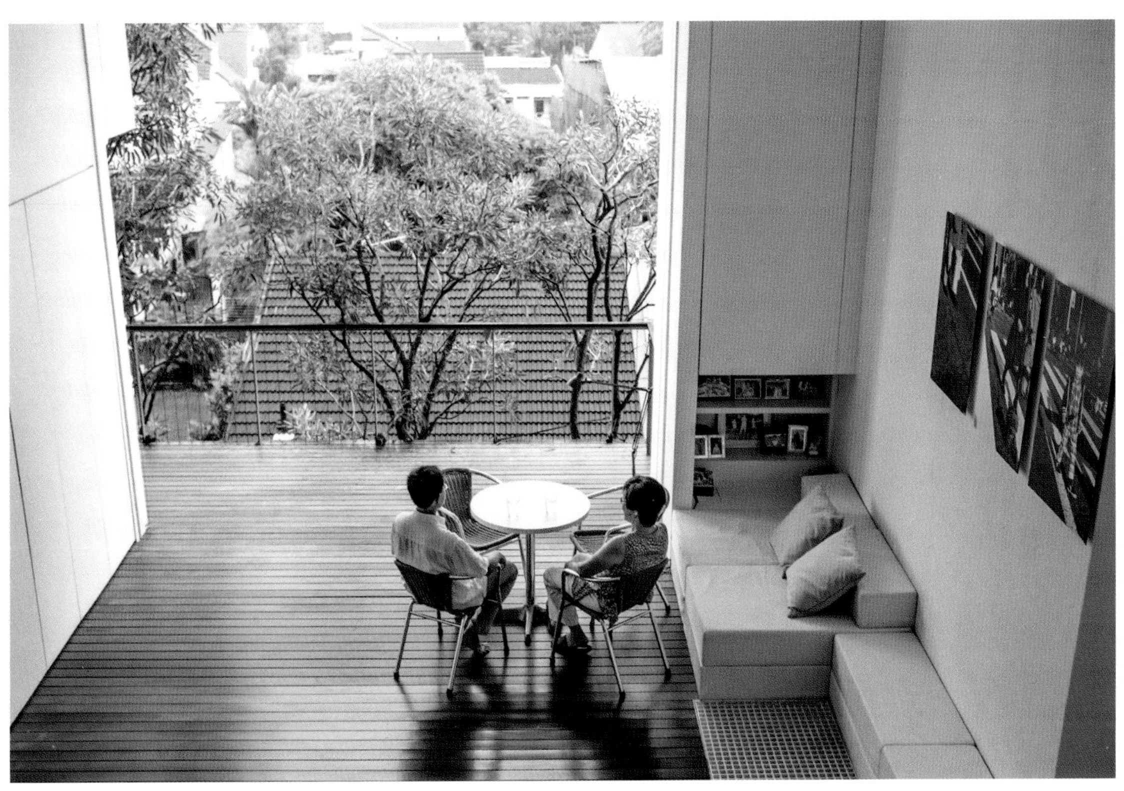

Opposite Seen from the dining room, the water garden is visually calming while also providing natural ventilation.

Left The terrace sitting room enjoys panoramic views and draws in plenty of natural light.

Below The driveway and carport, which has its own rooftop garden.

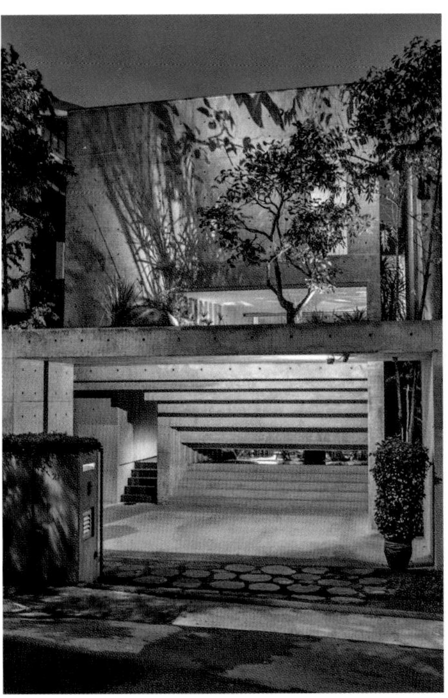

celebration of living in a tropical climate—of living *with* the climate rather than railing against it.

The clients are grandparents of three children, including twins. They had already decided to retire in Penang, but when the twins came along they reconsidered their plans and decided to retire in Singapore to be close to the children and to support their parents who both lead busy professional lives. They asked Chang Yong Ter to look at their Penang house to get a feel of how they liked to live. Coincidentally, the two sites were similar in that both sat on high ground with panoramic views over the neighbourhood. The clients wanted a concrete house and privacy at the front and down the side where the neighbours are very close.

The use of concrete has led to some virtuoso counterpointing of finished and off-form concrete. At the front, the house presents almost as a bunker, giving little away, but is softened by the garden on top of the carport, with a dracaena tree snaking up through the roof from inside the house. The porch itself is like a telegraphed 'ziggurat', with stepped concrete retreating back to an open slot, beyond which is a lush garden. This glimpse of something beyond the house façade sets up a mood of anticipation, which is teased out by the indirect arrival sequence—to the side, over a timber walkway and into a vestibule before turning right into what seems like a tropical paradise.

What we had glimpsed from the outside is finally revealed as a verdant tropical garden with water cascading into a koi pond. To the left, the house unfolds through a central 'thoroughfare' with dining area, sitting room and expansive elevated deck with panoramic views. This water garden is not just wonderful to look at and calming to hear, but with its large, slightly splayed slot opening it also plays a major role in cooling the house because it draws in prevailing winds over the water and greenery to naturally cool the house.

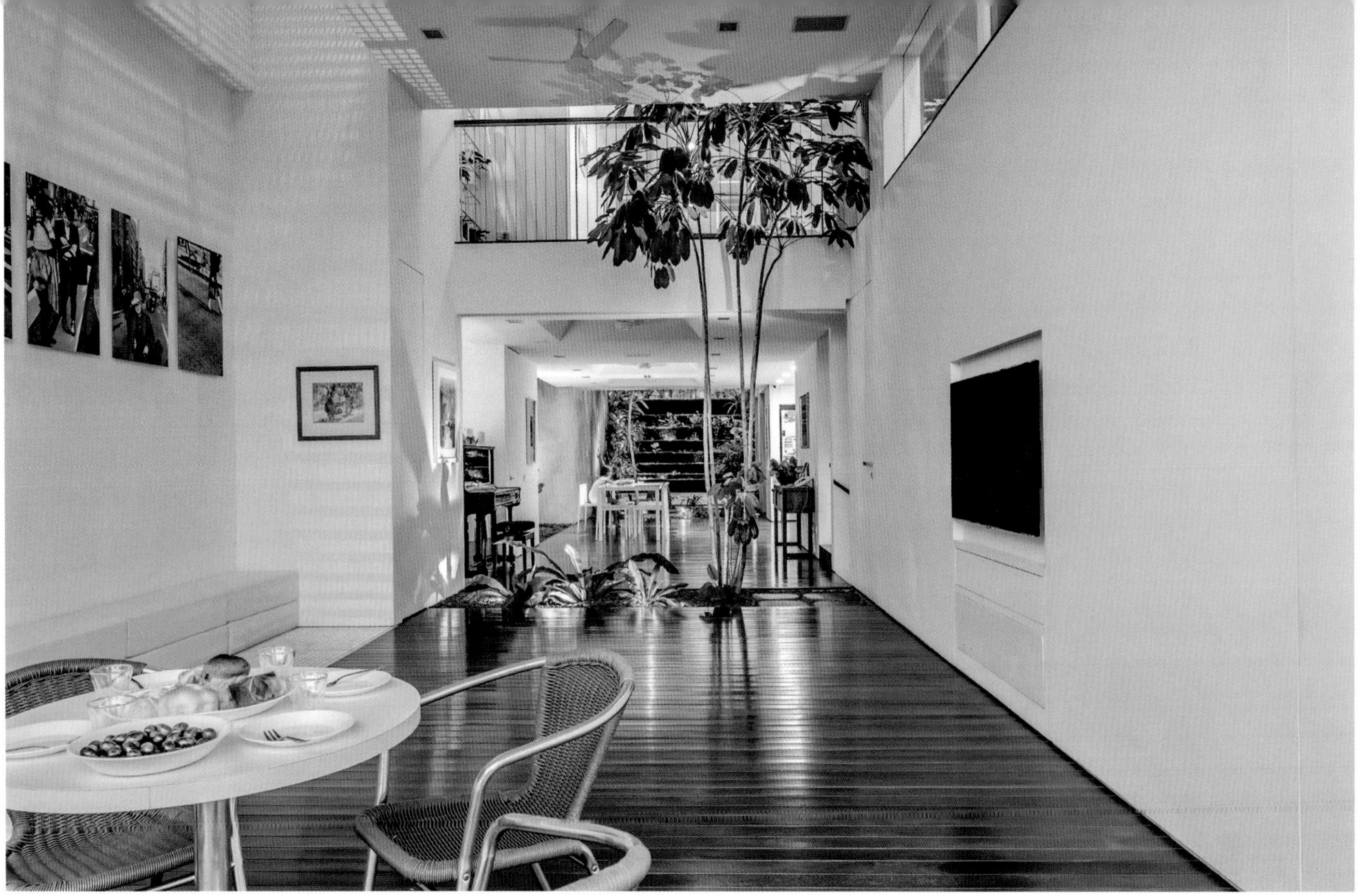

Above Looking back from the terrace sitting room with the Level 2 link and the children's bedroom.

Below The terrace sitting room on Level 1.

Right Looking down from the carport with the water garden and Level 2 link above.

The water garden combines with the thermal mass of the concrete shell to keep the house cool at all times, several degrees cooler than the outside temperature. This is part of a larger strategy to reinterpret the tropical house. Hence, we have recessed spaces protected from direct sunlight, overhangs, timber screens and a strategy to bring the landscape into the house, both through the tropical garden and by the use of plants and airwells as 'separators'. The free-flowing spaces are accordingly connected yet separated—just as the family is separated but connected.

The programme of the house basically follows the four levels, one of which is a rooftop garden. The basement includes the maids' quarters, a laundry (a shute for collecting and delivering laundry connects all four levels), a guest room currently used as a kids room and music room, storage and two rainwater harvesting tanks, one for drinking, the other for

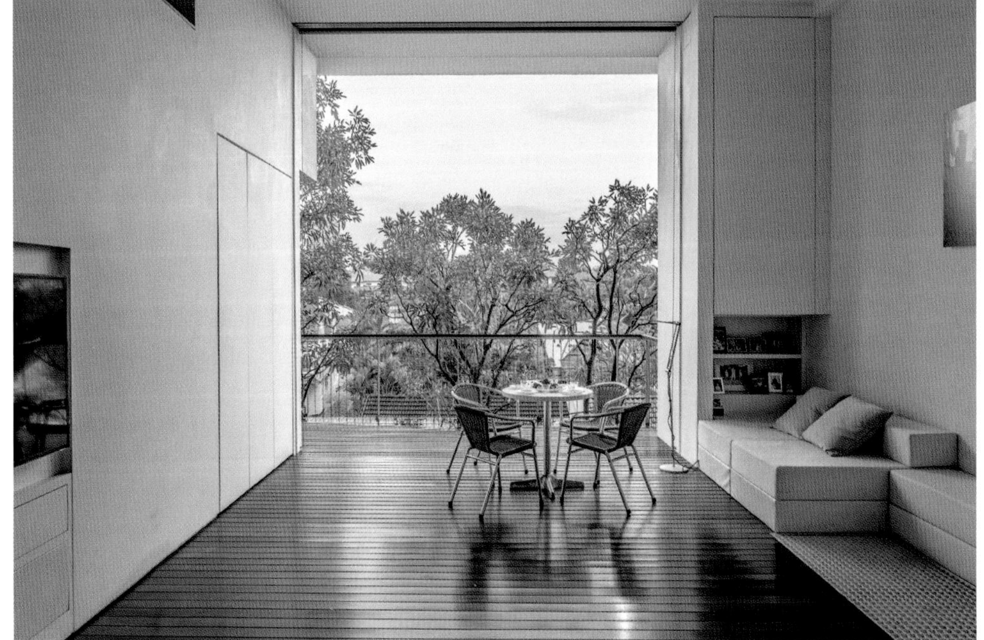

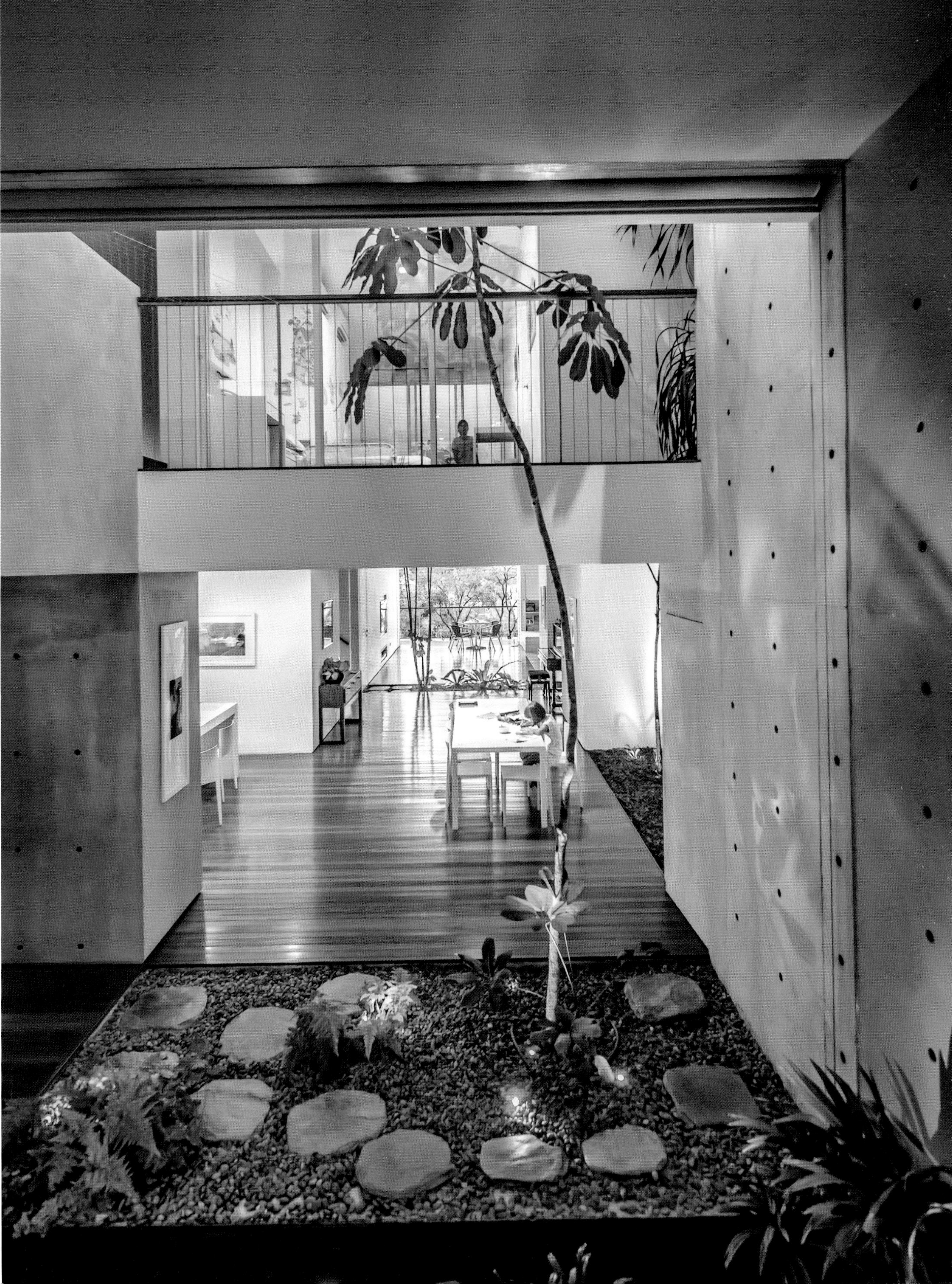

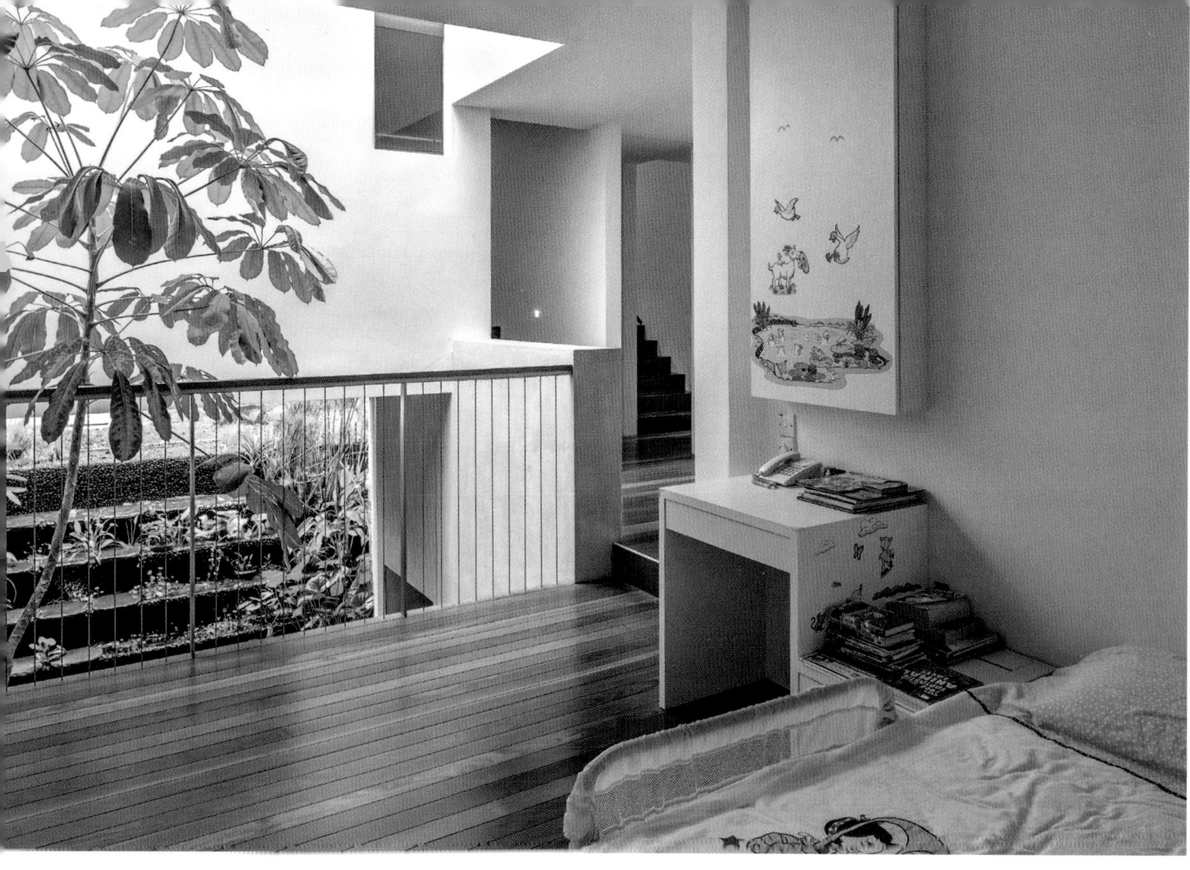

Left The Level 2 link and children's bedroom.

Above right The children's playroom on Level 2.

Right Plans.

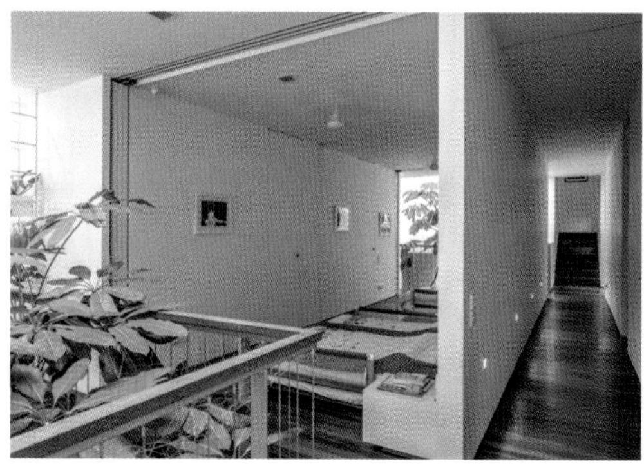

Above The children's bedroom is a self-contained box with a linking corridor down the side.

Right The attic office opens to its own courtyard.

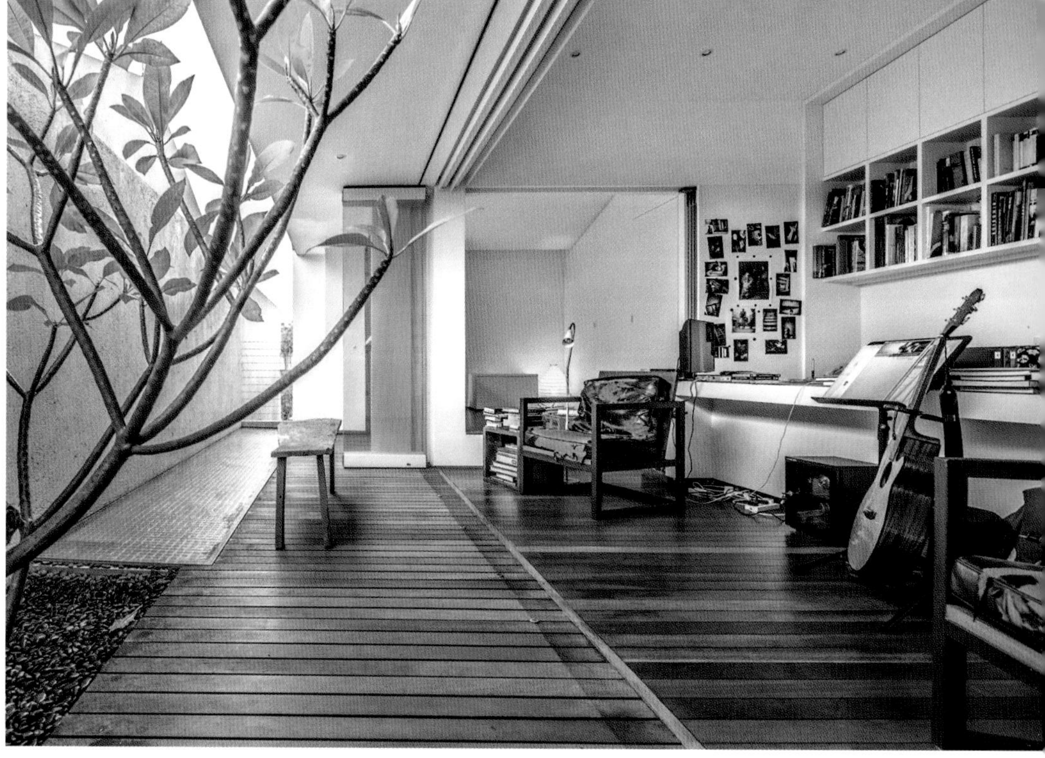

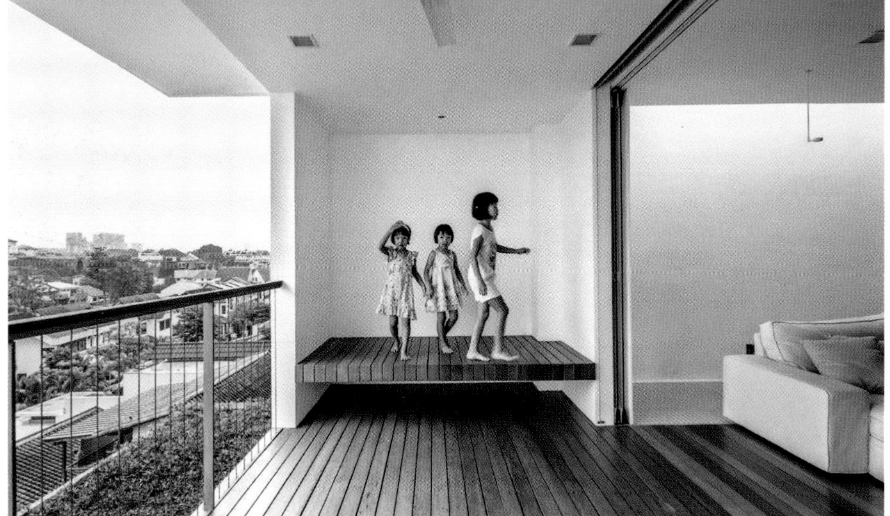

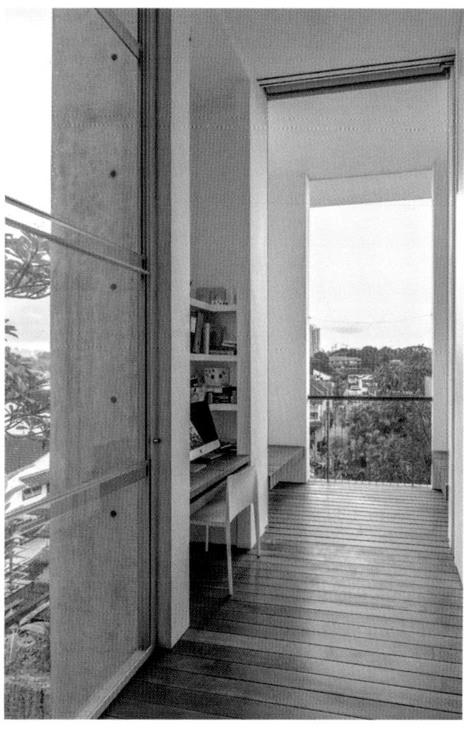

Above The home office extends off the side linking corridor on Level 2.

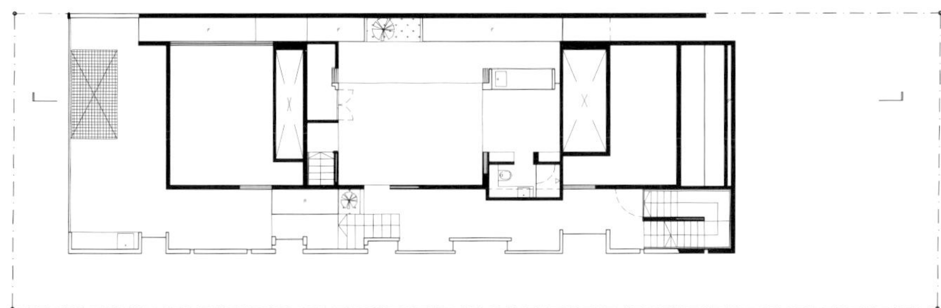

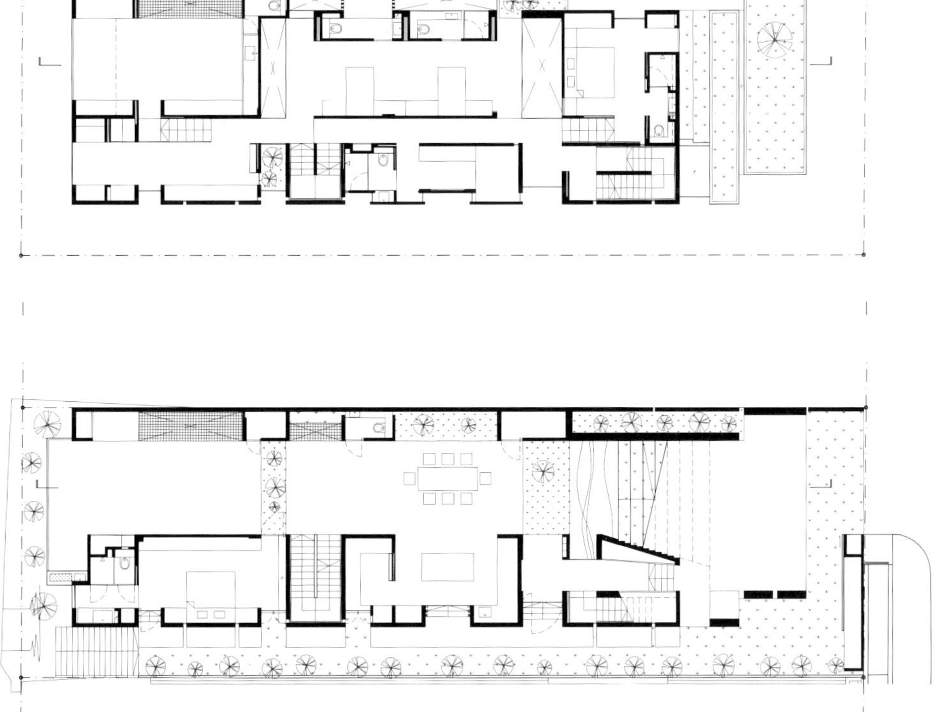

irrigation. Level 1 includes the dining room, the wet and dry kitchens—and a special outdoor in-ground fountain for feet washing—along with the grandparents' quarters. Level 2, which has two voids, is almost a mezzanine with views down to the entry level. The children's room appear to 'float' in the middle. The parents' quarters are on the street side of the building, while on the other side there is a library with study spaces for the whole family, another deck and a family room. Level 3 is the attic where the son, who is a photo-journalist, has his office and studio, a lateral space with sliding glass doors that open on to a deck. This is a self-contained space with a bathroom, pantry and separate access stairway from the ground floor exterior.

Clearly, this is a house which is environmentally highly sustainable. It is a case study in how to build for a tropical climate, enhancing the quality of life, reducing dependency on non-renewable resources, and optimizing the use of renewables for cooling, fresh air, light and water.

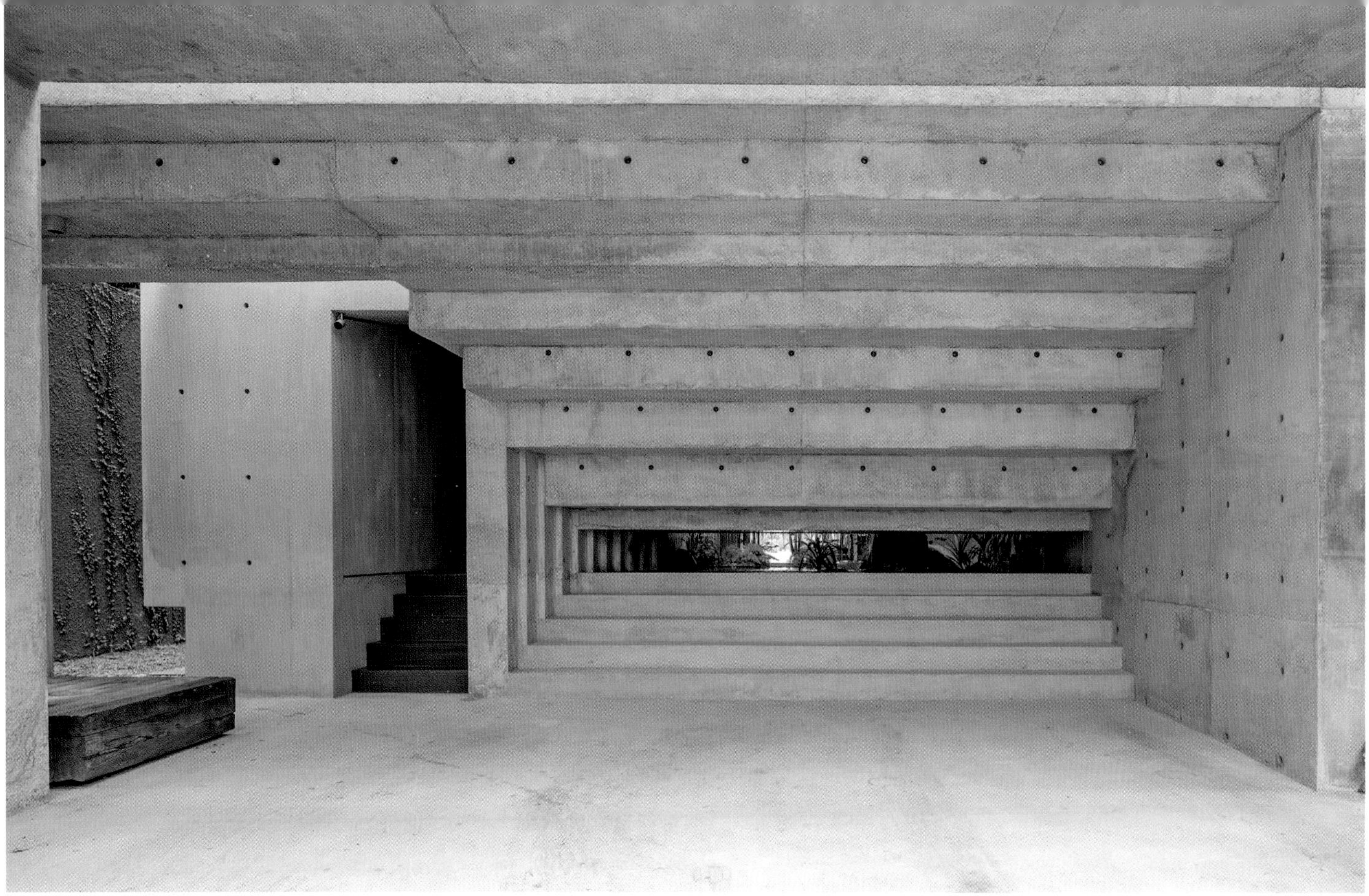

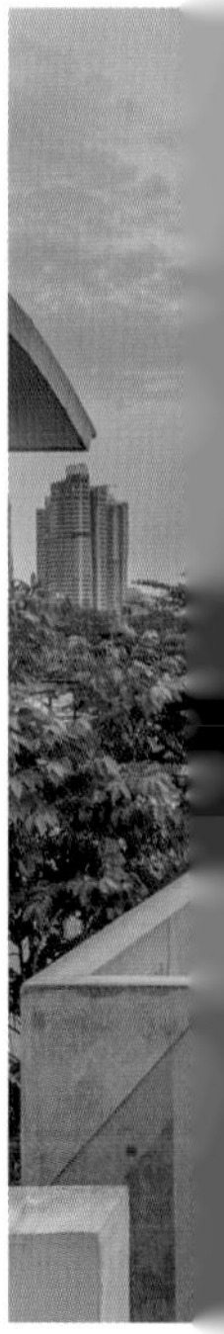

Equally fascinating are the strategies for sustaining family life over a long period of time. This is a multi-generational house that brings three generations together while recognizing a twenty-first century need for privacy and independence. At the same time, the house is designed to allow changes over time, with rooms planned to be combined or separated for different uses and as the children move through different stages of their development.

In the words of the architect: 'The house characterizes the family: its solid front belies an interior that is open and transparent; beneath its cold concrete shell is a sanctuary of heart-warming dwelling spaces; and its stoic monolithic presence conceals a constantly cool environment that is responsive to the tropical climate.'

Above From the carport, inverted concrete steps lead the eye to the open slot of the water garden.

Right The sound of gently running water adds to the soothing calm of the house.

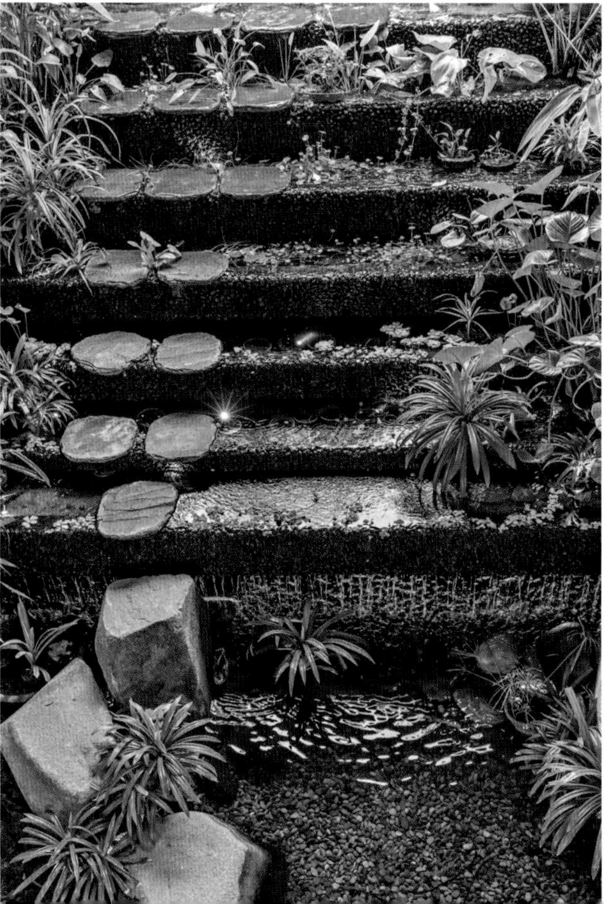

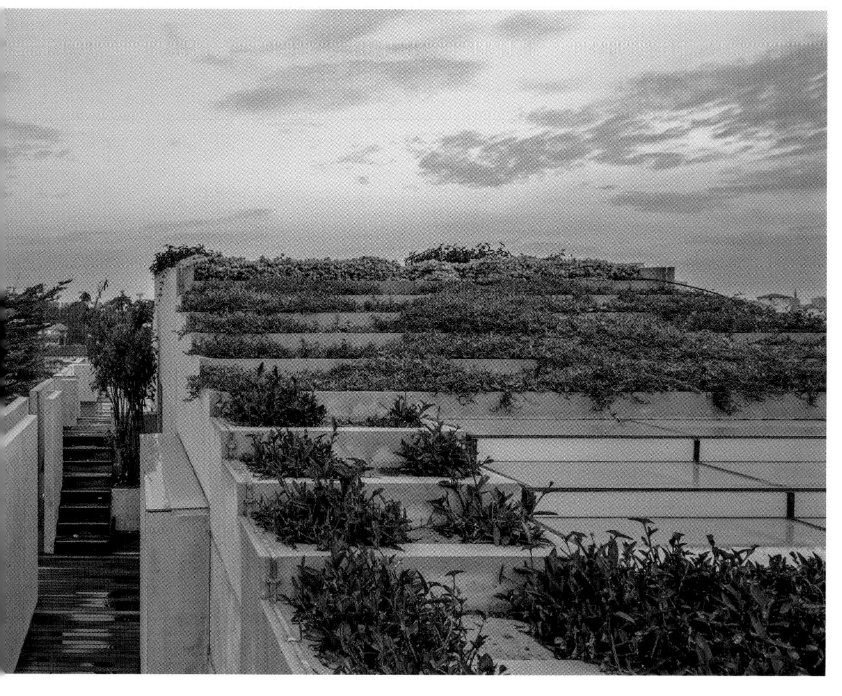

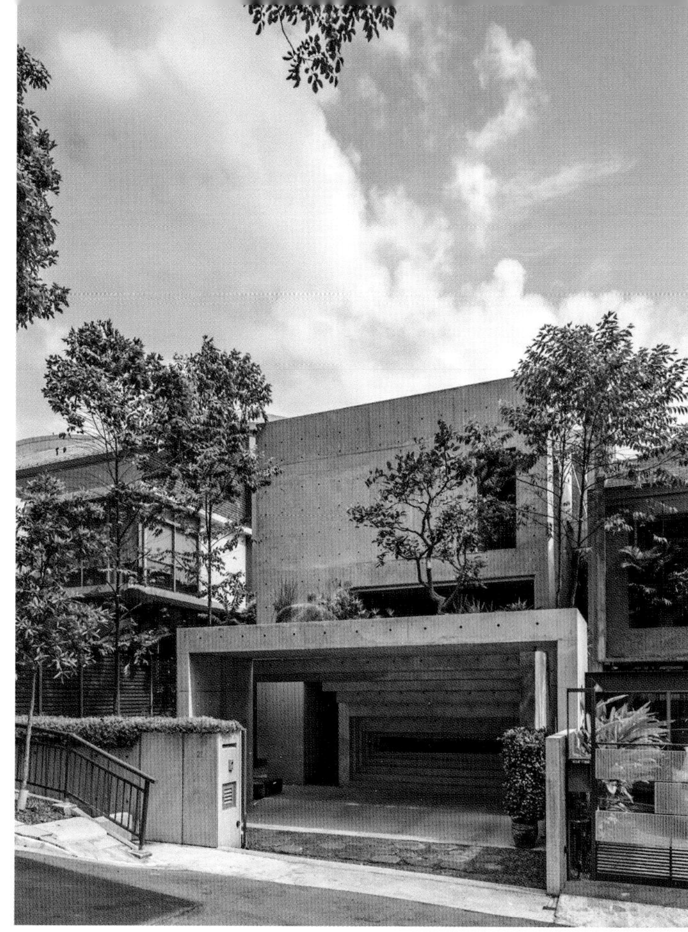

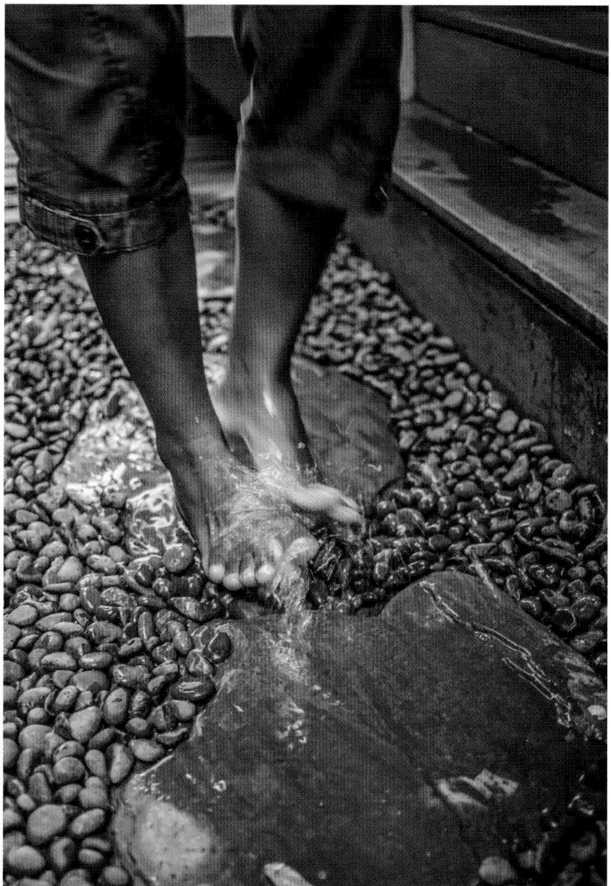

Above left The roof garden contributes to cooling the inside of the house.

Above The house shares the same scale as its neighbours but enjoys total privacy.

Left The small foot fountain outside the wet kitchen.

Right A green interior wall.

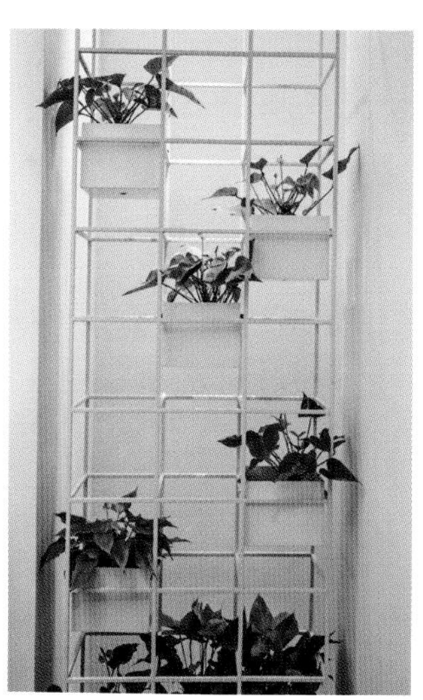

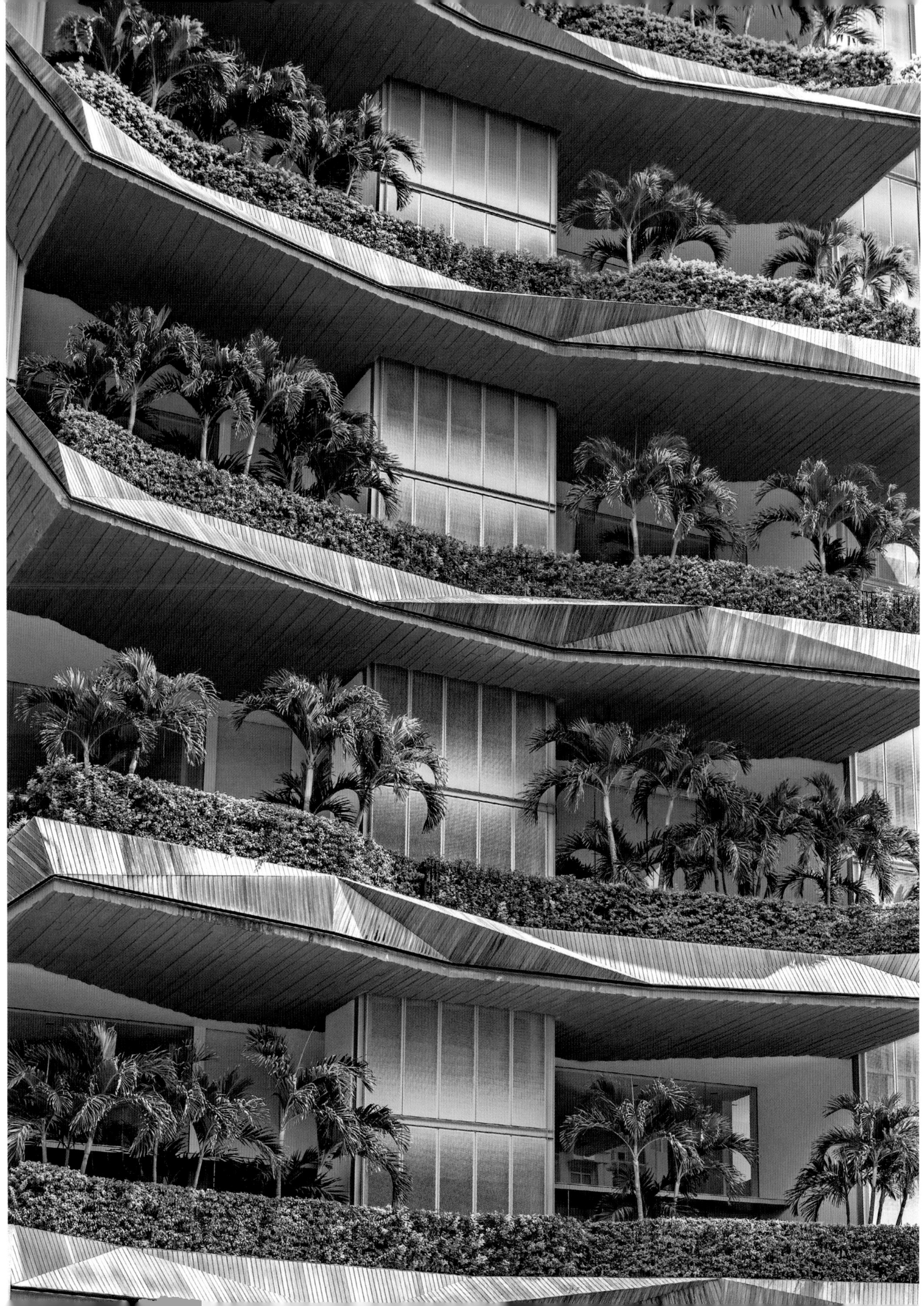

OLIV APARTMENTS
W ARCHITECTS

'We find ourselves constantly adapting to the URA building regulations, which are always changing for the better in terms of what they try to achieve for different building types and for the city.'—MOK WEI WEI, ARCHITECT

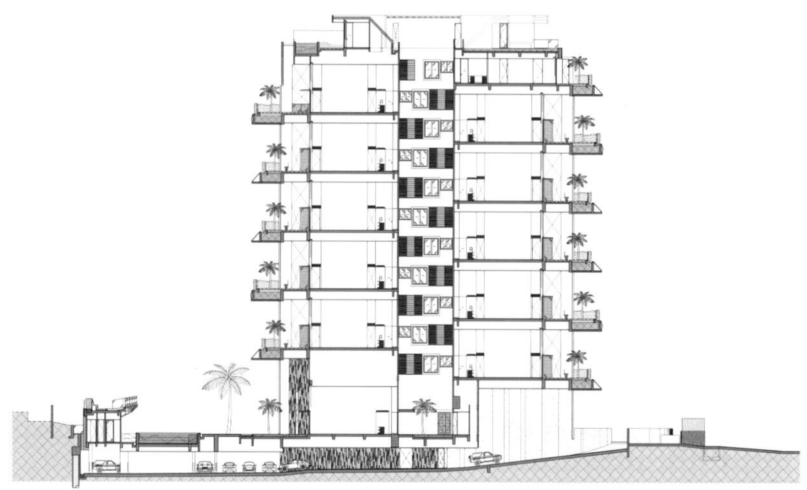

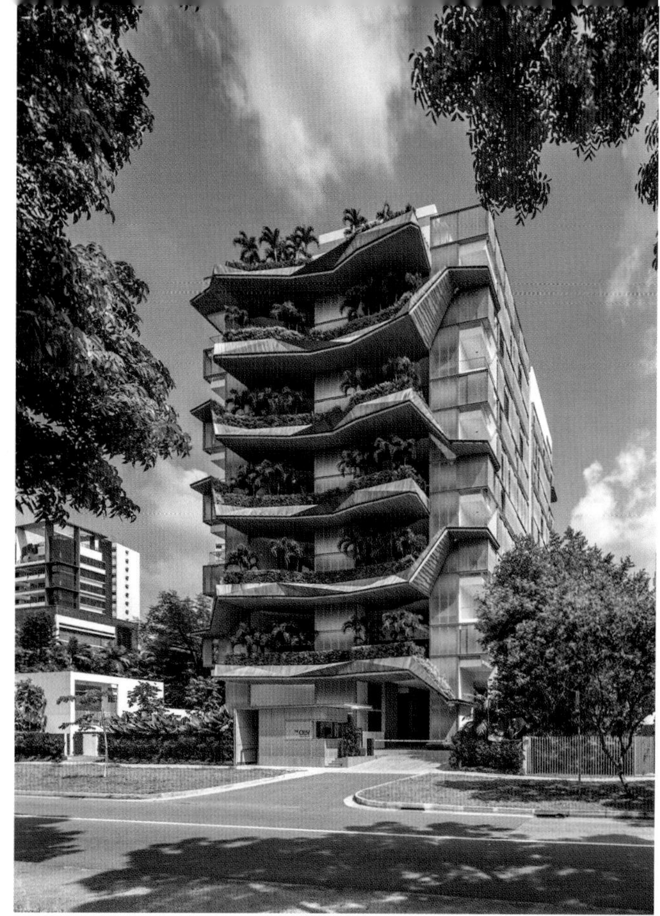

Opposite The architect refers to the irregularly shaped sky terraces as 'compositional topography'.

Above From the street, the building appears as a combination of vertical landscape and sculptural object.

Left Section.

It is no secret that in Singapore, as elsewhere, architecture is often a game played with the regulating authorities. Any regulation, no matter how well intentioned, is a constraint. Regulation is about standardization whereas residential architecture strives to individualize. Well, not always. In the last ten or so years, there has been a marked trend in Singapore away from looking just like your neighbour (only bigger) towards more individuality.

It is one thing to do this with a landed property, but multi-residentials are almost by definition standardized. Apartments 'house' people, they do not provide a home. Apartments, as Jonathan Poh comments elsewhere in this book, are 'nests'. Turning an apartment into a home is a constant challenge. One trend is for developers to leave the interiors of apartments as a *tabula rasa* to allow future owners to make their own decisions about internal layout.

Another issue is that apartments do not have a garden. In Singapore, where 85 per cent of the population lives in multi-residential buildings, the government's response has been to turn the entire city-state into a garden. Here, as elsewhere in the world, there has also been a greater emphasis on providing more amenities at ground level by way of compensation.

This new apartment building in one of Singapore's most affluent neighbourhoods is an example of a new trend to create vertical landscapes so that the apartments do not simply look out to the landscape but actually become a part of it. This is more than simply a case of having a balcony with some pot plants. The trend really began with 'green walls', popularized by Frenchman Patrick Blanc, who was the first to solve the maintenance issues of keeping the greenery alive. The Oliv Apartments have taken this trend to a new level of sophistication by a creative interpretation of the sky terrace regulations and by some imaginative planning, resulting, unsurprisingly, in Best Residential Award at the MIPIM 2014 Awards and a 2014 German Design Council Iconic Award.

In Singapore over the last decade, there has been a gradual loosening of the regulations regarding Gross Floor Area, from a situation that discouraged

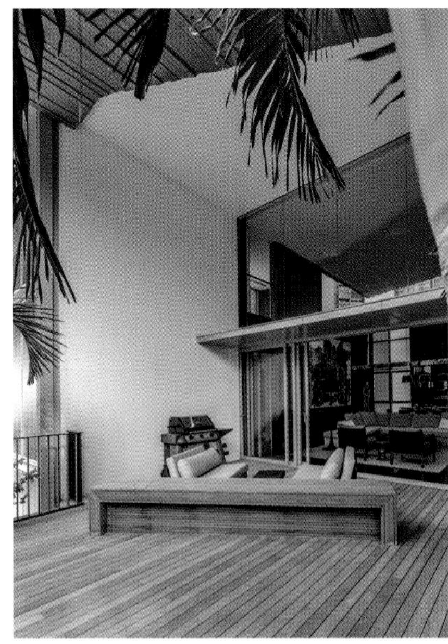

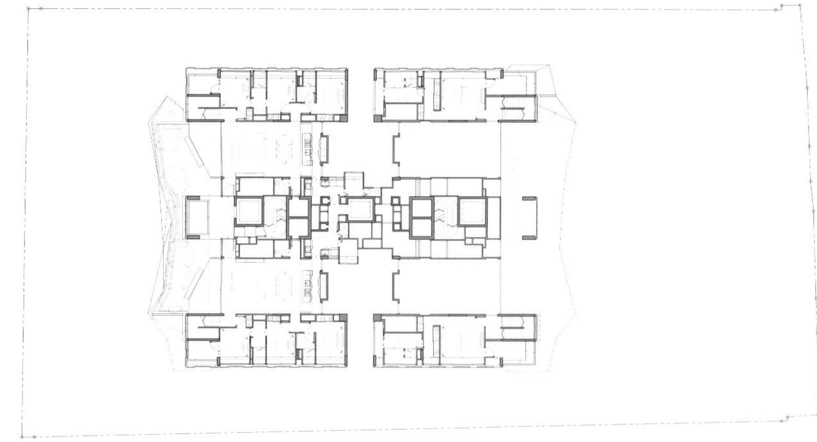

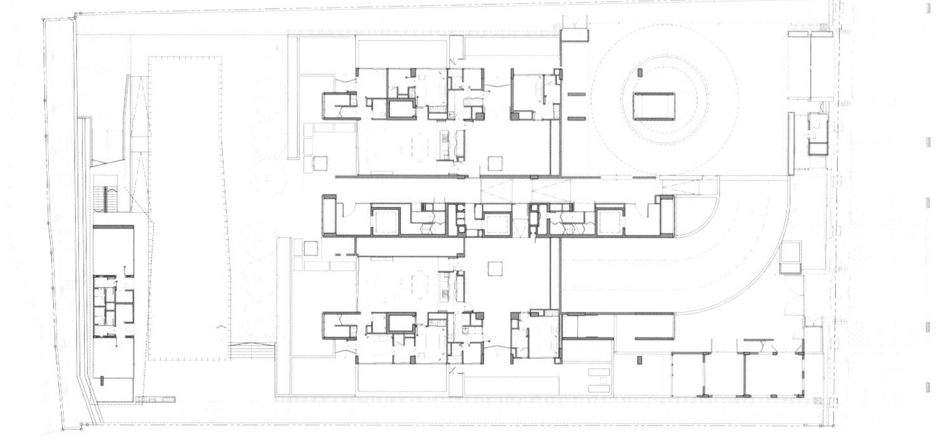

balconies of any kind through semi-enclosed outdoor space (using sliding screens) through to the situation now, which encourages sky terraces two to three times bigger than previous outdoor spaces.

In order to get this space, these areas have to be communal. Mok's solution was to link pairs of apartments (because two units is the minimum to qualify as communal) whose private and shared spaces merge into a single sky terrace. The greenery that results provides privacy. These space are irregularly shaped, double-height (seven metres) and 65 square metres in size, with the balustrades hidden within topiary green hedges to further the idea of living in a garden. The terraces are inked vertically by sloping parapet walls inspired by origami shapes.

Off-form concrete is used for the terrace soffits, with the floor and the edge made from balau timber, a dense tropical wood suitable for outdoor use, which will turn a silvery grey to complement the concrete.

From the street, the overall effect is of a vertical landscape in which the building takes on a powerfully sculptural form. Inside the apartments, there is a feeling of living in a landed house because the maisonette typology (two storeys in a single apartment) is so strongly supported by the greenery. This feeling is reinforced by the depth of the terraces—four metres from the front of the terrace to the sliding glass doors of the apartment—which provides privacy and reduces glare. The depth and greenery also enable the units to remain fully open, drawing in fresh air, cooled by the green terraces.

The building is twelve storeys high and contains twenty-three apartments, including two garden apartments and three penthouses. The 'origami' green walls are on the front and rear façades. On the other elevations, operable perforated aluminium screens provide a skin for the building. The typical apartment is a double volume, with the downstairs open plan and a kitchen along the rear separated

Top left The sky terraces offer a four-metre setback enhanced by the natural warmth of timber decking.

Top Third storey apartment plan.

Above First storey plan.

Opposite above left A typical apartment steps up to create separate sitting and dining areas.

Opposite above right From the sky terrace, it feels as if one is living among the trees.

Right Looking towards the terrace, the setbacks and greenery ensure not only shade but also privacy from neighbouring apartment buildings.

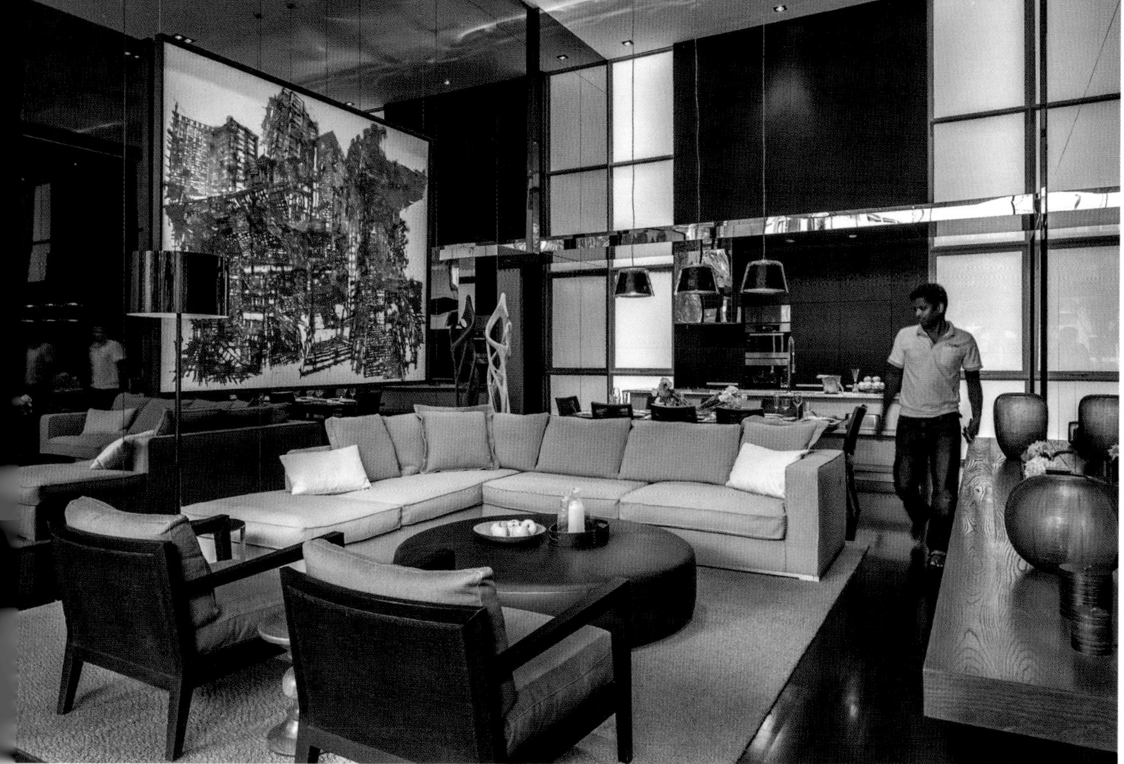

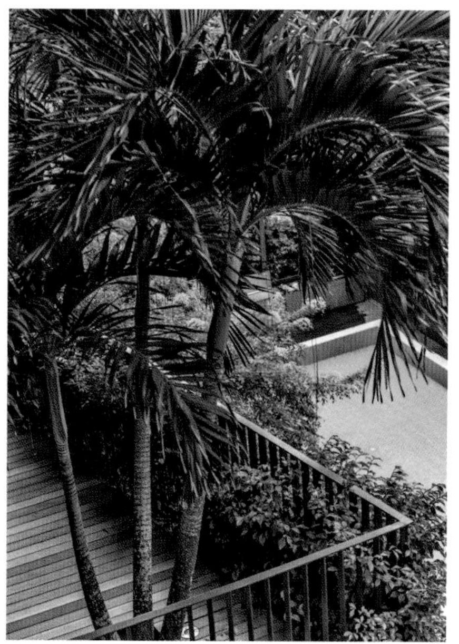

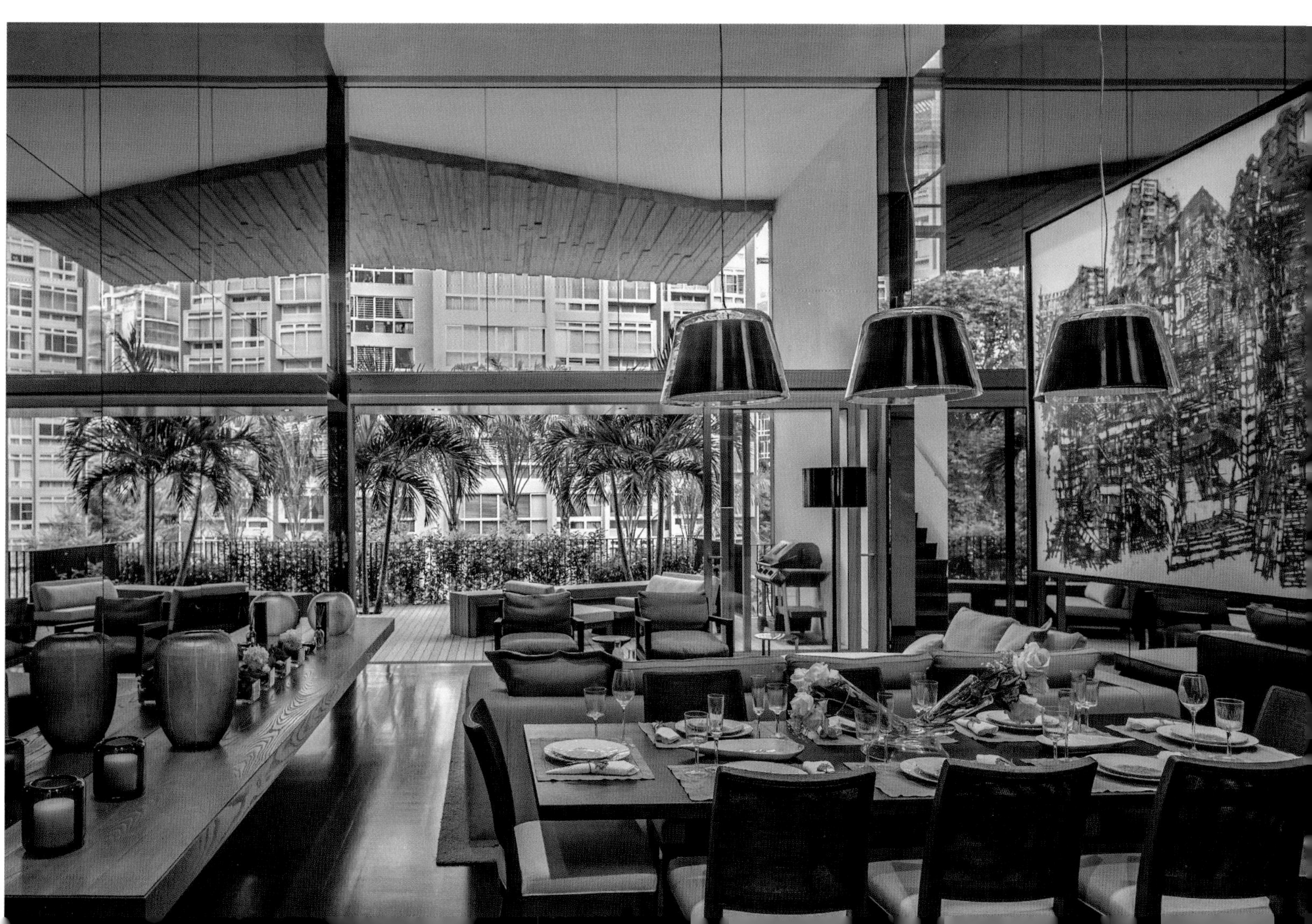

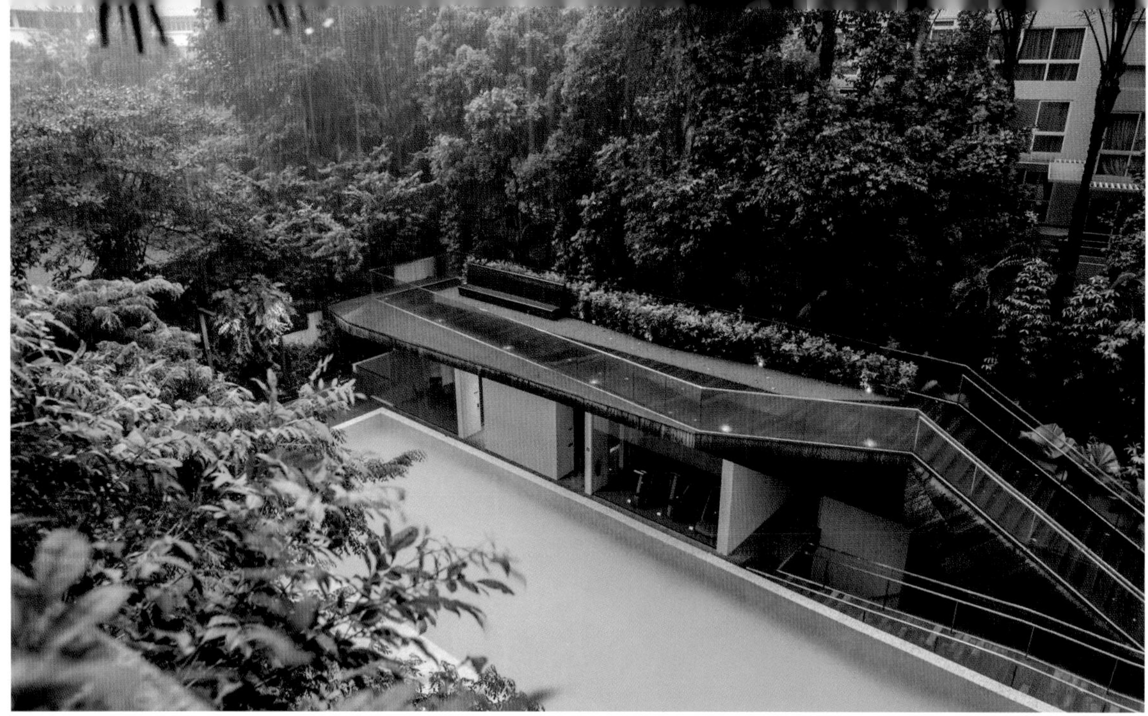

Left The undulating 'origami' form of the building is continued with the green roof to the pool pavilion.

Below left The sky terraces and interiors form one continuous space.

Below The theme of openness to the outside is continued in the bathrooms.

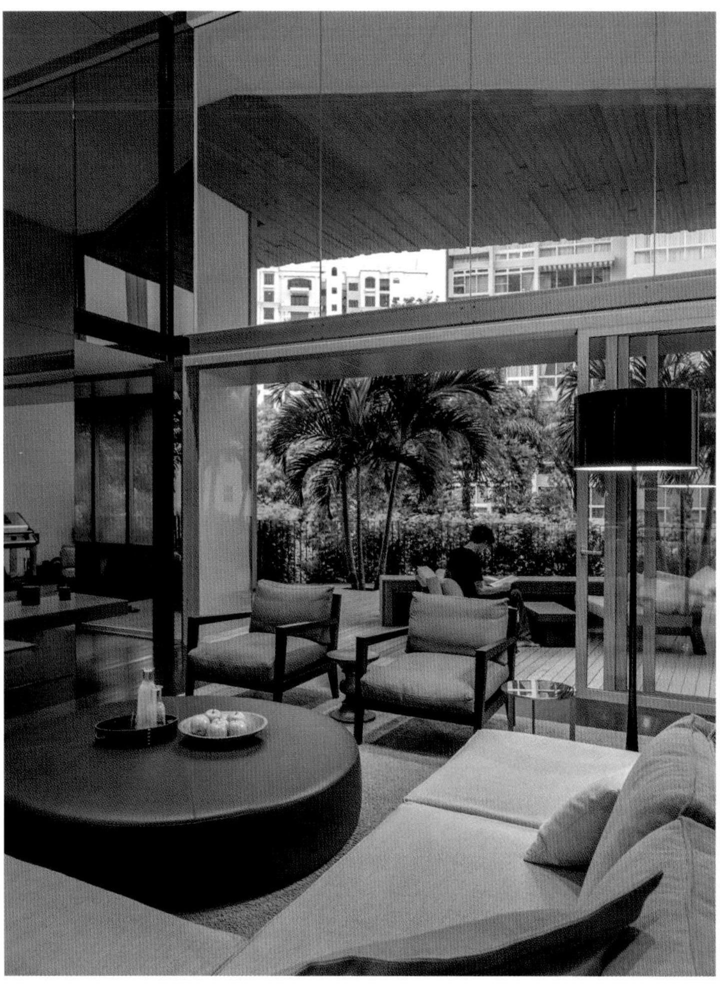

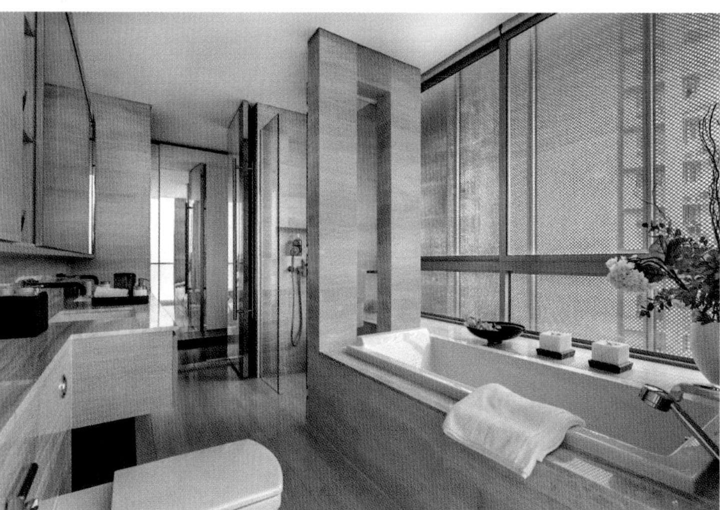

Opposite above The bedrooms on the upper level are private, yet still connected to the main living areas.

Opposite below The bedrooms typically connect with the outside and seem to dematerialize, becoming one with the outside landscape.

during cooking by a trimless sliding glass screen from the living/dining area. This level also contains a wet kitchen and maid's quarters. The private areas, consisting of three bedrooms, are upstairs where the landings look down into the living/dining space and where the master bedroom is somewhat elevated, giving it a greater degree of privacy.

The Oliv Apartments have an environmentally sustainable pedigree, and the shared spaces promote a greater sense of community than is normally the case in apartment buildings. But an important part of their sustainable credentials lies in the way they explore new ways of 'home-making' in multi-residential developments through greater individuality and by promoting the feeling of living in a landed house.

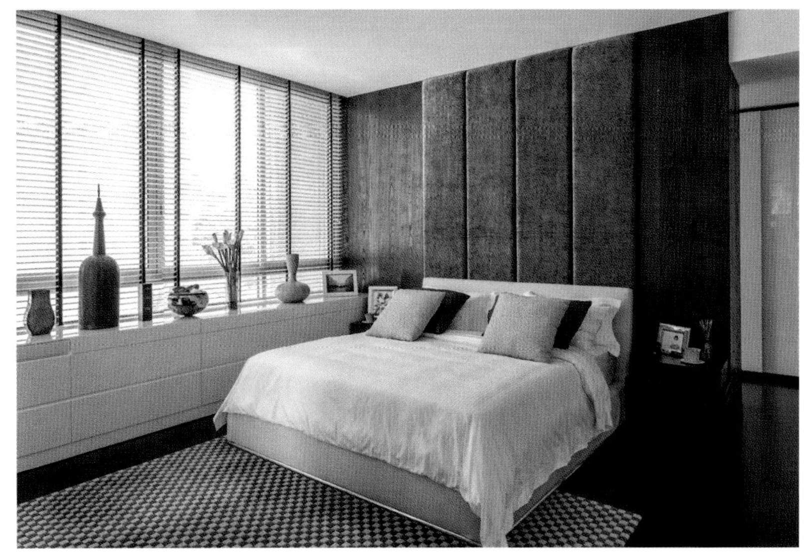

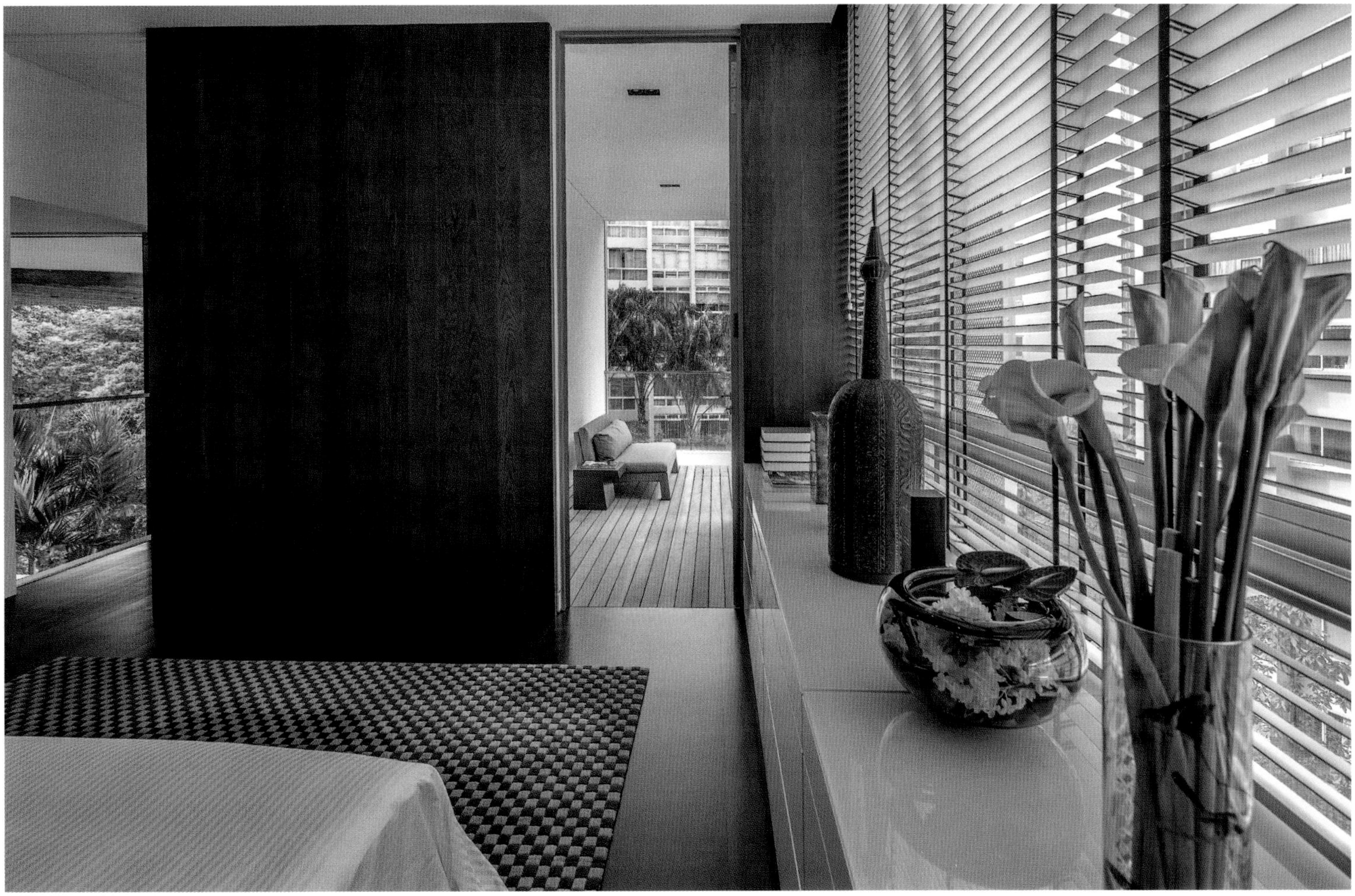

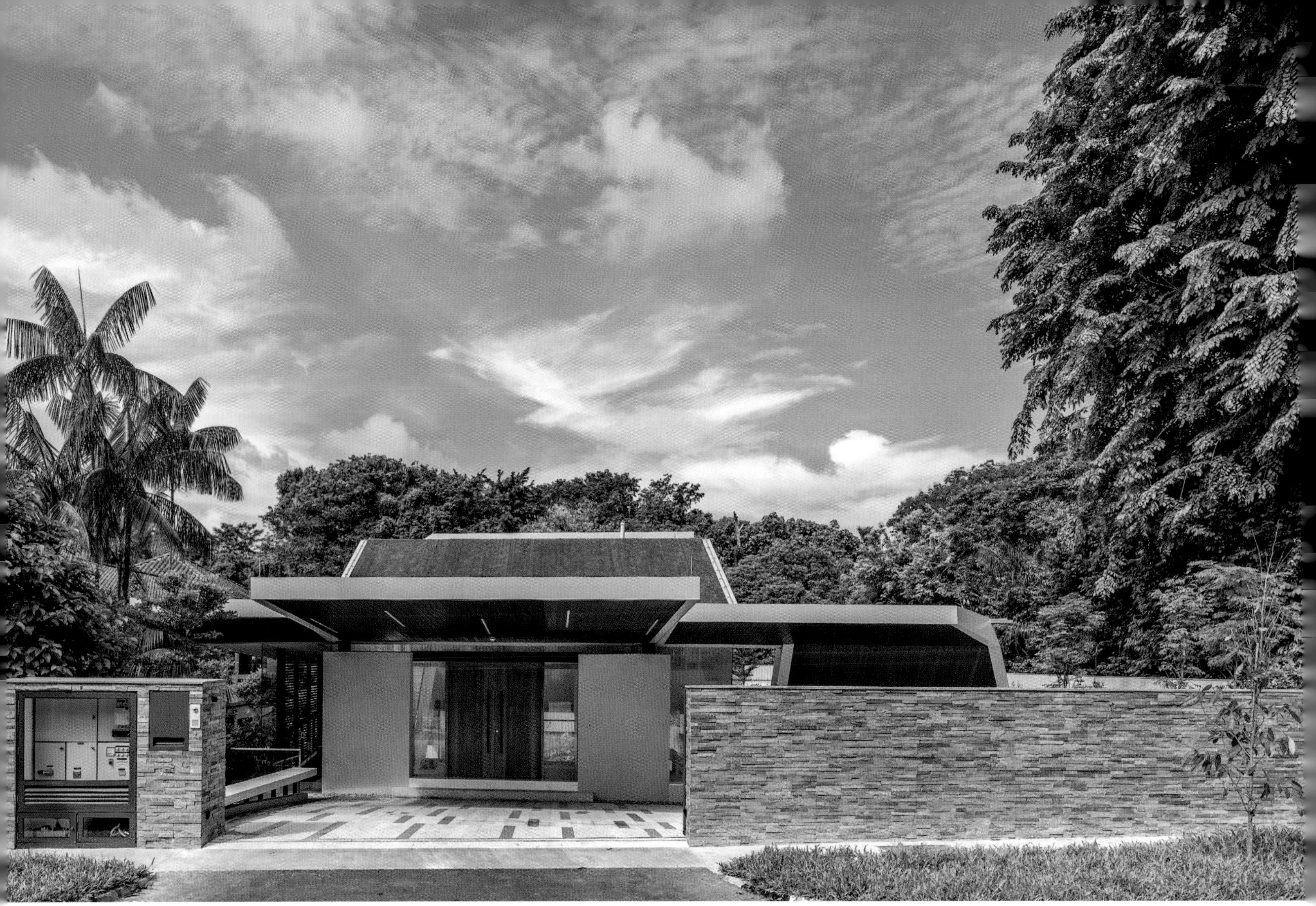

ANDREW ROAD HOUSE
A D LAB

'The whole building form was designed to bring light and wind in but also to provide a shield against the sound.'—WARREN LIU, ARCHITECT

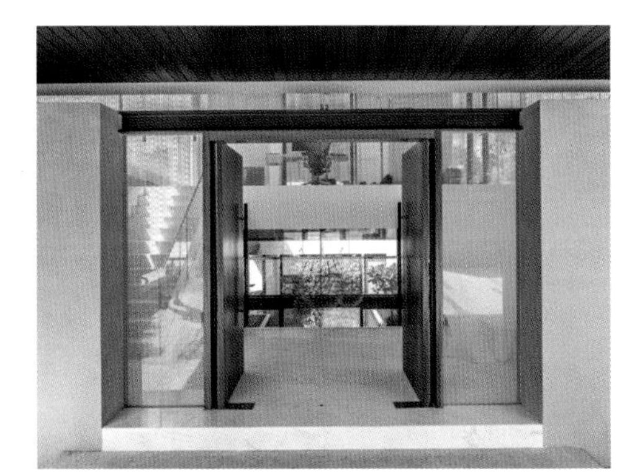

It was a great corner site in a relaxed and leafy neighbourhood but it was opposite a very busy elevated expressway. Noise levels would be unsustainable. The architects came up with a solution that took advantage of the undulating topography, where the plots are often one storey below street level and the houses are entered at the second storey. This solution, however, raised another problem, which the architects, Warren Liu and Lim Pin Jie, chose to see as an opportunity to create a truly sustainable home.

This is a multi-generational home. The clients are highly successful professional people who entertain a great deal. Part of the challenge was how to accommodate the parents without any loss of privacy for them when the clients held their functions. The solution to this issue was ultimately driven by the solution to other problems.

To address the problem of noise, the architects created a sunken garden courtyard, with the kitchen, dining and entertainment spaces, along with the parents' quarters, forming a basement that wraps around the courtyard in a C shape. The long swimming pool, with its glittering mosaic-tiled surface, becomes a water feature as part of a tropical garden. The house is thus a cluster of pavilions. One is the dining/kitchen pavilion in the sunken courtyard. Another is the entry pavilion. Here, at the entry, one either goes up to the client's home office, a glass room with its own idiosyncratic circular washroom, which surveys the entry and the courtyard below, or down to the basement level where there is a large open living room, a guest bedroom and the A/V room.

At the opposite end of the courtyard is the bedroom pavilion. Apart from the parents' bedroom and bedrooms for the children who will come along one day, this includes the master bedroom and its phenomenal 'shower room' on the upper level. Fritted glass is used in the two glass pavilions to insulate them from the traffic noise and give a significantly lower shading coefficient, but this insulation is not necessary elsewhere. However, sinking the courtyard raised the problem of how to get air into the basement area, both for cooling and for dealing with dampness and humidity. The solution was a series of shaped porches that collect prevailing winds and scoop them down into the basement area.

Opposite the dining/kitchen pavilion, a screened timber bridge runs the length of the property at the entry level. This shields the house from an overbearing next door property but also provides private access for the parents when there are guests. This

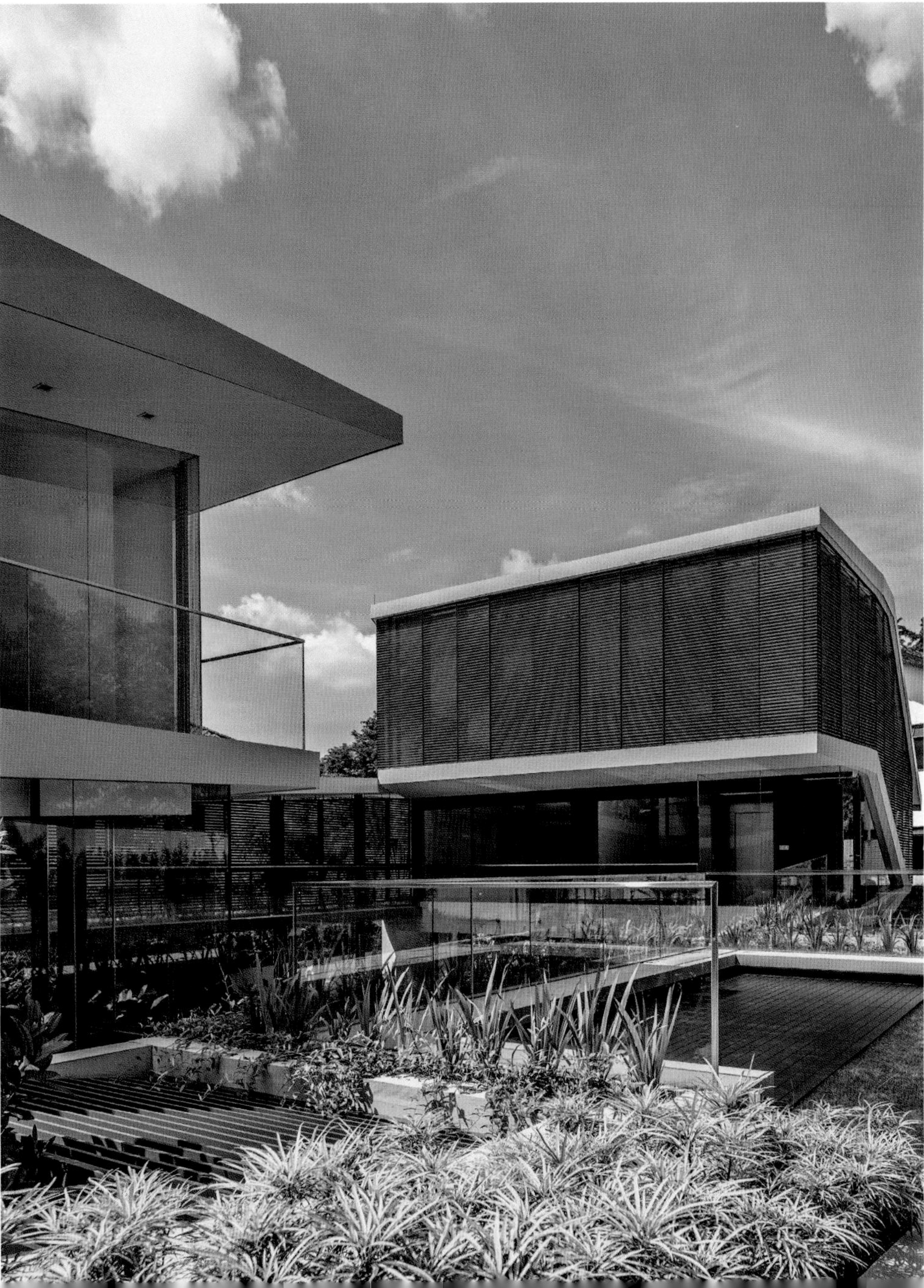

Opposite above The discreet entry to the house does not give any indication of what will be discovered inside.

Opposite below Once the two handsome entry doors are opened, the entire vista through the house is revealed.

Right A rooftop garden links the two pavilions on one side.

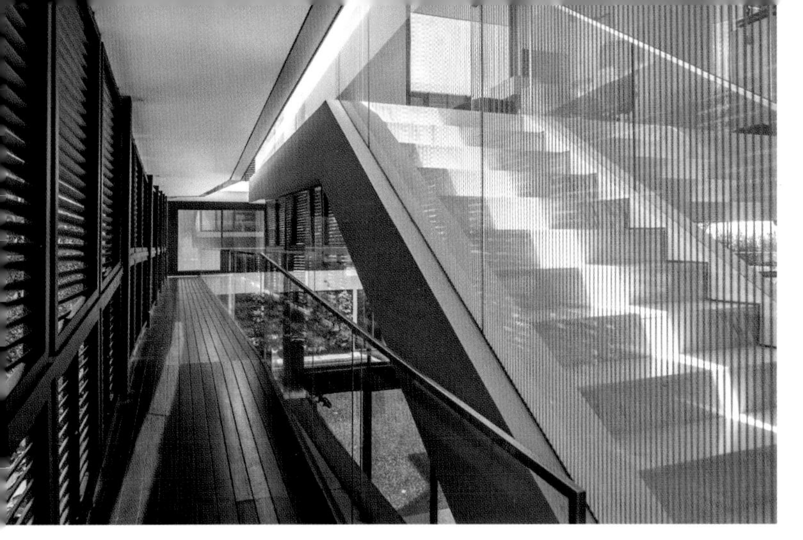

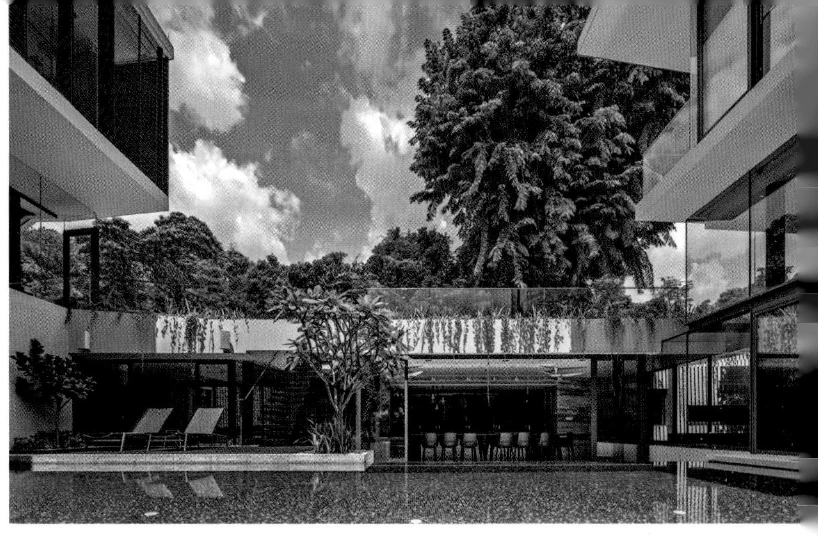

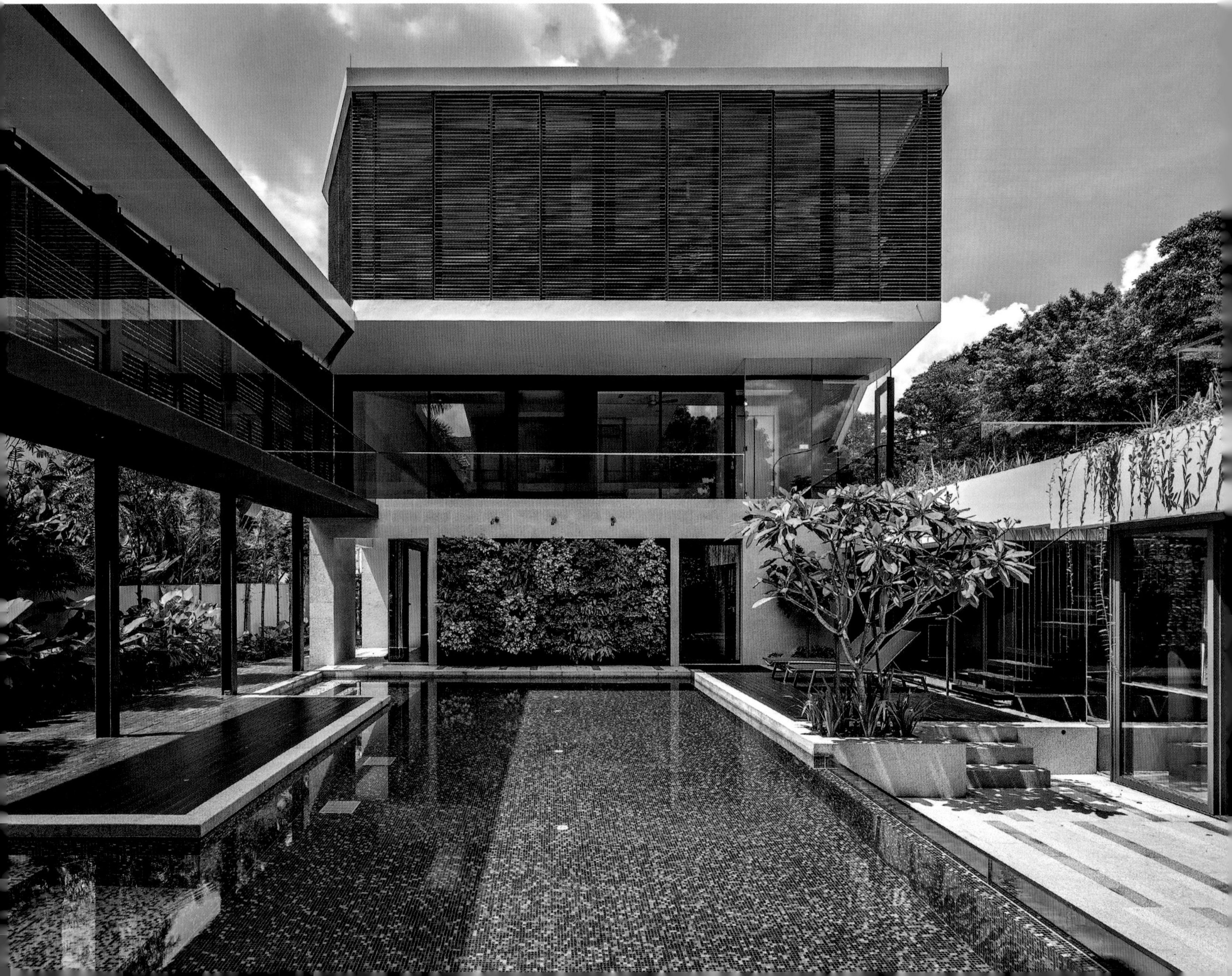

Far left A screened timber bridge links the parents' quarters to the entry.

Left A view of the basement living/dining area across the pool.

Below The bedroom pavilion is located at the end of the sunken garden courtyard.

Right Plans.

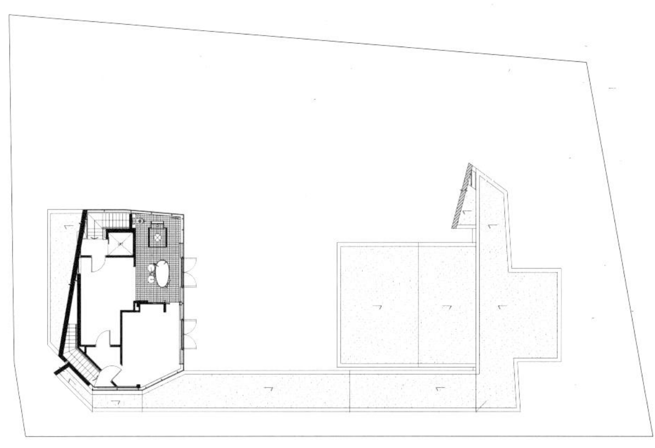

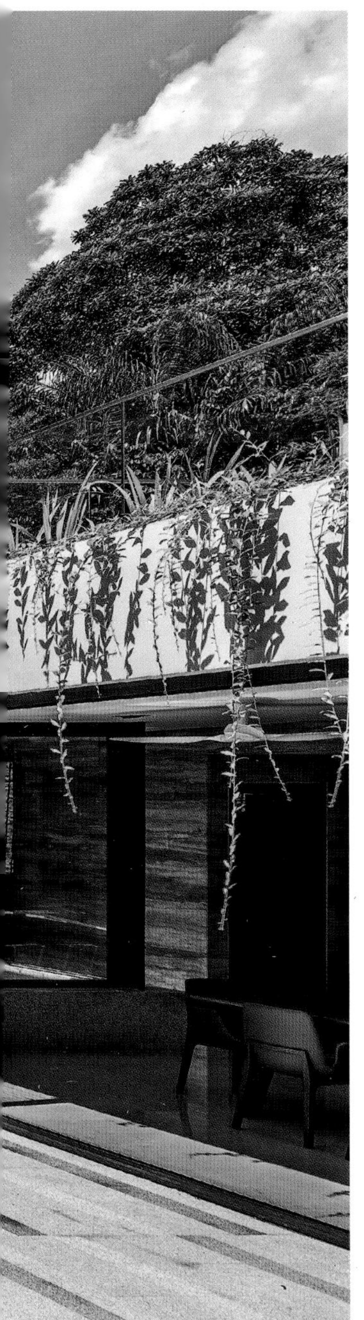

complements the circulation planning in the bedroom pavilion, which is organized around spaces to enable people to avoid bumping into one another.

Above this bridge and above the dining/kitchen pavilion are sloping green roofs which, seen from the upper levels, make the house look as though it has a landscape. In fact, says Warren Liu, it feels like the whole house is a piece of landscape. 'We wanted to make it look as though the land was more prominent than the building,' he says. It also helps to moderate the scale of the building to the point where it has a 'non-presence' compared to other houses in the neighbourhood.

There is a theatrical quality to this house because it offers so many vantage points, mainly looking down, to observe comings and goings and the activities in the courtyard. It is akin to Shakespeare's Globe Theatre where spectators (other than those in the pit) looked down from timber galleries to the open thrust stage. For their part, the architects talk about 'choreography' in reference to the elaborated circulation of the building, where people can sometimes be seen and at other time be hidden, and where passing through the building offers fragmented views to counterpoint grand vistas.

The house exemplifies the new approach to multi-generational housing in Singapore, with its heightened awareness of balancing the desire for community in the family with the need for privacy and independence, in other words, sustaining the extended family in the context of rapidly changing social mores.

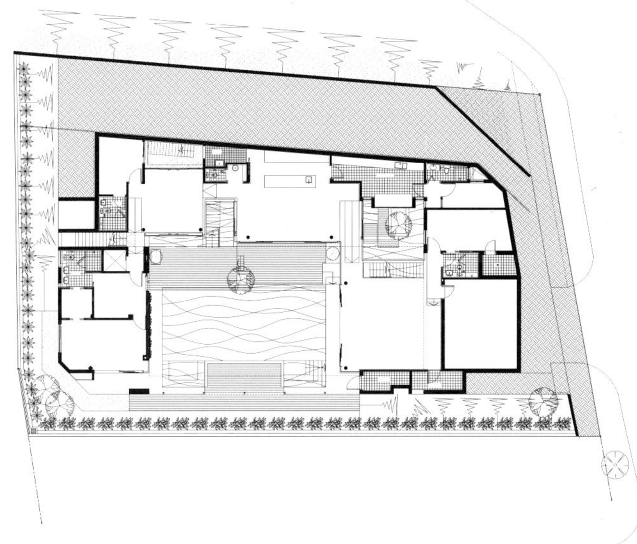

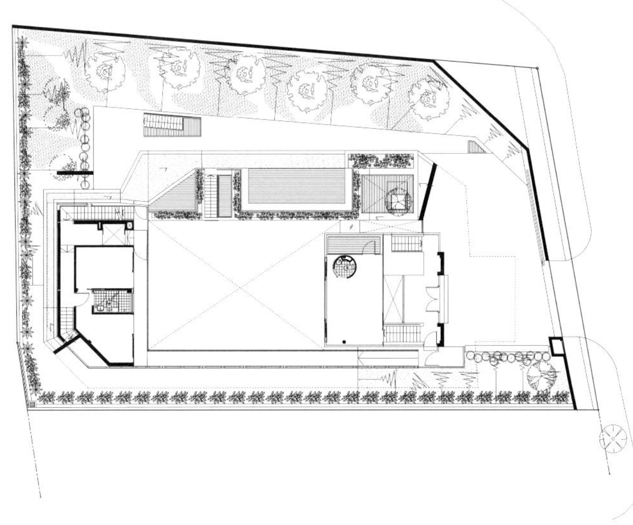

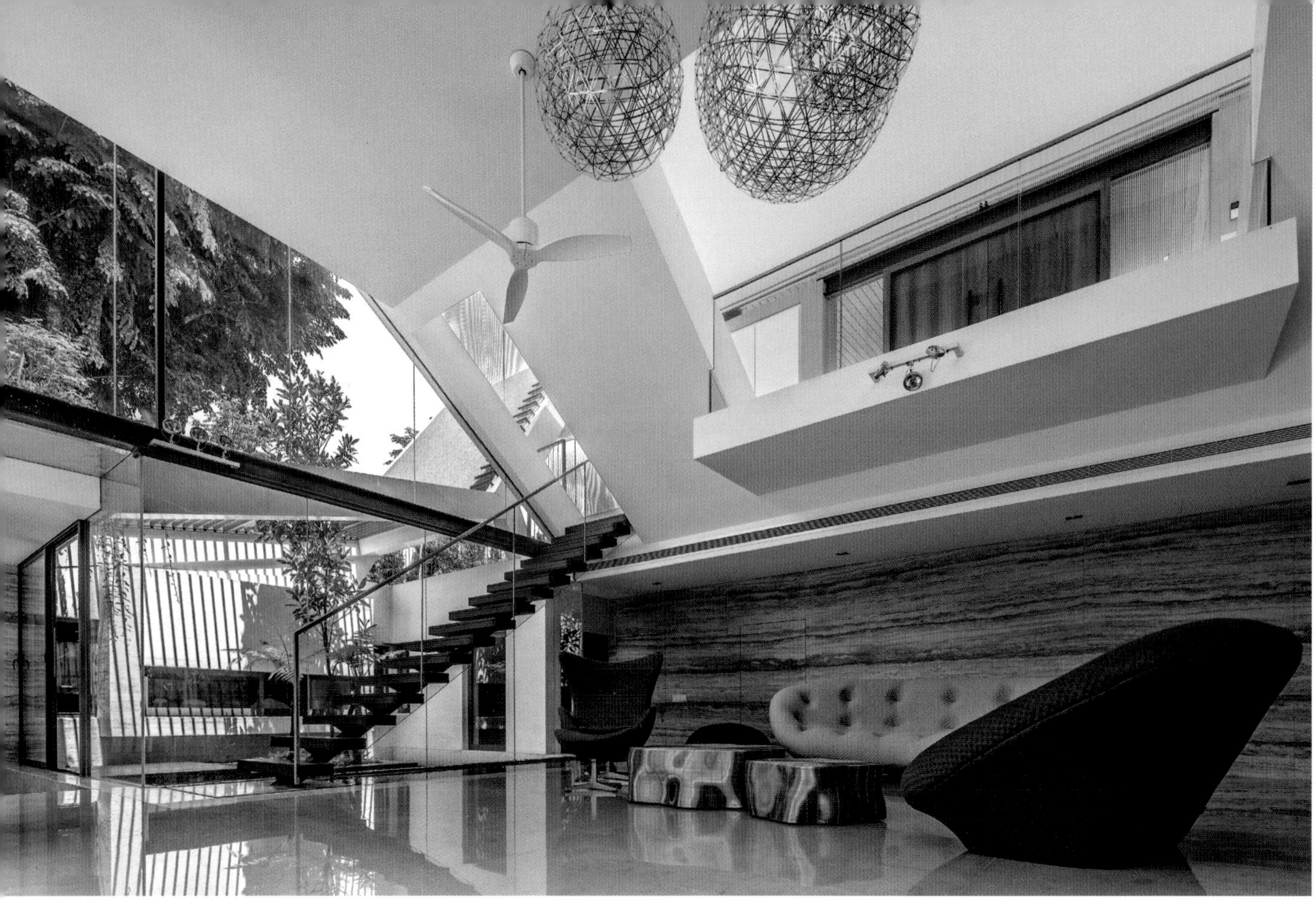

Above A spacious sitting area occupies the void below the entry lobby.

Right Looking down into the sitting area at the entry end of the basement garden court.

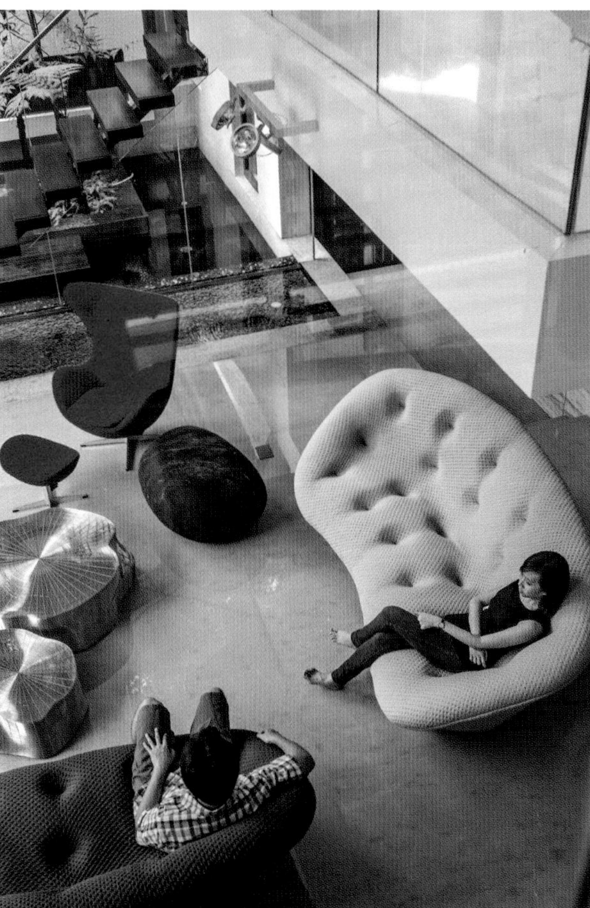

Opposite above The sitting area offers a dynamic perspectival view down the pool.

Right Looking back towards the entry along the timber-screened bridge, with the home office above the entry lobby.

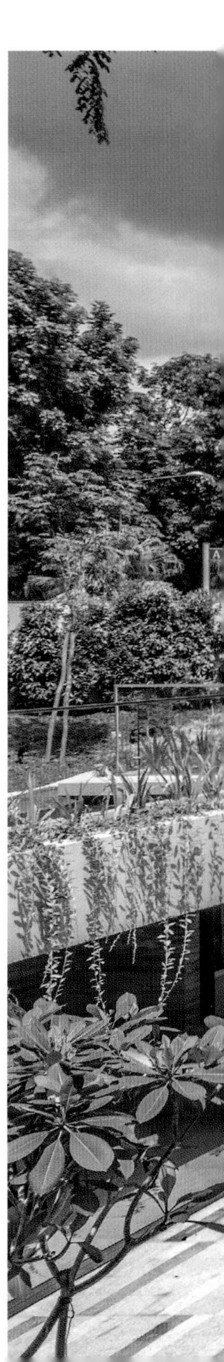

The house can also be seen as a harbinger of a new sustainable issue only just appearing on the horizon, namely, recognition of the deleterious effects of noise in an increasingly noisy world and the need for noise abatement strategies to protect people's well-being.

Finally, the house has substantial environmental integrity for its passive cooling and cross-ventilation strategies, along with its successful harvesting of natural light.

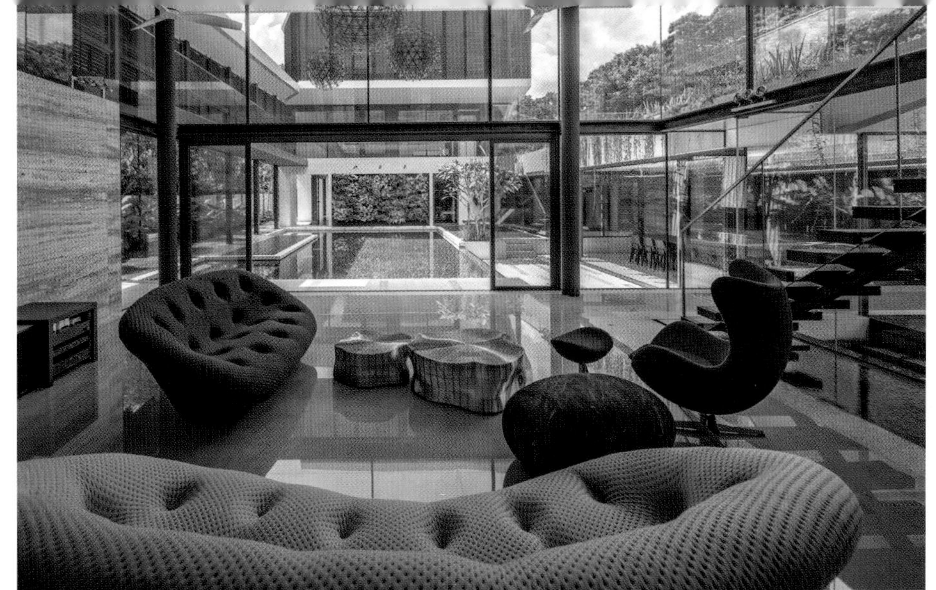

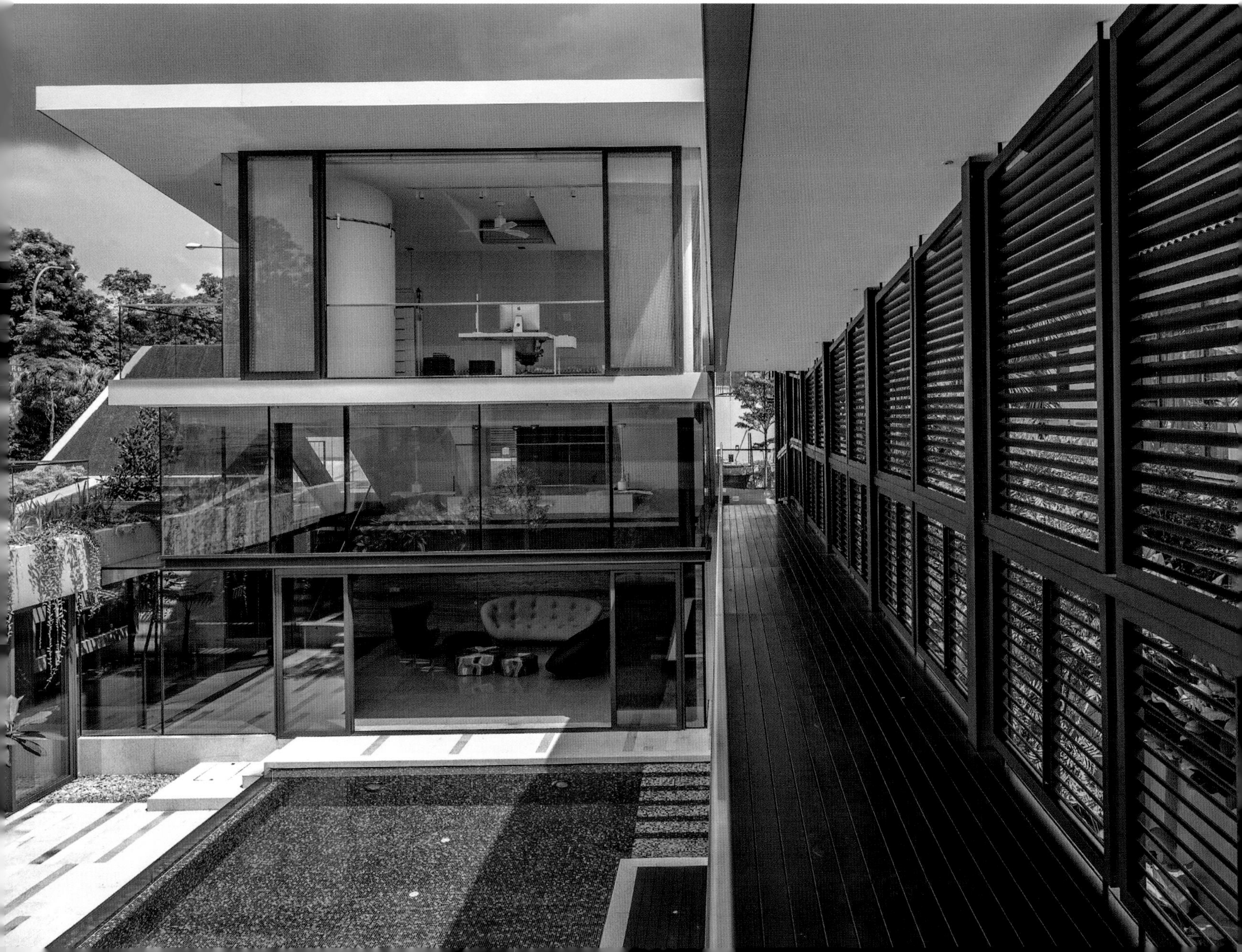

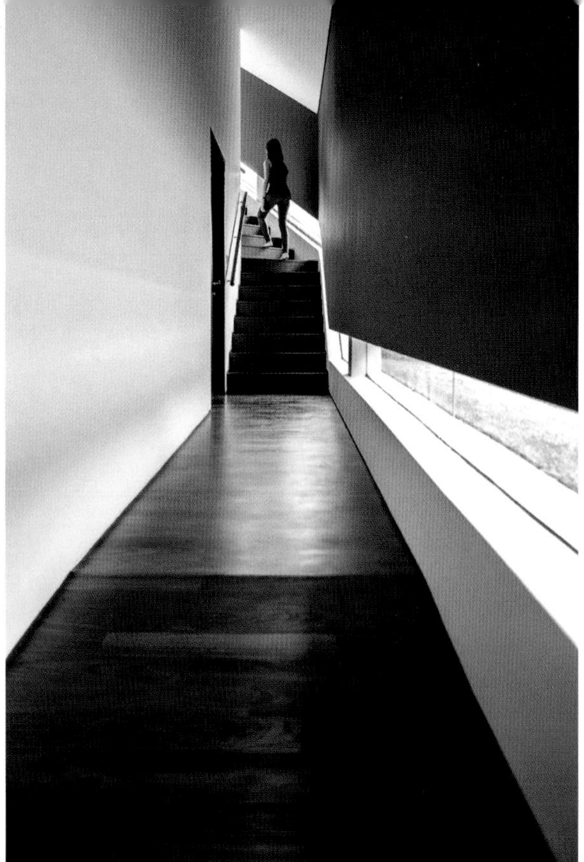

Right A striking feature of the home office is its idiosyncratic circular powder room.

Opposite below left The en suite for the master bedroom is a study in luxury.

Opposite below right The master bedroom has richly toned timber flooring and screens.

Right An elegant timber stairway at the rear of the bedroom pavilion links each level.

Below Looking back along the roof garden and a slanted porch that draws air down into the basement area.

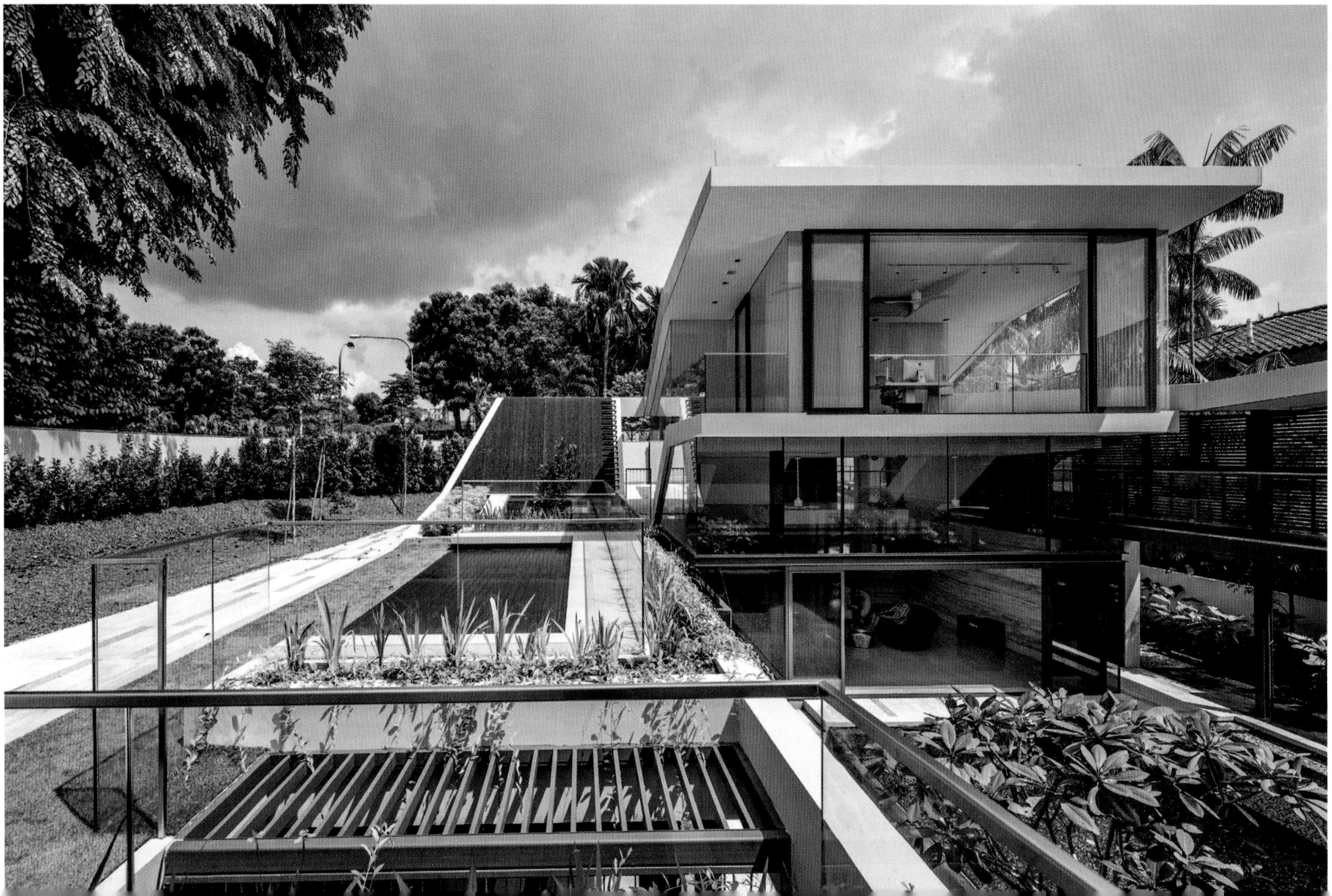

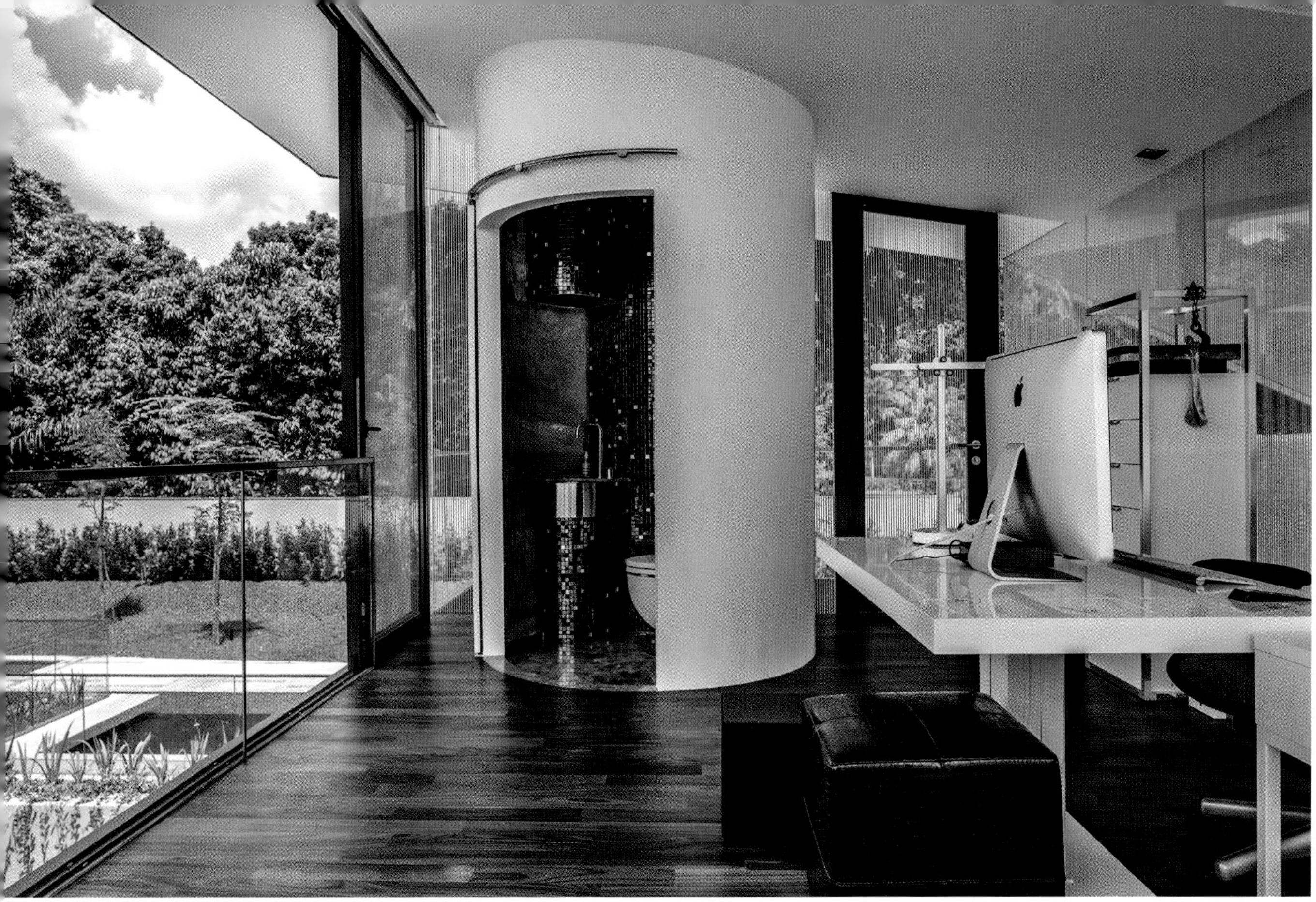

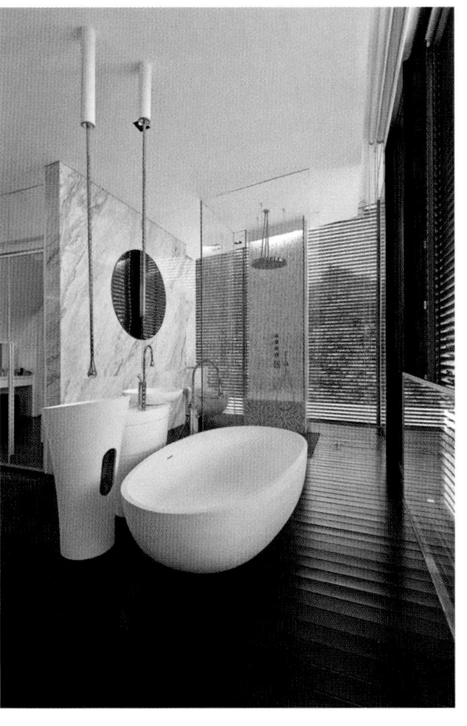

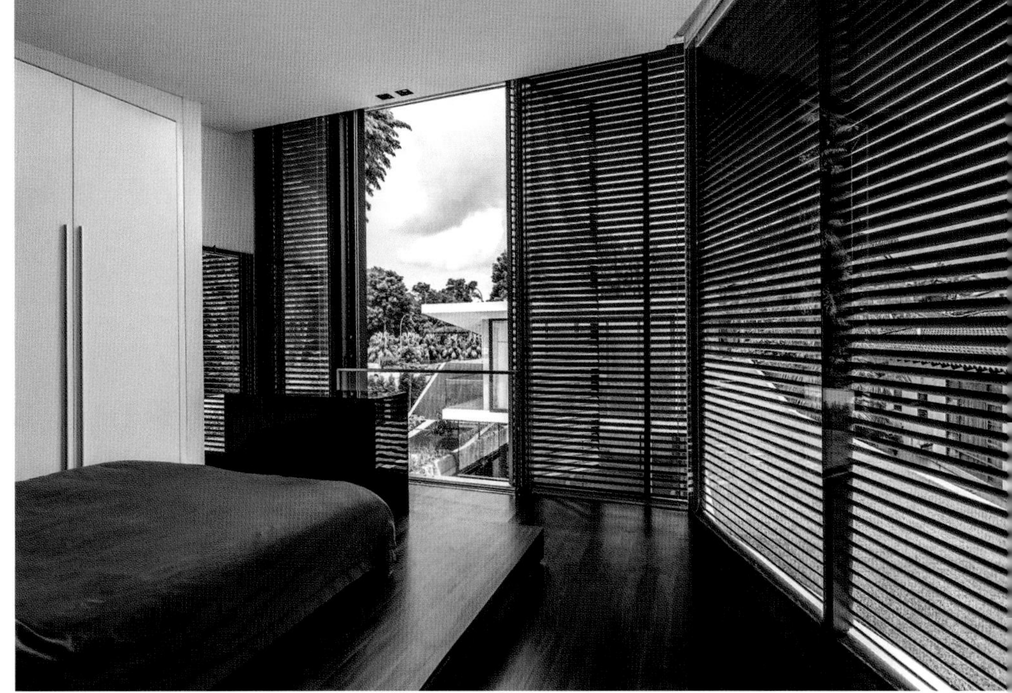

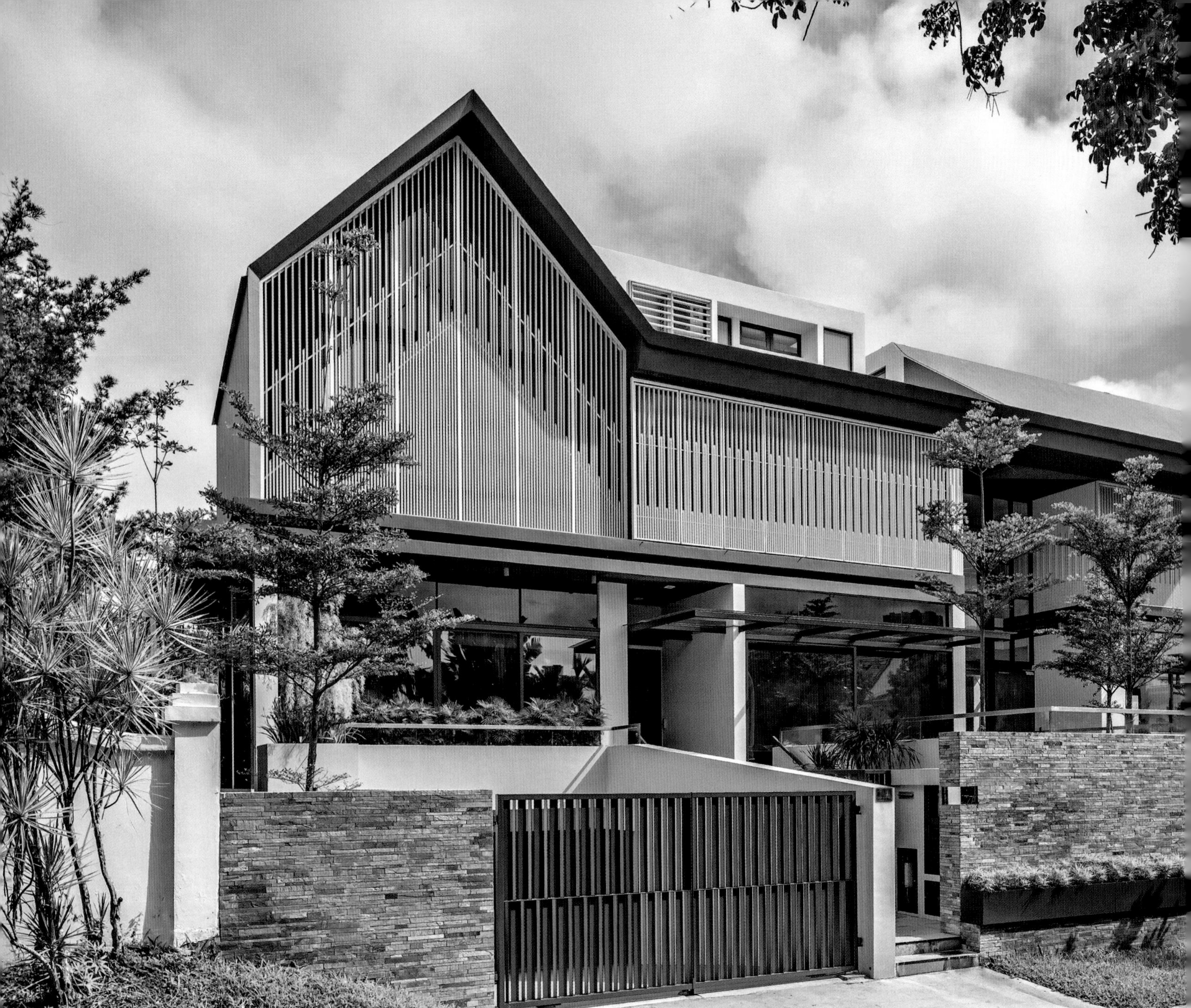

HOLLAND GROVE HOUSE
A D LAB

'To allow them to live happily together, looking at each other, but having their own privacy, we created this courtyard in the middle.'—DARLENE SMYTH, ARCHITECT

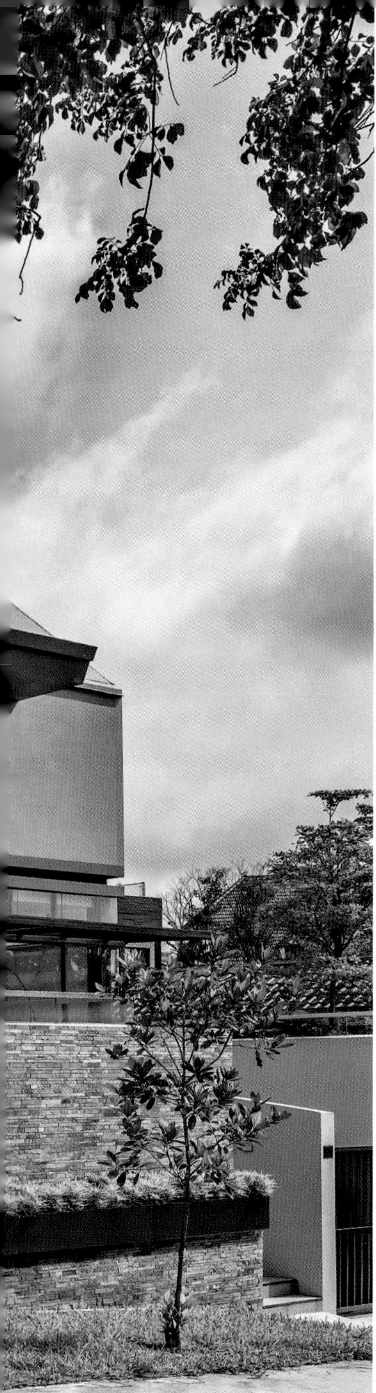

In an environment of constantly rising property values in Singapore, keeping the family together has become as much an economic strategy as a part of the tradition of the extended family. Pooling resources enables a better quality of life, while parents with young children have grandparents available more or less on demand to help with the care of the children. The extended family as an economic and social unit is not new but the multi-generational house has certainly become more prominent. What is different is the degree to which such houses are custom-designed, making them multi-generational in two senses. First, they are designed to accommodate at least three generations of a family, allowing for changing needs as children grow up, and, secondly, they are often designed in a 'timeless' way to allow for multiple owners as they are on-sold.

While the extended family might have a long tradition, it is a tradition that lives on in a rapidly changing world where as much as families may want to stay together, and as much as they see benefits in staying together, a younger generation also demands a greater degree of privacy and independence.

This house is an excellent example of how a multi-generational house has been designed to be economically, socially and personally sustainable, not to mention environmentally responsive.

The family had lived in the original bungalow since the 1980s. The idea was to build a new house that was essentially semi-detached—two houses in one. One son with his young family would live in one house, while his parents and an unmarried younger son would live next door. Physically, the two houses are connected, yet separate. Likewise,

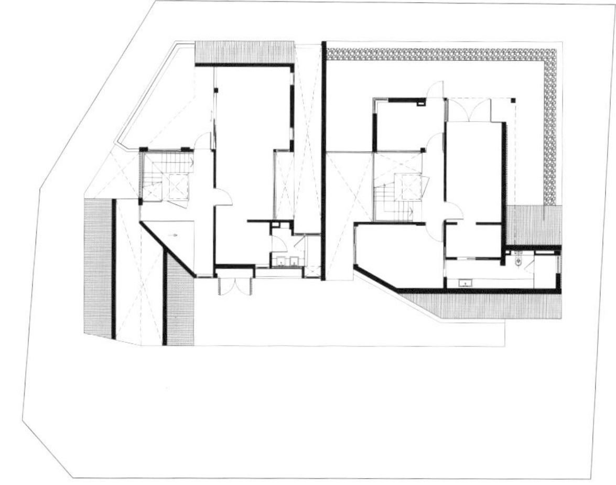

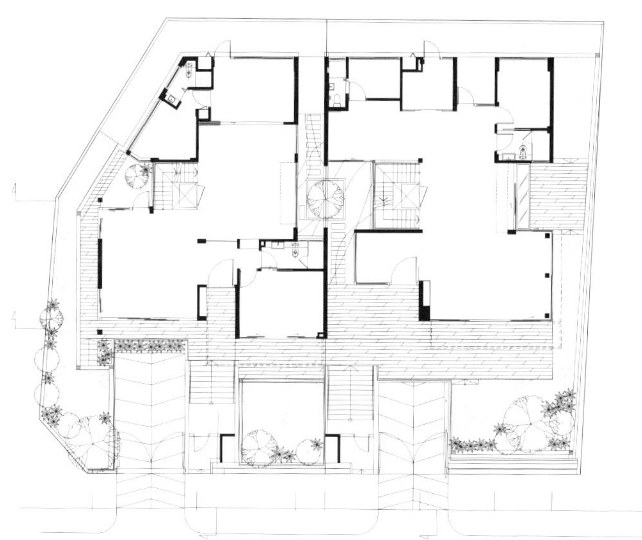

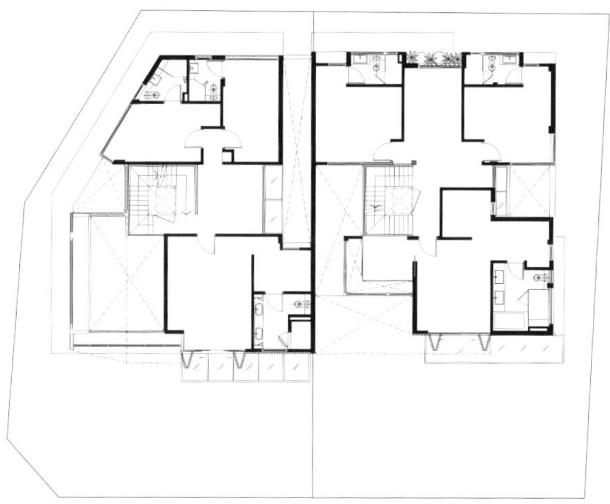

Above left The street elevation of the house, with its double-pitched roof, maintains the silhouette of the previous house.

Right top Attic plan.

Right centre First storey plan.

Right bottom Second storey plan.

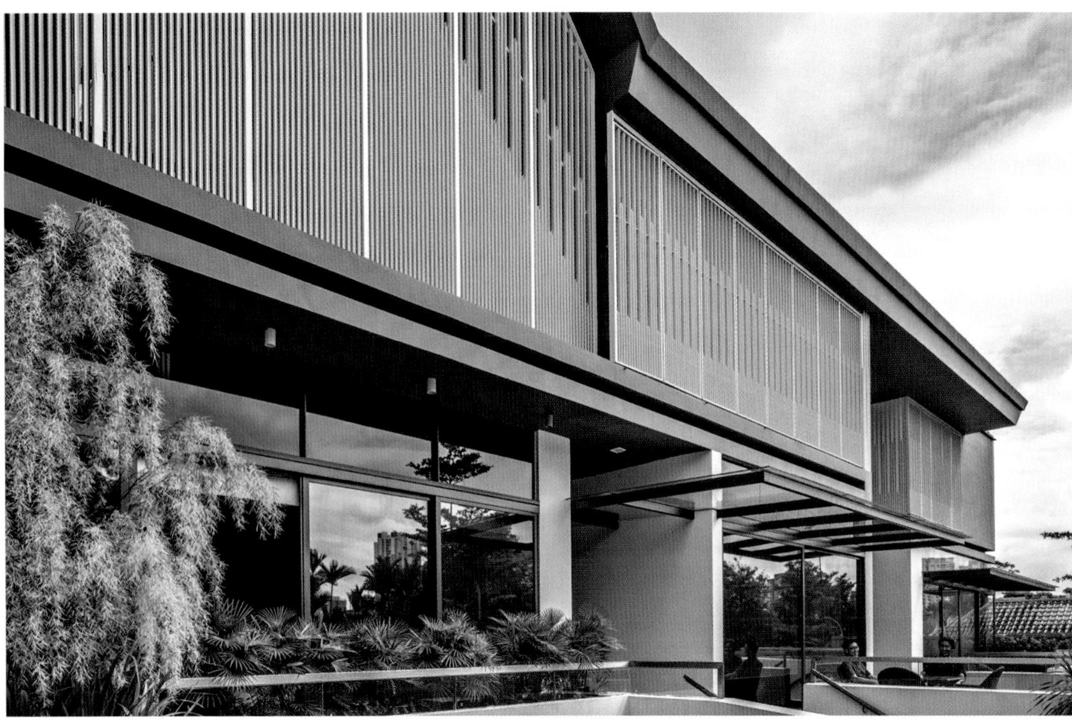

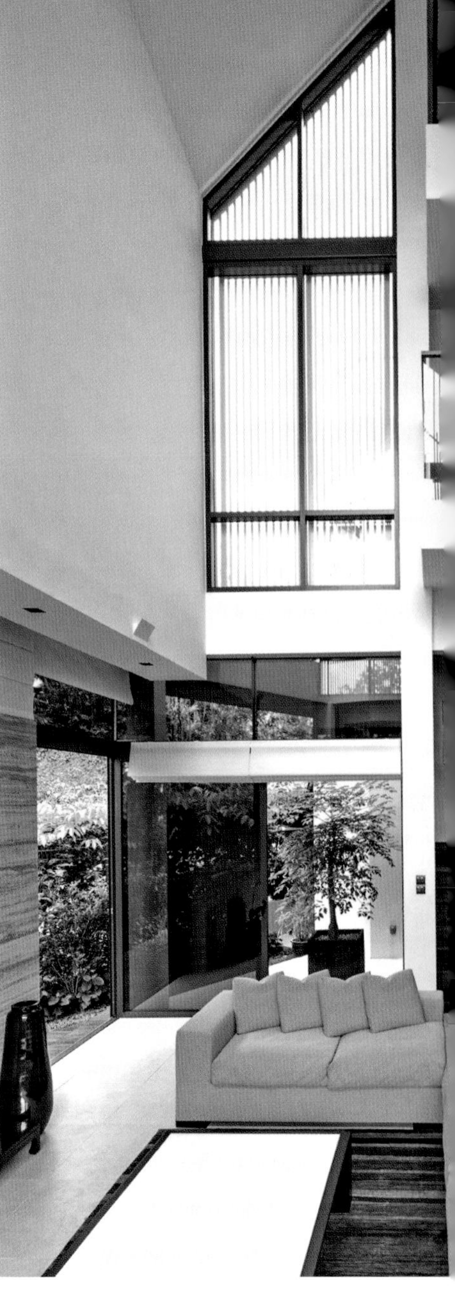

in terms of the continuity of family memory, they are separate yet connected.

It is a new build, but the new house, with its double-pitched roof form, retains the silhouette of the former house. Similarly, in plan and in the way the house is filled with light and a sense of being, a part of the garden maintains the memory of how it was to live in the old house. For example, the indirect way one enters the grandparents' home replicates the former house. This creates a sense of connection over time and contributes to the feeling that this is a family home which embodies that family's history and how each generation develops from the one before. It underlines how the home can sustain the family which, in turn, sustains our sense of who we are.

A potential problem for this particular scheme was that a semi-detached house is expected to have a party wall without any openings in that wall. The architects, Warren Liu, Darlene Smyth and C. J. Foo, argued that here was a father and a son who wanted to live together and were happy to have an opening between the two units. Eventually, the plan was approved on the understanding that if the house were to be sold, any openings would have to be filled.

The aim was to design something which looked like one house but with two entrances. There are three points of connection. The first is at ground level where the two units share the front garden and deck. There is also a common basement/car parking area. Inside, on the entry level, the houses are connected by a shared water garden, with a meandering plan and tropical vegetation, allowing visual connection between the two units.

The water feature becomes part of the arrival sequence to the son's house, which is scaled down somewhat compared to the parents' house, mainly to create more room for the family. Entry to the parents' house, on the other hand, is through a double-height living space. Only then do we turn right, past the powder-coated aluminium sun screen, and move into the body of the house. Here, on the ground floor, the grandfather has his office looking out to the garden. This room has its own en suite bathroom to enable it to be converted into another

Above left The garden and front terrace connect the two independent houses.

Above The married son's house looking back towards the connecting courtyard.

Right The double-height living room of the parents' house, with its cathedral-like acknowledgement of their faith.

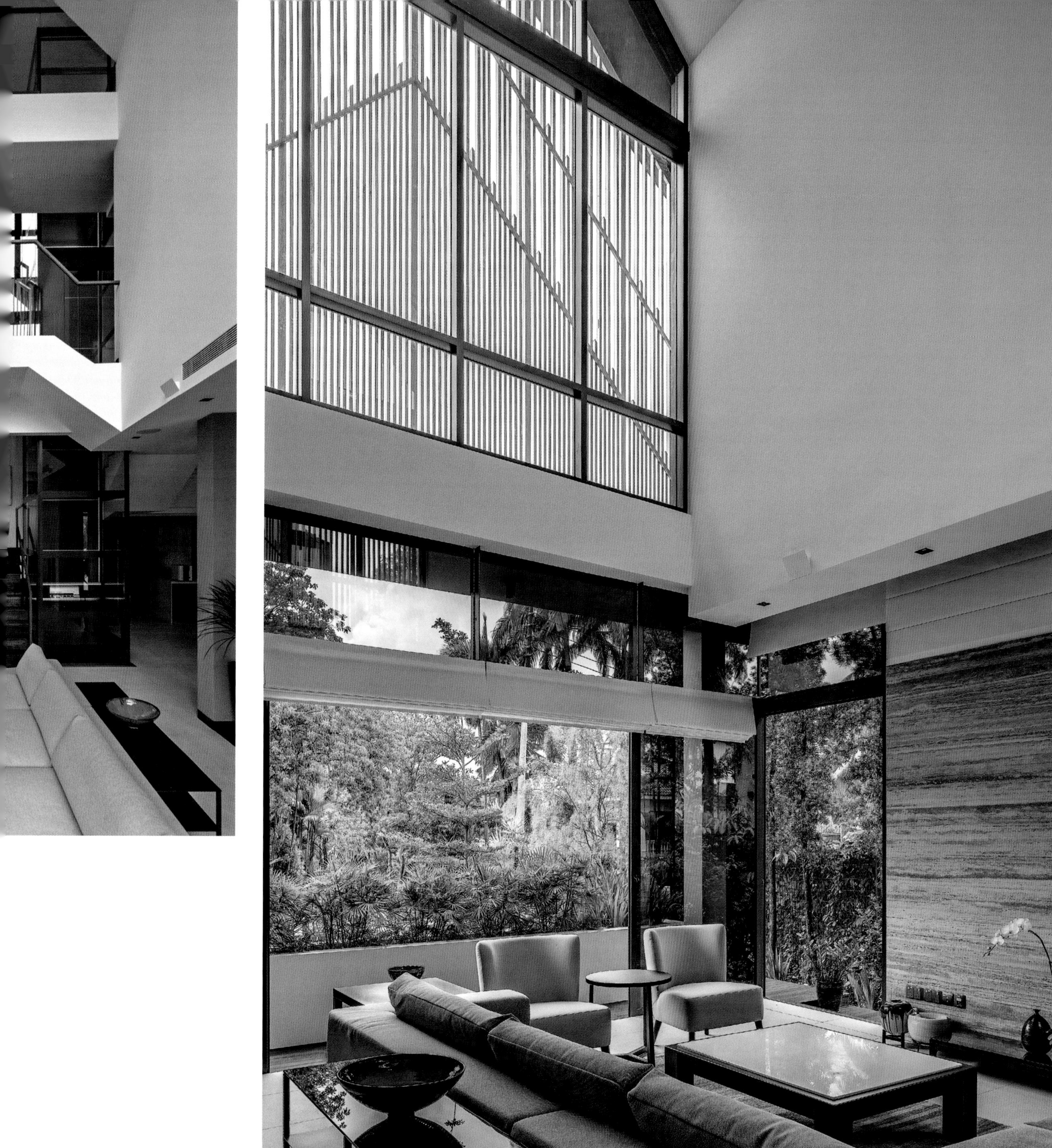

bedroom in the future. The son also has his office at the front to allow surveillance of the front garden, but on the upper level. Both houses have travertine feature walls in the entry rooms to create a sense of arrival and communicate a degree of ritual.

The house is oriented to capture prevailing northeast and southwest winds. All the openings are diagonal in order to channel these breezes, including the water feature that acts as a natural cooling agent.

The unmarried son lives in what the architect describes as 'a cool pad in the attic'. Here is an example of how adult children are being encouraged to stay at home by having quality accommodation designed to suit their lifestyle and, at the same time, provide privacy. Here, the son has an impressive outdoor shower where the fossil stone wall is continuous with the courtyard wall. The fossil stone, in a different finish, is used on the inside part of the bathroom as well.

Below Looking back towards the parents' house along the connecting timber deck.

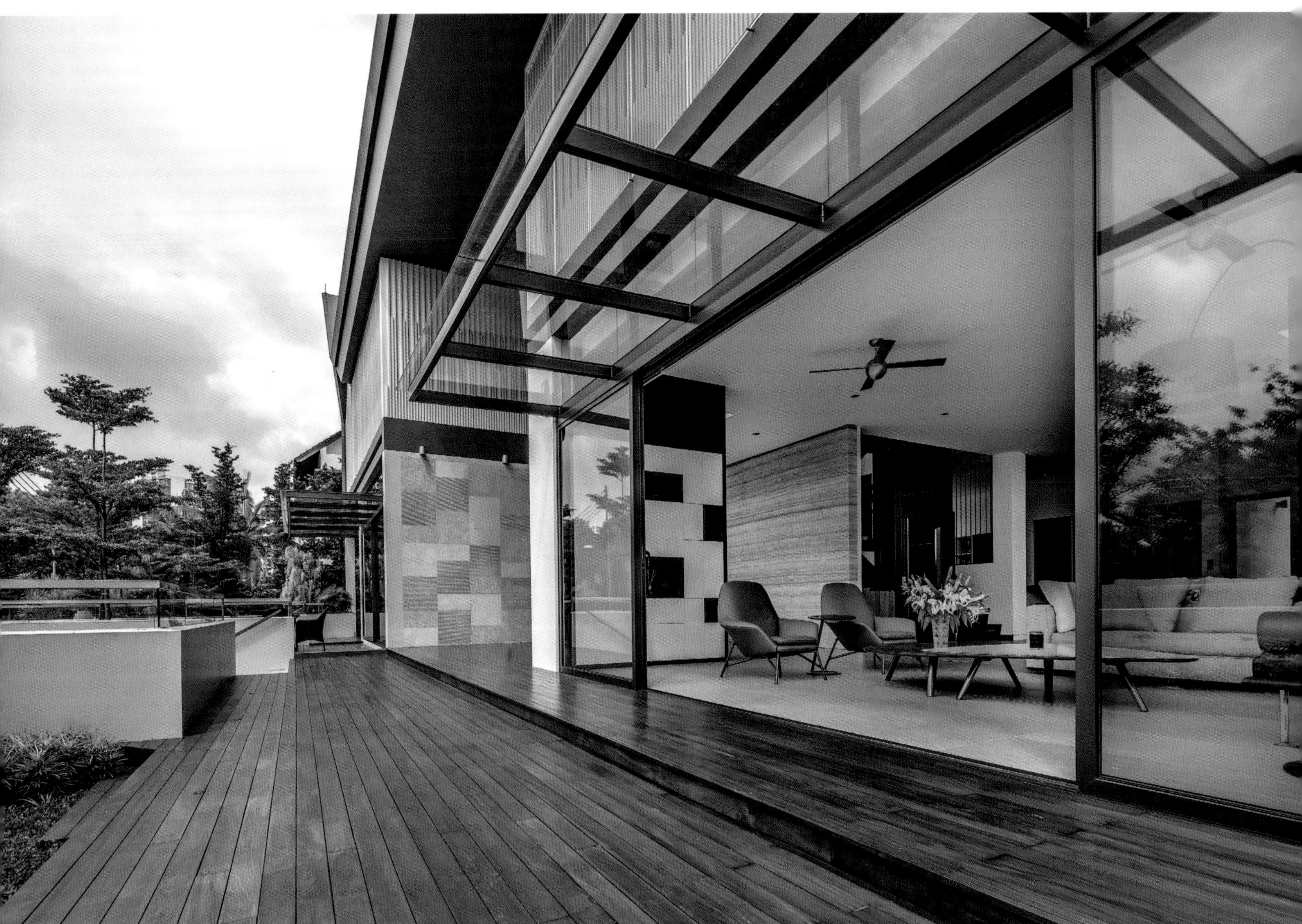

Right The garden court that connects the two houses.

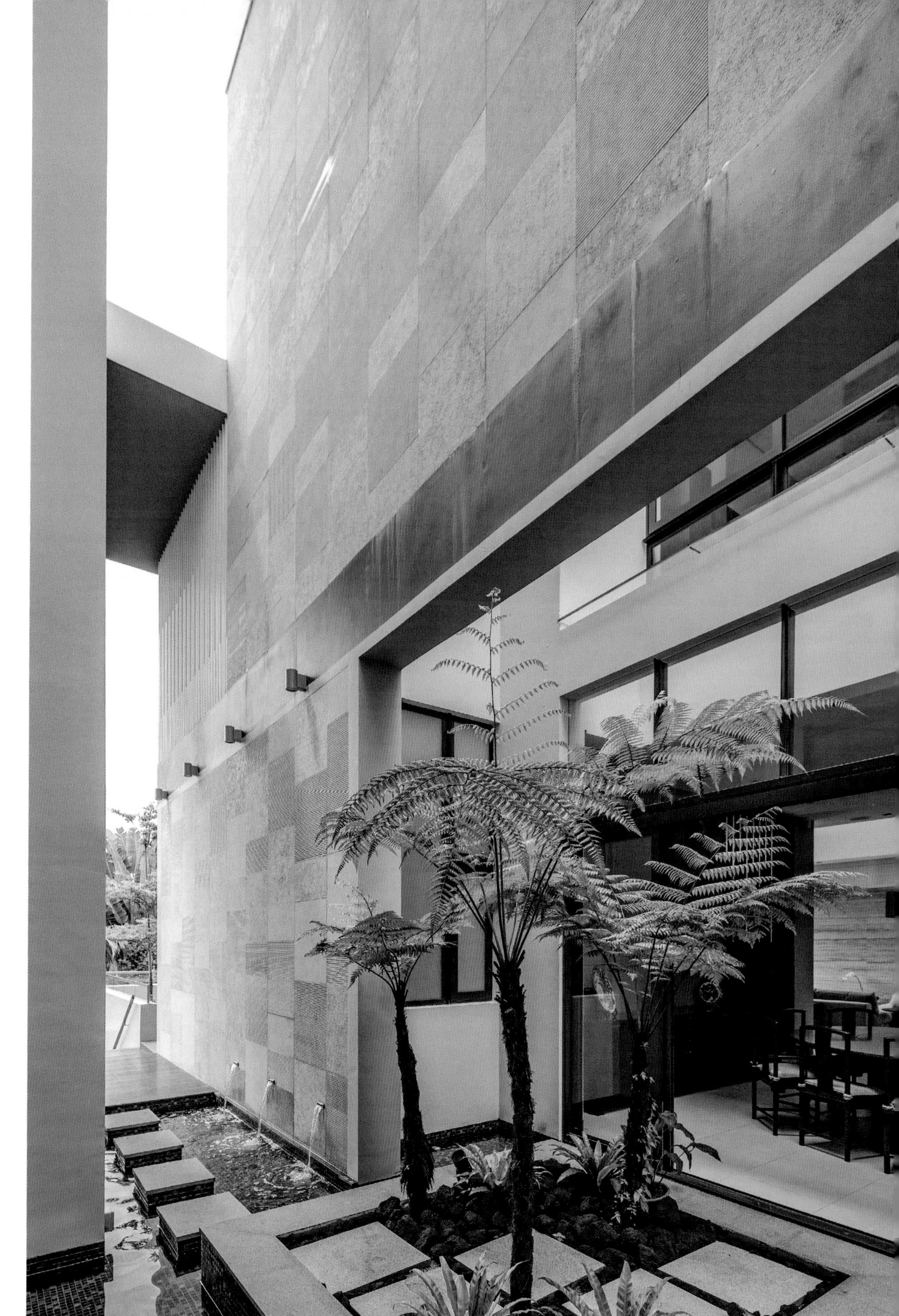

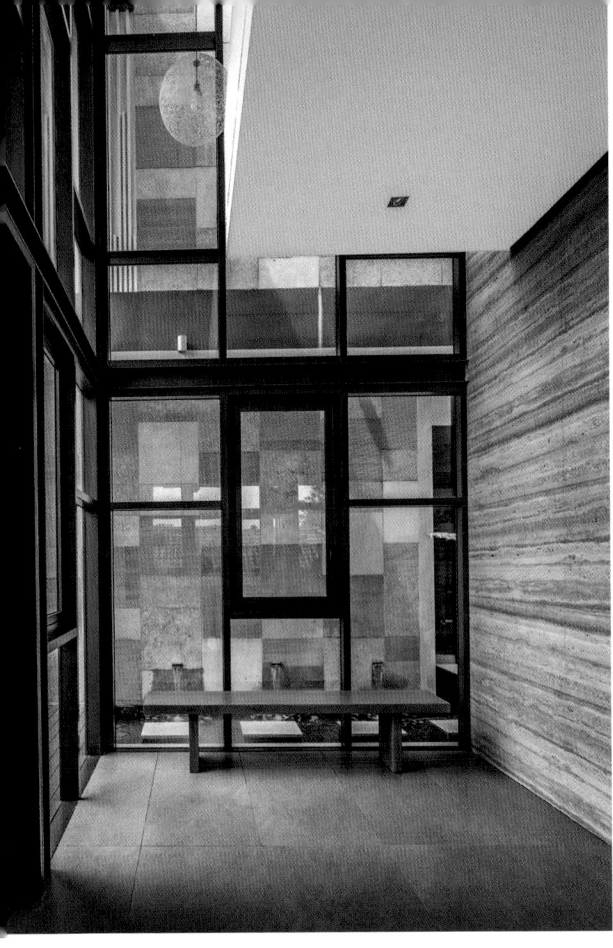

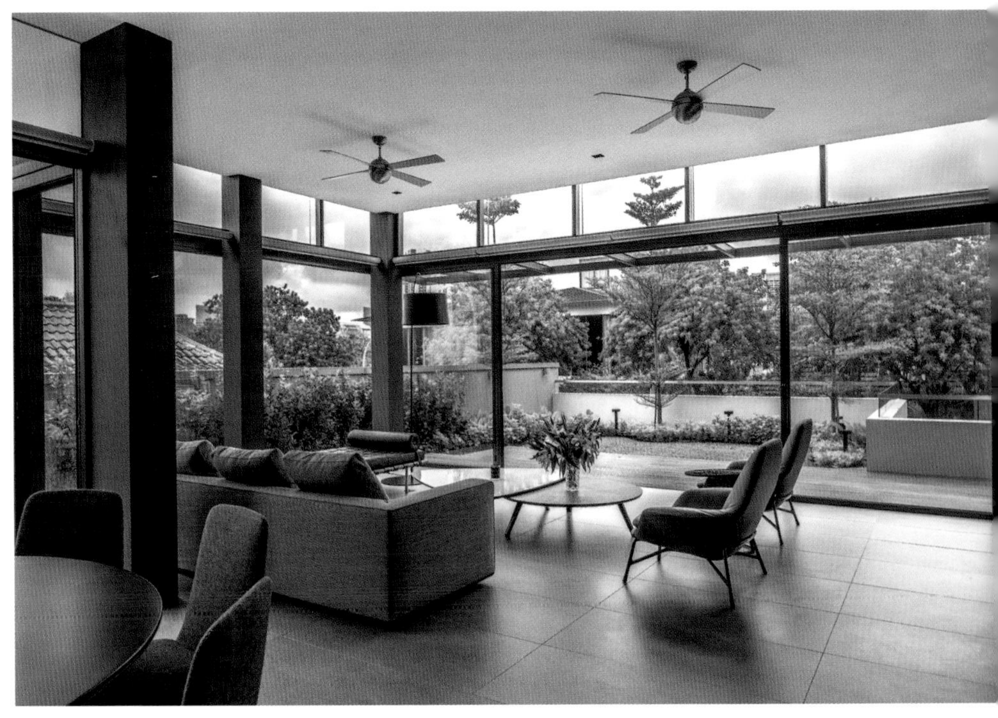

Above Double-height spaces are a feature of both houses.

Below The master bathroom has finishes that allow for ageing users.

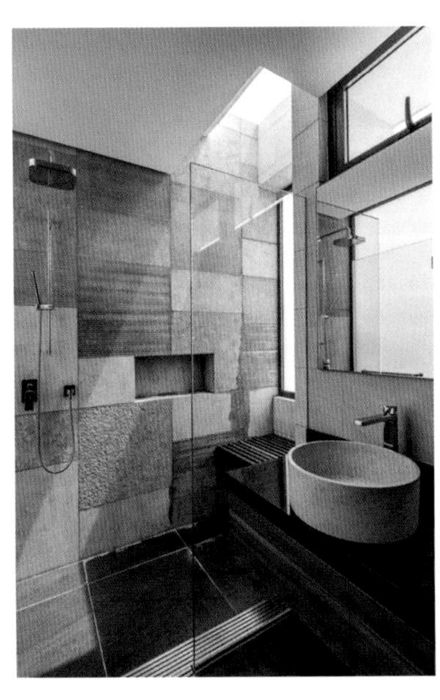

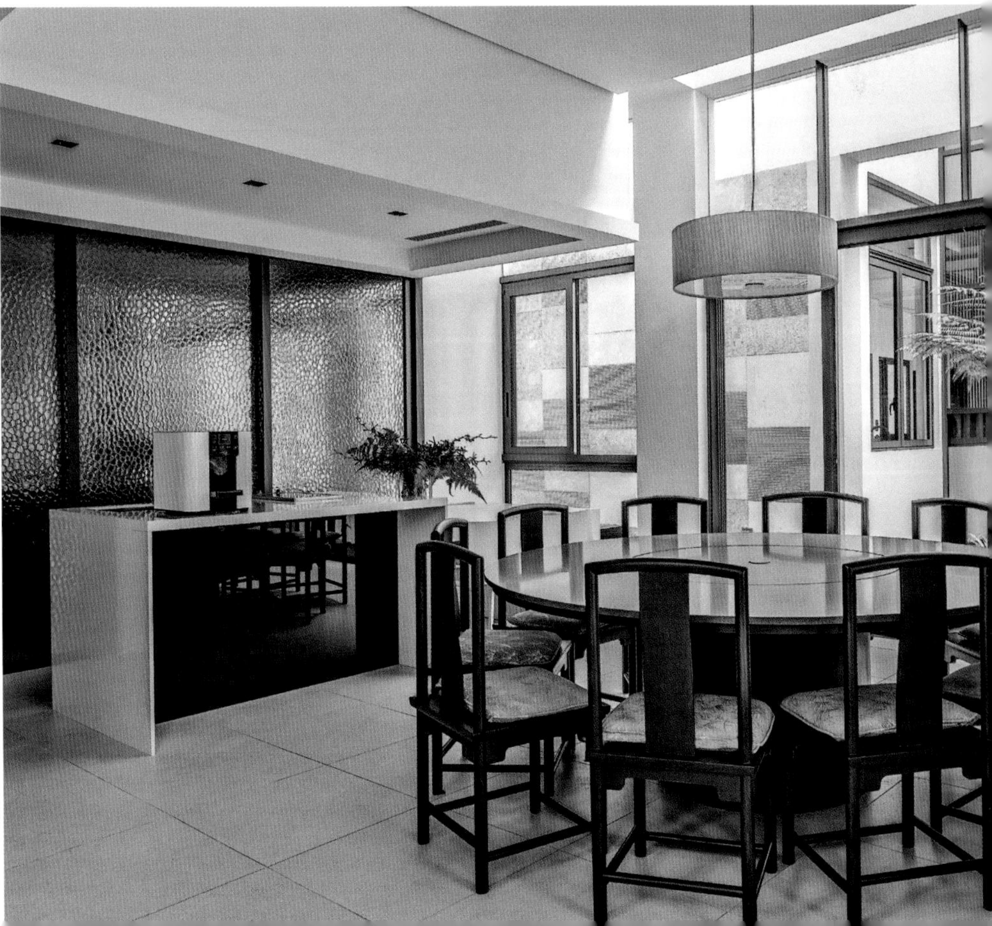

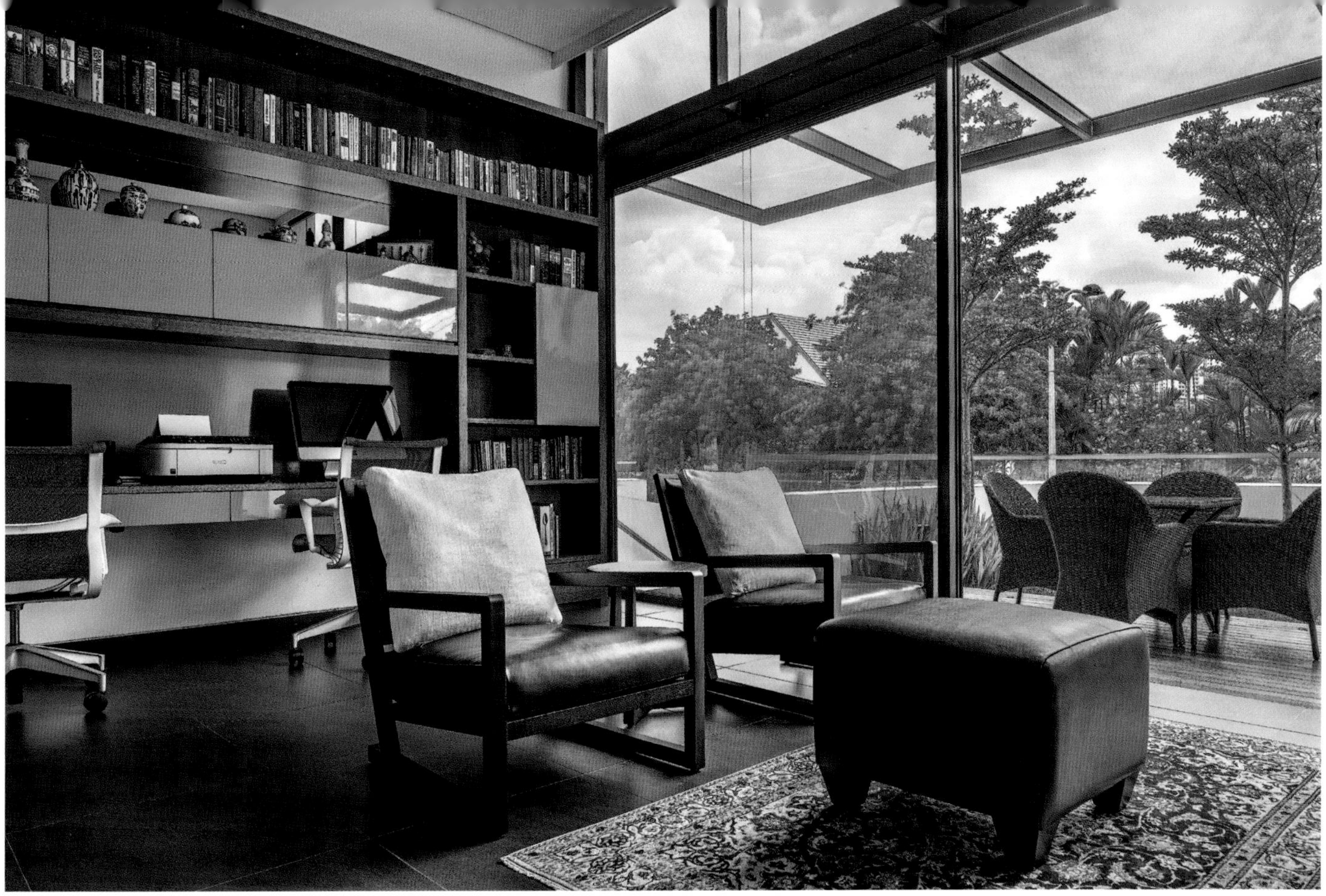

Above The home office in the parents' house.

Right The unmarried son enjoys a penthouse-like apartment on the top floor of his parents' house.

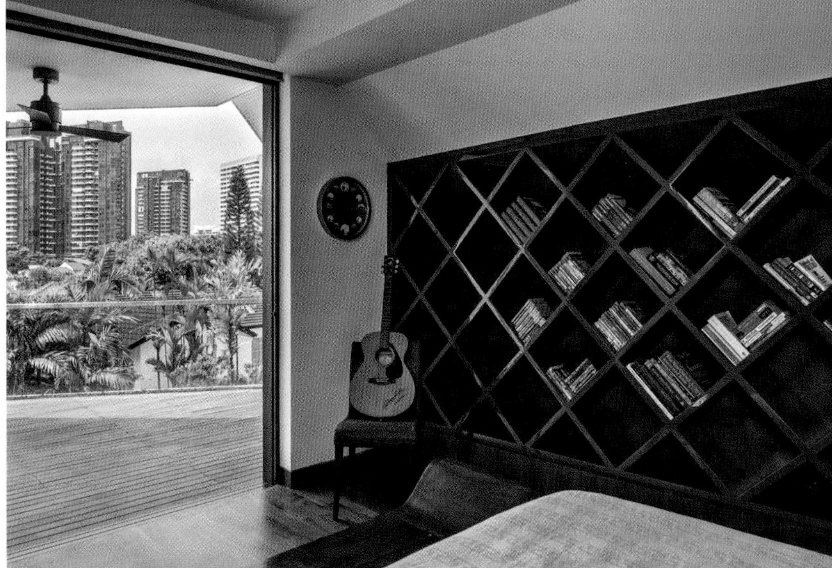

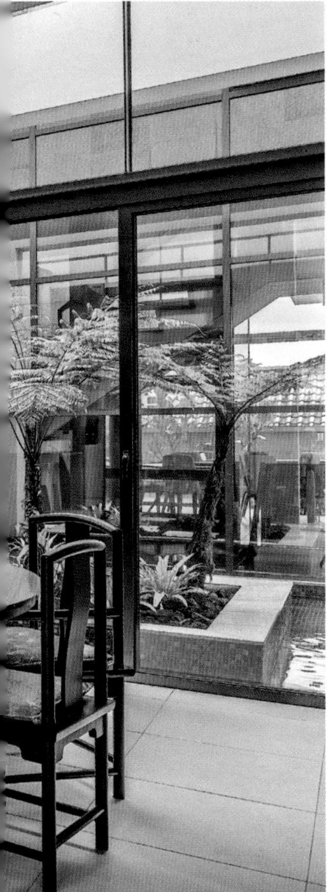

Above centre The linking courtyard acts as a cooling element for both houses.

Left The dining space in the parents' house has views across the garden court to the son's house.

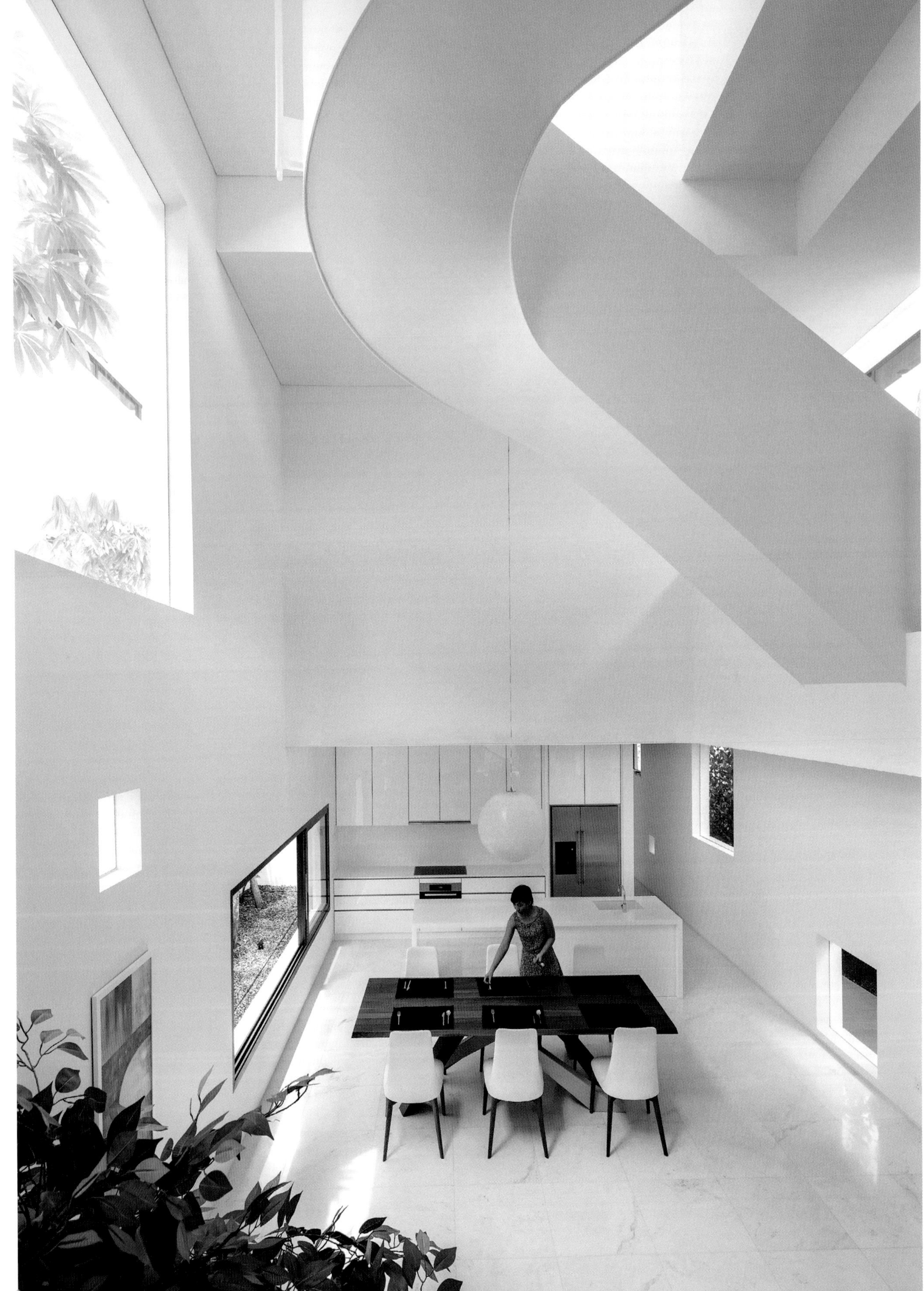

SEMBAWANG LONG HOUSES FORMWERKZ

'We could have done two at the front and a third at the back connected by a driveway. But we thought that would be a waste because the back is where the view is. We wanted to equalize it.'—ALAN TAY, ARCHITECT

Opposite The houses follow the form of a traditional shophouse but with a reinterpretation of the central lightwell.

Below Rear short sections.

Bottom The three houses present as a family of buildings.

These three houses are in Singapore's commuter belt of Sembawang. In contrast to the suburbia surrounding them, however, they back on to state land with a forest of mature trees stretching into the distance. 'Borrowed landscape' like this is a dream in Singapore, so the architects decided to make the most of it, in so doing optimizing density on the site and ensuring that each of the three houses had access to the view.

The plot is framed on one side by a terrace house and on the other by a semi-detached house. Conscious of the importance of relating to the neighbours—being a 'good neighbour'—the architects decided to reference the neighbouring typologies in a subtle way. They did this by designing a contemporary reinterpretation of the Singapore shophouse or courtyard house. This involves long, narrow volumes with an atrium in the middle—the equivalent of the central courtyard in the shophouse—to draw in light. Each of the atria has a tree growing up towards the top of the house.

A courtyard house is typically limited by a party wall. Here, there is no such restriction as each house is free-standing. The architects followed the general plan and proportions of the shophouse except for the fact that each house is entered in the middle of the house after walking down the side.

Each house has three floors and a basement. The two outer houses have basically the same plan but the middle house is organized differently, with the architects 'using the middle one for the outer two to react to'. This was their strategy to avoid

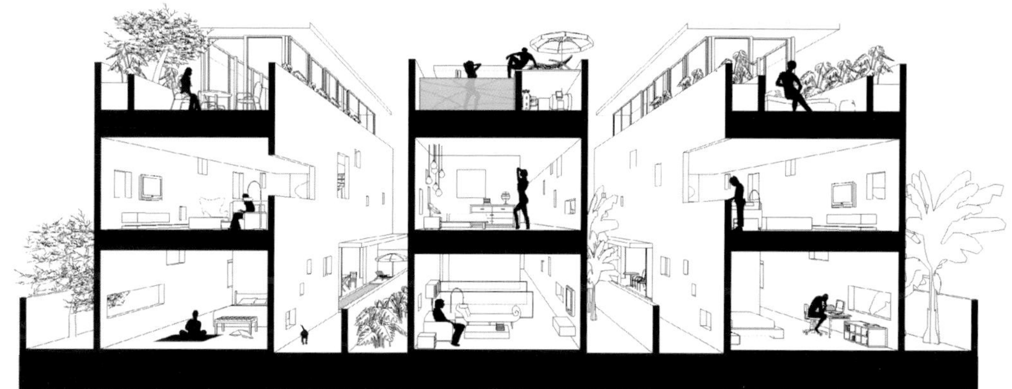

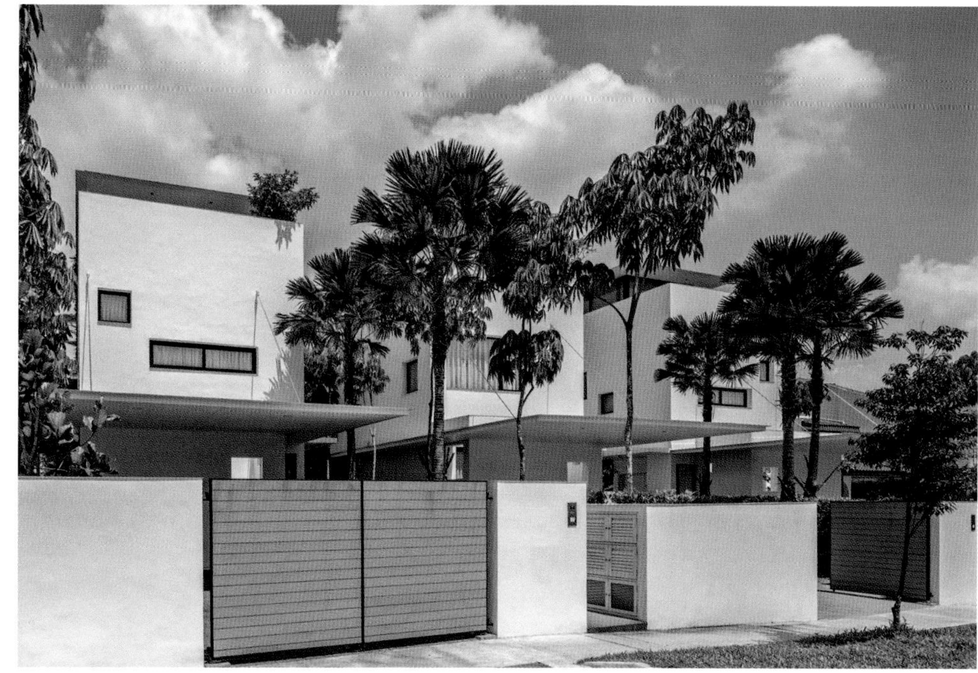

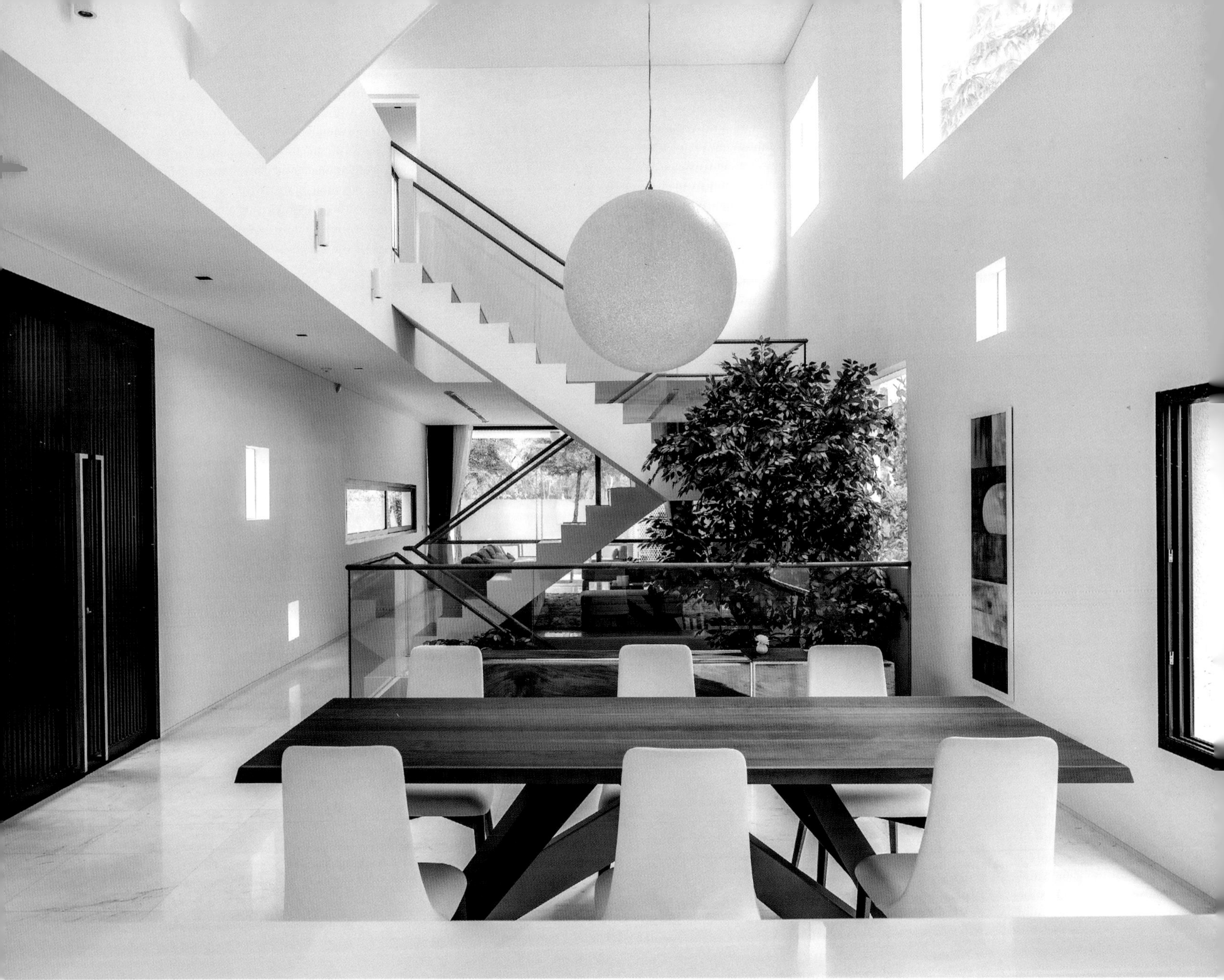

standardization, allowing each house to have its own individuality. In the middle house, the living area is upstairs whereas in the two flanking it, it is downstairs. Hence, they do not overlook each other.

Bringing greenery into the house with indoor gardens and atria with trees in the centre is typical of Formwerkz. Just as typical is the firm's creative fenestration. This creativity with windows—seemingly endless variations in size, height and shape—is used here to serve several purposes. It supports the strategy of individualizing each house but it is also a tactic for driving greater privacy given that the houses are very close together (just four metres separates them). With such a variety of windows, the houses can face each other without being intrusive. But, says Alan Tay, the variety in the fenestration also 'creates different viewpoints'. These are viewpoints to the outside gardens. But the variety also sets up a rhythm throughout the houses, generating a filmic experience as one moves

Above The central lightwell is served by a connecting stairway beginning in the basement.

Opposite above The rhythm of the windows is echoed in the way dark-toned doorways and window frames punctuate the glistening white space.

Opposite below The house offers vertiginous views down through the central void.

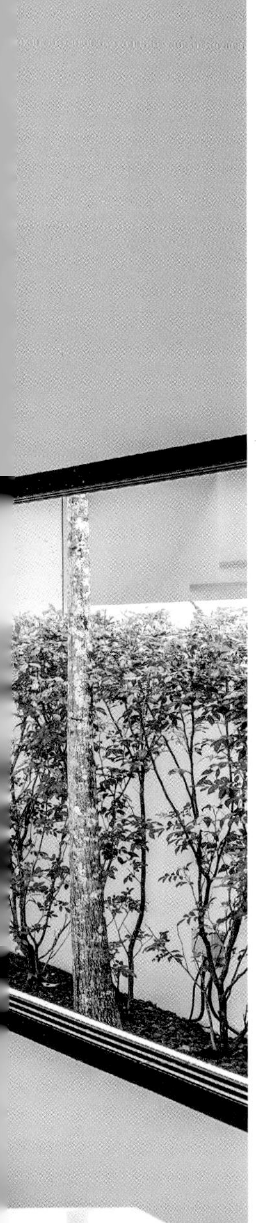

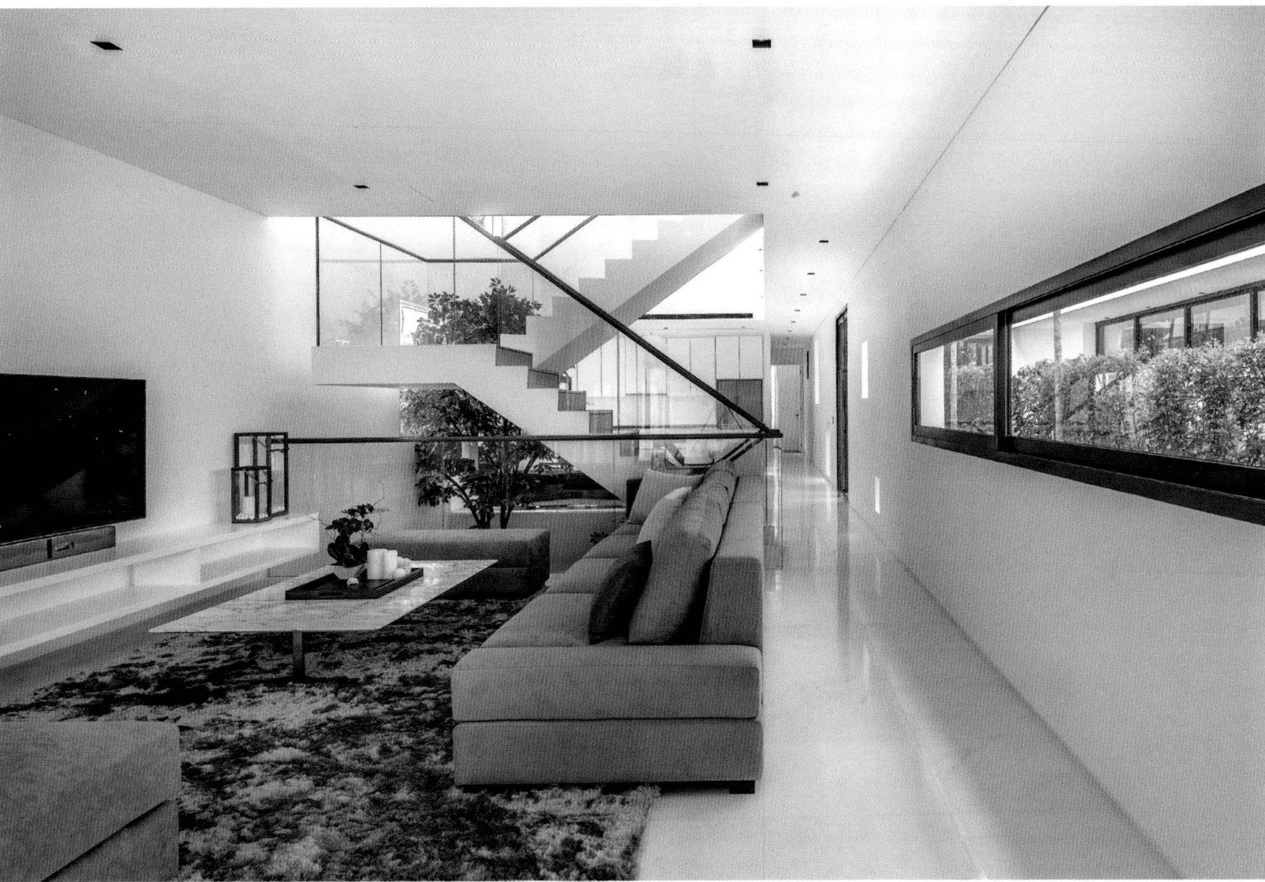

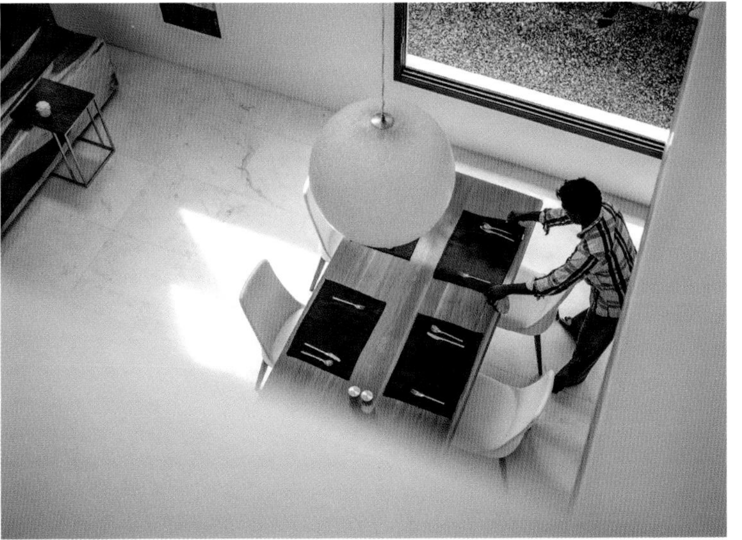

along what might otherwise be a predictable and unremarkable journey through the house, a risk when replicating the shophouse plan. This filmic quality is generated by the sequences of glimpsed views and by a constant play of light and shadow.

The houses allow for multi-generational occupancy, with the parents' room at the front with its own water feature courtyard, and the master bedroom at the rear with views to the state land. The side houses have their swimming pool running down the side so that it becomes a water feature. The middle house, however, has the pool on the top where a spiral staircase links the pool deck with the lower level. One enters the pool deck through a glass pavilion and the pool thrusts out towards the view, culminating in an infinity edge.

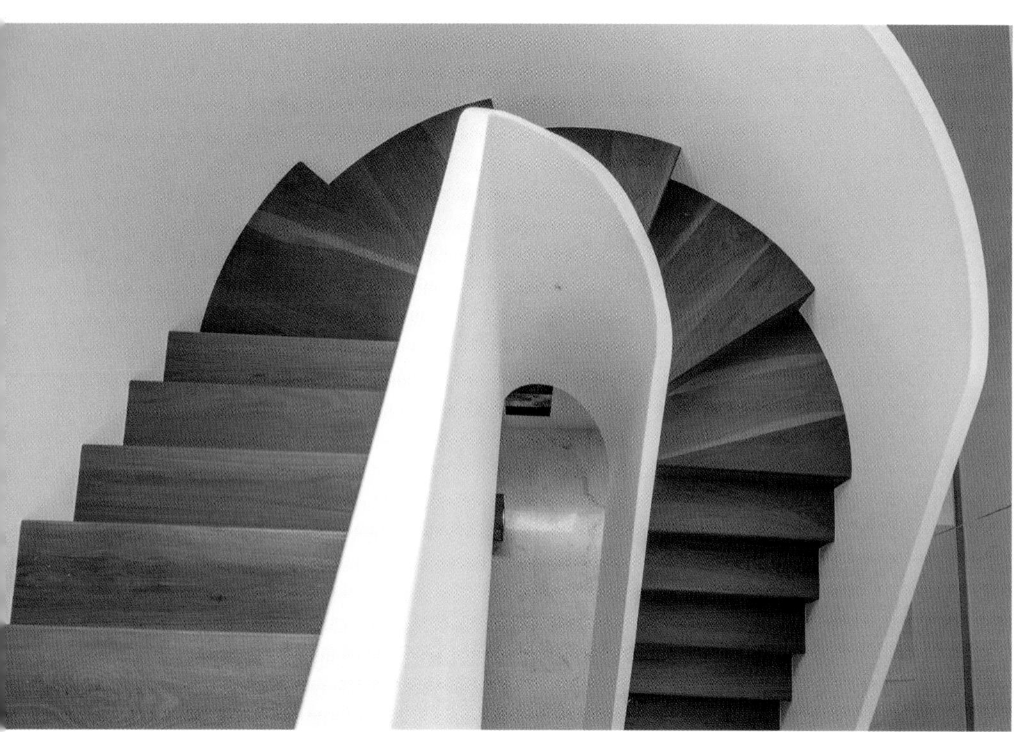

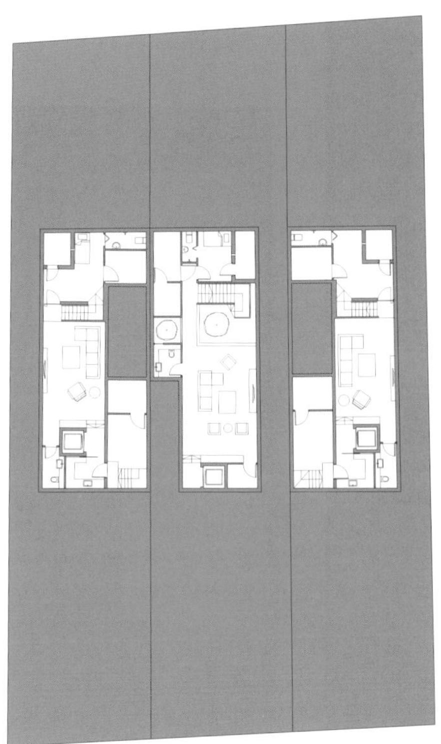

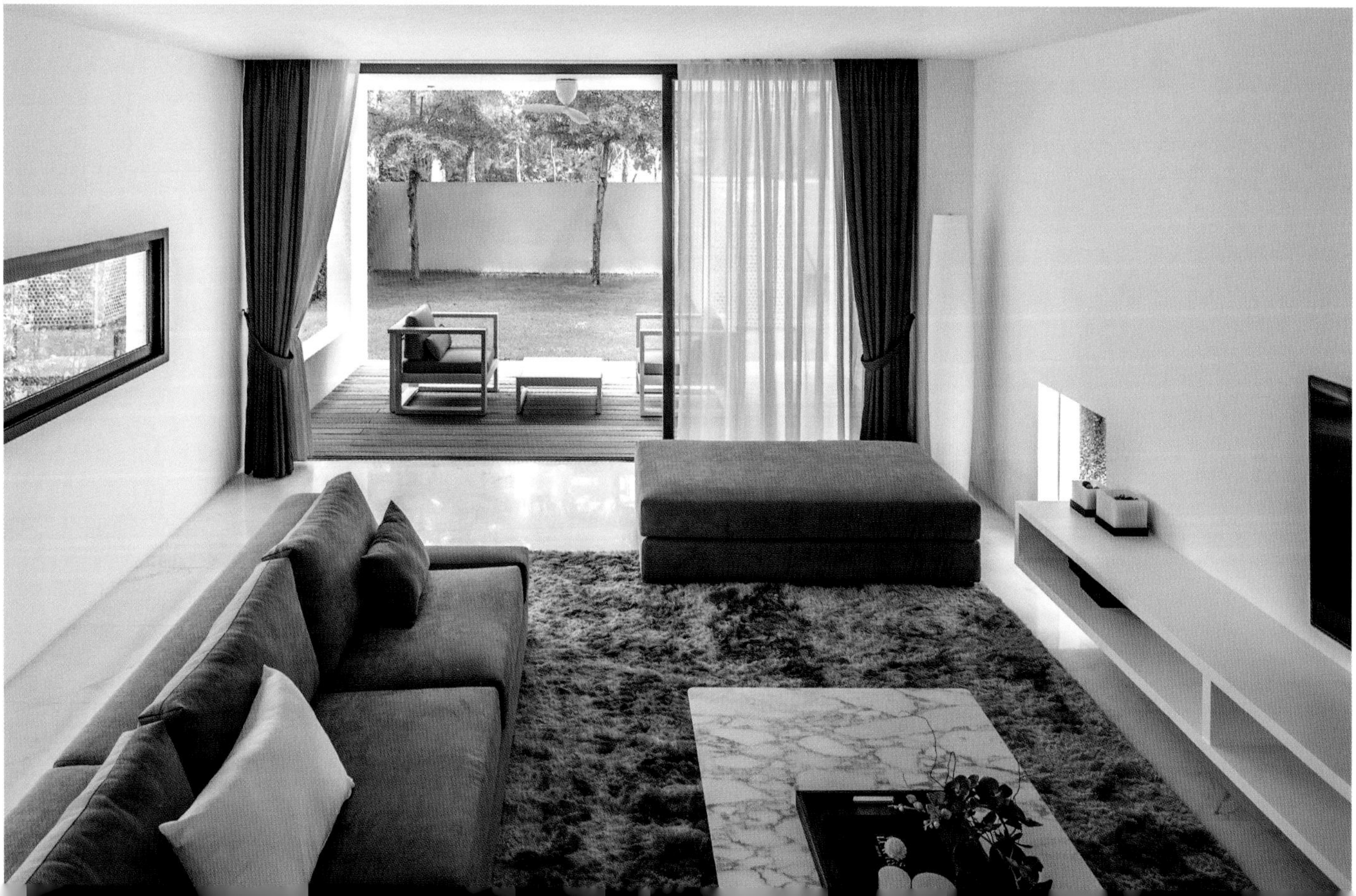

Far left The overall white palette is warmed by timber flooring.

Left Site plan.

Below left The living area spills out through a covered terrace to a walled garden courtyard.

Right Multiple sources of natural light soften the white palette.

Below Plans.

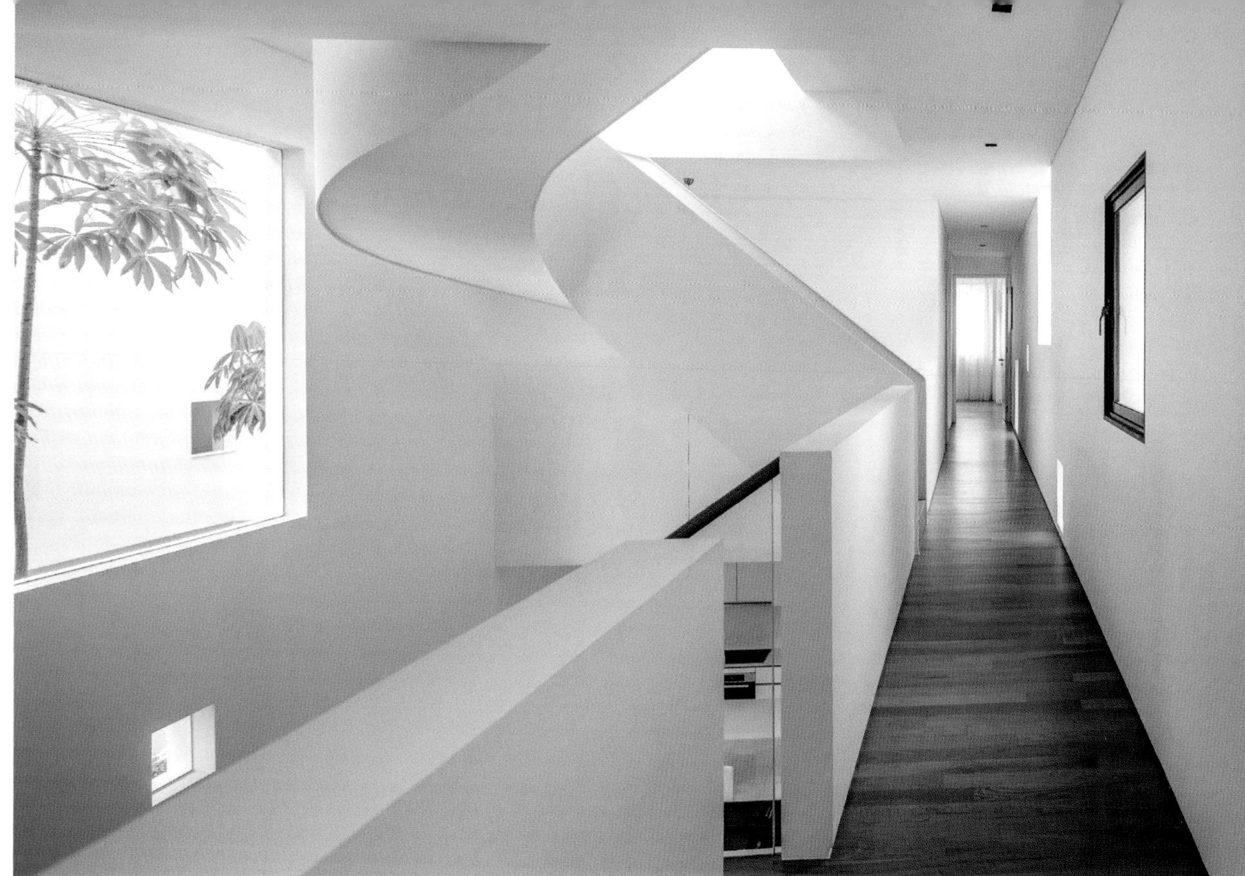

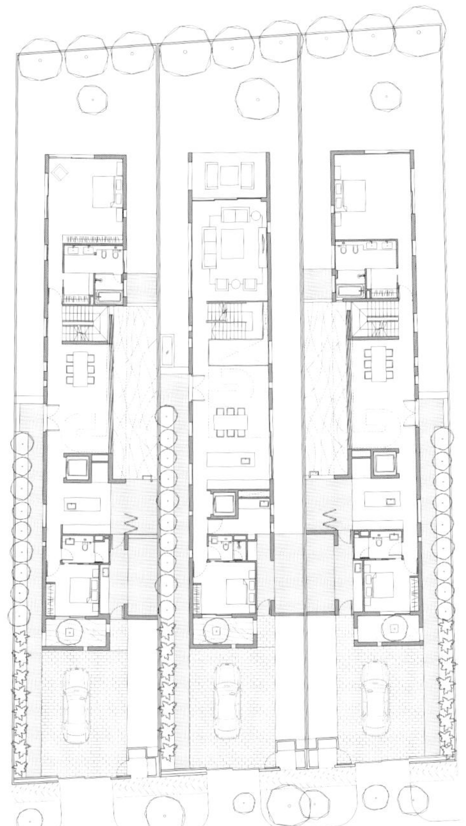

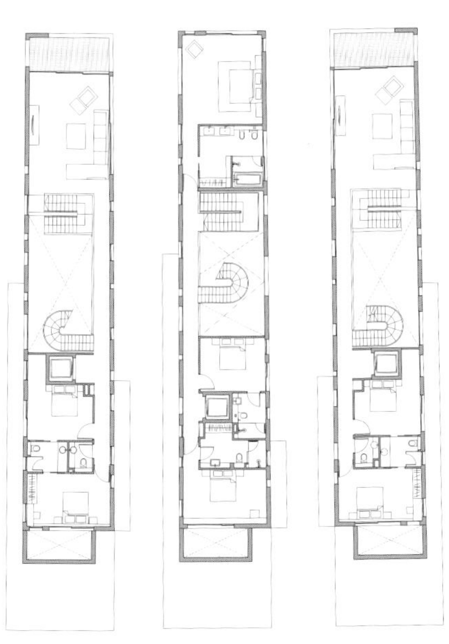

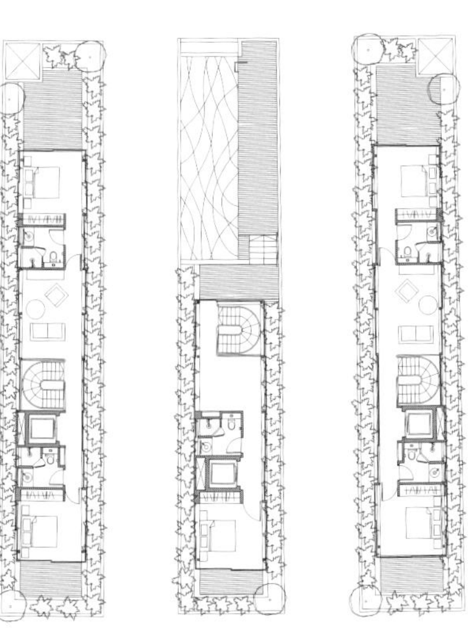

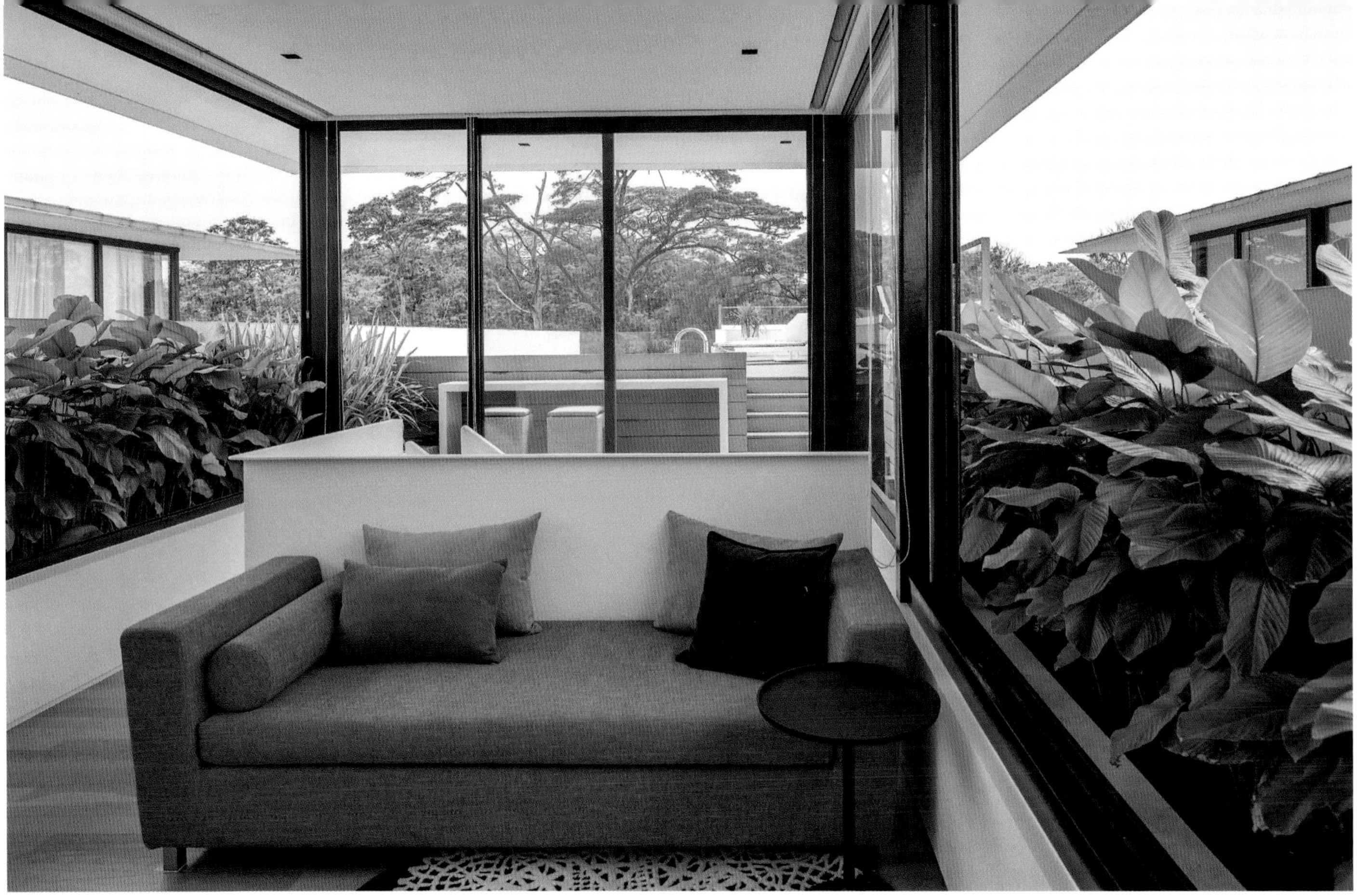

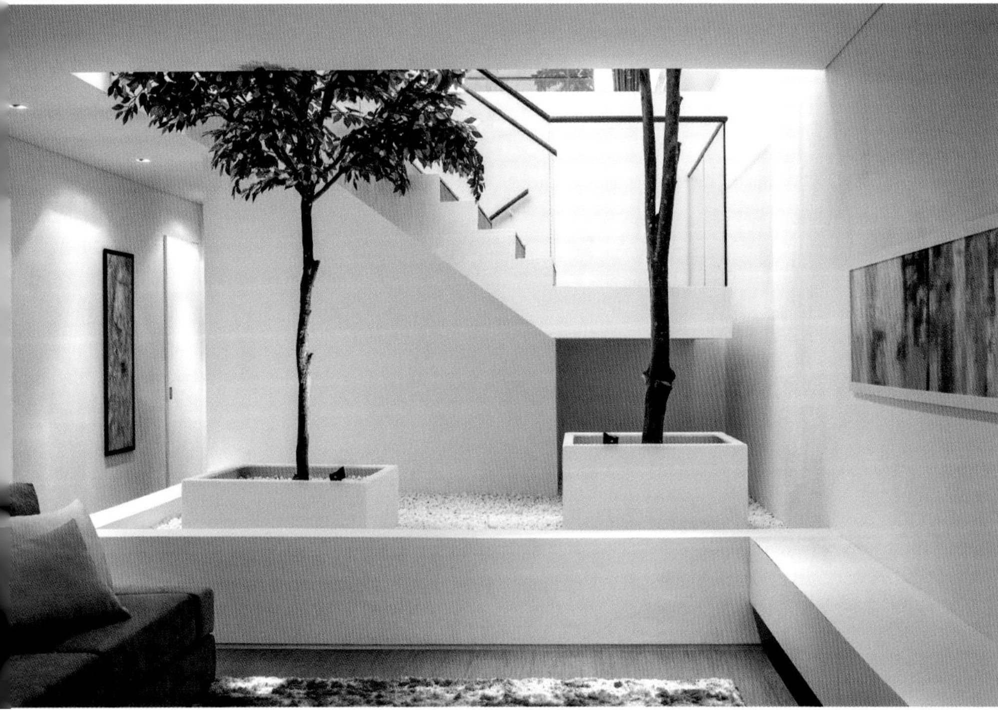

Above The swimming pool pavilion in the middle house is wrapped by tropical foliage.

Left Trees grow up through the central void.

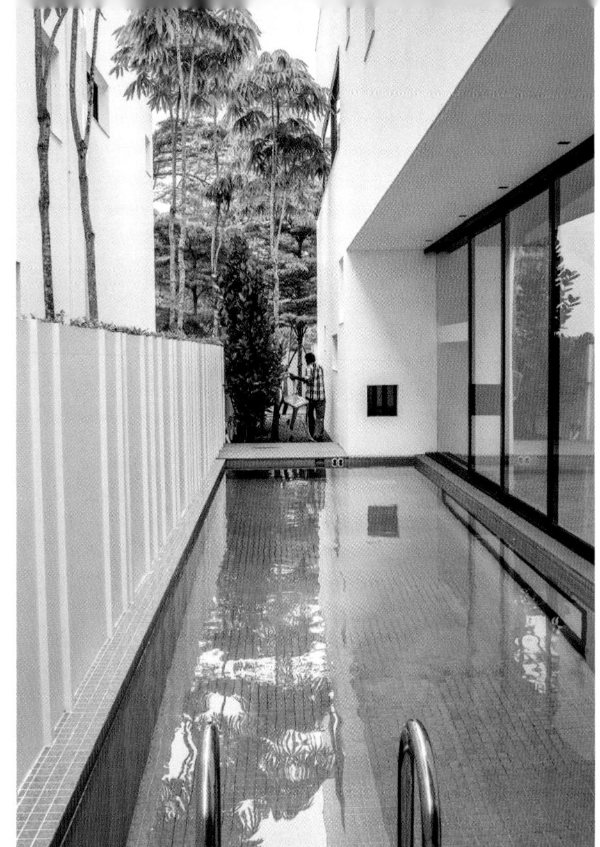

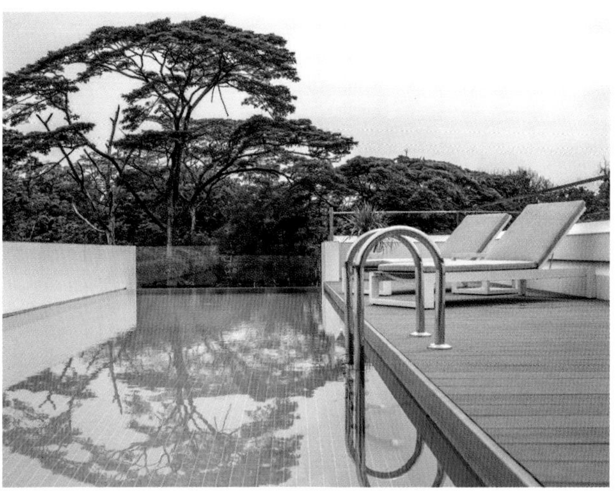

Left The two side houses have pools running down the side, doubling as cooling water features.

Above The middle house has a rooftop pool with an infinity edge embracing the reserve at the back.

Below The pool and its pavilion in the middle house.

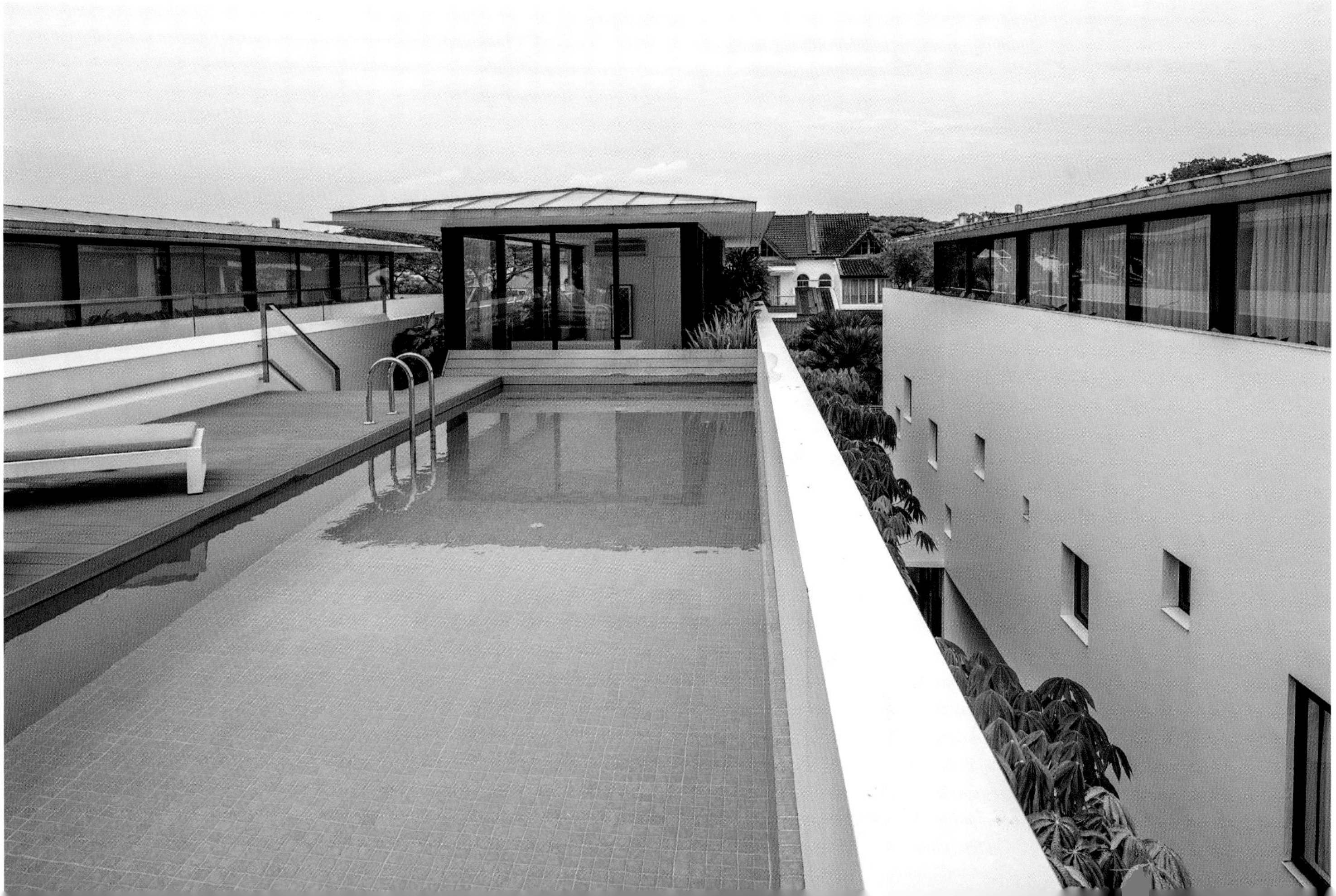

TREE HOUSE
FORMWERKZ

'We realized that it made sense to place the private spaces below so that you could have a more intimate relationship with the gardens. You are more private on the ground floor, whereas upstairs you are more exposed, more open.'— ALAN TAY, ARCHITECT

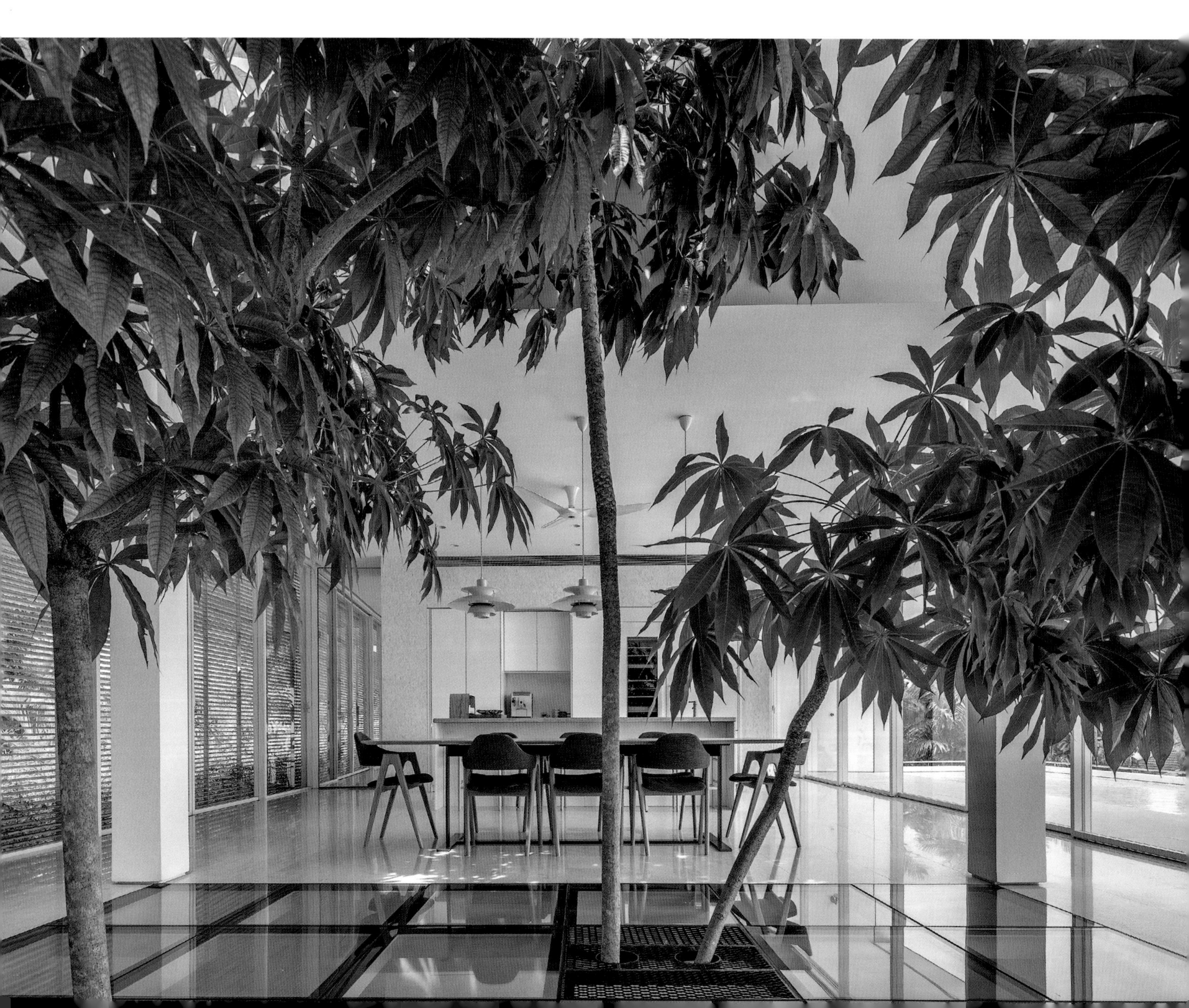

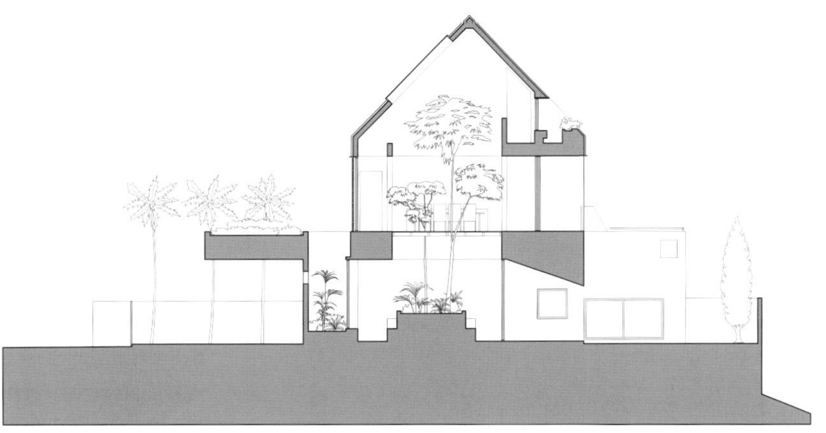

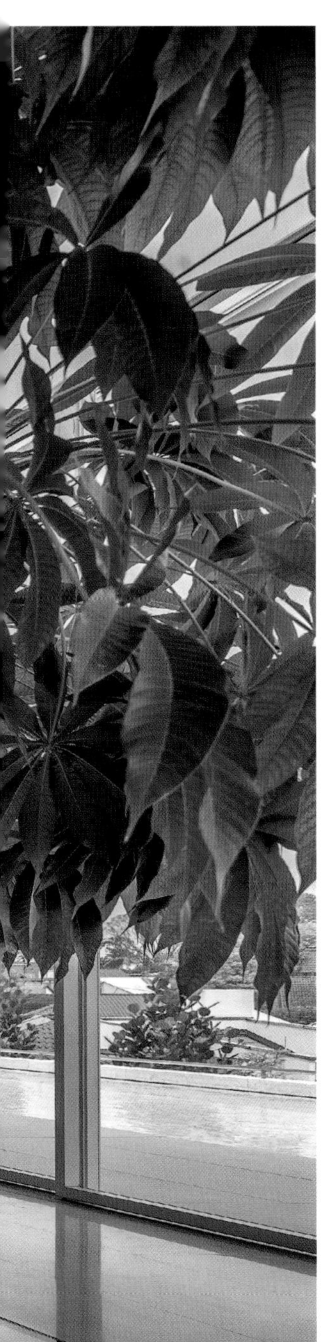

In linguistics they are called 'signs', defined by the *Oxford English Dictionary* as 'a thing indicating or suggesting a quality or state'. Signs tend to be repeated because they embody enduring values, they signal a way of life, the things that matter. They are crucial to how we communicate with our environment and with one another. Architects use them all the time, which is why we can often quickly identify the work of a particular architect. They will repeatedly use a certain device or variation of it to communicate what matters to them and their clients.

With Formwerkz, look for trees, windows and inversions as signs. This is not lazy repetition but the manipulation of certain principles to fit the programme of individual clients. And it serves multiple purposes: perceptual, emotional and functional. Signs in themselves are sustaining because they embody common and enduring meanings: because they are common they help to sustain communities; because they are enduring, they provide continuity and connection over time.

This house is in an unusually broad street in suburban Singapore. Its rear elevation enjoys panoramic views out to green precincts but also to some fascinating urban roofscapes. A timber screen on the street façade suggests a house turning its back on the street in order to open up to this grand view, not to mention 'borrowing' the lush landscape of its next door neighbour.

The house respects the scale of its neighbours by having the first storey as a large, solid base and the second storey as a lighter, smaller glass pavilion. This scaling reflects the strategy of inversion. Reversing common practice, the ground floor is for the bedrooms where they can be private and where they enjoy direct access to the gardens that surround the house. The second storey glass pavilion opens on to a terrace and pool delineated by a 'smokers bench'. This level contains the living, dining and wet and dry kitchen areas and leads up to an attic with small family spaces and an entertainment room with an intriguing stepped 'ziggurat' timber structure for watching movies.

The pavilion, save for the external screen on the street side, is completely transparent. It effectively dematerializes, filled with light, tempered by the Louis Poulsen lights over the dining table and the trees which thrust up magically through the middle of the floor.

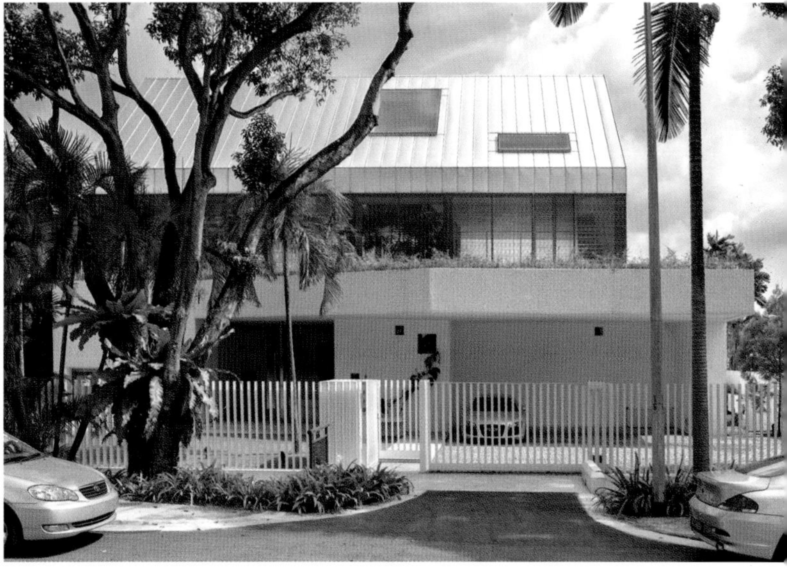

Opposite The living/dining pavilion and pool deck are on the second storey but enjoy trees growing up through the centre of the house.

Top Long section.

Above The second storey pavilion is screened for privacy from the street.

The trees link the three levels of the house but also serve to diffuse the intense tropical light, not just in the pavilion but downstairs as well where they soften and modulate the light. The trees also bring the garden inside as part of a network of gardens and courts that creates the sense of living in the garden.

The bedrooms all enjoy their own, essentially private, garden court. The sense of connection between the inside of the house and the outside garden areas has enabled the architects to keep the bedrooms relatively small and functional, freeing up space elsewhere. This brings into play the strategy of varying the fenestration—windows of different sizes and shapes organized in a seemingly random way. At one level, this creates a visual rhythm for each room, avoiding the monotony of standardized fenestration. It is also a strategy for drawing in light while maintaining privacy. At the same time, it is a creative alternative to accessing the view. Rather than revealing everything at once, the varied size and organization of the windows, which include low-set extended rectangular windows, provide tantalizing edited glimpses of the garden.

Taken together, these strategies suggest perhaps an overarching strategy—one of surprise. This is a house that can never be taken for granted because nothing is perfectly predictable. Apart from the environmentally and socially sustaining aspects of the house, this is also part of its sustainability agenda—to prevent living in the house becoming purely habitual. The fluid connection of internal and external spaces, the visual rhythms and the constantly changing prospect, give this house—like the Sembawang Long Houses (page 70)—a filmic or musical character. If a house is to be truly sustainable in an emotional sense, then it needs to provide for continual perceptual renewal.

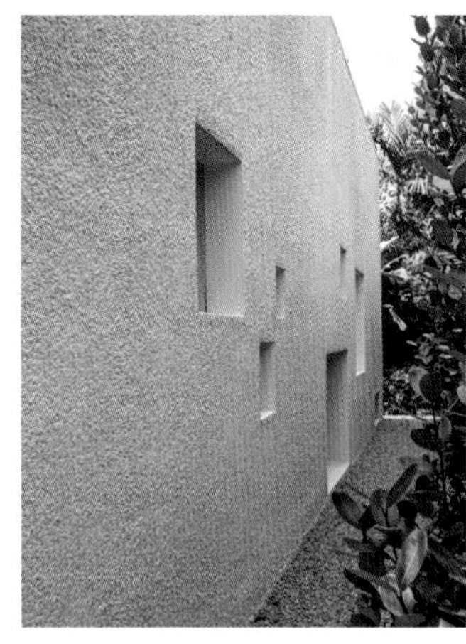

Above The architects' fondness for varied fenestration gives the façades a sculptural quality.

Below The street elevation provides a sheltering overhang for the carport with an elevated garden wrapping around the second storey pavilion.

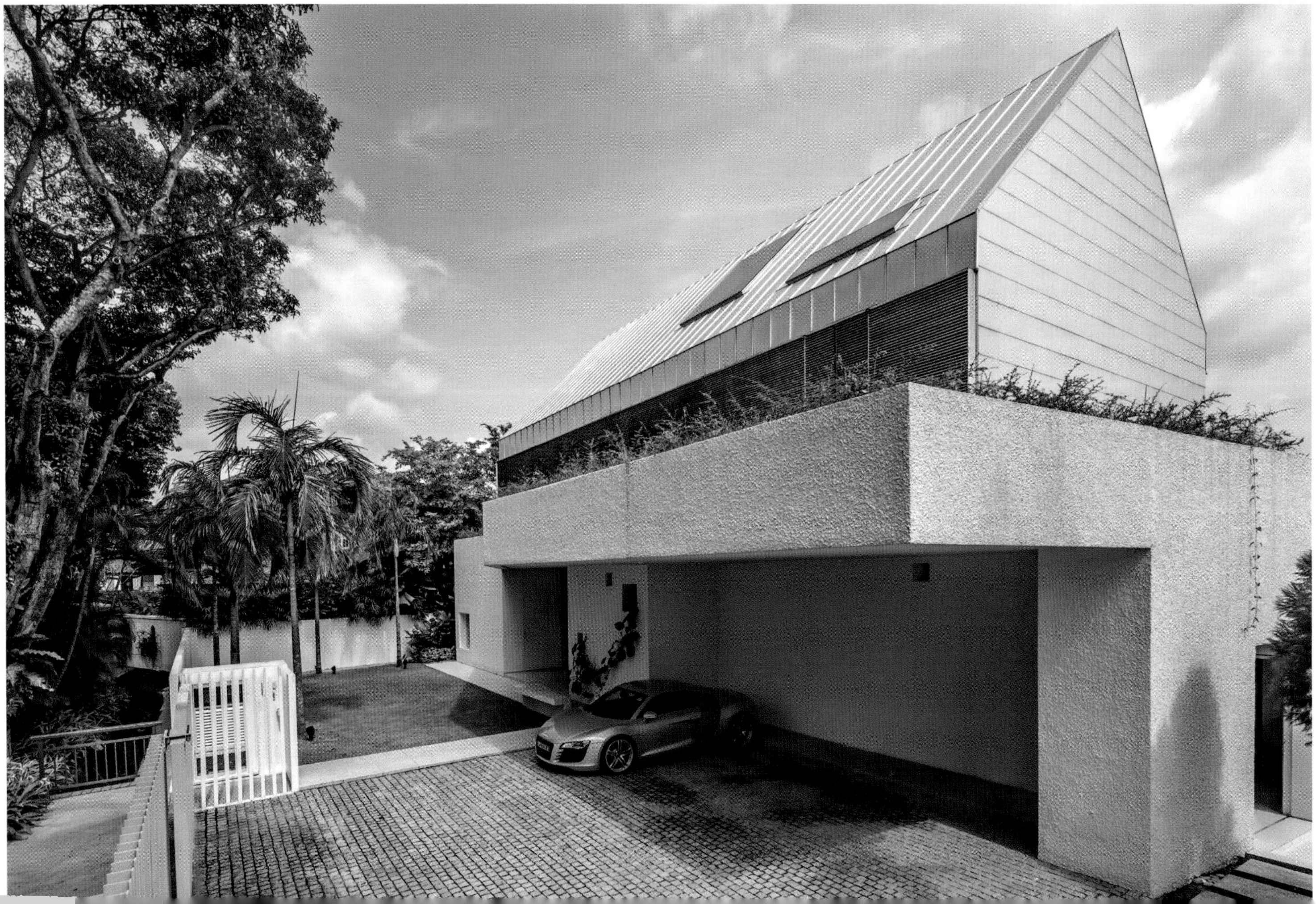

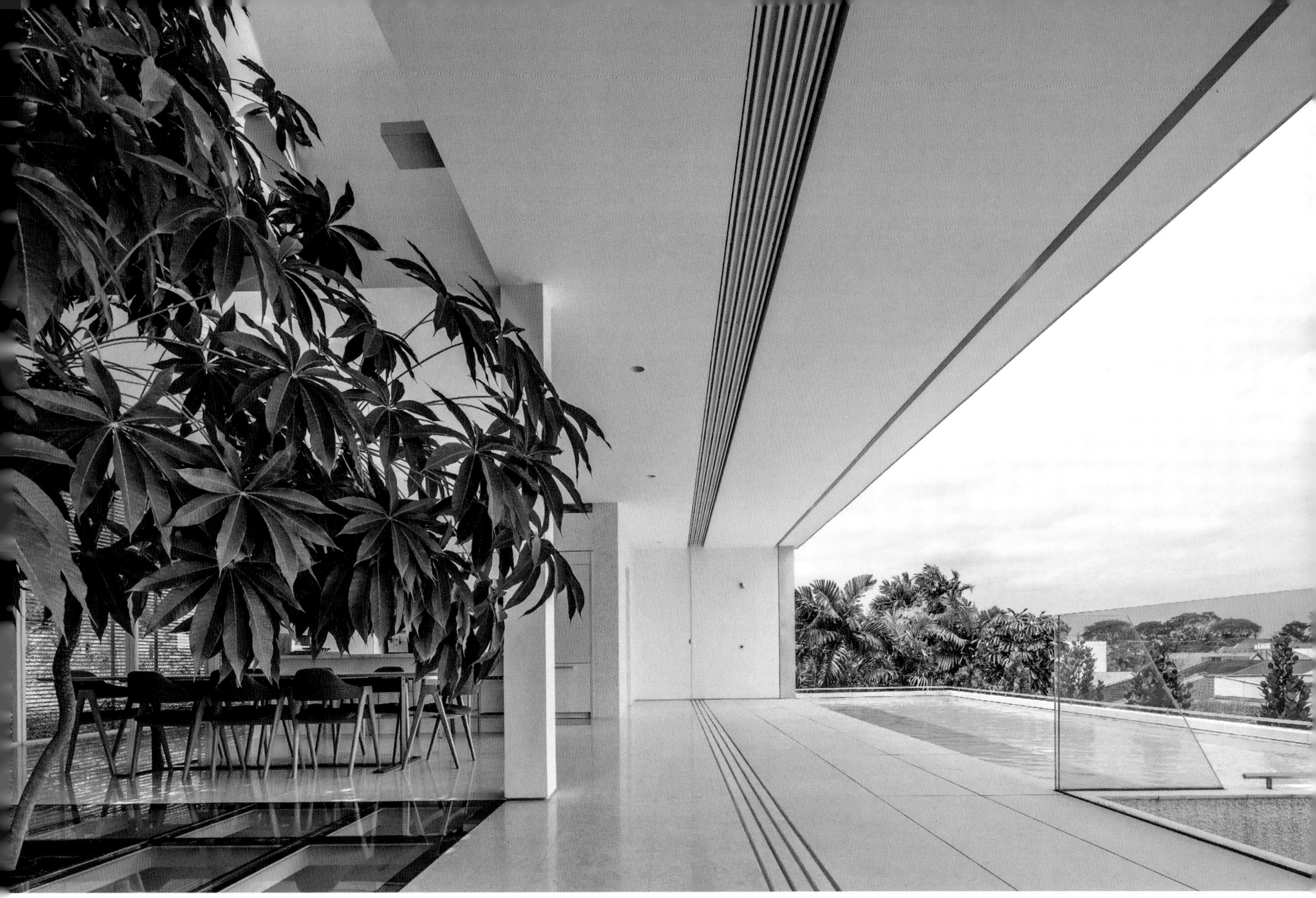

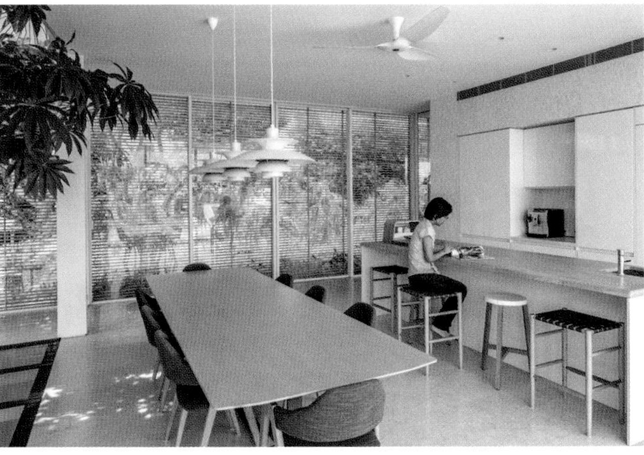

Above The living/dining pavilion opens up to form a single space with the pool terrace.

Left The living/dining pavilion also contains a breakfast bar.

Right The greenery of the living/dining pavilion and the skylight, which draws light down to the entry vestibule.

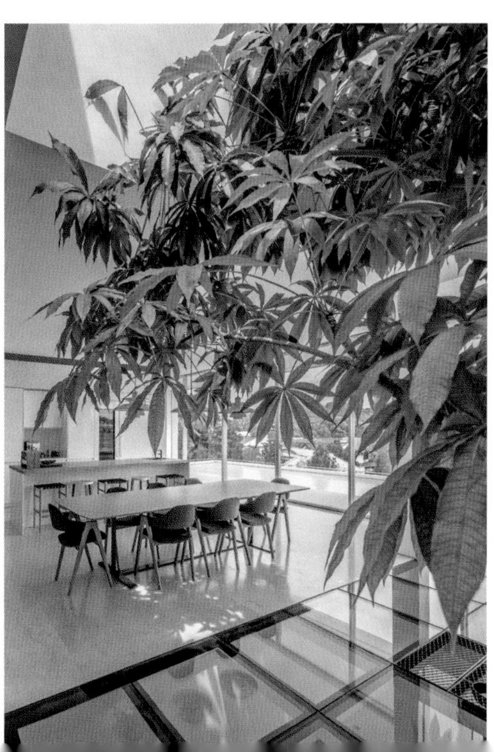

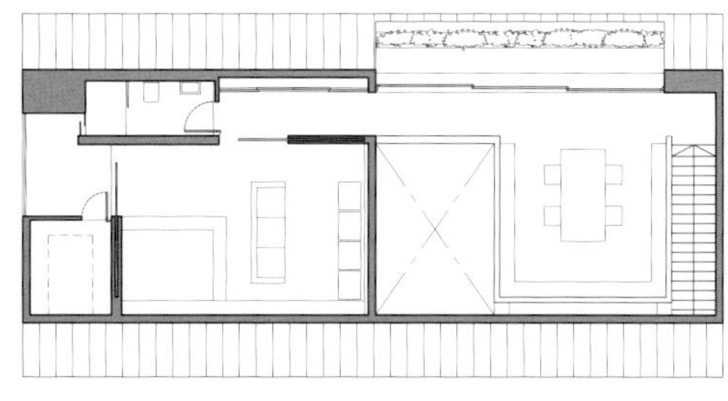

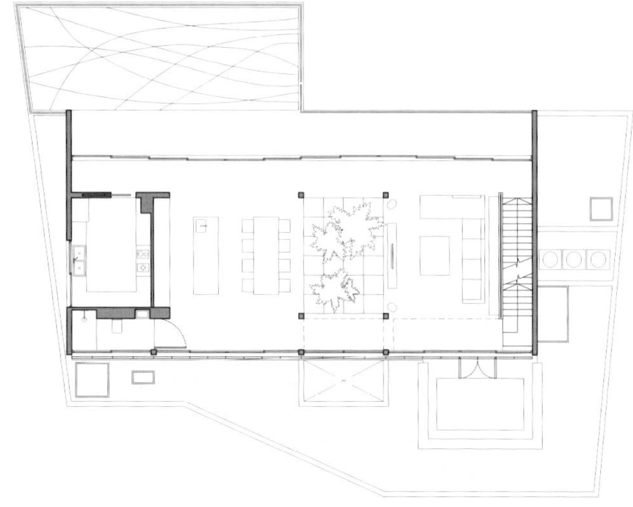

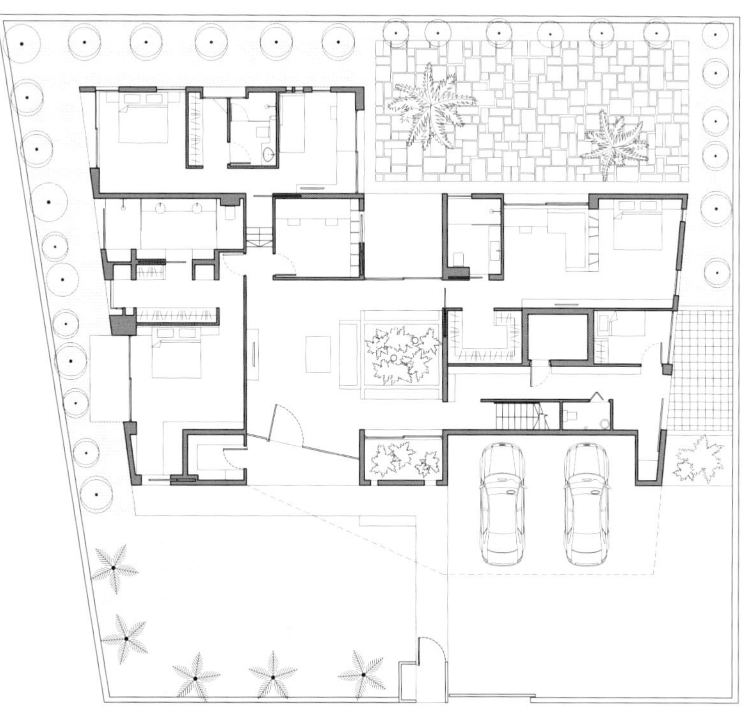

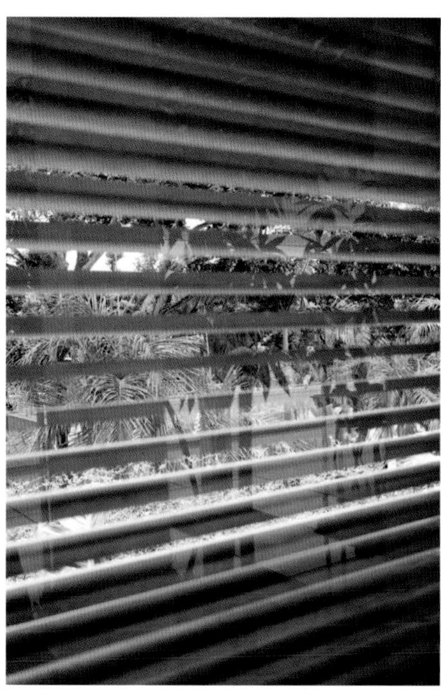

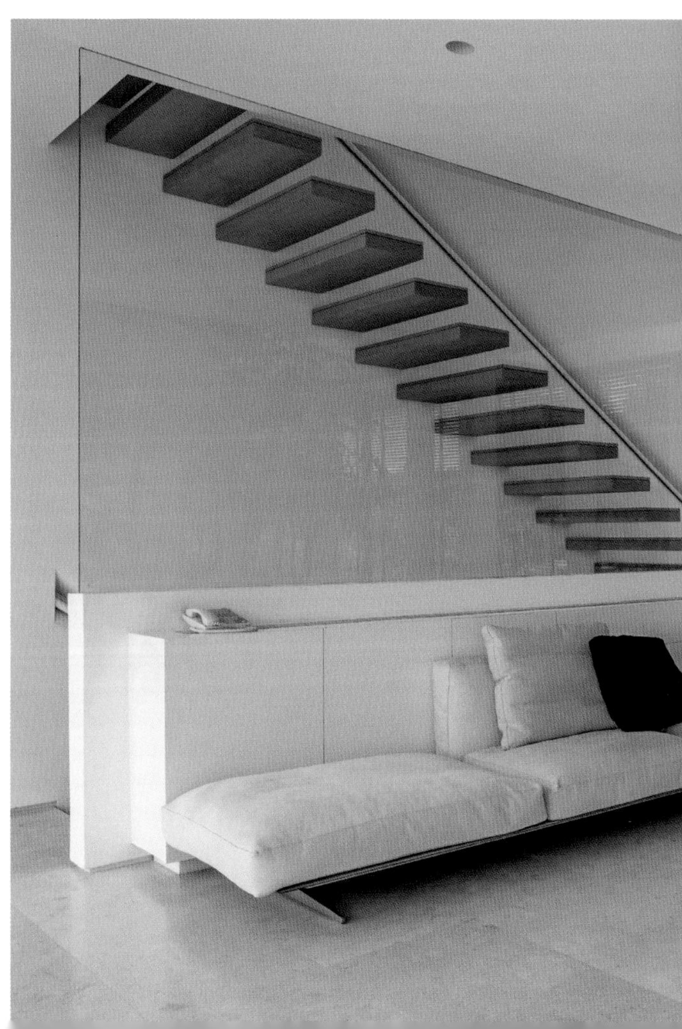

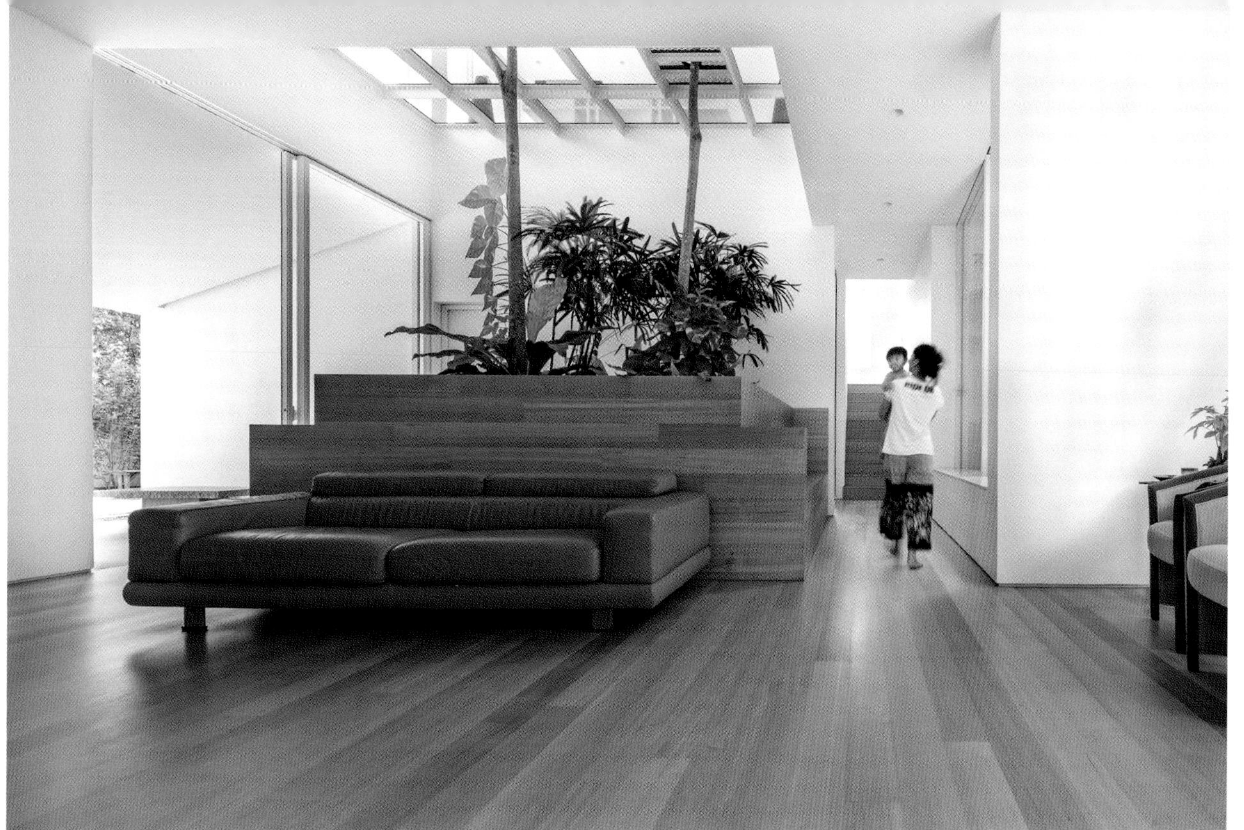

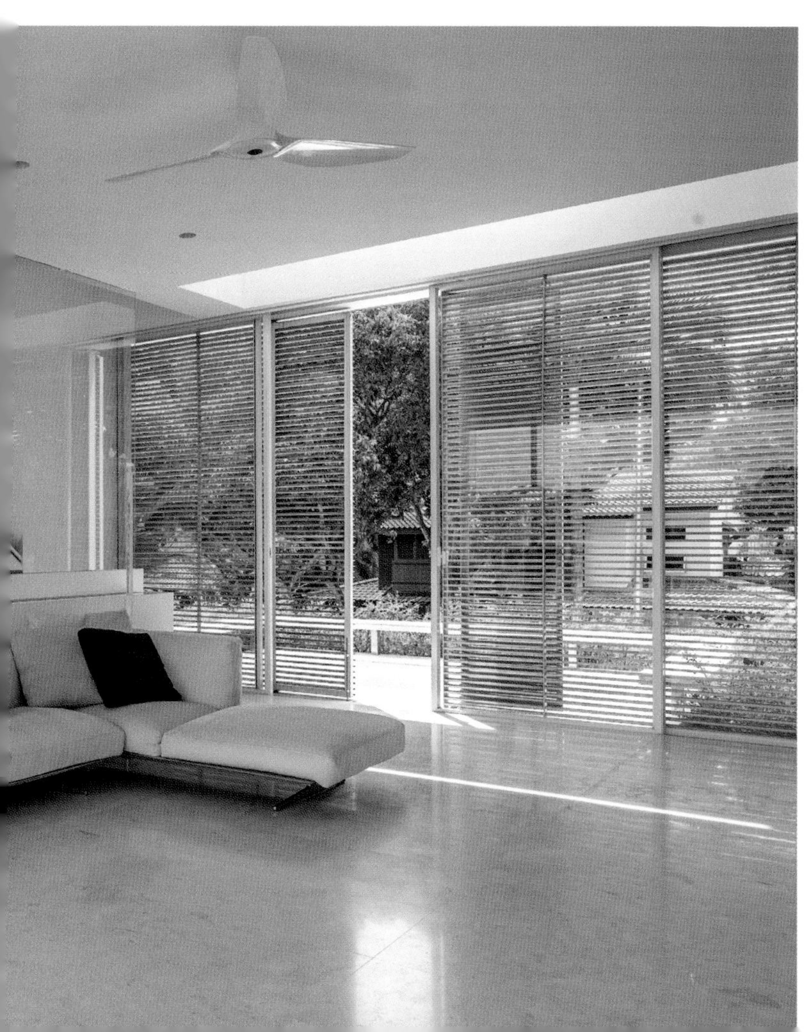

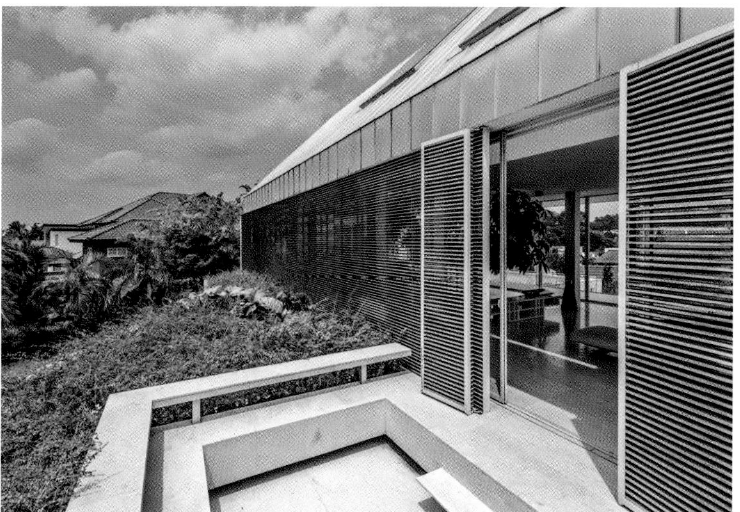

Opposite far left Attic, second storey and first storey plans.

Opposite above A detail of the screen that filters light into the living/dining pavilion.

Top The entry vestibule, with plantings and trees growing up through the middle of the house.

Above The living/dining pavilion also leads to an outside terrace on the street side of the house.

Left The entry vestibule.

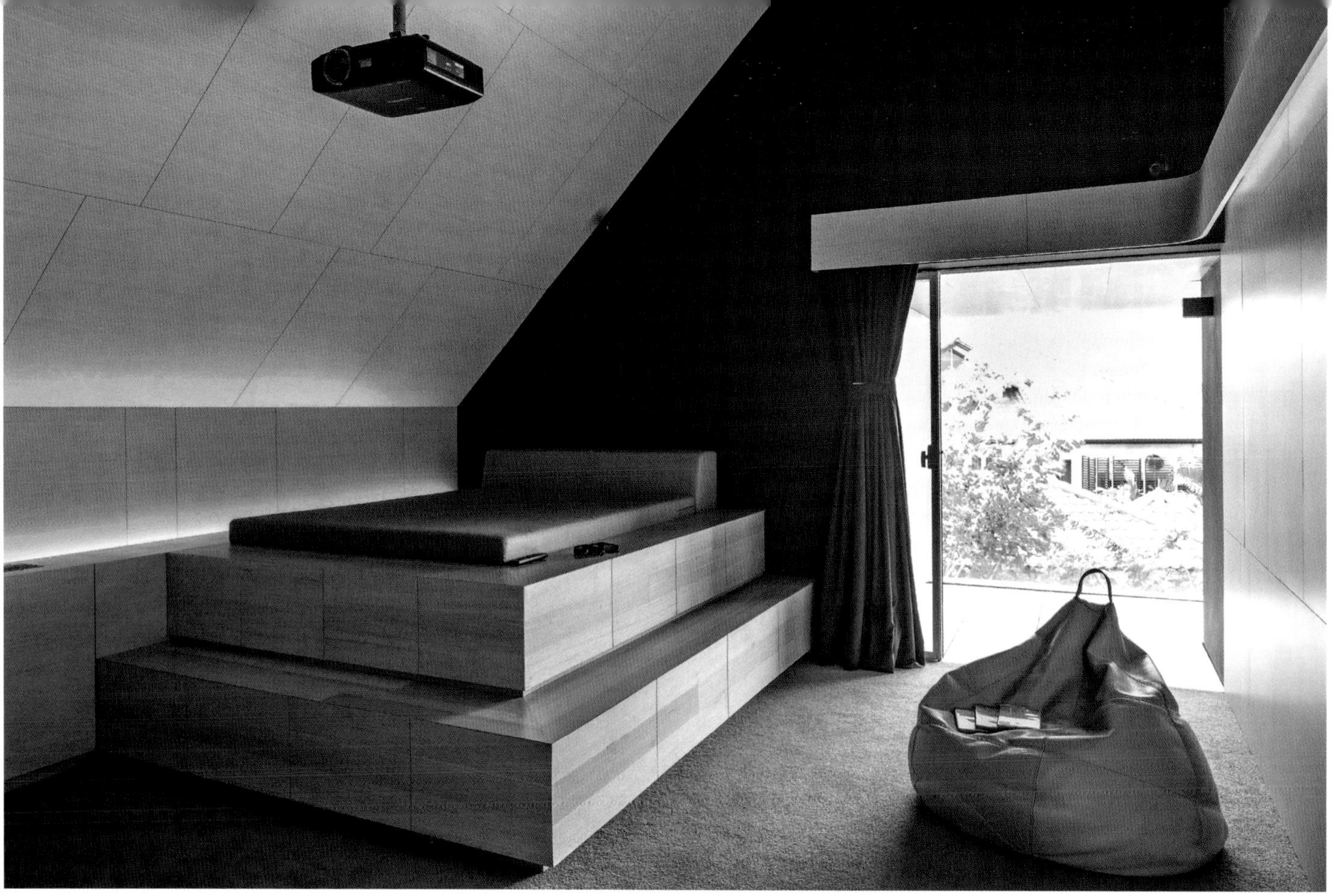

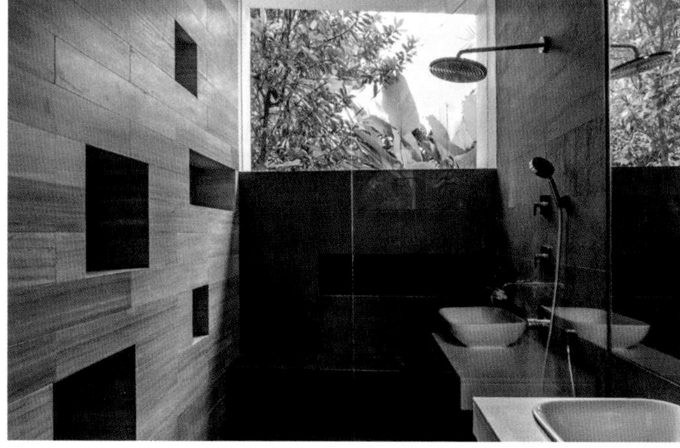

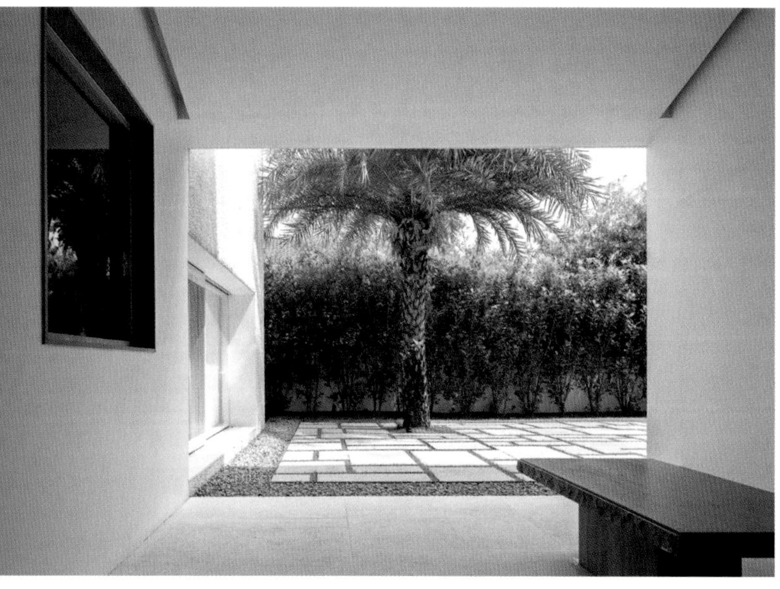

Top A 'ziggurat' stepped seating unit is an unusual feature of the entertainment room in the attic.

Above Wall recesses in the master bathroom echo the exterior fenestration.

Left Contrasting white and green gives the ground floor terraces an almost Mediterranean feel.

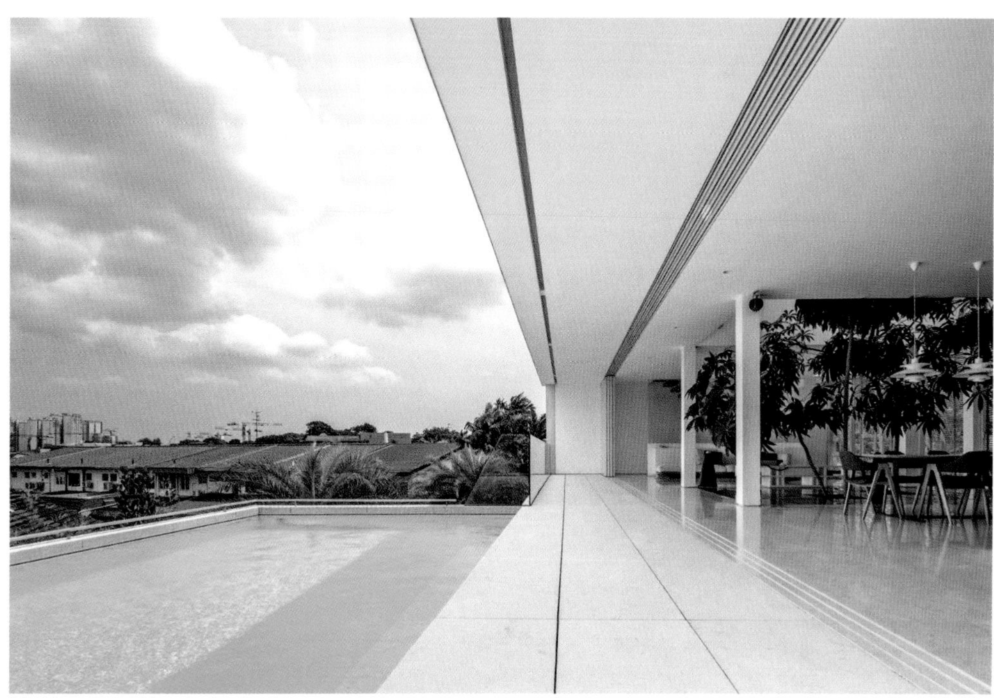

Right The pool terrace offers panoramic views over the neighbourhood.

Below The master bedroom has its own dense tropical garden.

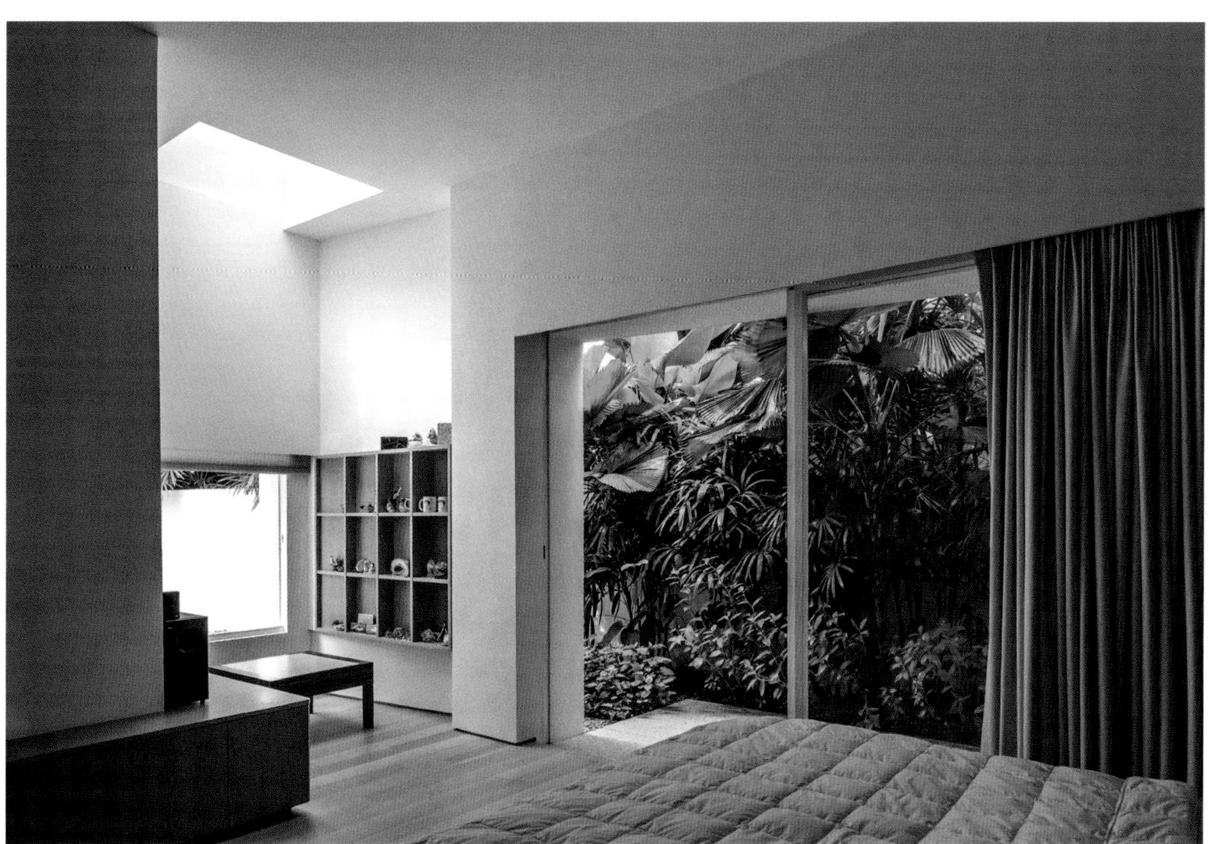

THE CORAL HOUSE
GUZ ARCHITECTS

'Choosing the architect was choosing a vision. If you see other projects by Guz, there is consistency. There are several themes. One is that everything looks at the garden, everything is green, everything has openness.'—OWNER

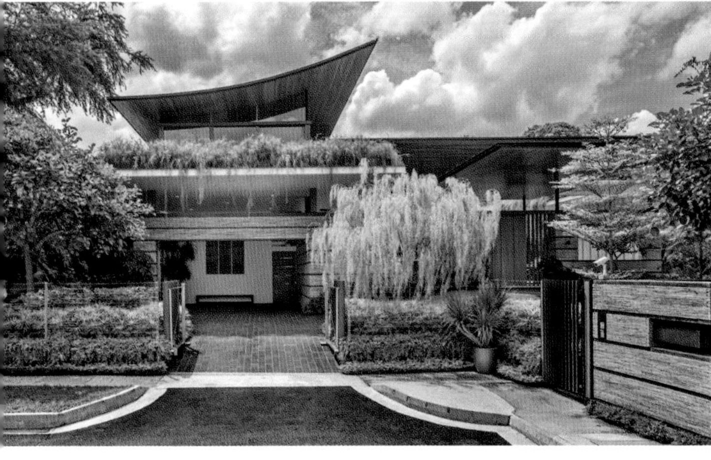

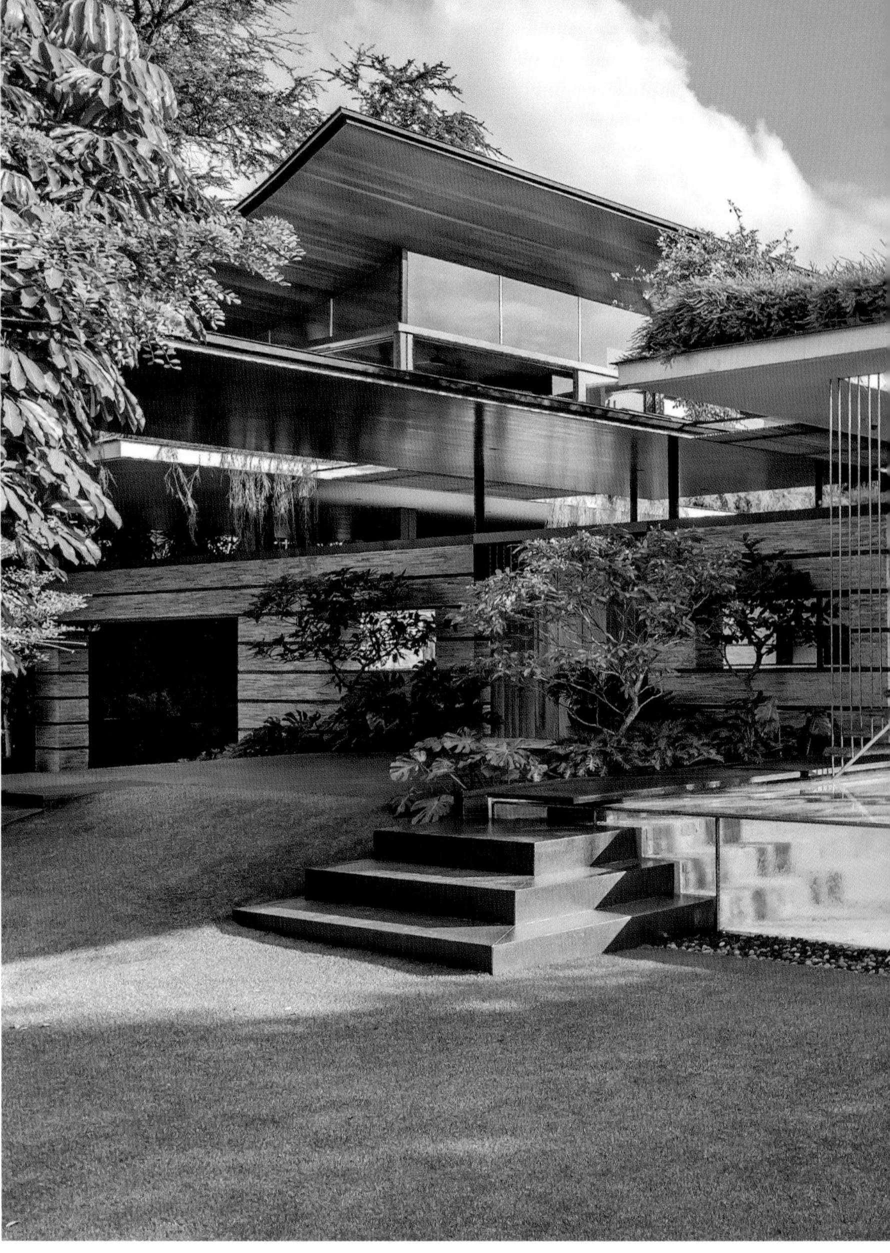

The clients had earlier approached Guz Wilkinson to design a house, which he declined to do. But 'after a year's courtship' he agreed to do this house, the first the clients had built for themselves. 'He doesn't do it for the money,' the clients point out. 'He must look at the place, the people who he is going to work with. He's quite selective.'

The brief was quite simple: a house for a family with three children and visiting in-laws, a master bedroom plus three other bedrooms, wet and dry kitchens, a pool, and so on. Because the clients did not relish the idea of being 'cooped up in an air-conditioned room', there was clearly the desire for a house where inside and outside blended and where there would be livable open spaces. The idea was to celebrate living in the tropics but be able to enjoy ample contemporary amenities.

The result is a courtyard house embraced by a tropical garden—'embraced' because this is a house where form dematerializes into a continuous series of spatial and sensual experiences. At ground level, the garden meanders, linked by water features, constantly suggesting different paths and possibilities. But—and this is a hallmark of Guz Wilkinson's work—the garden also floats upwards to rooftop gardens, a tree penetrates an oculus, the open garden pavilion, which appears to float over water, has a rooftop garden where even the steps leading up to the roof have green under-treads of artificial grass.

Looking down from the master bedroom, the garden is a tropical paradise, which also 'borrows' abundant landscape from the neighbourhood and Bukit Timah hill in the distance.

The experience hints strongly of a Chinese stroll garden, a gentle progression from the public realm

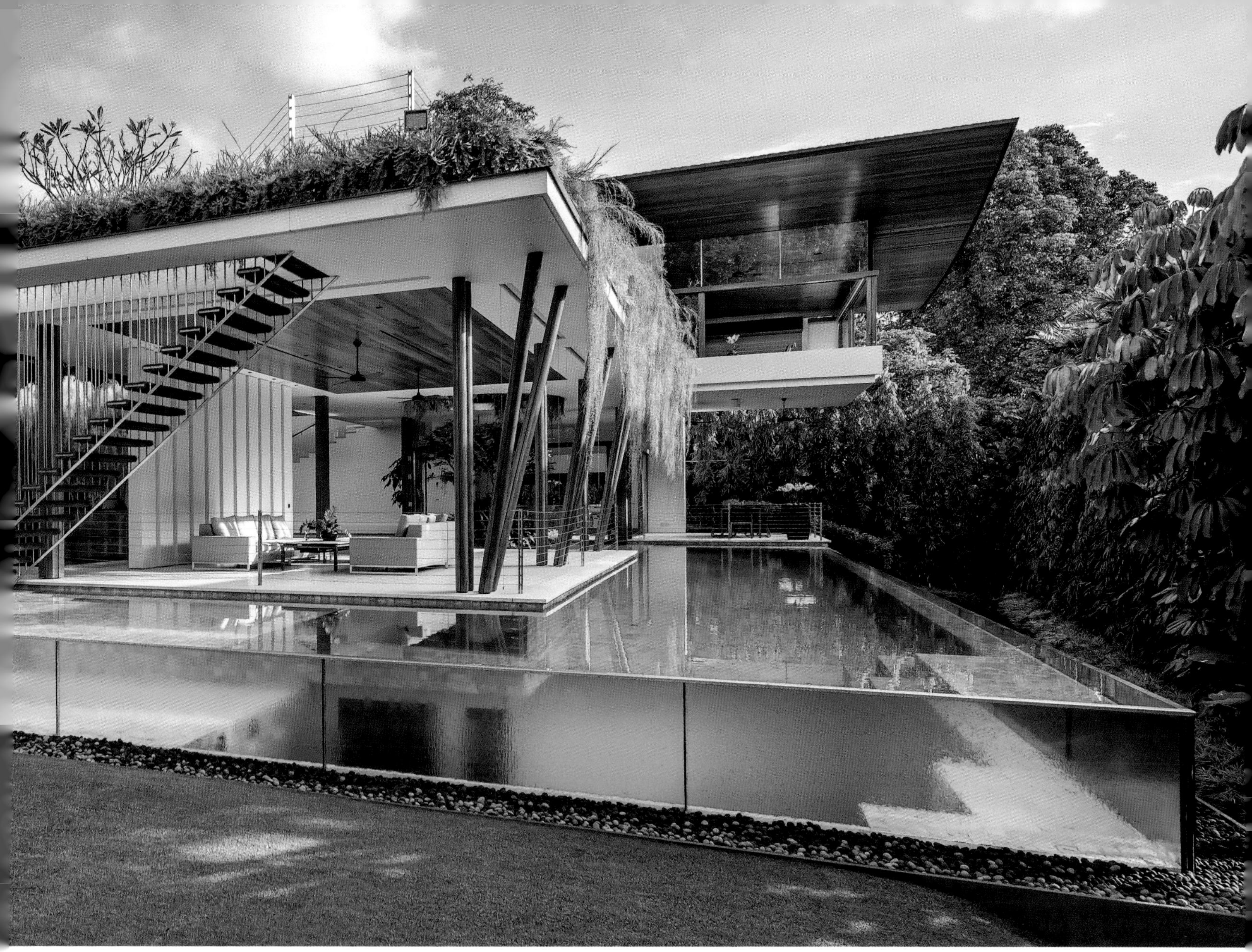

Opposite The driveway entry to the house.

Above The pool pavilion appears to float on the transparent pool that wraps around it.

Right The pedestrian entry to the house is under a grand overhang and through a portal that sets up a great sense of arrival.

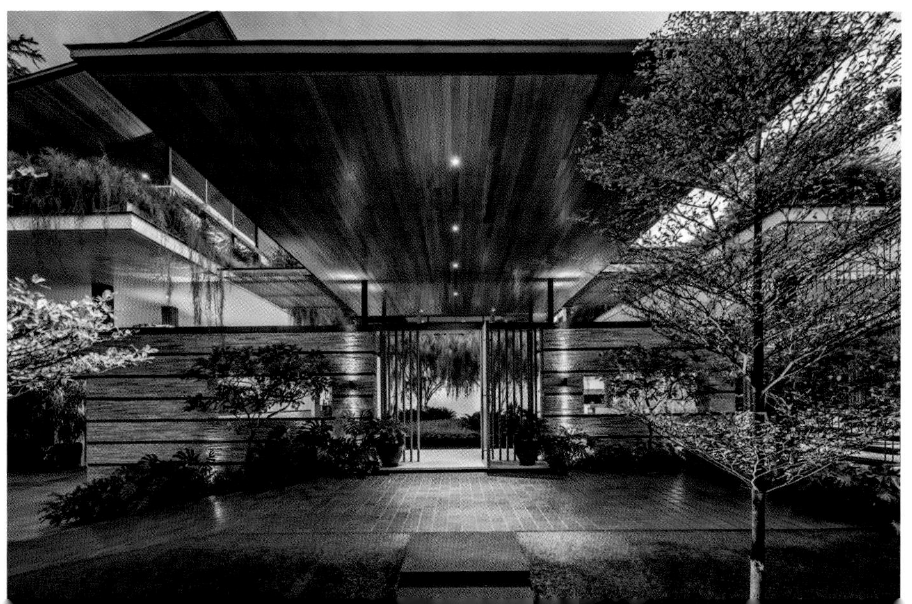

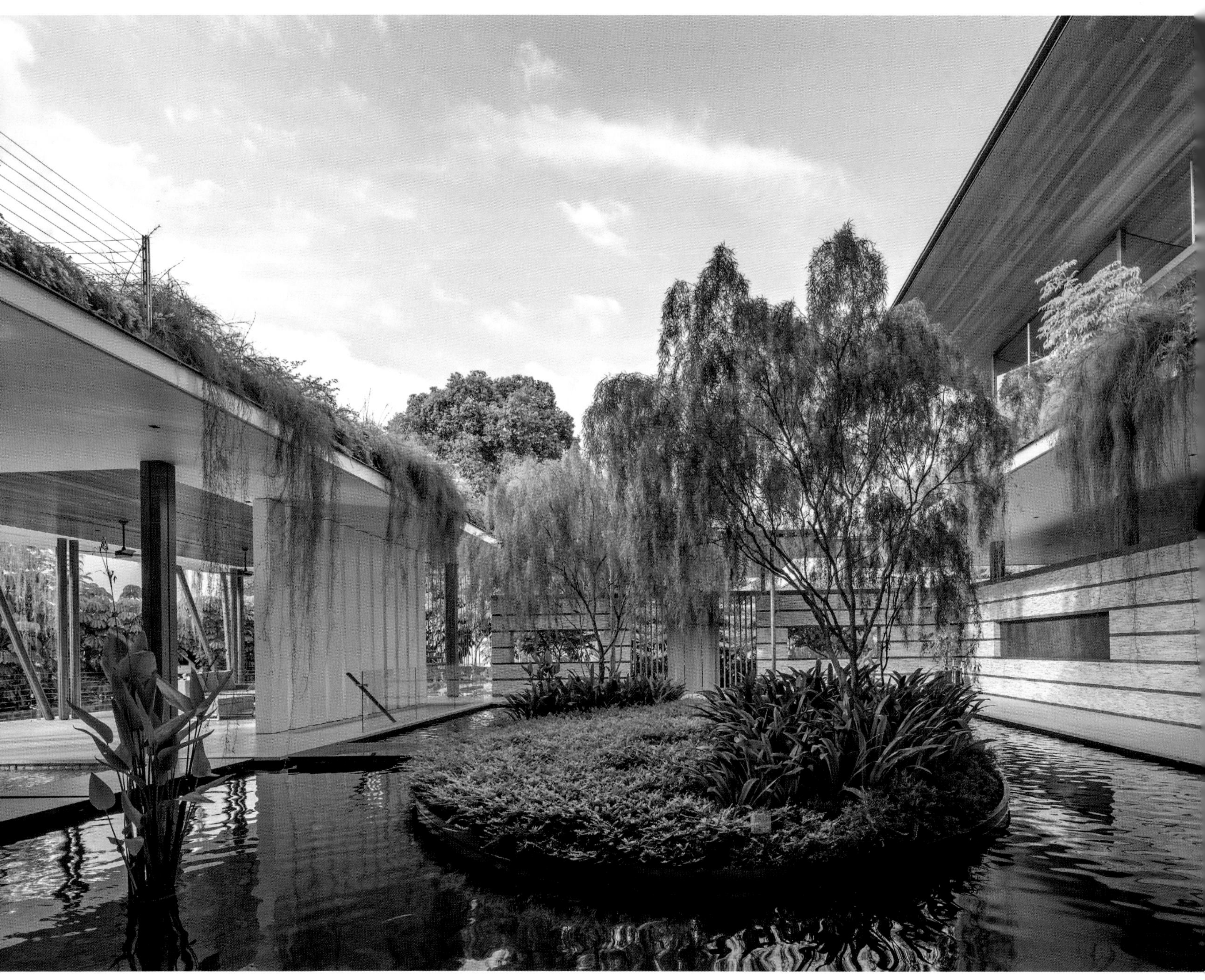

Above Between the pool pavilion and the house a willow tree grows up from a verdant island in the pond.

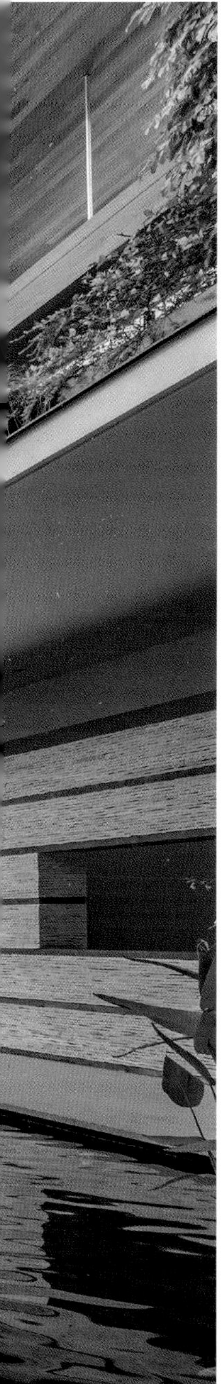

into a calm and sheltered private domain. This sequence begins at the gate where the entry is under a low 'floating' roof; indeed, the 'floating roof', where the roof does not touch the walls, is a feature of the whole house. Then we pass a pond with a small island in the middle reached by stepping stones. To the right is the 'floating' outdoor entertainment pavilion, while straight ahead is a willow tree, just to reinforce the mood of tranquillity.

The house appears L-shaped but is basically two pavilions linked by timber galleries on both the ground and upper levels. The pavilion to the left of the entry has guest amenities on the ground floor, with the children's 'dormitory' above. This has a handsome horizontal window overlooking the courtyard and the rooftop garden and, apart from bedrooms, contains the children's common room.

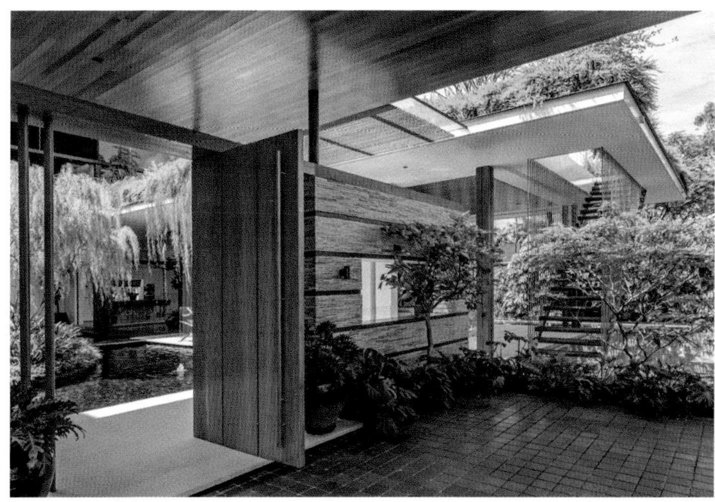

Above Passing through the beautiful double timber doors at the entry, one moves into a magical tropical garden.

Below A tree thrusts up through an occulus in the pool pavilion roof.

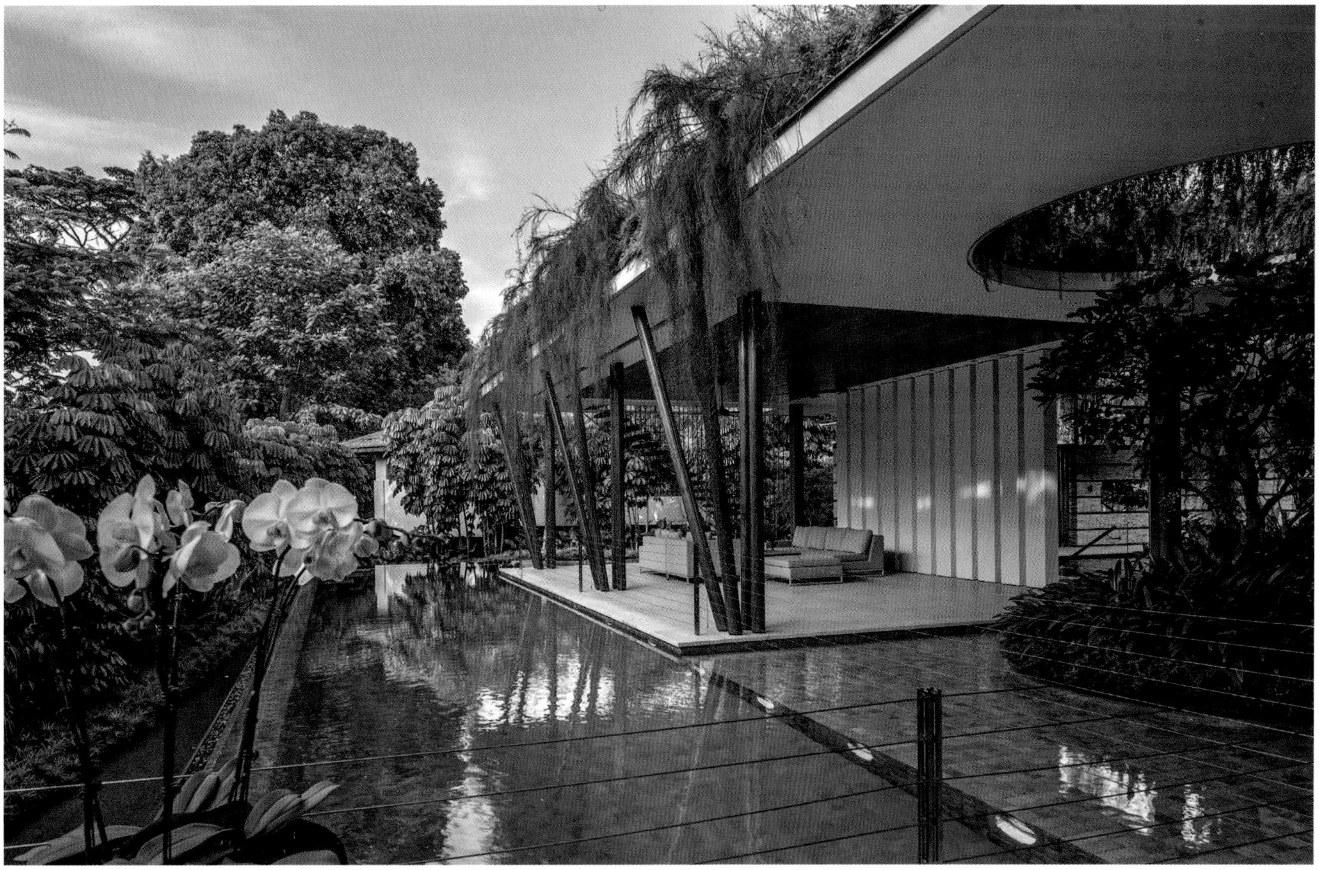

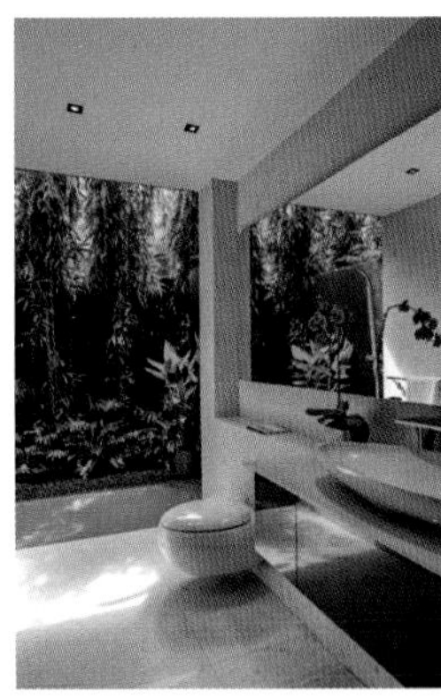

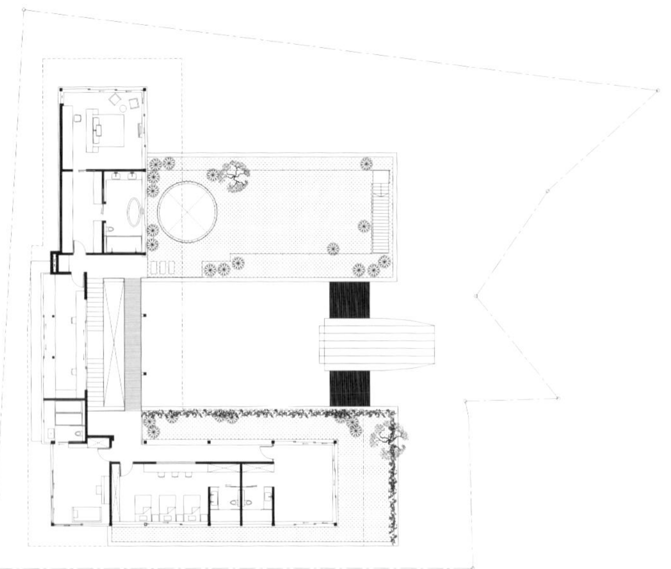

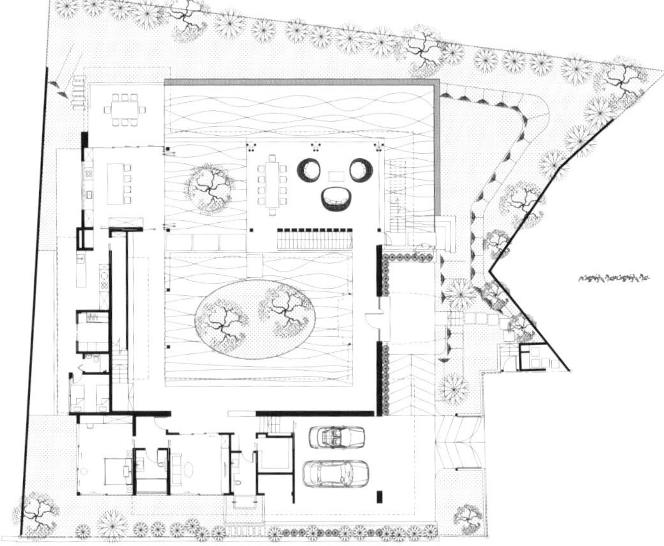

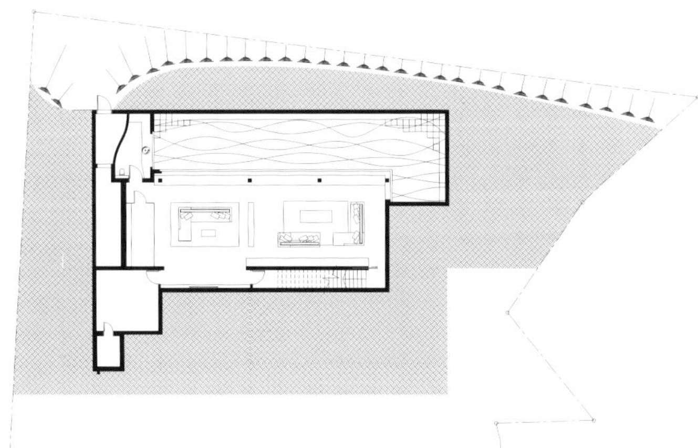

Above The bathroom for the guest bedroom celebrates living in a tropical garden.

Right top Second storey plan.

Right centre First storey plan.

Right bottom Basement plan.

Opposite The tree pushing up through the oculus joins a lush roof garden.

This also acts as a television room for the family, part of a strategy to deliberately isolate the television that does not feature highly is this family's day-to-day life.

The other pavilion contains the master bedroom upstairs and the kitchen and dining areas below. The dry kitchen/pantry has a breakfast bar but the actual dining area is outside, an open timber extension off the pantry. It is in this pantry/dining area that the family members spend most of their time together.

This is a house where everything is pushed to the boundary in order to maximize open spaces and the semi-internal spaces connected to the garden. One result of this constantly unfolding sequence of spaces as interior merges with exterior is that everything feels bigger than it really is.

But one space really is big—the basement living-cum-media-cum-party room. At three metres deep, it is naturally cool, with enough natural light to mean that artificial lighting is not required during the day. A lot of this light is filtering through the 22-metre-long swimming pool. The basement is an underwater viewing room for the pool. The clients claim that the acrylic window is the biggest of its kind in Southeast Asia. An organically shaped banquette snakes its way along the entire length of the window. At the end of the room is a sumptuously tiled bathroom that looks down the length of the pool, diffusion from the glass providing the necessary privacy.

On the other side, the pool is lined by a sculptural quartz stone wall, which continues into the garden, adding to the textural richness of the landscape.

There is an interesting tension to this house: Is it enclosed or not enclosed? You are never quite sure. As a result, you remain alert, your perceptions heightened and, because of this, your experience of being here is intensified. It is as though you are inside and outside, up and down, in one spot but also in others, all at the same time—a kind of four-dimensional tropical Garden of Eden.

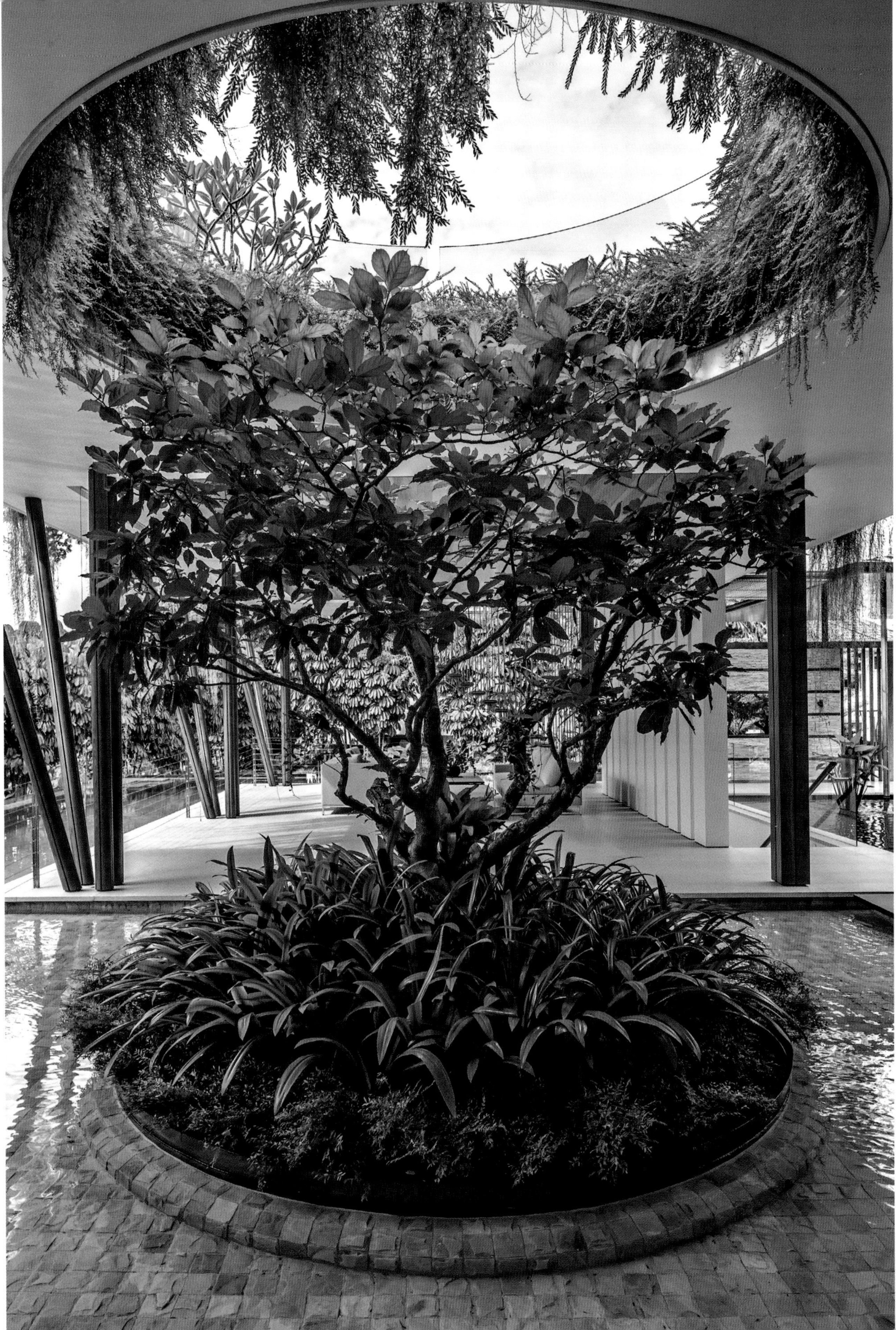

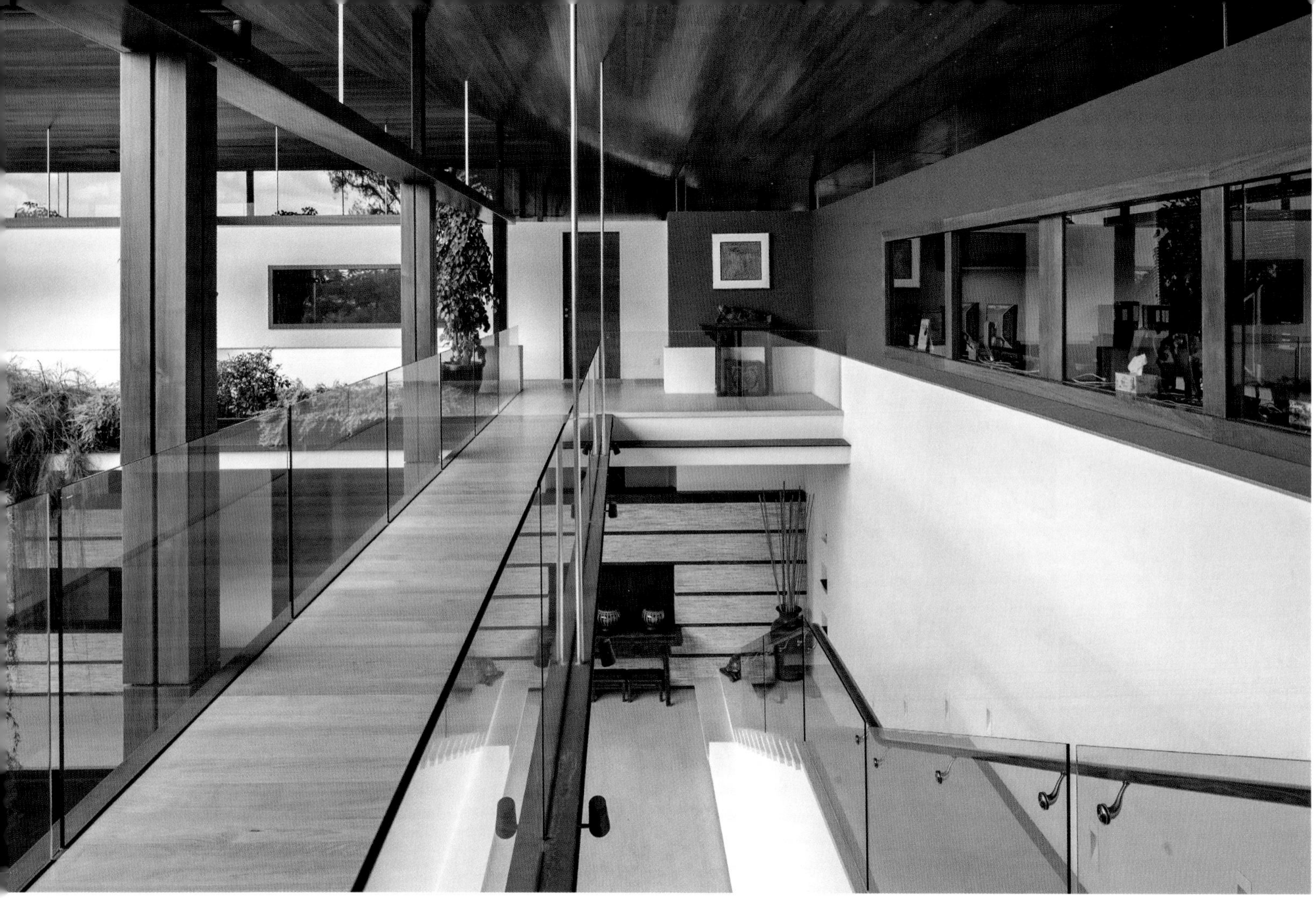

Above The bridge linking the two bedroom wings on the second storey.

Right A guest bedroom has its own private garden.

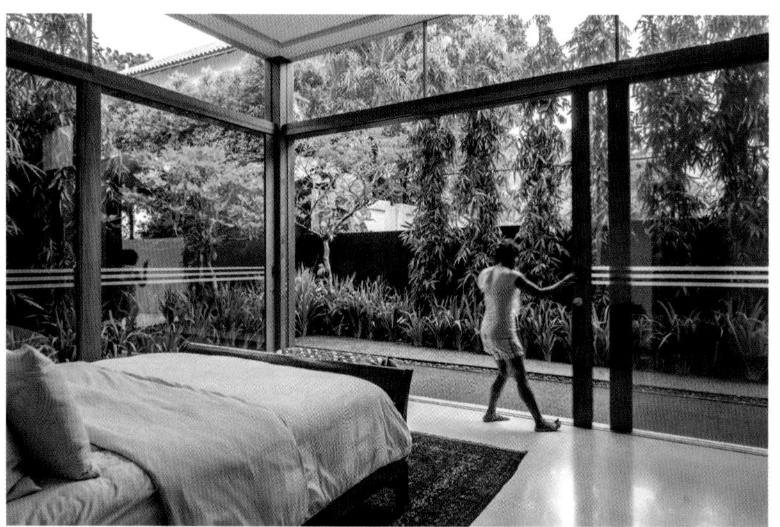

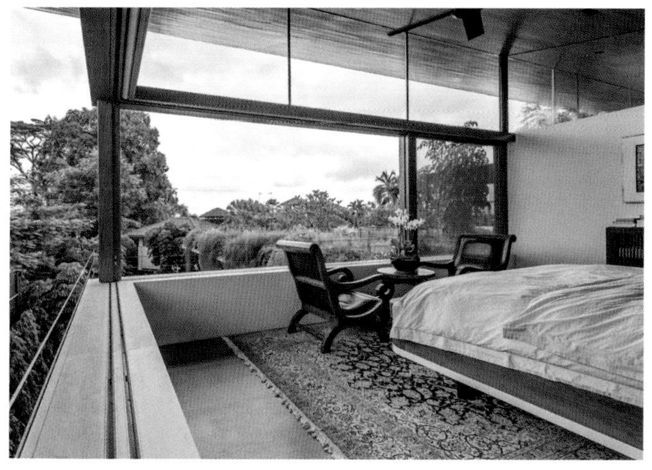

Left The master bedroom enjoys panoramic views, 'borrowing' a dense forest landscape opposite.

Right The bedroom levels of the house look down on elevated tropical gardens.

Below The roof garden can be accessed from the second storey connecting bridge.

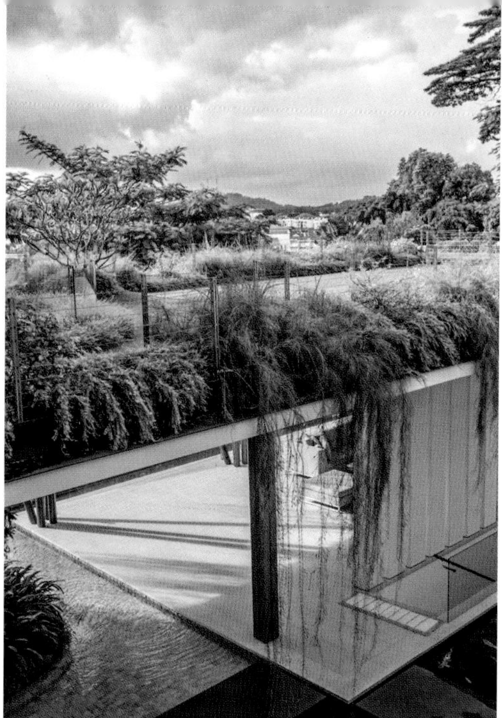

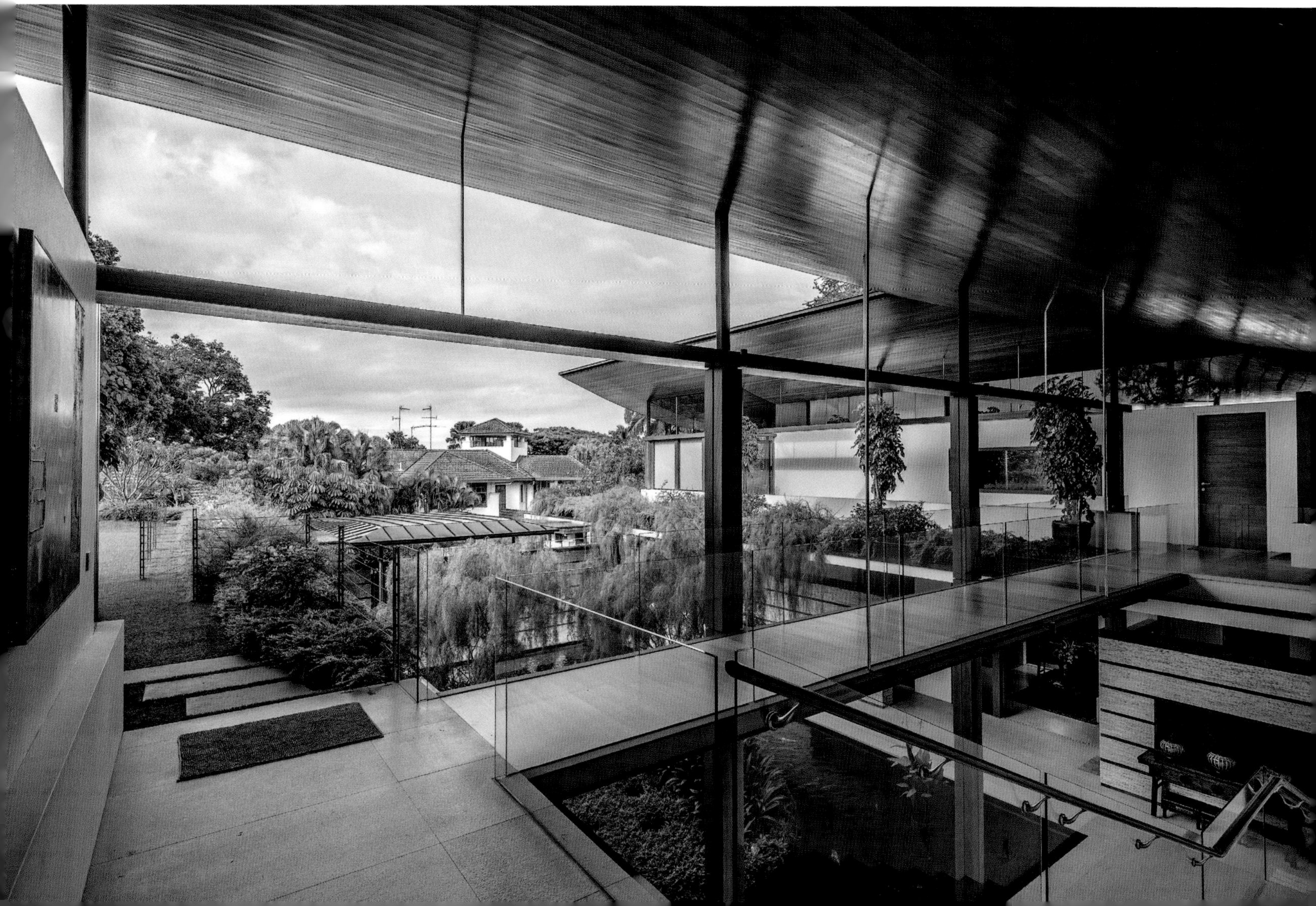

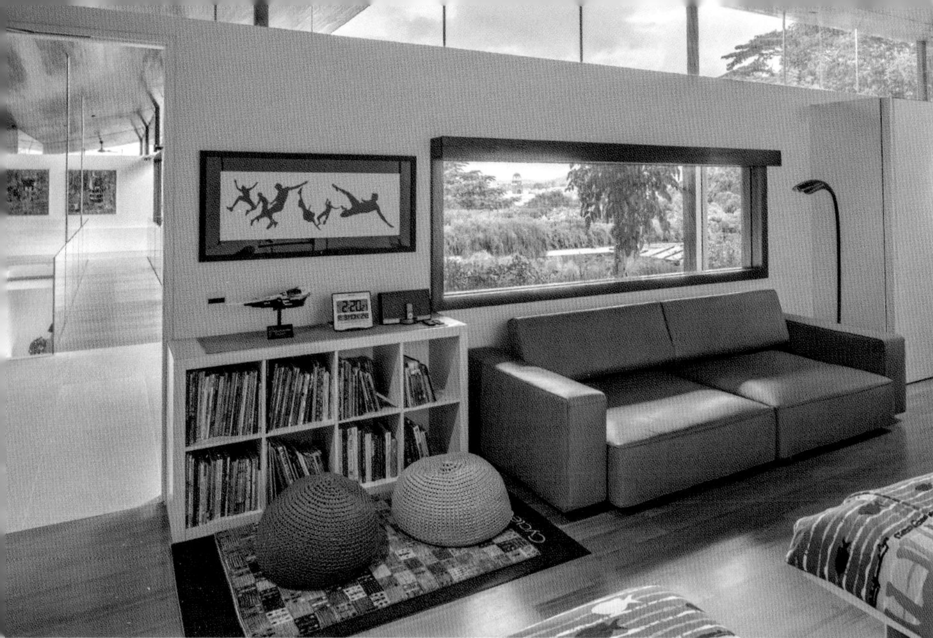

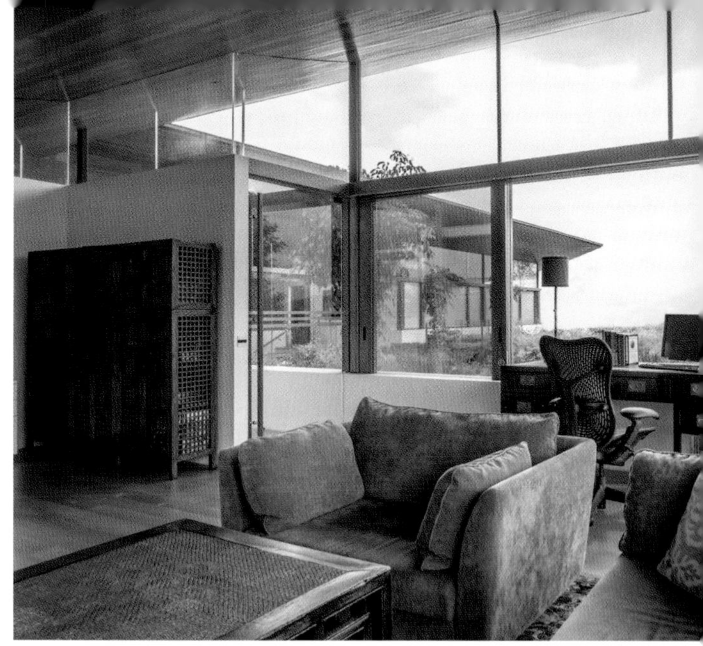

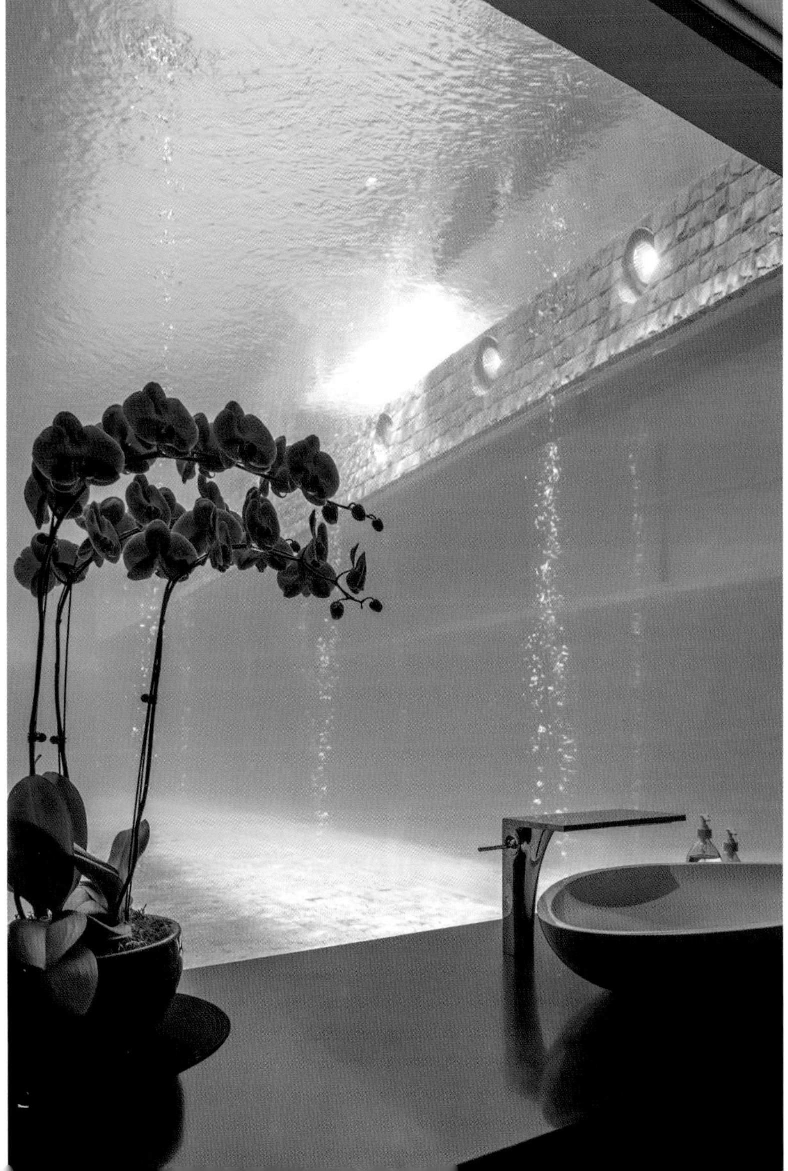

Above left The children's bedroom features a beautiful slot window framing the view.

Above The family room is located at the end of the children's wing on the second level.

Left The powder room in the basement looks directly into the pool, its acrylic window diffusing light for privacy.

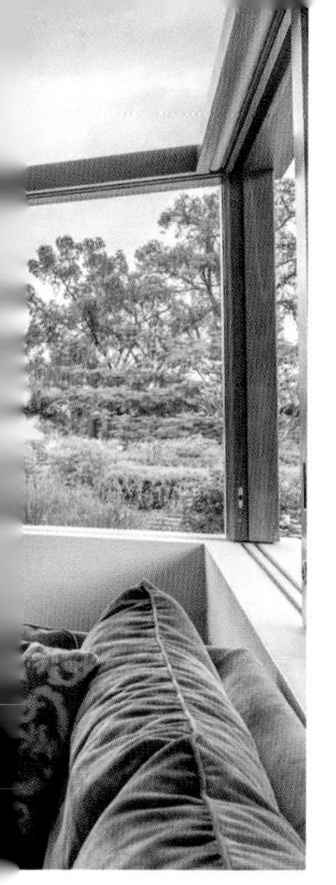

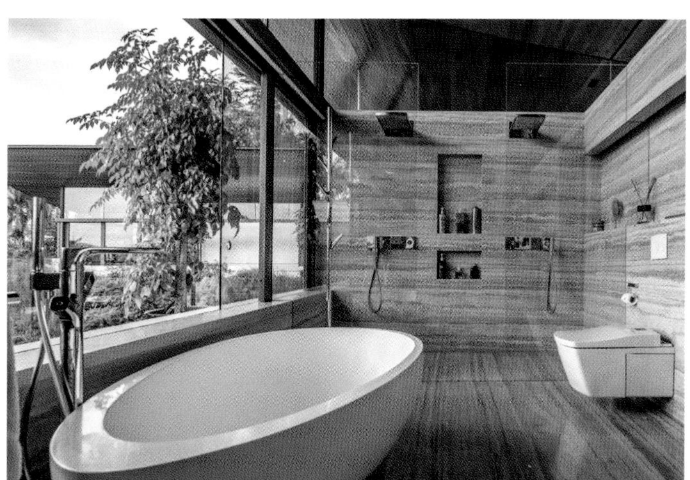

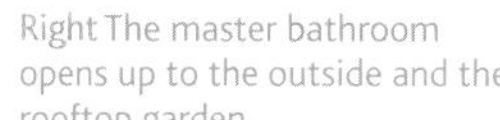

Right The master bathroom opens up to the outside and the rooftop garden.

Below The basement entertainment room is cooled by the pool, which filters natural light into the space.

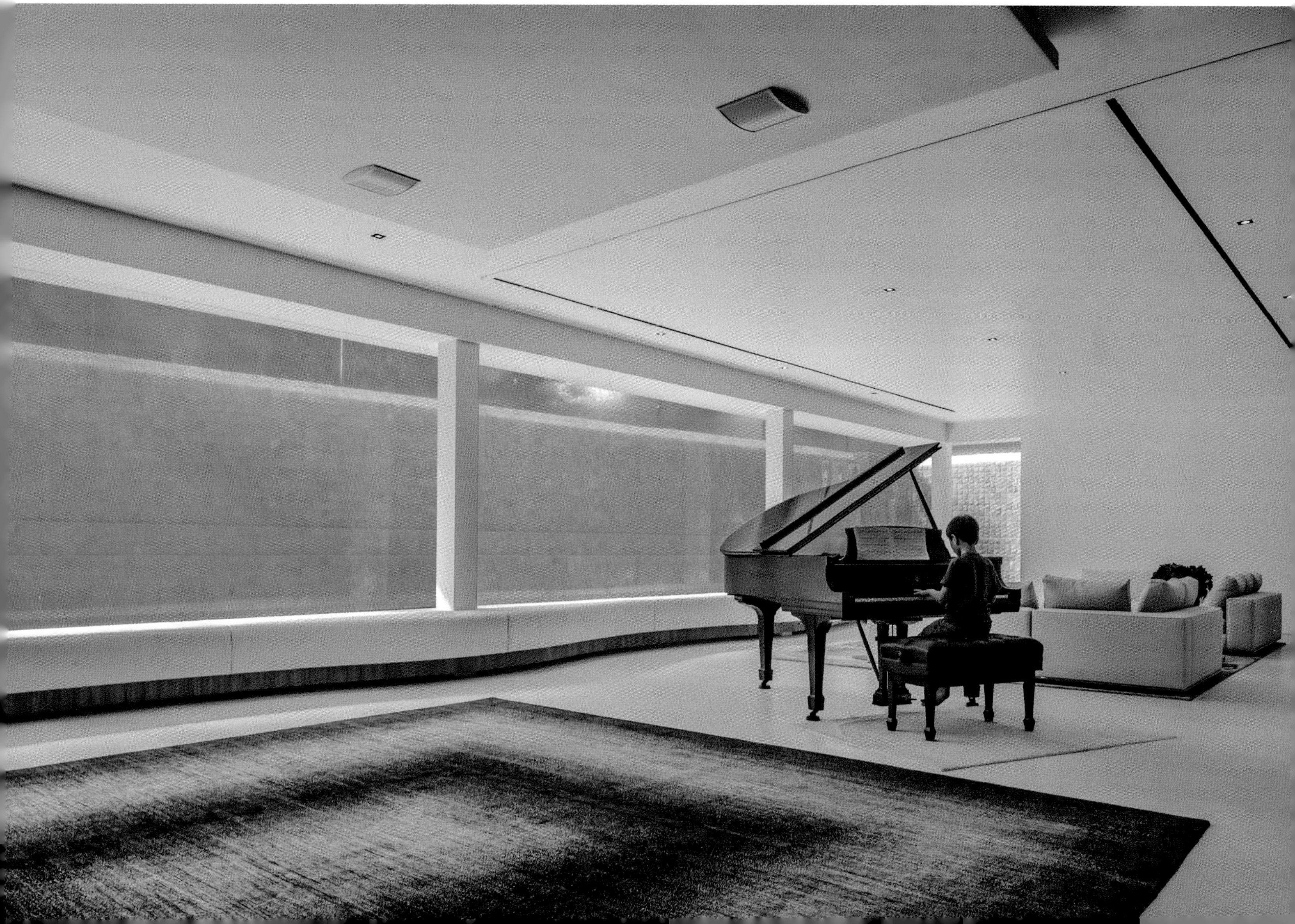

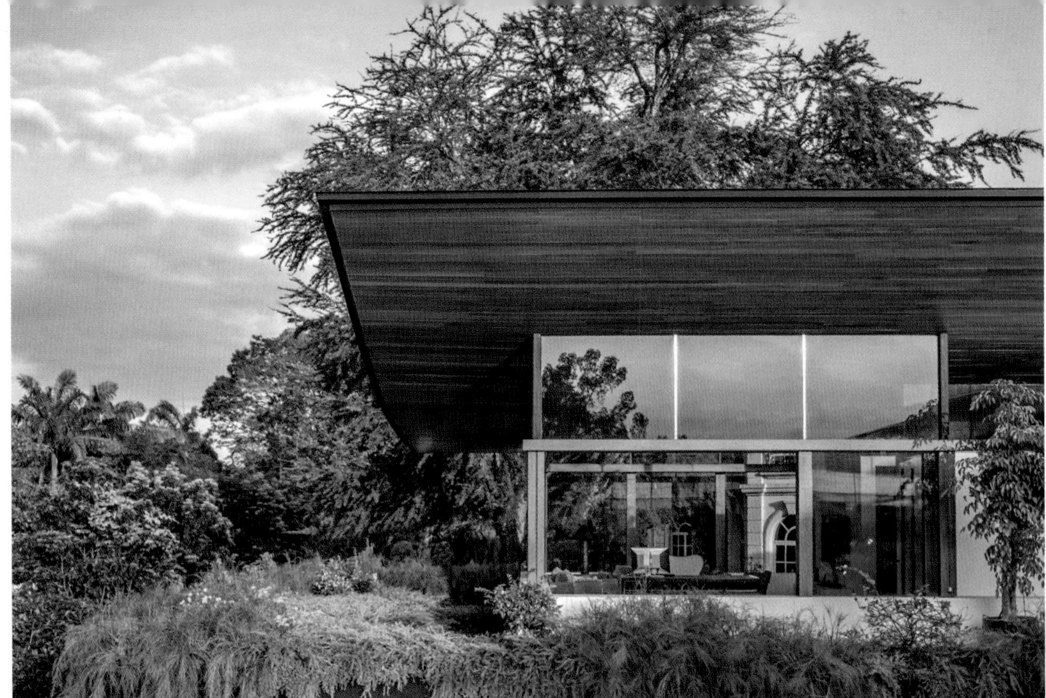

Right The dry kitchen and breakfast bar, with its outside dining terrace.

Below Looking down on the pool pavilion.

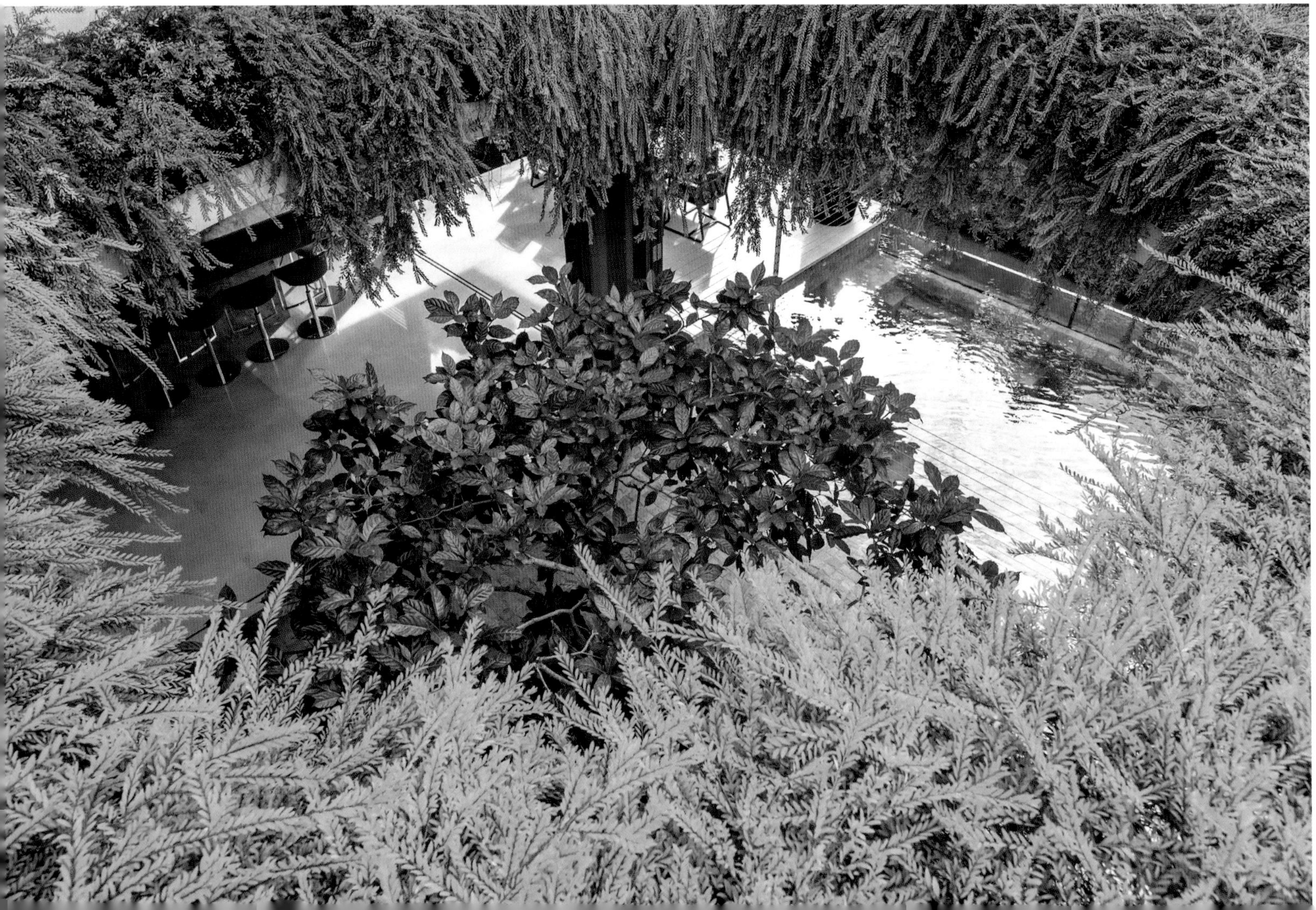

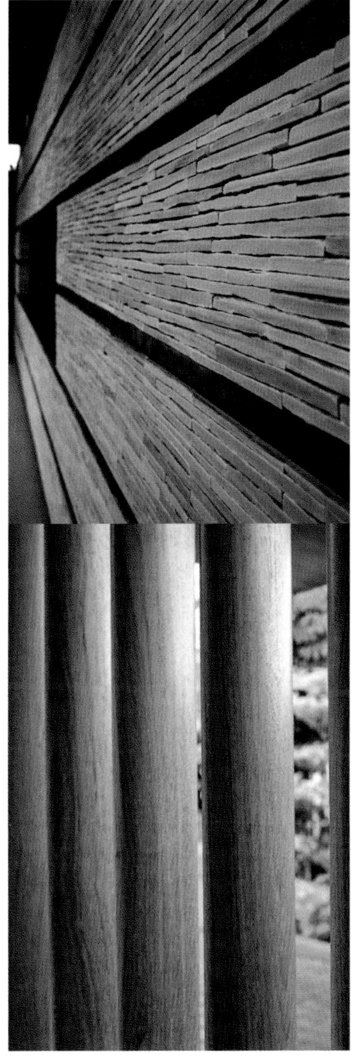

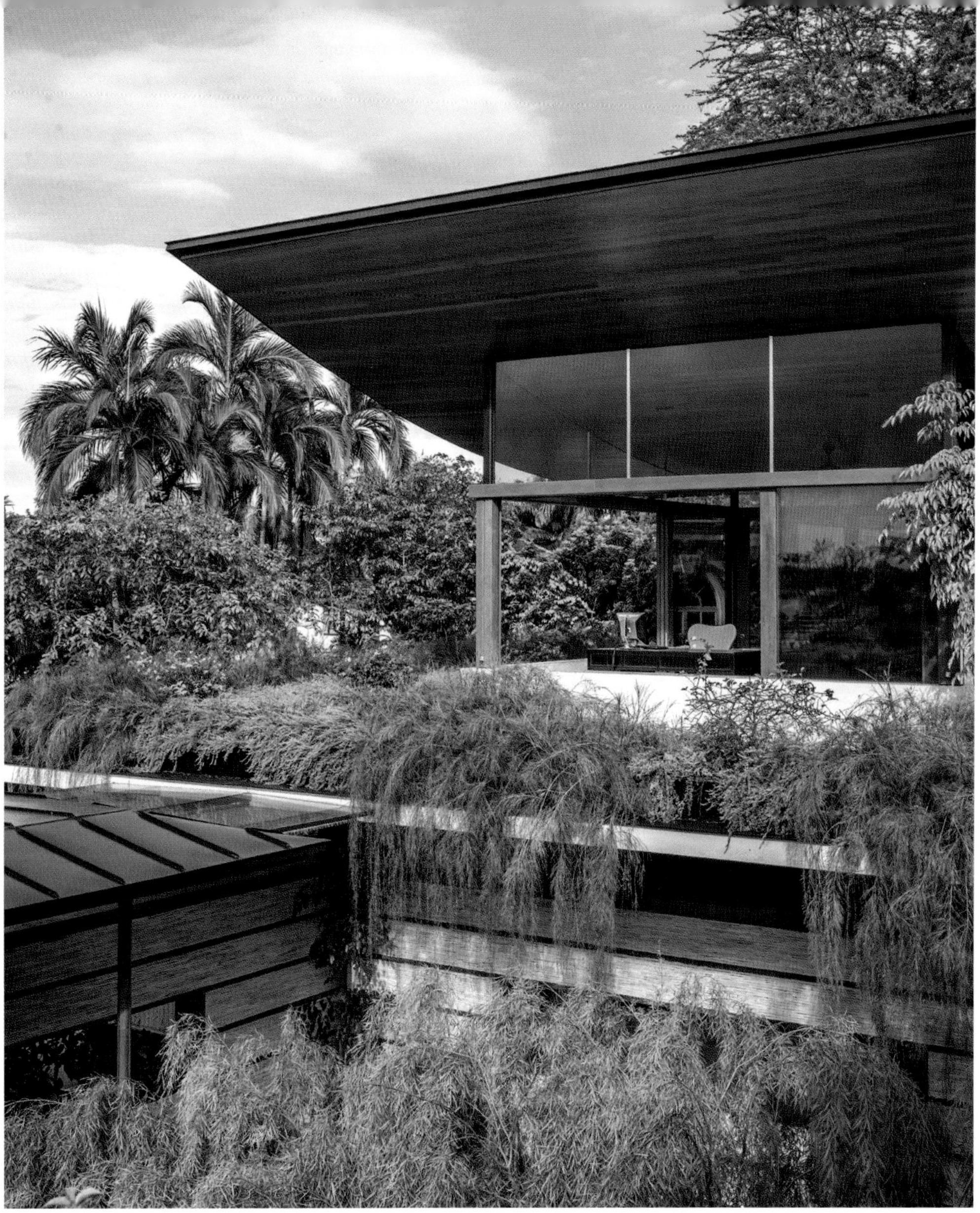

Top Detail of the entry wall.

Above Detail of the timber screen at the entry.

Above right The outdoor dining space and terrace are protected by a generous overhang and are cooled by the surrounding garden.

Right Outdoor showers add a touch of tropical sensuality.

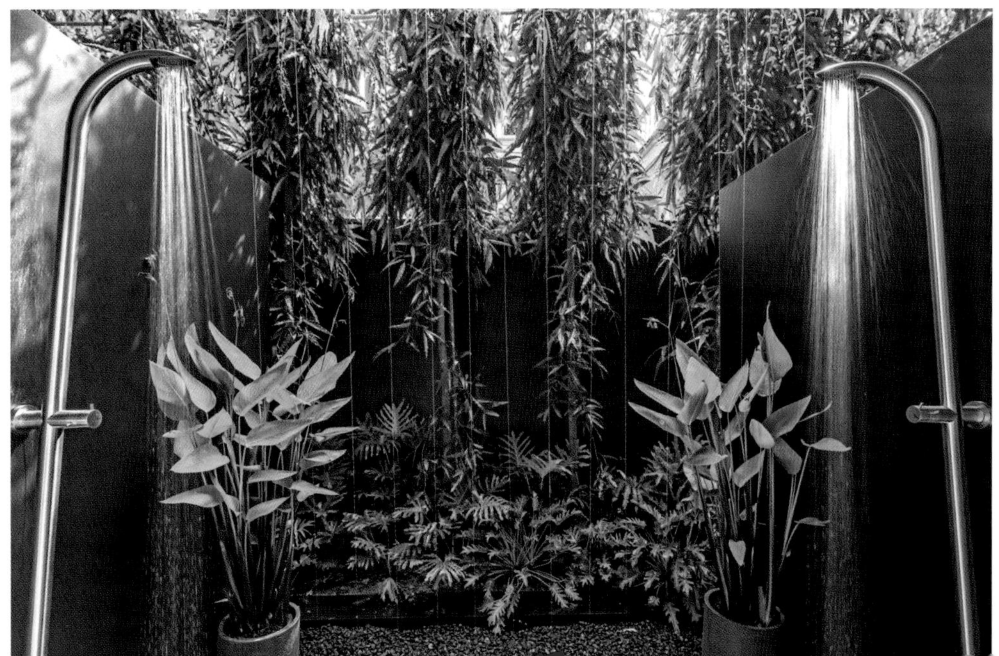

WATER LILY HOUSE
GUZ ARCHITECTS

'I am very happy because I have come to a stage in my life when I want a change. Home for me is very important. I wanted it for family. I wanted it for the children, for generations. Now we have four generations living in the house.'—CLIENT

Opposite The house takes advantage of its elevated site to lift even further up to capture views from the entertainment terrace and bedrooms above.

Below On the roof of the house at the rear is a secluded meditation pavilion.

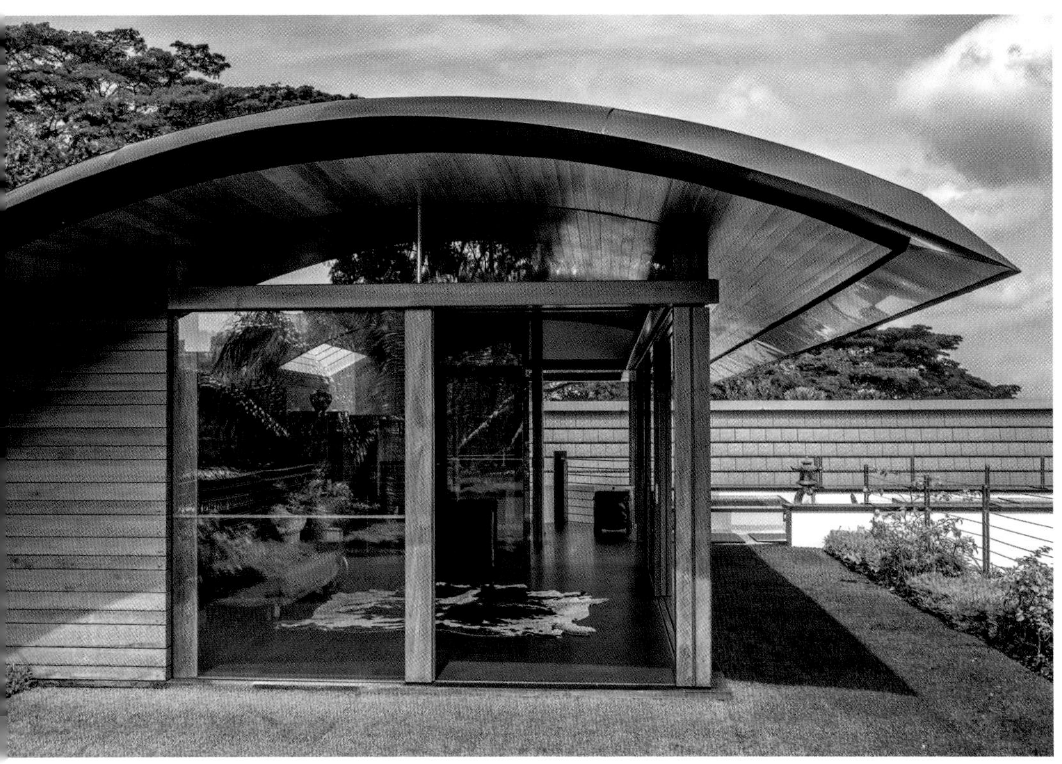

This is a multi-generational house accommodating three generations. Eight people live in the house, including three helpers. It is also a gathering point for the extended family (there can be up to twenty people present on weekends, including five grand-children) and a venue for entertaining. While the communal areas were important, it was also necessary to clearly delineate the public and the private domains—to be separate and yet together. At the same time, the clients wanted a home filled with light (their previous home on this site had been dark) where inside and outside came together and where there was a sense of limitless space. The other requirement was for generous entertainment areas. The architect has obliged with a dining space seating thirty-two served by a Ligne Roset modular table setting.

The clients did not want any dark areas in the house. They wanted lots of glass, including sliding glass doors. Hence, the house seems to dissolve into the gardens, drawing in so much light that artificial lighting is never required during the day. Although there is a lot of glass, the house never heats up because there is also adequate cross-ventilation.

One further function was important. Since the client is the agent for the international furniture brands Ligne Roset and Rolf Benz, and given the large amount of entertaining he does, the house acts as a kind of gallery for the furnishings. This is noticeable throughout the house but especially in the living pavilion. Because of the steep fall of the site at the front, the living pavilion, although on the entry level, is actually elevated, allowing panoramic views. It leads to a garden terrace with a shallow (one metre deep) swimming pool, which almost meanders around the timber deck, making it more of a water feature than a pool.

The house is organized around the central sunken courtyard and consists of three pavilions. The two main pavilions, like book ends, are linked by timber walkways on the first and second storeys. The third pavilion, which includes a music room, maids' quarters and the clients' private area, is at the basement level, defined on one side by the sunken garden courtyard and on the other by another outside garden space running the whole length of the building.

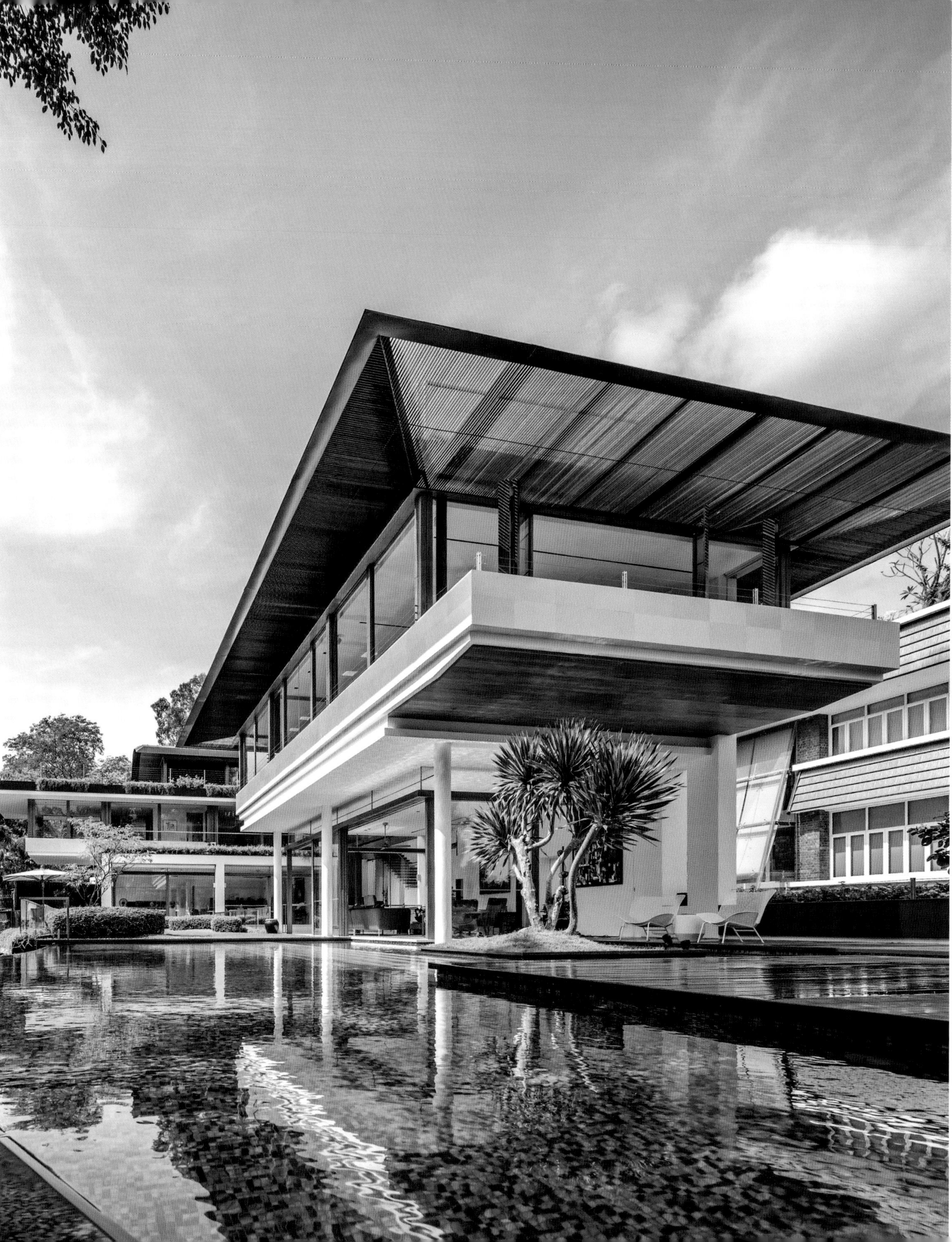

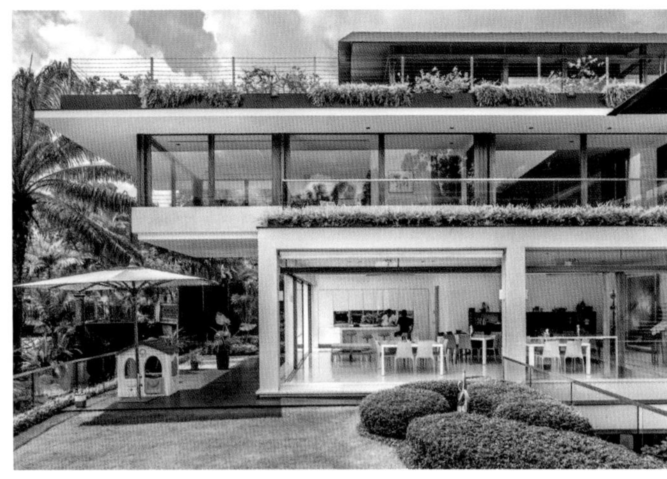

Left Looking towards the rear of the U-shaped house and the entertaining areas and meditation pavilion on the roof.

Below Looking towards the front, the house is revealed as really two pavilions joined by a double-height glazed link.

The house is entered through two substantial timber doors which, despite their size, give no hint of the light-filled and cathedral-like space within. Once inside, one turns either left to the living pavilion or proceeds straight ahead down the timber walkway overlooking the tropical garden courtyard below. This gallery is connected by an elegant stairway to the second storey walkway. The glazed balustrading of these galleries helps create an extraordinary transparency to this link between the two outer pavilions. At the end of the entry level gallery is the spacious dining area and dry kitchen and the daughter's quarters. In the attic area, there

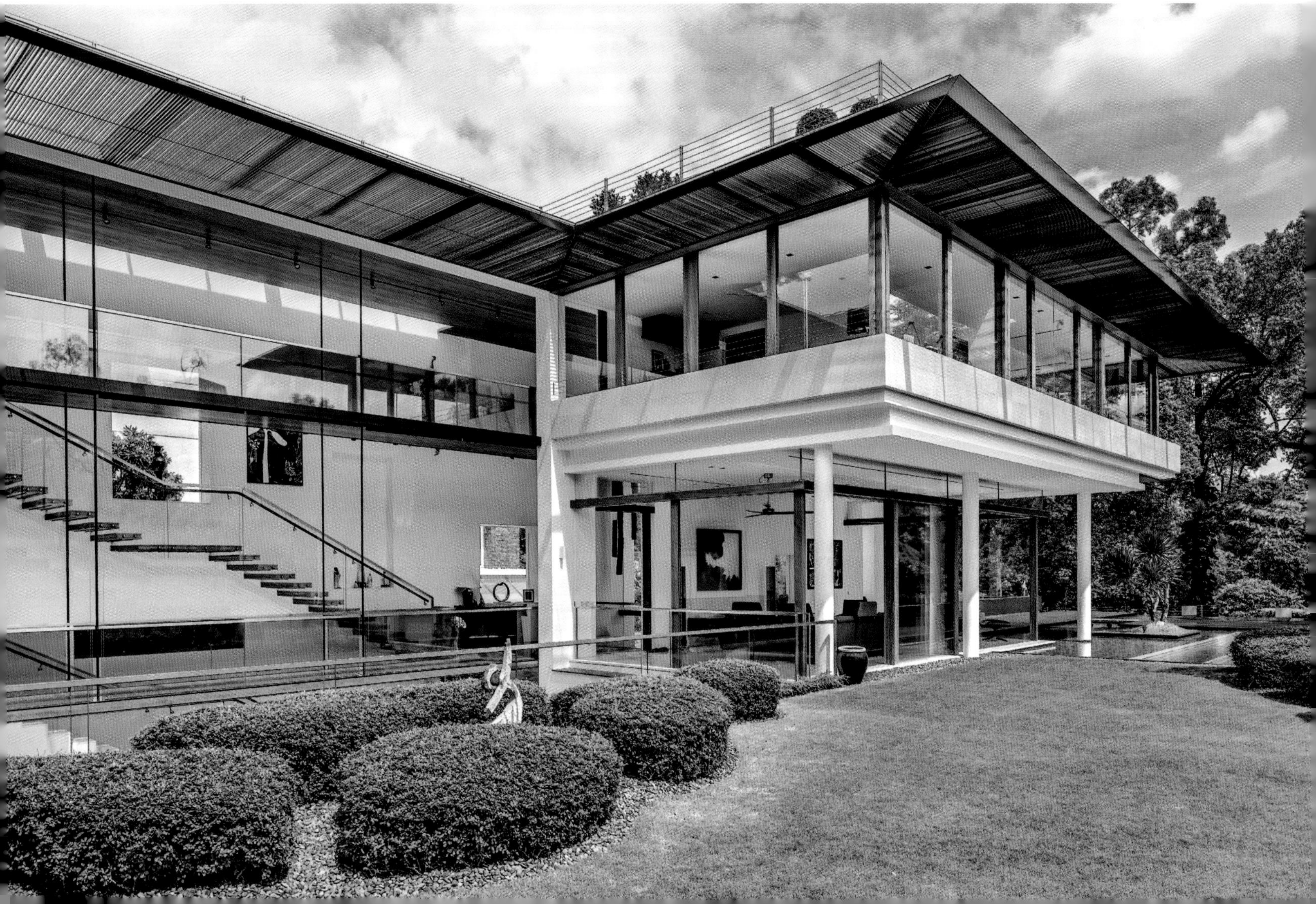

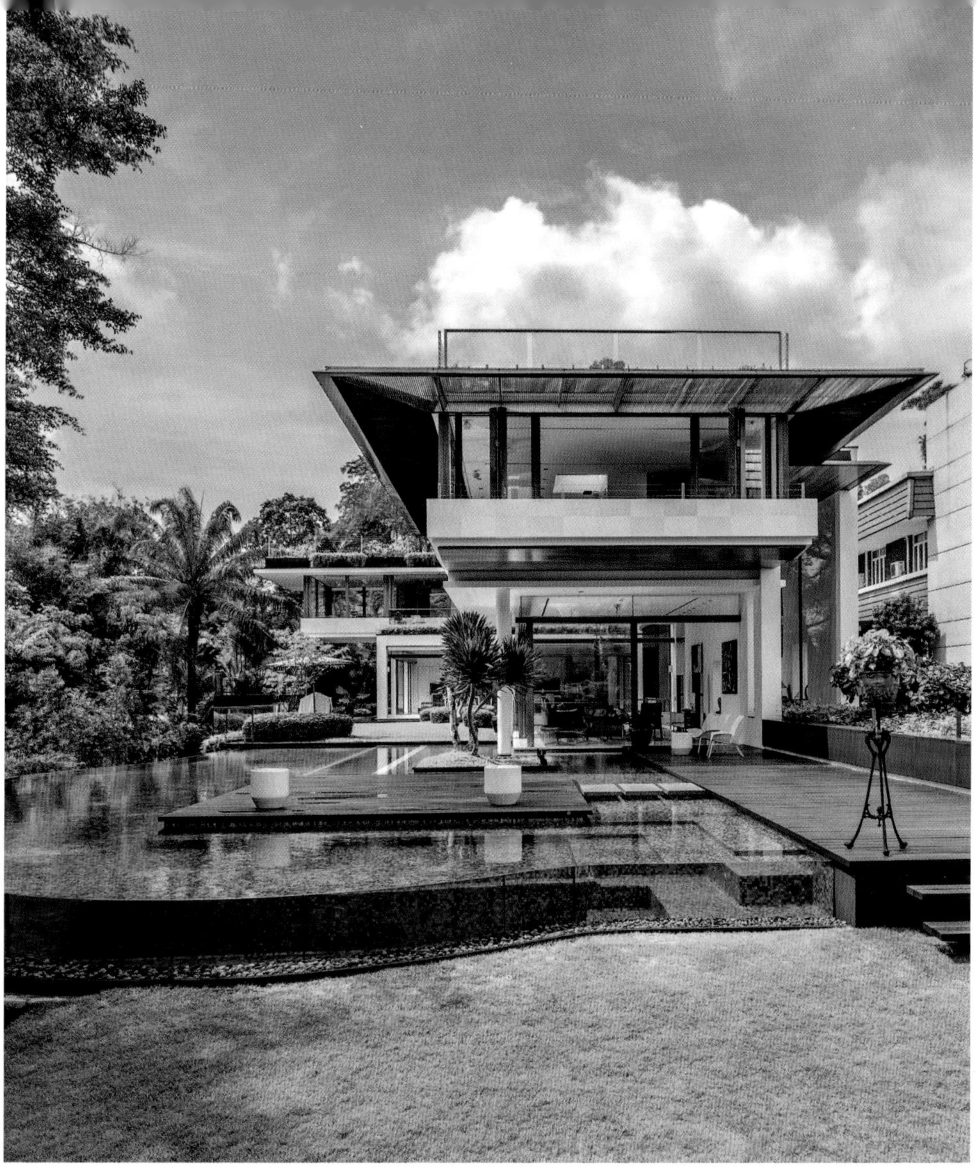

Left The family area with sitting room and pool terrace.

Below The rooftop walkway leads off the meditation pavilion.

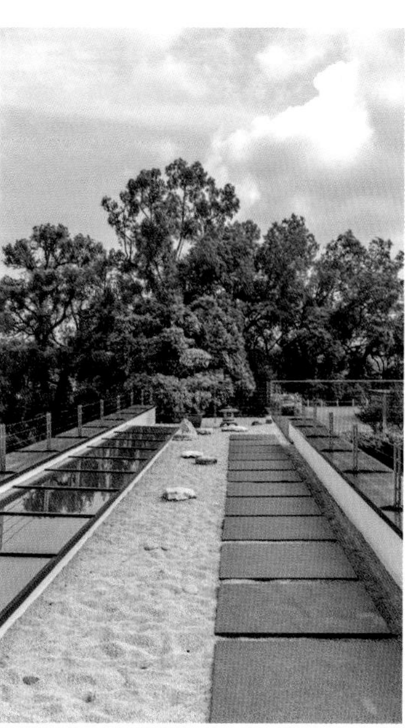

is a quiet space used for massage, meditation and reading the Bible. The son's quarters are above the living pavilion at the front of the building. Thus, the three units making up the family are clearly separated from one another, providing each of them with complete privacy whenever they want it. When the family comes together, it is invariably in the living pavilion and around the infinity pool.

Living in this house is a combination of living in the garden and in the landscape. There is not a single space that does not feel immediately connected to the outside, both physically and visually. This generates either a quiet, calming sense of intimacy with the natural world or a sense of liberation in the case of the elevated spaces with their panoramic views to the wider landscape or to other parts of the house. Filled with light and naturally ventilated, the house, with its covered walkways, open pavilions, water and lush greenery, cools itself.

In an environmental sense, the house is clearly sustainable. But its sustainability goes well beyond that. As an astutely planned multi-generational house that provides both privacy and community for its permanent residents while also accommodating large numbers of visiting family, it sustains family life with all the benefits that this brings to the individuals. It must also be wonderfully sustaining at the personal level. Apart from the privacy it affords, the private areas themselves contribute enormously to the well-being of the family.

This is perhaps best illustrated by the bathrooms. The grandparents' bathroom (and bedroom) look directly out across a pond to a private garden. It is hard to imagine a more serene experience than to lie in the Roman bath and feel as though one were floating in the pond itself. The daughter, too, has a bathroom which opens to the outside with an outdoor shower—a completely different experience for being not in a tranquil water garden but in the sky. On the other hand, the son's shower has been designed to respond to his love of the outdoors and physical activity. In the words of the client, 'This is not so much a house for show but for family use, because we like the family to come back here, enjoy ourselves and spend quality time together.'

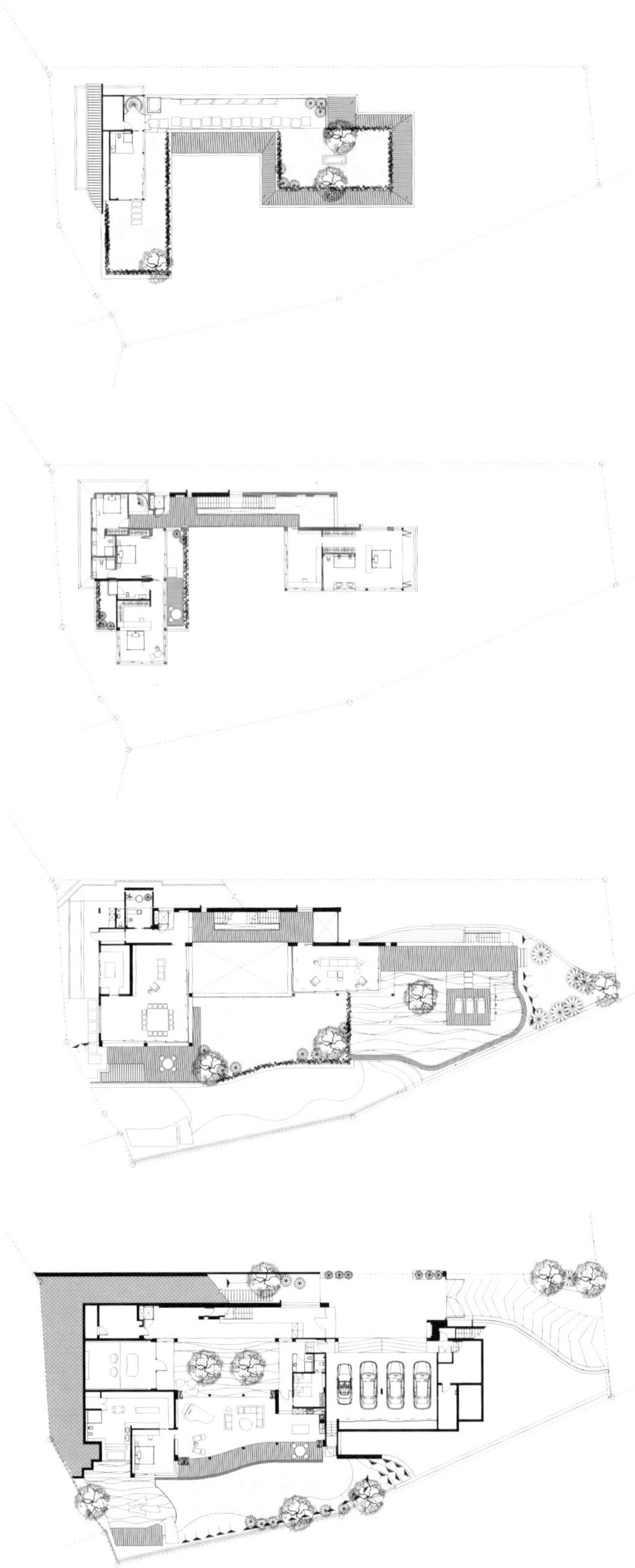

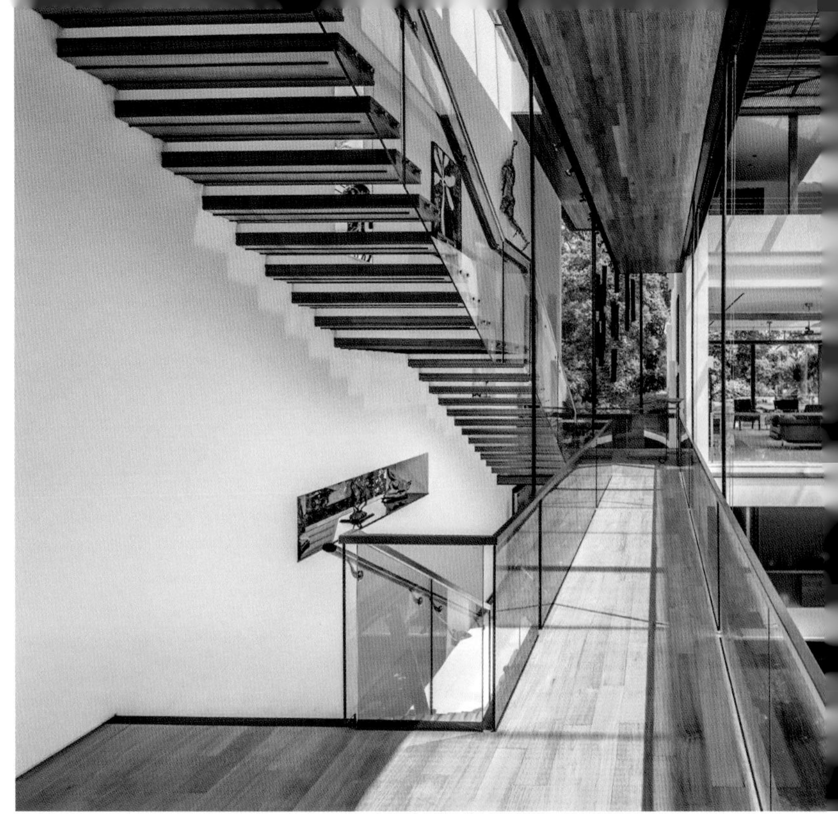

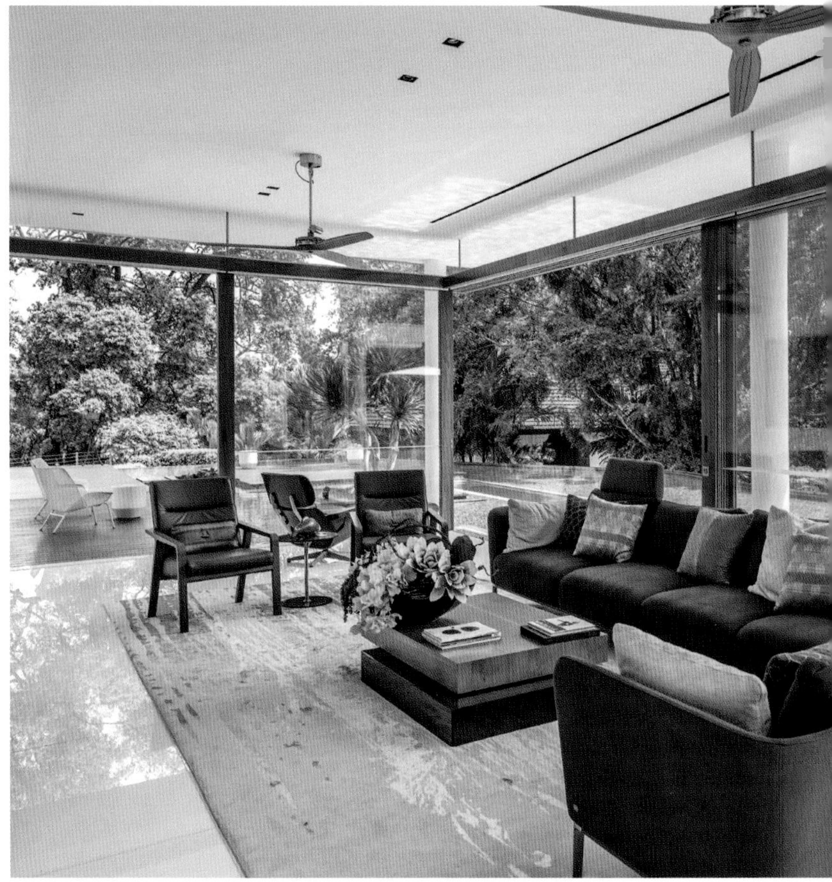

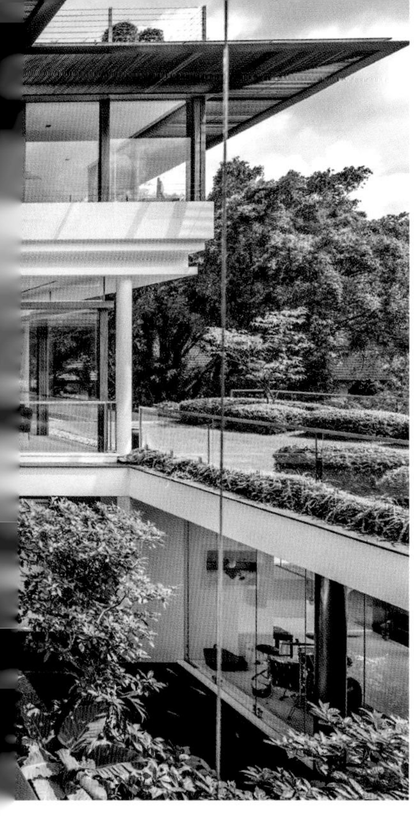

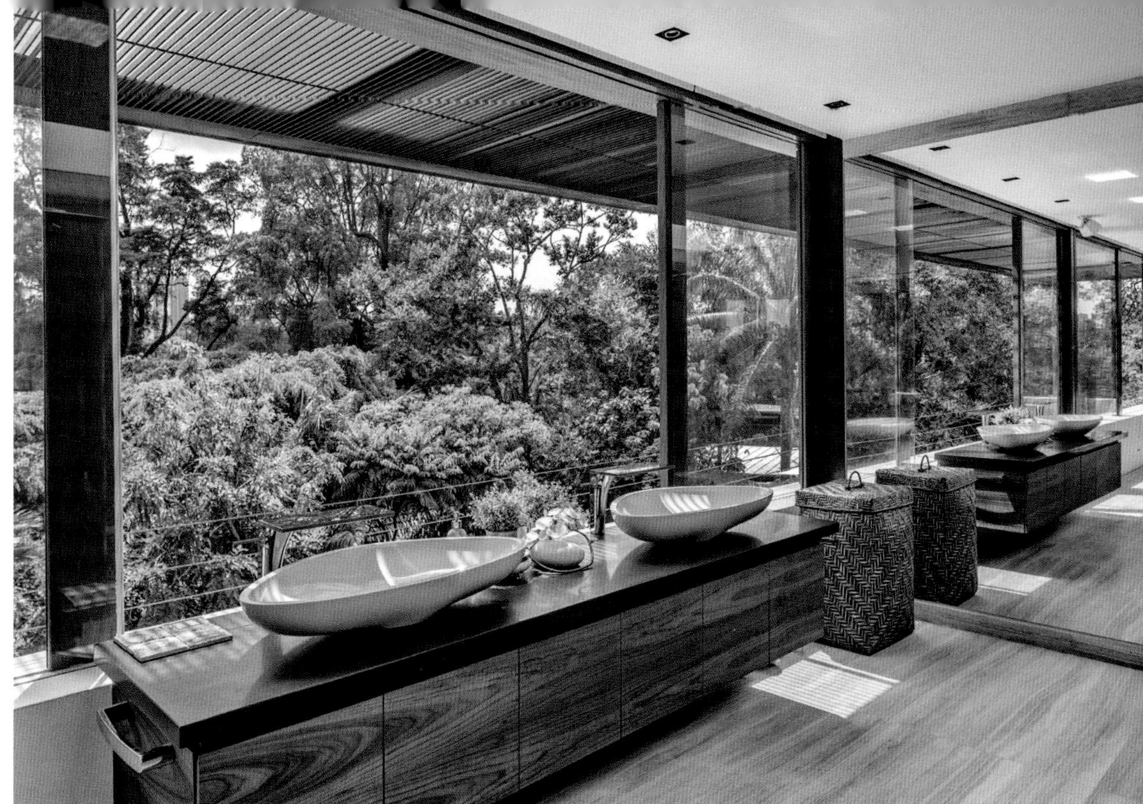

Far left Plans.

Above left The glazed link looks down into the basement garden, music room and master bedroom.

Left The family sitting room opens on to the pool terrace.

Above The en suite bathroom for the Level 2 bedroom at the front of the house.

Below The elevated bedroom at the front of the house.

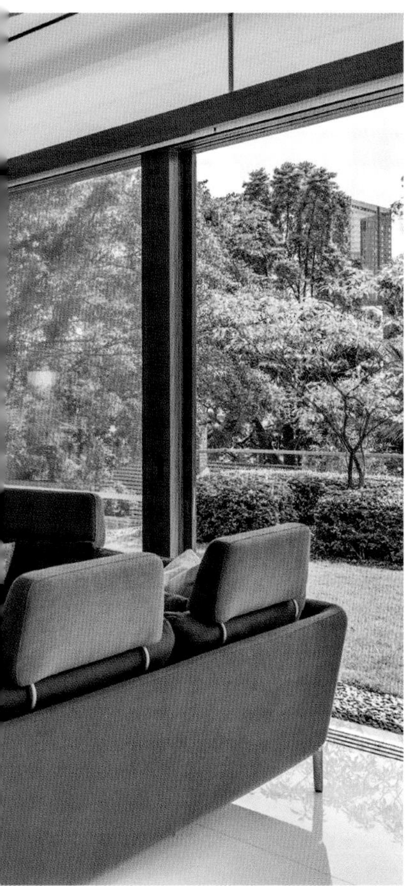

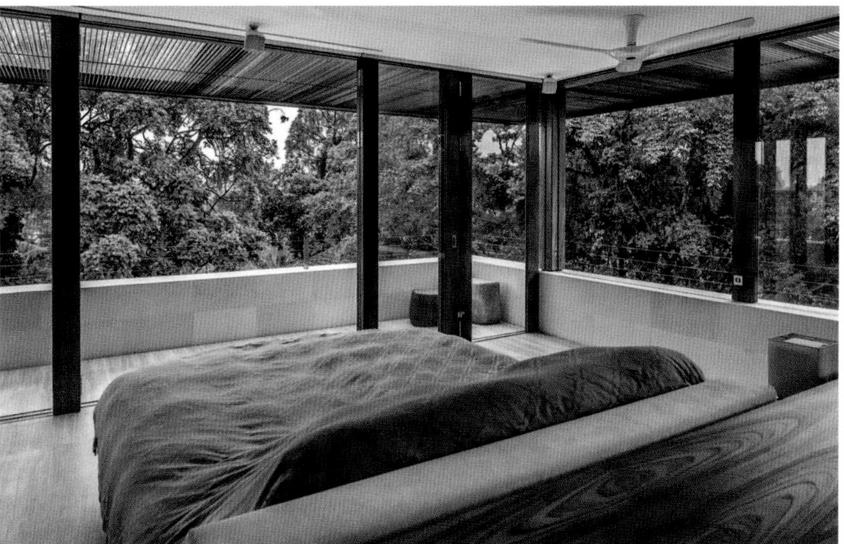

BELMONT ROAD HOUSE
CSYA

'We had to visualize what the company chief would need. So I looked back to times during the colonial period when the families would come out with a whole entourage of helpers. We used that as the basis for a company house. That was how we formulated the brief.'—SONNY CHAN SAU YAN, ARCHITECT

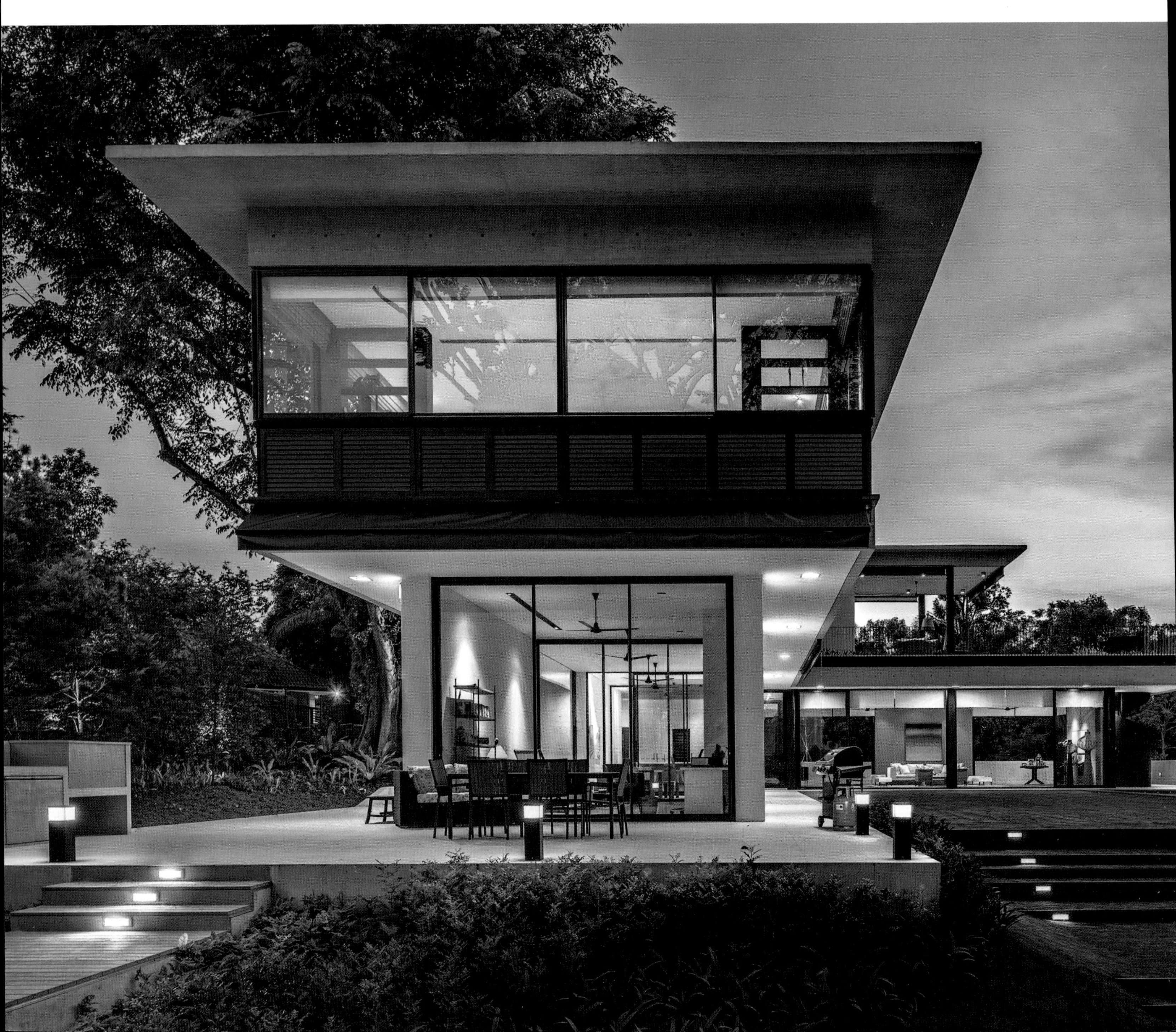

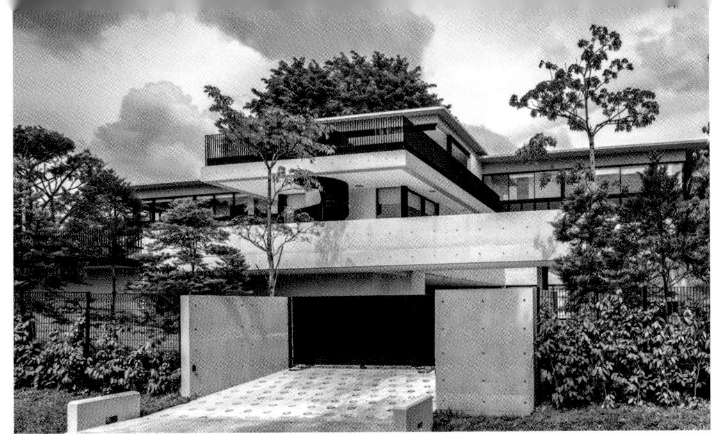

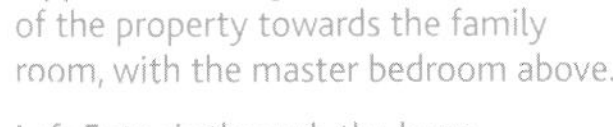

Opposite Looking back from the rear of the property towards the family room, with the master bedroom above.

Left Entry is through the huge basement car park.

Below Looking back from the pool towards the covered terrace on the left and the guest living room on the right.

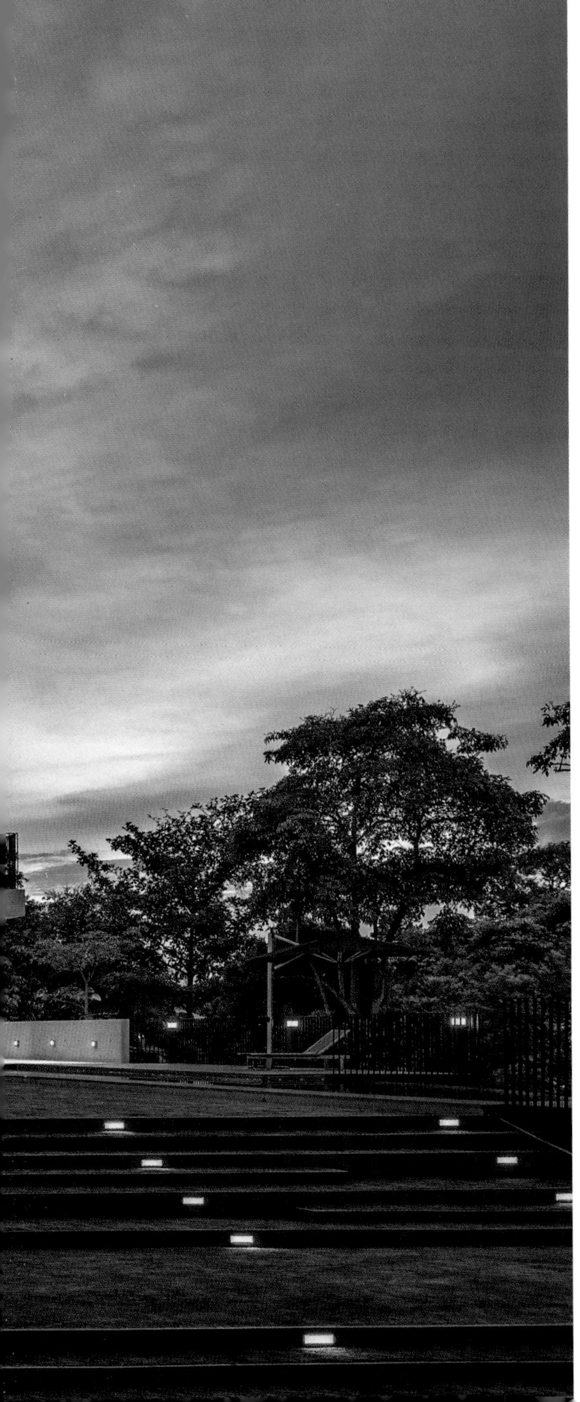

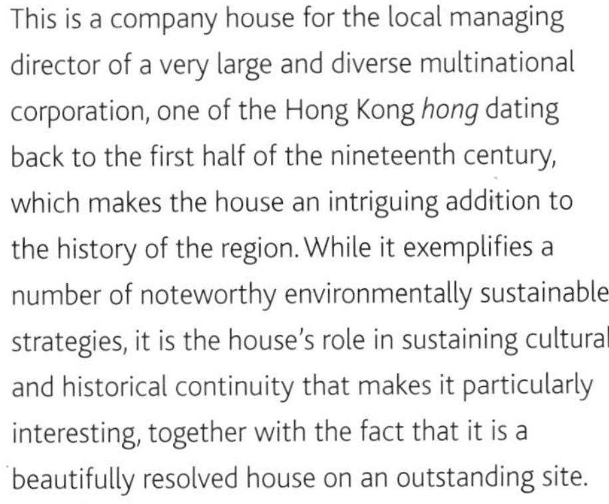

This is a company house for the local managing director of a very large and diverse multinational corporation, one of the Hong Kong *hong* dating back to the first half of the nineteenth century, which makes the house an intriguing addition to the history of the region. While it exemplifies a number of noteworthy environmentally sustainable strategies, it is the house's role in sustaining cultural and historical continuity that makes it particularly interesting, together with the fact that it is a beautifully resolved house on an outstanding site.

The house is in a tree conservation area and there are at least two significant trees on the site. Responding to these trees helped generate the plan of the building. The plot is elevated significantly above the road, which allows stunning views, but also created the opportunity for a spacious basement car park forecourt to provide guest parking when entertaining and so relieve pressure on the congested public roadway. Above this, the private and public wings of the house form a vague T shape, although the plan is predominantly an L shape with the swimming pool defining the long open edge and one of the trees acting as a focal point at the open short end of the site. The overall effect is of a large and expansive garden courtyard.

This effect is integral to the key design idea, which was to reinvent the colonial black-and-white

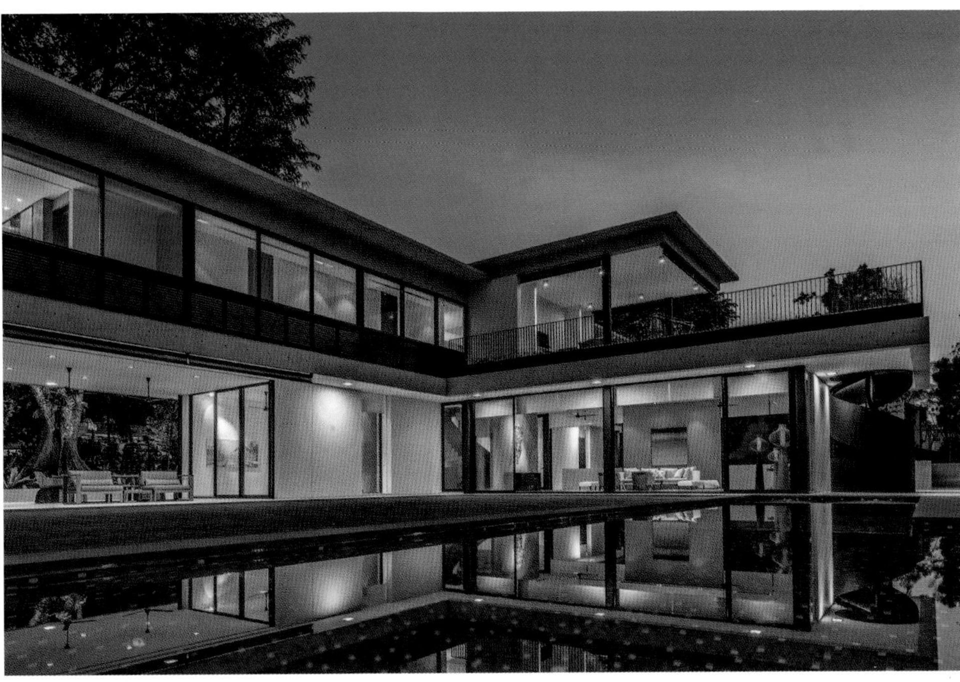

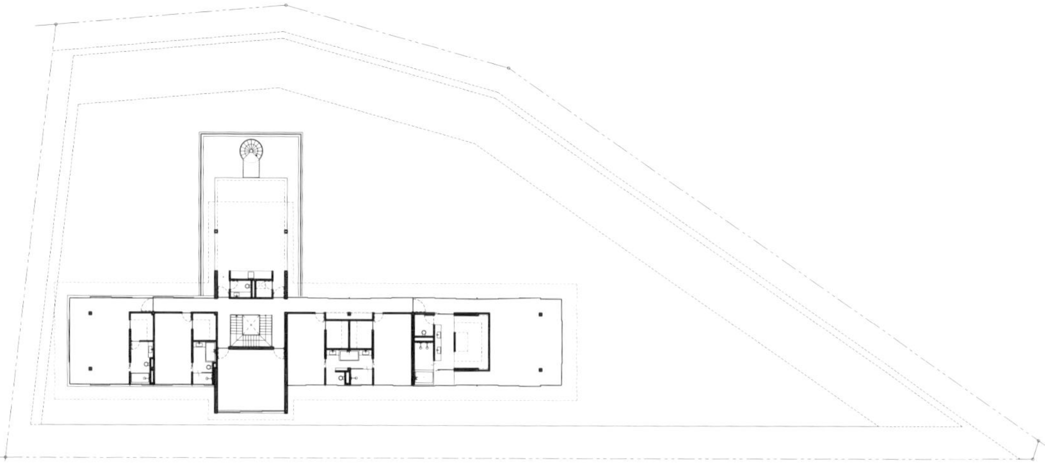

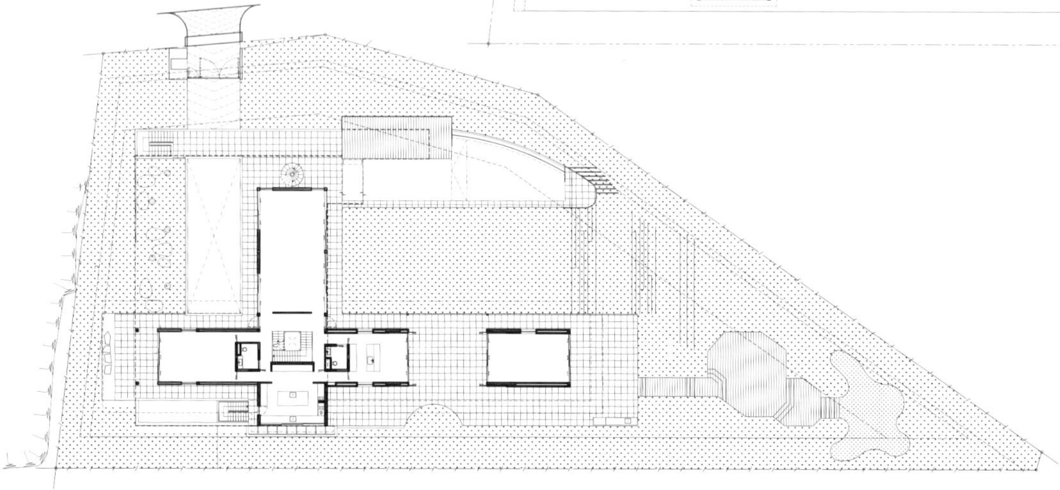

Above Second storey plan.

Left First storey plan.

Below left The breakfast bar opening on to the covered terrace.

Below The covered terrace, with one the significant preserved trees in the background.

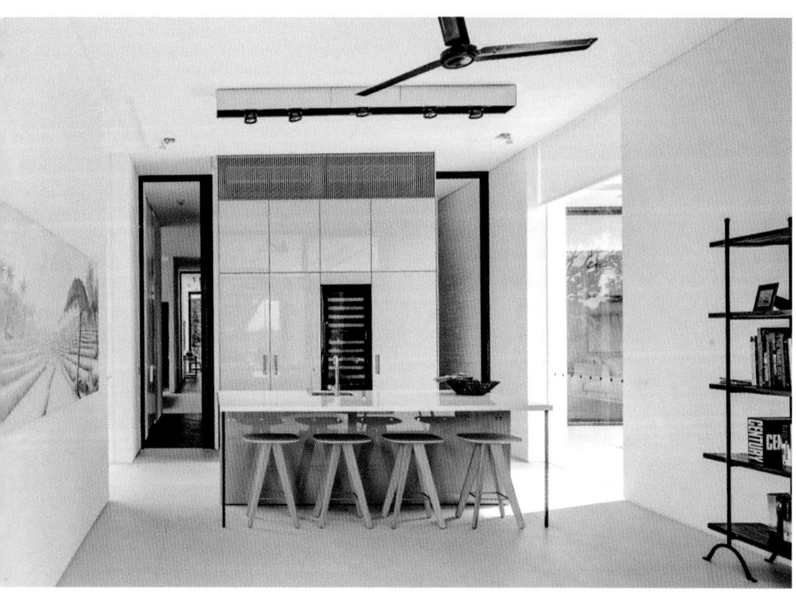

house as a contemporary company house. In this way, the house would not be simply just another Good Class Bungalow (over 1400 square metres in plot size) for a transient expatriate executive but be part of an evolving history and of its place, not just literally in the way it responds to its site and the climate but also metaphorically in the way it reflects its cultural 'place'. This, then, is analogous to the black-and-white house. Families would come for, say, a five-year tour of duty and then move on to be replaced by the next family, but the house remained as the constant denominator, accumulating in some intangible way its own history and contributing to the history of Singapore.

Despite its name—and the 'Tudorbethan' decorative elements that name reflects—the black-and-white house was, in fact, an intelligent

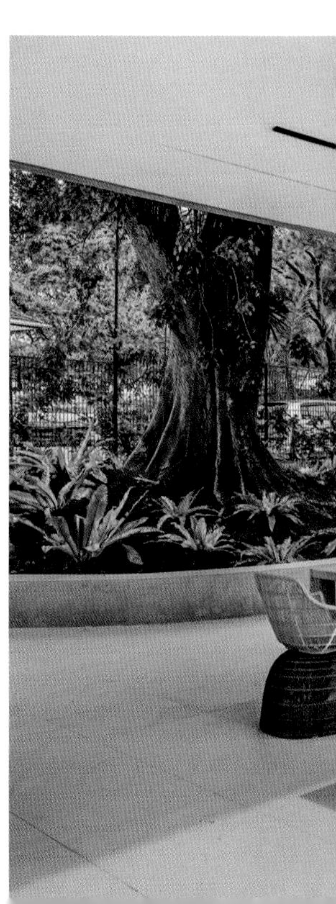

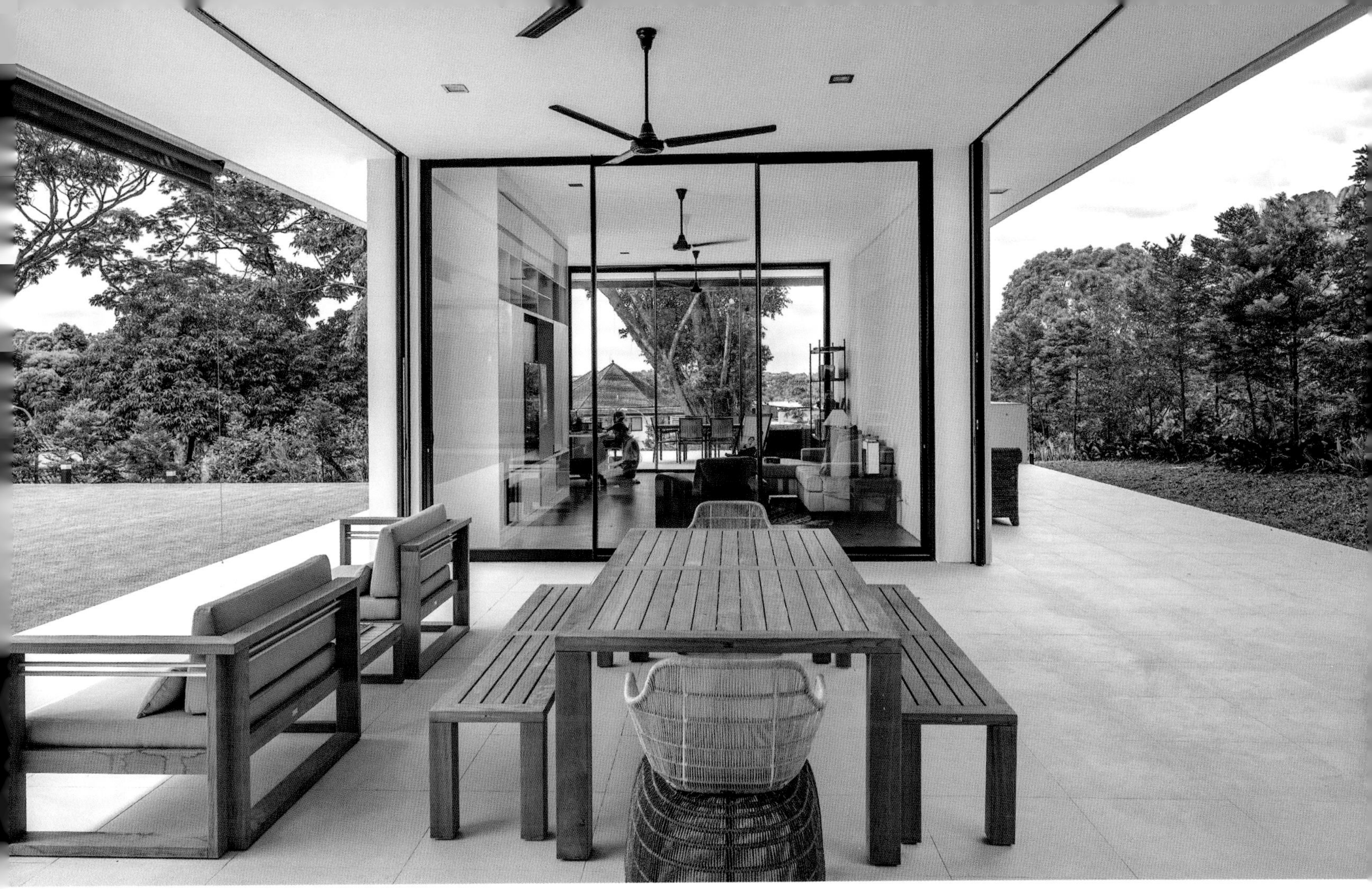

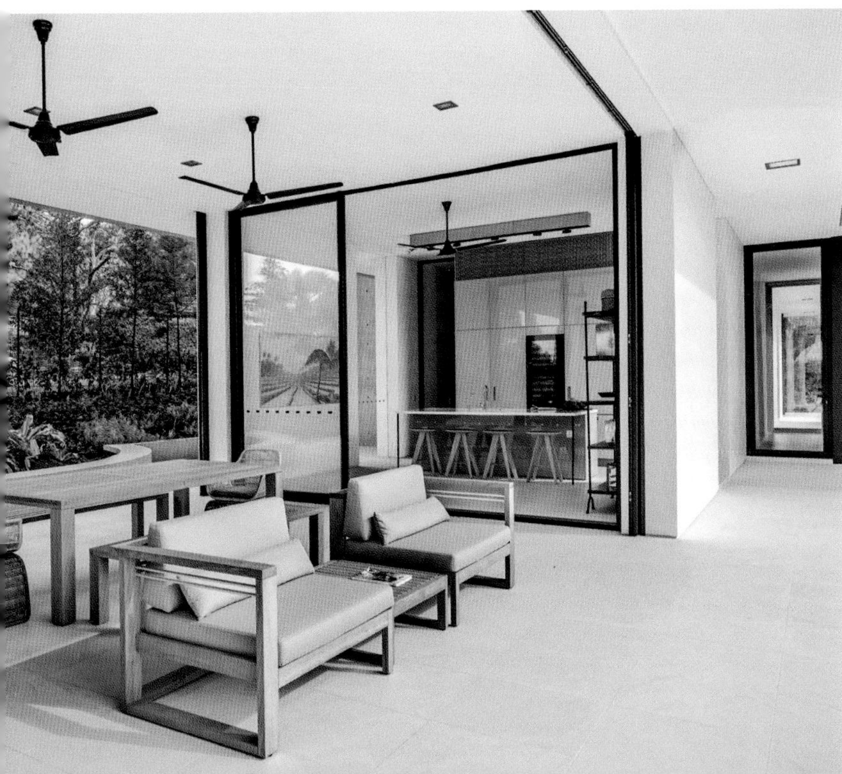

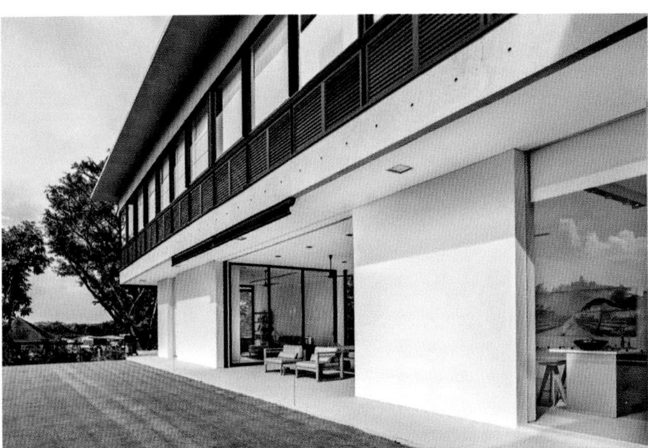

Top The covered terrace looking towards the family room is a contemporary version of the traditional tropical verandah.

Above The enfilade of dark-toned windows and louvres suggests the colonial black-and-white house.

response to living in a tropical climate and its design is an eclectic mix of local and Indian vernacular traditions with the various colonial adaptations of those traditions. This house needed to be both a family home and an entertainment venue. As a venue for company functions, it needed a certain grandness. As Sonny Chan points out, wherever you are in the house you see a panorama, across the grounds of the house and beyond.

The private and the public areas are well defined. In fact, guest entry does not need to be through the main house. It can be by a grand spiral staircase from the car forecourt leading first to the courtyard level (and the 'public' pavilion with the main living area and dining room) then up to the entertainment deck on Level 2. The long side of the L shape is a family wing. On the courtyard level, this consists of a pantry leading to a completely open terrace and then to an enclosed family room, which can also be opened up completely to the garden. This sequence of spaces recalls the deeply shaded recesses of colonial verandahs where interiors and exteriors merged to create an effortlessly elegant form of tropical living without air-conditioning.

The family bedrooms are on the upper level of this wing, which is just one room deep. Hence, all rooms have either two, or in the case of the master

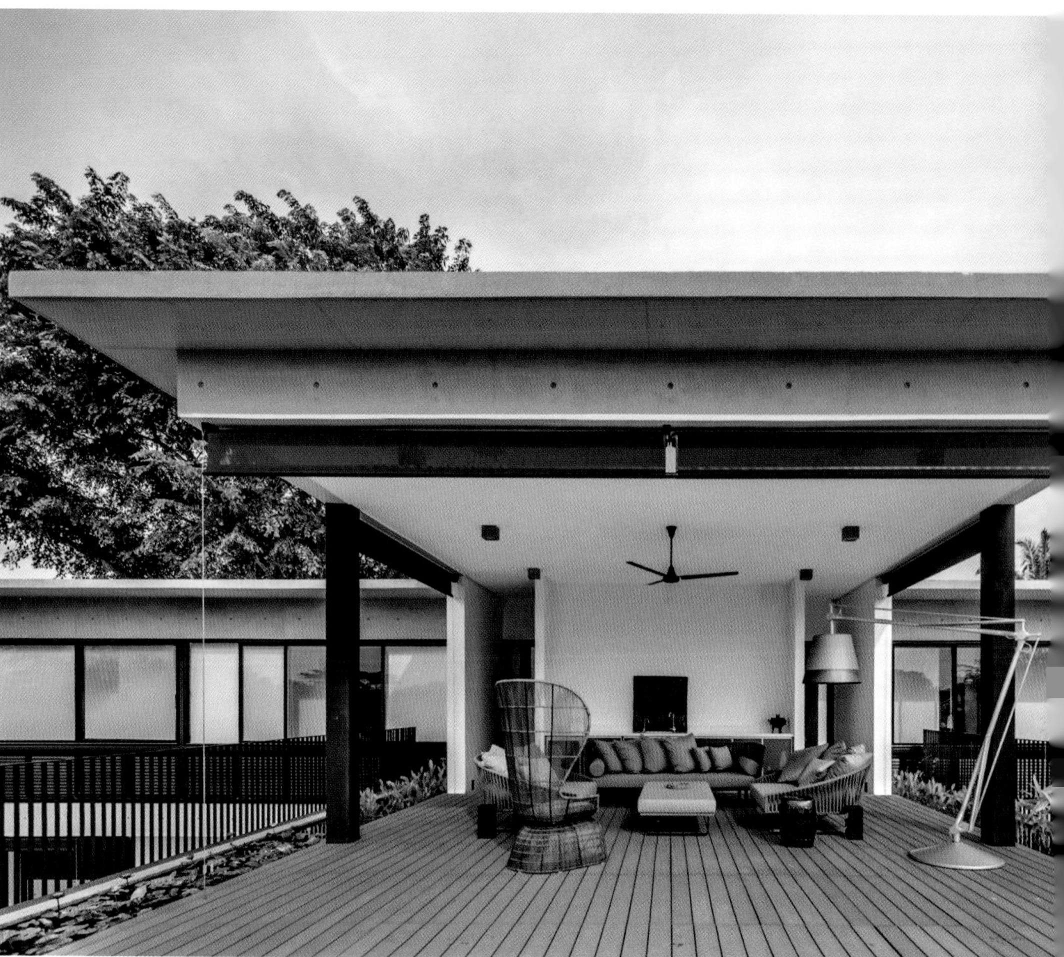

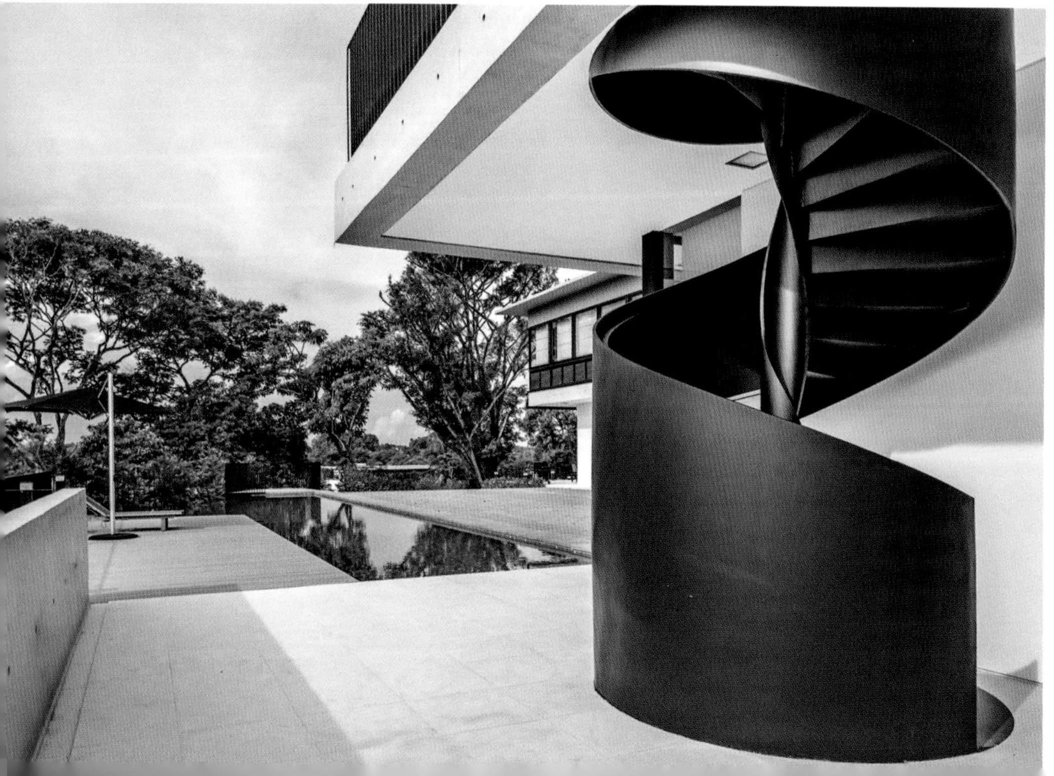

Above The outdoor entertainment deck and cabana on the second storey are defined by a perimeter water garden.

Left The black steel spiral stairway winds its way up over three levels, from the basement to the entertainment deck.

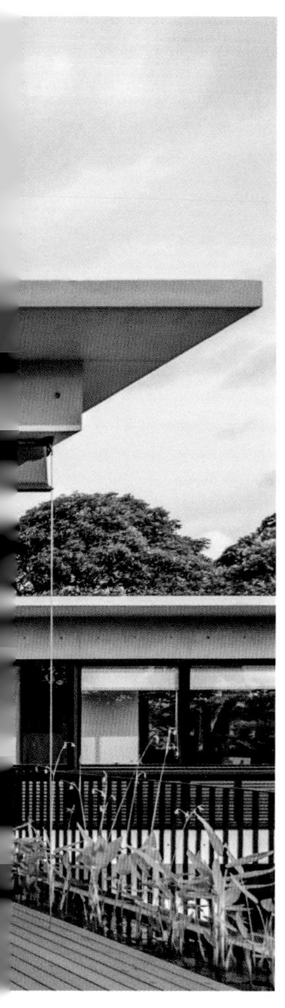

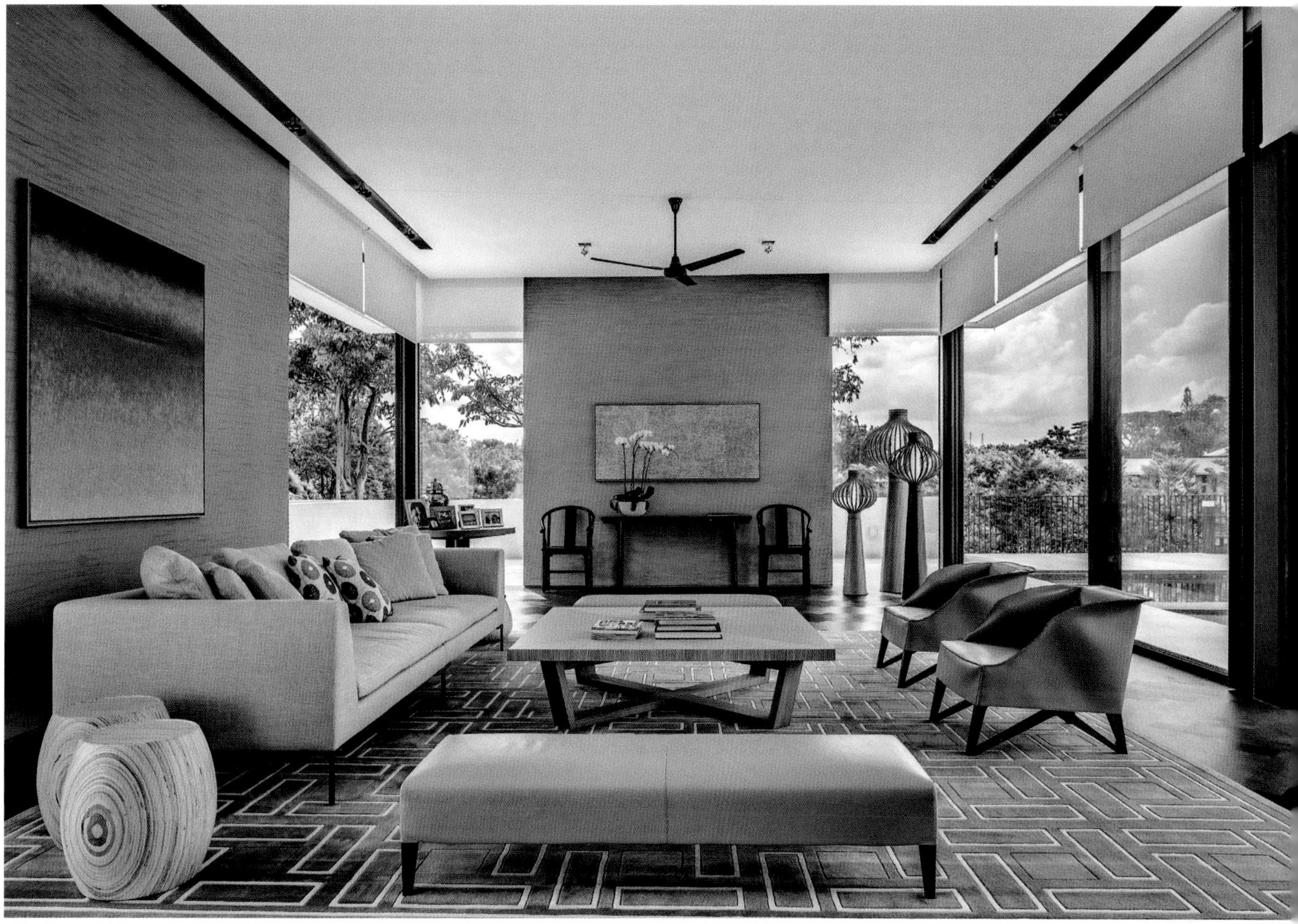

bedroom at the end of the wing, three sides exposed to the outside to enable generous cross-ventilation. The bedrooms are linked by a gallery, an enfilade of windows and operable powder-coated black louvres. The outside wall is a mix of white render and fair-face, off-form concrete which, together with the louvres, suggests a reincarnation of the colonial black-and-white house.

Two guest bedrooms are similar in plan but smaller than the master bedroom and its impressive skylighted master bathroom. They are also upstairs, separated from the family bedrooms by the central sky-lit, dark-stained oak stairway. Beneath the guest bedrooms on Level 1 is the main dining room, with floor-to-ceiling windows and doors leading out to its own courtyard and lawn.

The highlight of the public domain is the outdoor entertainment deck located above the main living space. Here, a cabana leads out to a timber deck—actually a green mark product of recycled plastic and woodchip—with a perimeter water feature and garden and sensational views down into the lower courtyard and across the neighbourhood.

This is a house that combines environmentally sustainable features—extensive use of natural light, cross-ventilation, indoor/outdoor living and recycled materials—with a subtle celebration of cultural continuity. Like the black-and-white house it takes its inspiration from, it sustains a sense of connection with the past and with a tradition that has helped form contemporary Singapore.

Above The grand living room, which is used for entertaining guests.

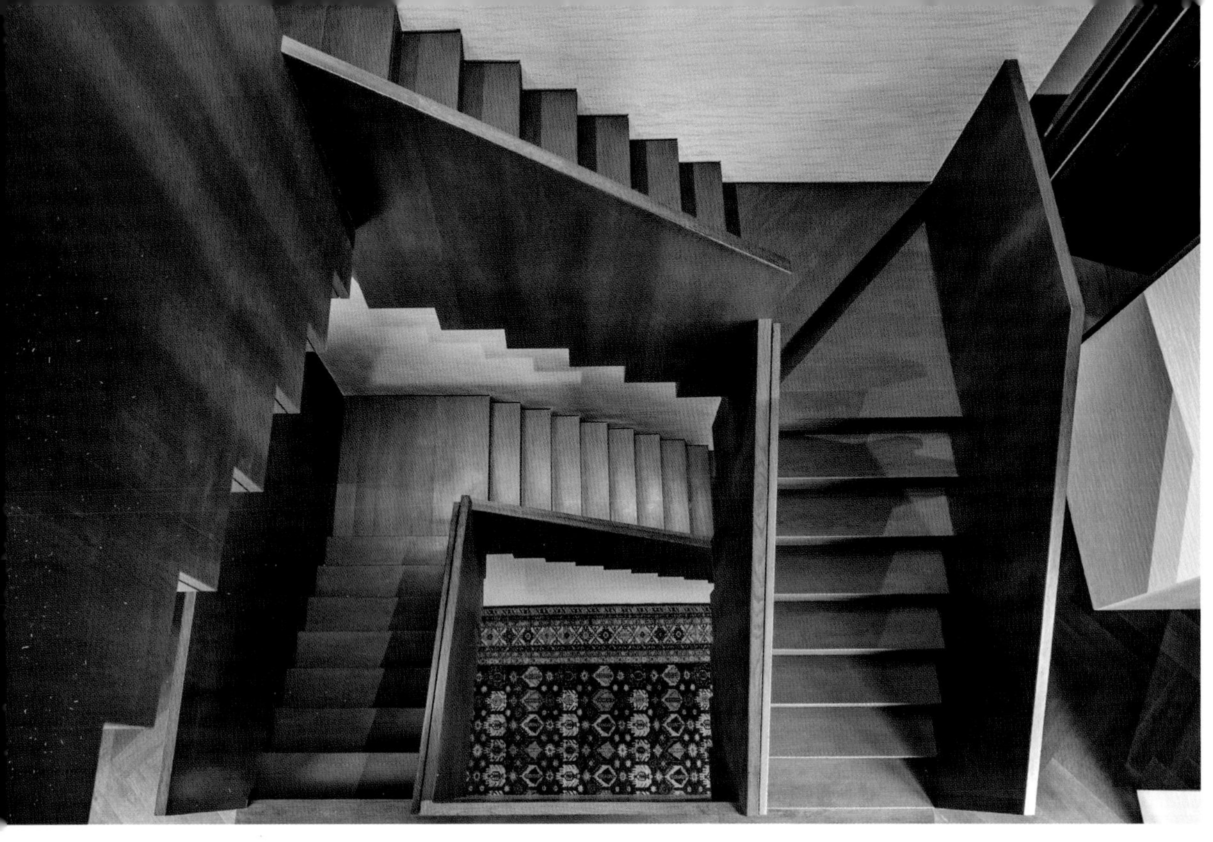

Left The dark-stained oak stairway through the middle of the house also divides the private and public domains.

Below left The dining room for guests looks out to its own garden courtyard.

Below The central stairway at the first storey.

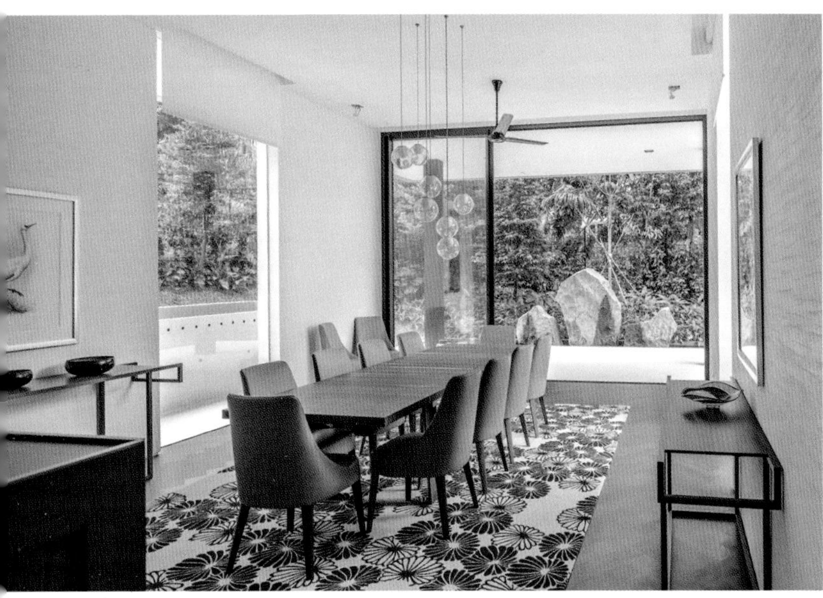

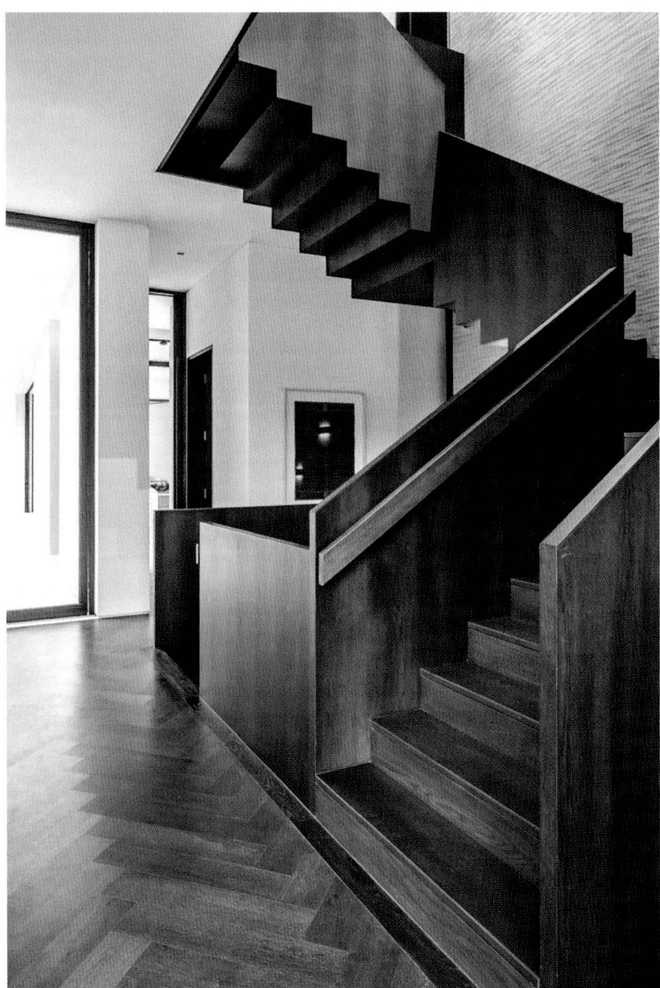

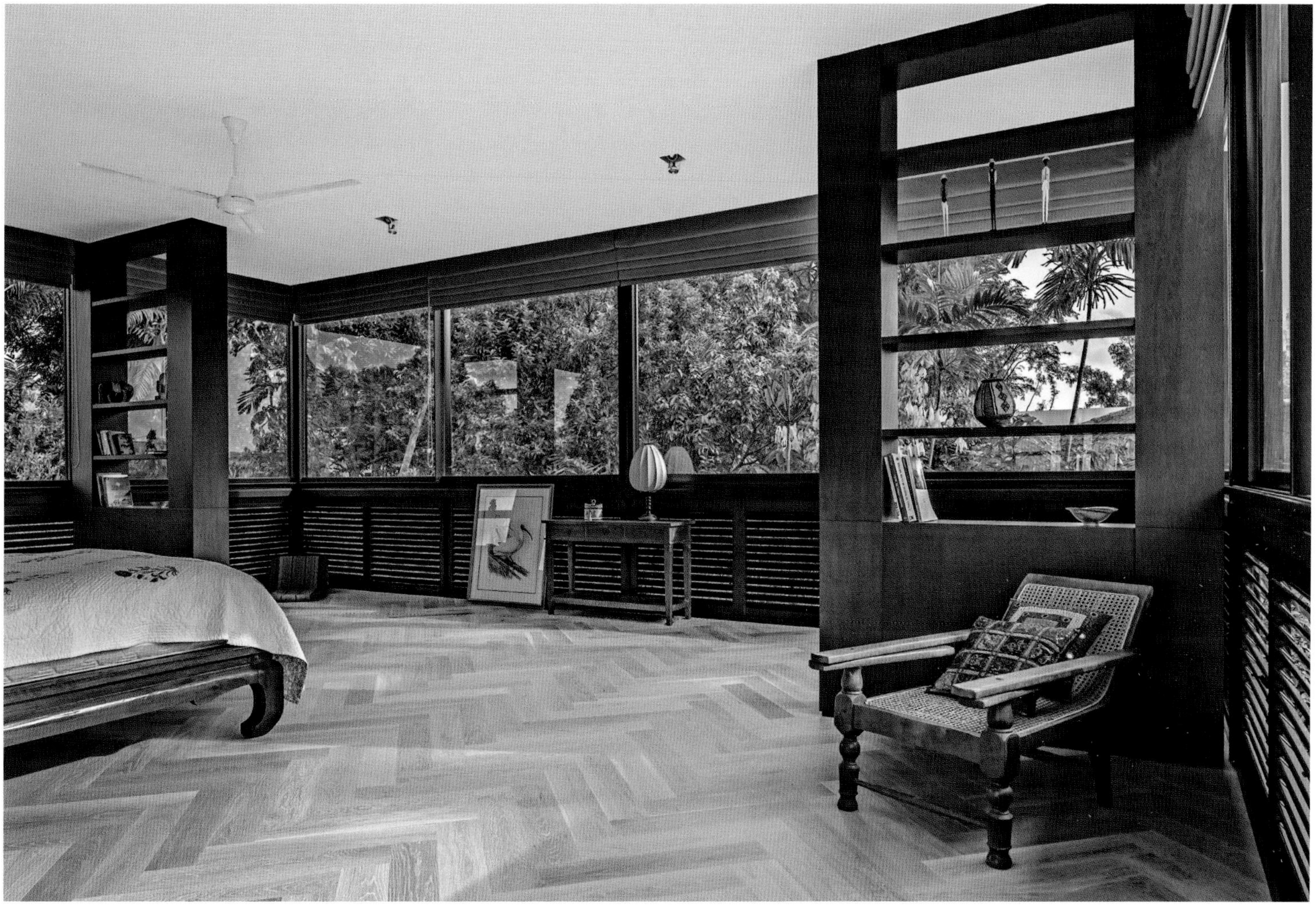

Above The master bedroom has a banquette spanning the length of the far wall.

Right Looking back towards the house from the rear of the property, with the two significant preserved trees.

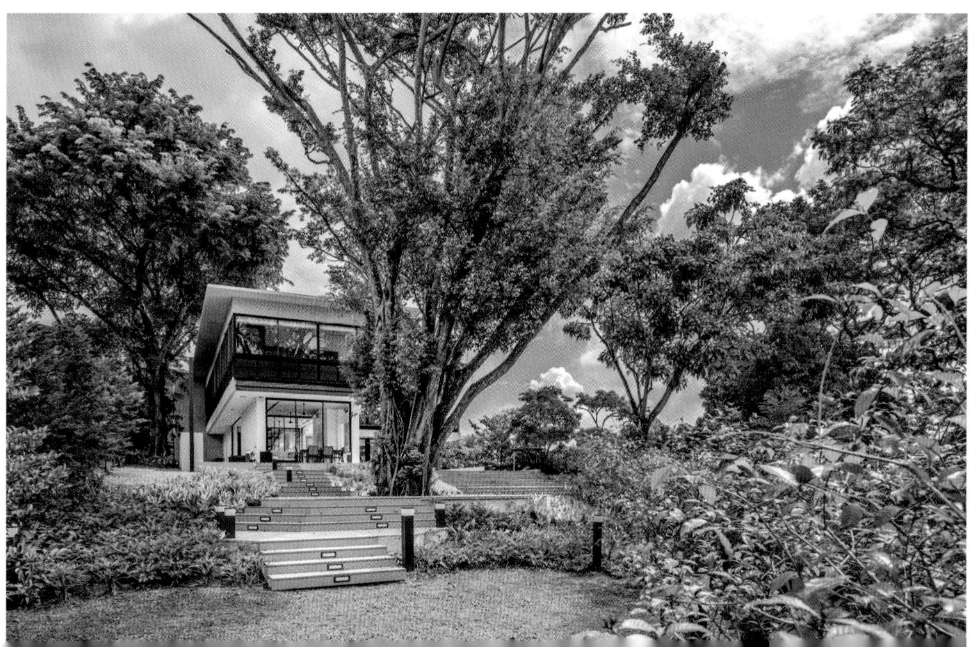

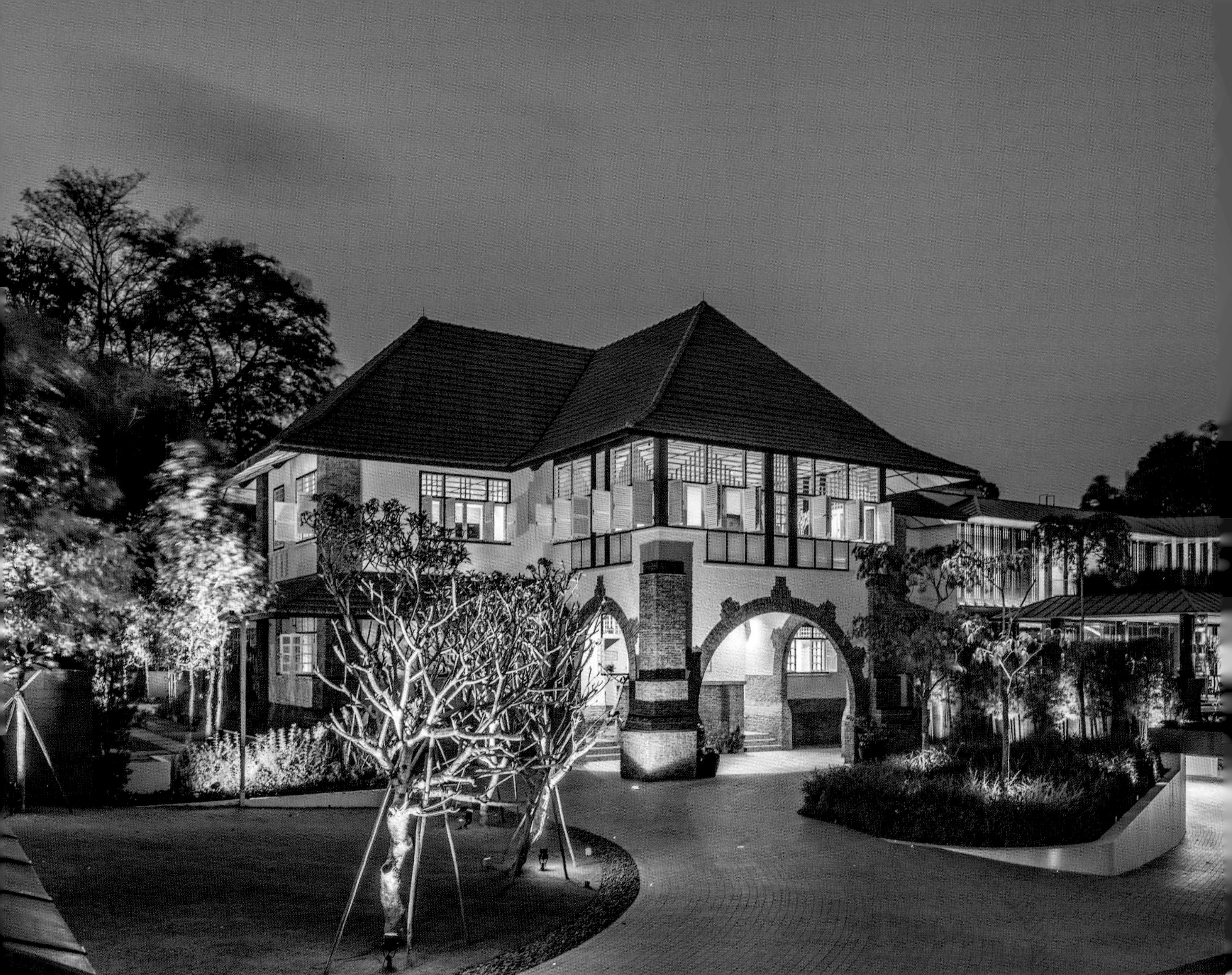

CHATSWORTH PARK HOUSE
ECO:ID ARCHITECTS

'My father said that he wanted this house to bring longevity, not just to individuals but to relationships, longevity for generations to come.'—CLIENT

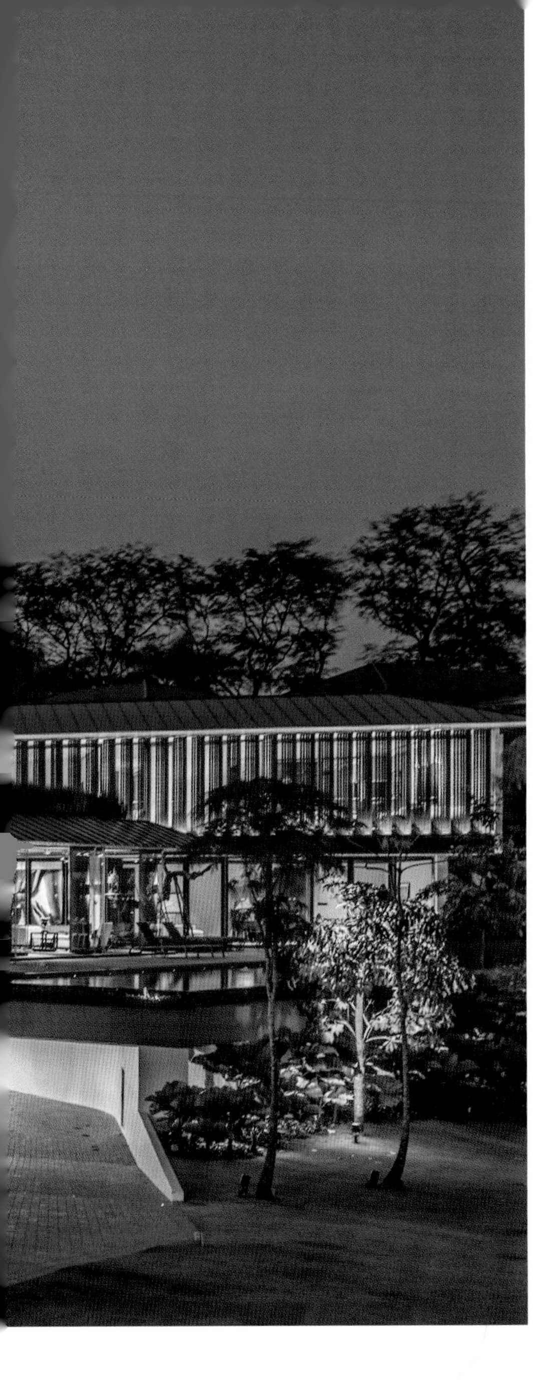

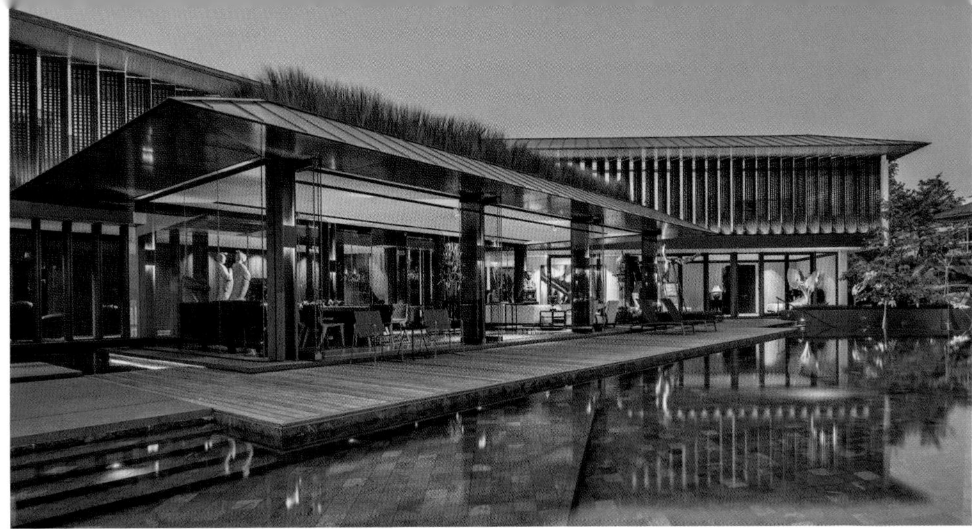

In his magical book *The Poetics of Space*, Gaston Bachelard comments that 'the house is one of the greatest powers of integration for the thoughts, memories and dreams of mankind.' In this sense, the house—the home—is the single most sustainable thing any of us is likely to have in our lifetime. The house is a repository of memories, and memories sustain us over time. But a house at any given moment in time is also crucially sustaining because it is a shelter, a refuge, and a site where families support one another and generate the meanings which enrich individual lives.

This house consists of the original house and an extensive recent addition. It is sustainable from several points of view. It is largely naturally ventilated and cooled by wide eaves, shutters, screens, water features and, in the case of the 'floating' living/dining pavilion, a rooftop garden,

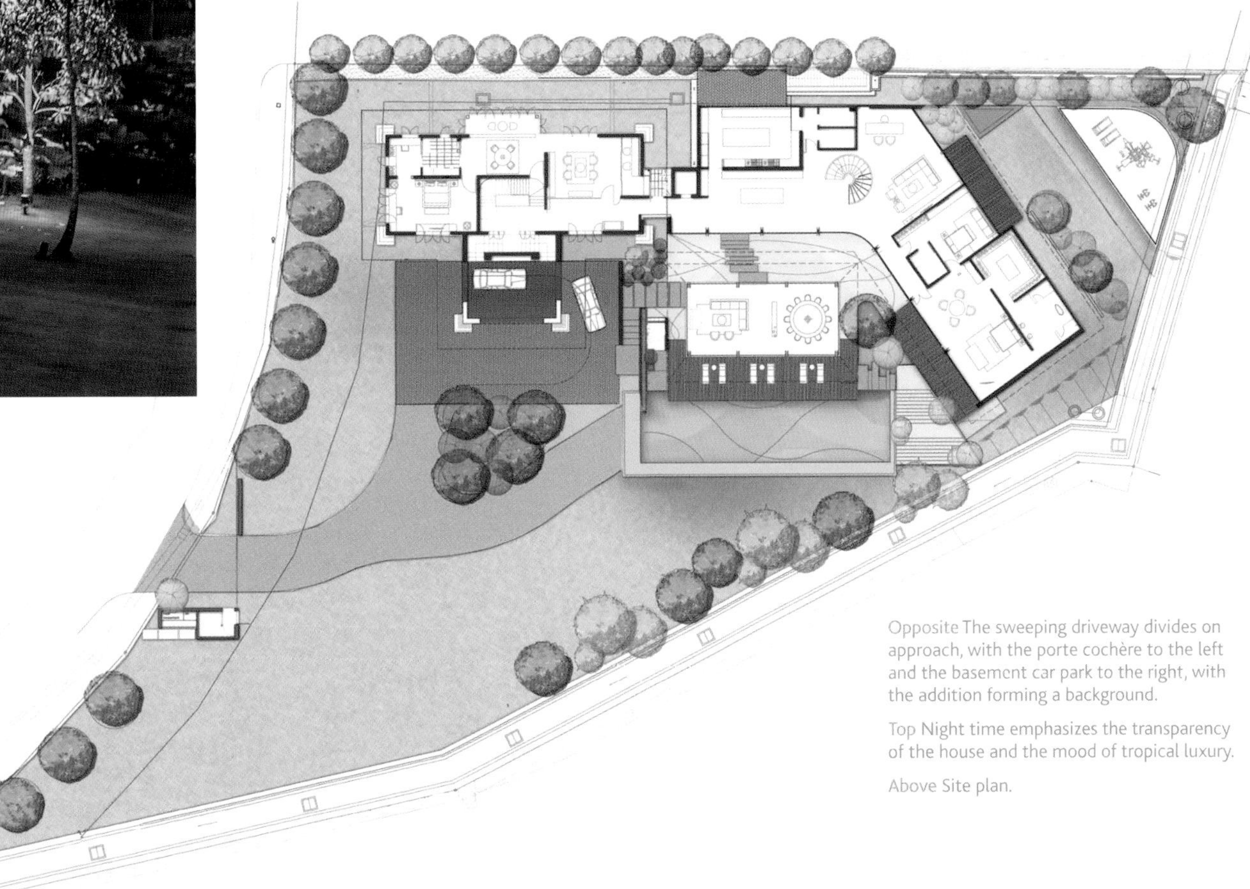

Opposite The sweeping driveway divides on approach, with the porte cochère to the left and the basement car park to the right, with the addition forming a background.

Top Night time emphasizes the transparency of the house and the mood of tropical luxury.

Above Site plan.

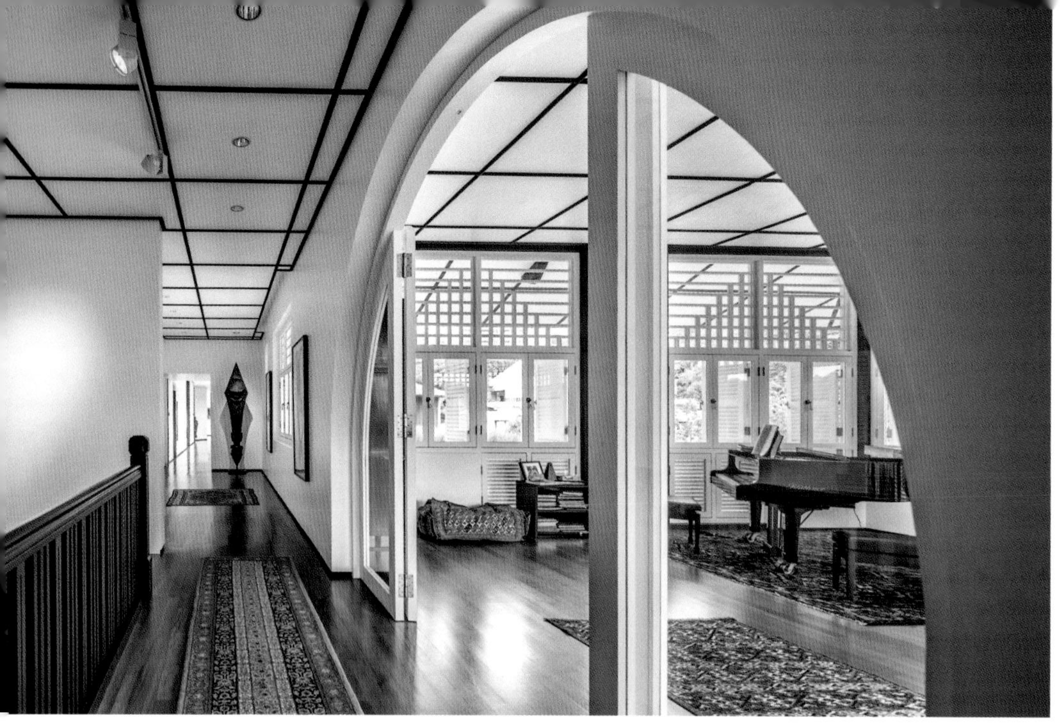

house residential projects, working only with clients for whom they feel a close affinity. For the addition, it was important for principal Sim Boon Yang to retain the integrity of the original Brewer-designed house. The idea was not to set up a competition between the two but to generate a conversation. There can be no conversation with a pastiche, so the addition is unapologetically contemporary. But there is a complementarity of scale and aesthetic. The addition maintains the roofline of the original, with the new façade aligning with the old. The screens and lattice windows are repeated in a contemporary form and the dark grey tone is subtly picked up—'like a shadow'.

The addition unfolds like a gently bended arm to create a kind of expansive casual courtyard. But the

along with rooftop solar panels. But it is the cultural and familial sustainability that is its outstanding feature. It is a family house and the client points out that it was built in the same year that her parents were both born. When she acquired the house, her parents came back together again after a long period of separation and the house now is home to three generations—the client, her two sons and her parents—and therefore sustains an extended family.

The original house, designed by Frank Brewer (1886–1971), was built in 1927. A number of Brewer's distinctive houses are found on this estate and this one has most of his characteristics. While it retains elements of Singapore's black-and-white houses (ventilation grilles, louvred shutters and the palette of contrasting darks and lights), its overall influence is from the Arts and Crafts movement (which began in Britain in the 1880s and spread across Europe and America), as expressed by Brewer: high-pitched tiled roof, deep eaves, buttressed walls and an arched porte cochère with brick voussoirs. Thus, the eclectic character of the house already had a story to tell. The addition is a new chapter in that story.

Eco:id is known for its quality hotels, resorts and multi-residentials. It is highly selective with its single

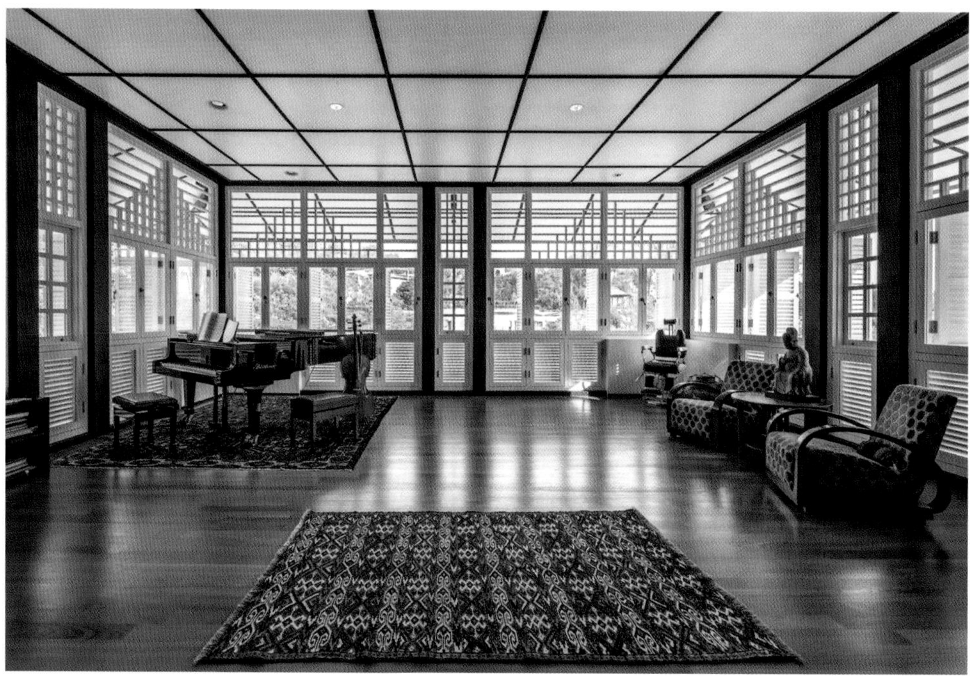

Top The music conservatory in the original house, with the corridor on the left linking old and new.

Above The conservatory enjoys an elegant symmetry because of the fenestration and the characteristic screens and louvres.

Right The Art Deco vanity mirrors in the master bedroom of the original house have vertical lightboxes.

Far right The corridor connecting the old and new wings also acts as a gallery for the client's extensive art collection.

Below The new entertainment pavilion appears to float over an expansive pond, connected to the main pavilion by a granite footbridge.

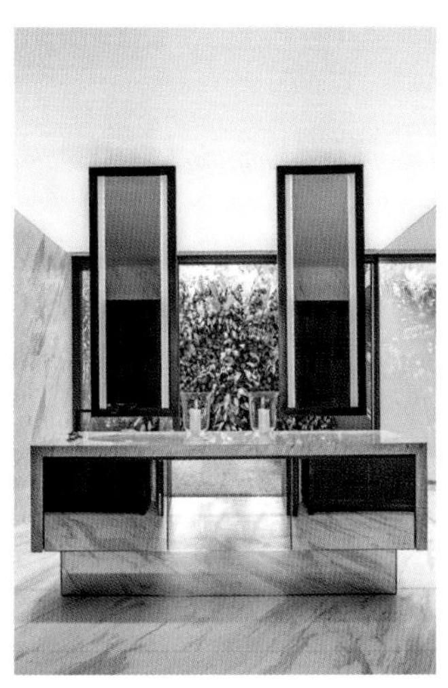

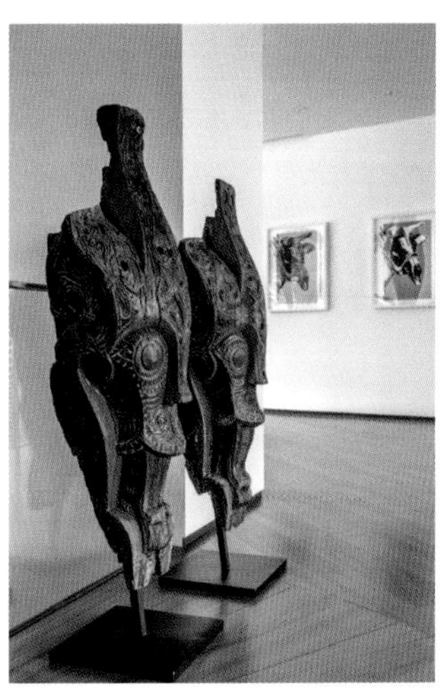

formal composition is enriched by the glazed living/dining pavilion, its roof aligned with the floor of the upper level of the extension, which extends out from the centre of the house, echoing the way the porte cochère extrudes out from the original house.

The progression through the house from old to new along two wide internal galleries can be likened to a journey. This journey is given added dimension by the living/dining pavilion that marks the middle of the link between old and new. It leads off from a breakfast bar, behind which is a substantial kitchen with large windows looking on to the Japanese garden at the rear, and is reached by crossing a granite bridge over a fish pond. The pavilion is as much an art gallery as it is a living/dining space, and the grand landscape beyond the timber deck

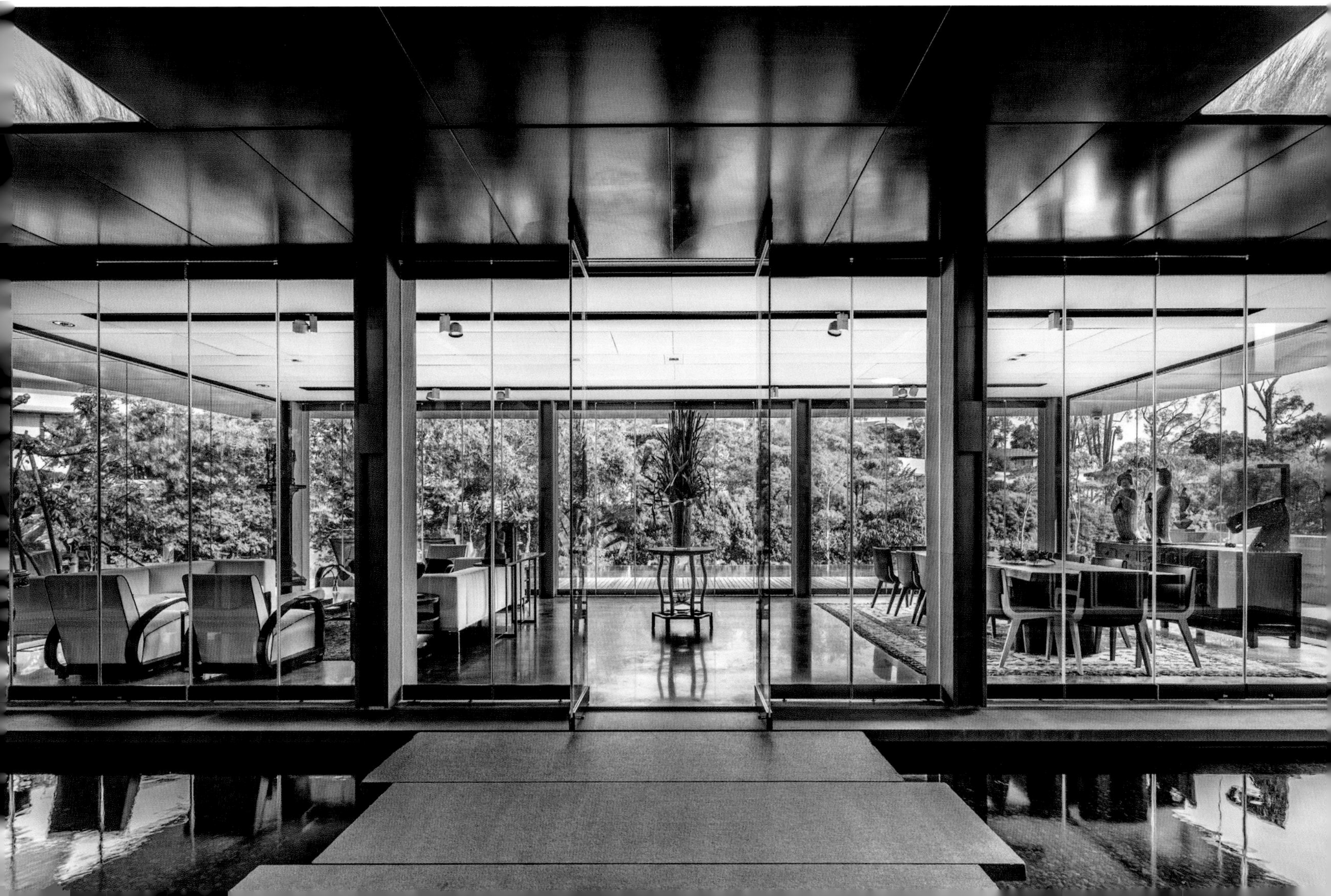

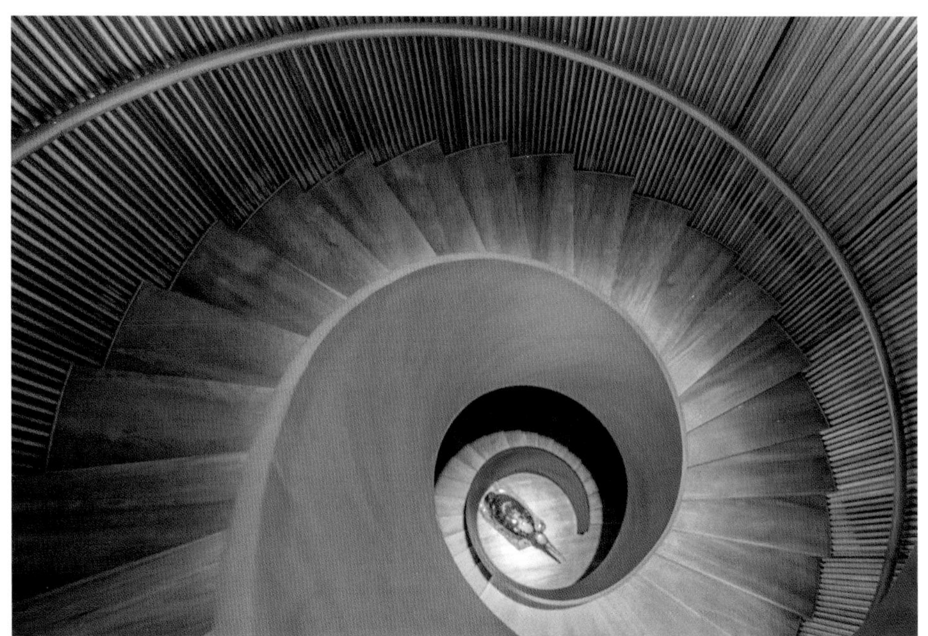

Right The staircase spirals down into the basement car park and entertainment room.

Below On the ground floor, a breakfast bar faces the footbridge to the floating living/dining pavilion.

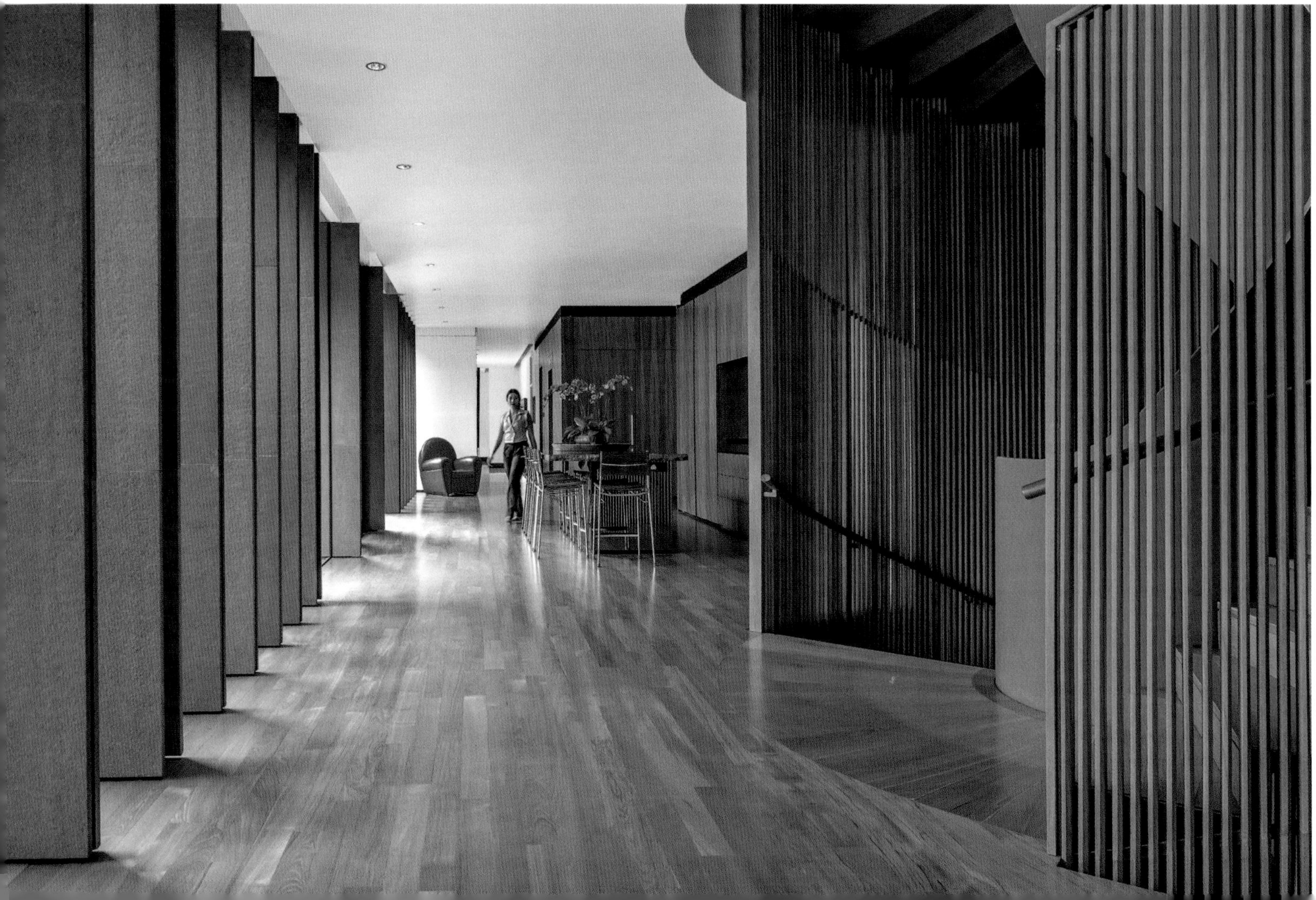

and swimming pool becomes part of that aesthetic experience—along with the specially reupholstered colonial-era armchairs which, like a delicate timber detail in the lift, reflect the Arts and Crafts sensibility of the original house.

The journey actually begins at the gate where the visitor first sees an undulating vista of lawn and trees. Then, as the driveway turns, the original house comes into view followed by the addition which, says the client, 'acts like a shadow of the original house'.

Residents continue to the underground basement car park but guests still enter through the original house. The client and her mother live in the old wing where the front room, above the entry, has been converted into a conservatory. Opposite is the master bedroom where everything is panelized to conceal the storage spaces. The bedroom also houses a home office, which is also integrated as a piece of joinery. The link to the bathroom features vanity mirrors with vertical lightboxes, picking up again on the Art Deco mood of the building.

The central part of the building acts as a link to the 'men's wing' where the two sons live on the upper level and the grandfather has his own 'apartment' on the ground floor. This is essentially a gallery space—although there is a business centre on the upper floor and the kitchen below—where the two levels of the addition are connected by a lift and a handsome spiral staircase with a timber screen and micaceous iron oxide balustrade. The gallery is wide, and the sunlight filtered through an enfilade of operable vertical louvres makes it an ideal space for the client's art collection. On both levels, at the point where the addition elbows around to the various bedrooms, including a guest bedroom with its own pantry, there are TV/sitting rooms with views out to the Japanese garden of trees and bamboo and where even the neigbour's swimming pool is successfully 'borrowed' as part of the landscape. The bedrooms themselves look out past terraces to the main garden.

This house is culturally, socially and environmentally sustainable. It is an example of a strategy for sustaining the extended family by taking an existing site and developing its capacity to accommodate several generations, simultaneously providing privacy and the opportunity to be together. Through the sensitive way in which it has brought old and new together, it is also an example of how a sense of continuity over time can be spiritually and emotionally sustaining for individuals, families and communities.

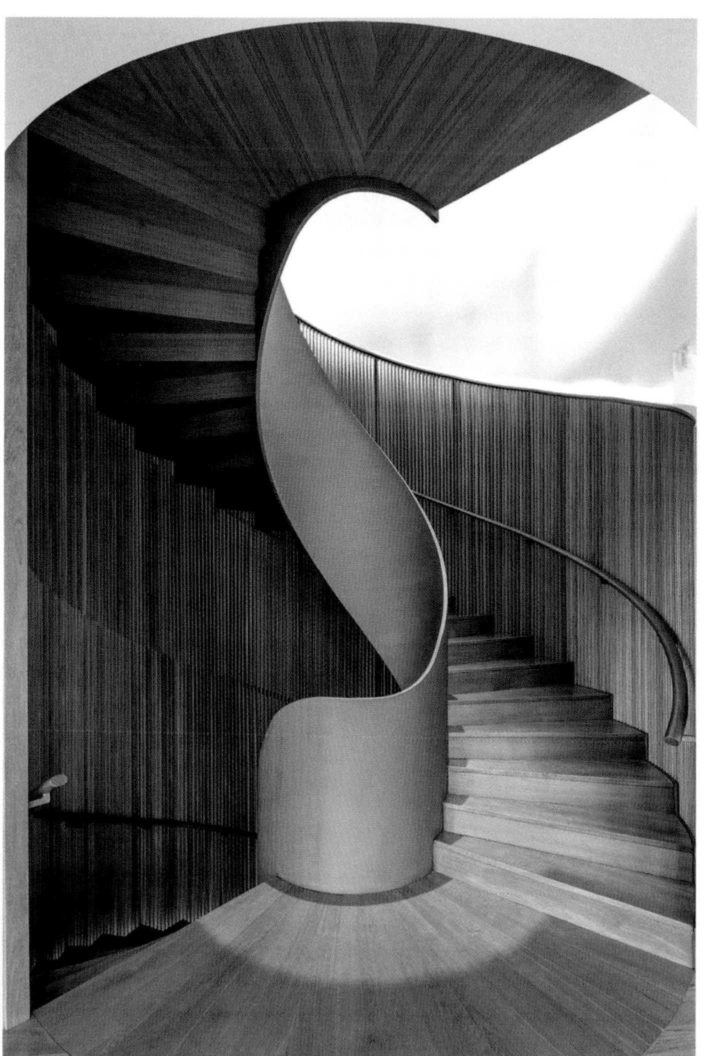

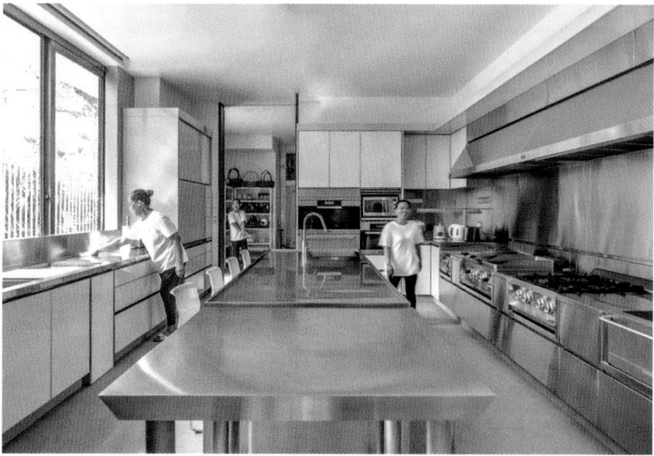

Left The splendid timber-screened spiral staircase connects the basement to the two upper levels of the house.

Above Behind the breakfast bar is a comprehensive kitchen.

Right A bathroom attached to one of the downstairs bedrooms opens directly to its own garden courtyard.

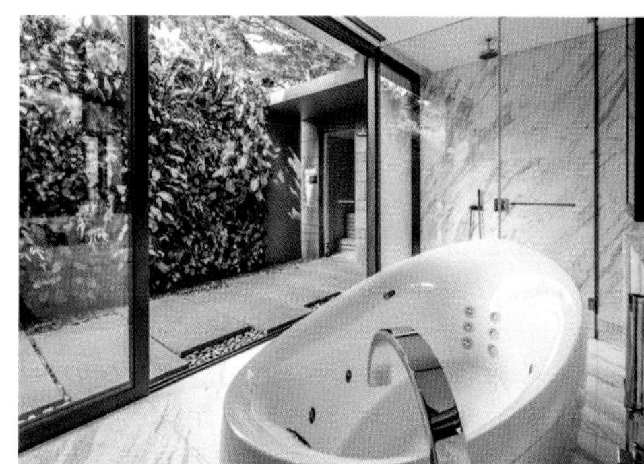

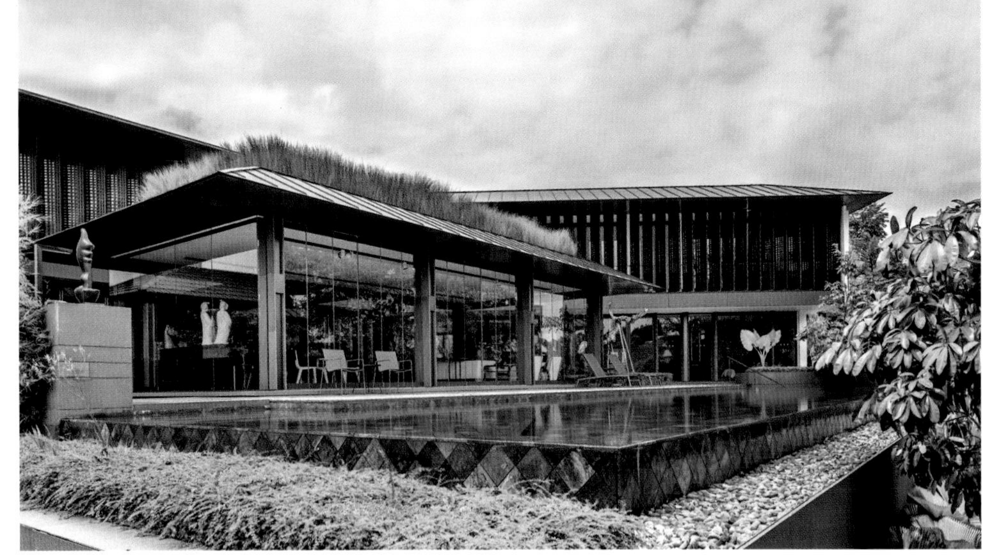

Left The living/dining pavilion, with its garden roof, leads out to the pool, which is elevated above the grounds of the house.

Below The living/dining pavilion is fully transparent, giving the impression that it is one with the landscape.

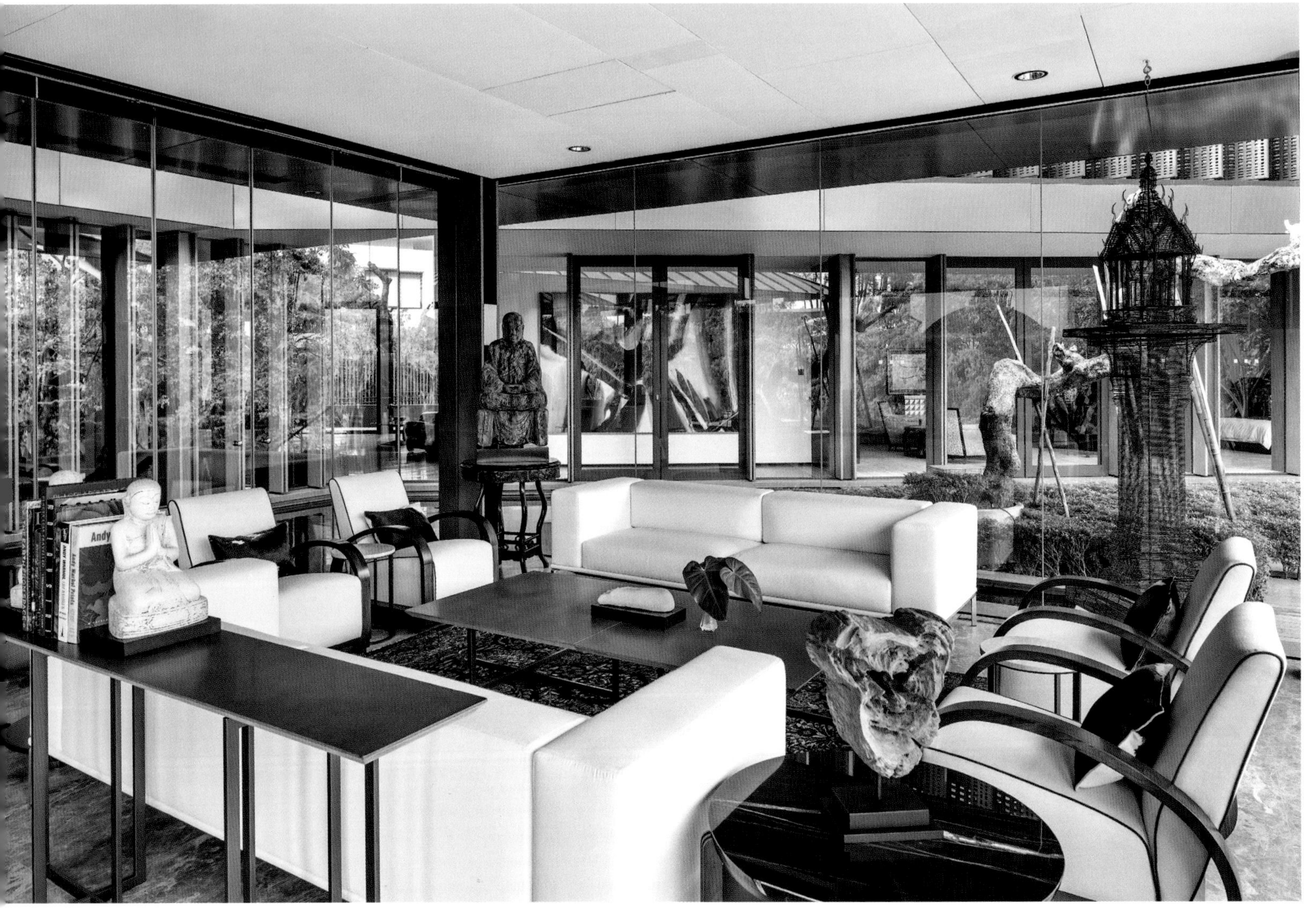

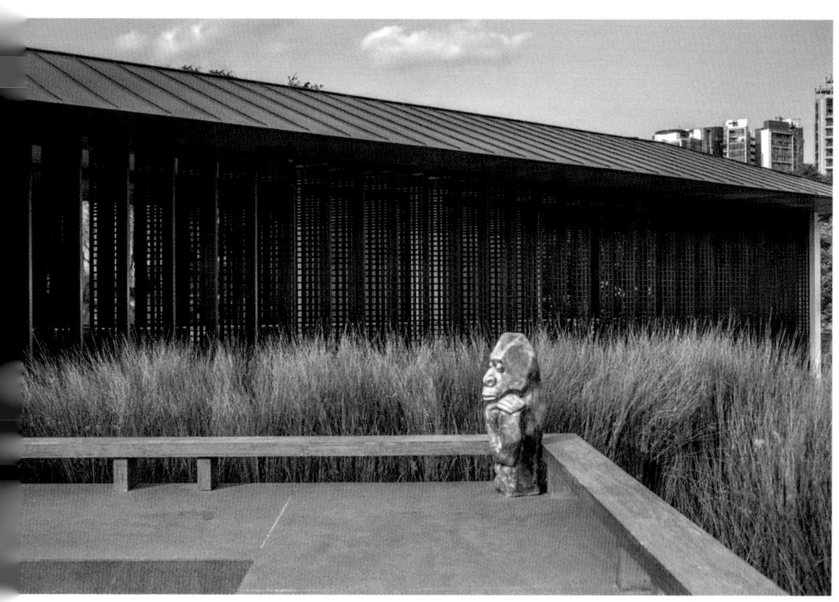

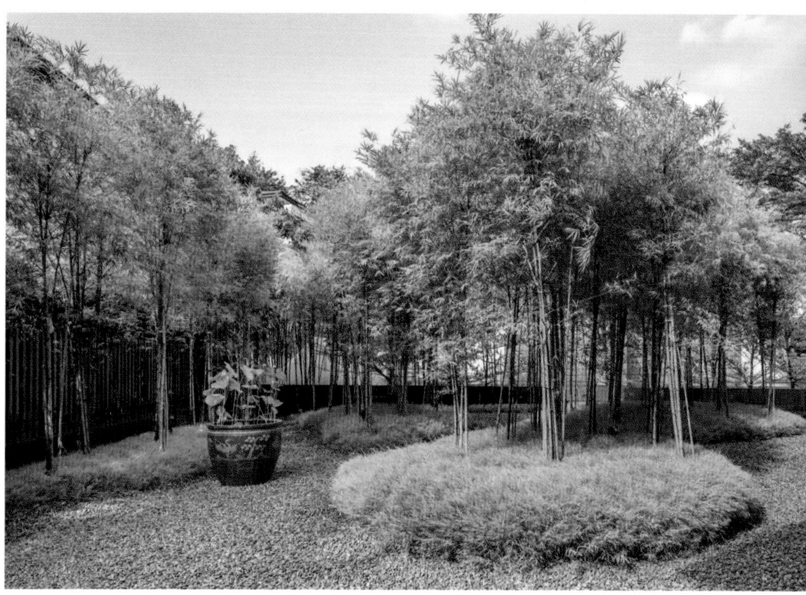

Above A view of the enfilade of vertical louvred screens.

Above right The Japanese garden behind the house.

Right The elevation of the pool, together with its infinity edge, makes the living/dining pavilion seem a part of the stand of mature trees around the edge of the property.

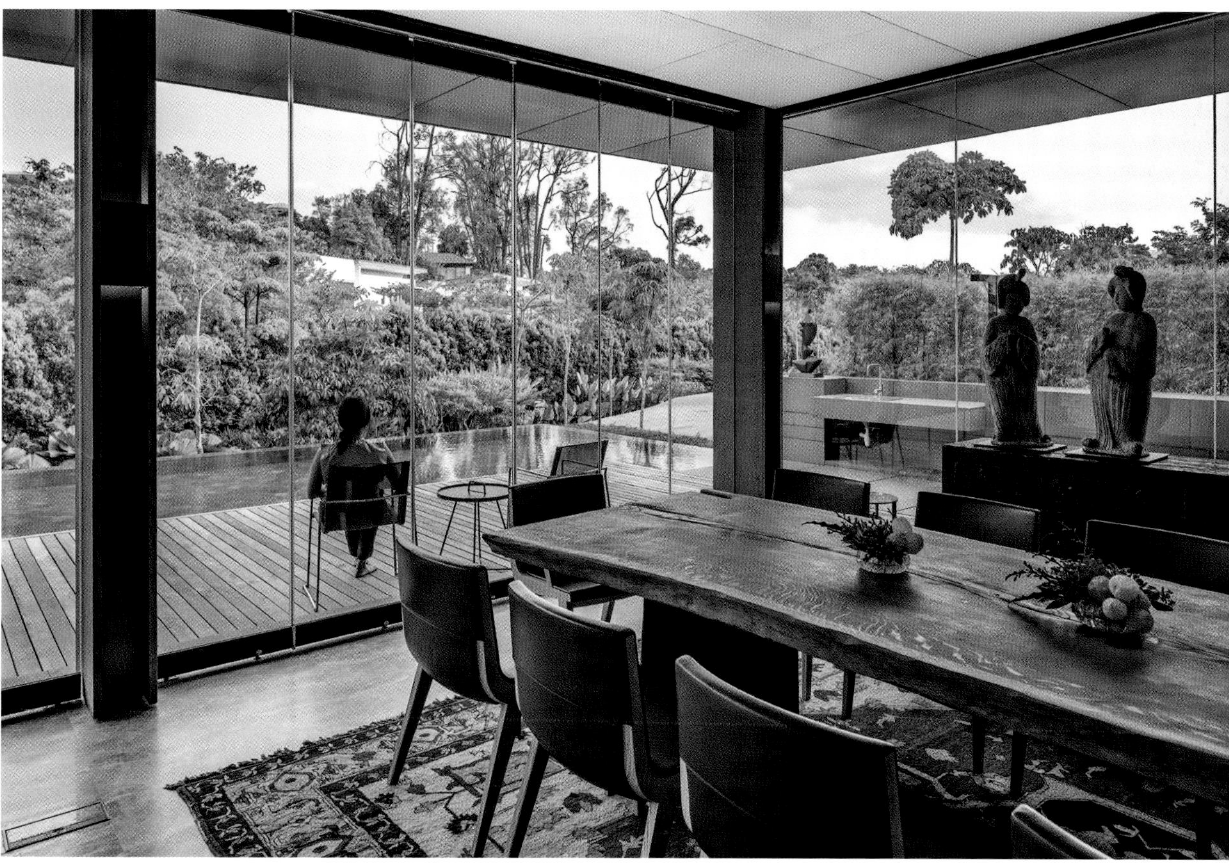

THOMSON HEIGHTS HOUSE AAMER ARCHITECTS

'They dreamed about going back to this retreat style where they can have a big garden and areas of plantings. So, it is a kampong house with some modern content and grandeur.'—AAMER TAHER, ARCHITECT

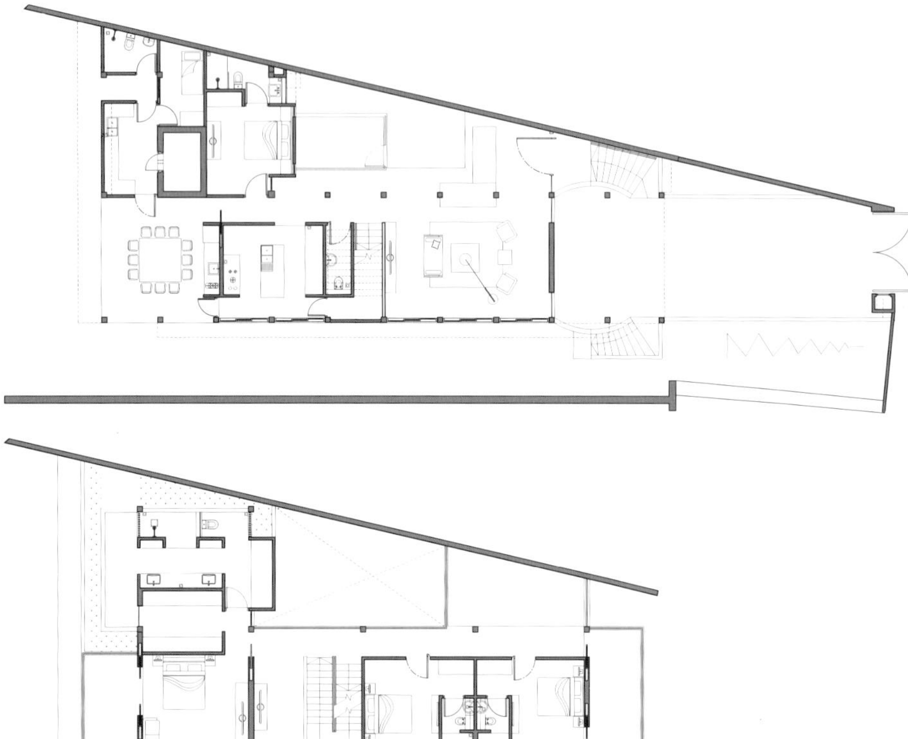

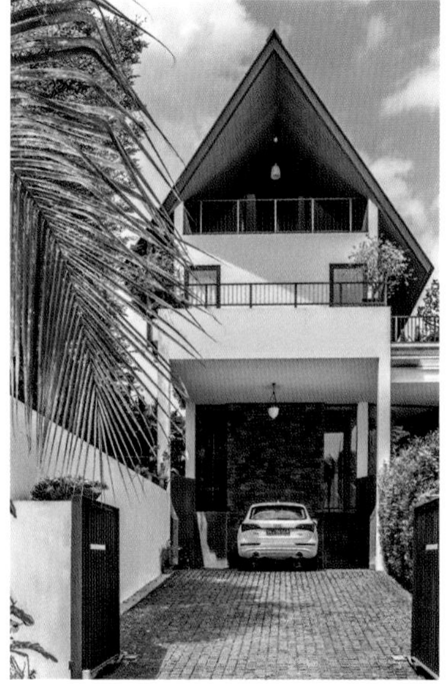

Left First storey plan.

Below left Second storey plan.

Above The house stands at the top of a short, steep hill, which makes its roofline all the more dramatic on approach.

Right Past the entry vestibule, the house opens up immediately, with the living room directly connected to the courtyard and a colonnaded link.

Opposite below A view from the living room to the courtyard whose trees make it an interior green landscape.

The kampong house has proven to be a fertile source of inspiration for a generation of architects taking up the challenge of designing contemporary houses in a tropical climate. Apart from the politics of sustainability, it is simply common sense to design for living *with* the climate, not in competition with it. One result is a new kind of luxury, not so much the luxury of the latest technology and its capacity to create a self-contained, quarantined world, but more the luxury of tropical living, of enjoying the luxuriant vegetation of a tropical garden. Along the way, architects have discovered that tropical living and a contemporary way of life are not mutually exclusive, a discovery that arguably began not with houses but with the 'Bali-style' resorts of Geoffrey Bawa, Kerry Hill and Peter Muller.

What is loosely termed the kampong house has been a useful model for at least three reasons: the look of the house, its environmentally sustainable features and its embedded notions of social and family living. This house is in an area which Aamer Taher describes as 'quite rural for Singapore'. It uses the kampong house as a model, an agenda driven as much by the clients as by the architects.

The house sits on a very steeply sloping site. Clearing this site and building a retaining wall meant that the budget for the house itself was limited. The result is a simple but richly intimate home. Not that it looks intimate at first sight. Approaching the house, it looks very imposing, almost cathedral-like, its roof typical of the traditional long houses of eastern Malaysia, high-pitched and tilted forward to provide shade. The back story is that this was originally a semi-detached house. Apart from the lack of light and ventilation, a semi-detached house does not

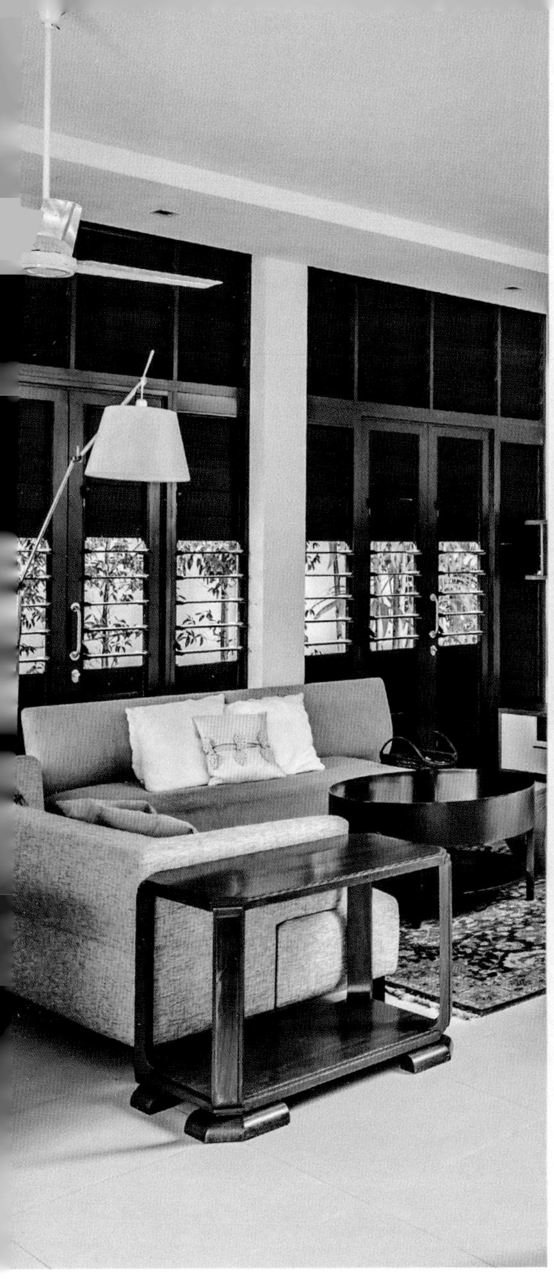

have the status of a free-standing house. Thus, the client asked for a new house, posing the problem, as architect Aamer Taher puts it, of 'how to detach a semi-detached house'.

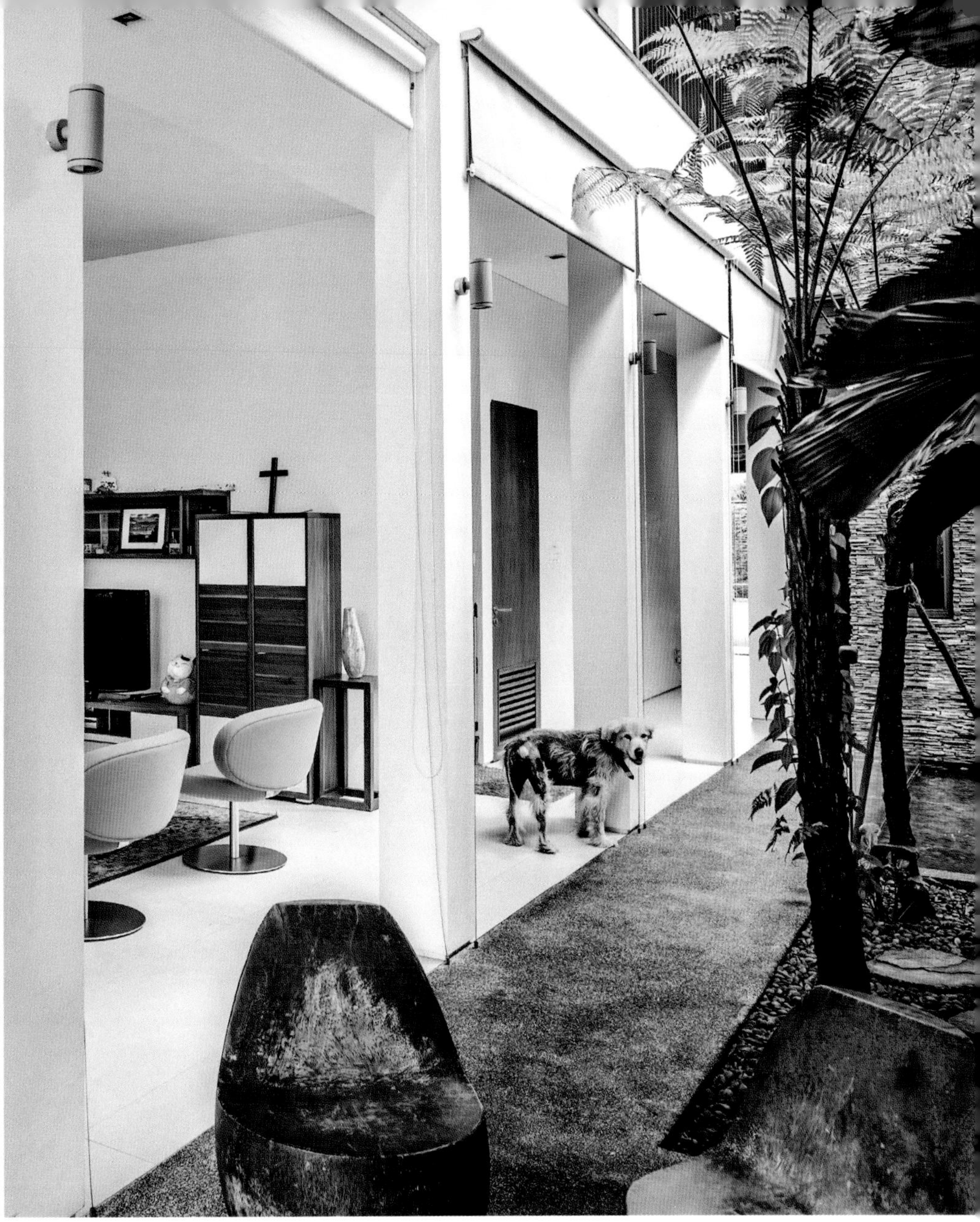

The solution was to construct a long rectangular block—the site itself is long, tapering from a narrow front to a wide rear with a significant level change—aligned with the site boundary and retaining wall. This block is independent of the party wall and contains all the main rooms of the house. The resulting rhomboid-shaped space between the main block and the party wall created

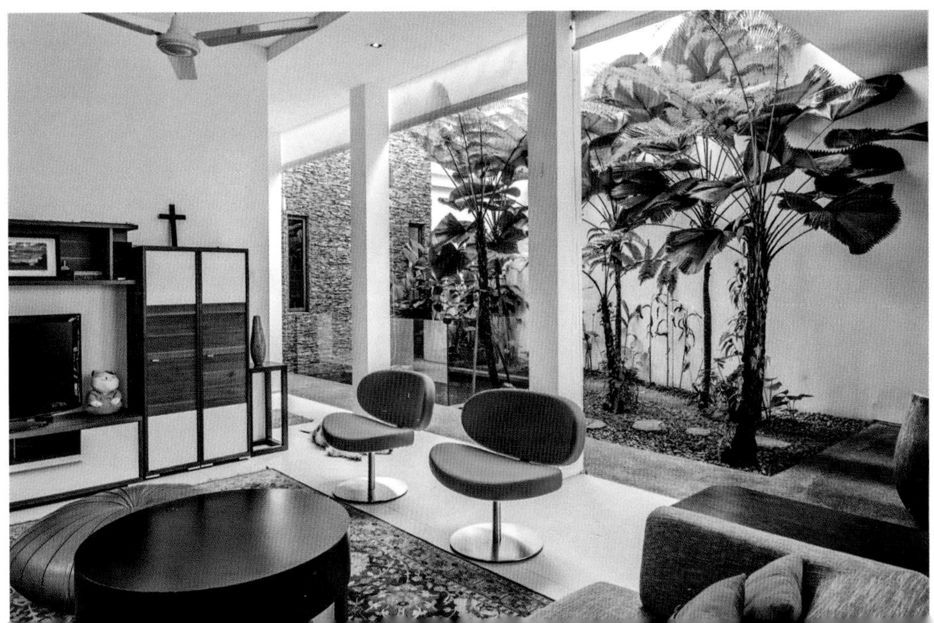

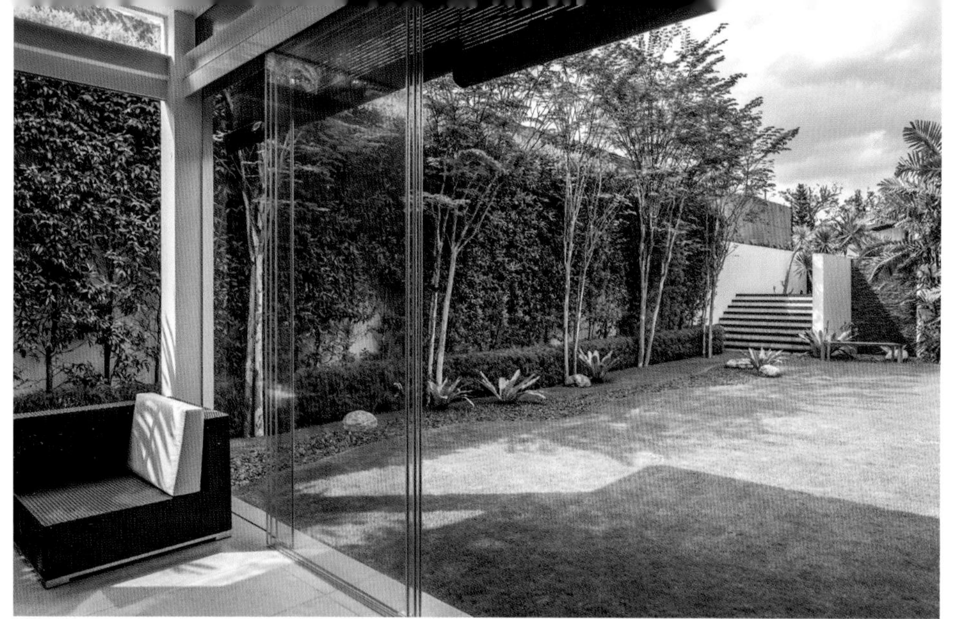

the opportunity for a water garden courtyard. This courtyard is an extension of the living room, making for a 'resort-style' open space of easy tropical luxury, defined on one side by the courtyard with its plunge pool and slate feature wall, and on two other sides by walls of operable timber louvres opening to the garden, which runs between the house and the retaining wall. The only part of the house that remains attached is the guest room and bathroom and maid's quarters behind the slate feature wall.

The open corridor on the entrance level, which links the living area to the kitchen, powder room, open terrace dining space and rear garden, is

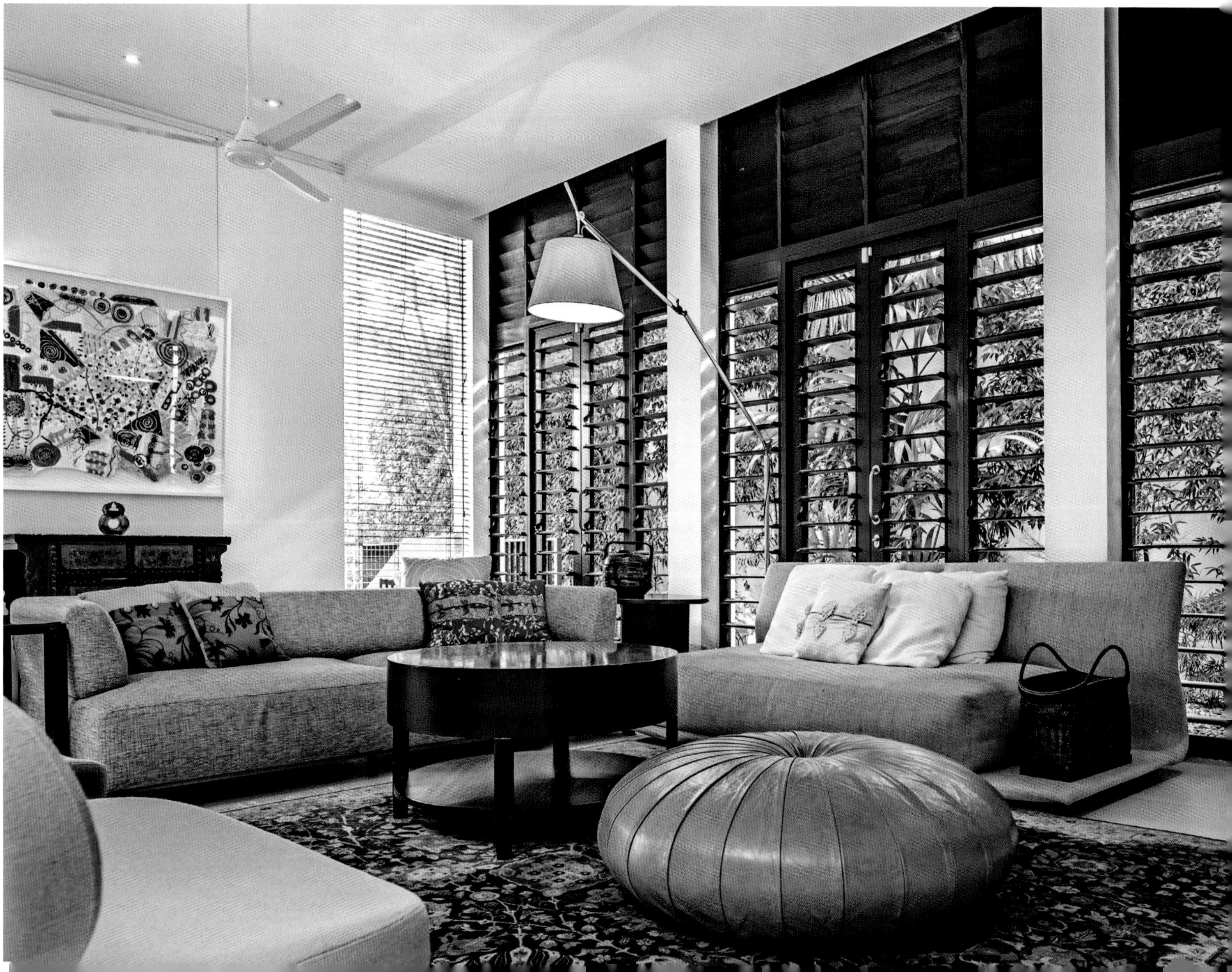

Opposite above The plot expands into a generous lawned area at the rear of the house.

Below left The living room has operable timber shutter screen doors that open to another green courtyard.

Below right The water courtyard has a plunge pool at the rear, outside the guest bedroom.

Right The side passage running past the living and dining rooms.

Far right above Long section.

Far right below Short section.

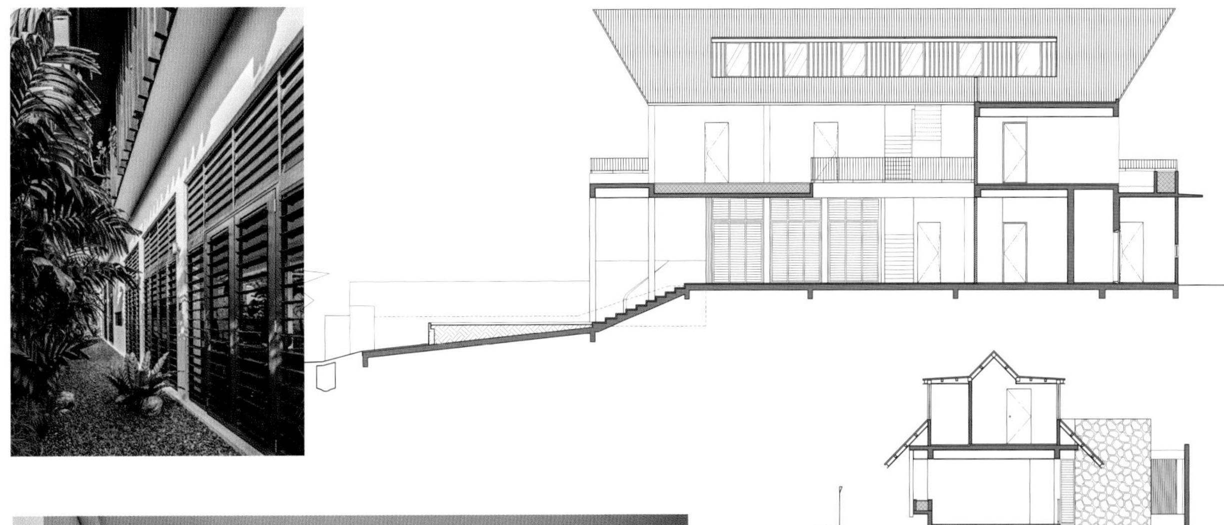

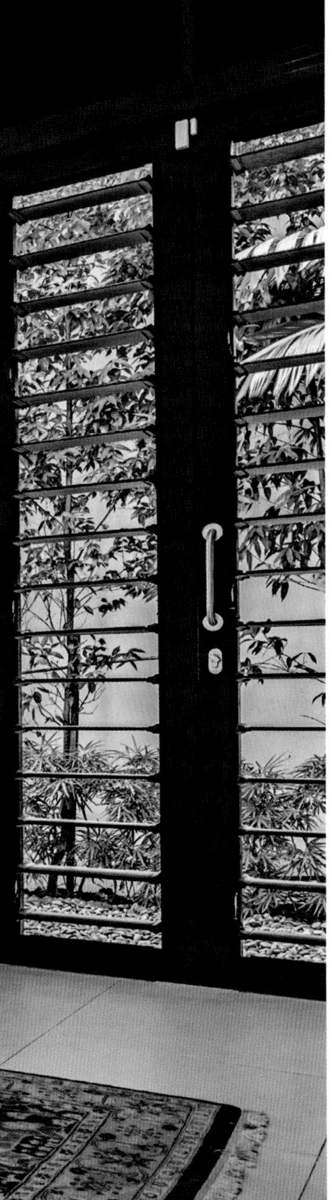

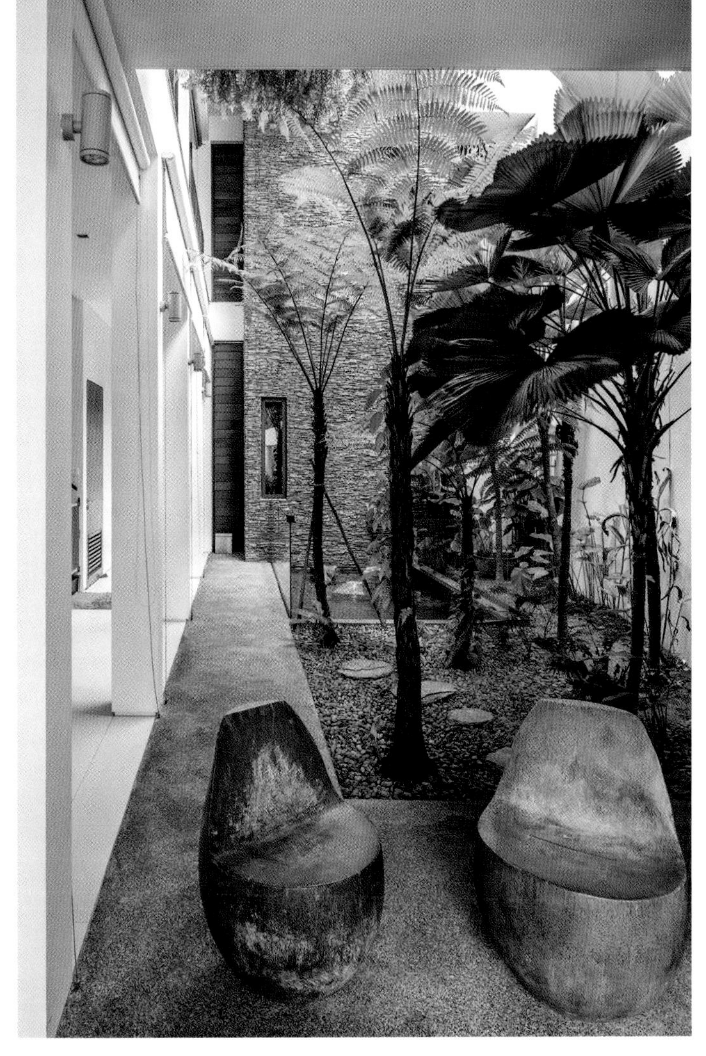

repeated on the upper level with a herringbone teak parquet gallery that links two children's bedrooms in the front part of the house with the central stairway and master bedroom, bathroom and jacuzzi at the rear. This gallery is open, shaded by an extended eave, and looks down into the courtyard garden, but also has its own upper garden. An attic level has the roof run the length of the house. This provides a dramatic A-framed ceiling, which also enabled extra rooms while still conforming to attic space guidelines.

Essentially, the house is completely open to the outside. This includes the bathrooms—'no wastage of glass or windows to clean, how we should live in the tropics'—which open to the elevated garden bed running the length of the retaining wall.

The house is a reinvention of the traditional tropical house. Simple in its planning and unostentatious in its choice of materials, it exemplifies an easy, resort-style tropical way of life, one that is entirely comfortable, drawing in ample natural light and requiring little or no air-conditioning.

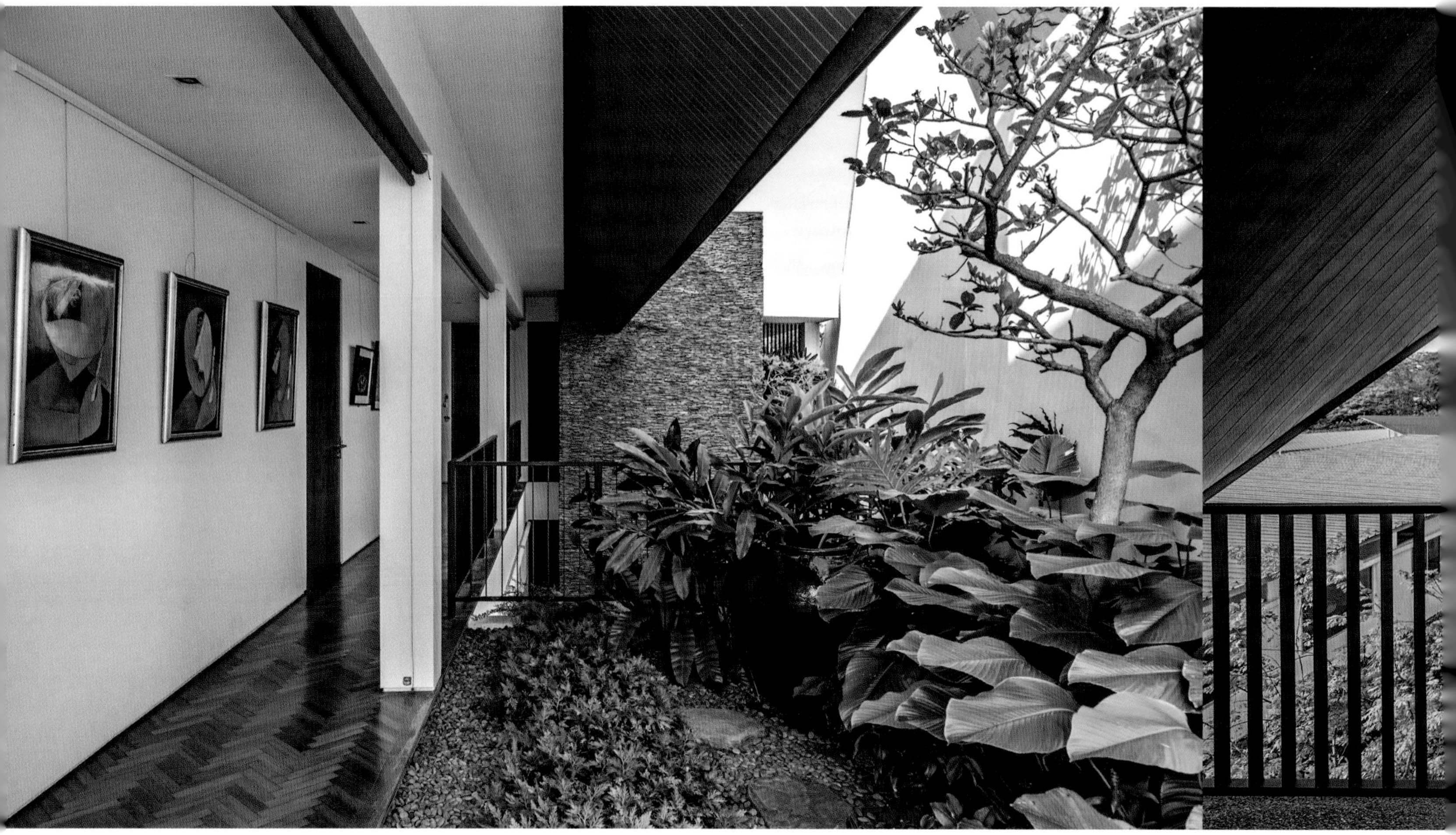

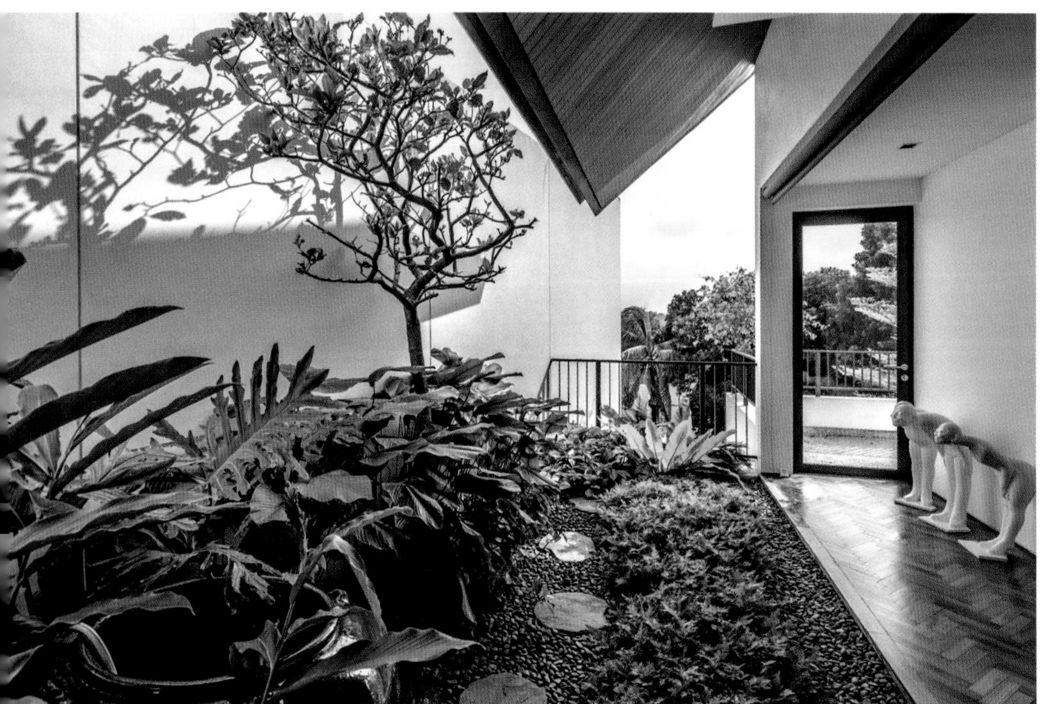

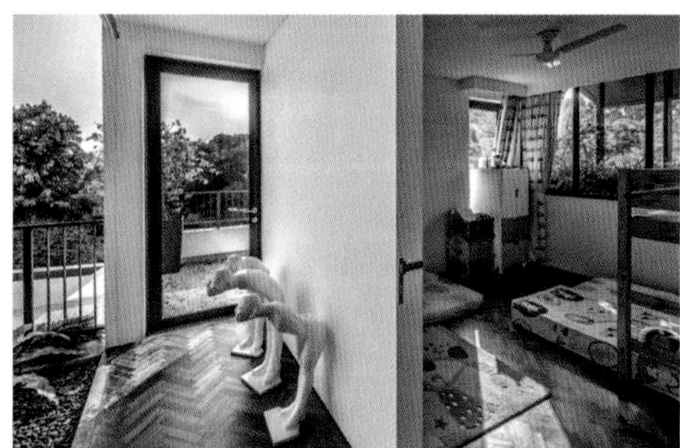

Above left The upstairs bedrooms are linked by a timber walkway that overlooks the courtyard below.

Above One of the children's bedrooms.

Left The second storey walkway culminates in an elevated garden.

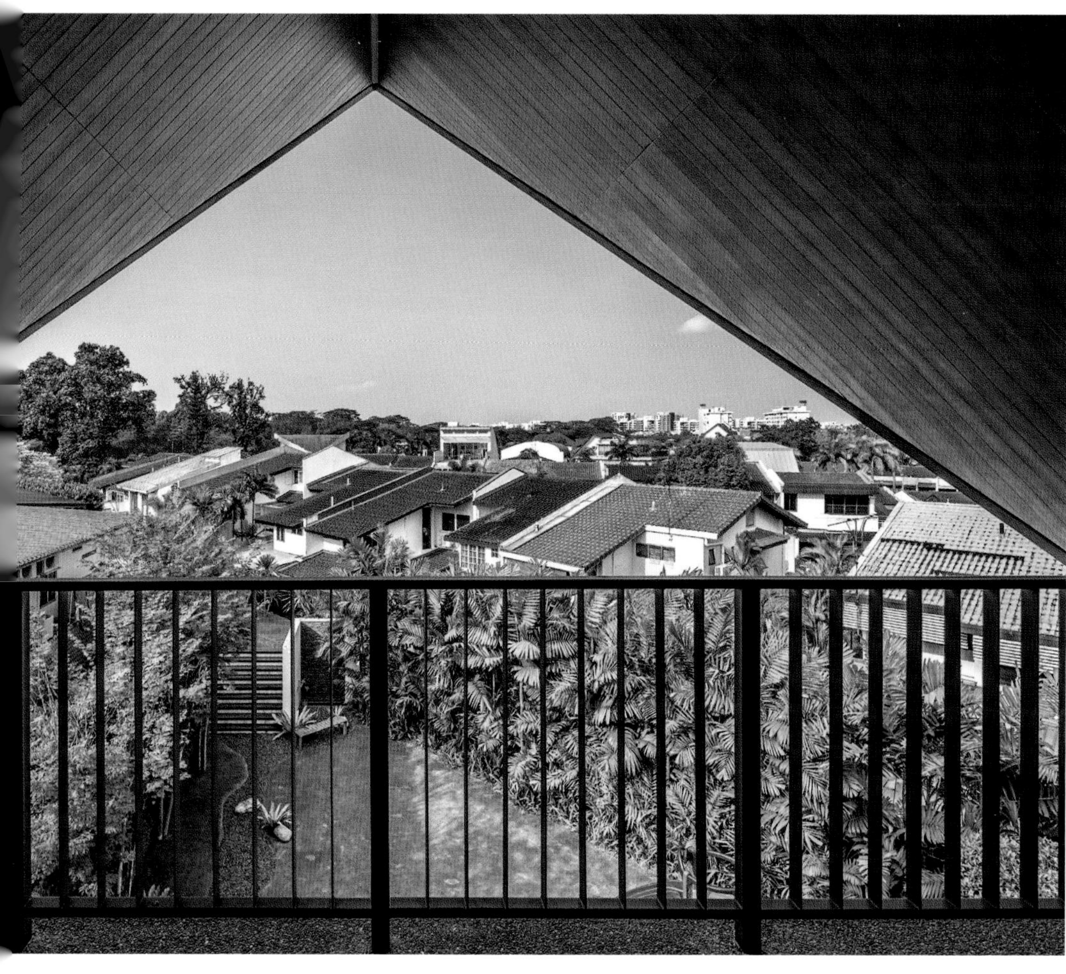

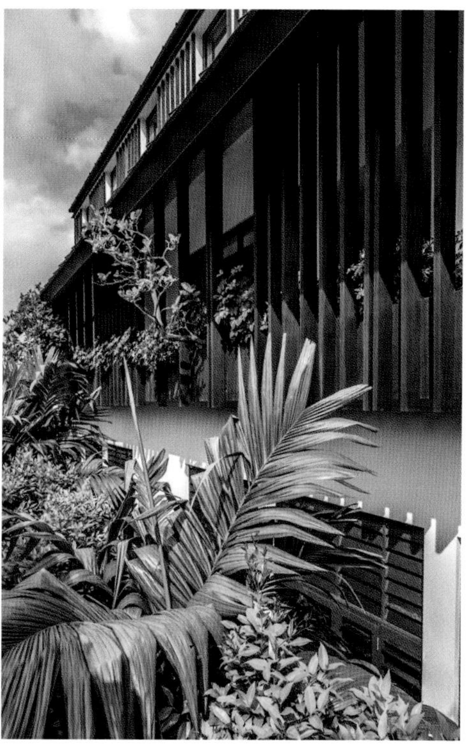

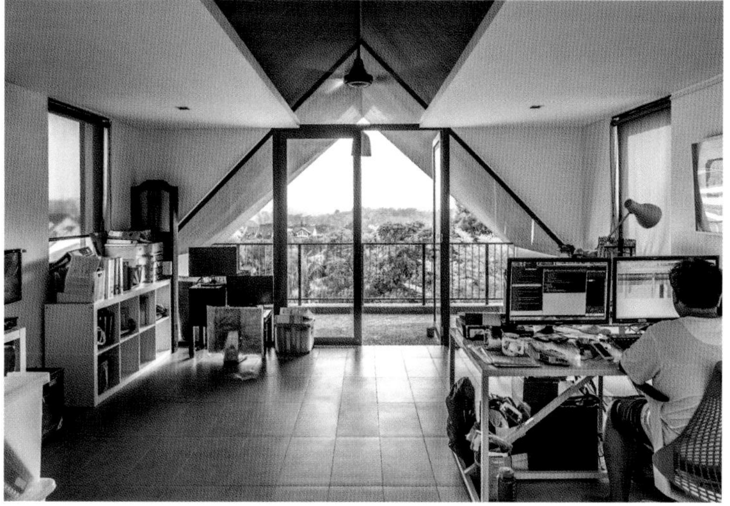

Above center A view from the second storey looking down into the rear garden and neighbourhood.

Above The free-standing side of the building is an enfilade of timber screens, reinforcing the metaphor of a traditional kampong house.

Left The pitch of the A-frame roof runs the length of the house, allowing for a large attic home office.

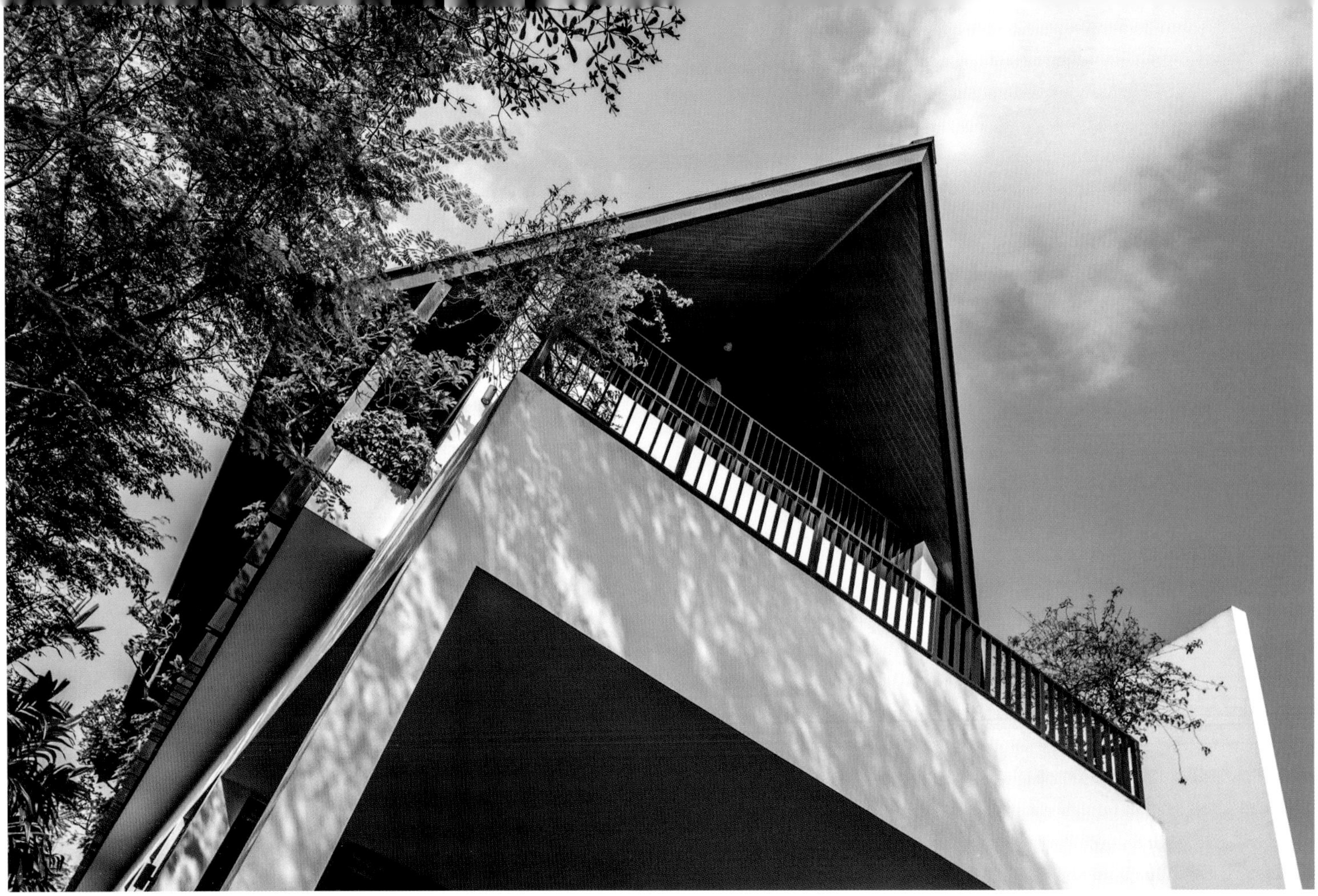

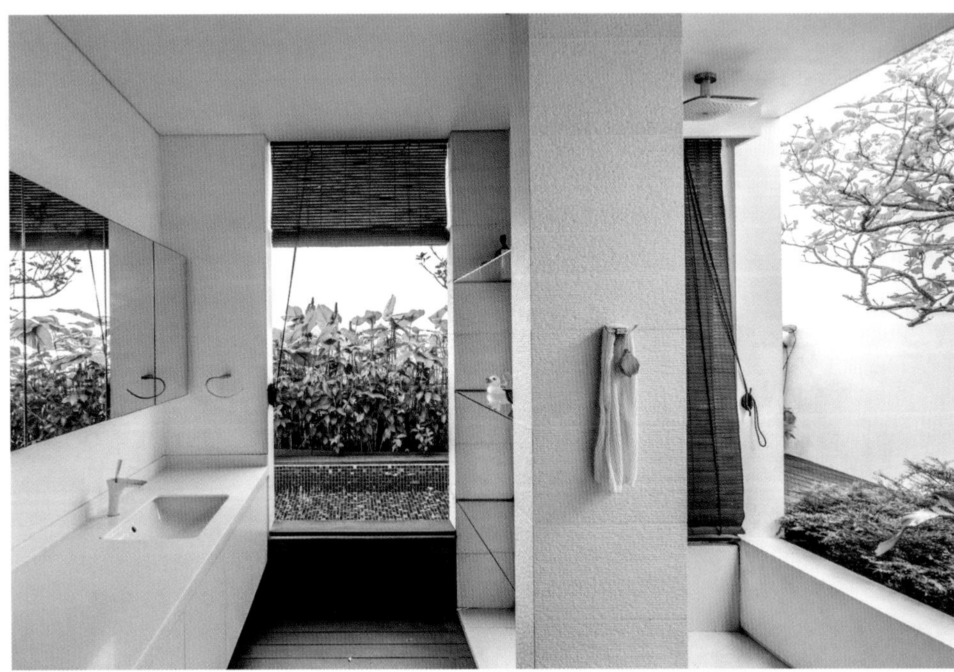

Above Looking up from the top of the driveway, the house has a dramatic cathedral-like presence.

Left The master bathroom leads out to the elevated swimming pool.

Below The swimming pool on the second storey is defined by a tropical garden running its full length.

Right Looking back to the house from the rear garden, with the dining room on the right.

Below right A view of the garden from the dining room.

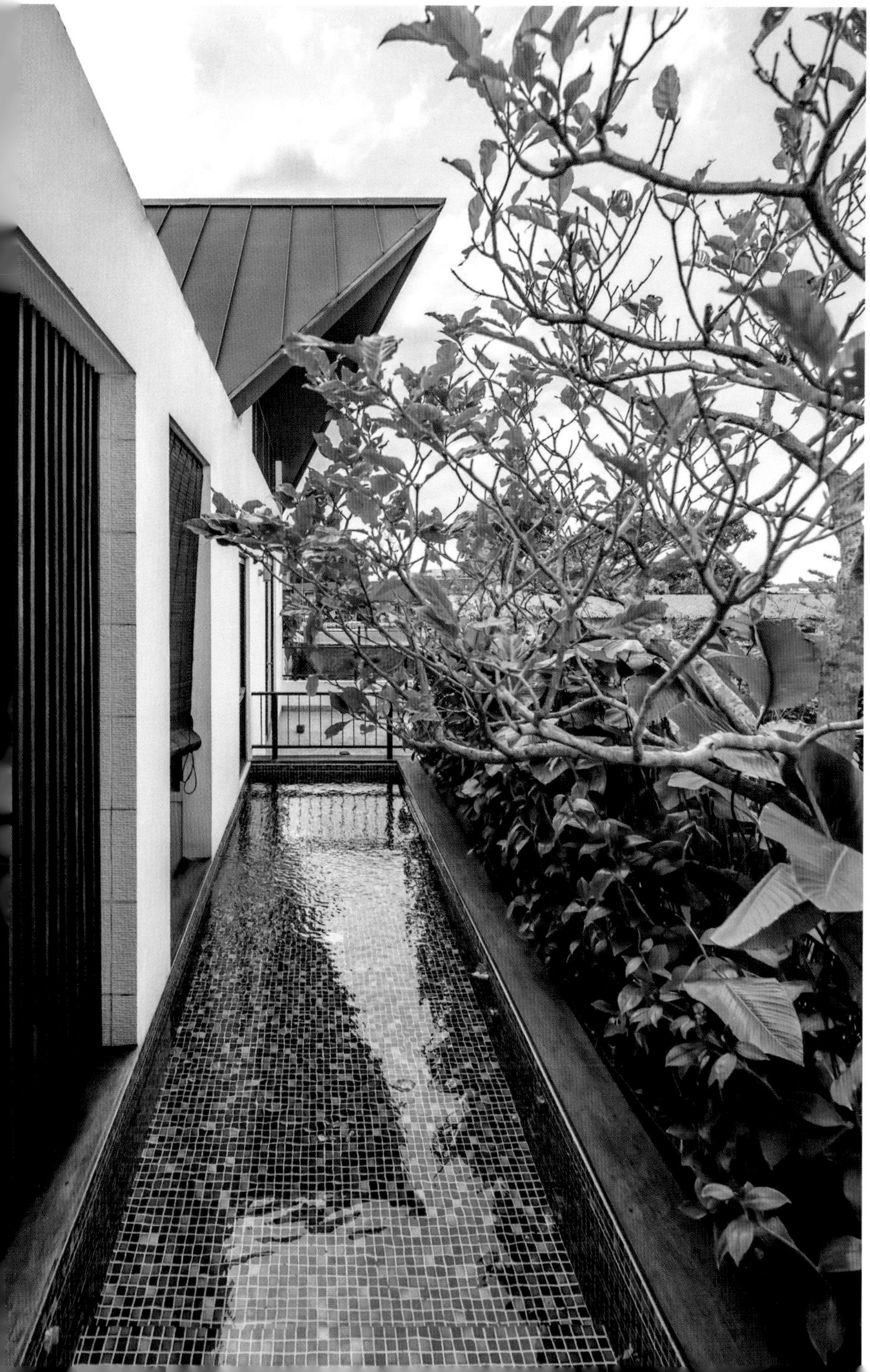

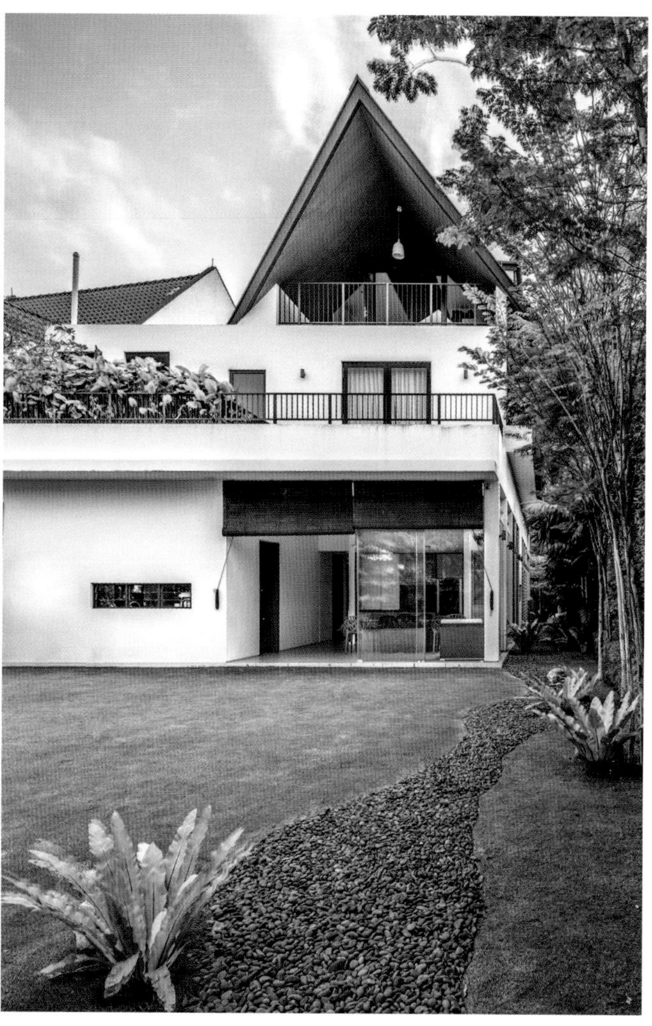

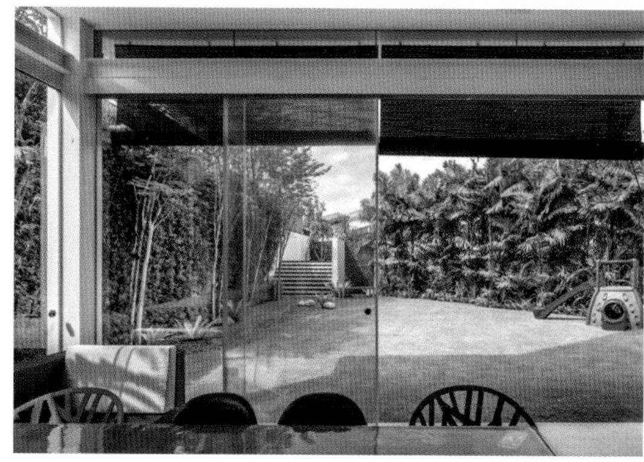

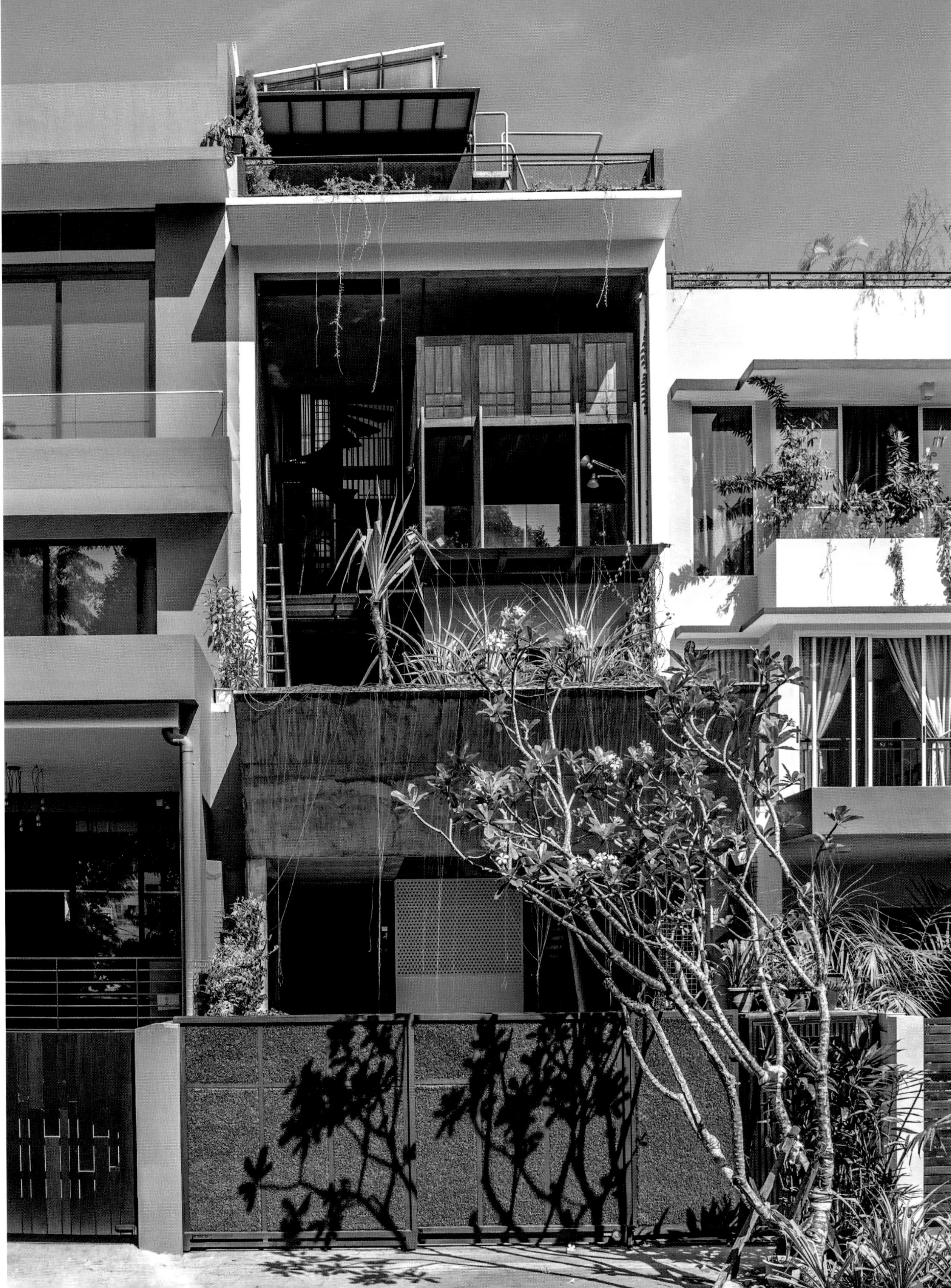

JALAN MAT JAMBOL HOUSE
ZARCH COLLABORATIVES

'It was quite organic and cost-conscious. My wife, also an architect, was the client, representing the end user's point of view. It was slow and easy. I kept it pretty private. My thinking cap was my architect's but I was really doing it simply as a home owner. I just wanted to do something for myself.'—RANDY CHAN KEN CHONG, ARCHITECT

This house is occupied by a couple, the architect himself and his wife. It is a 30-year-old intermediate terrace house located 400 metres from Singapore's port, and is designed to take advantage of the sea breezes. It is also situated opposite an institutional reserve that provides the opportunity to 'borrow' an expansive green landscape. And it is a house that started with a self-imposed challenge: 'What if the house had no windows?'

This experimental approach reflects the nature of Randy Chan Ken Chong's firm, Zarch Collaboratives, which is a multi-disciplinary practice with about 50 percent of the work being residential and the rest ranging from landscape design and master planning to interpretive centres, site-specific installations, theatre design and curatorial work. Behind the notion of a windowless house was the model of the kampong house, except that the result is not so much a kampong house as a kampong itself—a loose cluster of spaces assembled around a kind of small river.

Chan says it is still a work in progress but 'it also reveals what tropical living is all about'. It is also an exercise in sustainability. Sited on an east–west access, the house draws in natural light all day. Its general lack of windows ensures constant cross-ventilation. Although the master bedroom is enclosed to allow air-conditioning at night ('My wife kept me practical'), there is a window in the kitchen, a sliding glass door on Level 3 to protect against heavy rain and five round glass skylights to draw in light but keep out rain. The house makes extensive use of recycled timber and its bio-pool system cleans itself, cools the house and attracts and sustains native birds, while its fish take care of the mosquitoes. Twenty solar panels supply 40 per cent of the house's energy needs.

From the street, the façade of the house signals the intriguing spatial composition inside. A raw champfered concrete fascia attracts the eye but also reveals how the interior of the house is completely open. Perhaps Chan's work as a stage designer has contributed to a certain theatricailty in the

Opposite The street elevation is an arresting composition of voids and two-dimensional forms.

Below The ground floor space has a sunken music pit and a sitting area but it also acts as a gallery for the architect's art collection.

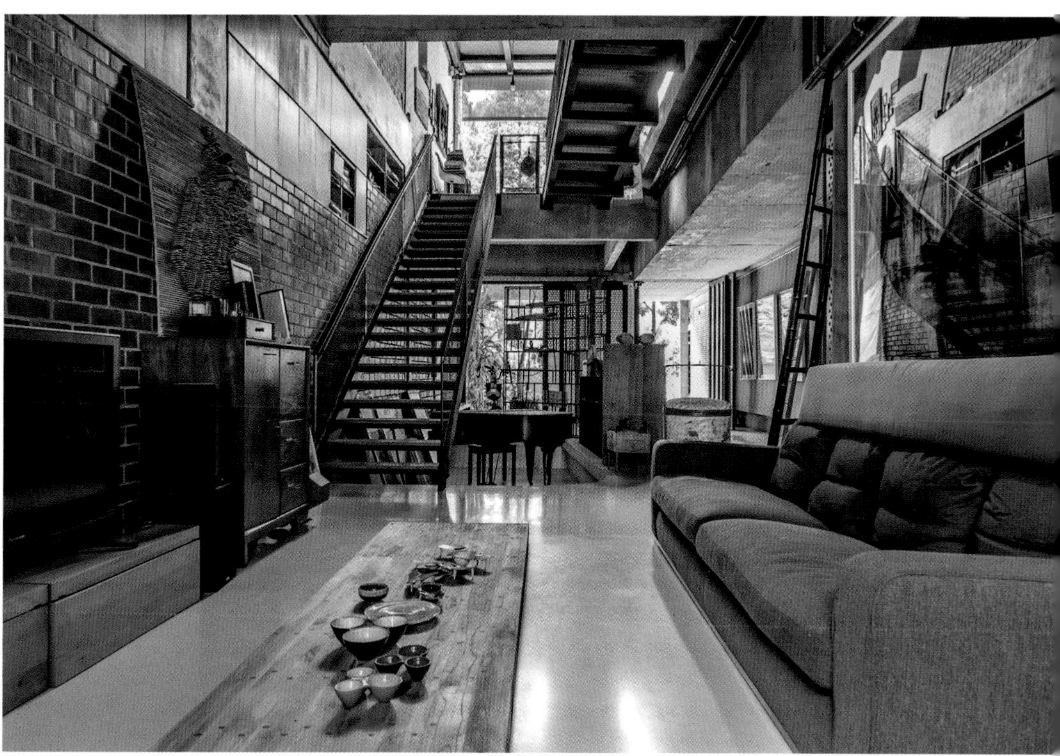

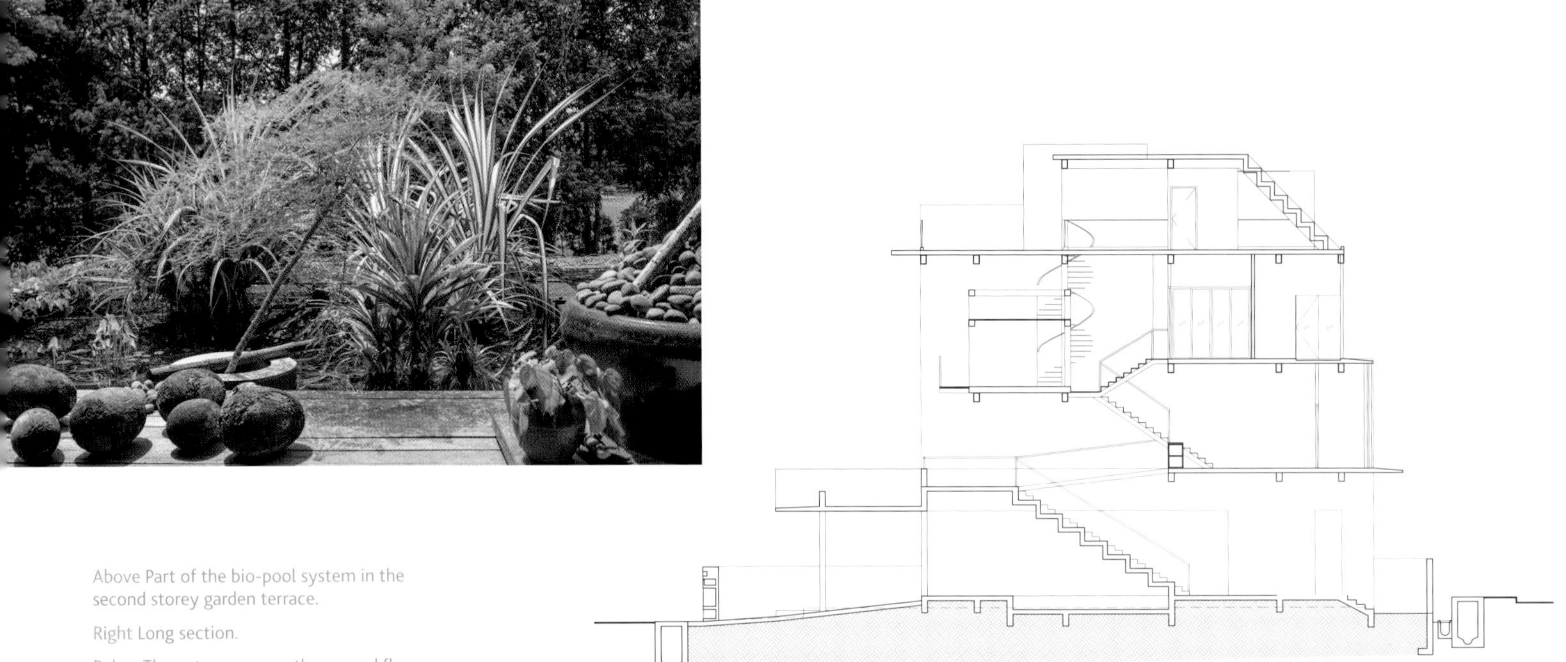

Above Part of the bio-pool system in the second storey garden terrace.

Right Long section.

Below The entry space on the ground floor.

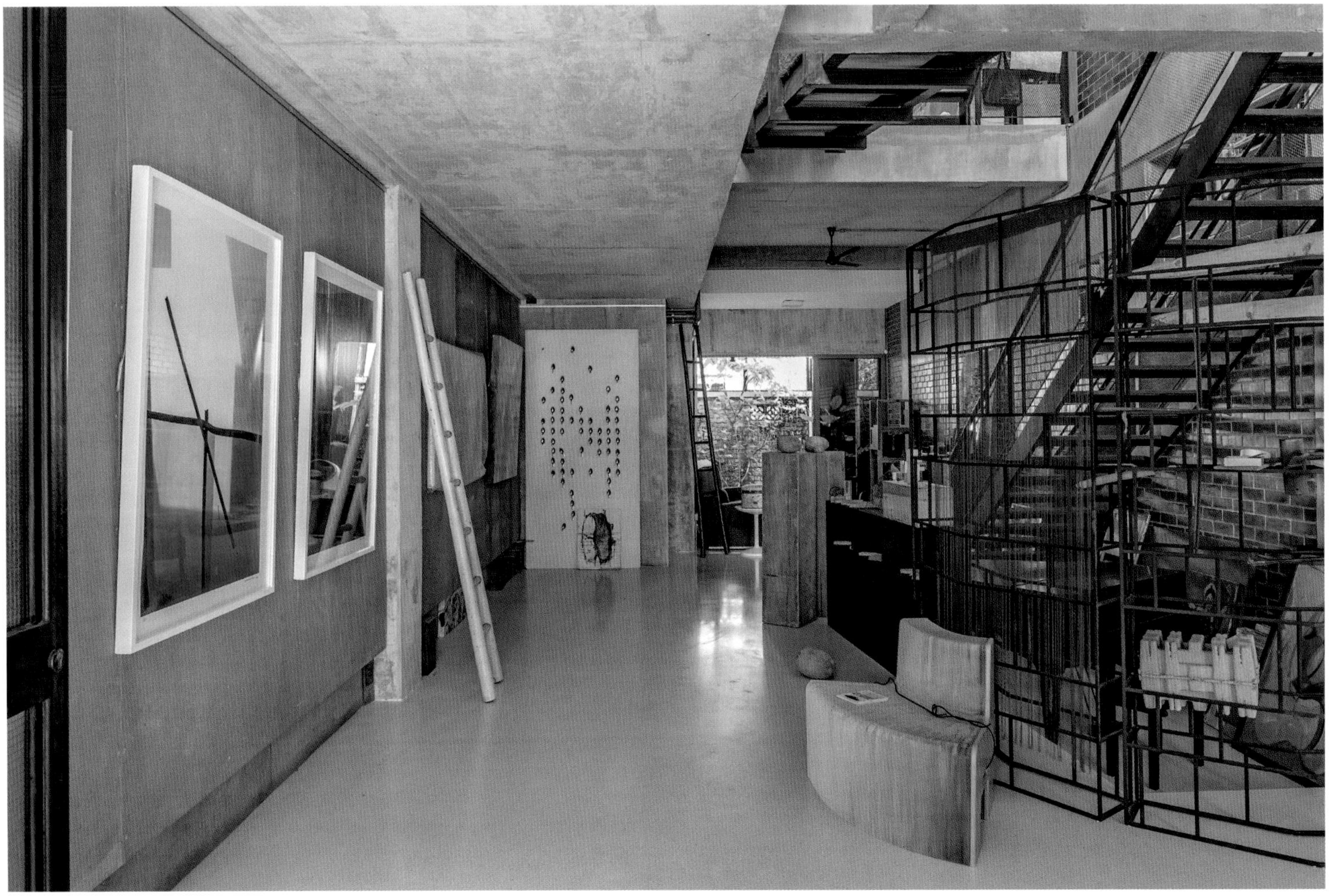

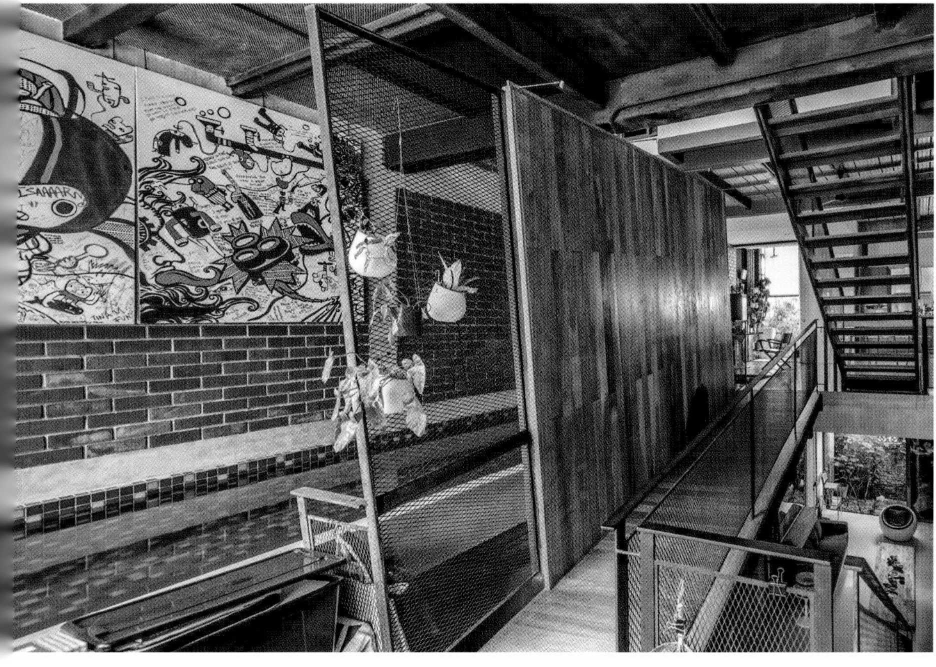

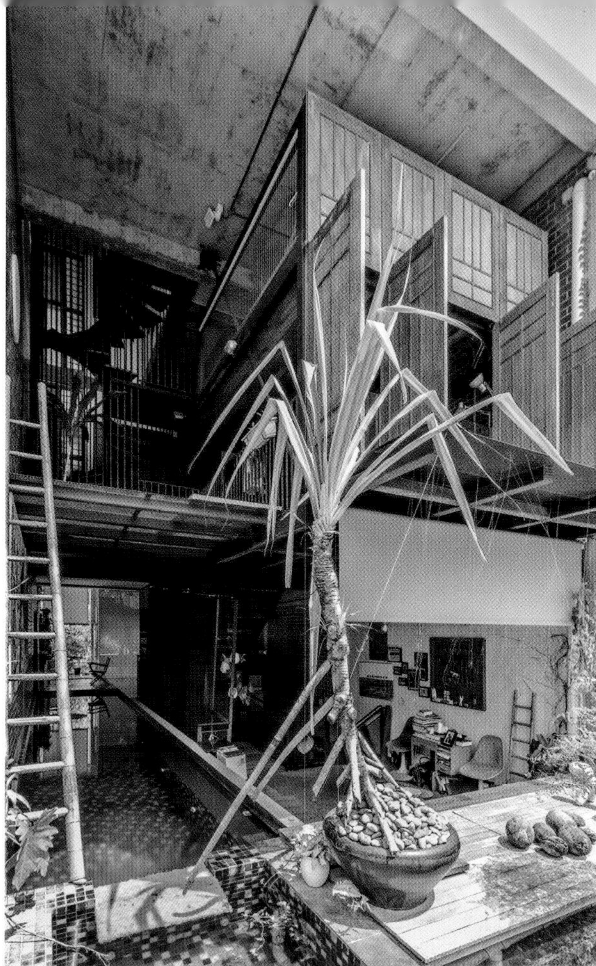

Above The pool, which runs down one side of the second storey, is separated from a walkway by a timber screen.

Above right The view from the second storey roof garden reveals the architect's 'primitive hut' on the intermediate level.

Right A view from the kitchen and dining area on the second storey of the pool running down the party wall on the right.

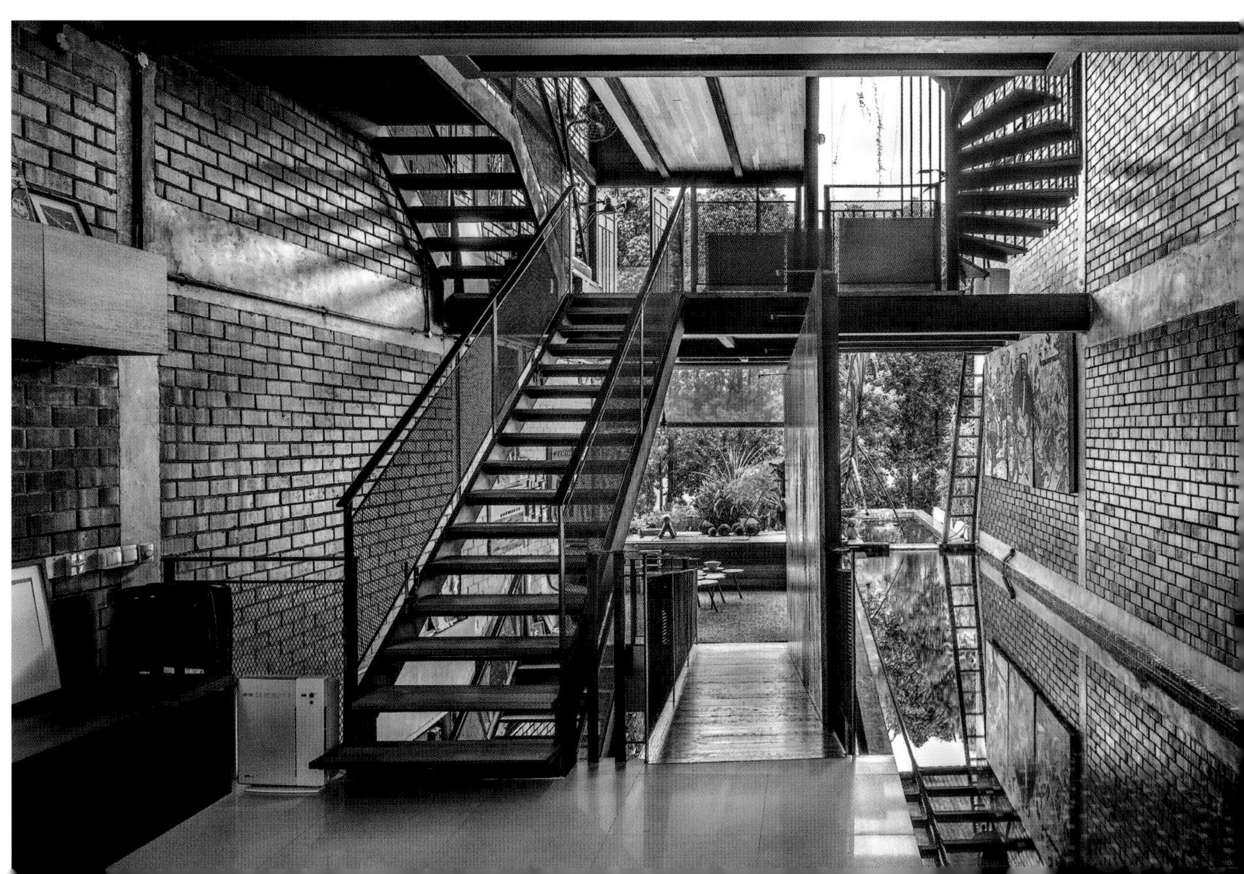

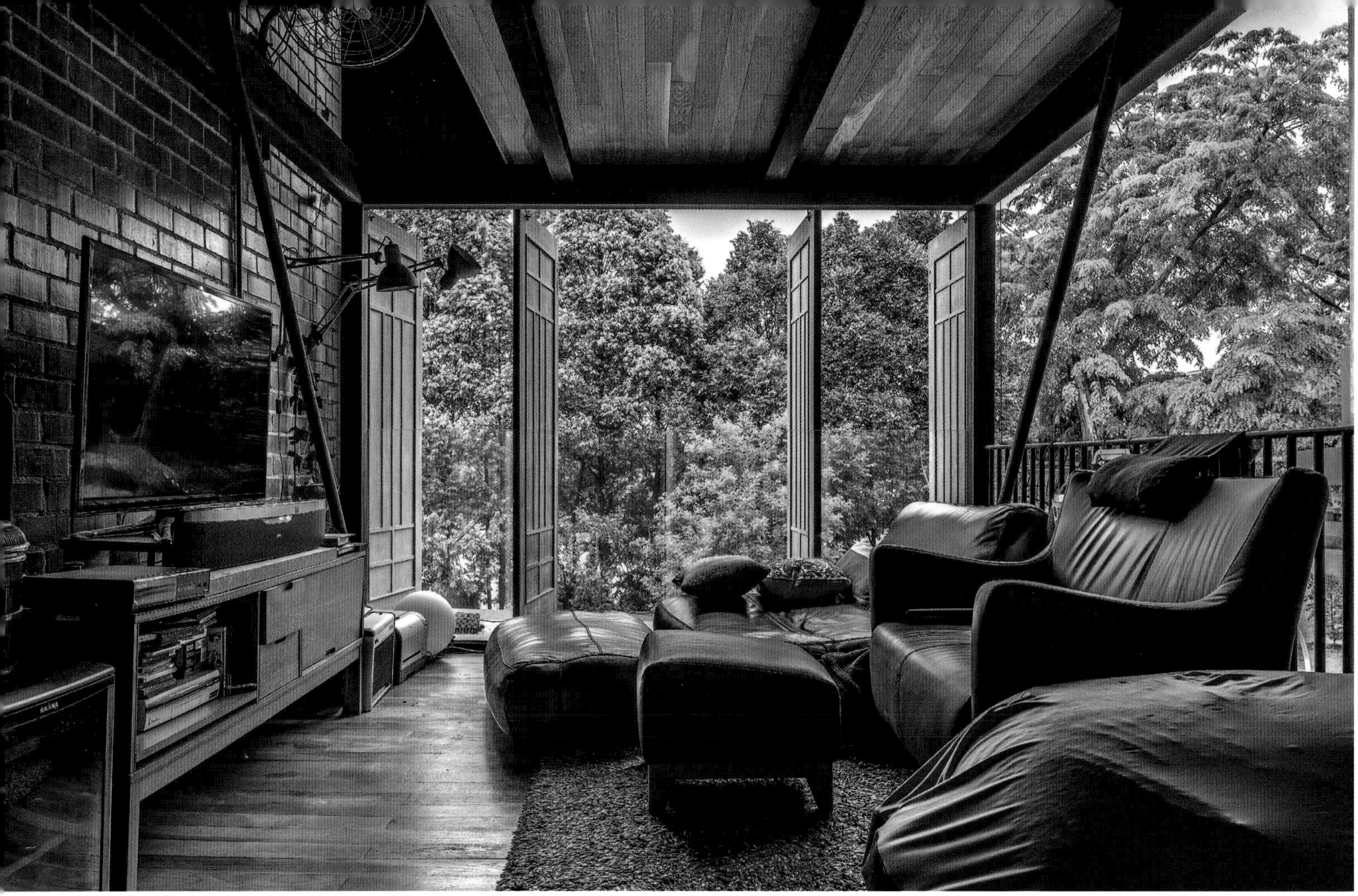

Above The 'primitive hut' on the intermediate level is a chill-out room both in the sense of relaxing and in the sense of capturing cooling sea breezes.

Below The dining area is compact, with a screen partly hiding the neighbours and an outside shower and powder room.

Below The tone of the elegant cantilevered kitchen bench complements the palette of the brick wall.

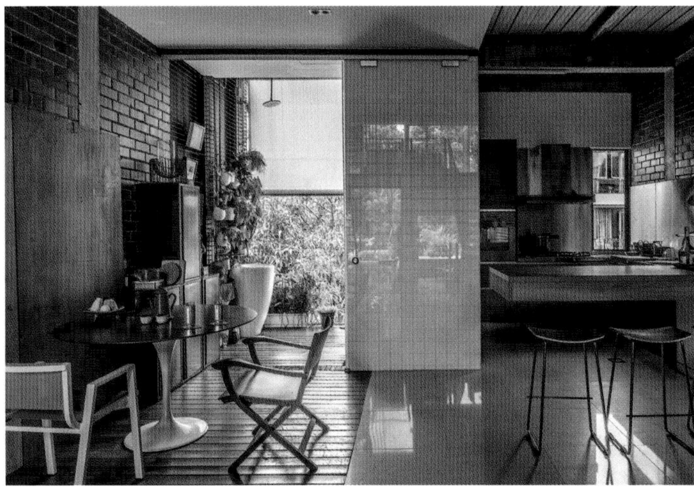

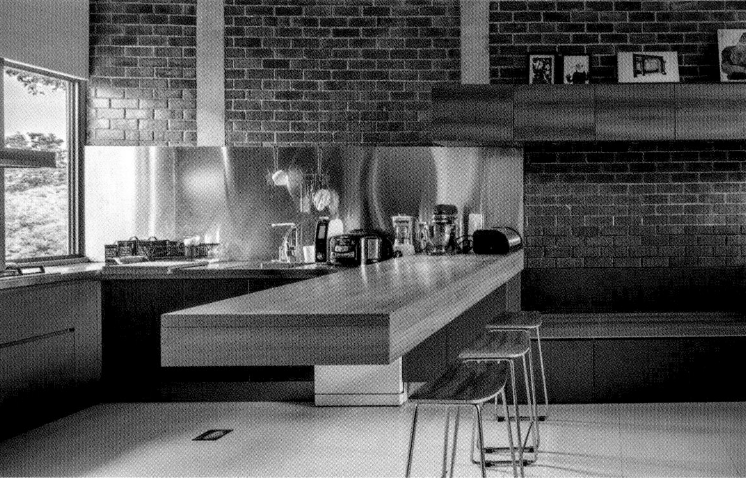

design, promoting the idea that we are getting glimpses of a micro-world inside—a theatrical quality augmented by the extruding timber box in the upper part of the building, which, in fact, is part of a kampong house imported from Malaysia.

This theatricality is continued inside where the only partially defined spaces constantly interact with one another to generate a perpetually evolving scenario.

There is an organic quality to the house, which probably reflects the way in which it evolved. Chan says he started at the third level with his 'primitive hut'. But at that stage he did not know what he would do with it or, indeed, with the whole house, which is 18 metres deep and 6 metres wide, with party walls on both sides. In the event, the ground floor has become a kind of anteroom featuring a sunken pit with a baby grand piano and much of Chan's art collection.

The real business starts on the next level. Here is the kitchen and an informal sitting and dining space reflecting the kampong inspiration—the furniture is Dedon outdoor furniture to cope with the humidity of an open house—along with an open shower recess and powder room. Also on this level are the pools, part of a patio space formed by the two-metre overhang above the entry. The 12-metre swimming pool runs from the living/dining space along the party wall of fair-face brick infill; otherwise the house is a steel and concrete construction. The pool is a focal point for the communal areas but also lends perspectival dynamism to the space,

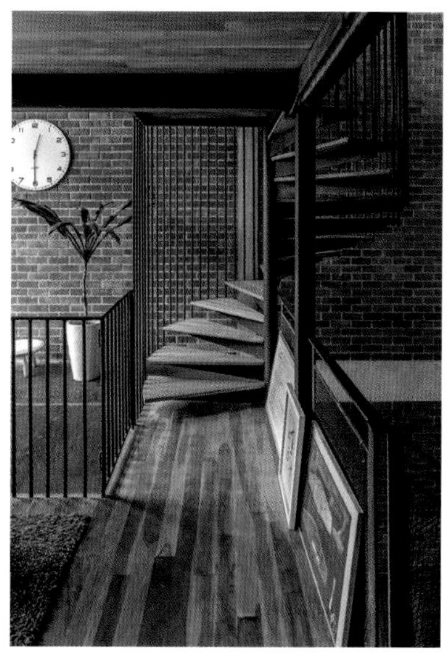

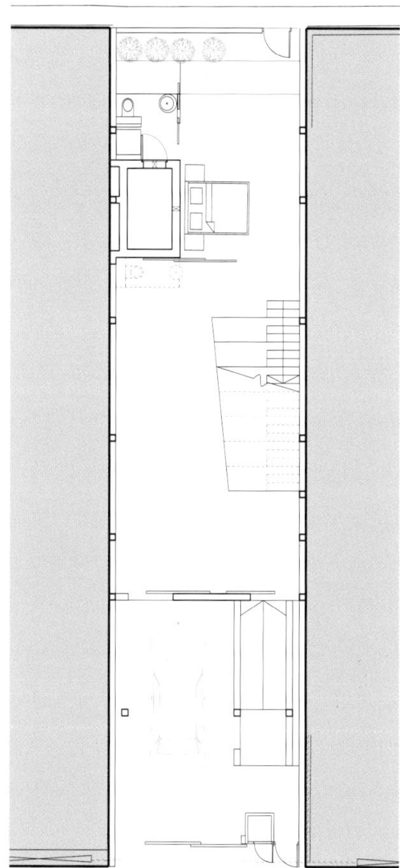

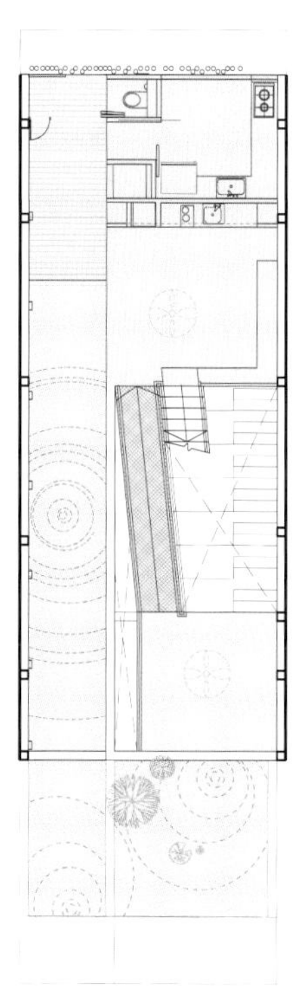

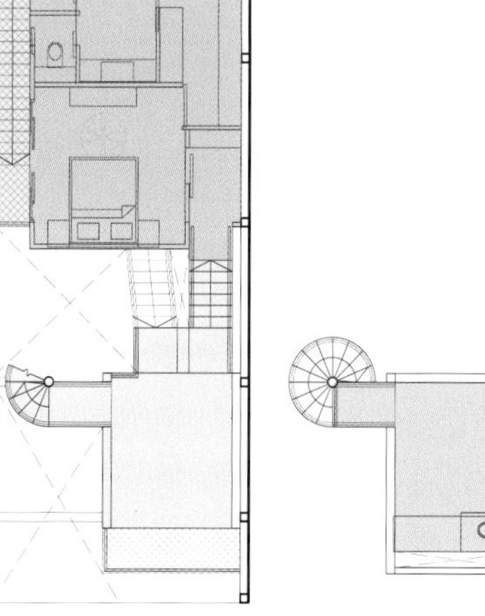

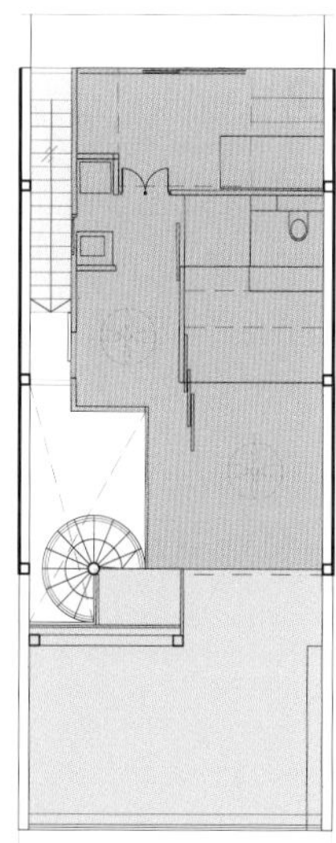

Top The timber walkway on the second storey, with a stairway leading to the intermediate and attic levels.

Above Ground floor, second storey, intermediate level and attic plans.

drawing the eye towards the reserve opposite. This pool links to two other pools on the patio to form a self-sustaining filtration system. This is an entirely natural system with the plants (pandana trees) and fish ensuring that the water, replenished by rain, is clean enough to be drinkable by the time it reaches the swimming pool.

Looking towards the patio from the living/dining space, there are four framed views, modulated by the changing light during the day, including the shafts of light coming down from the circular skylights. This visual dynamism is enhanced by the ramp and its angled timber wall going up to the next ('intermediate') level where it all began. Chan's primitive hut is now a small sitting room cantilevered off two diagonal steel struts. Opposite this, at the rear of the house, is the master bedroom. Further up is a home office and a roof terrace.

While the inspiration may have been the kampong house and while, in environmental terms, it is about as sustainable as it gets, this house is also an intriguing exercise in urban living, providing a rich domestic environment for a professional couple whose interest in visual culture is sustained as much by the constant stimulation of their house as by their collection of art.

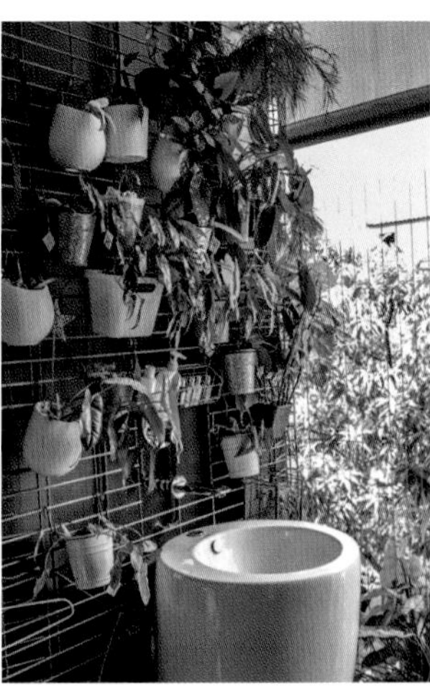

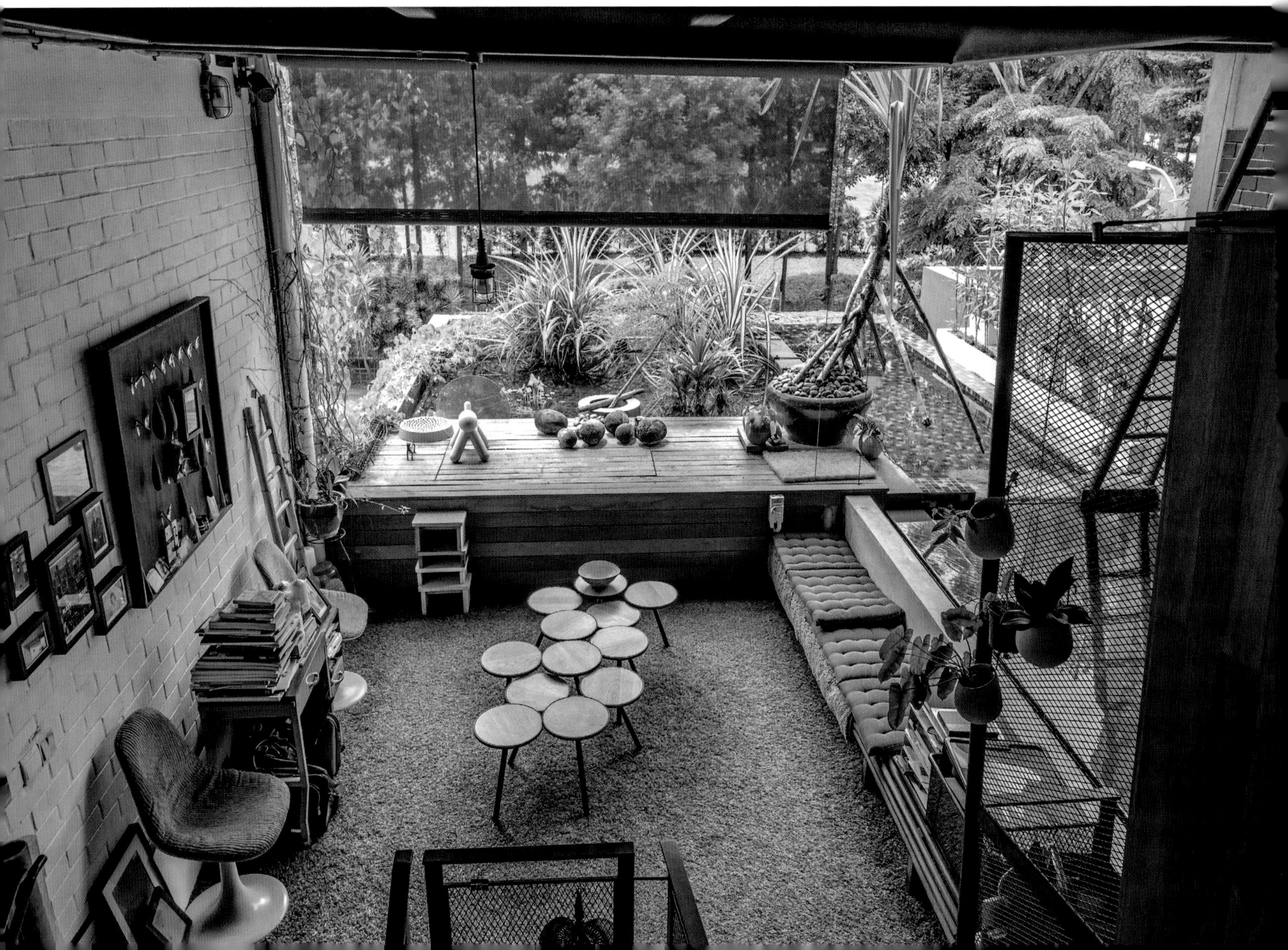

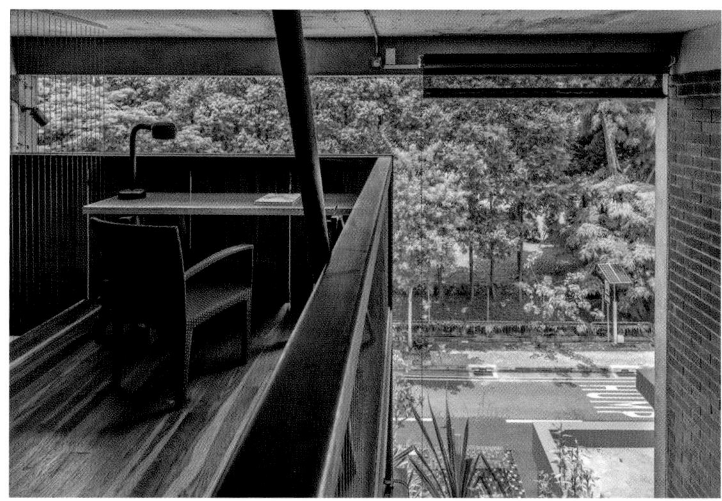

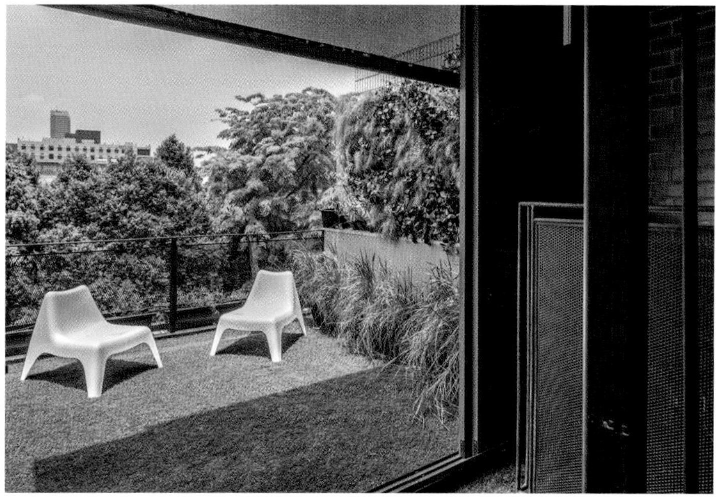

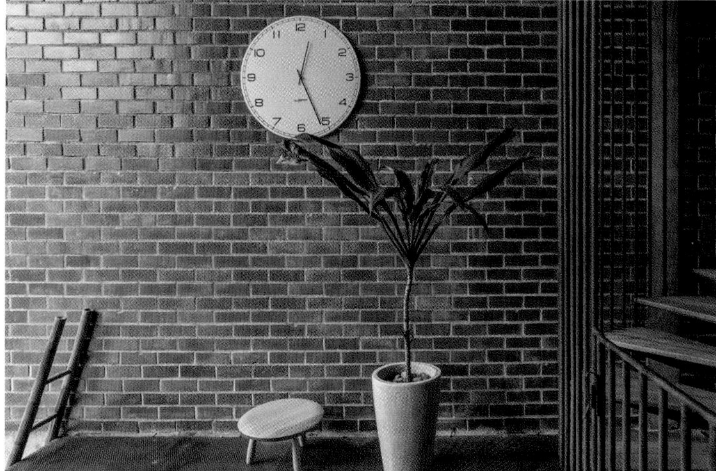

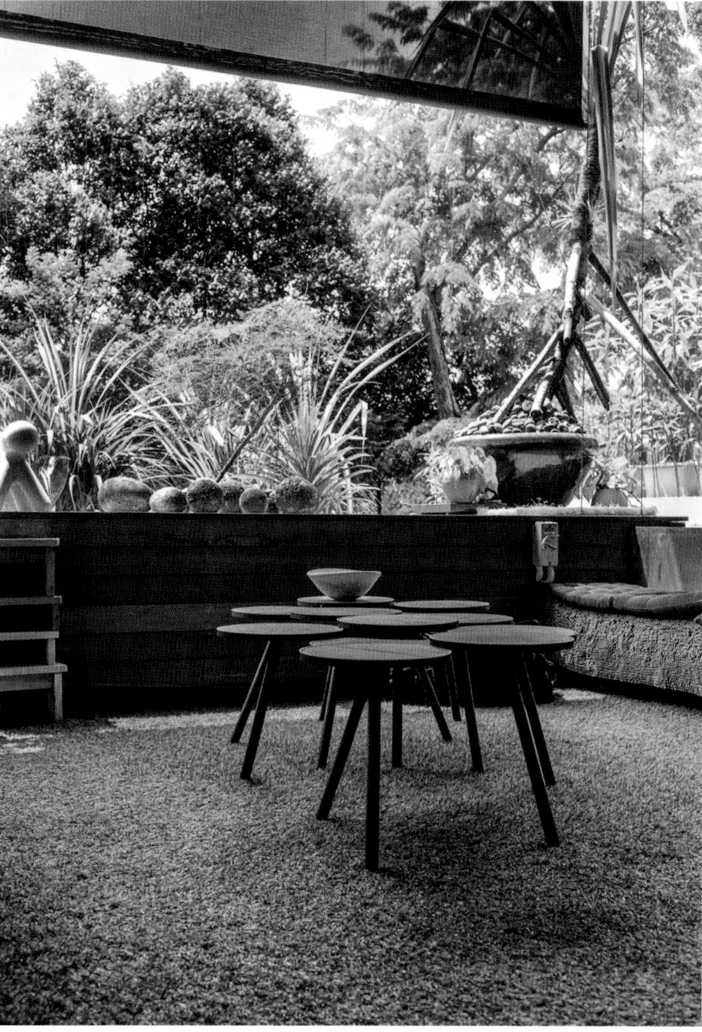

Left above The outdoor powder room off the kitchen/dining space brings the tropical landscape inside.

Left This view of the second storey space shows the water garden and swimming pool.

Top A view of the water garden from the home office.

Above The house is enlivened by decorative yet functional items, such as the clock and ladder.

Above right The roof garden on the attic level.

Right The sunken sitting room next to the water garden.

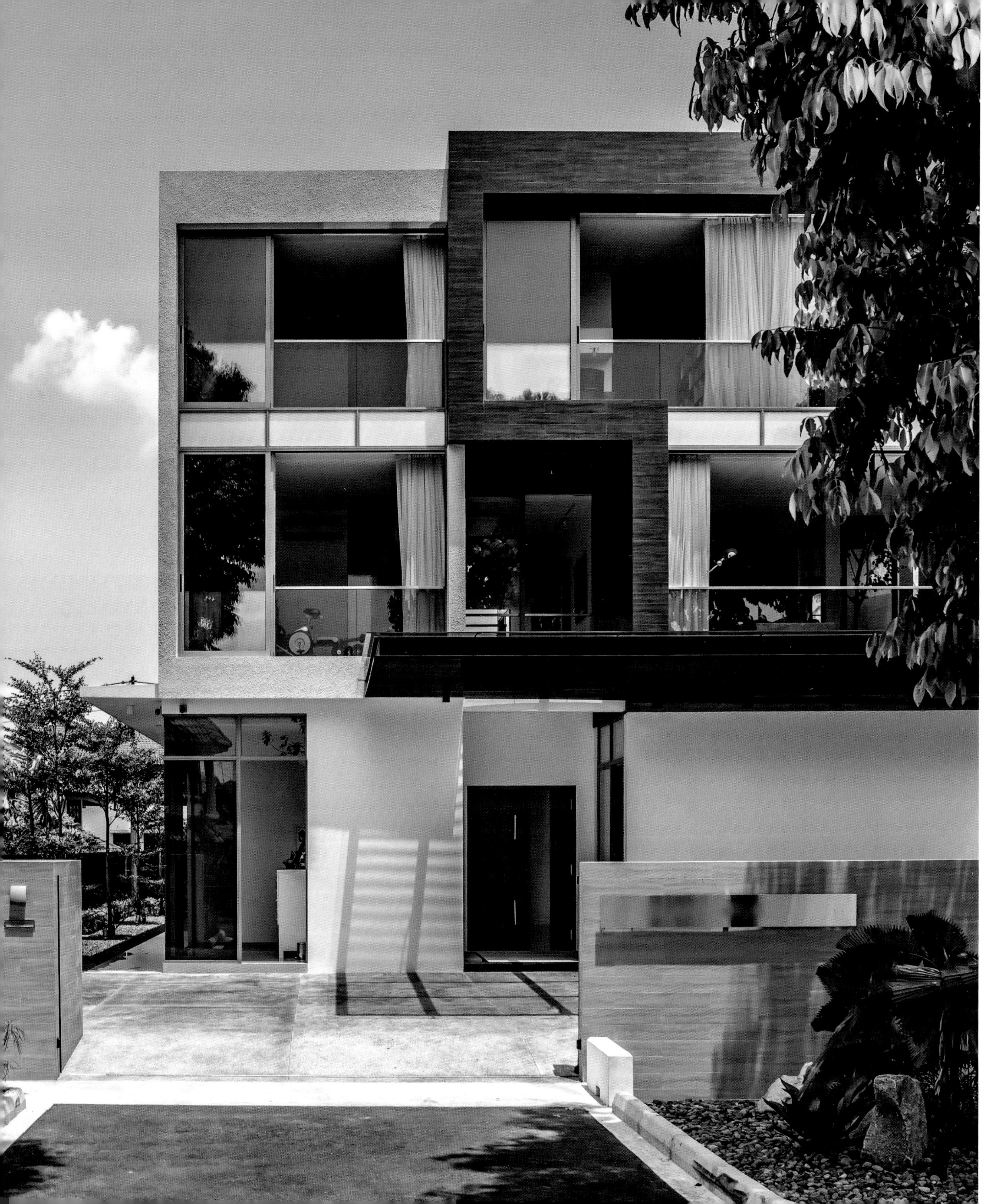

INTERLOCKING HOUSE
LATO DESIGN

'It is not a large plot of land and the owner wanted a big house, so there was not a lot of room to manoeuvre. It was built right up to the boundaries.'—LIM AI TIONG, ARCHITECT

This house is designed for two generations of a family along with their guests and in anticipation of a third generation of grandchildren. On the one hand, it is an example of responding to the challenge of designing a house to be shared by an extended family, keeping in mind the demand for higher levels of privacy than was once the case. On the other hand, the house tackles the challenge of how to provide a garden when there is no space for one. The result is an imaginative exploration of connection and separation.

The architect found his solution in the formal composition of the house. It is divided into two parallel but interconnected blocks on the second and third storeys. This is signalled on the street façade of the building where, on the eastern side, the owner's block and the son's block above are highlighted by the use of brown timber tile cladding, while the guests' block on the western side features a contrasting beige texture wall. Internally, the two blocks are separated by a naturally ventilated corridor with void spaces and a skylight. Hence, Level 2 is the master level with guest rooms while Level 3 is the domain of the son and daughter-in-law, their guests and future children. The common areas are on the ground floor where there is a spacious living/dining area, a kitchen entertainment room and an al fresco dining terrace.

Having clearly demarcated the areas of the house, the architect then realized there was a need to also connect them. The solution to this also became the solution to bringing green space into the house, along with additional light and cross-ventilation. The

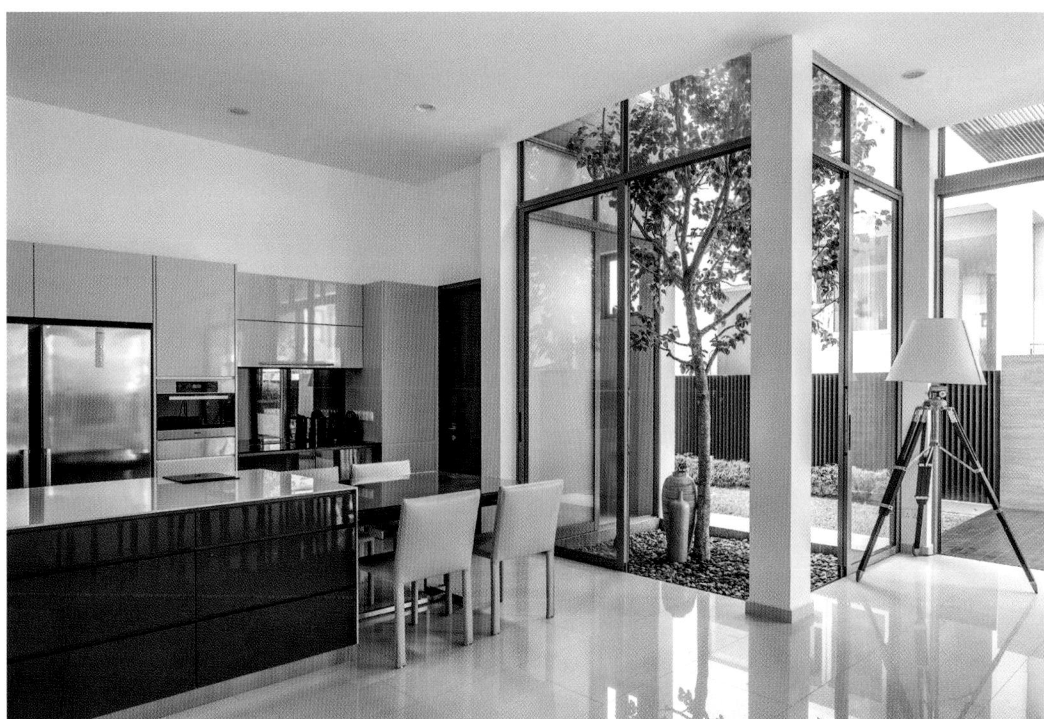

Left The two interlocking forms of the house are clearly visible from the street.

Right One of the garden voids next to the dry kitchen screens a powder room.

resulting connections, a series of four double-height garden voids, work both vertically and horizontally.

The first void is encountered at the entry to the house. Passing under an extensive screen canopy, the visitor transitions over stepping stones across a water feature at the base of the first double-height void, which can be viewed from the home office on Level 2. The second void is on the ground floor adjacent to the dry kitchen and powder room. This cuts into the main volume of the house, making the tall ficus tree a green highlight in the living/dining area. This void extends up through the second storey and separates the master bedroom from the master bathroom, providing cross-views modulated by the green of the tree.

The third void begins at the end of the corridor on Level 2. It has a water garden at its base and, again, brings a cooling, calming element into the body of the house while also providing panoramic views across the neighbourhood. This void can also be seen from the guest rooms, walk-in wardrobe and family area on Level 3. The fourth void begins on Level 2 and again features a tall ficus tree that can be viewed from the master bedrooms—it is effectively a part of the son's bedroom and sitting room—and both bathrooms on Levels 2 and 3.

Running down the centre of the house on Levels 2 and 3 is a corridor with full-height operable windows at both ends to generate cross-ventilation, with a skylight above to draw in light. The staircase, lift and rarely used guest bedrooms are all strategically located along the western side the house, protecting the rest of the house from the western sun.

This house exemplifies another strategy for the multi-generational home, namely 'pavilionizing' a single building, creating separate but connected domains for the different generations living in it.

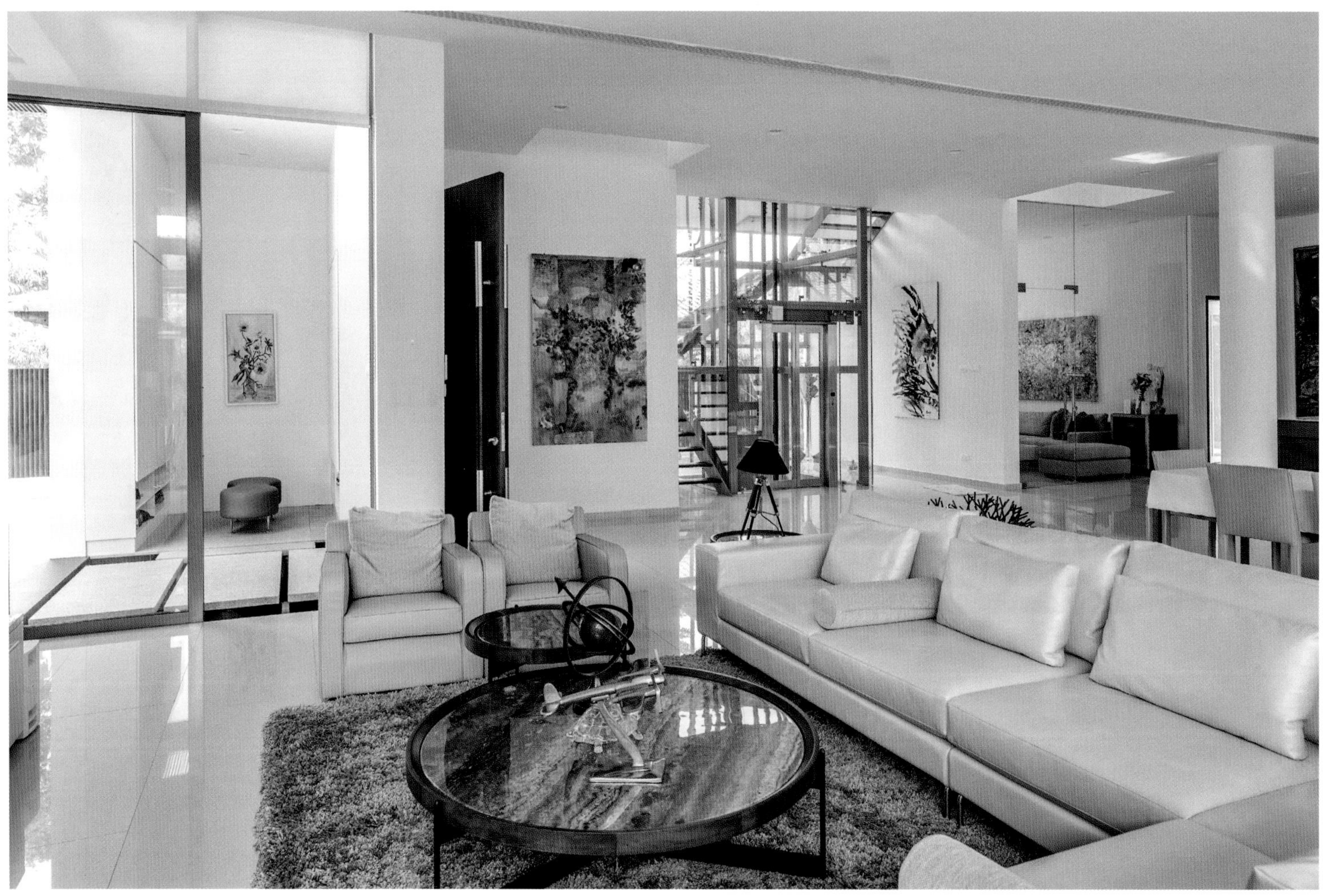

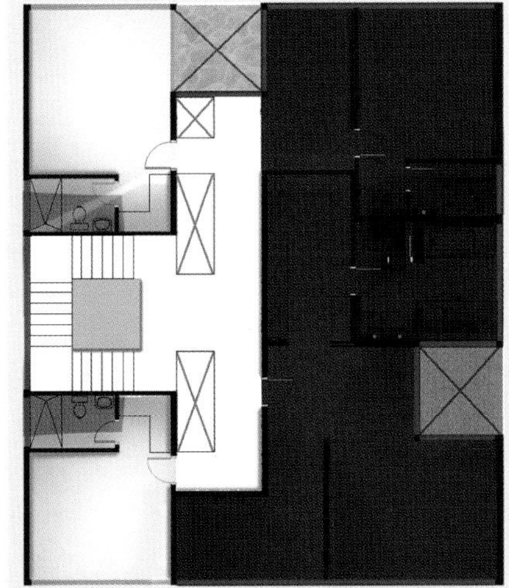

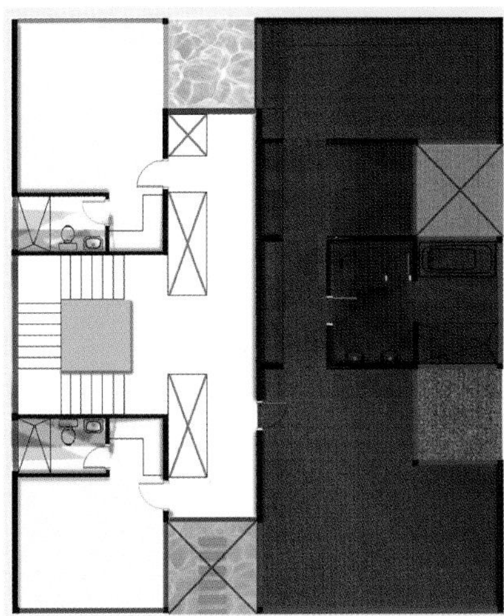

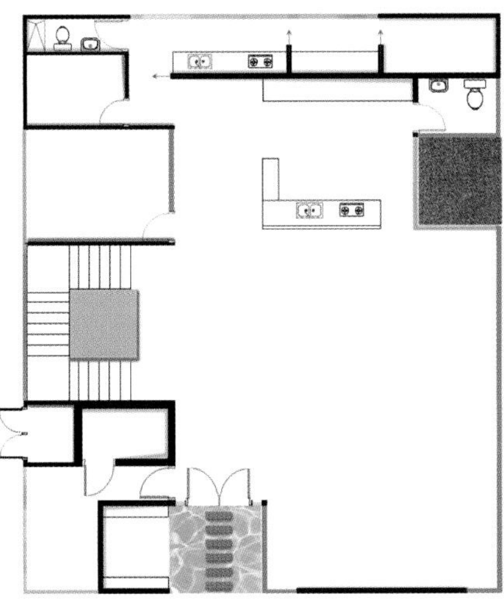

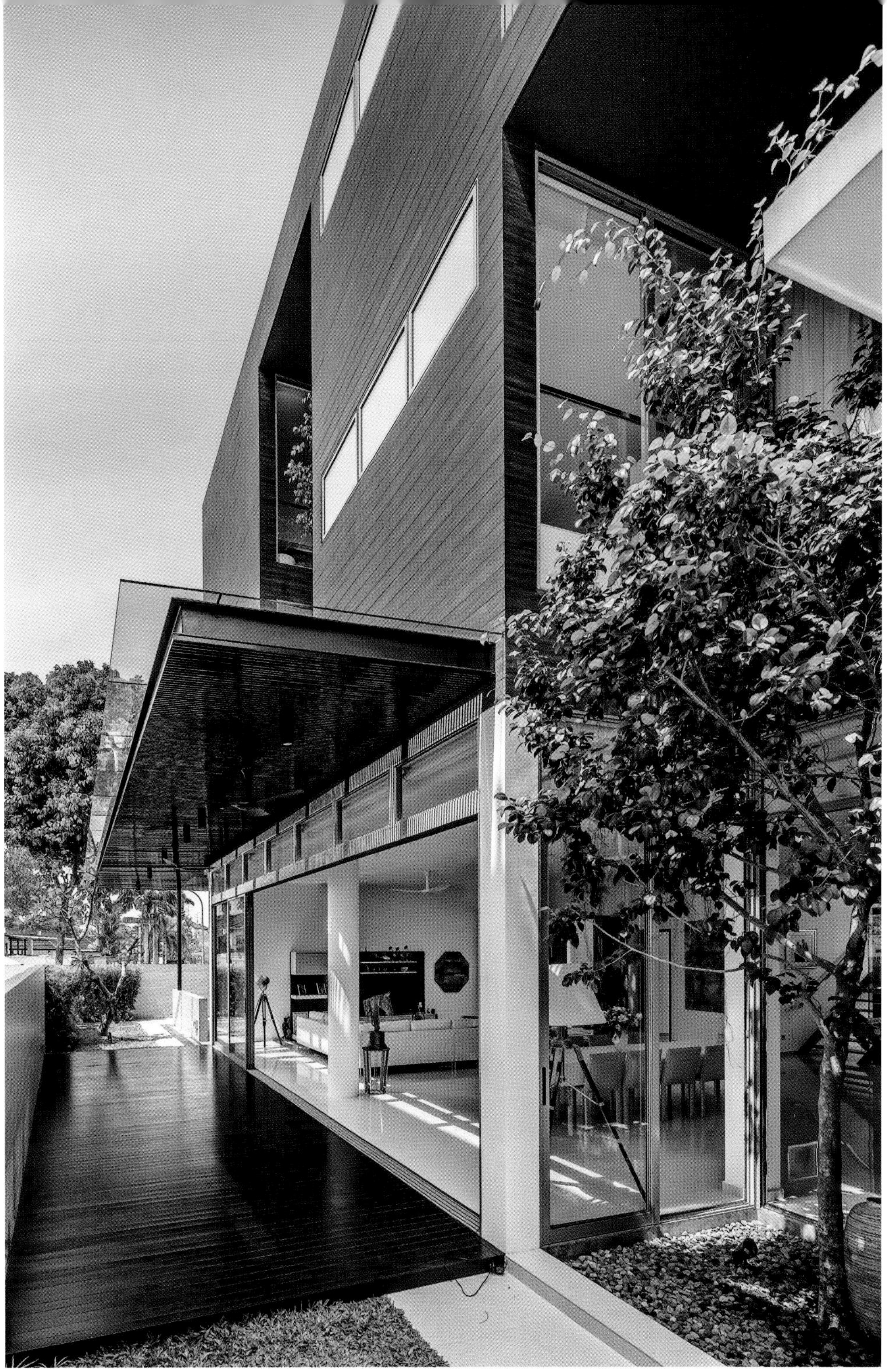

Above The outside dining terrace.

Opposite The living area, with the entry void to the left, the central glazed liftwell and a small sitting room.

Left Third storey, second storey and first storey plans.

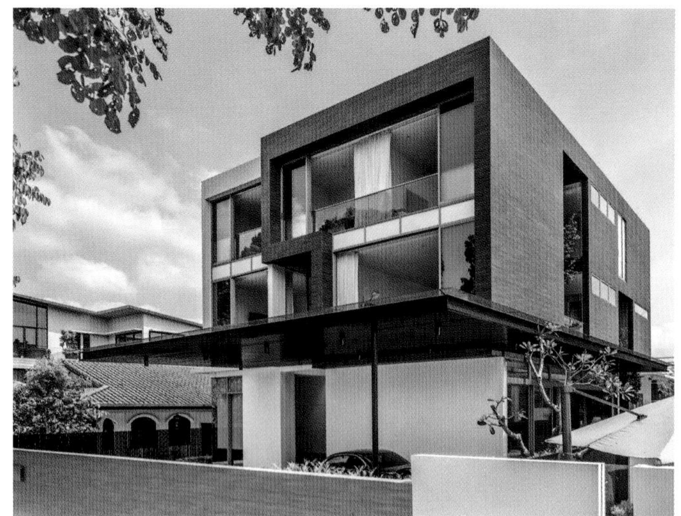

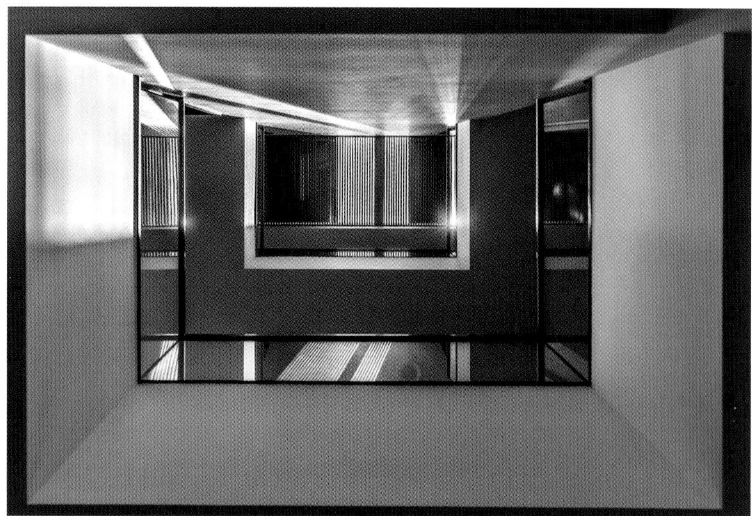

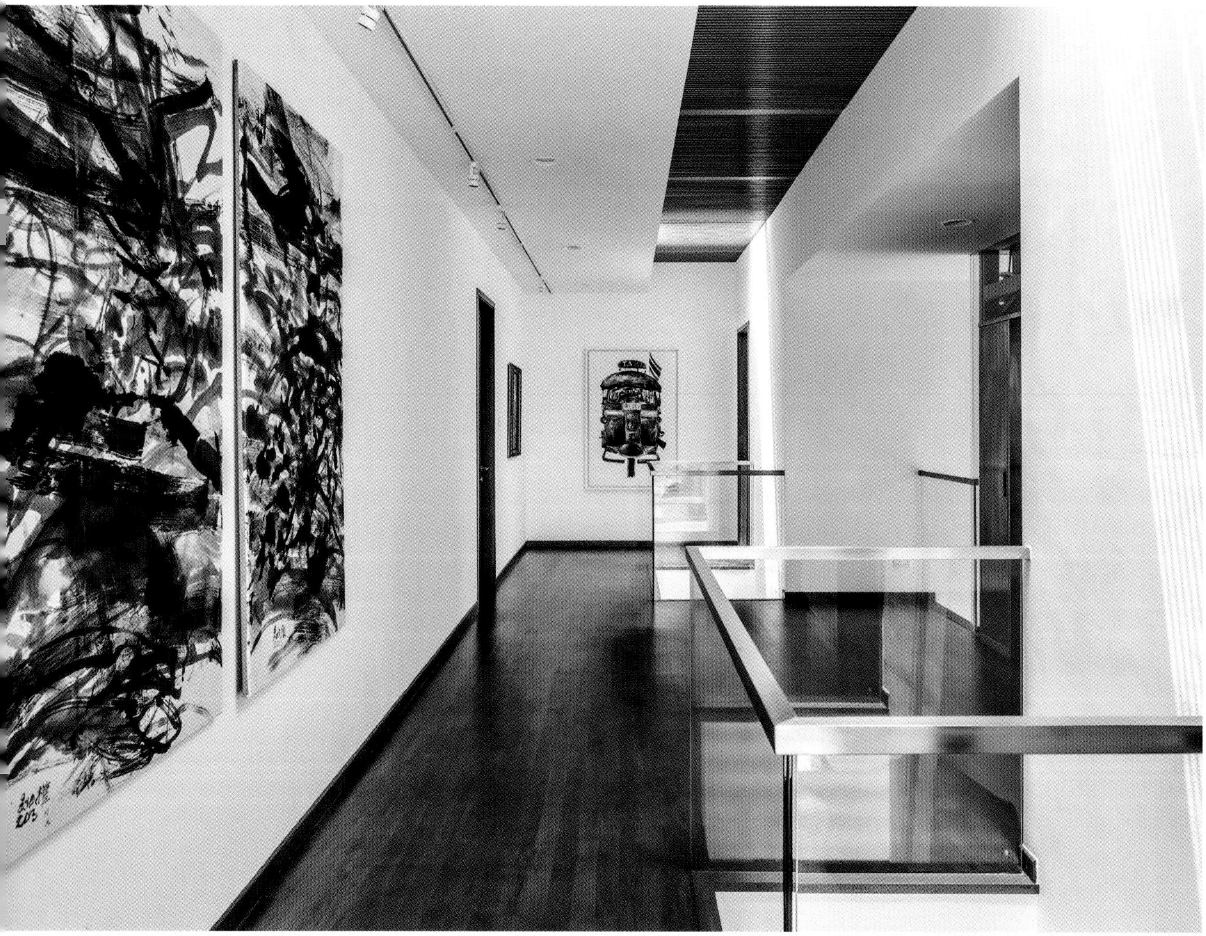

Above left The interlocking forms seen from the street, with the broad canopy forming the porte cochère and garden voids cut into the side of the house.

Above Looking up the central void to the skylight.

Left Generous timber lobbies surround the central void and link the bedrooms on the second storey.

Right The trees in the garden voids extend up through two levels.

Below The open master bedroom suite is set among trees in the void and by the 'borrowed landscape' outside.

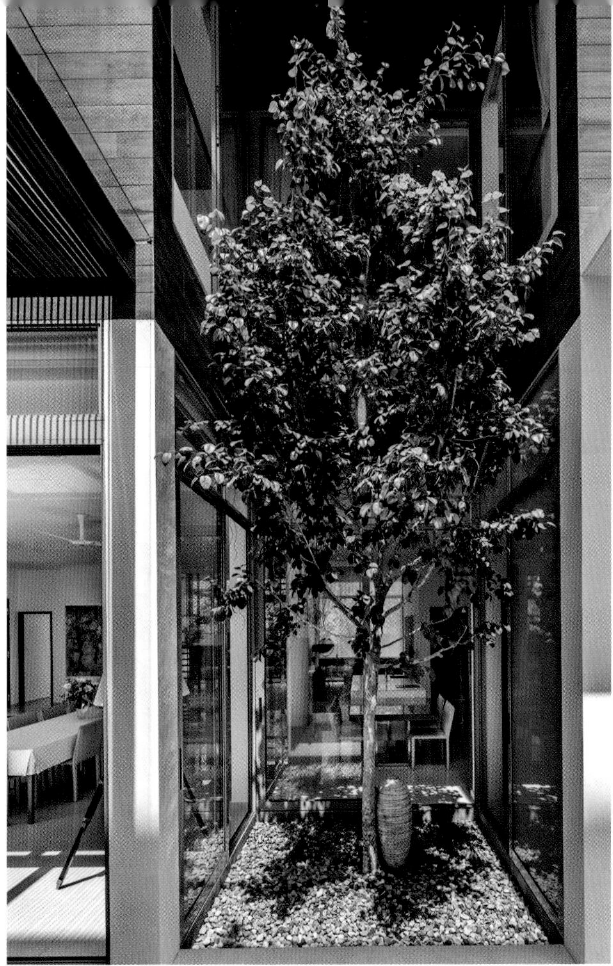

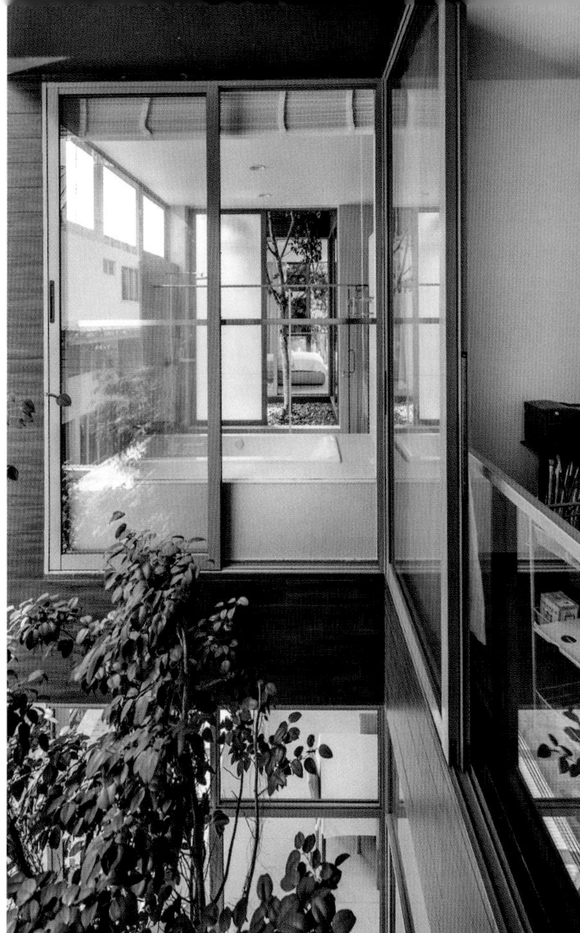

Above The bathrooms are highly transparent and also enjoy the greenery thrusting up through the voids.

Below A garden void on the second storey.

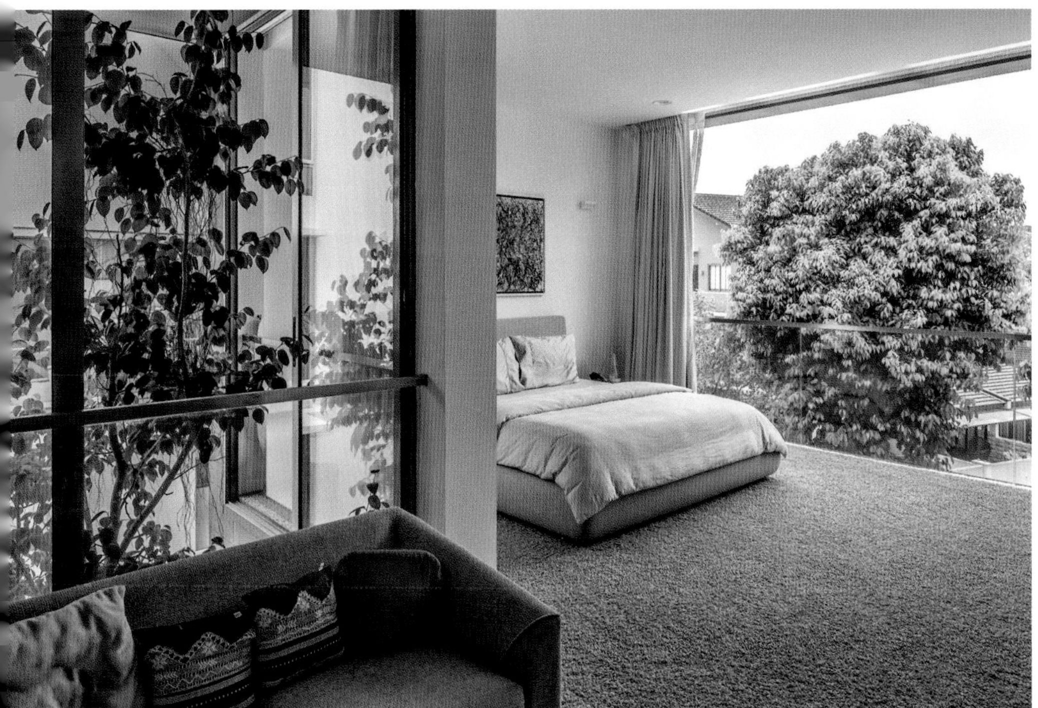

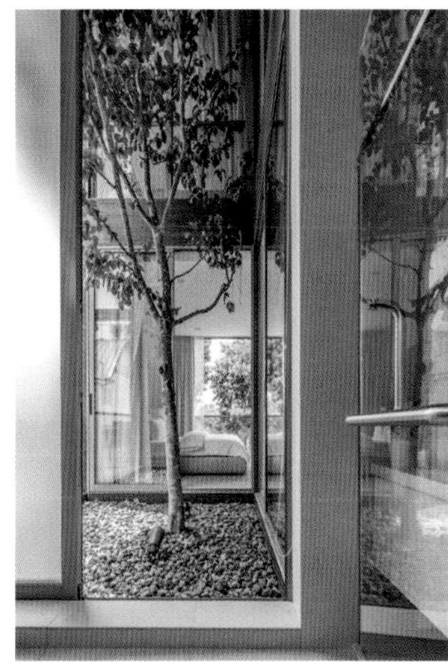

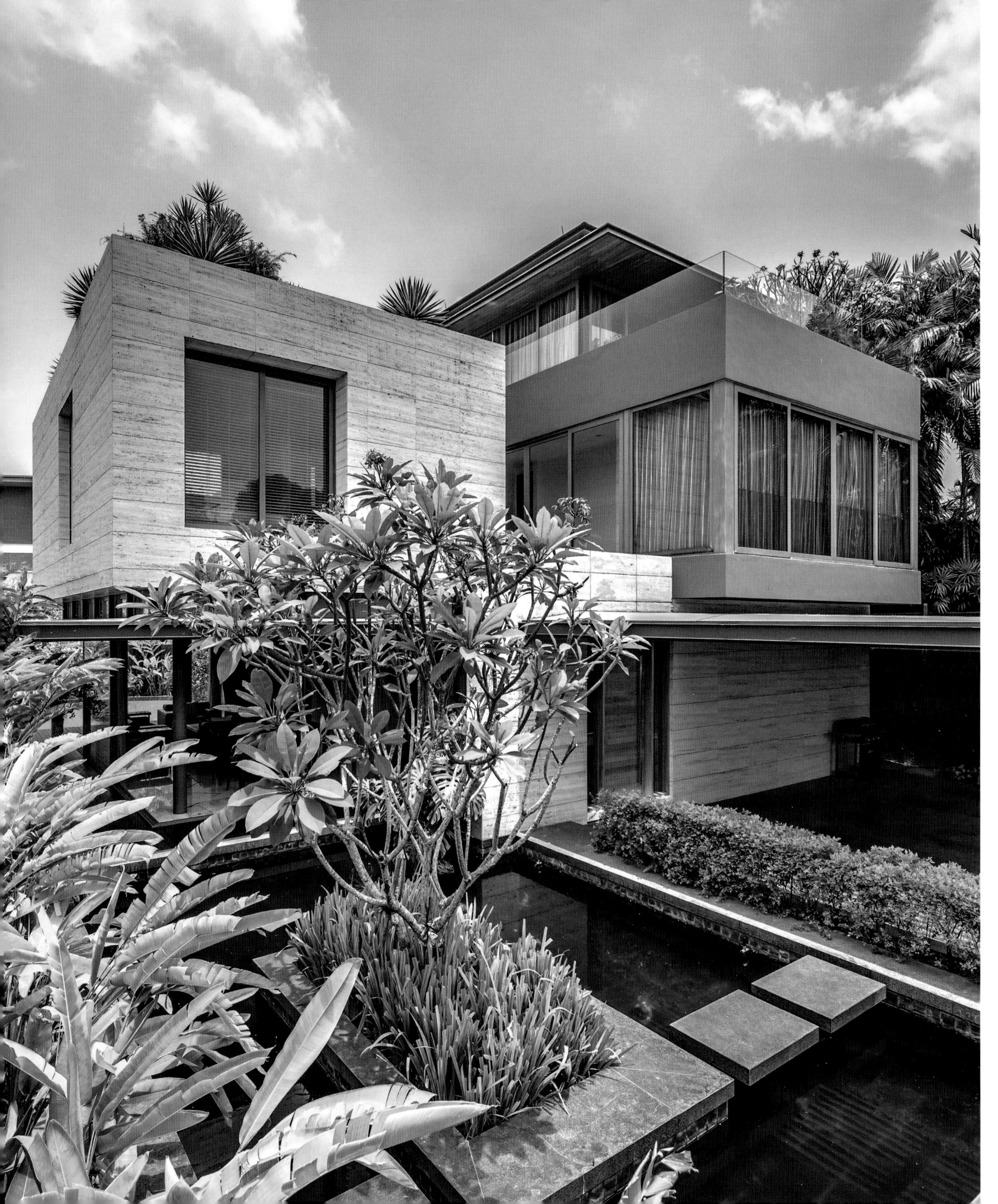

TRAVERTINE DREAM HOUSE
WALLFLOWER ARCHITECTURE + DESIGN

'This is the sort of thing you can't have in an HDB flat. It was a dream that some day I would have a house, I would have a big koi pond.'—OWNER

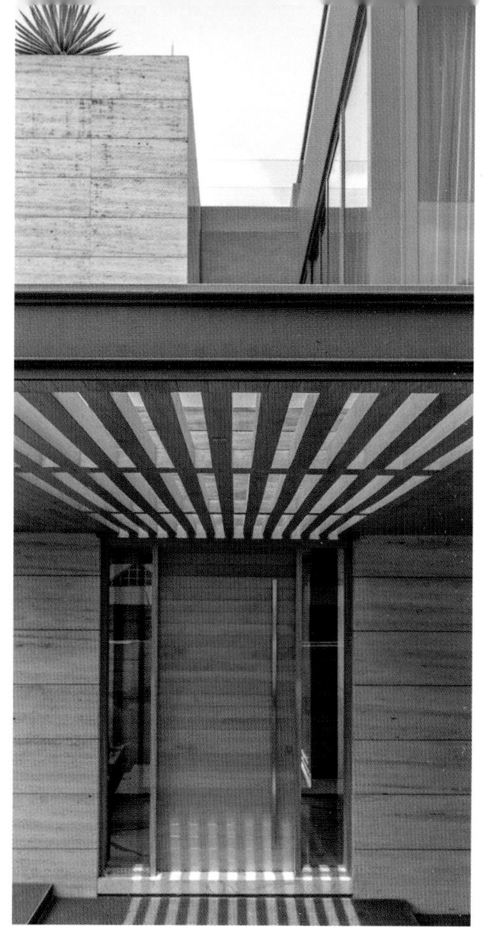

This house represents an imaginative and rather beautiful reconciliation of a number of competing concerns. In so doing, it highlights a number of sustainable aspects as well as some of the ways in which residential design in Singapore is responding to current social and economic trends.

For the client, the house is a memorable stage in a journey which began in a Housing Development Board apartment. It is the culmination of a dream, especially because it has enabled him to fully indulge his passion for koi. Notwithstanding the koi pond, the client was mindful of the resale potential of the house. In this respect, the house reflects a current preoccupation in Singapore—maximizing gross floor area and avoiding over-customizing new homes, thereby allowing for differing requirements from future owners. In this case, the architects also argued for 'a balance between future development and the current neighbourhood.... We have to protect the owner by building a size which he thinks is good, but not so big that the neighbourhood thinks it sticks out like a sore thumb.' A happy compromise was reached, the owner commenting that 'the design is just nice, we have enough rooms.'

As well as optimizing the site, the client wanted as much greenery as possible. This apparent contradiction was resolved by spreading gardens and water bodies throughout the house. The highly transparent living/dining space forms a pavilion that appears to float over water with the koi pond on one side and the irregularly shaped swimming pool on the other.

The key strategy was to build the house as two separate blocks. One is the living/dining pavilion, which has the master bedroom above it and a roof garden above that. Parallel to this is a longer block. This has a basement (another increasingly popular way of creating more space in Singapore), forming a void between the two blocks that are linked by glass bridges on Levels 1 and 2. The void not only draws light into the basement but at the bottom has a 'Japanese garden' running its length. The basement also accommodates an entertainment room, including a huge fish tank with 12-year-old arajuana fish, and the maids' quarters.

Level 1 houses the kitchen, laundry, wet kitchen and a guest room at the rear, overlooking the pool. Level 2 is the children's domain, while the Level 3 attic area includes two potential guest rooms, one with a timber deck, frangipani tree and neighbouring trees providing a privacy screen. This rooftop pavilion connects with the roof garden on top of the master bedroom. The wall of the master

Opposite The strategy of spreading gardens and water features all through the house is immediately apparent on arrival, with the koi pond seen from the entry.

Above The timber-screened porte cochère, with the entry door placed between the two pavilions of the house.

Below Long section.

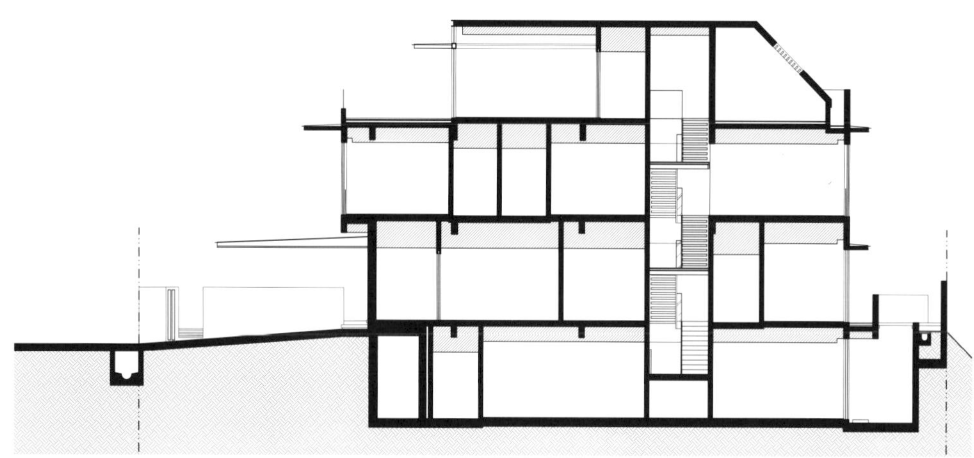

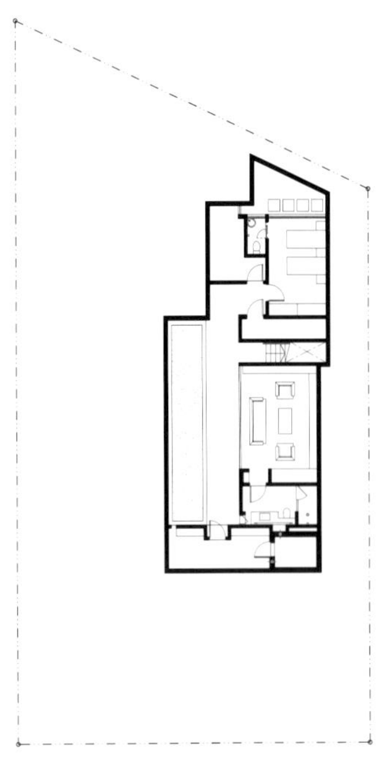

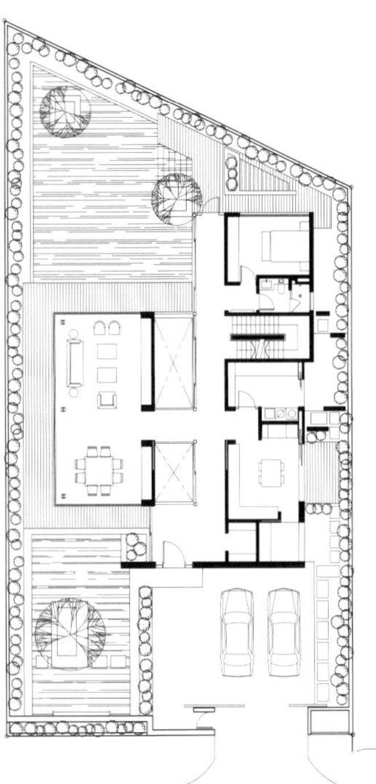

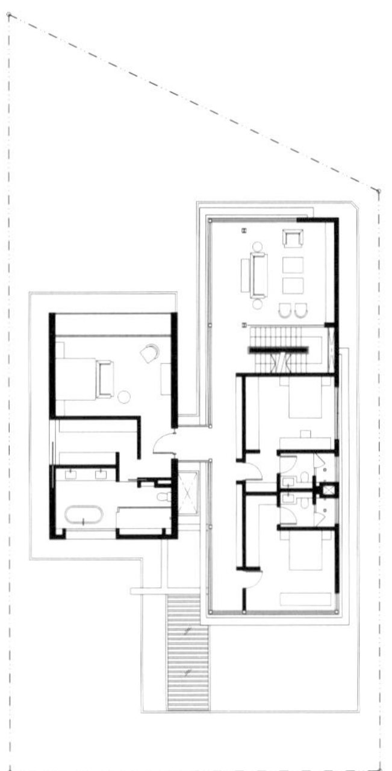

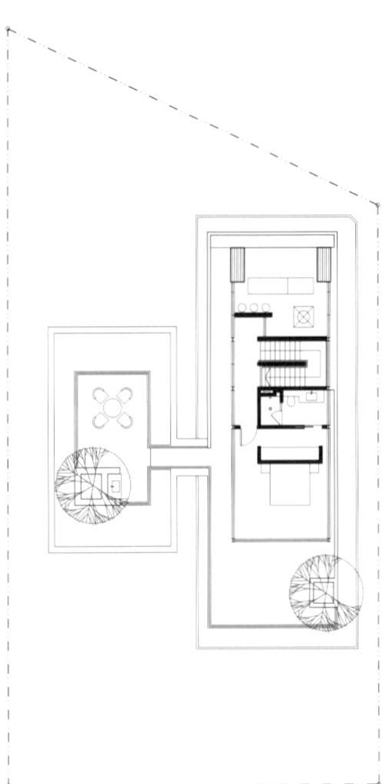

Above Plans of the attic, second storey, first storey and basement.

Left The living pavilion seems to float on top of the koi pond.

Below The basement entertainment room has a large fish tank.

Right The 'Japanese garden' in the basement area.

Far right Looking back down the swimming pool towards the living pavilion with the master bedroom above.

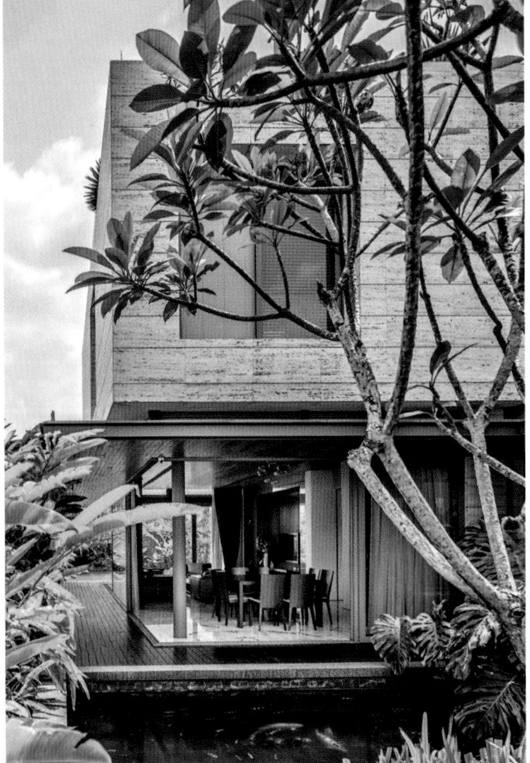

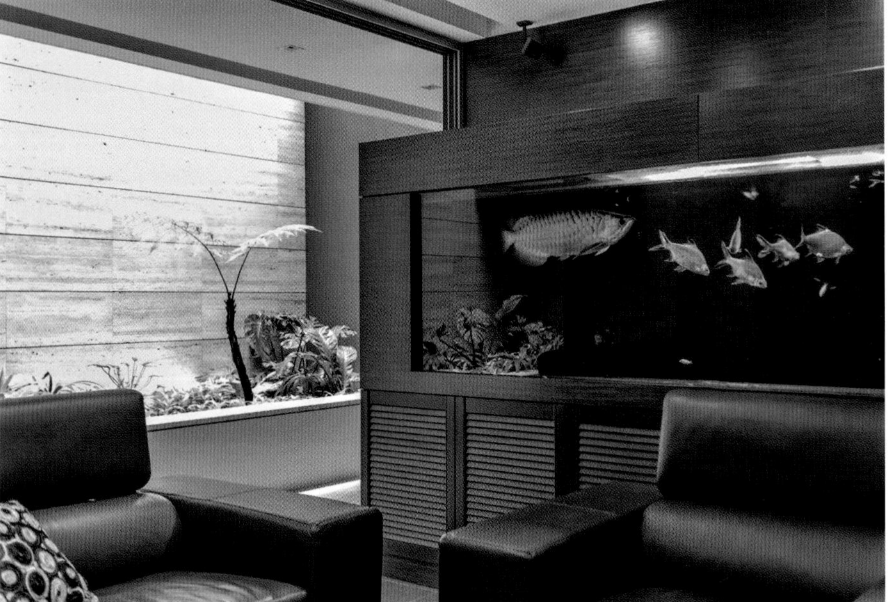

bedroom is 200 mm thick with a second layer to create an air gap for cooling. This is supported by the greenery of the roof garden, which also has an air gap between the timber deck and the concrete roof, thus helping to lower the temperature in the master bedroom by roughly five degrees.

Clearly, this is a 'green' house. The living/dining pavilion opens up on three sides to gardens and water. The void draws in natural light and generates cross-ventilation. The rooftop garden adds another cooling layer. Architect Robin Tan Chai Chong argues, however, that architects have always been environmentally sensitive and the issue is to look at sustainability 'in a holistic manner'. The task of architecture, he maintains, 'is to balance consumption ... we try to minimize consumption.' This house illustrates his point. The client wanted

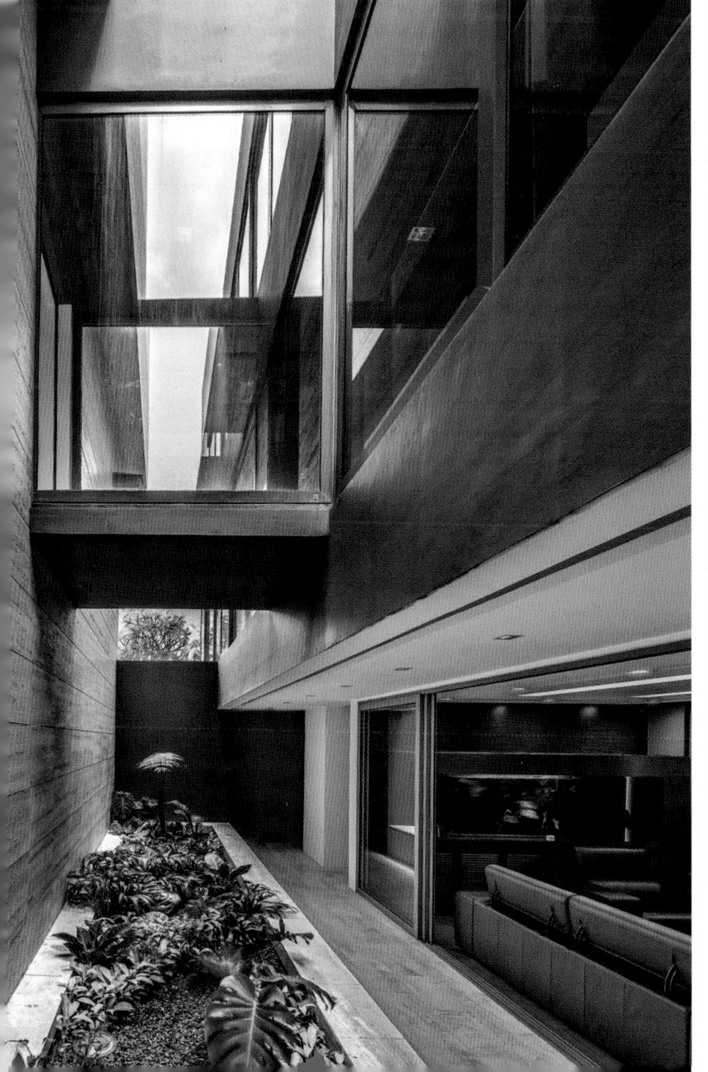

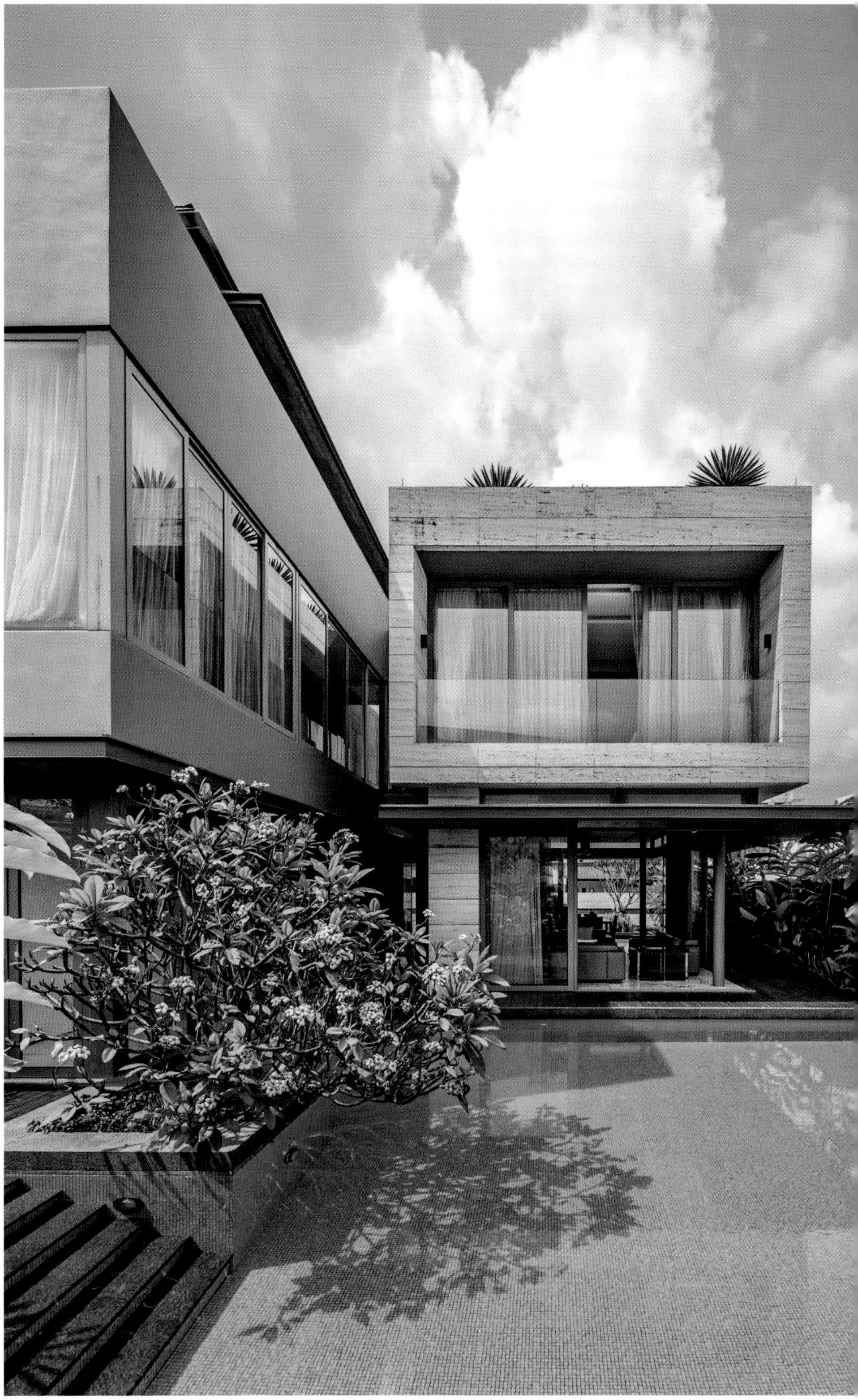

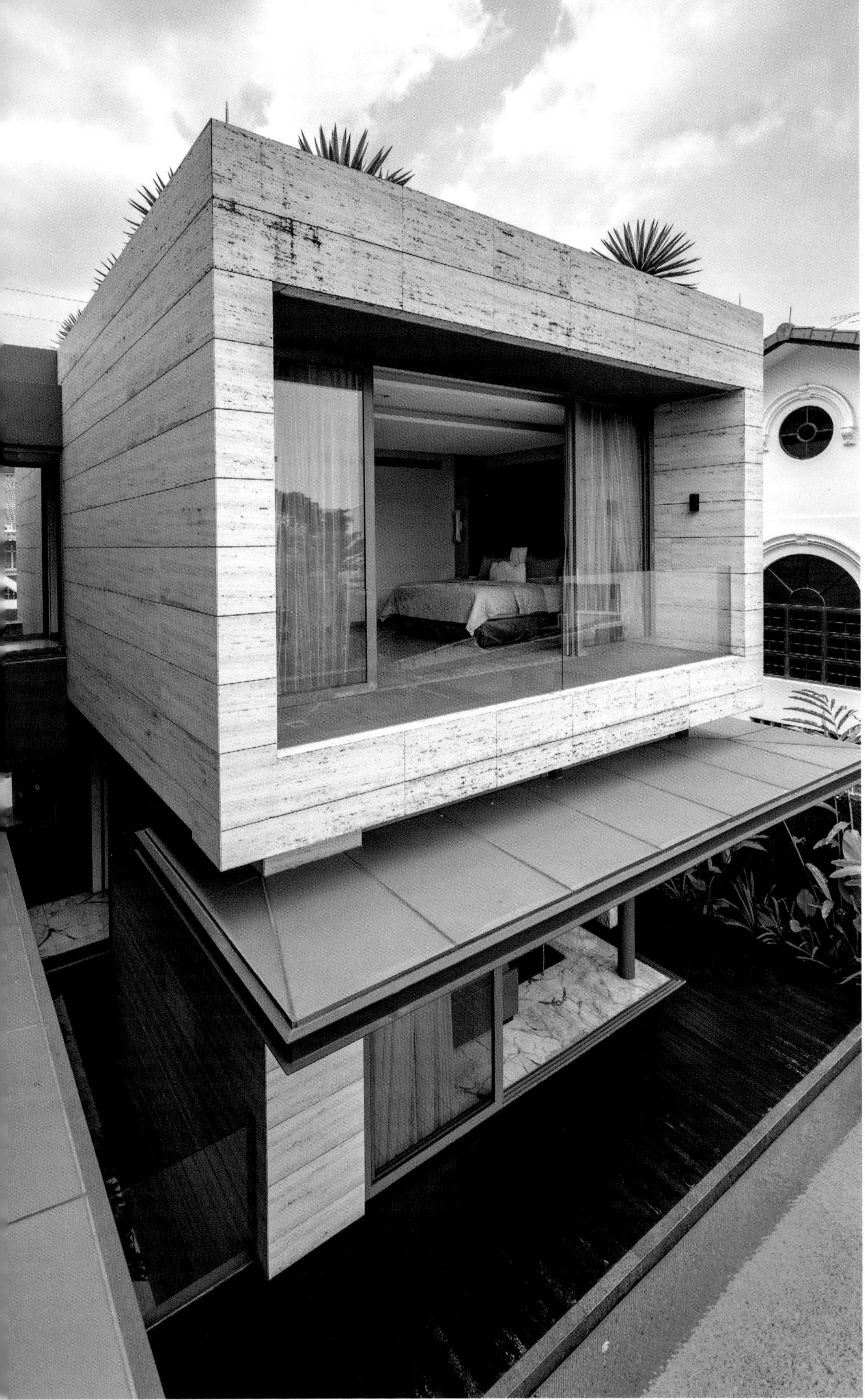

Left The master bedroom sits as a self-contained box above the living pavilion, opening up completely to the outside.

to clad the house in marble but the architects suggested the more modest, and arguably more beautiful, travertine. The client accepted the recommendation, especially as he was able to draw a connection between this material and his own happy memories of touring Italy. In fact, he sourced all the travertine at a cost far less than would have been the case if purchased in Singapore.

The travertine now gives the house much of its character, signalled on approach from the street by several layers of travertine that 'suggest a tenuous threshold between the outside and the inside'. This loose assembly of forms, punctuated by garden beds and points of transparency, makes the house a 'good neighbour' in that it does not stand out in the street. The warm, soft texture of the travertine helps here, giving the house a degree of tasteful reserve.

This compositional character is continued inside where the constant interplay of solids, voids, textured surfaces (different kinds of travertine are used inside and out), 'green' and 'blue' spaces, and the visually engaging irregularity of the pool all combine to provide a range of experiences, from the intimate and private through to an easy communality. In short, this is a house that is highly sustainable in so many ways, from the 'green' to the personal and familial.

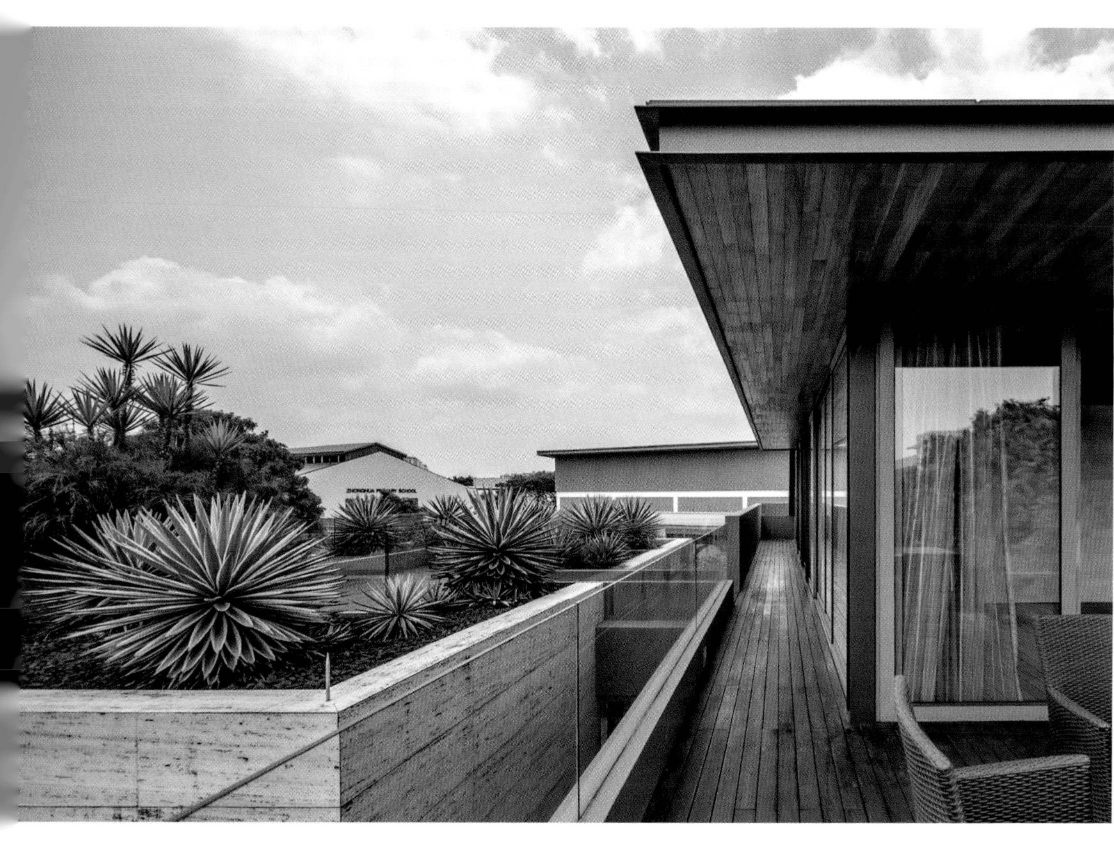

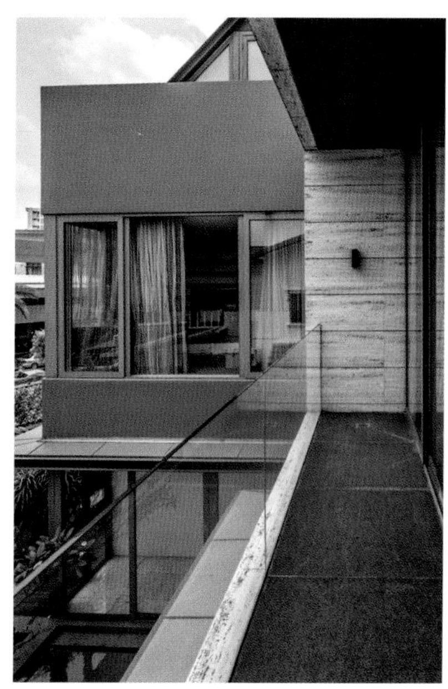

Above The roof garden of the attic area above the master bedroom.

Above right The attic has a number of multi-functional rooms, including a guest bedroom.

Right Entry to the master bedroom is across a glass-enclosed bridge.

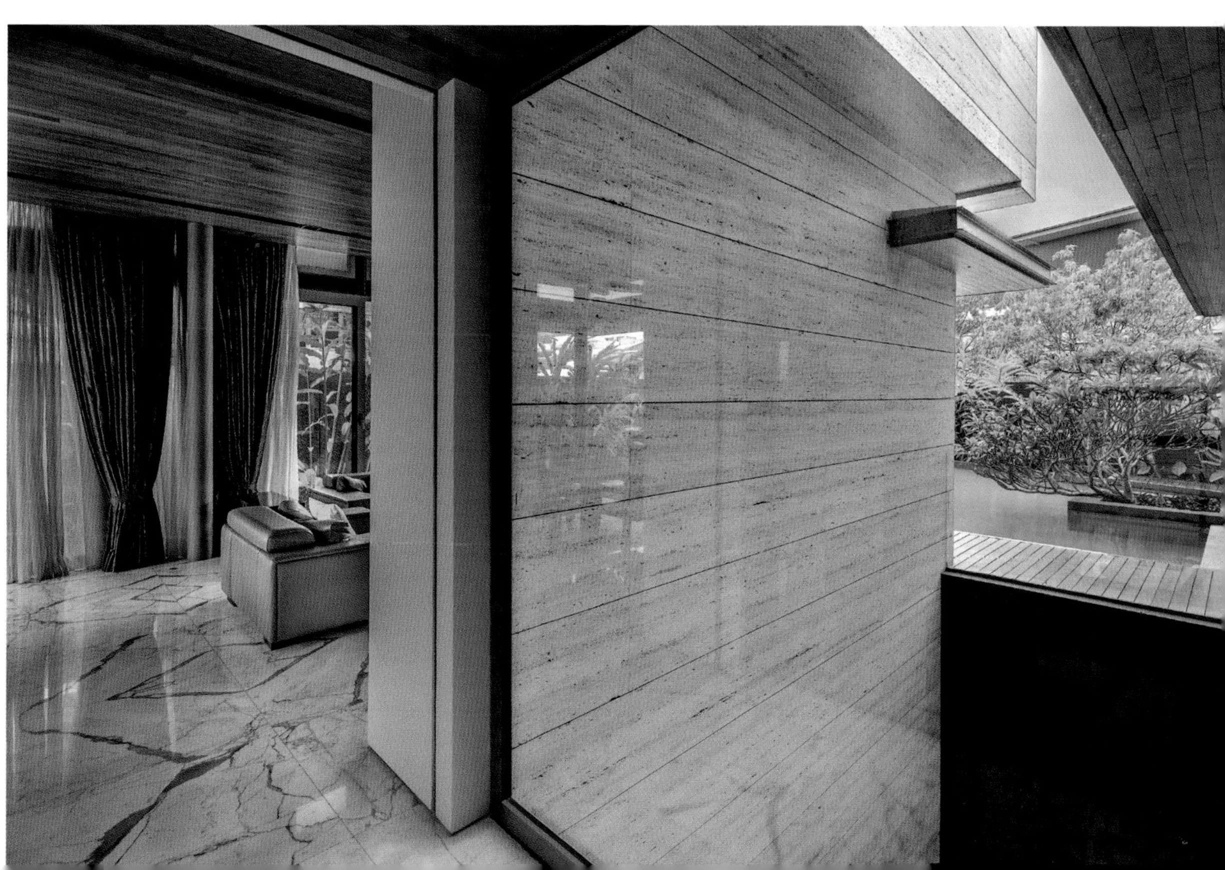

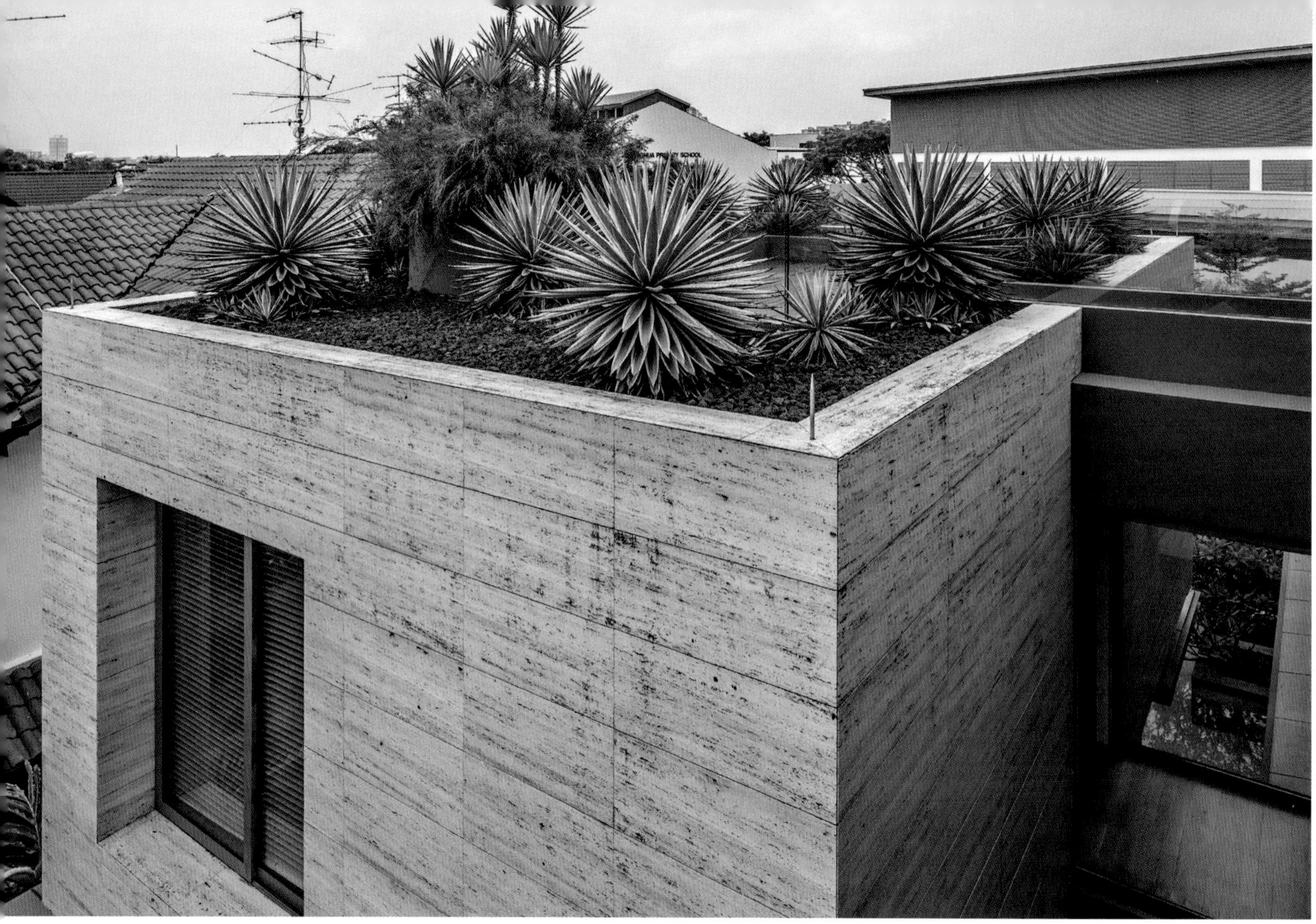

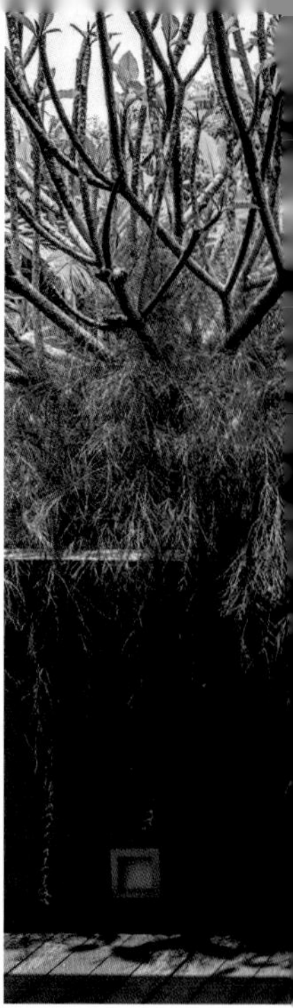

Above The rooftop garden helps to naturally cool the master bedroom below it.

Below The master bedroom.

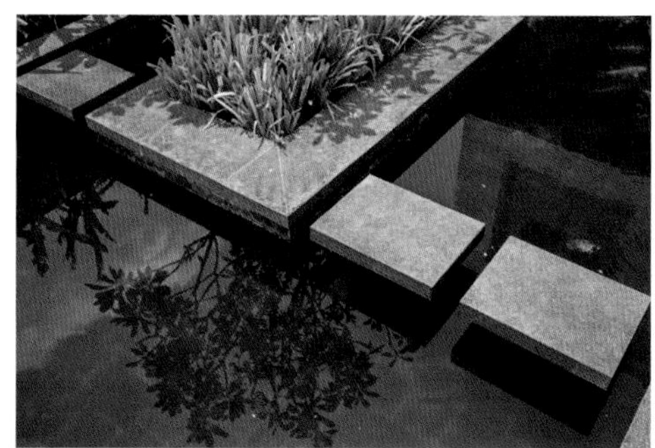

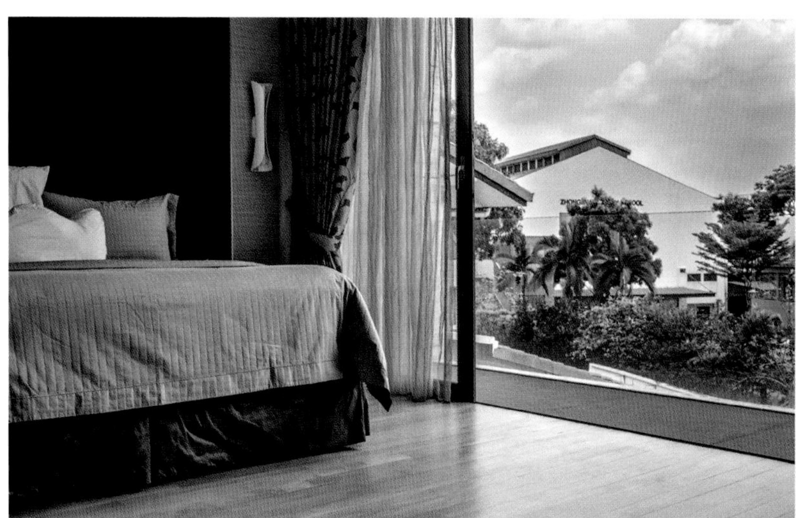

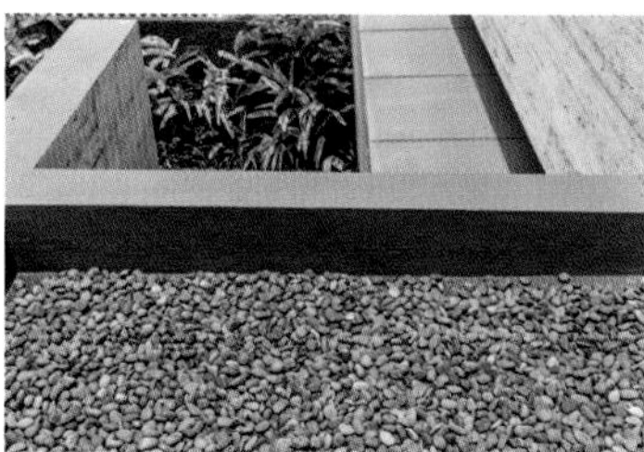

Above Floating pavers across the koi pond.

Left The green voids draw light into the whole house, especially to the basement.

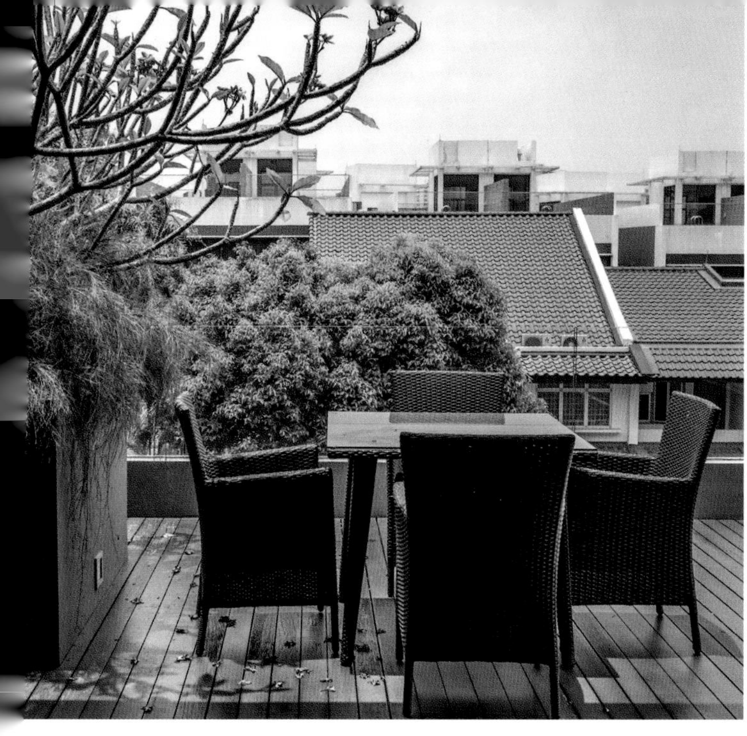

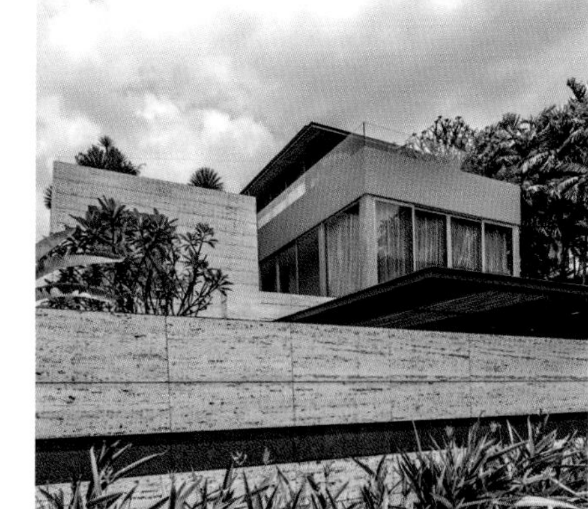

Left An outdoor sitting area in the attic.

Right The extended travertine street wall begins a series of layers of travertine, setting up a juxtaposition of solid and transparent.

Below Seen from the street, the house presents as an assembly of solid blocks, voids and garden spaces.

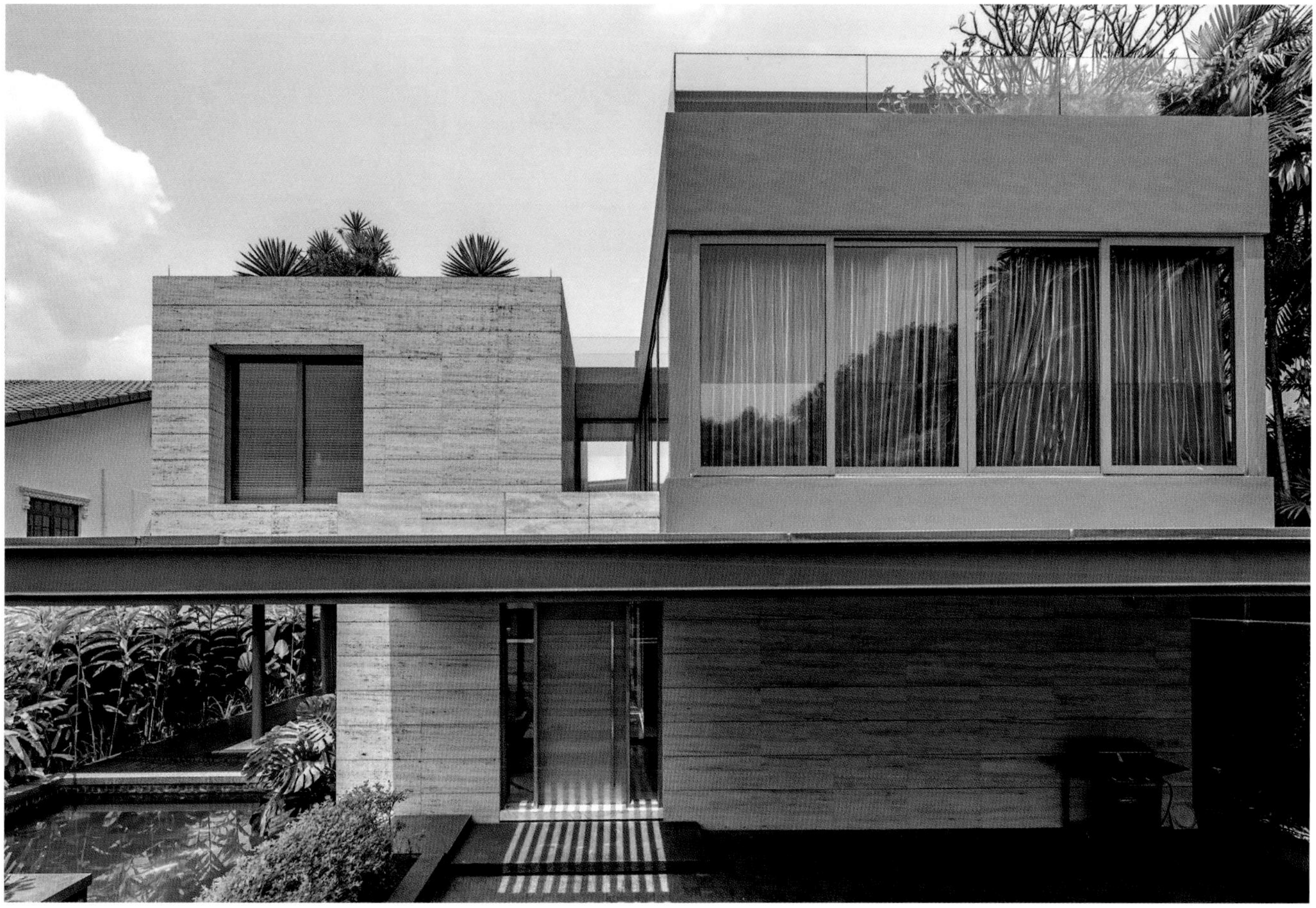

BARNSTORM HOUSE

'We wanted at least a double ceiling and a big entertaining area, preferably all in one—kitchen, dining room, nice open space to the garden—but we had no idea he would come up with this. Also amazing is the shutter idea, the roller blinds, which is why it is called the Barnstorm House—there are no walls.'—OWNER

This is a house that is highly distinctive and very welcoming, but without in any way imposing itself on the neigbourhood. In fact, it lends character to its immediate context and has won the approval of its surrounding neighbours. In other words, it is a 'good neighbour'.

Despite the cathedral-like space of the open living, dining and cooking area, which is its most immediately noticeable feature, this house is actually very restrained—in the way it presents to the street, in terms of its size (1000 square metres), in the materials it uses and in the way it does not 'take over' the site. An existing stand of trees was left untouched, and to an important extent the house responds to those trees, embracing them as part of the experience. Effectively, from the street, the house 'dematerializes', its structure blending into its context.

Indeed, the client points out that the choice of materials (bricks, plywood, iron instead of stainless steel, no expensive custom-made kitchen joinery, a concrete island for the outdoor dry kitchen bench, just some parquetry in the bedrooms and bricks instead of tiling for the living/dining floor) brought the building costs in at roughly 30–40 per cent less than houses of comparable size.

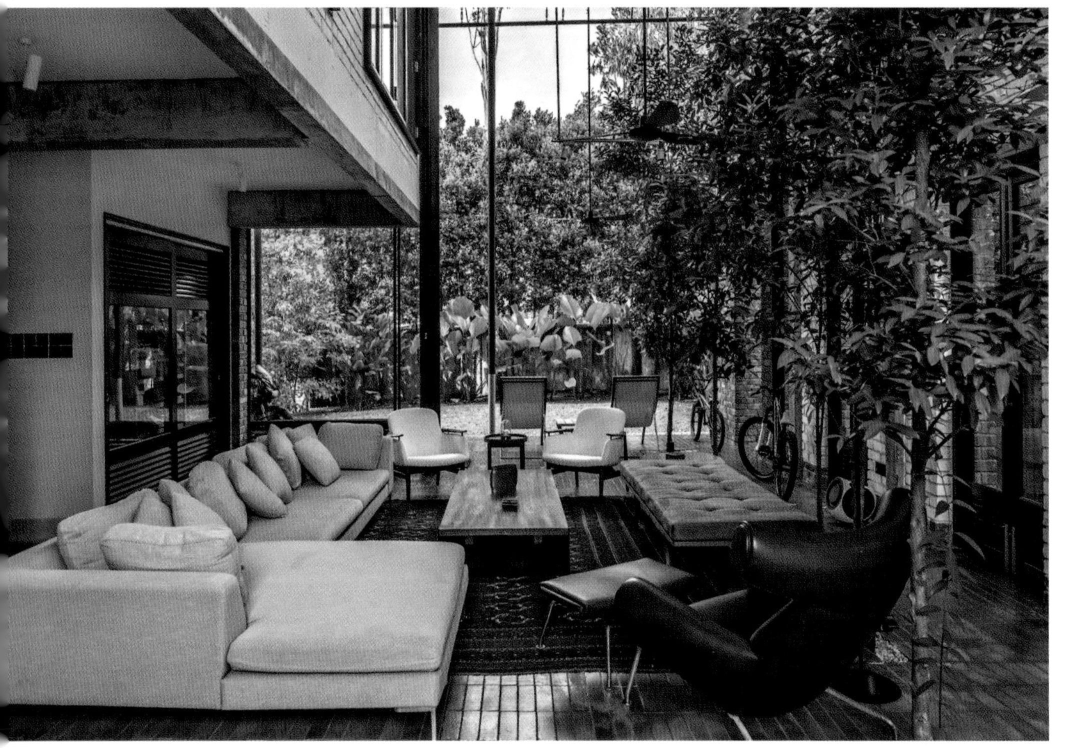

Indeed, the trees, the burnt brick outer wall of the 'barn', the greenery inside the barn space, the through view, the transparency of the main house and the doors and fenestration, which suggest a long-established vernacular house, all combine to create a 'lived in' feel, the sense of a house well settled into its place, almost an organic part of that place.

The suggestion of a barn is clear enough in the large, open volume and its high-pitched tiled roof and skylight. It is less a room than a space with a roof. The barnstorm idea, however, is slightly more subtle, referring as it does to the colloquial American term of informal political campaigns and theatrical performances that would swing through rural areas using barns as impromptu venues. The idea here is that this is a space for entertaining and where cooking and dining have their own theatricality. Attention is drawn discreetly to this from the street in what the architect refers to as 'the act of being somewhat invited to *see* and of being *seen*, albeit tactfully and within the limits of appropriateness'.

The barn is largely open. A roller shutter system gives protection when needed from the rain and folding customized doors can be opened for greater air circulation. A green jasmine trellis screens the neighbours at the back, while at the rear of the main house where the wet kitchen is, an operable corrugated roofing system can be opened to generate more light and air.

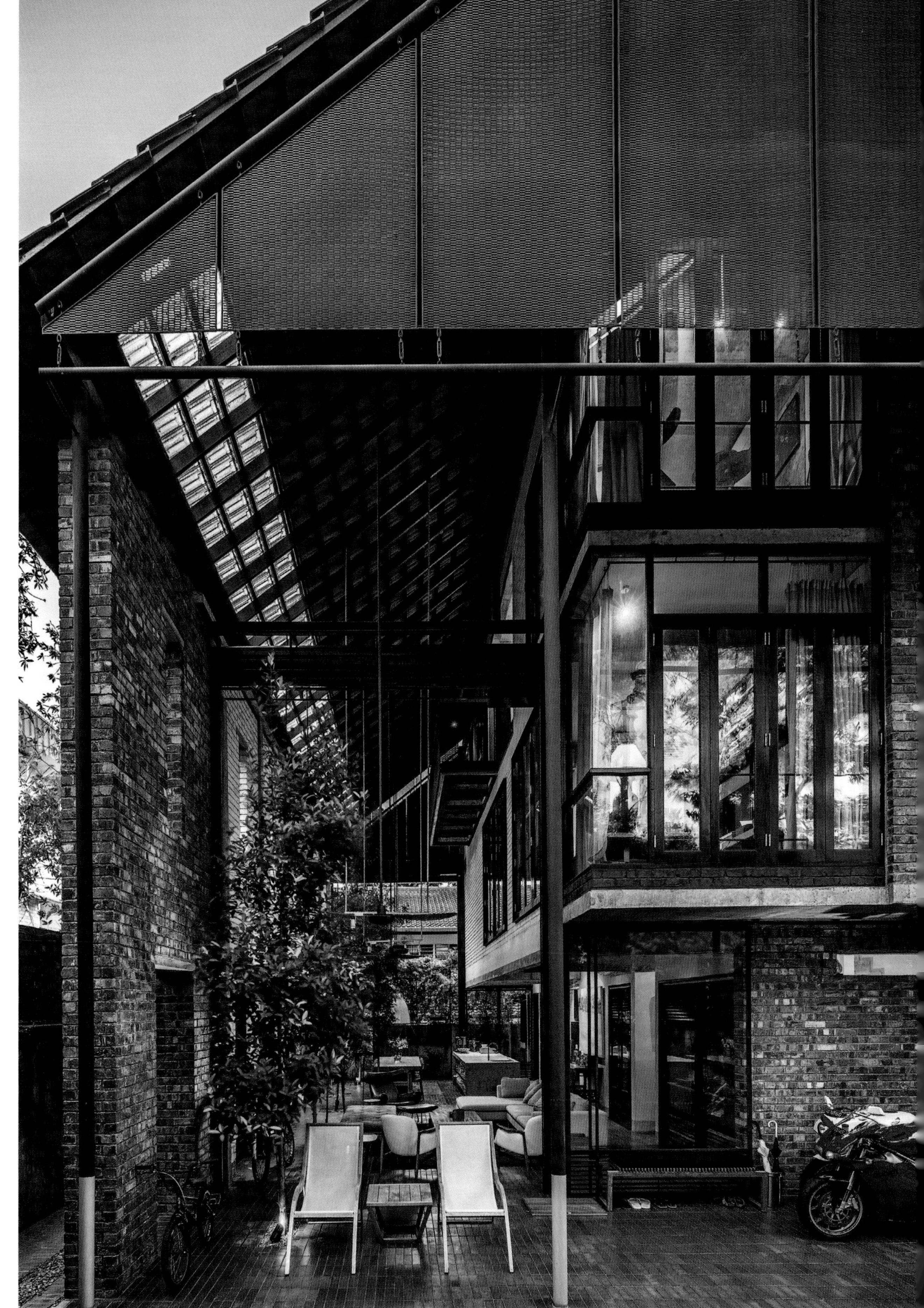

Opposite The outdoor living/dining area looks towards the street.

Right The living/dining space is a grand space, rich in materiality, with a barn-like quality that gives the house its name.

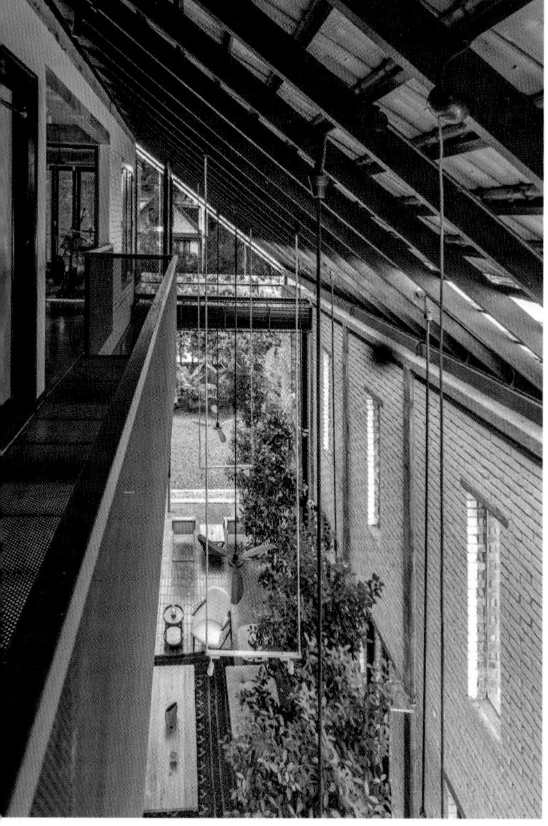

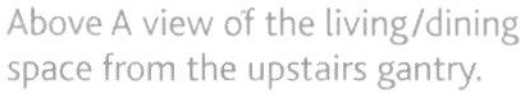

Above A view of the living/dining space from the upstairs gantry.

Right The living/dining area has a dry kitchen, which is a part of the space and its theatre.

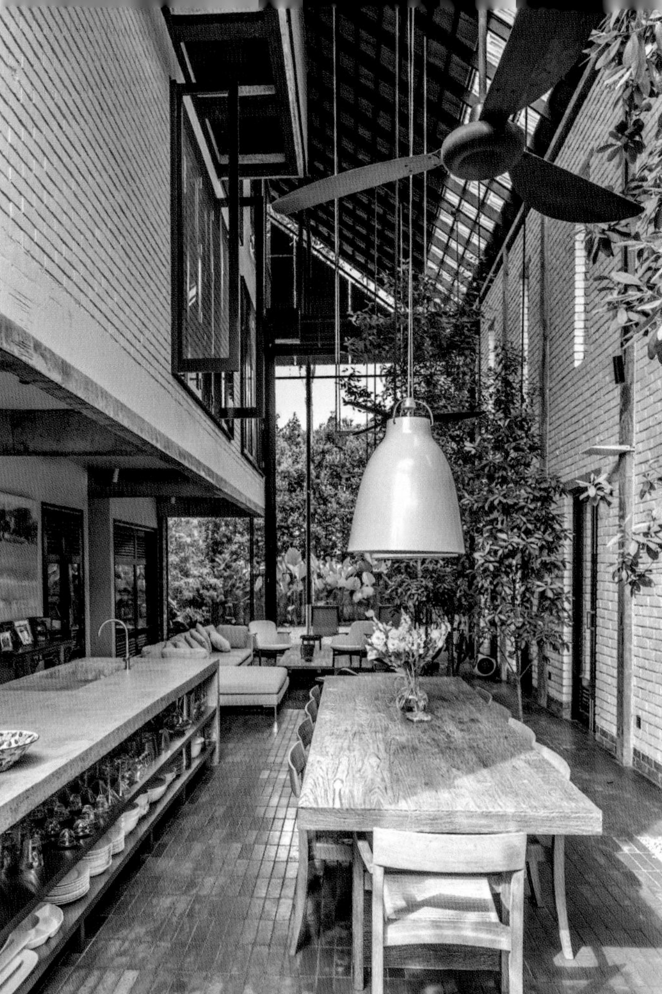

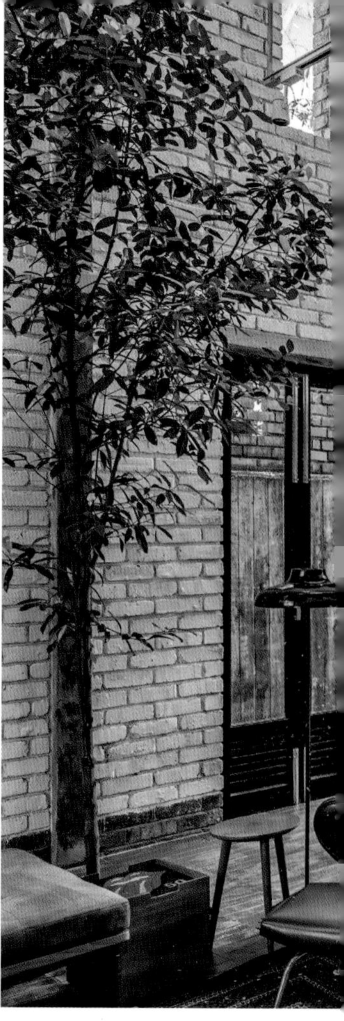

Right The burnt brick outer wall takes on an edge of sophistication by the use of black window frames.

Far right The concrete island bench is an example of the use of simple, even industrial, materials.

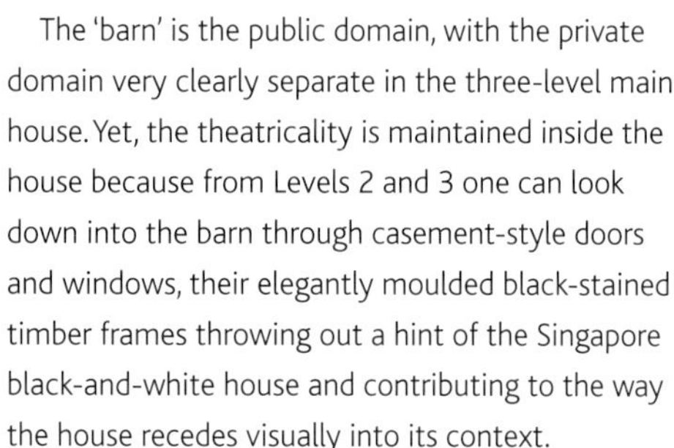

The 'barn' is the public domain, with the private domain very clearly separate in the three-level main house. Yet, the theatricality is maintained inside the house because from Levels 2 and 3 one can look down into the barn through casement-style doors and windows, their elegantly moulded black-stained timber frames throwing out a hint of the Singapore black-and-white house and contributing to the way the house recedes visually into its context.

This is a house which is as big as it needs to be. Rich in nooks and crannies and intriguing little journeys, it provides all the rooms and amenities initially requested as well as high levels of intimacy.

Level 2 includes the laundry, TV sitting room and master bedroom (with its 120-year-old carved timber bed from Solo in Indonesia) and attached bathroom (with a customized concrete 'Roman' bath set into the floor). Level 3 features bedrooms, linked by a steel gantry, for two sons, a music room and a small TV room. The bedrooms draw in light from skylights and are cross-ventilated through their attached bathrooms, which are almost completely open. Overall, the house is ventilated by the barn. The owners report that they use very little electric light or air-conditioning.

This is a house that illustrates how sustainability is less about choice of individual materials or even strategies and more about an overarching ecological approach. The choice of simple materials—in fact, the very simplicity of the key idea of the barn—has meant a house that is restrained in what it consumes. It is also restrained in the way it co-exists with its neighbours and with the existing site. It is restrained in its need for artificial lighting and cooling. And it is highly sustainable at the personal and social level.

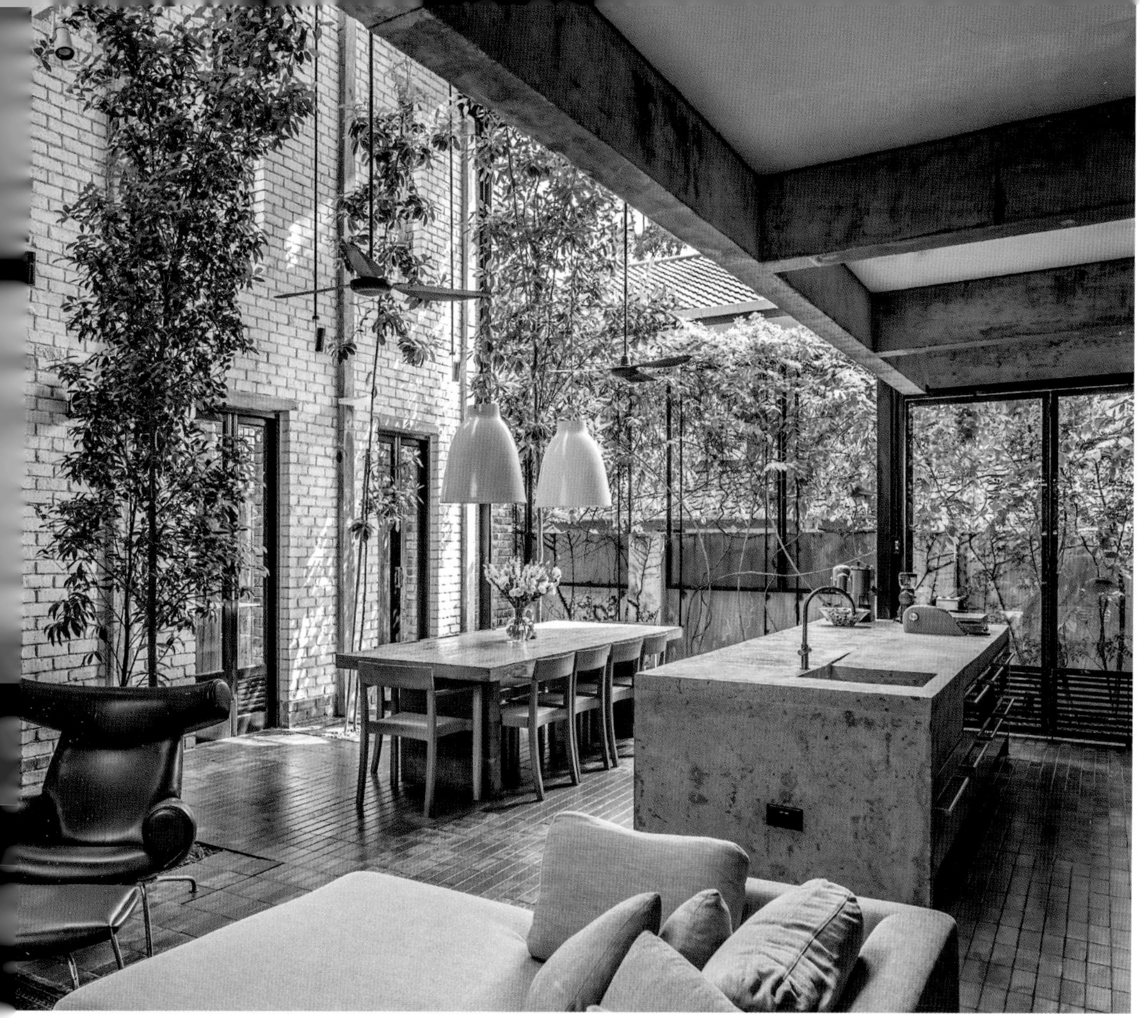

Left Connection with the outside is emphasized by bringing trees into the space.

Below The 'barn' space combines formal settings with informality.

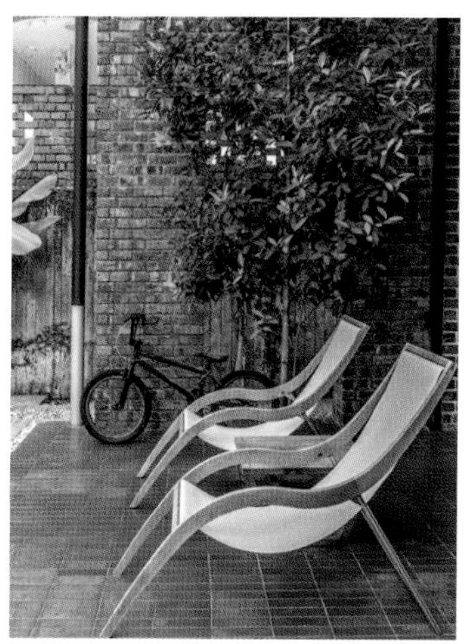

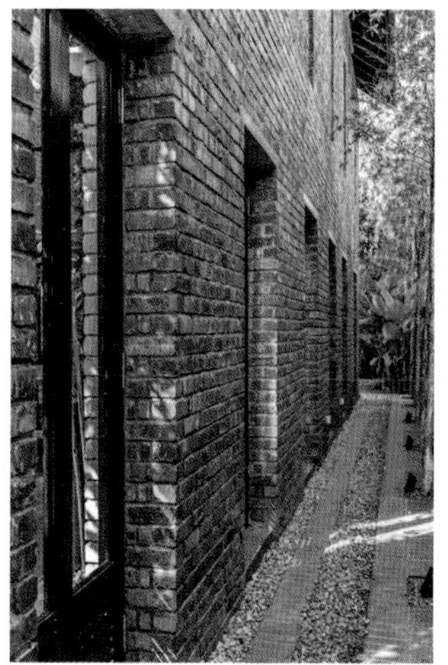

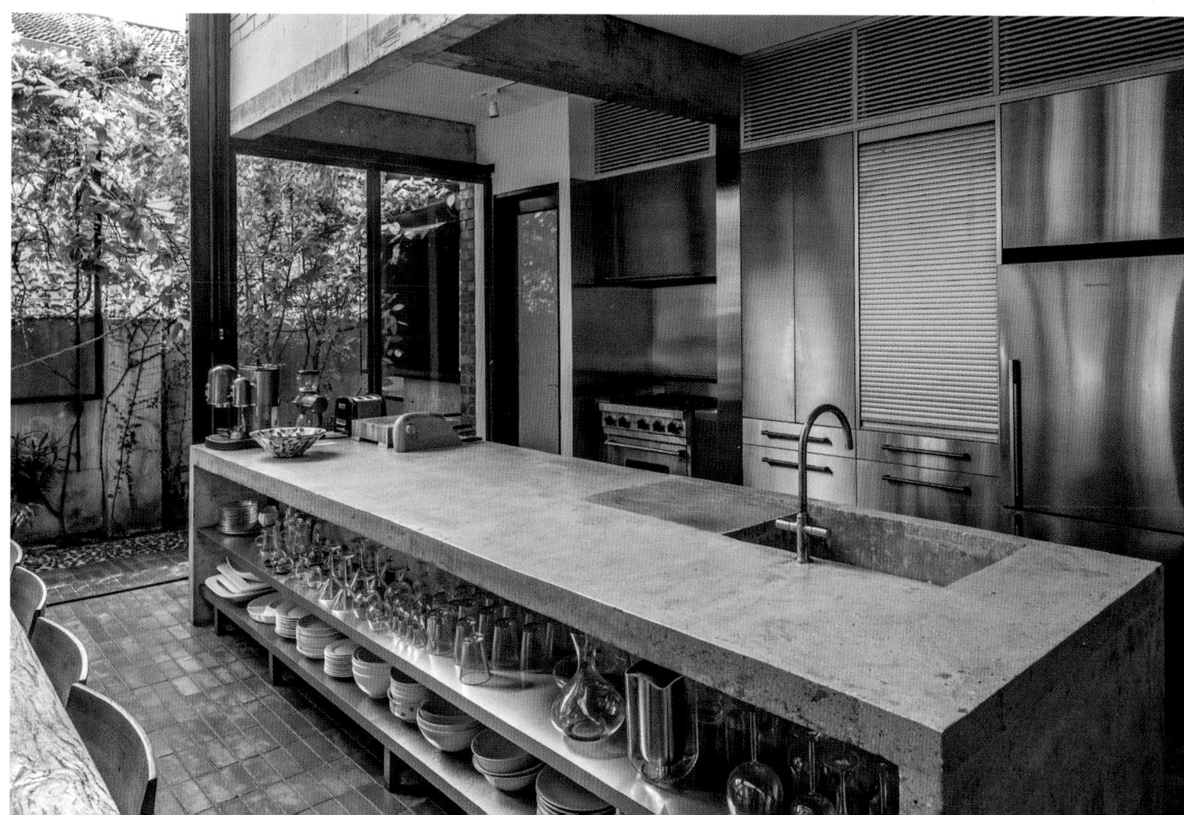

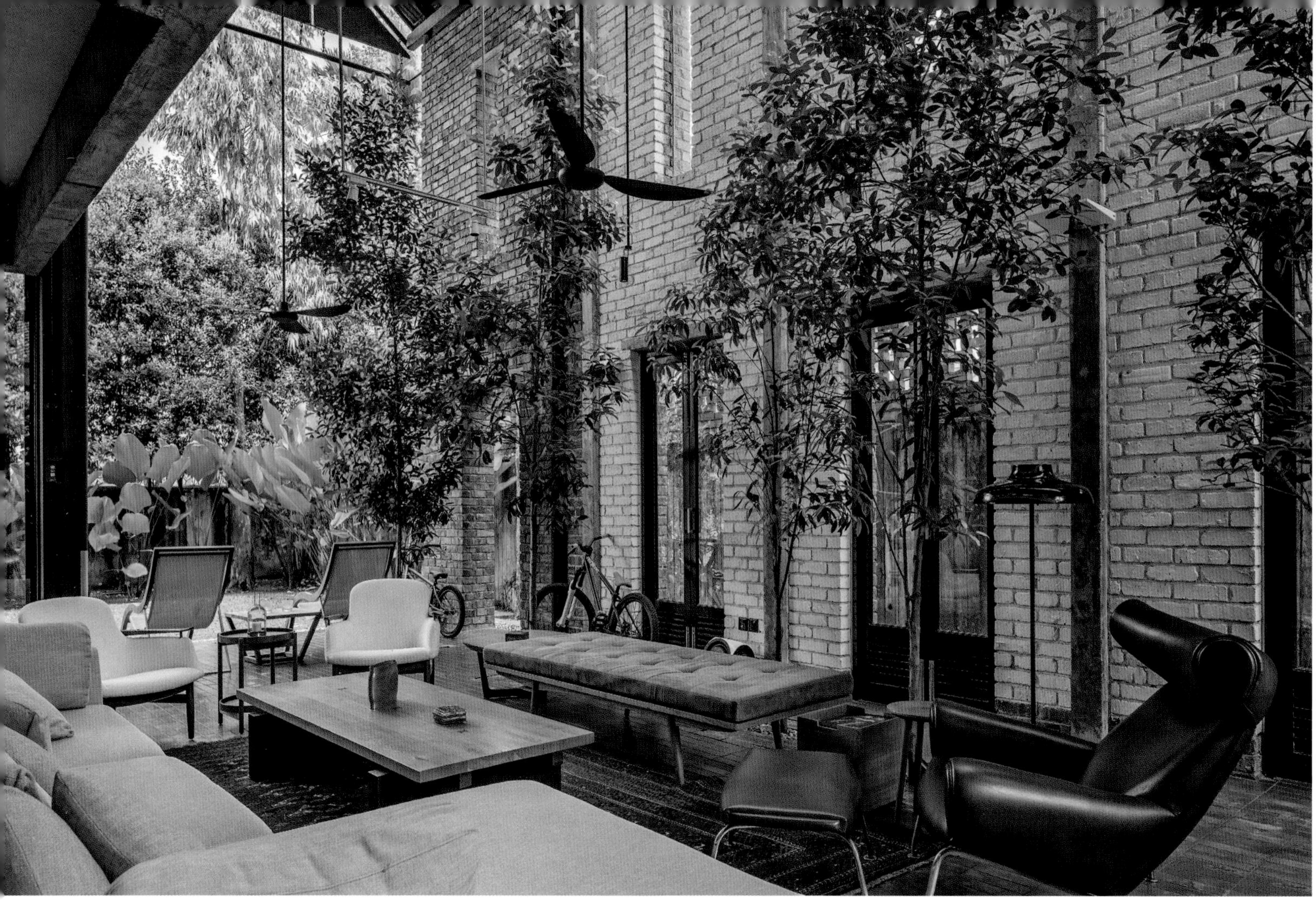

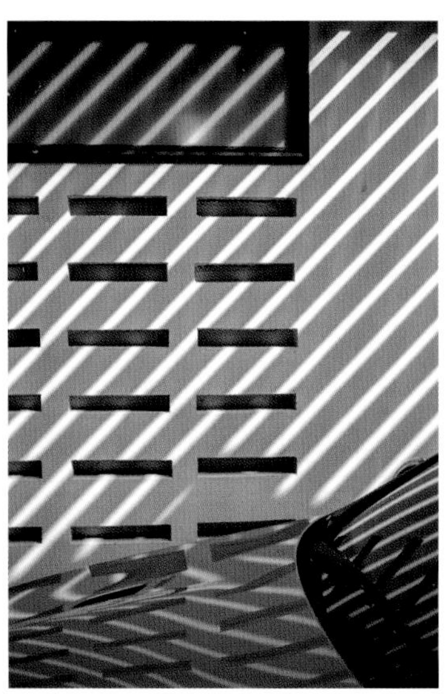

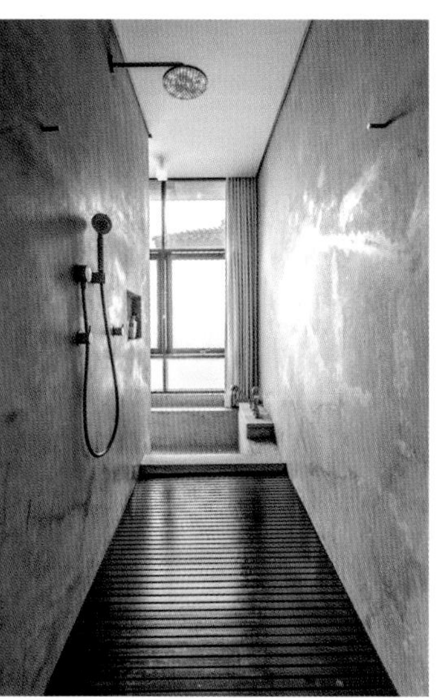

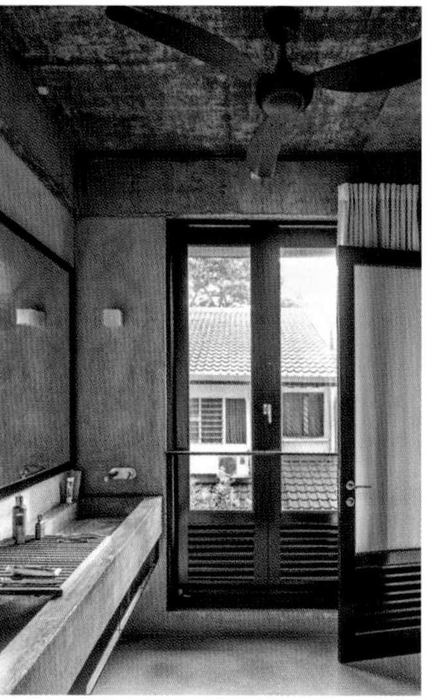

Above Looking towards the street, the outdoor living room has surprising privacy because of the stand of mature existing trees in front.

From far left Natural light is drawn in through many sources, often indirectly, generating delicate shadow patterns. The shower stall in the master bathroom (centre) as well as the rest of the master bathroom (right) achieve elegance through simple materials and overall restraint.

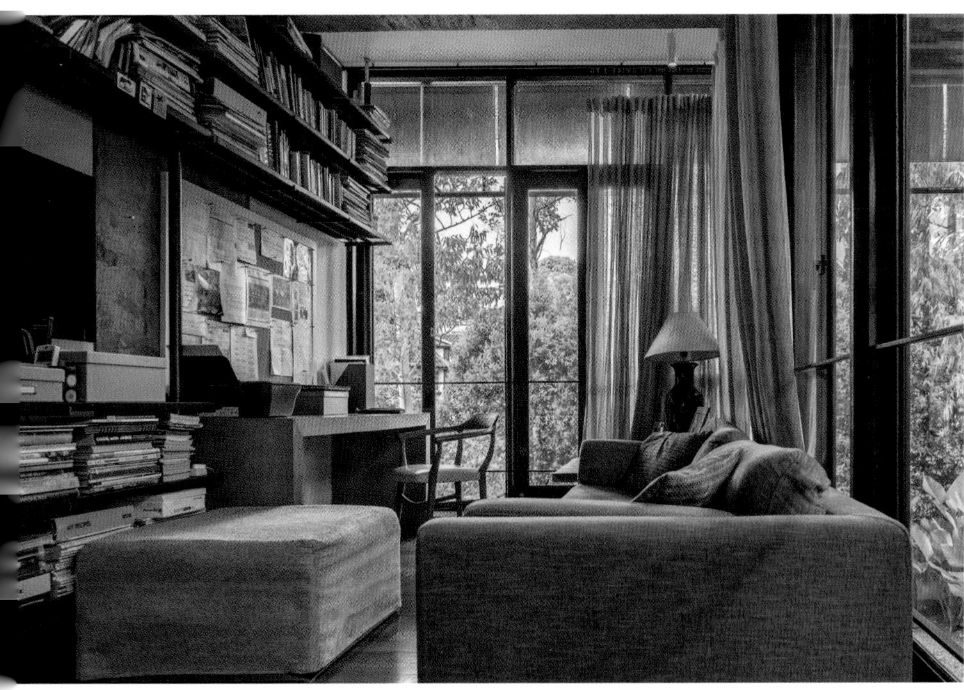

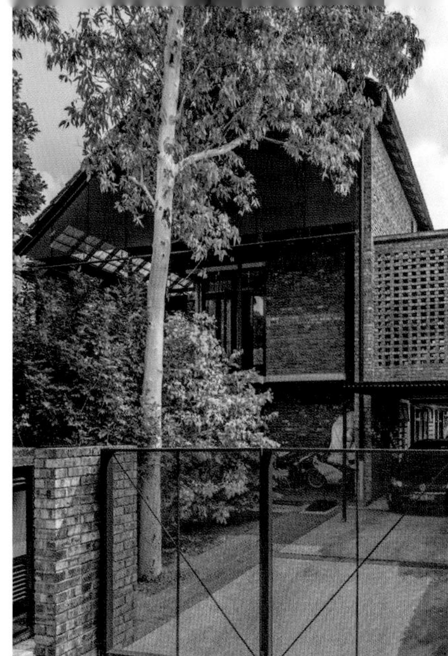

Above From the street the house presents as an intriguing puzzle.

Left The home office, glazed on two sides, is on the second storey.

Below Windows and trees emphasize the barn's verticality.

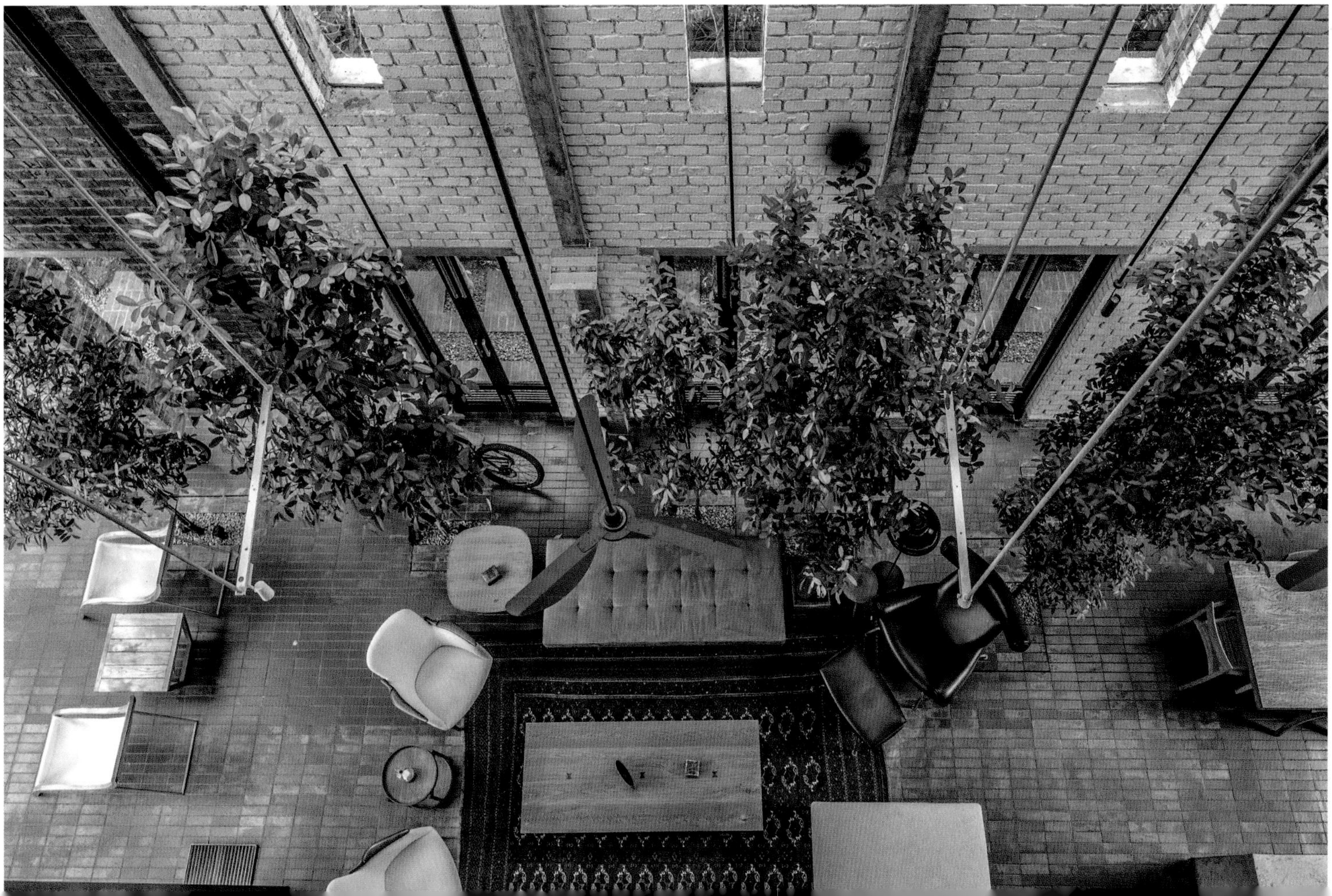

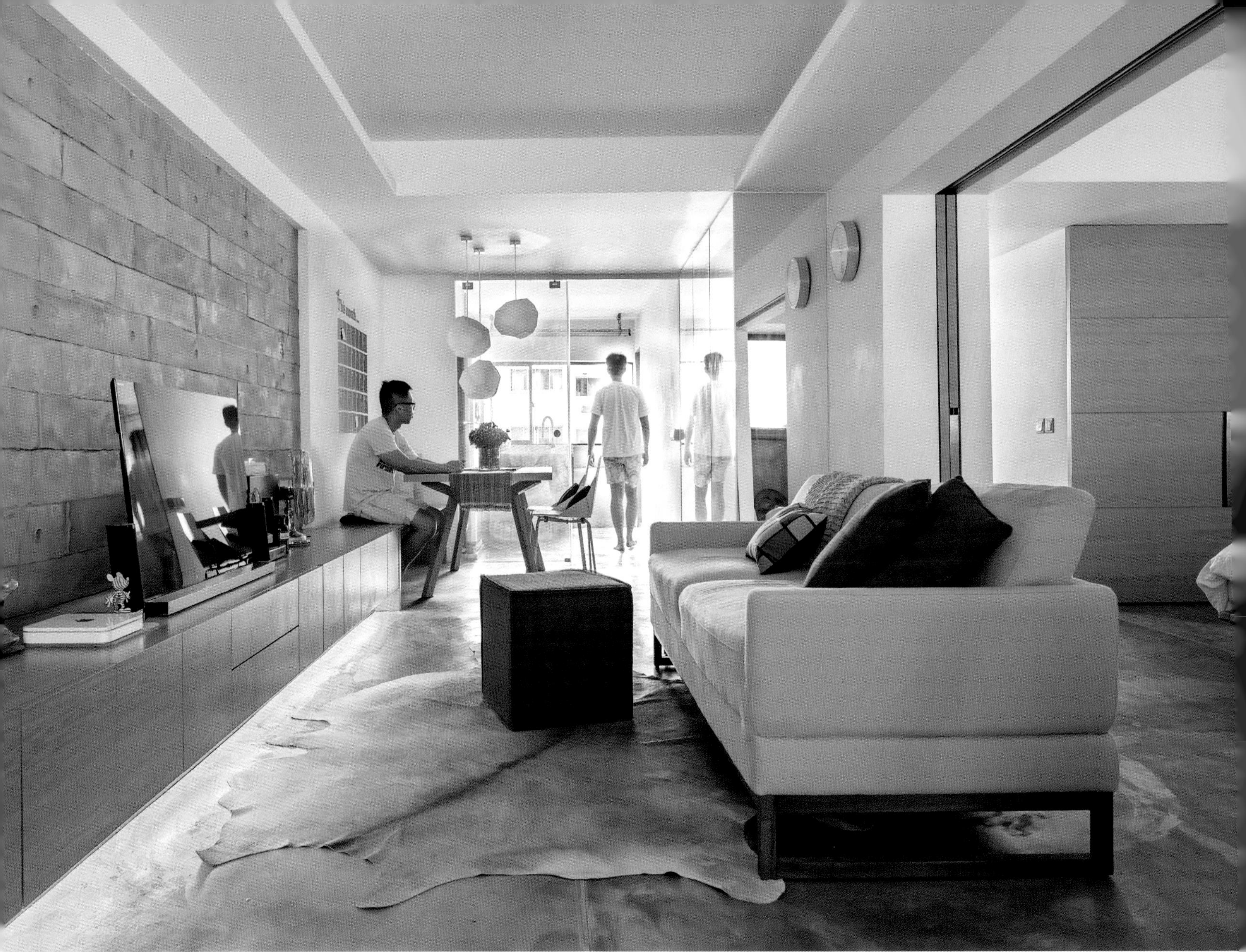

DAKOTA APARTMENT
JONATHAN POH

'What most buyers of second-hand properties like to do is buy a flat like this because of its versatility. Many of the walls are non-structural and so a lot of the younger generation buy this kind of flat in order to renovate it. This is what I did here.'—JONATHAN POH, ARCHITECT

Above The sliding doors of the bedroom can be opened up to create one single space.

Above right This HDB apartment block is slightly different from others in that it is angled, creating cross-views and a greater sense of community.

Right The living space looking towards the entry now enjoys much higher levels of natural light.

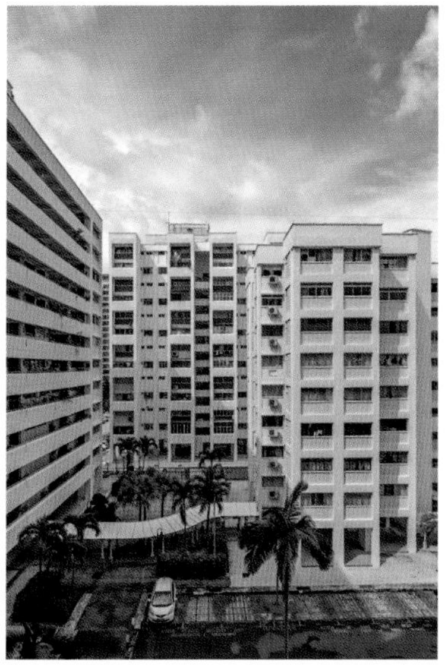

The high-rise towers of the Housing Development Board (HDB) public housing are symbols of modern Singapore. On the one hand, they represent the government's commitment to provide a roof over every Singaporean's head. On the other, their brutal matter of factness expresses the utilitarianism so often associated with the island state. Ironically, this mass public housing is increasingly contrasted with the much earlier example of the pre-war Tiong Bahru Estate (initiated by the HDB's colonial predecessor, the Singapore Improvement Trust) with its low-rise organic buildings that mixed European Art Deco urbanism with the local urbanism of shophouse architecture at street level, making for an aesthetically pleasing, livable and textured neighbourhood with a genuine sense of community.

Time not only generates nostalgia but creates new economic imperatives. With the cost of housing rising continually, HDB apartments, while themselves also constantly appreciating in value, are significantly more affordable than condominiums. Condominiums will always face outwards, providing light, breeze and views, whereas the typical HDB apartment is a gun barrel configuration: dark, stuffy and claustrophobic. Happily, HDB apartments are now enjoying a second lease on life and offering an alternative to the highly unsustainable option of demolition and rebuild.

Housing affordability, compounded by the shortage of affordable land, is now a major issue in Singapore and fuelling a hot property market that the government is currently trying to cool. In

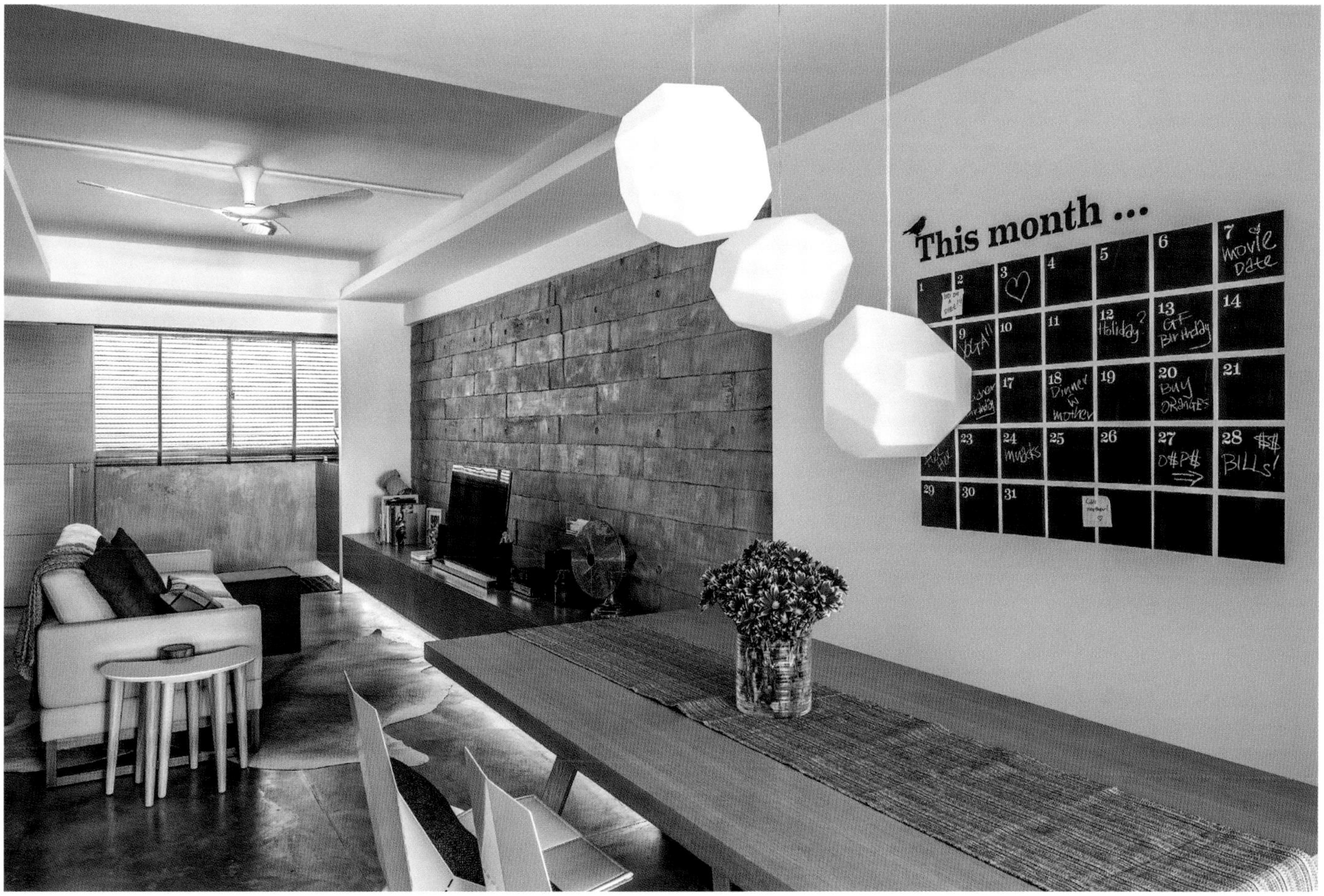

Below The bedroom, like the living space, uses hidden lighting to generate a soft, all-over light in the apartment.

Bottom A view from the bedroom to the living room where subtle detailing creates a sophisticated feel.

Right The home office in the bedroom is a clever optimizing of space and can be closed off.

Far right Plan.

Opposite below Warm timber detailing softens what was previously a harshly functional space.

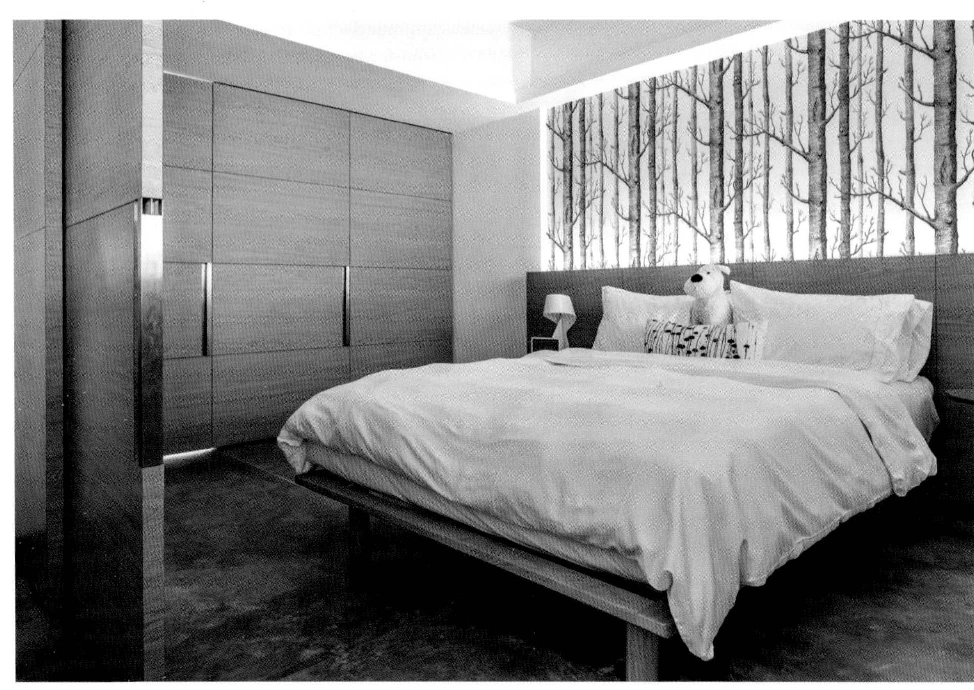

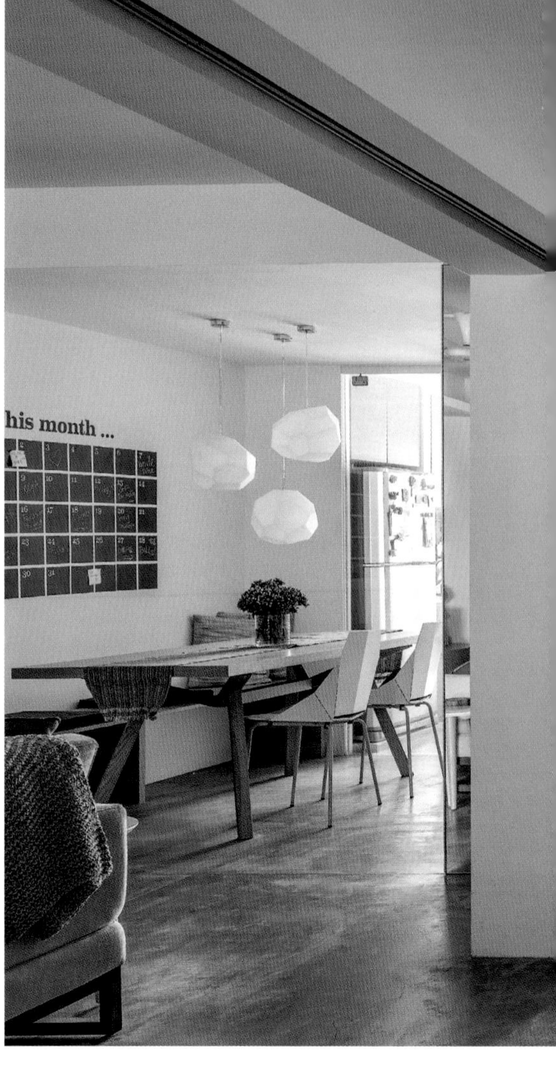

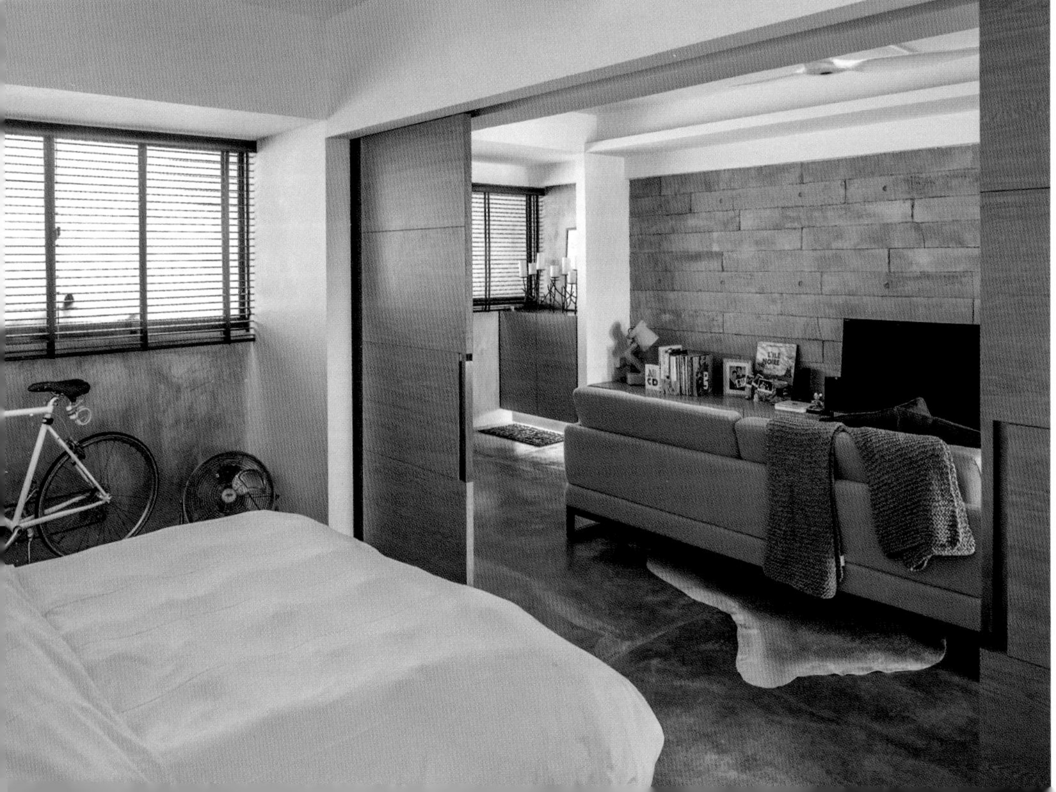

Singapore, as elsewhere in the world, the people most affected are those trying to enter the property market for the first time—and this despite the long-standing government policy in Singapore of ensuring that everyone has a roof over their head. As architect Jonathan Poh comments: 'The government actually gives us this privilege of having this nest as our apartment.'

There is now a secondary market for HDB apartments because they are increasingly sought after by a younger cohort. One reason is that they represent an investment, although not so much for their rentable potential, since this implies another property to live in. A more important reason is that they are affordable. This is supported by a growing sentimental value as the island state approaches its fiftieth birthday. These once despised 'brutalist' buildings have begun to embody a cultural

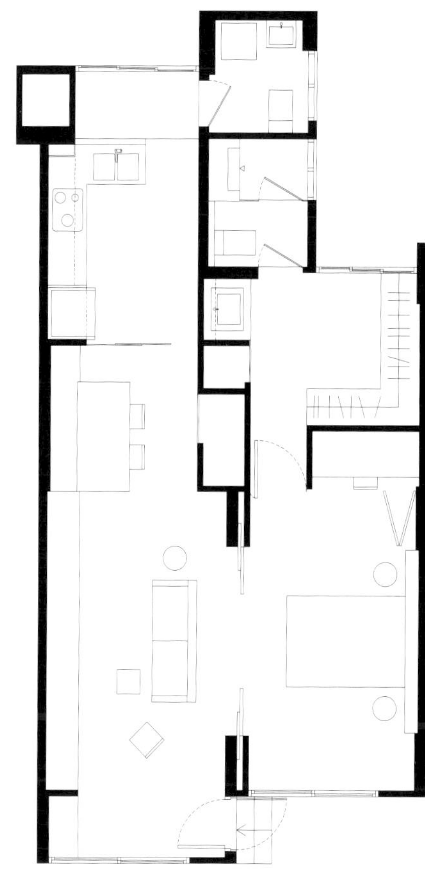

history that Singapore has largely lacked until now, but for which there is a growing hunger.

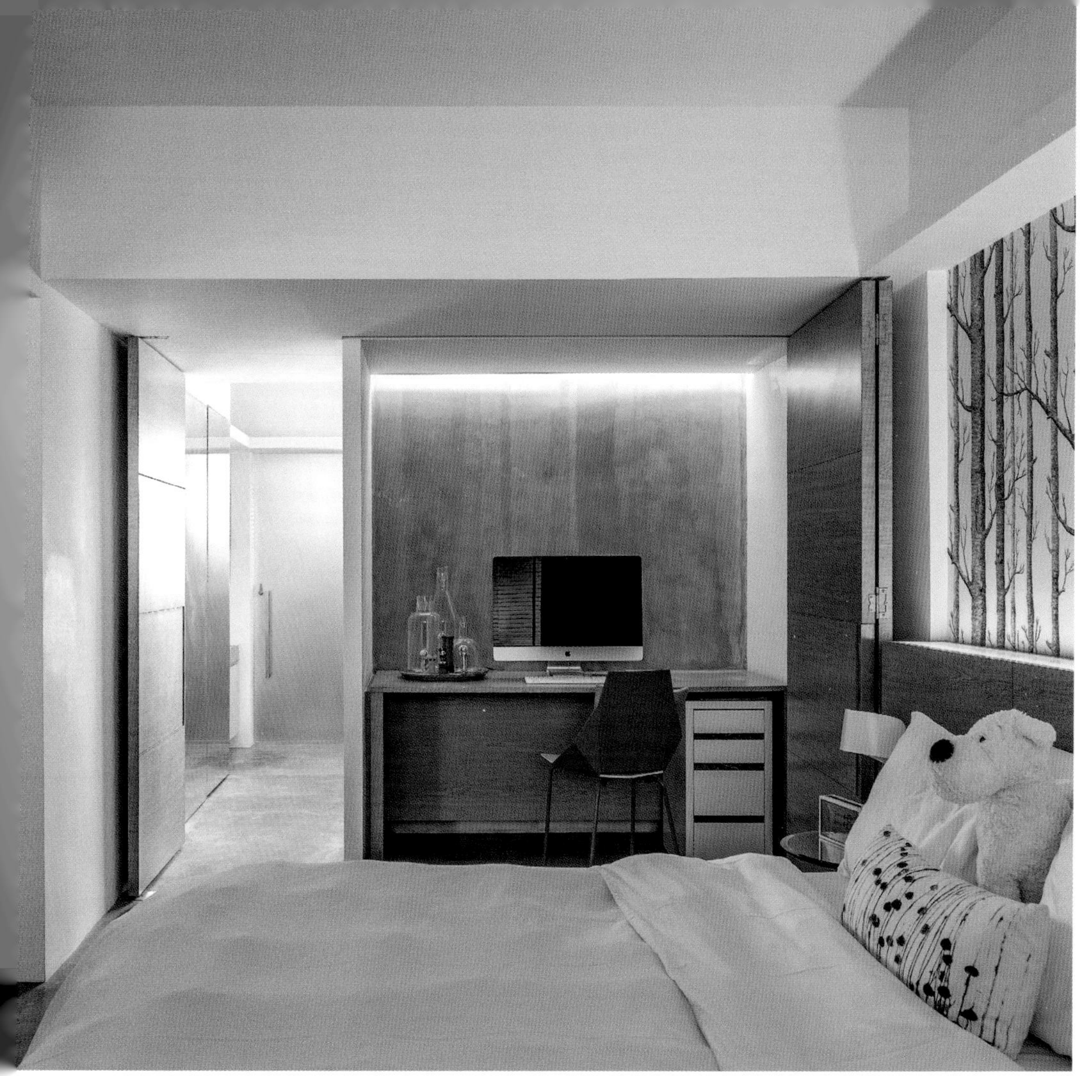

This late 1970s apartment complex is in the Dakota district of Singapore, which includes raffish Geylang and upmarket Katong. It is near an MRT station, which made the location attractive to Poh and his partner. But the building, like any HDB apartment, brings with it issues of privacy, especially in this development which is angled, unlike the more typical rectangular 'slab' blocks, so that there are cross-views added to the typical long, open corridors. The 67-square metre apartment previously housed a three-generation family in two enclosed bedrooms, a living room, kitchen, store room, laundry and two bathrooms—one really just a powder room.

Poh bought the apartment with the aim of reconfiguring and refitting it for a contemporary

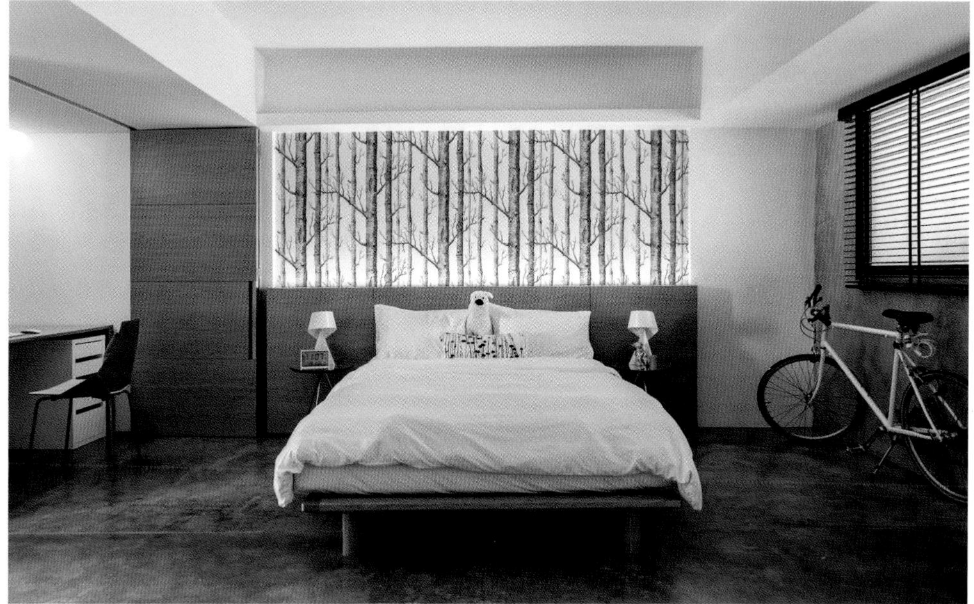

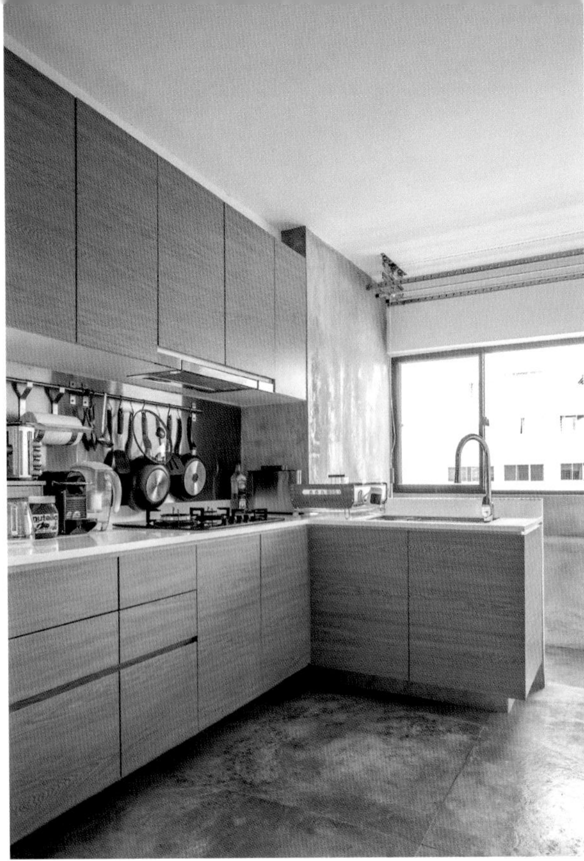

lifestyle. The result, he says, 'is adequate for two people—one more would tip the scales'.

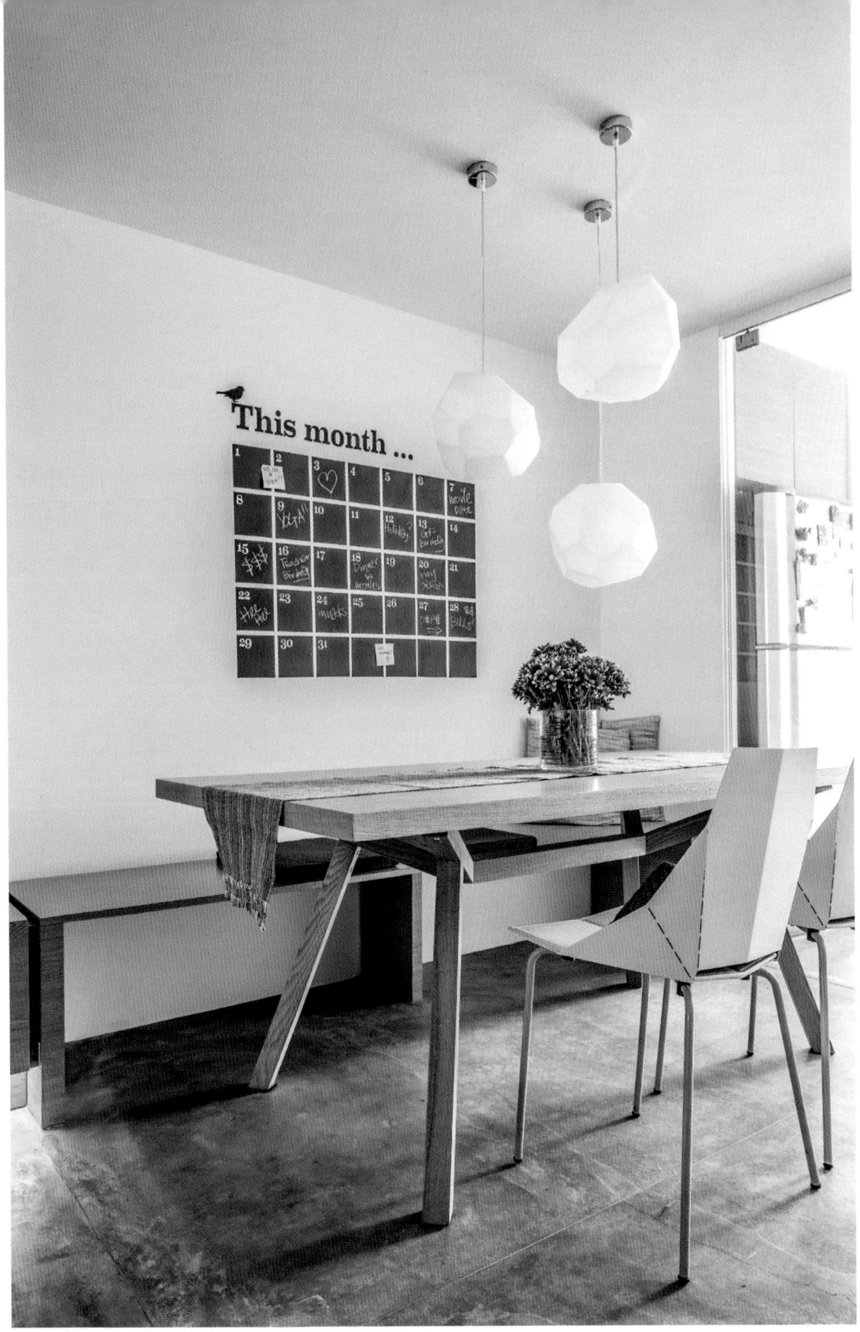

The key to the transformation lay in the non-structural walls. Poh removed most of these to create an open plan, a long, sleek and light-filled single space. The bedroom and living room are now connected but can be closed off when necessary by oak laminate sliding doors. Similarly, a small home office off the bedroom can be hidden by sliding panels. A modern kitchen has been installed, which can also be closed off from the living/dining area by a sliding glass door, keeping the cooking smells out but allowing light in. This space also includes a washing machine and dryer and the renovated powder room.

Typical of a younger lifestyle, Poh and his partner eat out most of the time. Hence, the kitchen is smaller than the original, allowing more space for a separate dining area. The original division of the apartment into two sections has been retained to a certain extent because storage joinery separates the dining and kitchen spaces from the second bedroom (used as a walk-in wardrobe) and the main bathroom and toilet. An HDB apartment typically combines shower, toilet and wash basin but Poh was able to create two areas connected by a clear glass door, separating toilet and shower from wash basin and vanity. He has also given this wet area a modern aesthetic by hiding the pipes, typically left exposed, using refined finishes (mosaic tiles, polished concrete and white render) and hidden slot lighting. Indeed, apart from a pendant light over the dining table, most of the lighting in the apartment is concealed, contributing to its clean, open and spacious feel.

Above left The kitchen is remarkably spacious and can be closed off from the dining room by a sliding glass door.

Above The dining space is well lit by natural light streaming in through the kitchen.

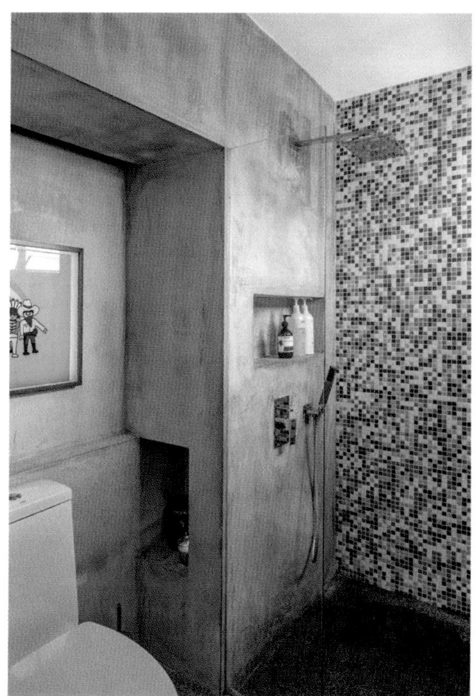

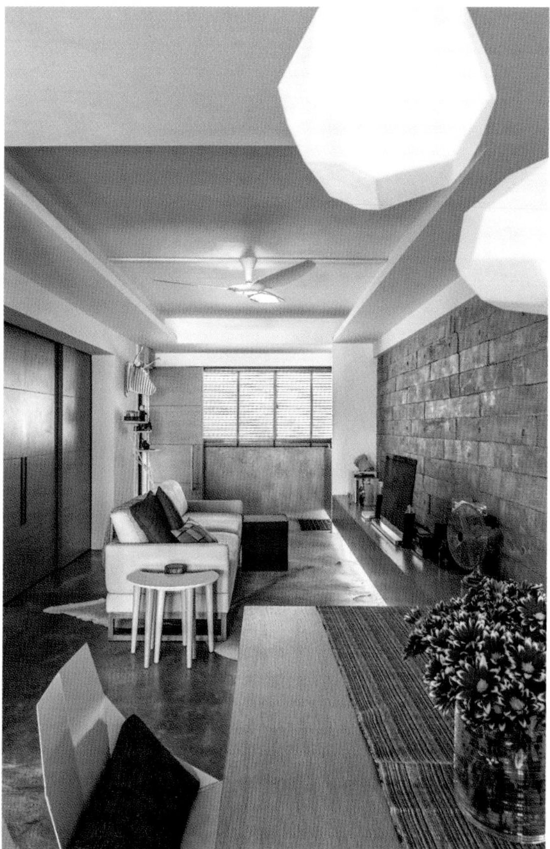

Far left The main bathroom has an industrial character, softened by the mosaic wall tiles and indirect lighting.

Left The extended single space mixes natural light with warm, indirect artificial light.

Below The hidden lighting underneath the credenza is less intrusive than direct lighting.

Privacy in the apartment remains an issue given the large number of people living in the whole complex, the cross-views and the volume of foot traffic along the corridors. This has been addressed by putting film over the windows and by installing a steel mesh front door, which offers visual privacy but allows significant through-ventilation, thus minimizing the need for air-conditioning. However, as Poh points out, while privacy can be compromised, there is also a sense of belonging to a community and thus he likens the building to a vertical kampong.

This apartment is an excellent example of how existing—and in the view of many, obsolete—HDB apartments can be 'recycled', obviating the need for demolition and rebuilding. New condominium apartments offer more light and are generally bigger but they are also more expensive and come with a standardized configuration offering less opportunity to personalize the apartment than a renovated HDB flat. Poh's exercise has shown how a typical HDB apartment can be reinvented for contemporary use and for new lifestyles, including by an environmentally more aware generation.

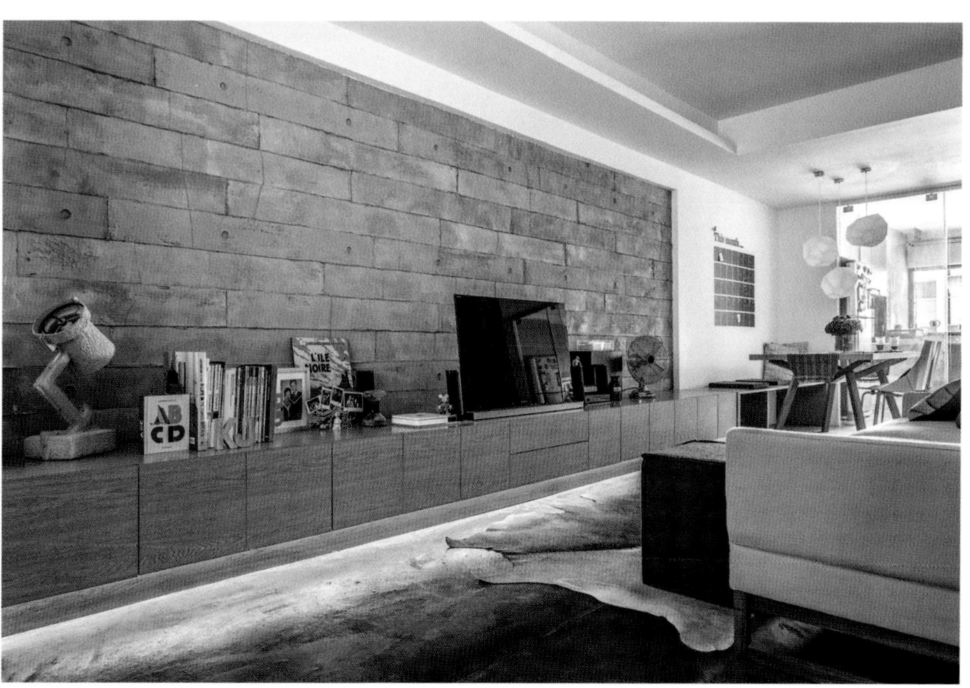

BAMBOO CURTAIN HOUSE
ECO:ID ARCHITECTS

'I don't use a lot of materials in my projects. I'm a modernist. I like to build the bones of a project with absolute clarity and simplicity and then add the tactile layers. The choices are also very logical.'—SIM BOON YANG, ARCHITECT

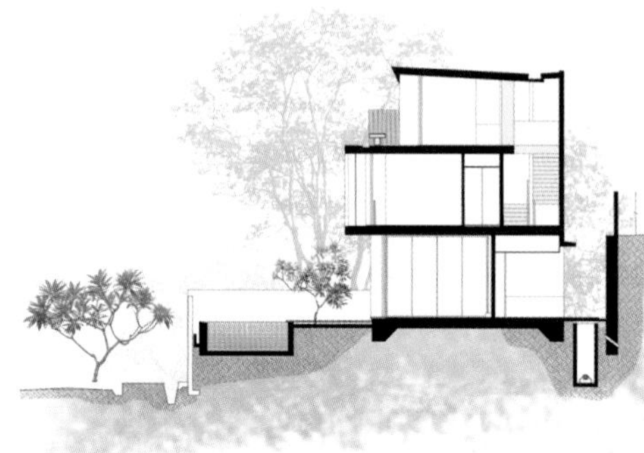

Above Short section.

Right Set on a rise, the house is raised above the level of the street by a concrete retaining wall, granting complete privacy to the first storey living/dining spaces.

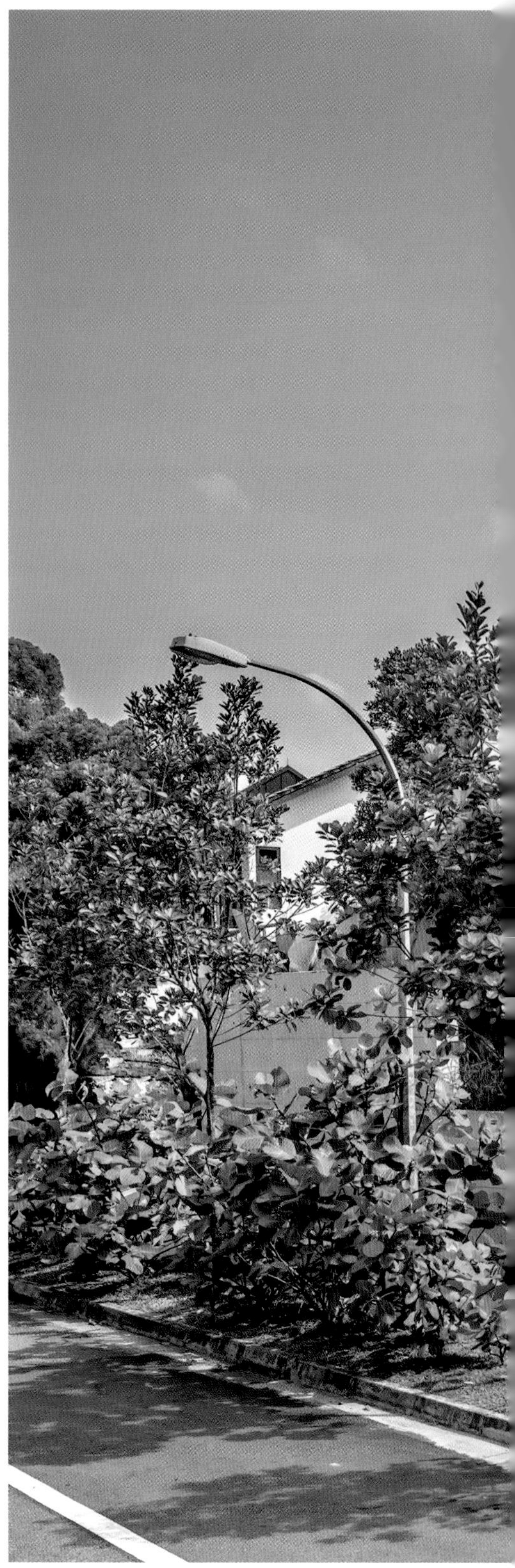

If any house is going to be sustainable, it will surely be an architect's own home. For those of us who are not architects, we can provide a brief to an architect, confident he will design a *house* for us that we can then set about turning into a home to sustain us and our family according to the way we choose to live. But an architect designing for himself is, from the outset, designing a *home* in which every detail will be an expression of what matters and what sustains him, professionally and personally. In addition, the house will almost certainly represent a kind of credo, an embodiment of the architect's architectural beliefs. Of course, the odds are there will also be quite a lot of experimentation—taking the opportunity to play with ideas that clients may not be willing to entertain.

All the above factors, along with a strong environmentally sustainable agenda, are true of this house designed by Sim Boon Yang, co-founder of eco:id Architects, for himself, his wife and their two sons. The house, however, is no prescriptive exercise. Its starting point is the site, which is in a green part of central Singapore and at the top of a rise where it captures not only panoramic views but also the surrounding greenery and any breezes that come its way.

The raised position of the house provides much of the privacy needed from the street, especially with the eventual maturity of the trees in front, which will provide a further screen. Hence, the fair-face concrete retaining wall, with the basement garage entry to one side and a garden bed on top running the length of the swimming pool, enables the first storey, with its terrace, living, dining and kitchen areas, to be completely transparent and the sliding floor-to-ceiling glass doors to be left open. A blade wall separates this area from the entry stairwell and landing leading up from the garage. Here, there is another kind of screen—a hanging bamboo curtain.

This bamboo curtain gives the house its name—and its distinctive façade—and is repeated on the second storey where it screens three bedrooms but not the master bedroom, which has a glass wall with an extruded frame set back beneath the extended

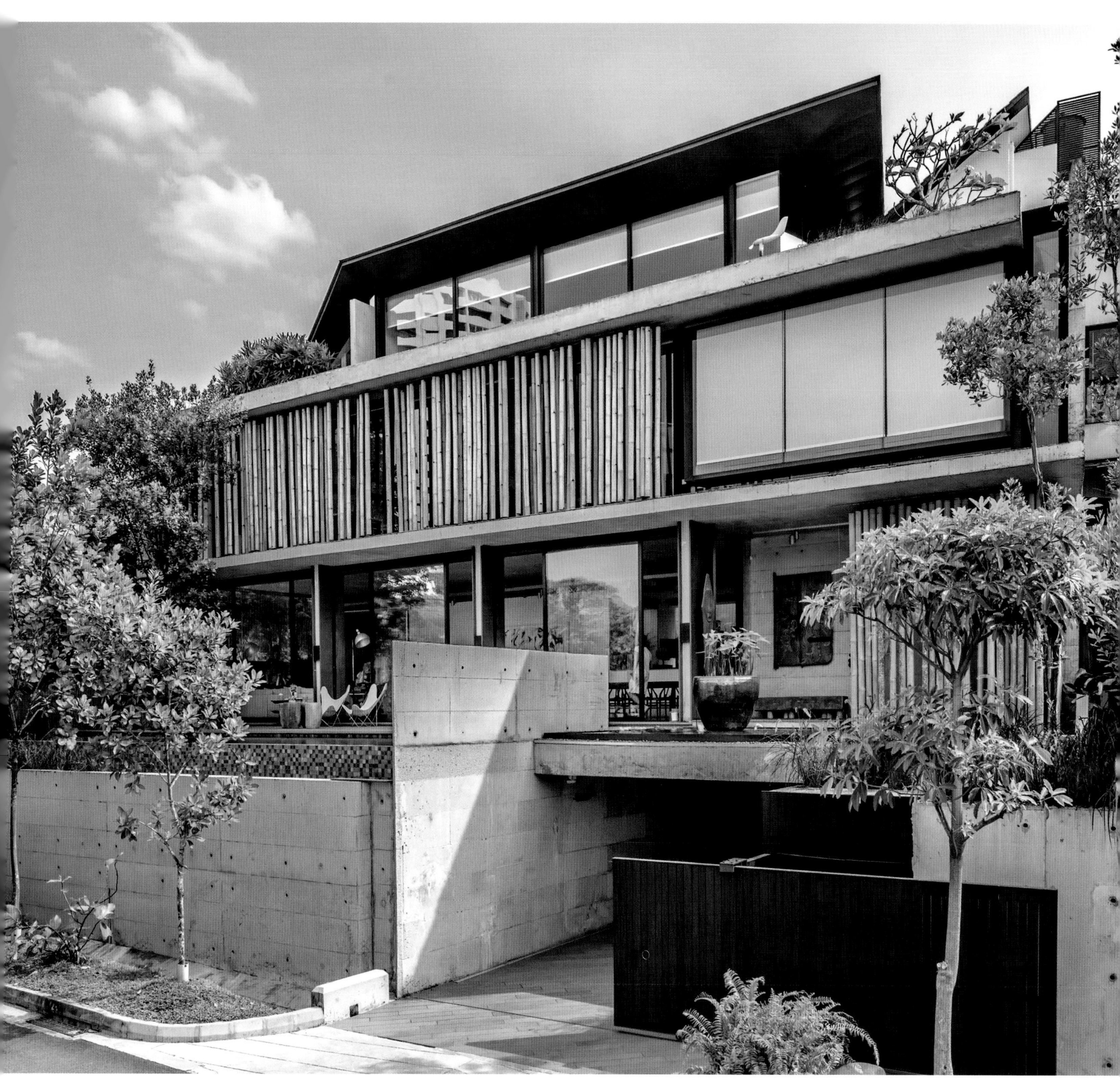

eave. This spans the width of the room, creating the impression of a neatly inserted box. The horizontal transparency of the powerfully rectangular glass wall contrasts with the tactile verticality of the bamboo screens next to it and below it, while the beautifully proportioned composition of white vertical and horizontal concrete planes with a floating dark-framed rooftop studio complete a stunning formal and material composition for the house's street elevation.

The image from the street is a mix of materiality and transparency: solid concrete, semi-solid bamboo screens and transparency of the first storey and second storey bedrooms. This tantalizing counterpoint is continued inside where spaces blend seamlessly with one another or have the transition from one to the other signalled in some way, as with the faceted directional wall leading into the kitchen and the rear garden beyond, a device repeated at the stairway leading to the second storey.

Sim is a passionate art collector and the house acts as a gallery for his collection, which includes framed paintings but predominantly cultural artefacts from around Asia, picked up on his many professional trips around the region. The transparency of the house works to highlight the character of these stone and timber pieces. Their materiality is emphasized, and simple, originally

Below An angled timber stairway leads to the second storey, the transition marked by some of the architect's collection of Asian artefacts.

Right The totally transparent living room.

Opposite below The living/dining space looking out to the terrace and pool.

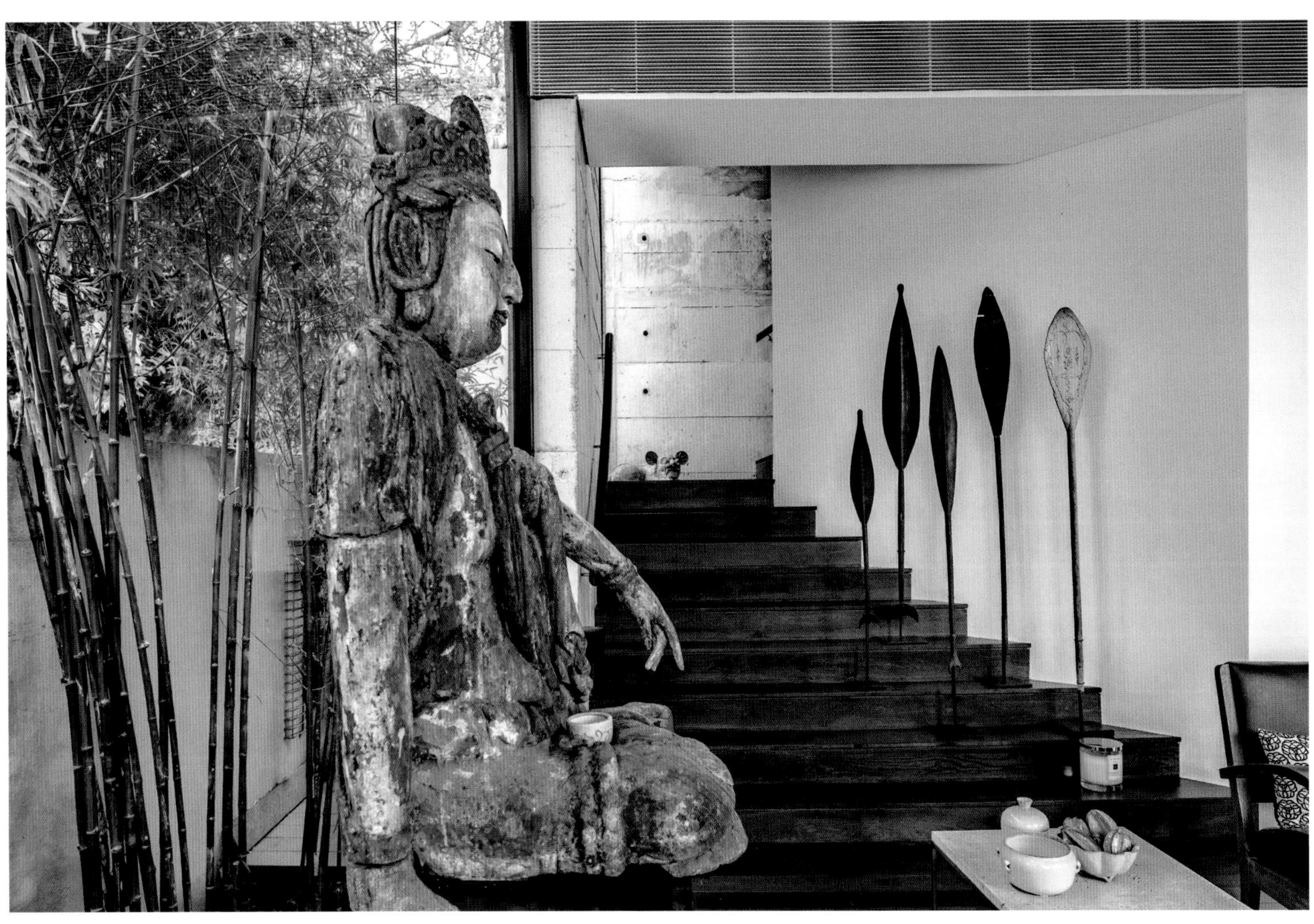

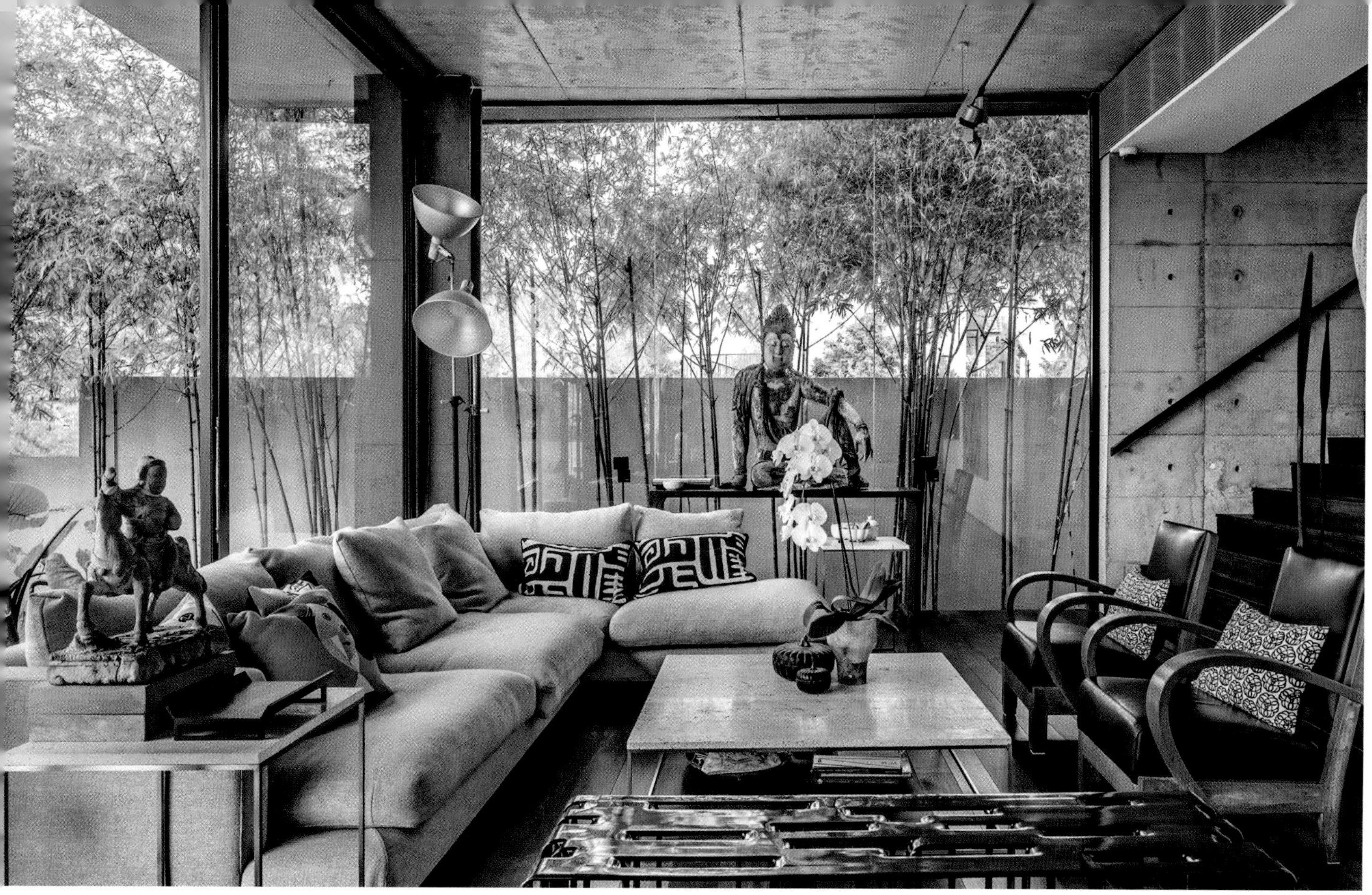

functional items, take on an added dimension. The architect varies the experience on the second storey where, at the top of the stairs, there is a light-filled double-height gallery. The bedrooms lead off this gallery whose dark oak-stained floor complements the carved timber bench but contrasts boldly with the light from the skylight and the light-drenched concrete wall.

The juxtaposition of the bamboo curtain and concrete signals from the street entry a conversation that continues throughout the house. The curtain itself—Javanese bamboo treated with boric acid—acts as a privacy screen and as protection from wind and rain. An unintended benefit is the music of the bamboo stems as they knock against one another in the breeze. This highlights the reflective quality of the house where the architecture of form and space integrates with the furnishings and decorative elements to generate this constant conversation of old and new, light and dark, solid and transparent, functional and

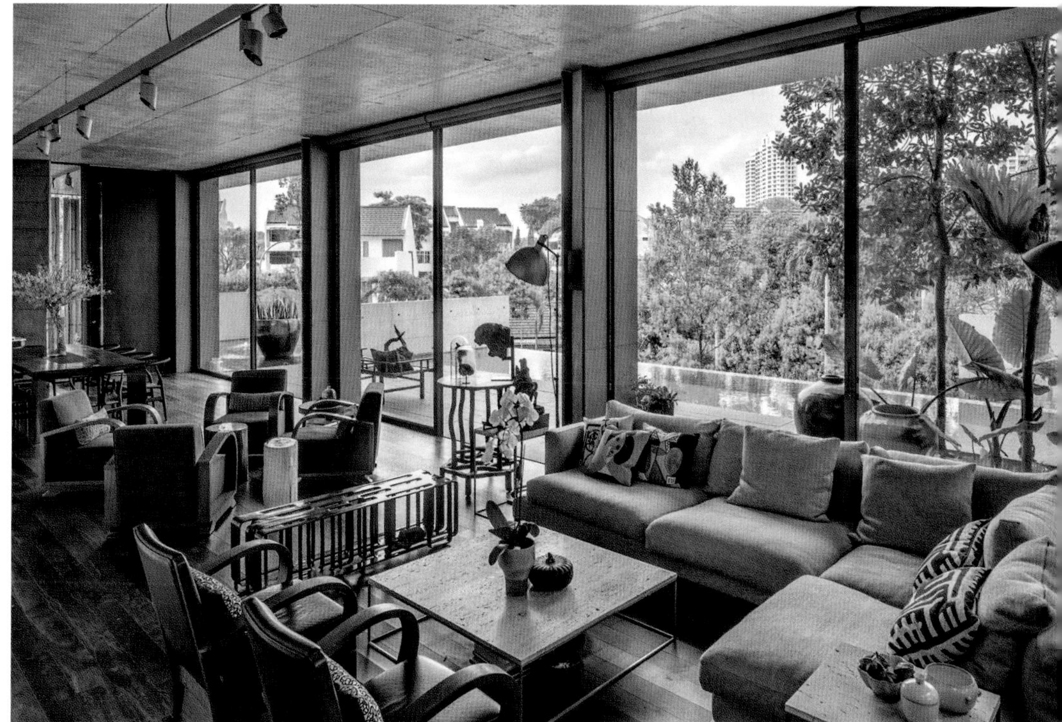

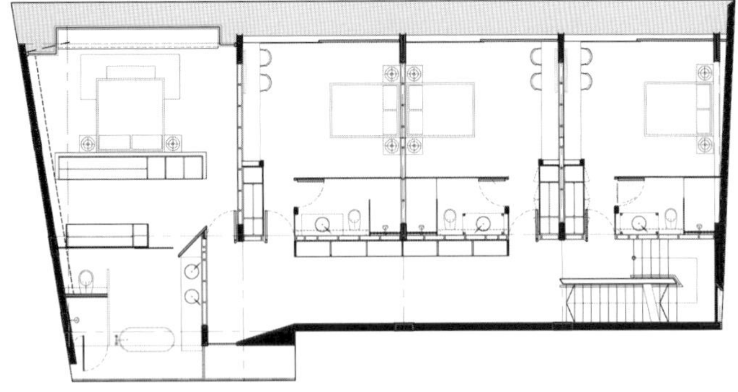

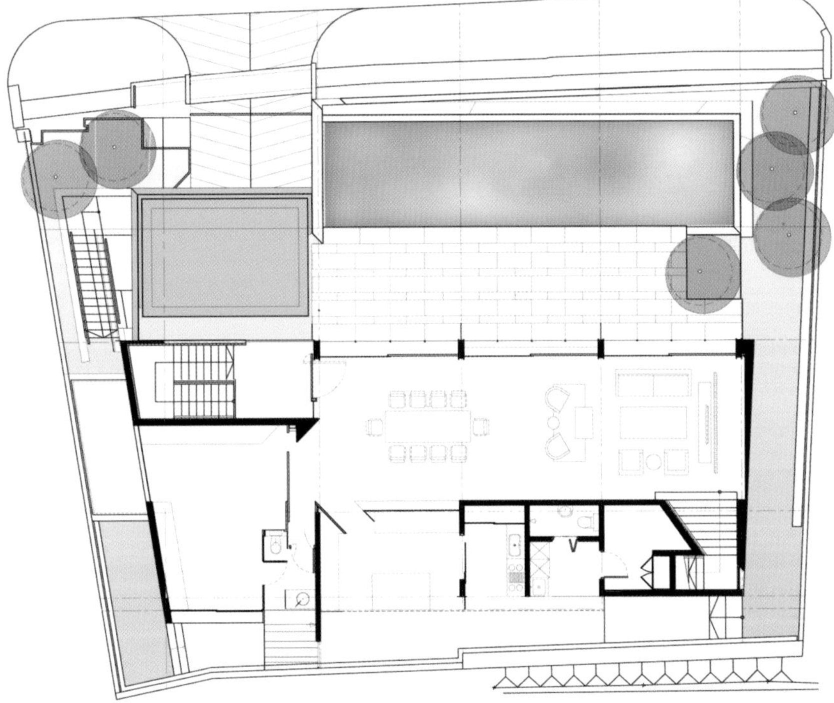

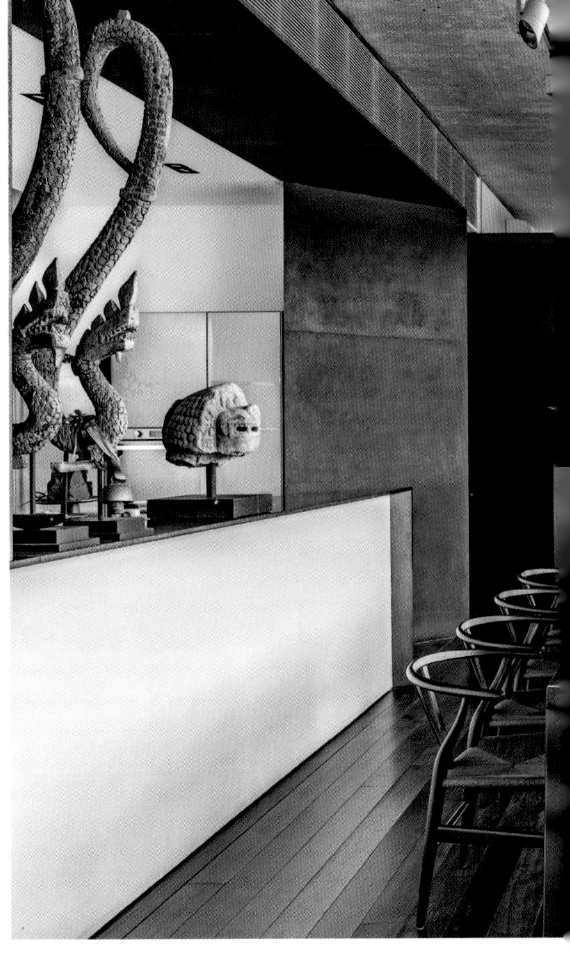

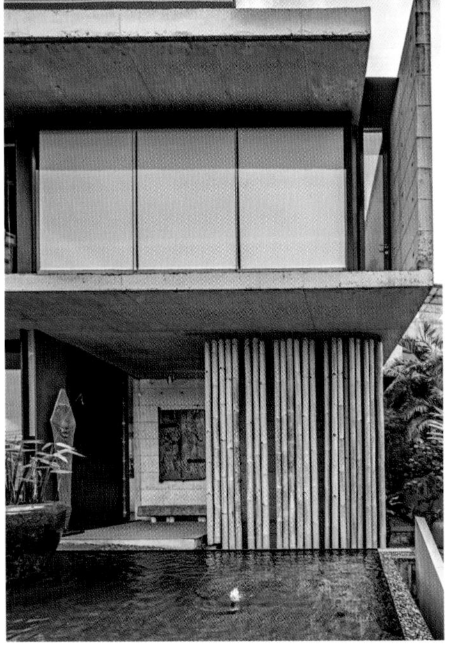

Above Plans.

Right The entry vestibule to the first storey, shielded by a bamboo screen.

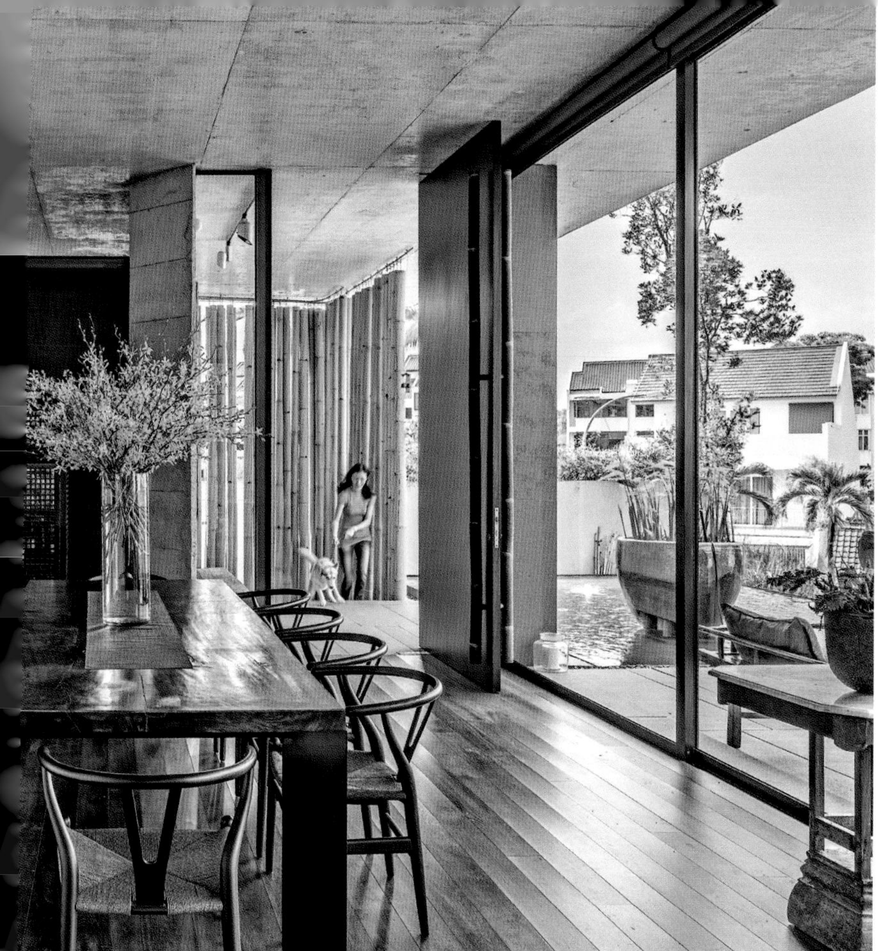

Left At the far end of the dining area is the bamboo curtain that screens the stairs to the basement car park.

Below The breakfast bar is part of a small courtyard, which draws air and light into the kitchen.

Bottom The master bathroom continues the theme of a bamboo curtain, with furnishings and fittings reflecting the artisanal quality of the art collection.

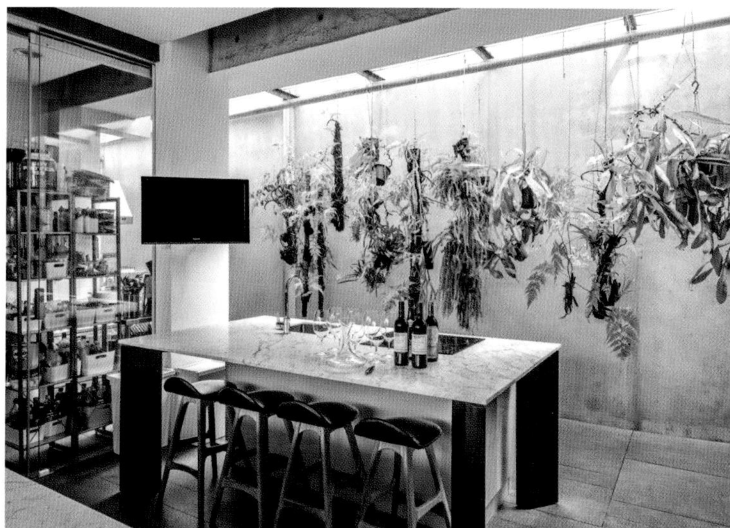

decorative. This is nowhere more apparent than in the master bathroom where bamboo is again used as a filter between inside and outside, contrasting with travertine finishes and contemporary fittings and complementing an informally cut bench from old lychee wood.

Environmentally sustainable initiatives include solid walls on the east–west façades for heat control, an overall openness that captures the breezes available from the house's elevated position, a water harvesting system and solar panels.

But it is sustainable in a number of other ways. Apart from the personal and environmental sustainability of the project, we can add cultural sustainability for the way in which the architect has collected a wide collection of artefacts from around the region, many of them originally purely functional (including hand-crafted furniture to complement custom-made pieces from recycled timber) and given them a new life.

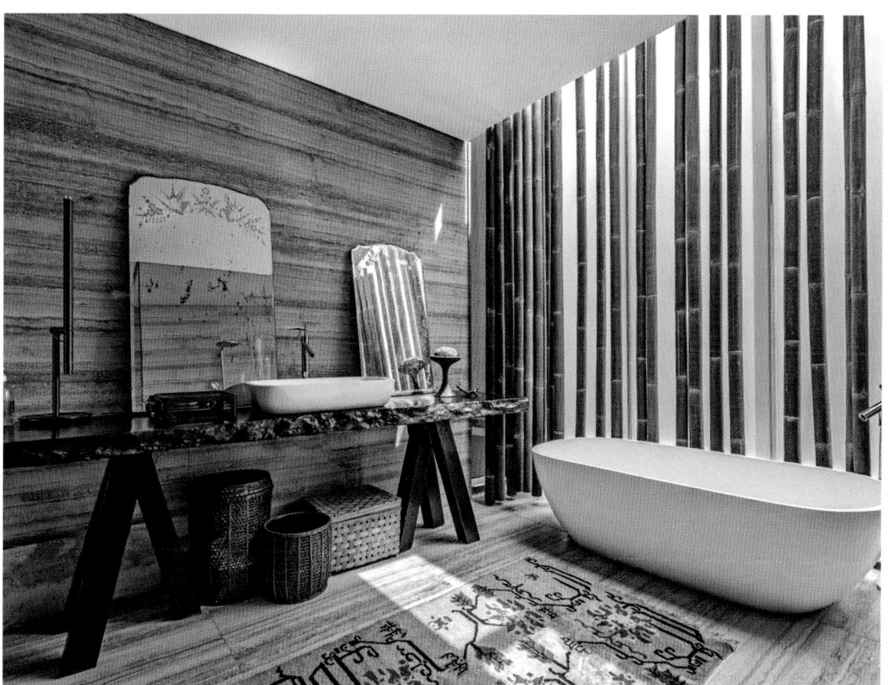

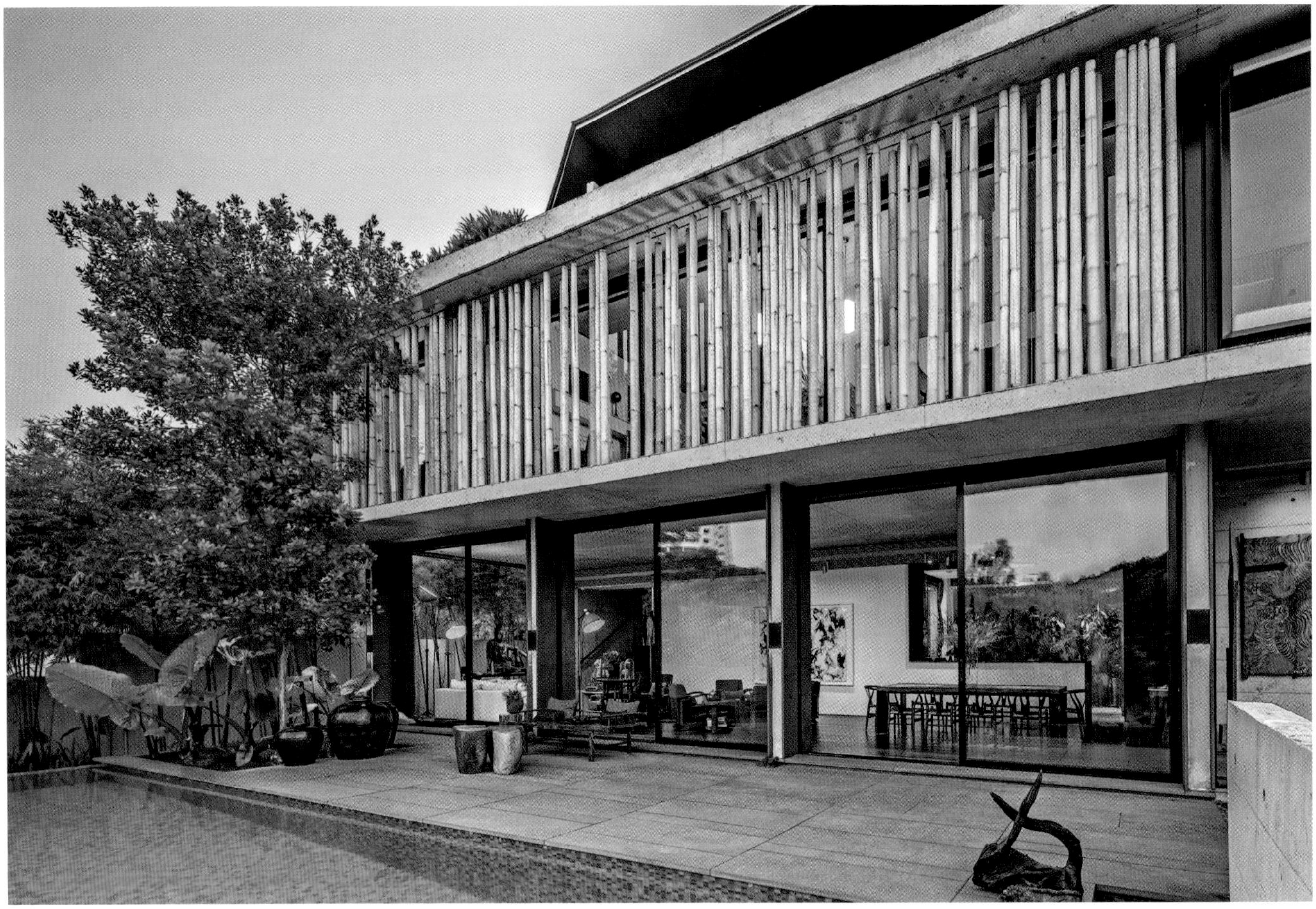

Above In contrast to the grounded, transparent lower level, the upper bedroom level seems to float in the air, achieving both character and privacy from the bamboo curtain in front.

Right The double-height gallery on the second storey is filled with light from the skylight. The gallery links all the bedrooms but also acts as an exhibition space for part of the collection of artefacts.

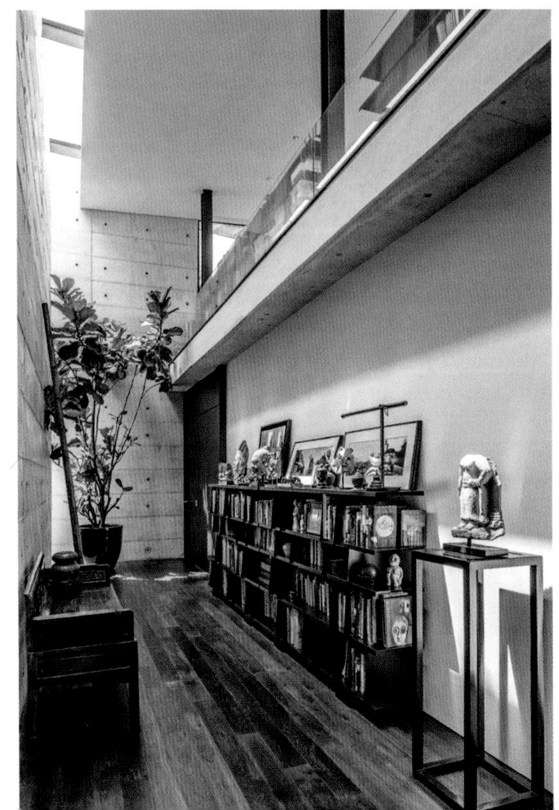

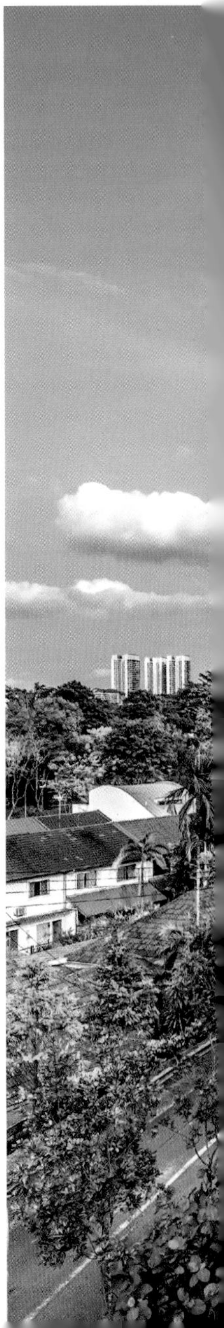

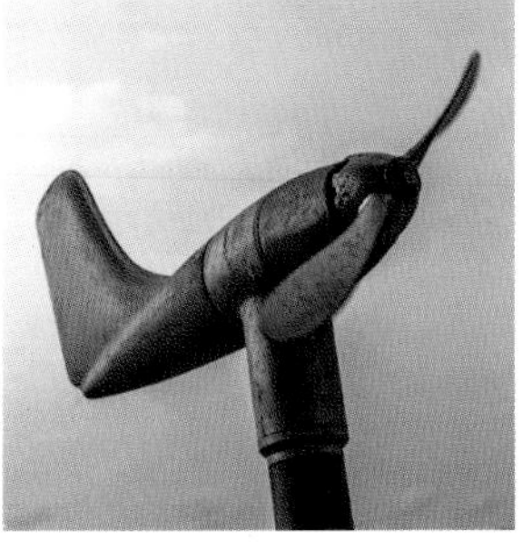

Left This wind gauge is typical of the whimsy that adds interest to the house.

Right The master bedroom has a full-length window for enjoying the view without any loss of privacy.

Below The attic level contains a studio/office opening to a terrace.

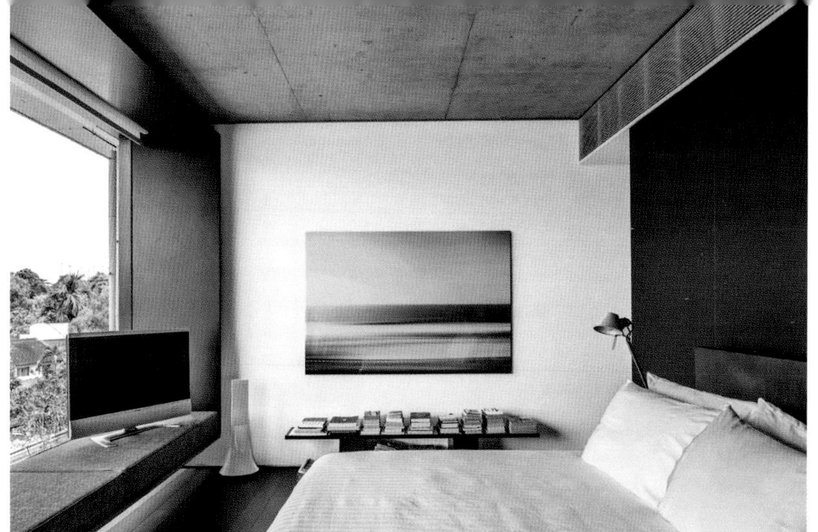

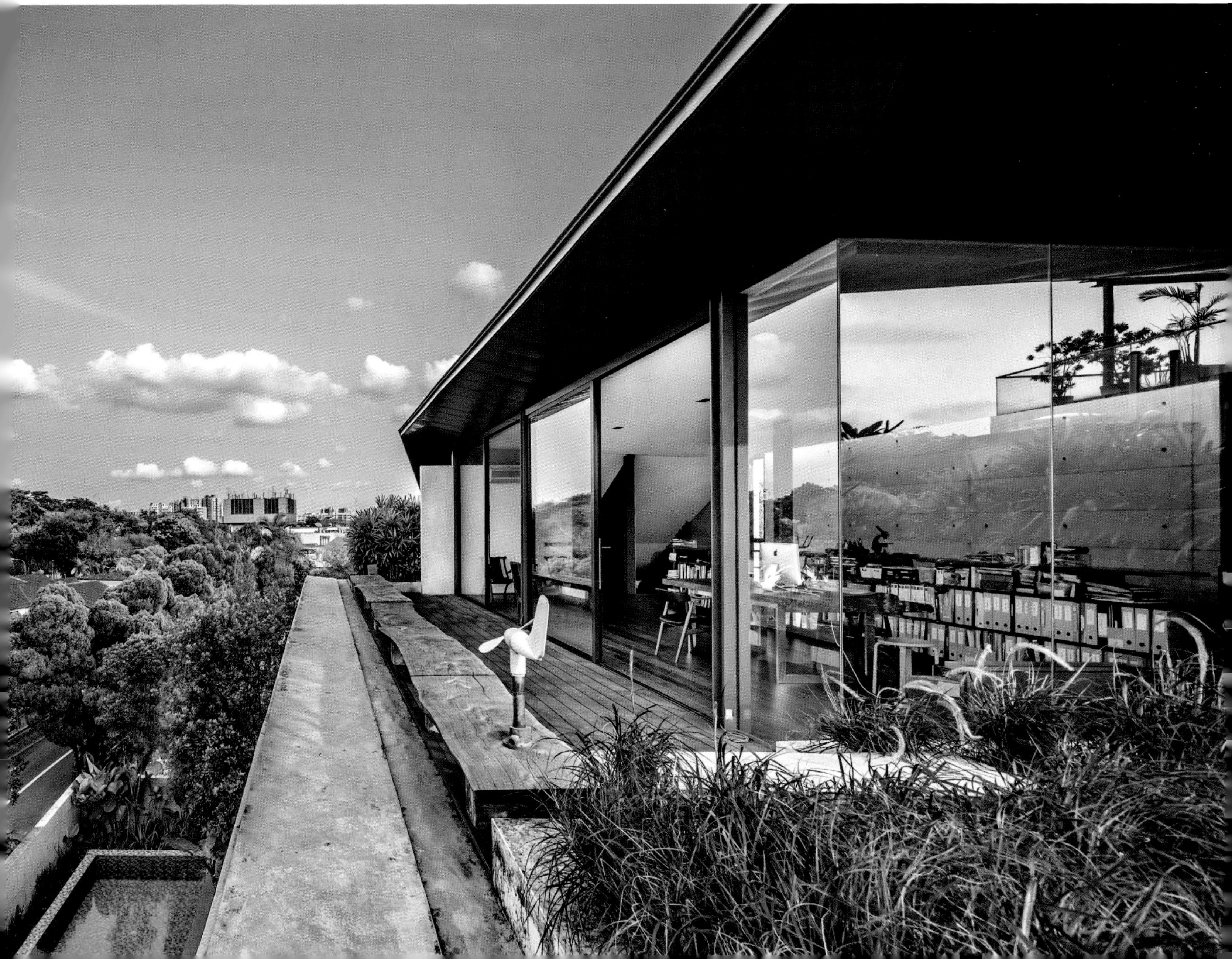

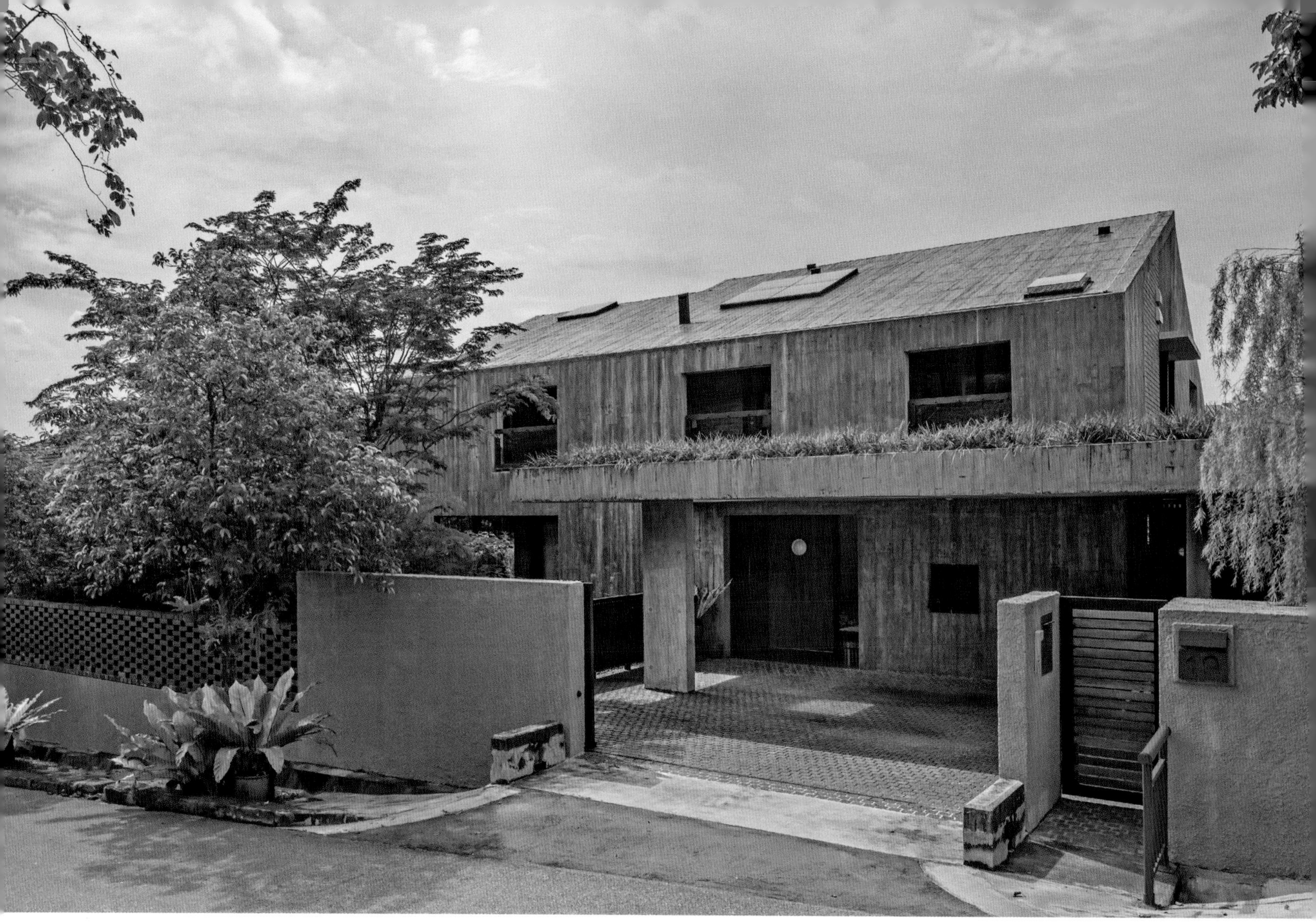

SUNSET PLACE HOUSE
IP:LI ARCHITECTS

'The owner grew up in this area and wanted to come back. So she bought the house. But by this time she was married with kids and wanted more than the original house could satisfy. She didn't need a lot more, so I said: "Why don't I just build a house within a house?"'—YIP YUEN HONG, ARCHITECT

Above Although the house has a new concrete skin, it maintains the profile of the existing structure. A perforated brick wall recycles original bricks to connect both with the neighbourhood and the original 'internal' house.

Opposite above The concrete canopy of the house entry provides shade while admitting light.

Right Openings in the concrete shell and small terraces help define the intimate garden spaces.

Yip Yuen Hong set up his practice ip:li in 2002 with his wife Lee Ee Lin. Prior to that, he worked with legendary architects William Lim and Tay Kheng Soon, and their questioning, explorative and often playful approach is evident in ip:li's work. The company is now recognized as one of the most innovative in Singapore, boasting President's Design Awards in 2011 and 2012, an SIA Design Award in 2012 and Designer of the Year in 2013. The firm is known for its formal imagination, but especially for its exploration of contemporary tropical architecture, and has gained inspiration from precedents such as shophouses, black-and-white houses and kampong houses.

This house is in a 1960s development notable for the use of a very beautiful deep red russet brick that lends the houses in the neighbourhood a common character. The original house was also a brick house and featured well-maintained dark-stained chengal timber flooring, strip wall panelling and staircase; chengal is a durable, fine-grained hardwood from Malaysia that is now almost impossible to source. Yip reasoned that there was no need to demolish the existing house and lose the bricks and timber. It was more sustainable to keep the house, to preserve the fine timber detailing and to retain the house's relationship to its neighbours in terms of scale and materials. 'I was insistent,' says Yip, 'on keeping the original profile so that it didn't become bigger than what it should be.' Hence, in scale and with its pitched roof, the new house sits comfortably with its neighbours.

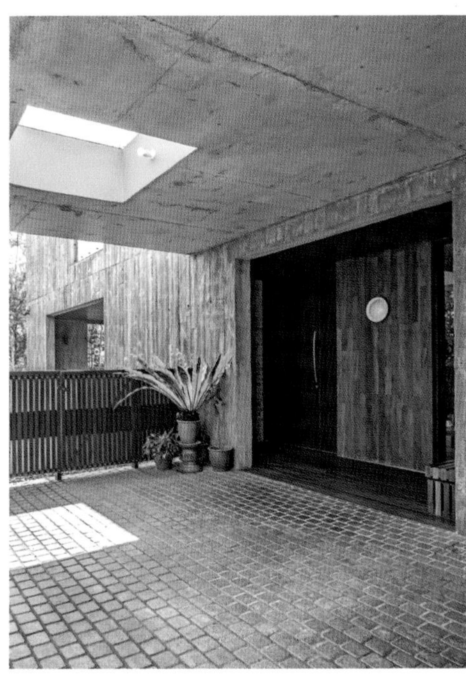

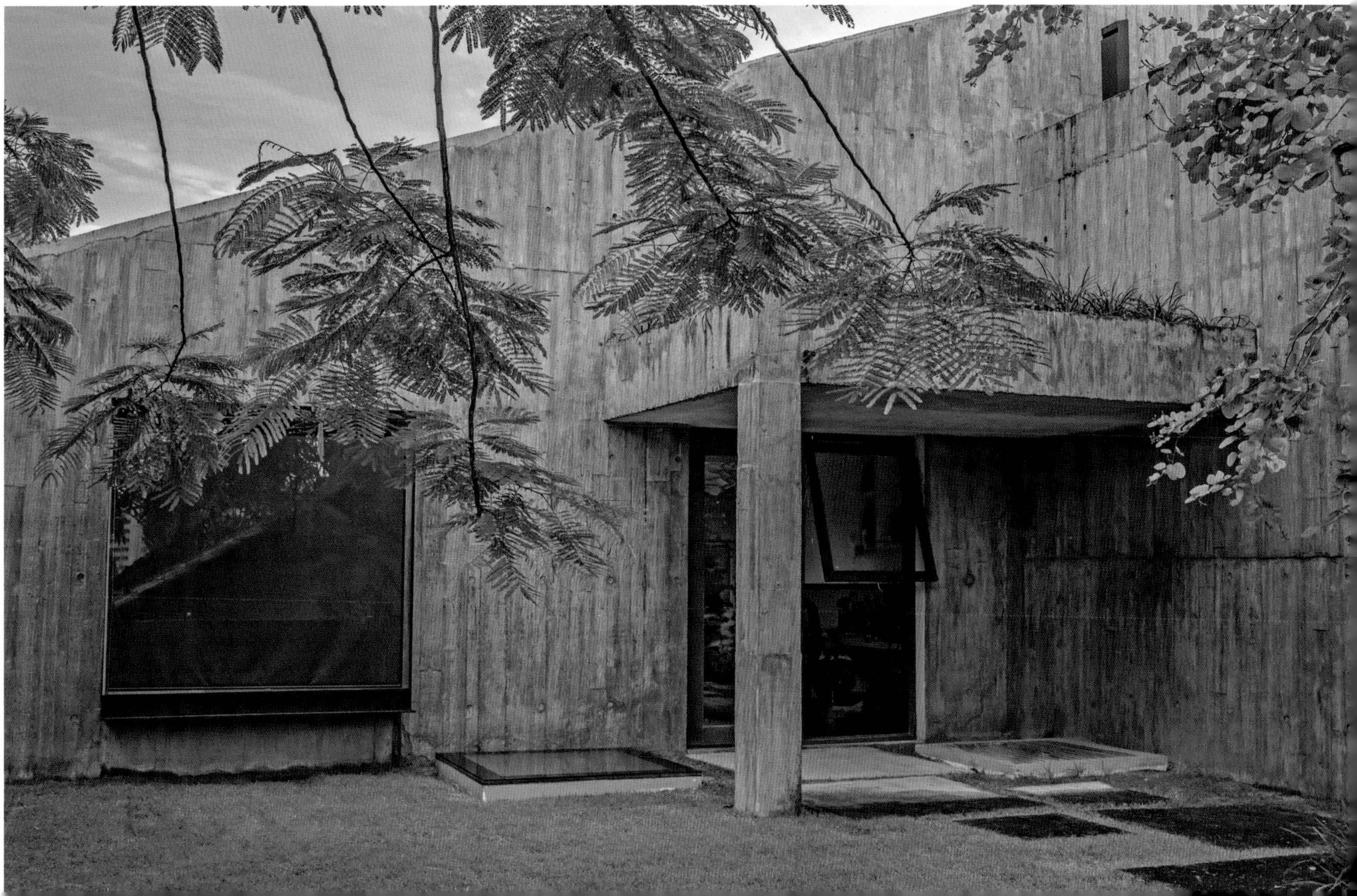

Building houses only as big as they need to be is not only a sound sustainable policy but has also been relatively rare in Singapore, at least as far as landed houses are concerned. In this case, Yip designed not so much an addition to the existing house but an organic extension that generated the

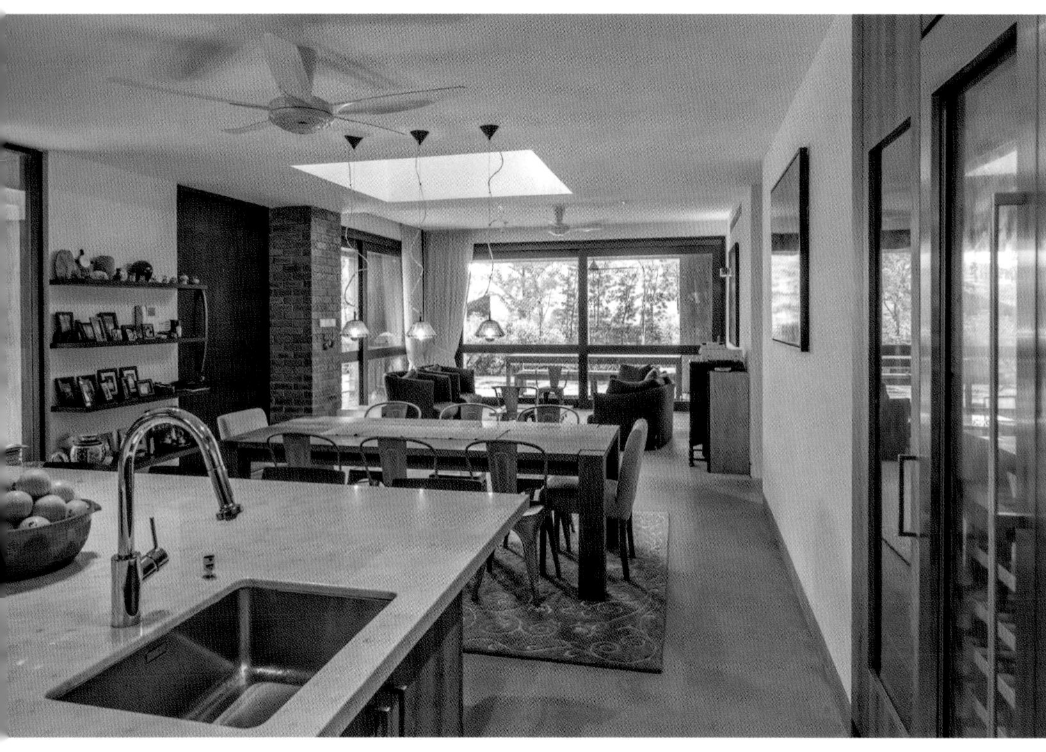

strips in the original house, again reinforcing the agenda of continuity, signalled from the street by the perforated brick wall (using the original bricks) cohabiting with the new concrete structure. With time, the concrete will weather, developing a more natural, aged patina in keeping with the original bricks and blending in with the landscape. 'The older it gets, the better it will look,' quips Yip.

At the entry level, the new shell has enabled the living/dining/dry kitchen area to be enlarged, especially when it is opened up to the patio spaces. Light is drawn into this enlarged space by an internal void created around the existing staircase. Windows on the inner and outer layers do not line up. Instead, they stagger, a deliberate strategy to draw in as much light as possible, at the same time maintaining privacy given the close proximity of the neighbours. This way people can see out but others cannot see in. The staggered window strategy is complemented by a variety of windows and doors, including an extruded glass cube.

extra space the client desired but maintained a sustainable scale and a sense of continuity with the original. Yip was able to achieve these while simultaneously addressing another important issue. 'If you look at the design of the original house,' says Yip, 'it wasn't really tropical. For example, the windows don't have enough overhang.'

The solution was to build a concrete shell around the original house. This provided new patio and balcony spaces on both the ground floor and second storey, together with new rooms at the back. The intermediate patio and balcony spaces help cool the house, while the new structure also provided the opportunity for new garden areas at different levels, including elevated garden beds, also generating natural cooling while also creating a tropical house that is a part of its landscape. Openings have been cut out of the concrete shell to create these intermediate spaces, which serve as a transition between the old and the new house and between the outside gardens and the interior. The board-marked concrete shell references the chengal timber

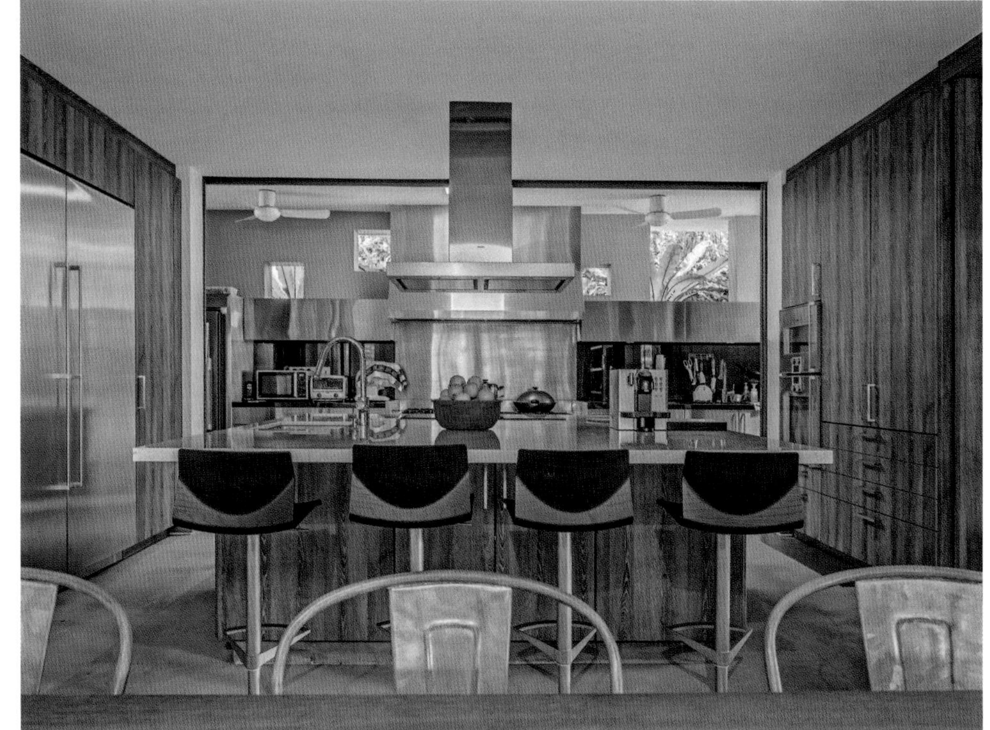

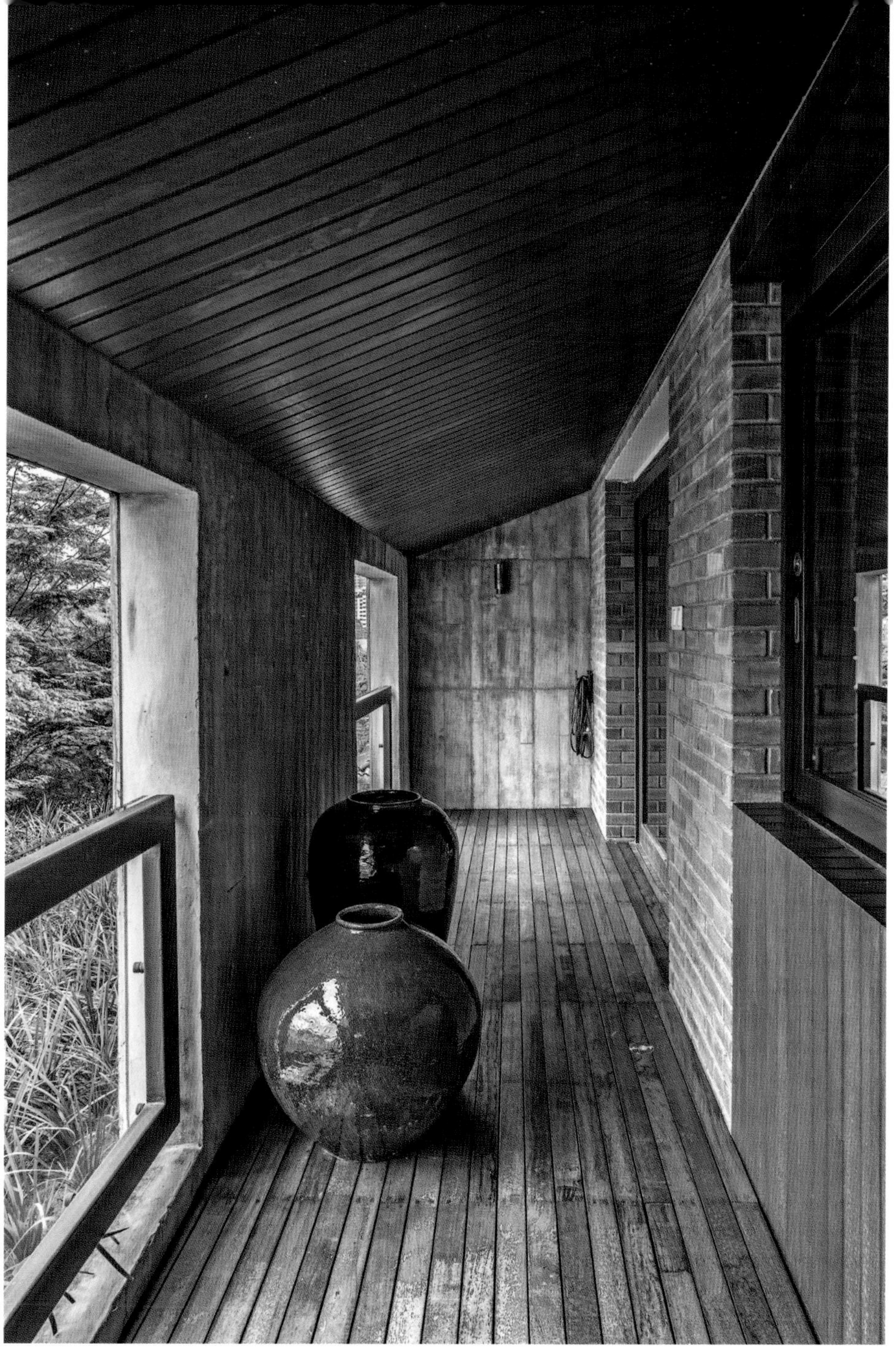

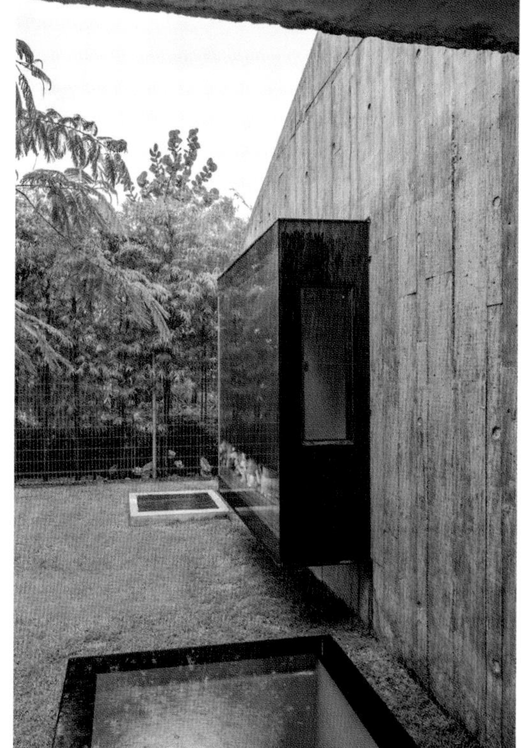

Left The new shell has enabled setbacks that have become shaded balconies.

Above An elegant black extruded window forms a bay window inside.

Below The original chengal flooring and joinery give the house character and maintain a connection with its history.

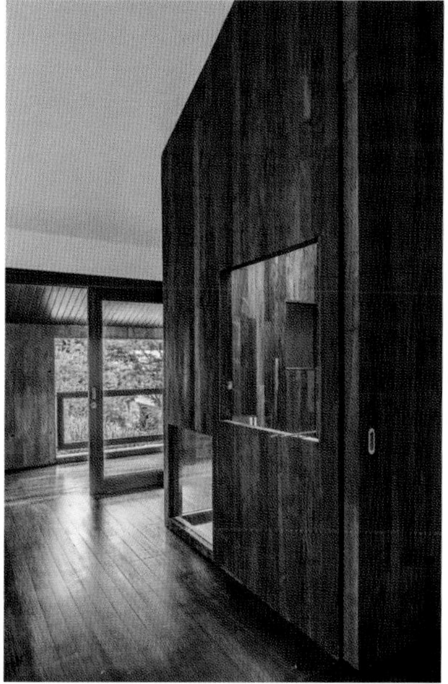

Opposite above A view of the main living/ dining space from the dry kitchen.

Left Timber joinery and industrial elements contrast with the contemporary, especially the state-of-the-art dry kitchen.

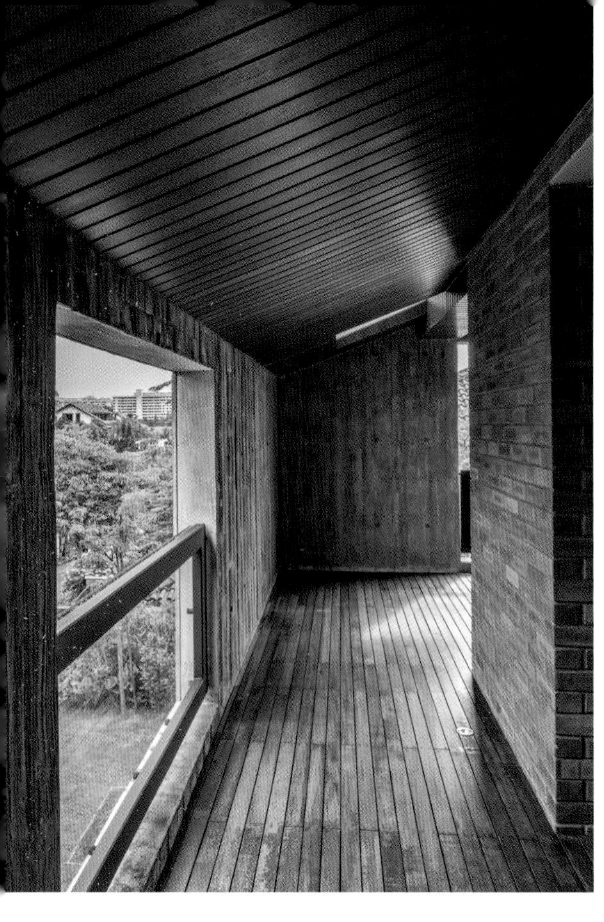

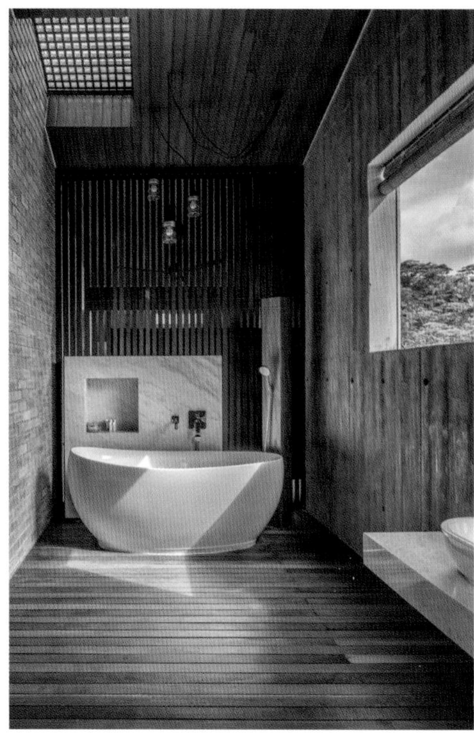

Far left The recycled timber deck complements the original bricks as the Level 2 balcony turns to become a private balcony for the master bedroom.

Left An outdoor bath off the master bedroom takes advantage of the privacy provided by the deeply recessed balcony.

Below left Cut-outs in the concrete shell break up the façade.

Below The home office enjoys its own private outdoor space.

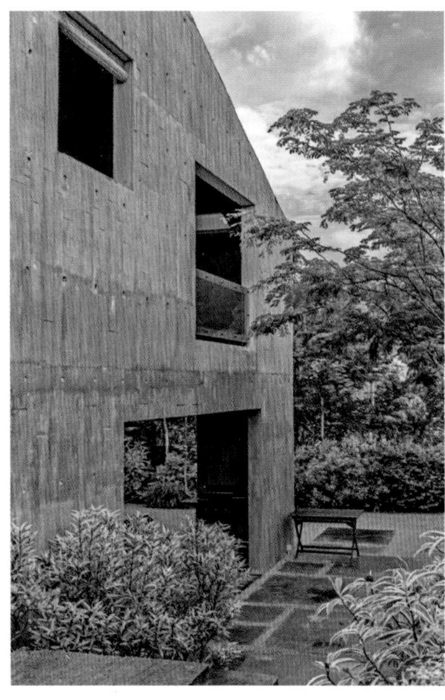

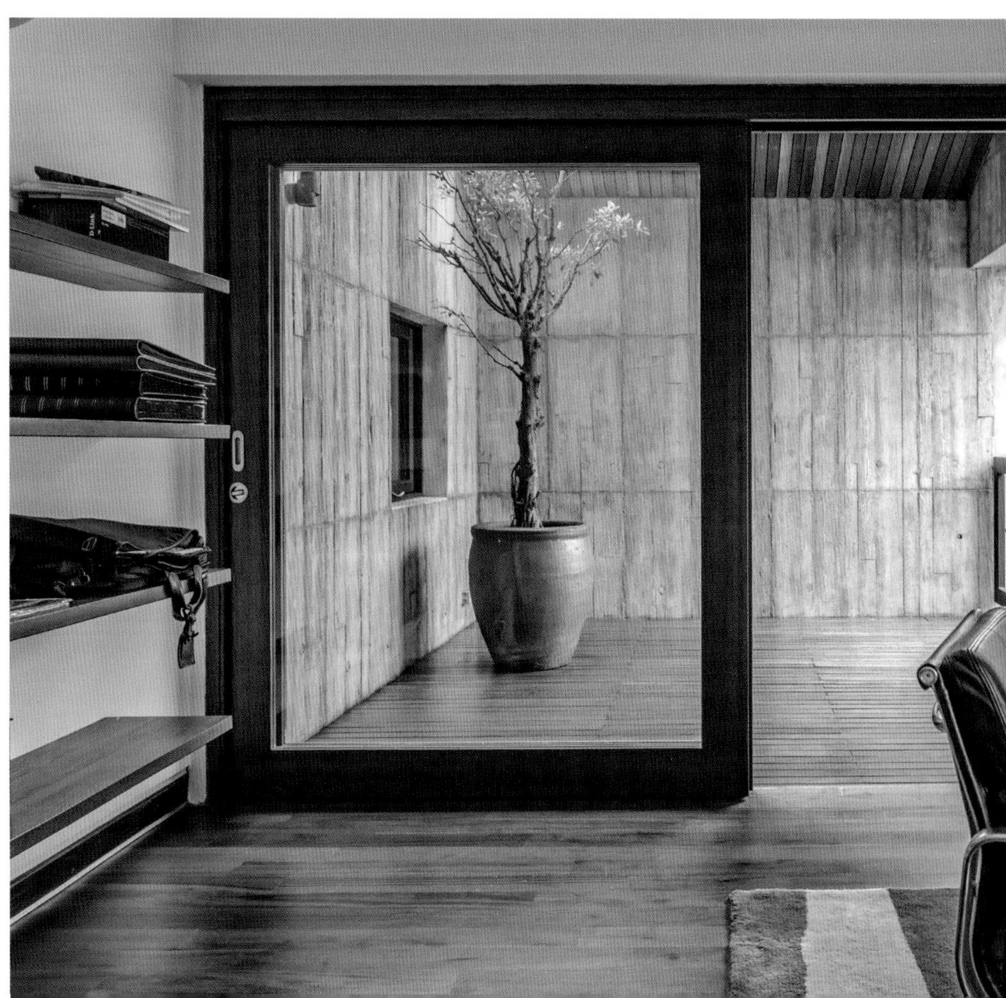

Right Like the perforated brick wall, timber batten screens provide privacy without giving the feeling of being enclosed.

Below right Looking up from the basement courtyard to the timber screen skylight and ingenious timber window.

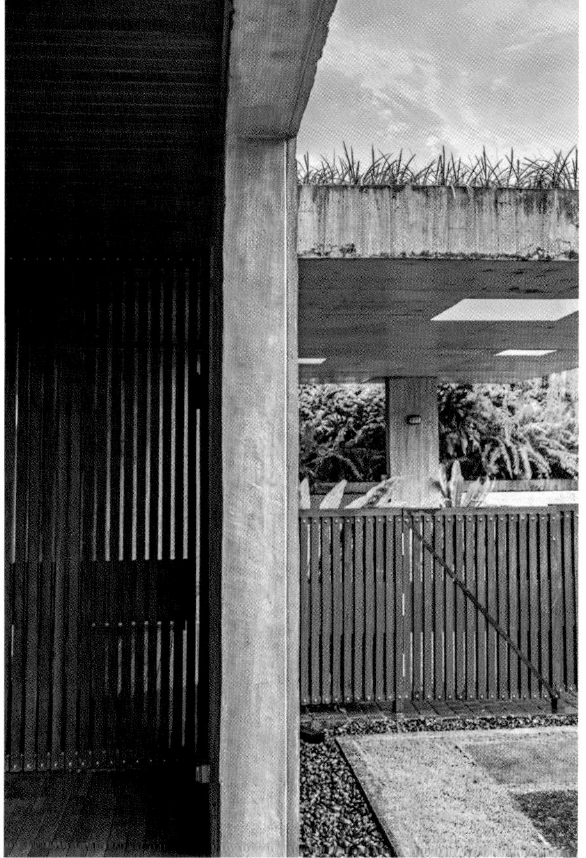

Downstairs, the basement has been enlarged to include the maids' quarters, laundry and guest rooms overlooking a sunken courtyard lit by a natural skylight. This means the courtyard is partly open and partly covered. Level 2 is the private domain of the house, with bedrooms for the parents and two teenage sons. Here, the new shell has enabled the architects to design open bathrooms. The master bedroom, for example, has its own private terrace and an outdoor bathroom with views of its own garden. The boys' rooms feature hatched bay windows, each with a view of the rear garden, contributing to an overall sense of endless nooks and crannies and surprise views to the outside.

Extending an existing house and recycling beautiful and now rare materials is an environmentally sustainable agenda, in this case complemented by a personal and cultural agenda of sustainability, brought together in a house that has been designed to adapt as the family develops.

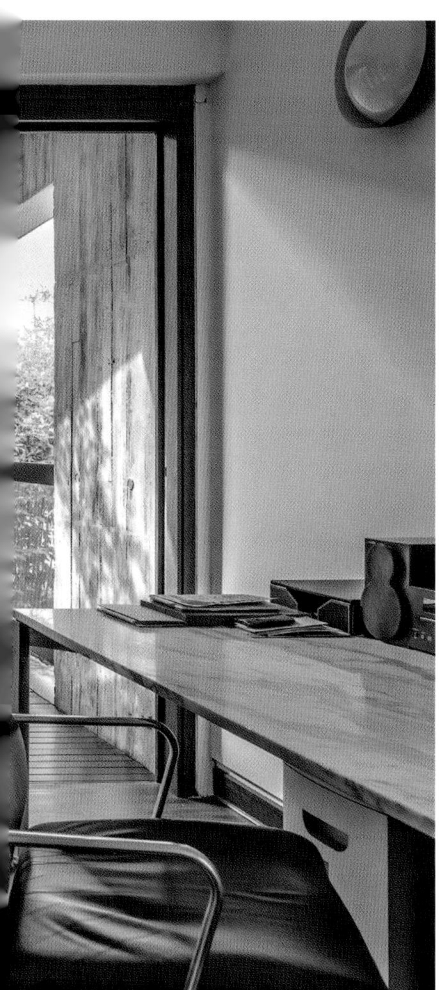

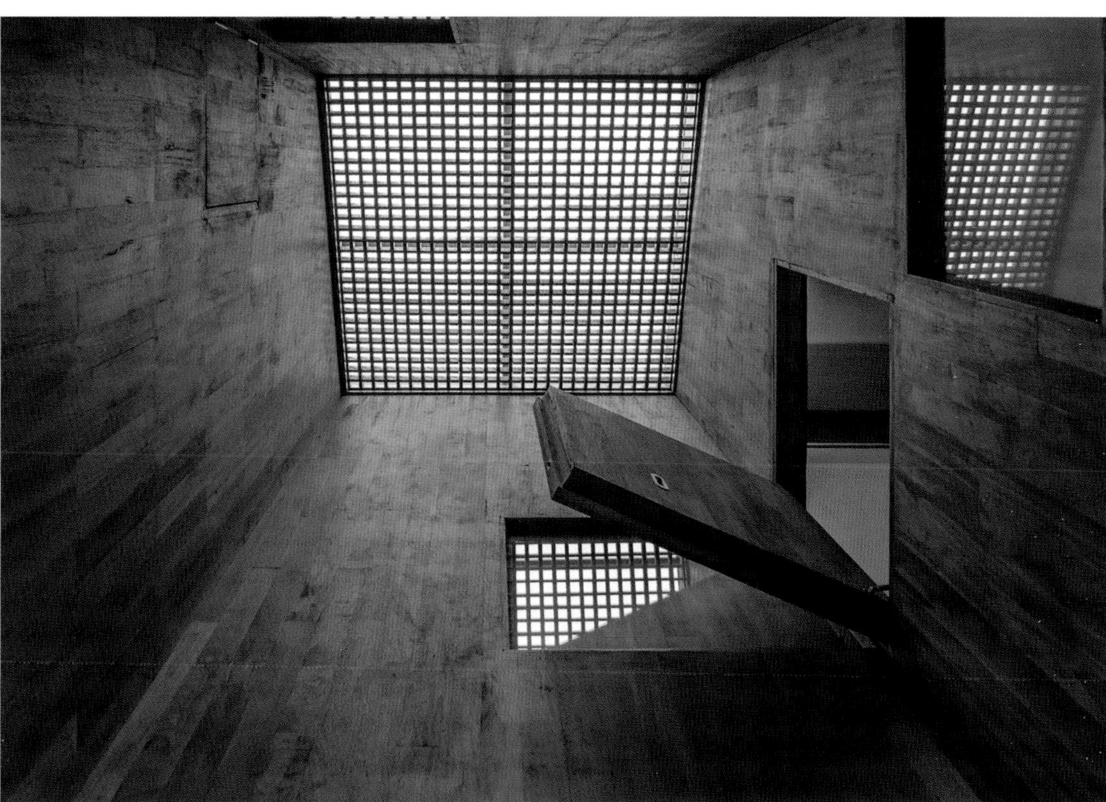

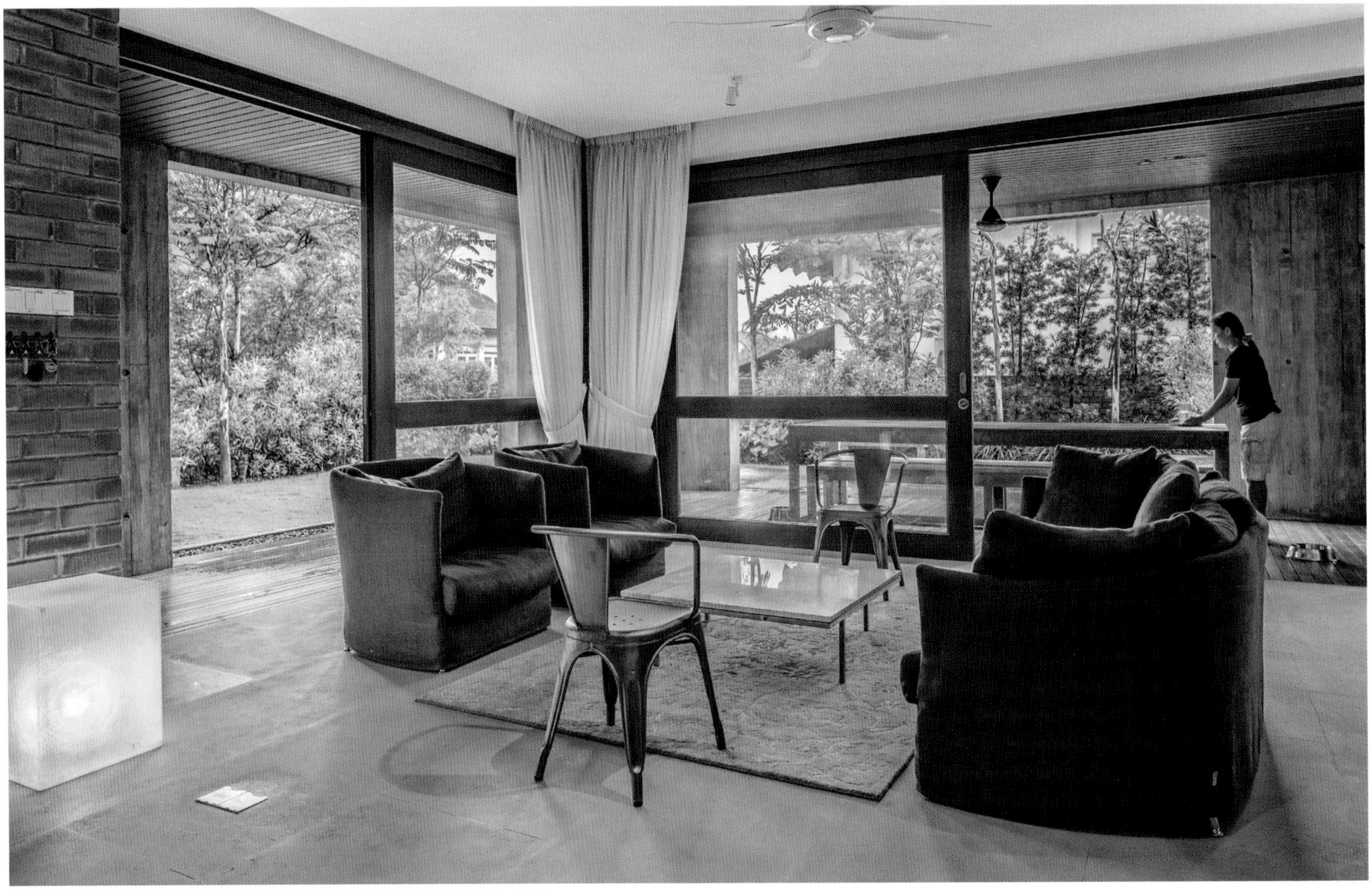

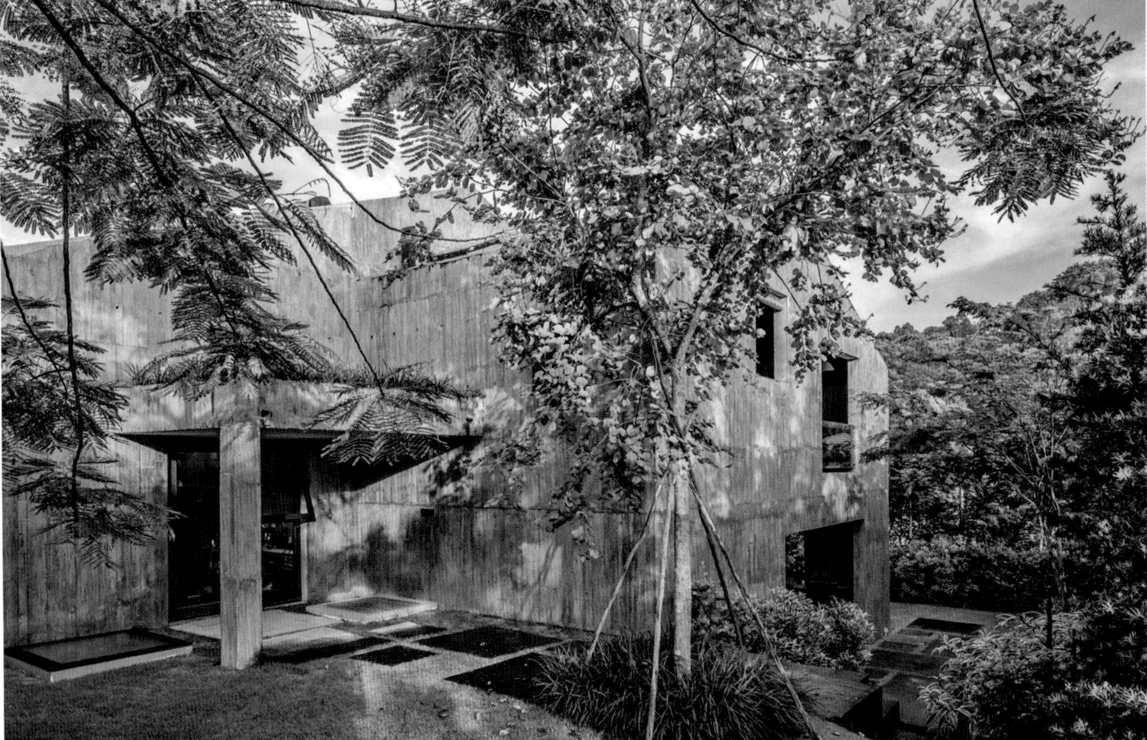

Above The living area now opens to a broad recessed wraparound terrace.

Left The terraced slope offered opportunities to break the garden up into intriguing smaller spaces.

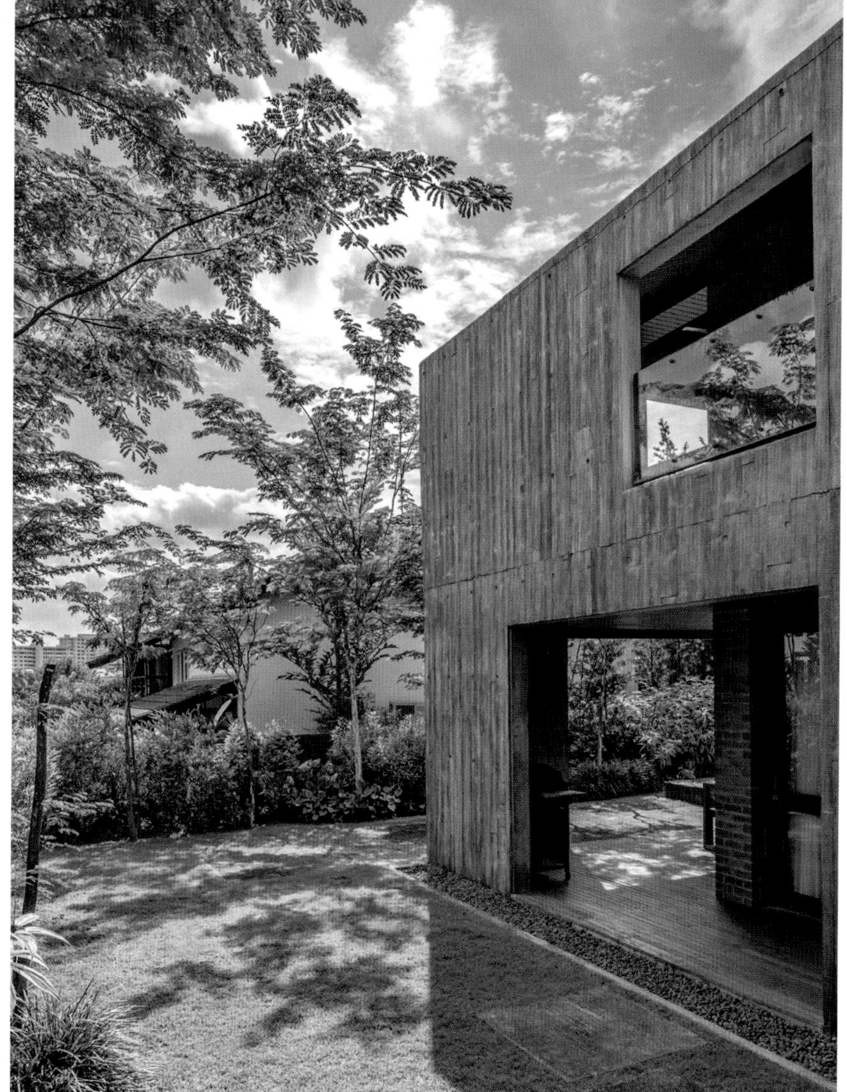

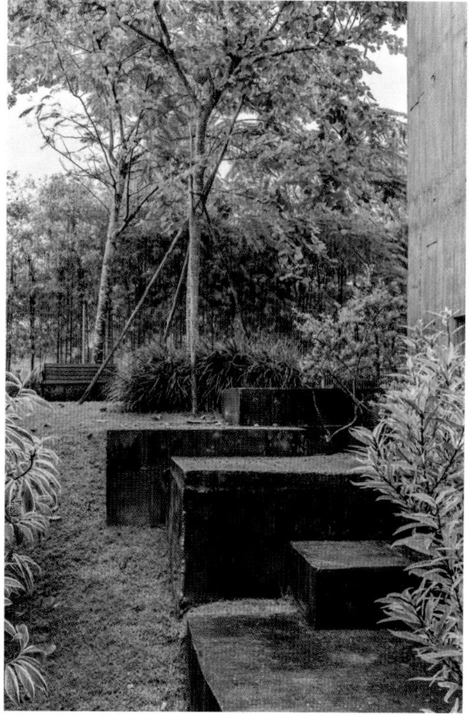

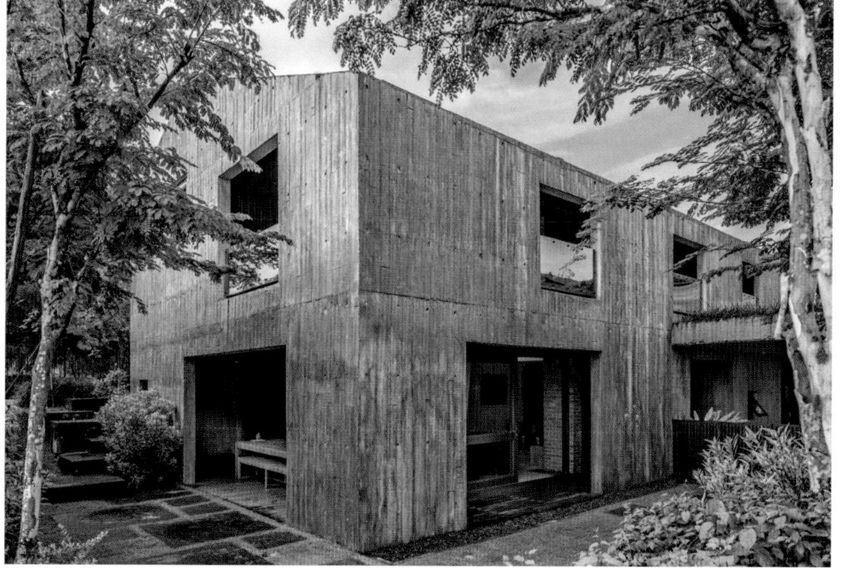

Above left The well-shaded terrace off the living area.

Above View towards the rear garden.

Left A view back to the living room terrace, which has a long wooden table and benches for outdoor dining.

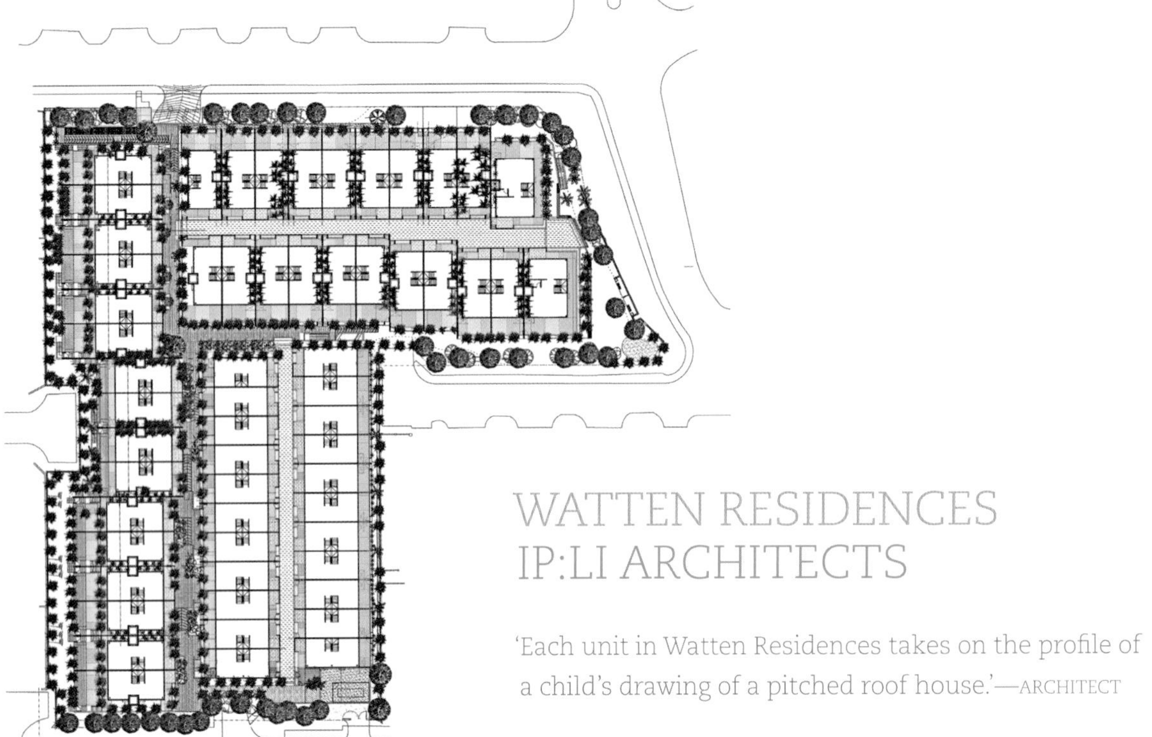

WATTEN RESIDENCES
IP:LI ARCHITECTS

'Each unit in Watten Residences takes on the profile of a child's drawing of a pitched roof house.'—ARCHITECT

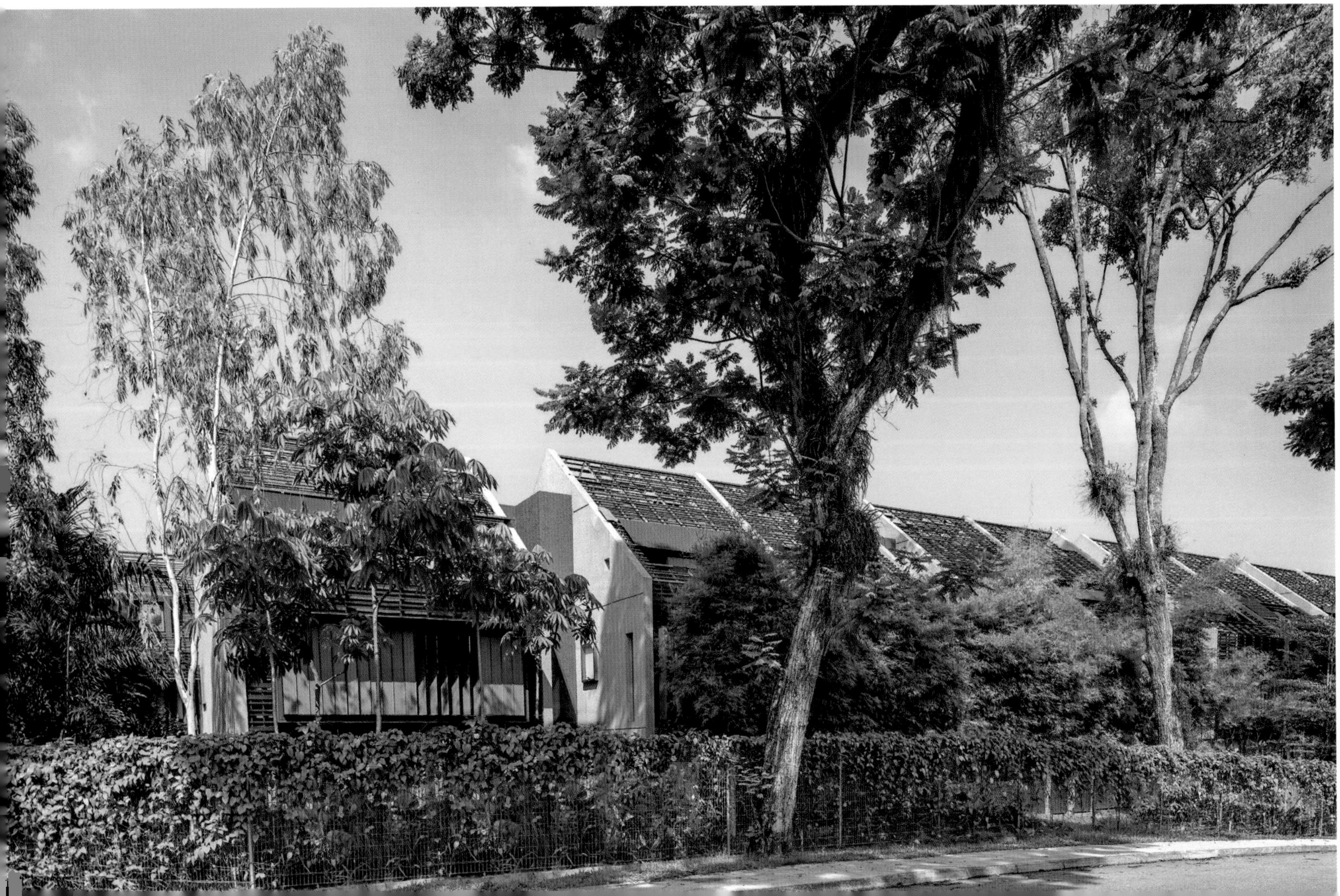

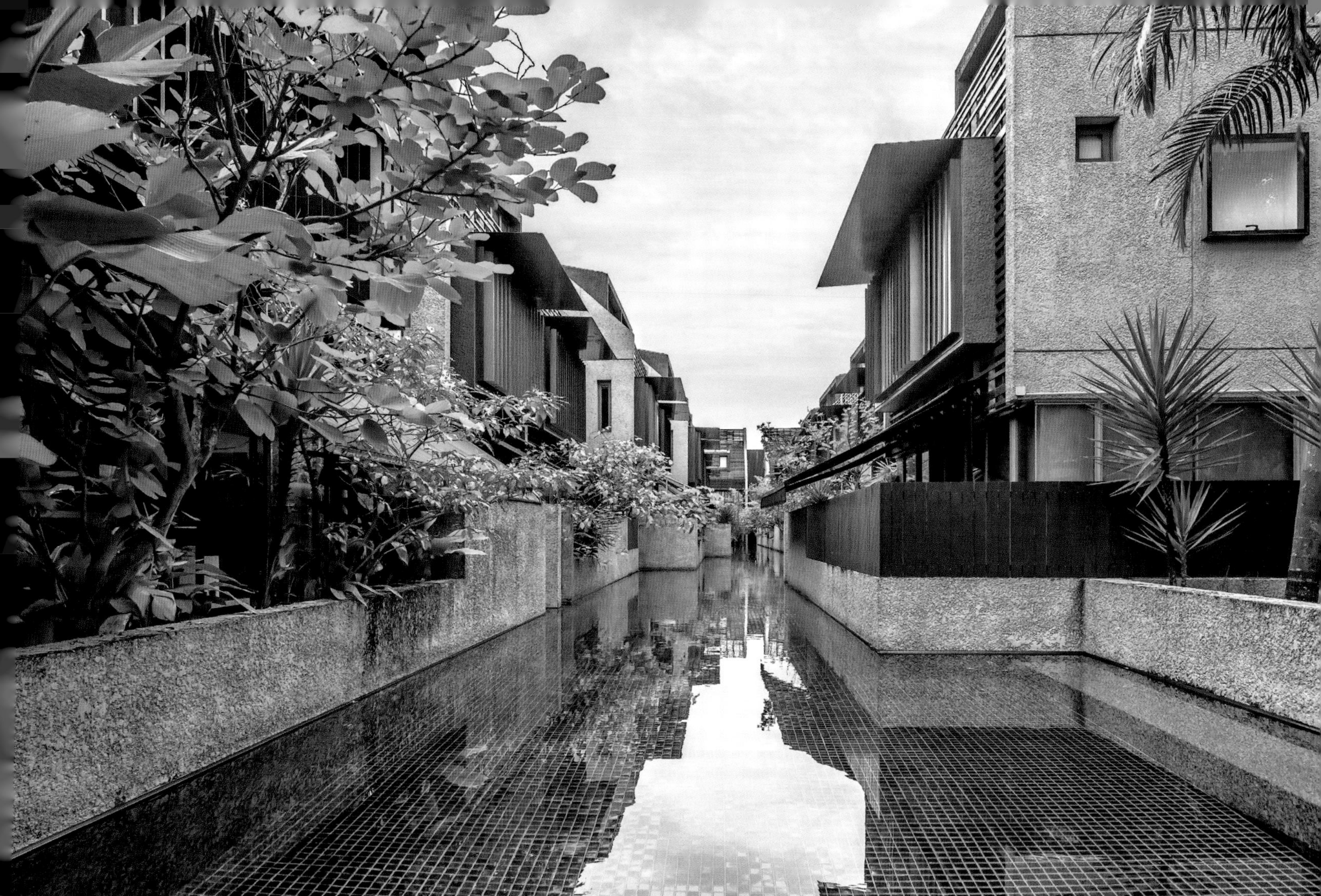

Living in multi-residential developments can often seem completely unsustainable: lack of privacy, noise from the neighbours, standardized, impersonal apartments and a lack of access to green space, especially one's own green space. It is the perennial challenge for architects to address these issues given the obvious spatial and economic constraints. One model that is gaining in popularity is cluster housing. This aims to bring together the privacy benefits and prestige of a landed property with the amenities typically available in a condominium. The amenities usually include some private green space as well as extensive community green space. In addition, there will likely be swimming pools, gymnasiums, outdoor exercise areas and equipment and common outdoor entertainment areas, including cabanas. Typically, each unit will enjoy two basement car parking spaces, making ground-level activities free from cars. Finally, they will be gated communities with 24 hour security.

The Watten Residences are generally typical of the cluster model although at a mid-price level and, with 59 units, of relatively high density. Despite the size, however, the scale has been kept small and there is a remarkable diversity of common spaces throughout the development. The result is a complex with many moments of intimacy and where the individual units are themselves private, with a sense of living in a landed house.

The architects are known for exploring ways in which traditional kampong living can be adapted to a contemporary way of life. Here, they begin by

Opposite above Site plan.

Opposite below From the street, the complex is screened by layers of greenery, creating a village-like ambience.

Above The mood is of a village on the riverside where the central waterway doubles as a swimming pool.

hinting at a continuity with Watten Estate, a 1970s housing development previously on the site, with extensive use of sputter texture finishes and 'utilitarian, hole-in-the-wall windows'. More broadly, though, the aim has been to create a feeling of living in a village on the edge of a small stream. It is reminiscent of a much admired development in Singapore, Gilstead Brooks, by WOHA Architects, which was included in my earlier book, *25 Tropical Houses in Singapore and Malaysia* (2006), where individual units have a small garden with direct access to a meandering waterway culminating in a swimming pool. Watten Residences applies this model on a much larger scale and on a more complex site.

From the street, the complex is largely screened by levels of greenery. Once inside, it becomes clear that the complex looks inward rather than towards the street. The complex consists of five tightly clustered rows of units, which make optimum use of the available site but without any sense of claustrophobia. On the contrary, the feeling is of an intimate, human-scaled village. Two pairs of rows face one another across a water feature, which doubles as a swimming pool. These pairs form a T shape and are separated by a pedestrian thoroughfare. The fifth row runs the length of the T-shaped aggregation, separated by a walkway.

The lush tropical vegetation and waterways might suggest a kampong, but putting aside the vegetation, this could easily be a Middle Eastern desert town or Mediterranean hill town. The intimate walkways that link the village are both public and private and are narrow enough to allow opposite houses to shade one another.

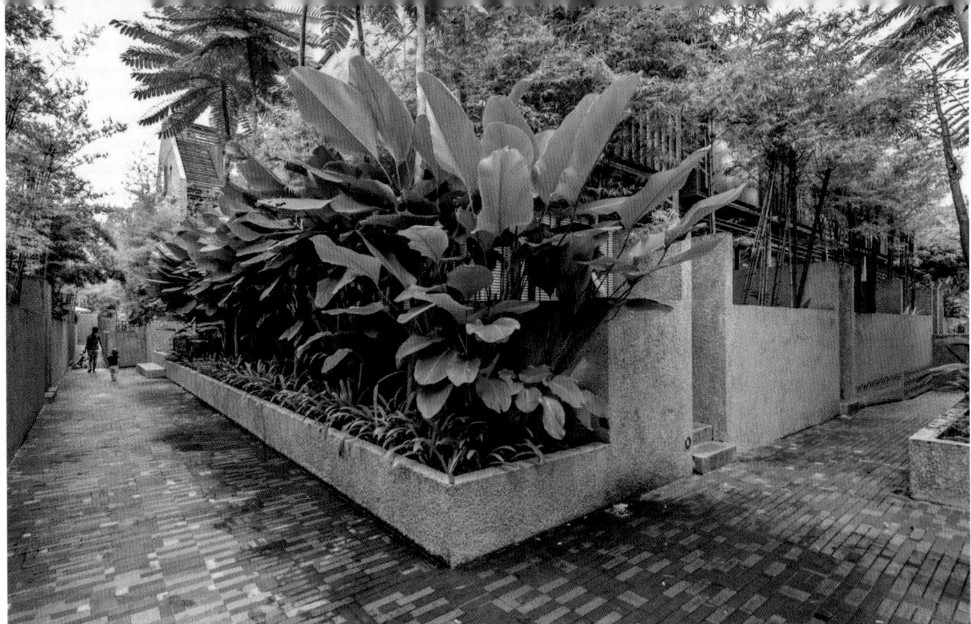

Above The abundant greenery also provides privacy from the village streets.
Below left Cross-section of the complex.
Below right Timber trellises on the roofs allow for vertical greening.
Opposite above Plans.

The child's vision of a house that the architects refer to is a simple and emblematic version of the house as an archetype, which again triggers a sense of something very traditional, very vernacular.

A typical unit has four levels, beginning in the basement where there is parking for two cars and bedroom space. The ground floor level is the public level, with living/dining areas leading to small, green terraces on either side, one going directly to the waterway. The next level and the attic contain bedrooms. With this kind of density, privacy

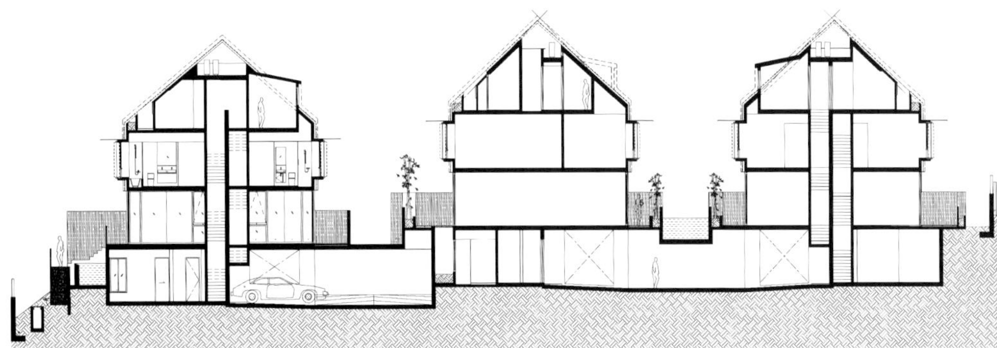

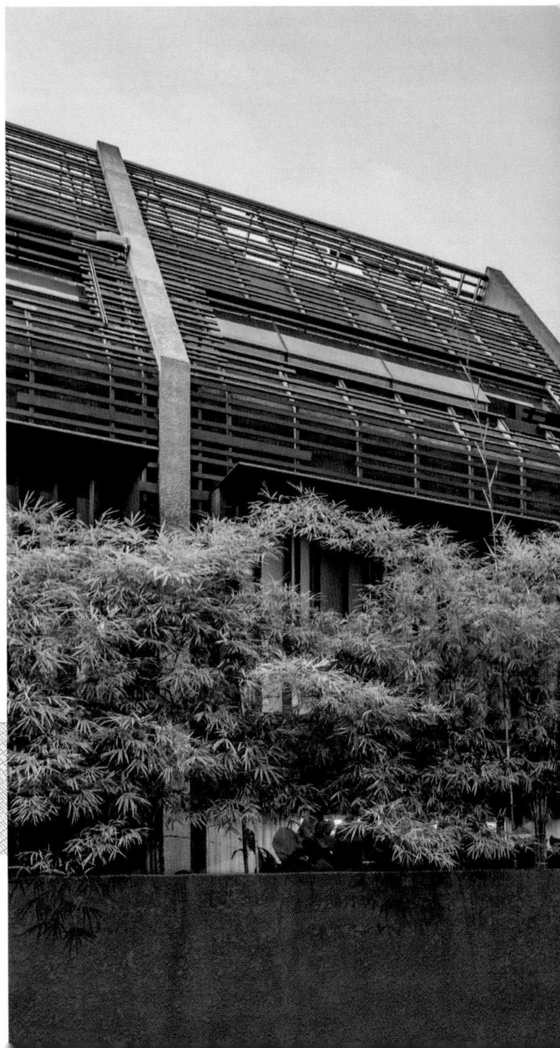

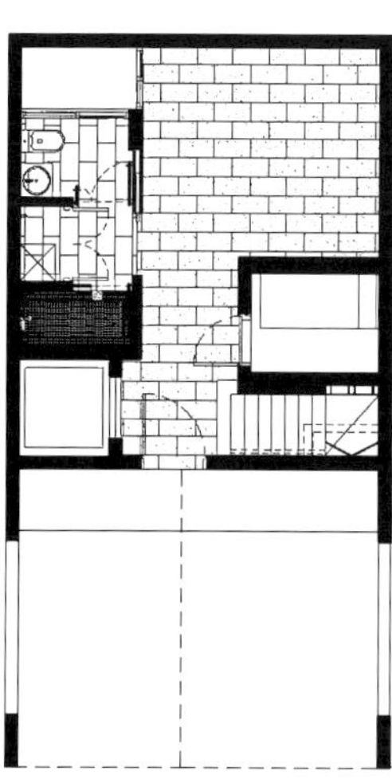

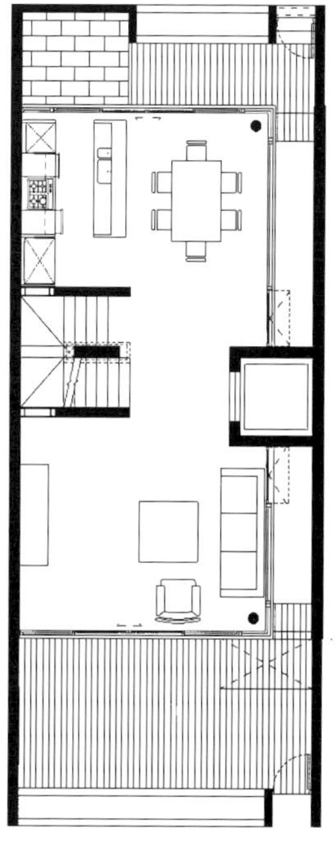

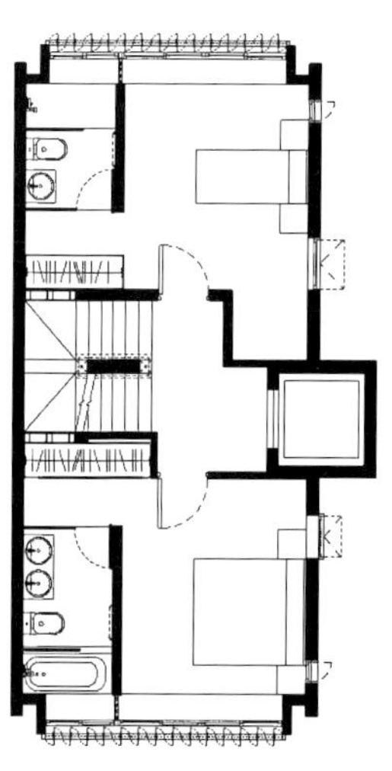

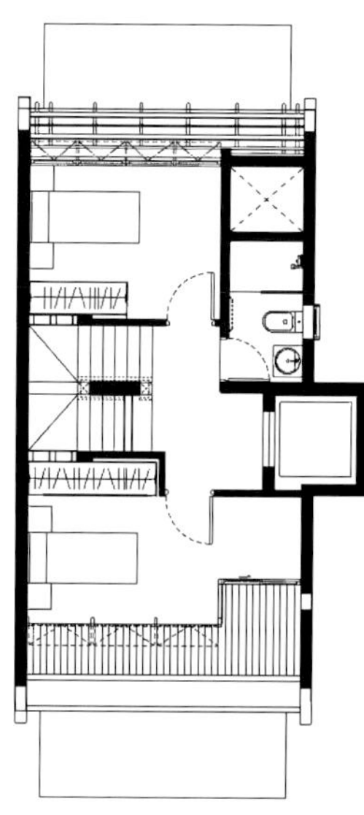

becomes an issue, the challenge being to create privacy without losing the sense of belonging to a community or feeling too constrained physically. The greenery does both these things—creating coherence but also providing privacy screening. Timber trellises for creepers on the roofs and second storey walls is a strategy for vertical greening, adding to the coherence of the complex and acting as a passive cooling device. Blade walls and vertical timber louvres provide further privacy screening.

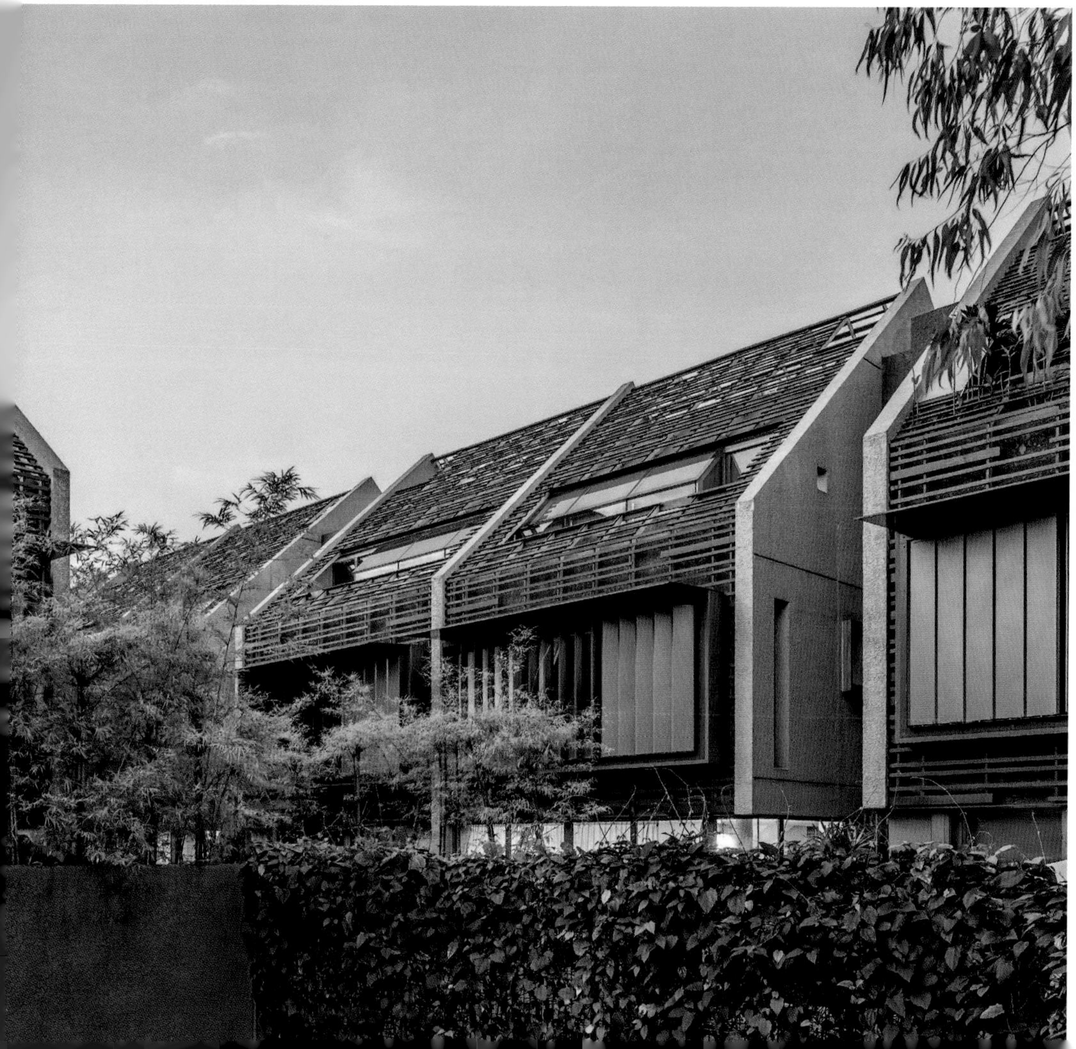

Watten Residences is a particularly adept and sensitive response to the ongoing Singaporean challenge of creating higher densities in the land-strapped island state, at the same time encouraging a sense of ownership, individuality and access to greenery, light, fresh air and water. This goes hand in hand with the aim of balancing privacy and community. The Singaporean government has long stressed the importance of community if the island state, devoid as it is of natural resources, is to sustain itself in the long term. Increasingly, however, changing mores have led to a growing demand for more privacy and autonomy, a demand which architects and developers are responding to in increasingly creative ways.

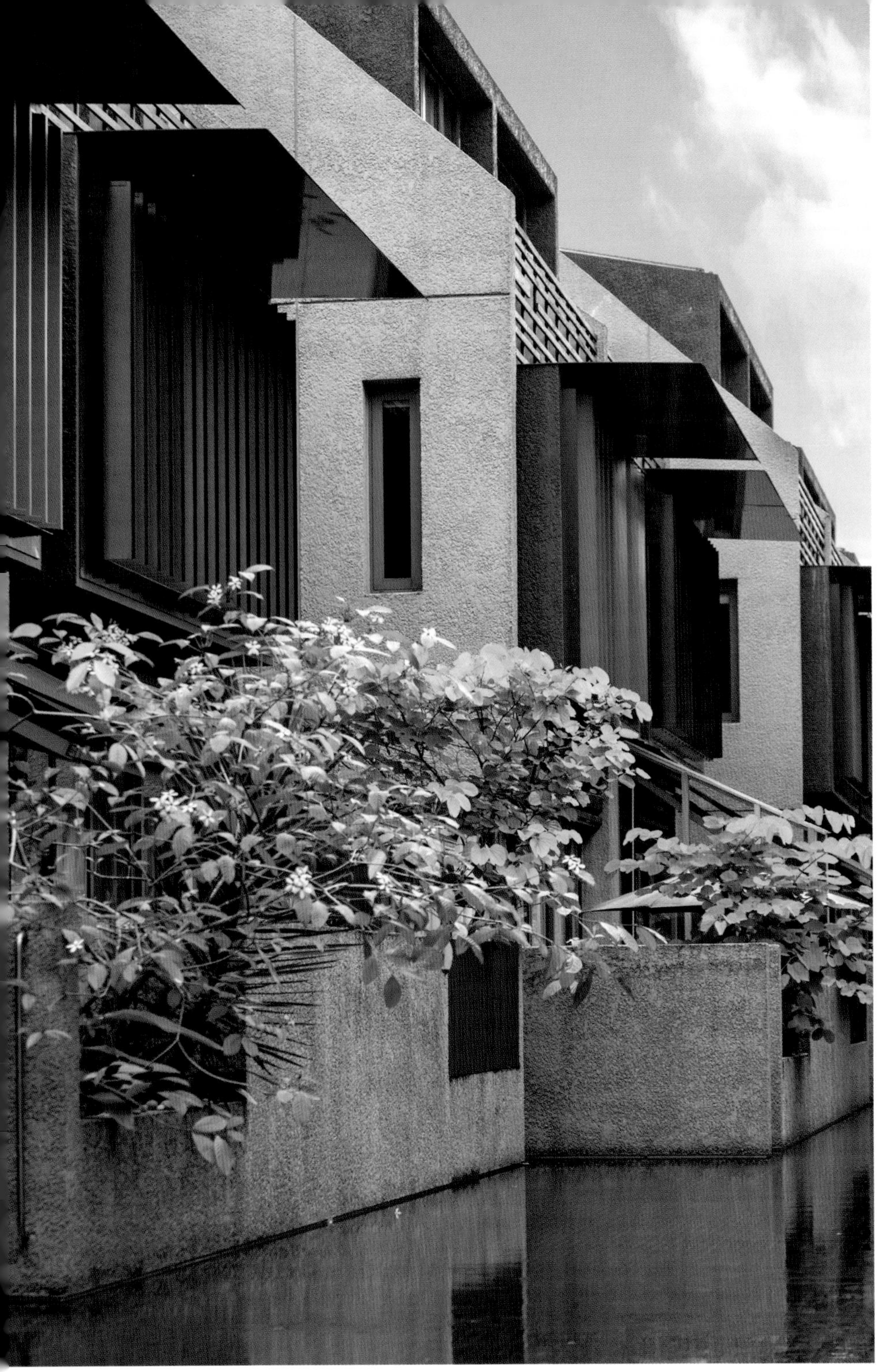

Above The faces of individual units are enlivened by a variety of screens and windows.

Right Different materials provide a textured palette.

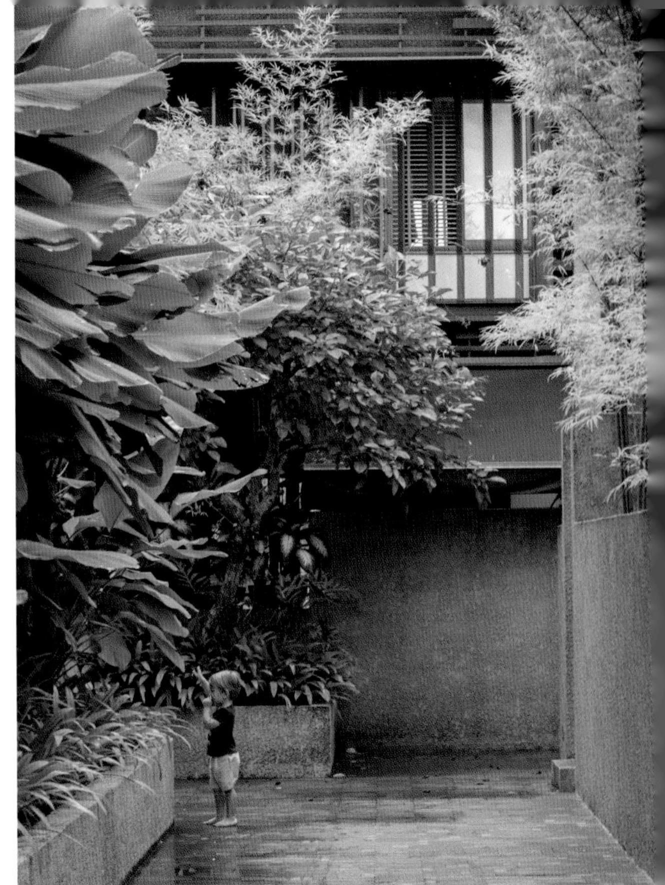

Above The 'canyon streets' are cooled by greenery and the close proximity of the buildings.

Right Reflections off the water enhance the textural finishes of the buildings.

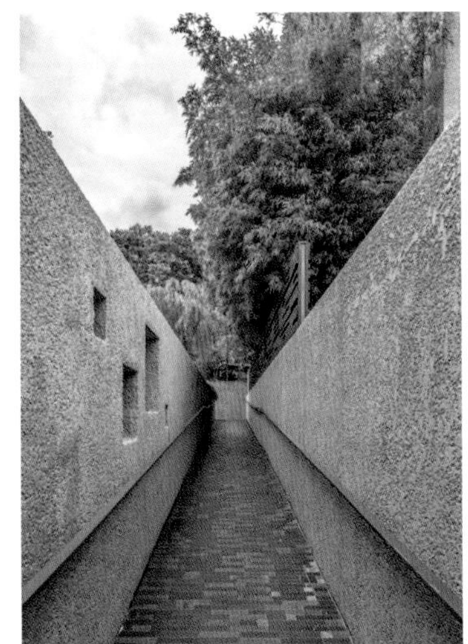

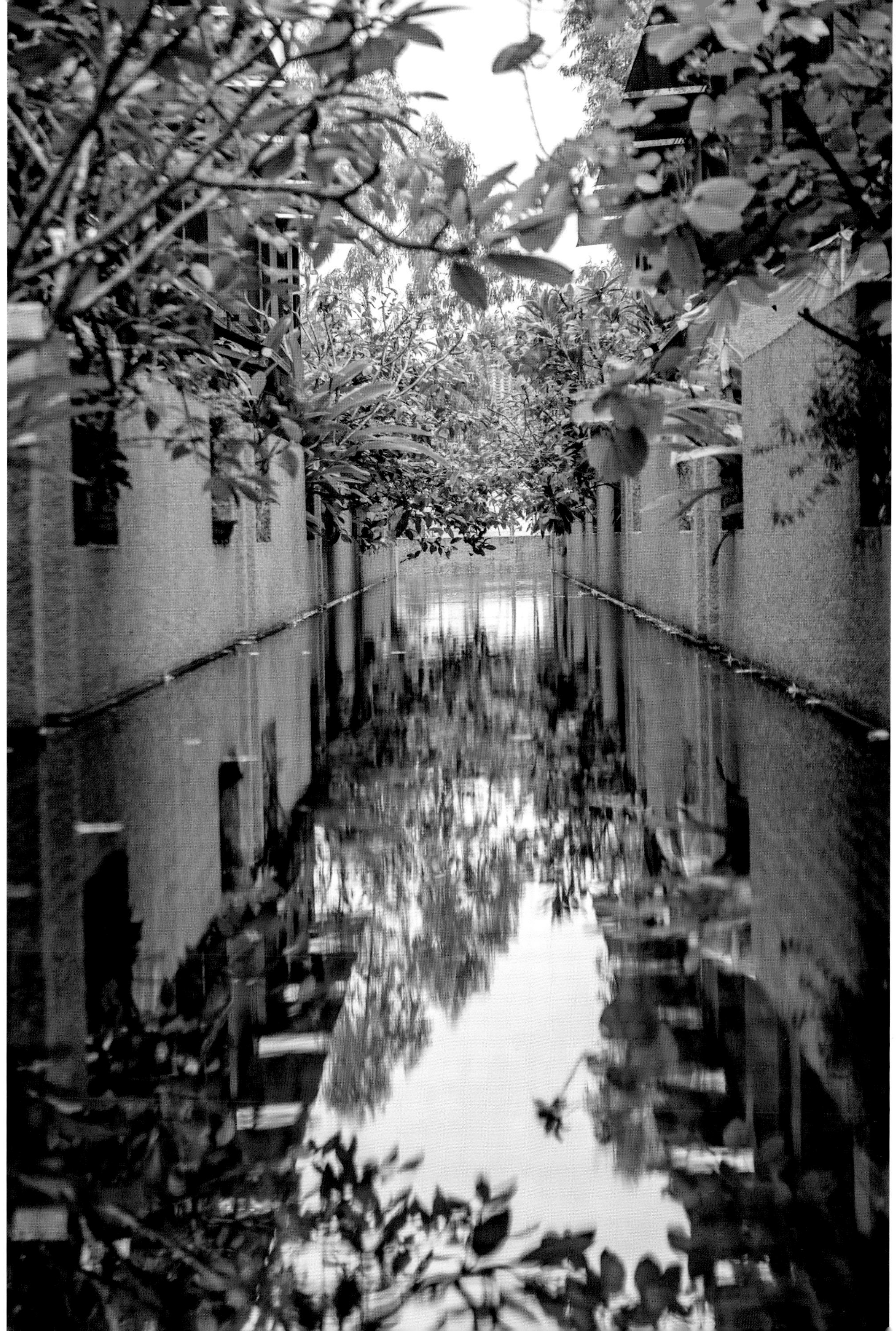

THE GREEN COLLECTION
RT+Q ARCHITECTS

'The intent was to design an alternative type of architecture as a visual counterpoint to the prevailing standards of aesthetics in Sentosa.'— ARCHITECT

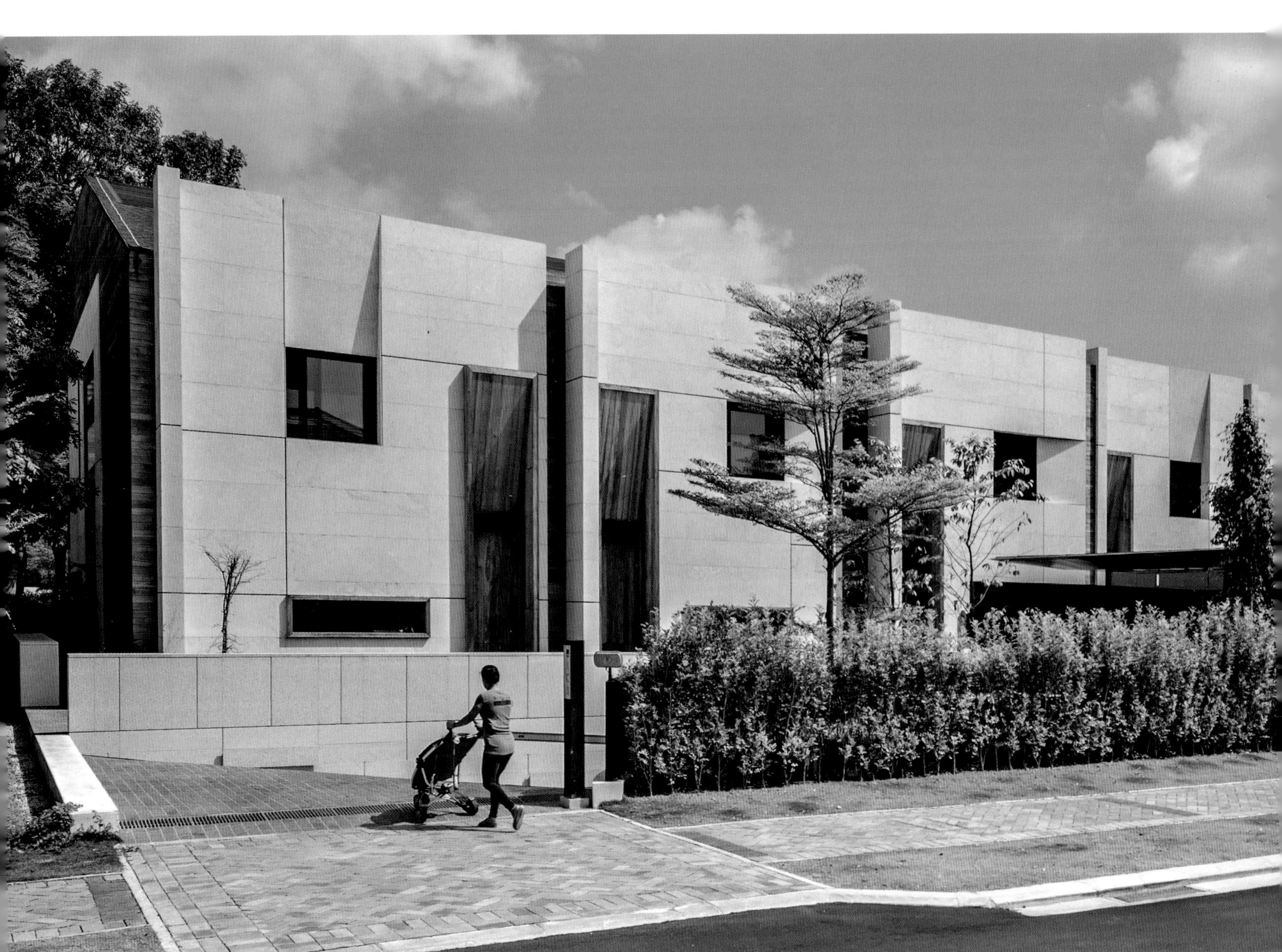

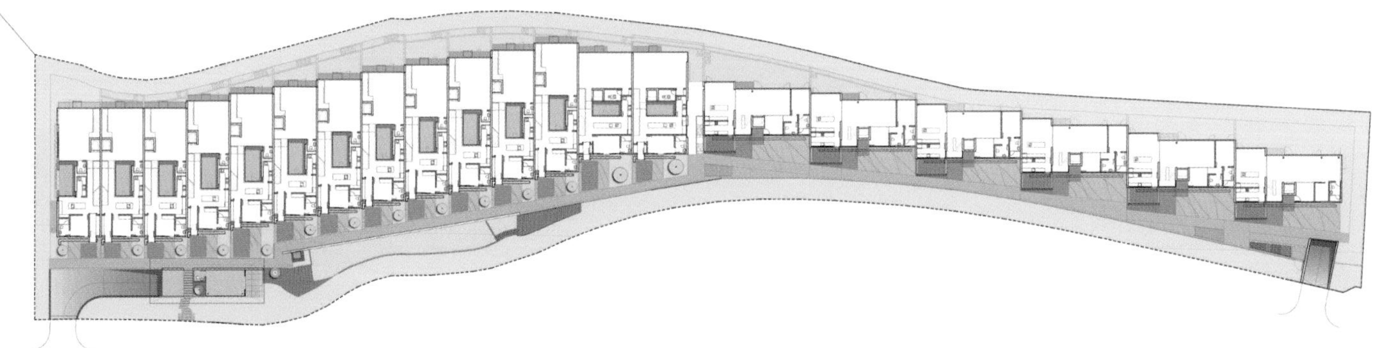

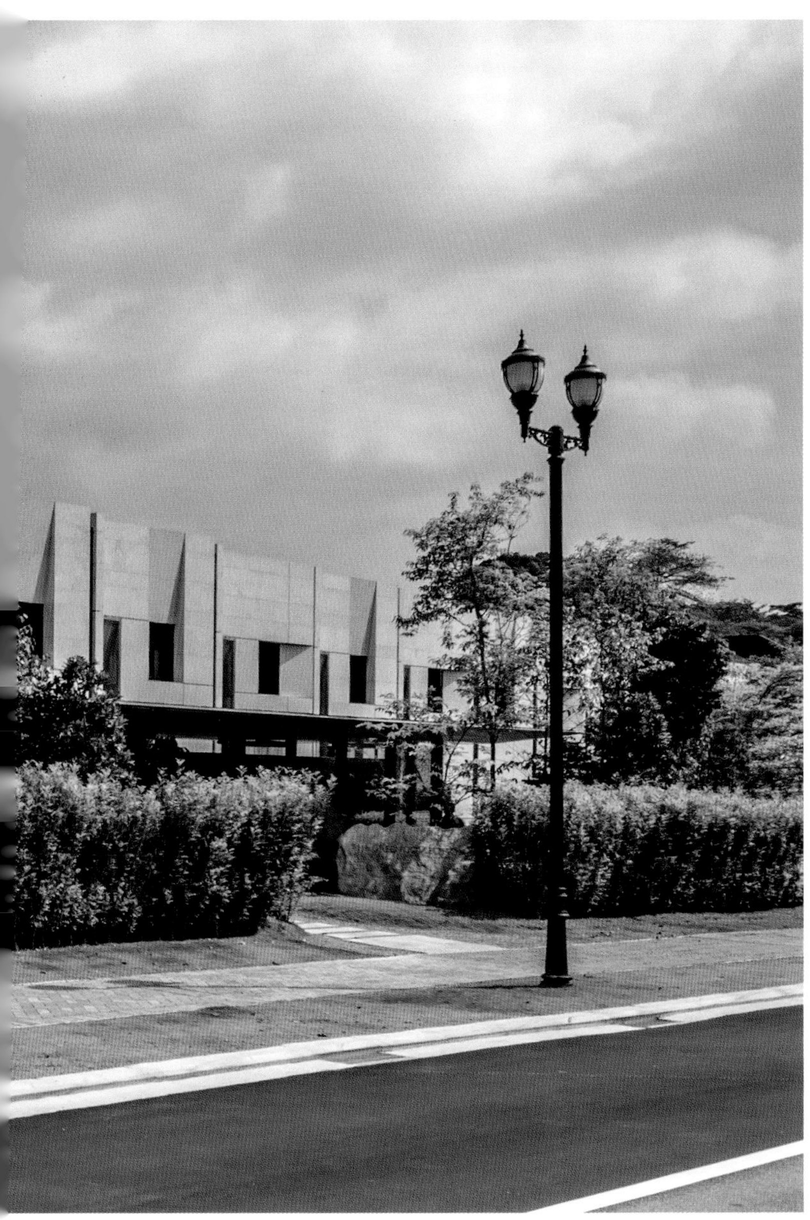

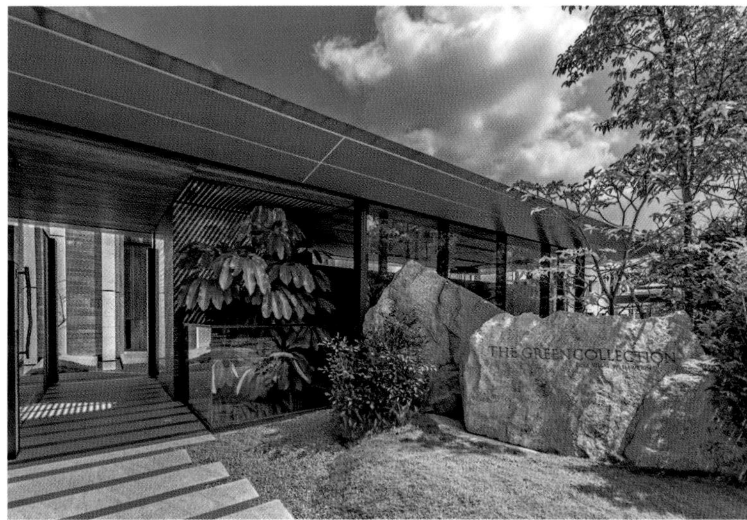

A joke doing the rounds about Sentosa Island is that it is a place where you cannot park your car on the street but where you are welcome to park your money. Although it may be only a fifteen minute drive from downtown Singapore, very few people actually live there. As the only part of Singapore where foreigners can buy freehold land, there is a lot of money invested in the bricks and mortar but not a whole lot in building a true community.

This award-winning development addresses this issue, aiming to create a living community. It is an example of cluster terrace housing—optimizing the site while giving individual units a sense of individuality and access to green space. In this case, individual units have very little private outdoor space. Even the deck, water feature and small plot of lawn at the entry to each unit is as much public as it is private. The rear decks and courtyards off the

Opposite From the street, the fenestration, vertical slots and timber doors give the façade a sculptural quality.

Top Plan.

Above The complex is screened from the street by greenery and the low horizontal plane of the reception and community pavilion.

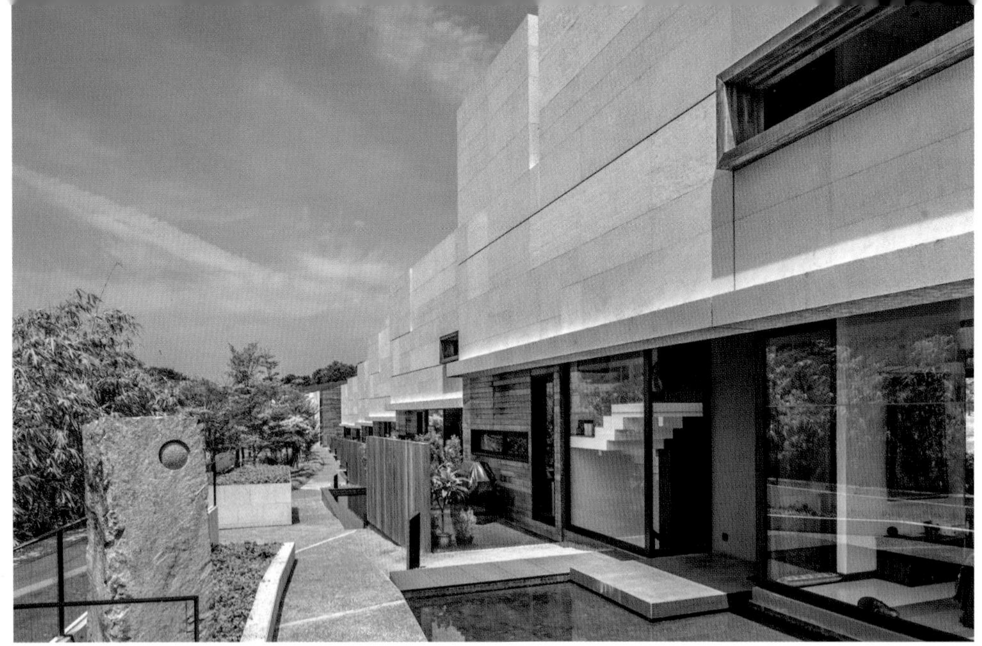

Left Behind the streetside greenery, ponds and floating pods and footbridges enliven the façade.

Below A landscaped pool meanders down towards the community activities pavilion at the front of the complex.

Opposite above The massing of the building is constantly broken down to create a sense of individuality.

Opposite below Individual swimming pools are at the rear of the complex, overlooking the golf course.

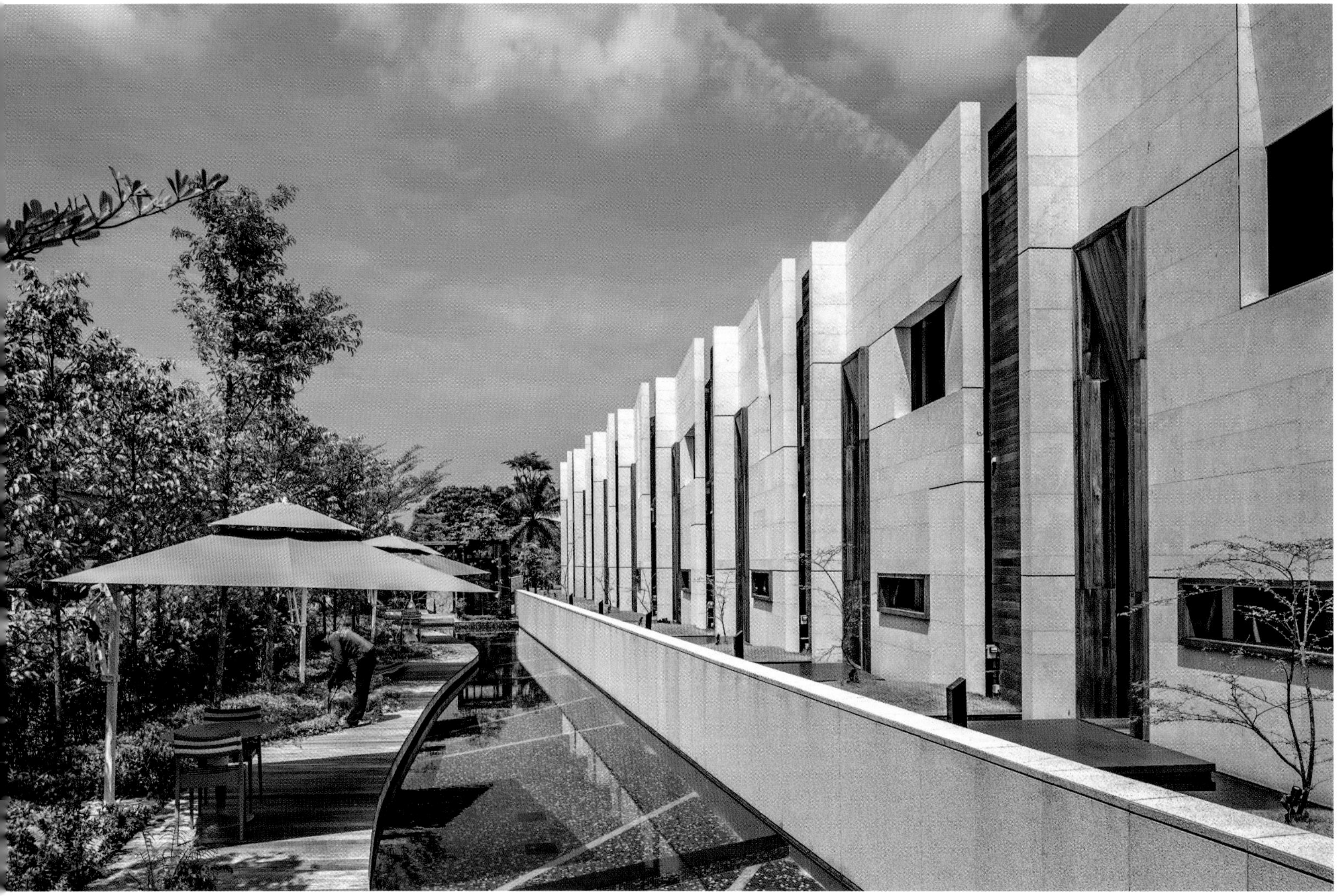

ground floor living areas are, however, more private. But the real *coup de théatre* is the communal space on the street frontage and the 'borrowed scenery' at the rear.

Like most cluster housing, this is a gated community, with entry either by car through the basement car park or by foot through the concierge building. A wall and trees screen the street side elevation. But there is also an exquisite meandering pool with landscaping by Shunmyo Masuno. The legendary Japanese landscape architect and Zen Buddhist monk has here created a typical blend of the contemporary and the traditional, providing a Zen garden as a place for reflection and contemplation. A community activities pavilion is attached to this garden.

At the rear, however, the complex enjoys unprecedented borrowed landcape: the Tanjong

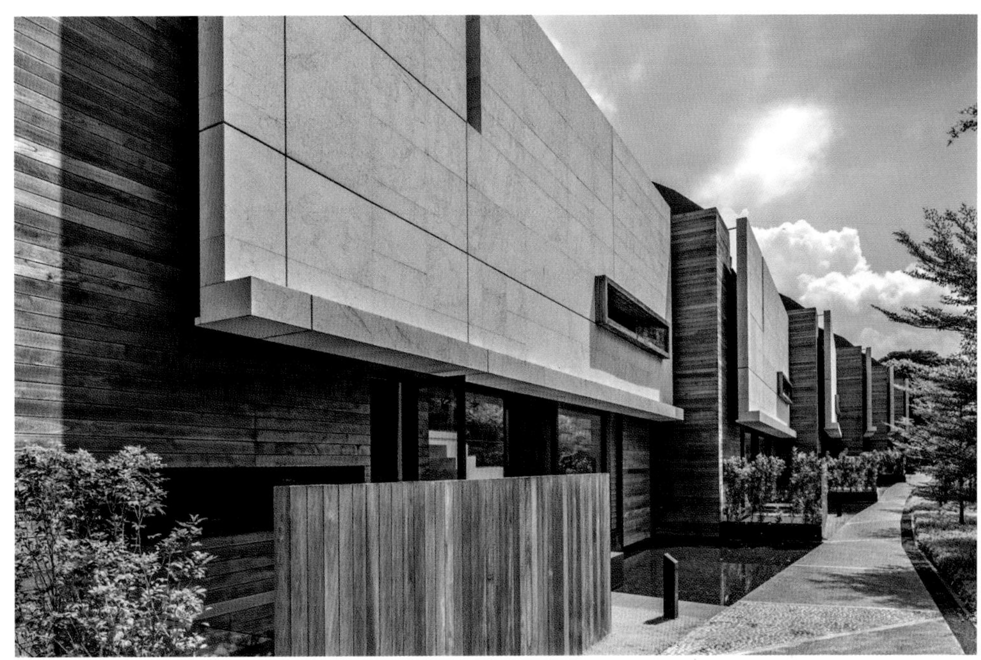

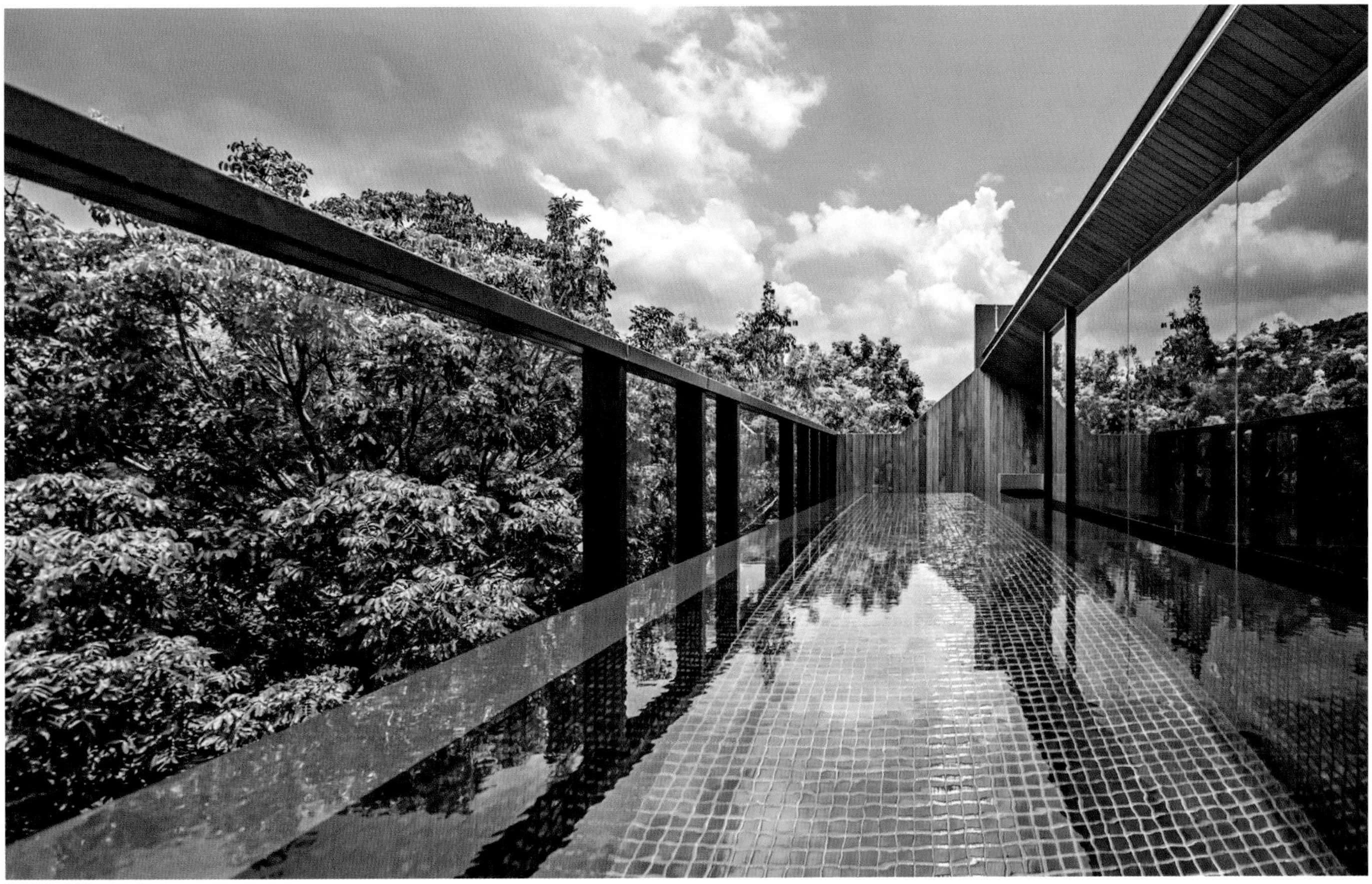

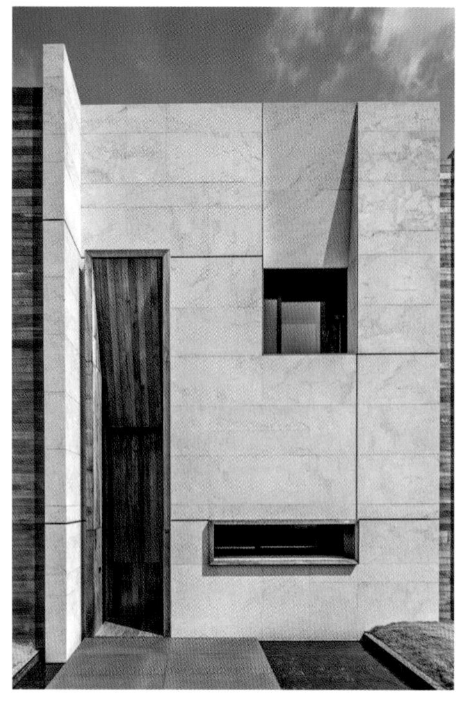

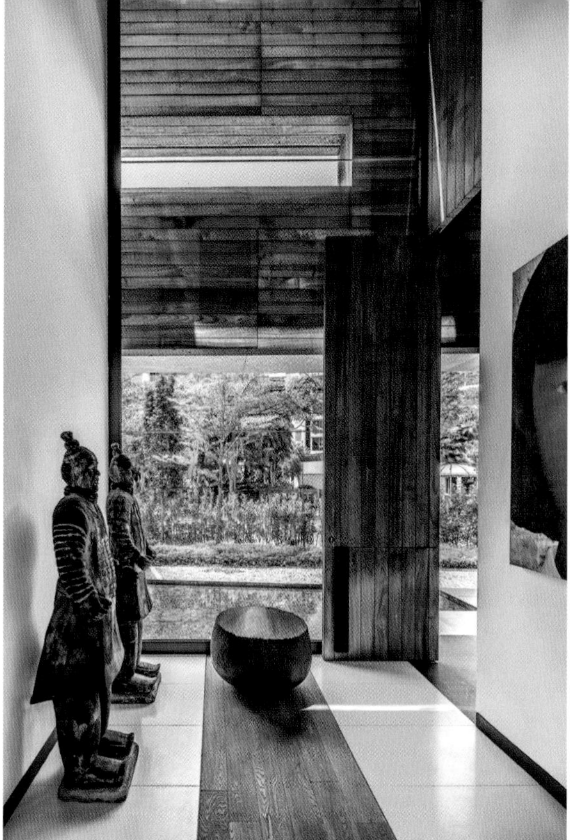

Far left The concrete façade, massive timber entry doors and varied windows create a sense of antique monumentality.

Left From inside looking down the entry corridor where the huge timber door contrasts with the horizontal slot window.

Below The community pavilion.

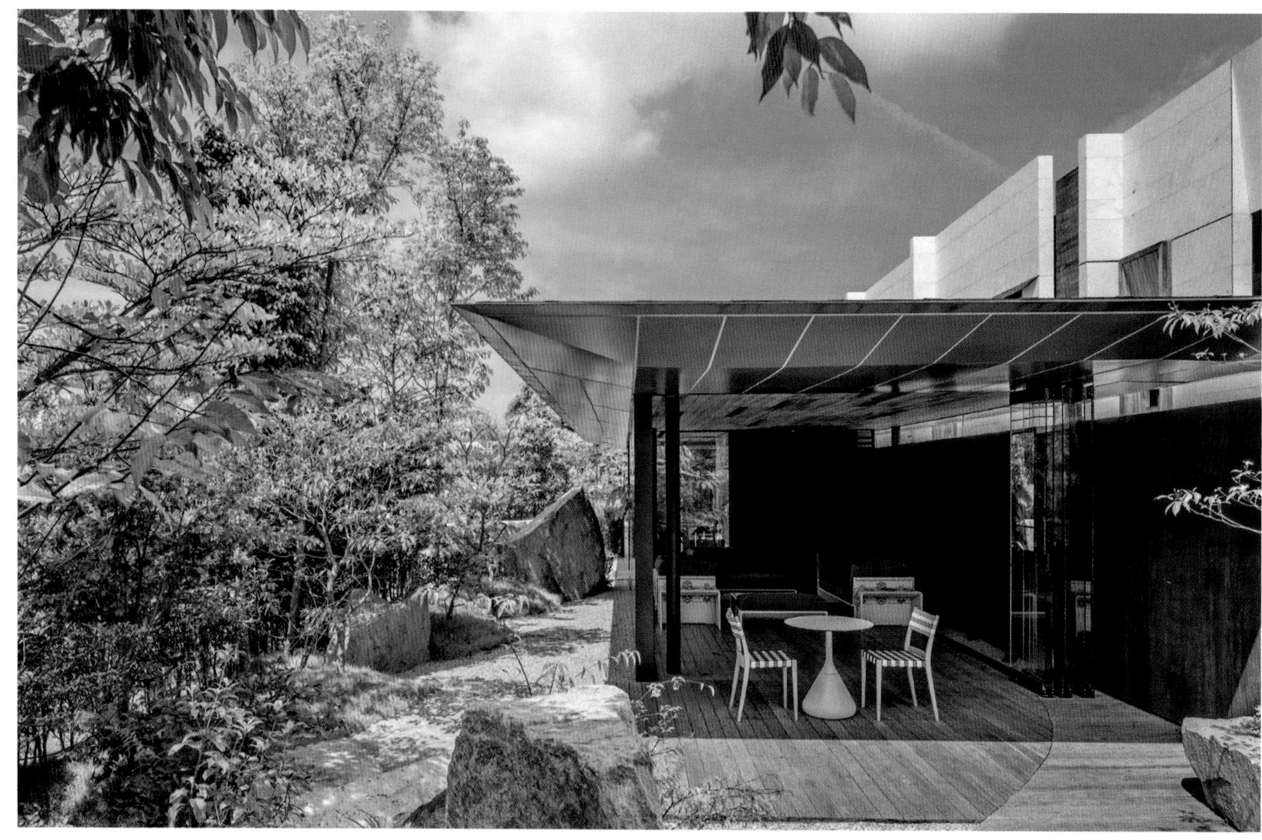

Right A full-height naturally lit void forms the centre of each unit.

Below Section.

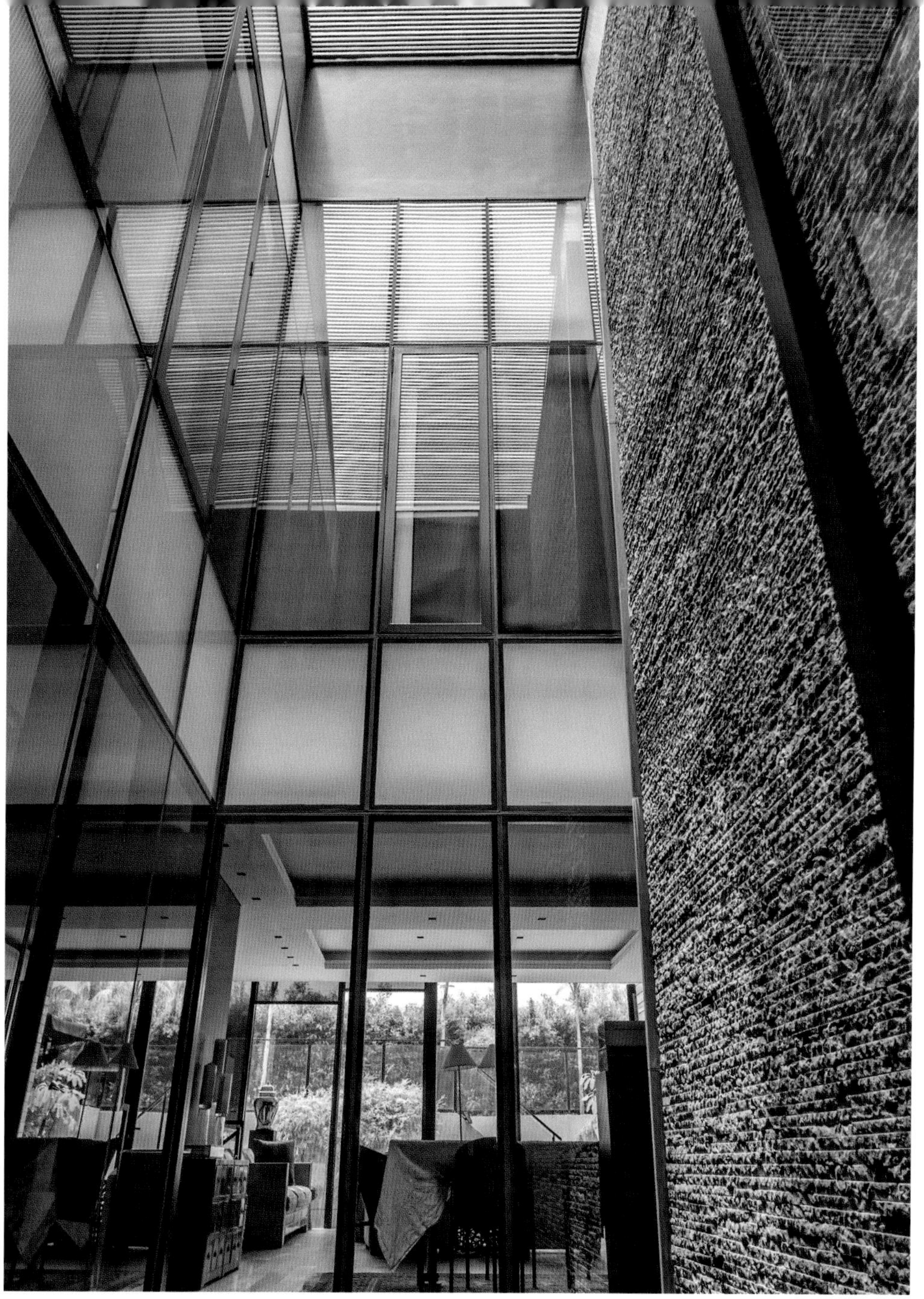

golf course. The rear of the terraces opens directly on to this sublime view of golf greens and forest, the best possible antidote to any sense of claustrophobia caused by living in a party-walled terrace complex.

Like Masuno's landscaping, the architecture of the terraces also suggests a blend of the contemporary and the traditional. There is a hint of classical monumentality to the façades with their concrete blockwork, faceted second storey windows set back into the wall for shading, and horizontal rectangular windows on the ground floor extruded to create visual variety but maintain privacy from the public walkway in front. Majestic double-height timber entry doors are also set back within timber frames, with full-height timber screens signalling the demarcation between units.

The monumental façade hints at a secret hidden behind it, which will be revealed only after passing through the grand portal. The secret, of course, is the magnificent view across the golf greens. But this is not revealed immediately on entry. Inside, there is a glass void drawing light into the interior. To one side there is a timber stairway to the upper level bedrooms, unseen from the entry. Straight ahead is a small flight of steps leading up to the living/dining space. It is only after a journey through the house that the view is fully revealed, with the rear of the house a transparent glass skin.

Apart from actually encouraging people to come and live at Sentosa, the Green Collection, in its architecture, landscaping and restricted palette of materials (echoed on the inside by Kelly Hoppen's

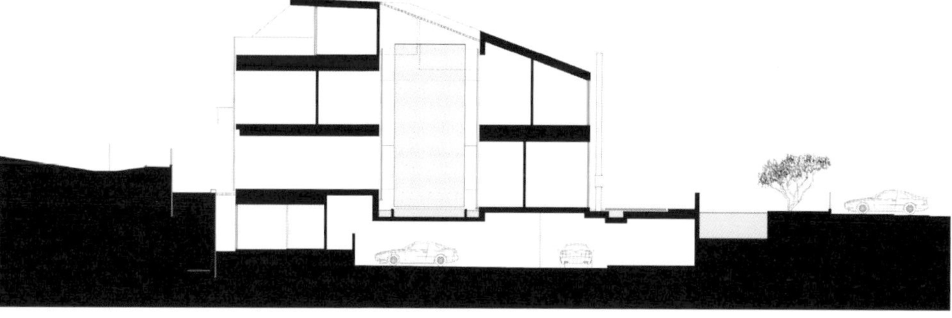

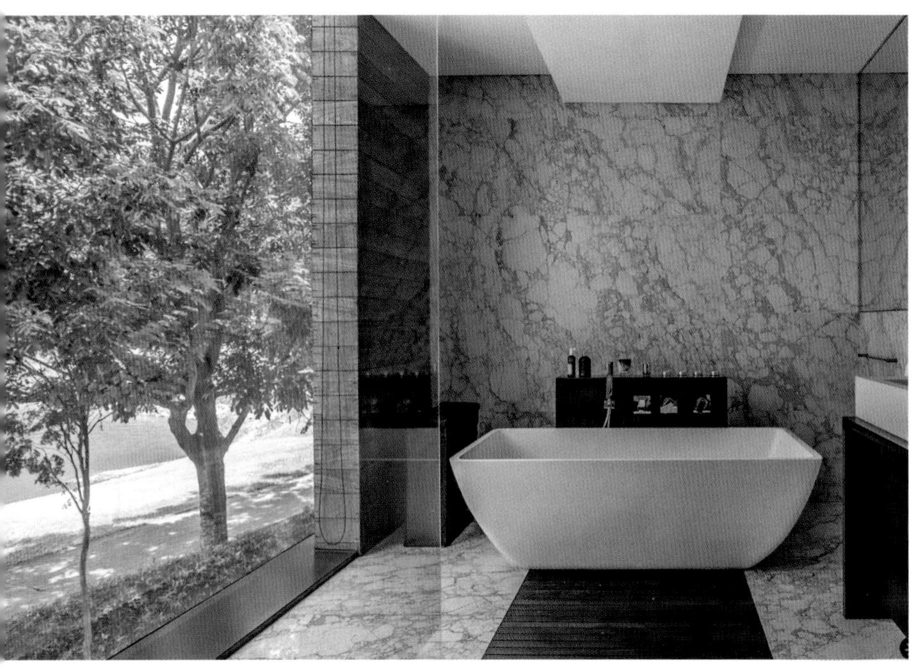

Left The master bathroom overlooks the golf course.

Below A view of the living/dining space and kitchen. The stairs lead to the upper level.

Bottom left Plans.

Bottom right The glazed lift to the basement car park.

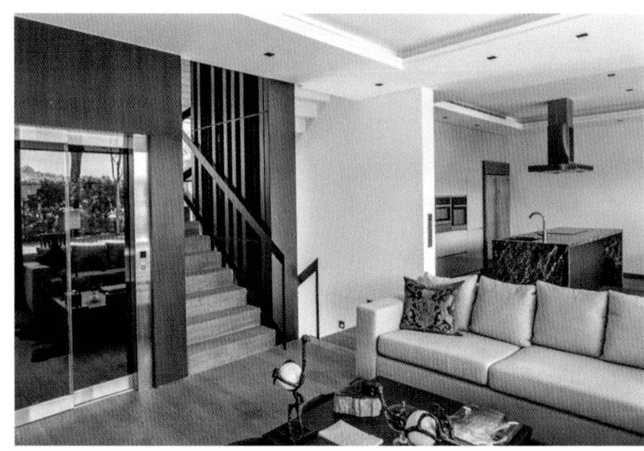

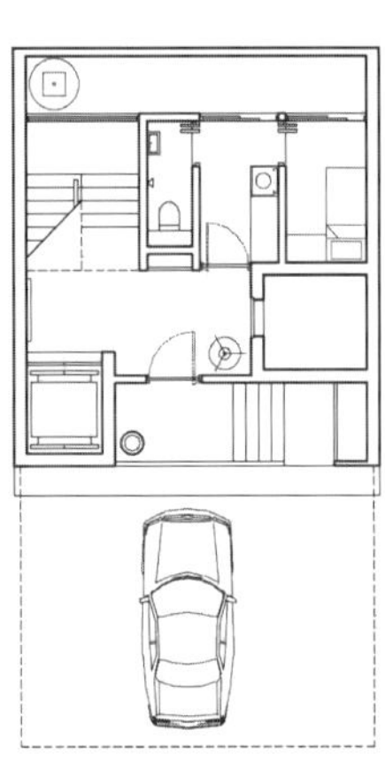

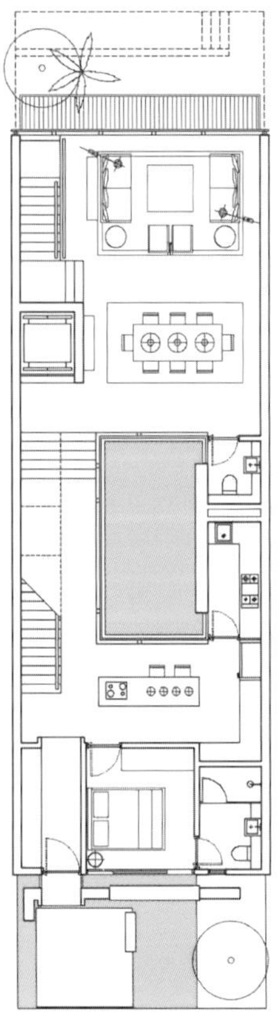

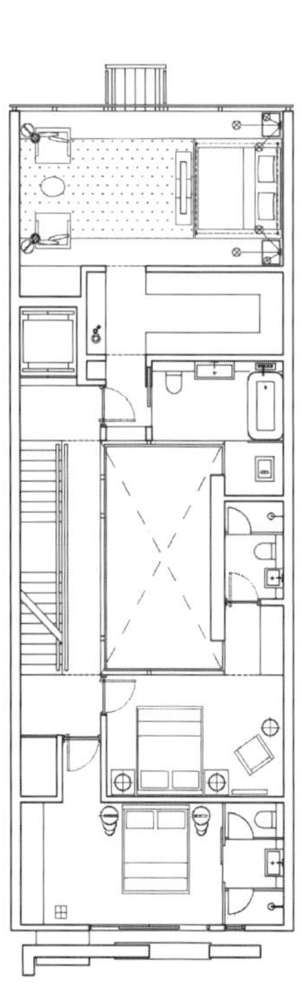

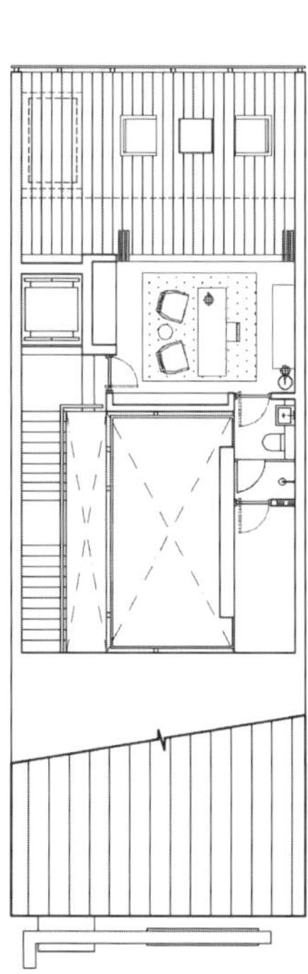

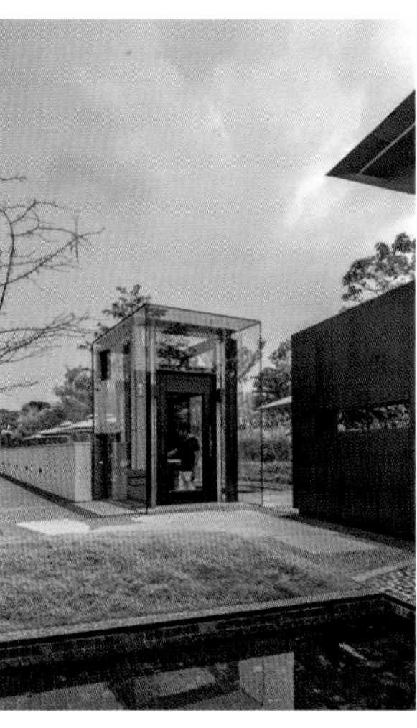

interior design) challenges the uniformity of Sentosa's rigid guidelines governing setbacks, roof profiles, materials and colour palette. Paradoxically, there is more than a hint of 'look at me' architecture on Sentosa, prompting the architects of the Green Collection to conceive of the complex as a 'back-drop to the existing physical environment, with fewer moves but bigger moves'.

The Green Collection is an excellent example of the growing interest in cluster housing, a strategy that is sustainable in a number of respects. It aims to make multi-residential living more sustainable, not just in the usual way of optimizing available land for higher densities at affordable prices but also in the various ways it creates the sense of living in a place with its own character (in other words, a home) and offers the amenities both of a landed house (green space, light, air and landscape views) and a condominium.

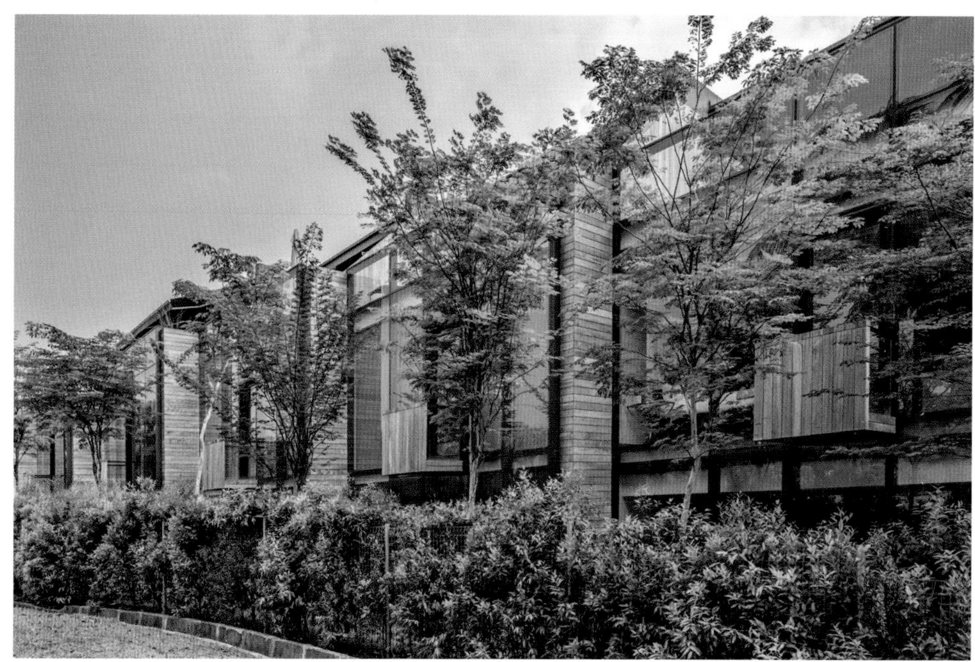

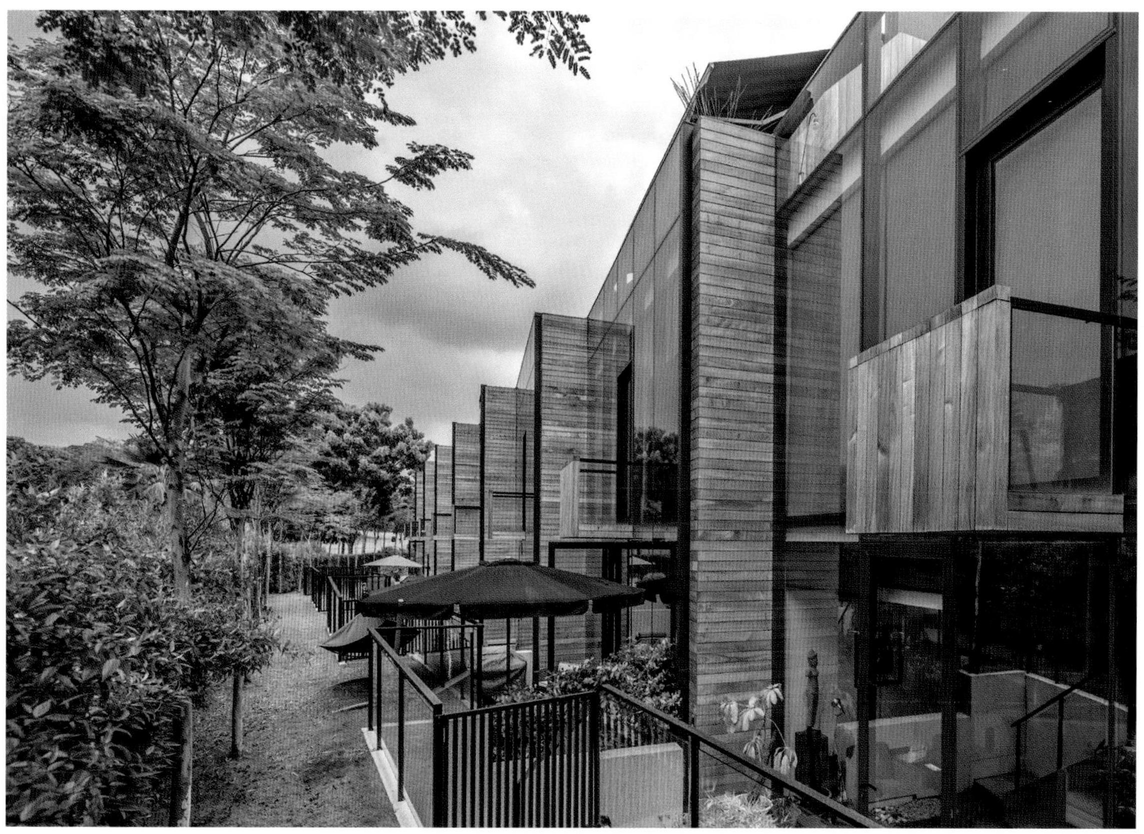

Above Trees and hedges separate the rear of the complex from the golf course.

Left The massing of the building is constantly broken down, along with a variety of materials, to create an endlessly varied façade.

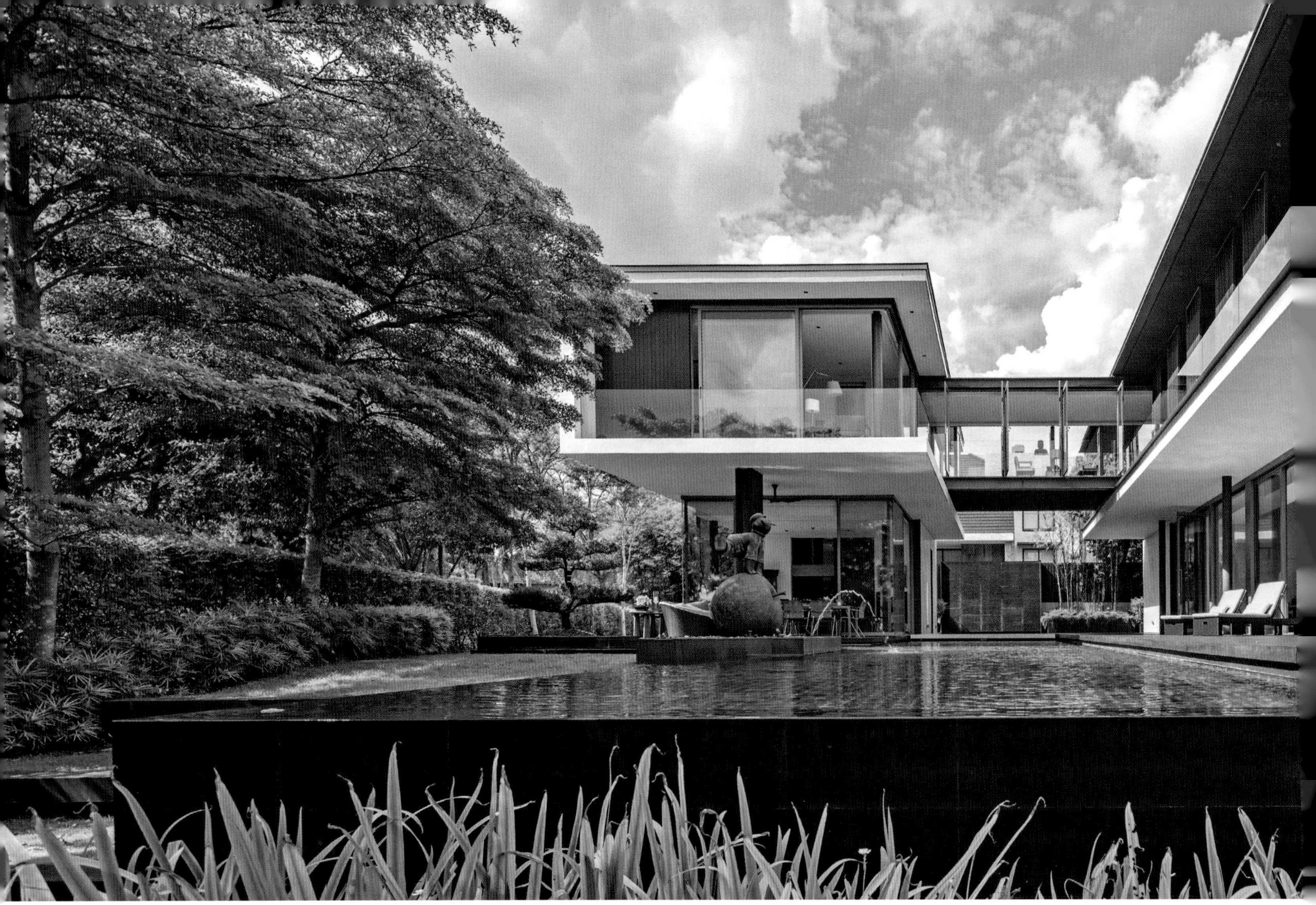

VERANDAH HOUSE
RT+Q ARCHITECTS

'The house does not really have a front door, save for the basement. The main front is actually the whole thing.'—ARCHITECT

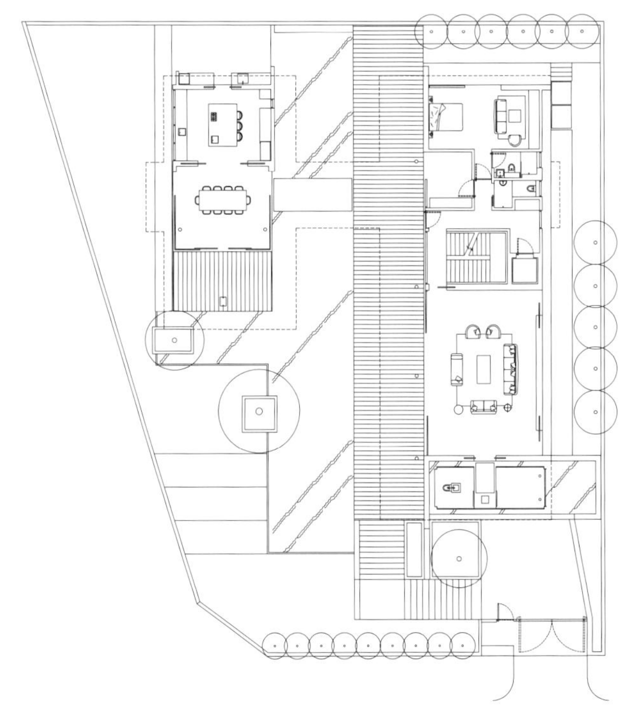

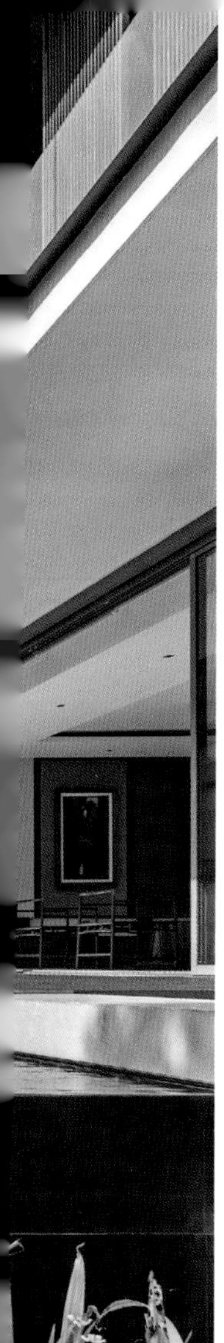

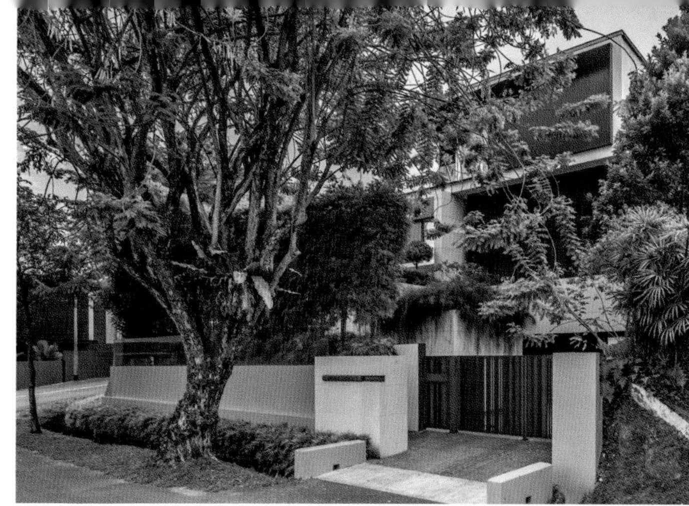

This house would seem to confirm the old adage that a man's home is his castle. Occupying a corner site, the house sits high above the road, epitomizing the Frank Lloyd Wright principle of refuge and prospect. On the one hand, it commands its locality like a castle or citadel, impregnable to attack—except that this lofty position is less about keeping watch for interlopers and more about having access to the panoramic views. On the other hand, it is definitely a refuge, a place to withdraw to and reconnect with oneself and the family after a day of dealing with the outside world. Just as Wright saw refuge and prospect as key to the sustainability of the home, so this house is about sustaining three generations of a family while also being an ideal venue in which to entertain guests.

The occupants drive in to a basement car park and enter the house through a vestibule and stairs to the first storey. Guests, however, are more likely to experience a very different arrival sequence, one which only reveals the house after a journey starting at the left of the basement entry and up a flight of steps. Initially, the house confirms its first impression as a citadel. The driveway is protected by a sculptural steel screen gate. Above this is a timber screen box (the first storey of the house) and above that another timber screen box with a large glass corner window and broad eaves (the second storey). Giving further texture to this street elevation are planters with trees set at different levels, part of an overall strategy for lush trees and bushes to provide a screen around the upper perimeter of the house. For the guests, now making their way up the garden steps, what is then revealed is the whole story of the

Opposite above After an extended arrival sequence, this is the view that is finally revealed to the visitor.

Opposite below First storey plan.

Above The elevation of the house and the greenery in front withhold a full view of the house until the visitor has progressed up the steps to the left of the gate.

Below The house consists of two pavilions linked by a glazed footbridge.

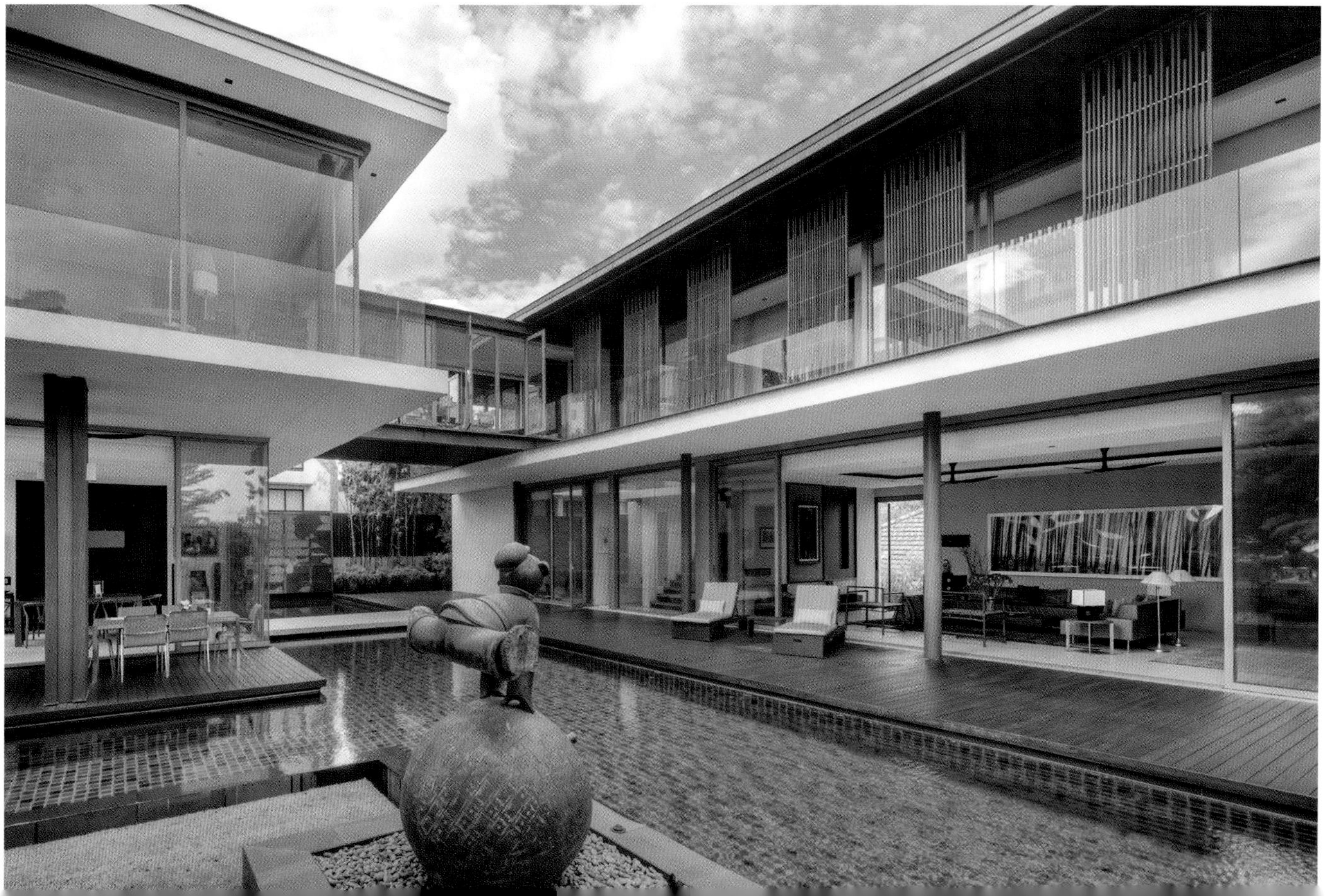

house in one dramatic image, a kind of panorama that begins with a lawn and tropical vegetation, then pans past a bizarre sculpture thrusting out over the pool, a 'floating' bonsai tree, an entirely glazed dining pavilion, the swimming pool and down the other side of the pool to the extensive living area, all forming a grand garden courtyard. The upper level of the house is screened, with the exception of a glass connecting bridge, by timber batten screens, and appears to float above the largely transparent and open lower level.

This is a multi-generational house and the planning clearly separates the parents's domain and the master bedroom over the dining pavilion from the children's bedrooms on the long wing of the second storey. The grandmother's quarters are at the far end of the first storey. Otherwise, this level

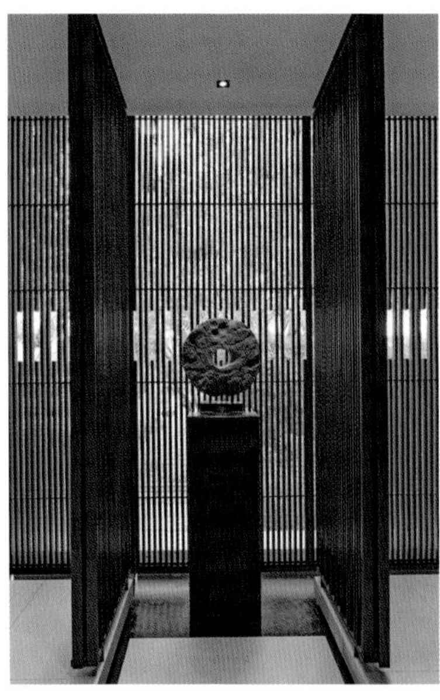

Left and right The powder room off the living space is a beautiful assembly of stone, water, timber screens and filtered light.

Below The expansive living space.

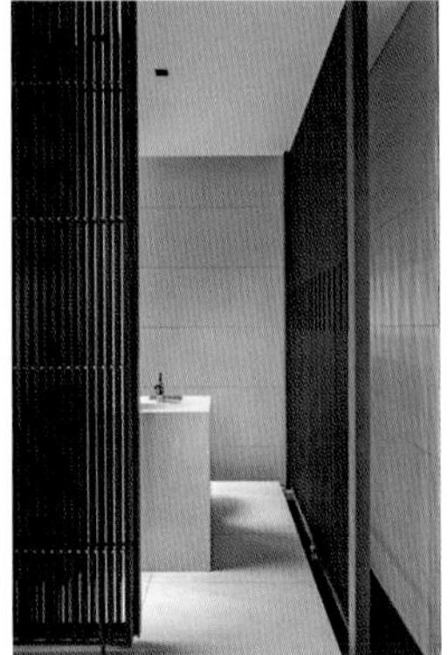

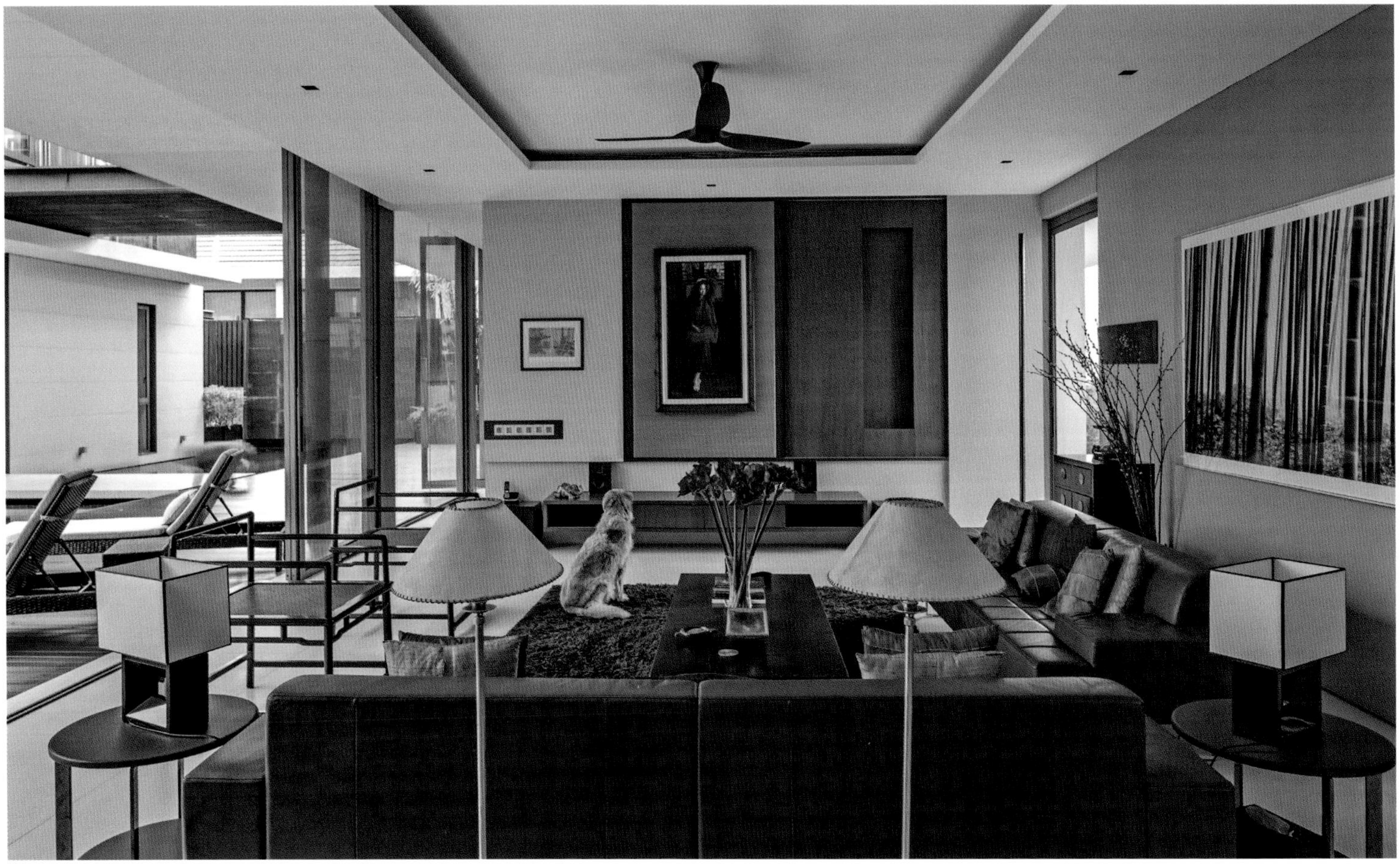

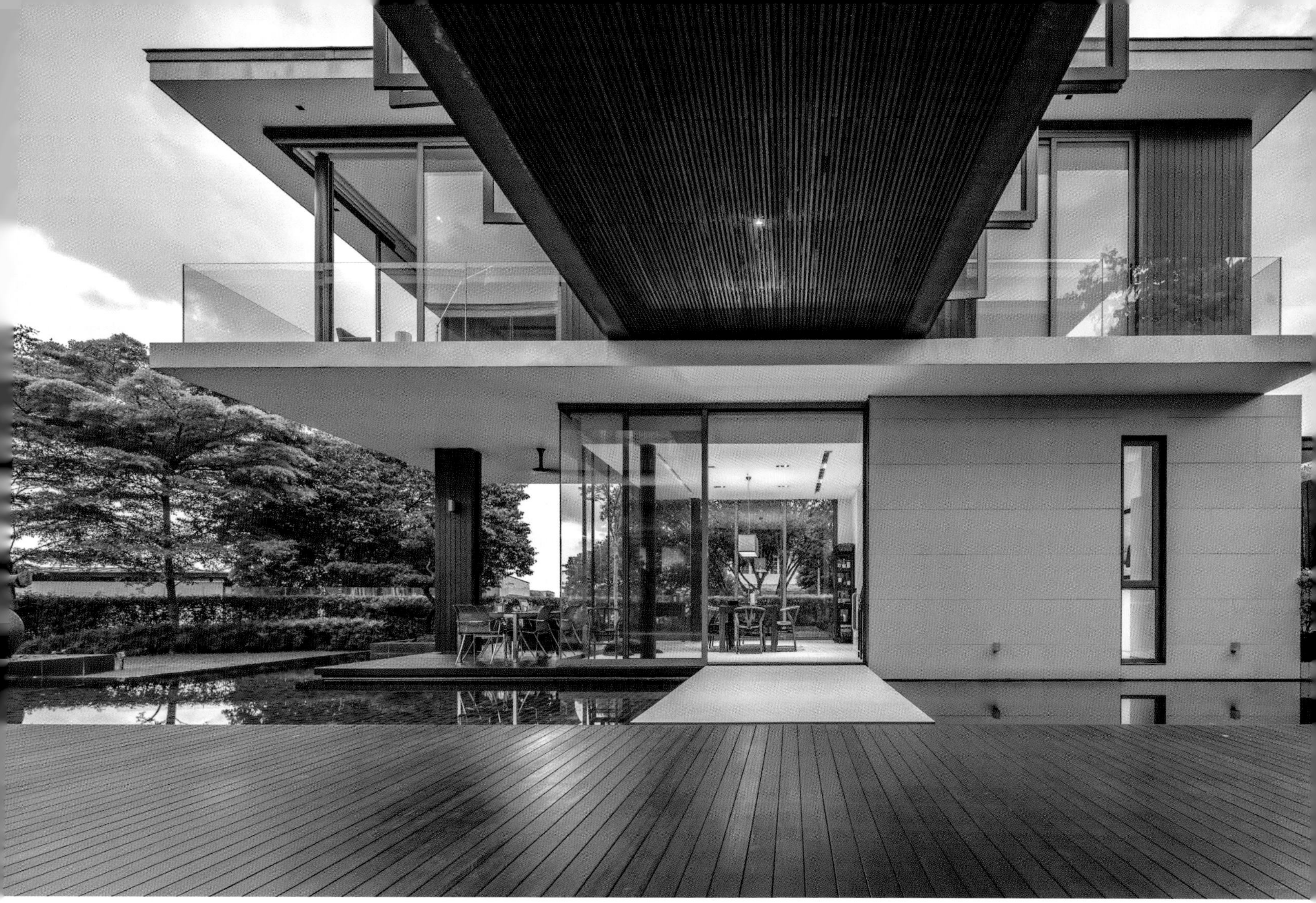

Above The dining pavilion is accessed by a footbridge across the pool.

Right The dining pavilion seems to hover over the water and opens up to an outdoor terrace.

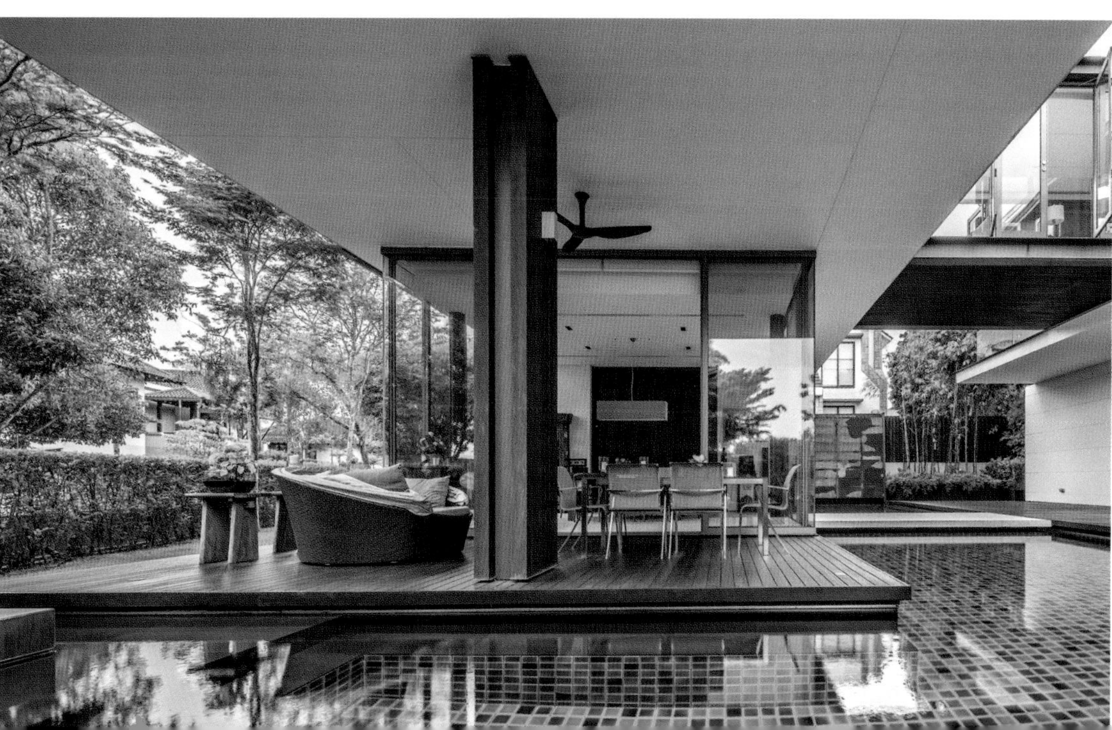

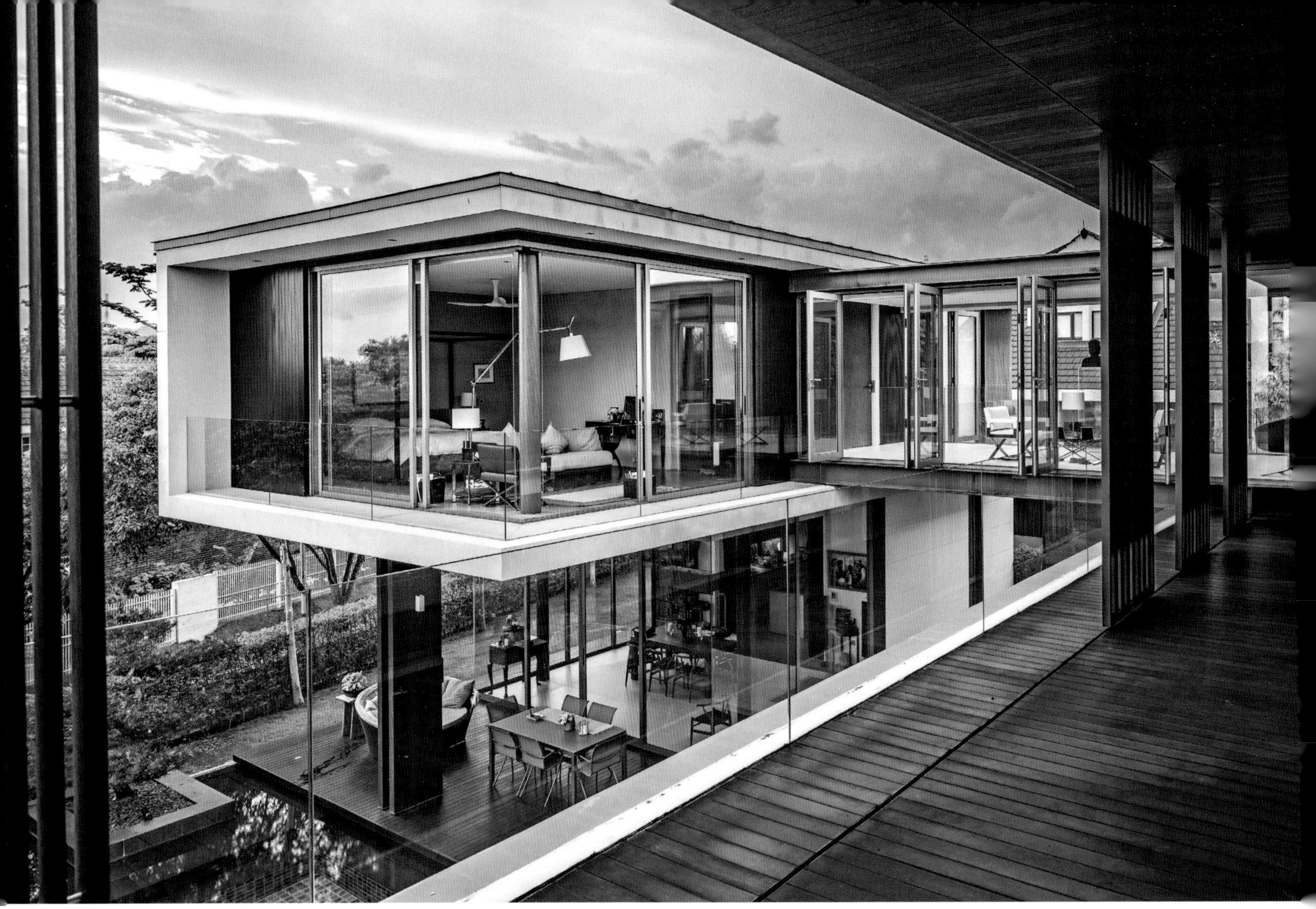

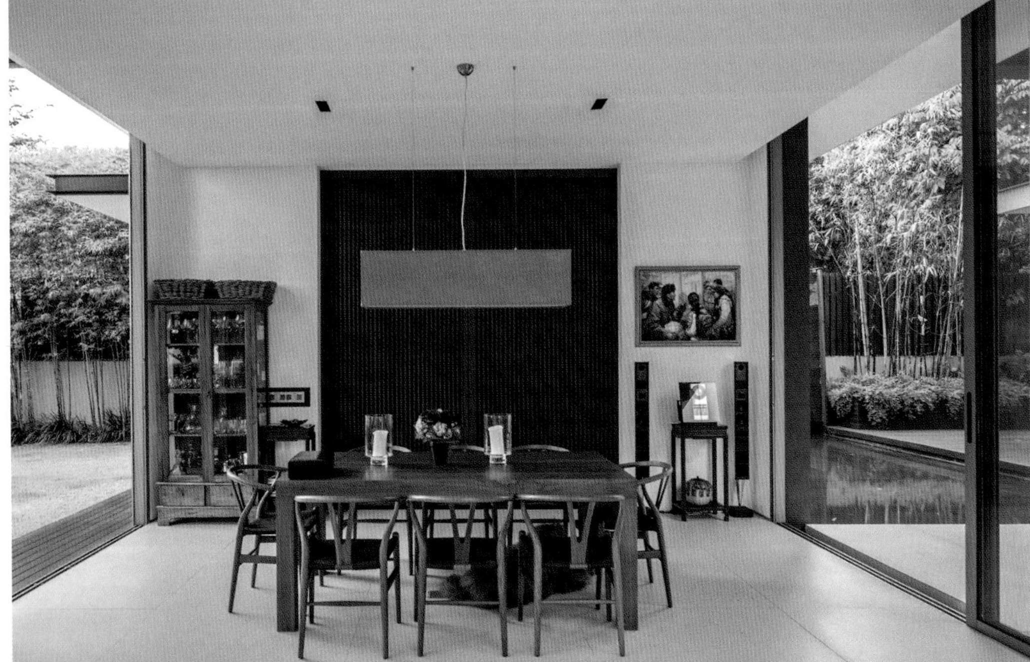

Above The master bedroom sits above the dining space and is accessed by the glazed footbridge from the other pavilion.

Left The dining room is fully transparent except for the rear wall beyond which are the wet and dry kitchens.

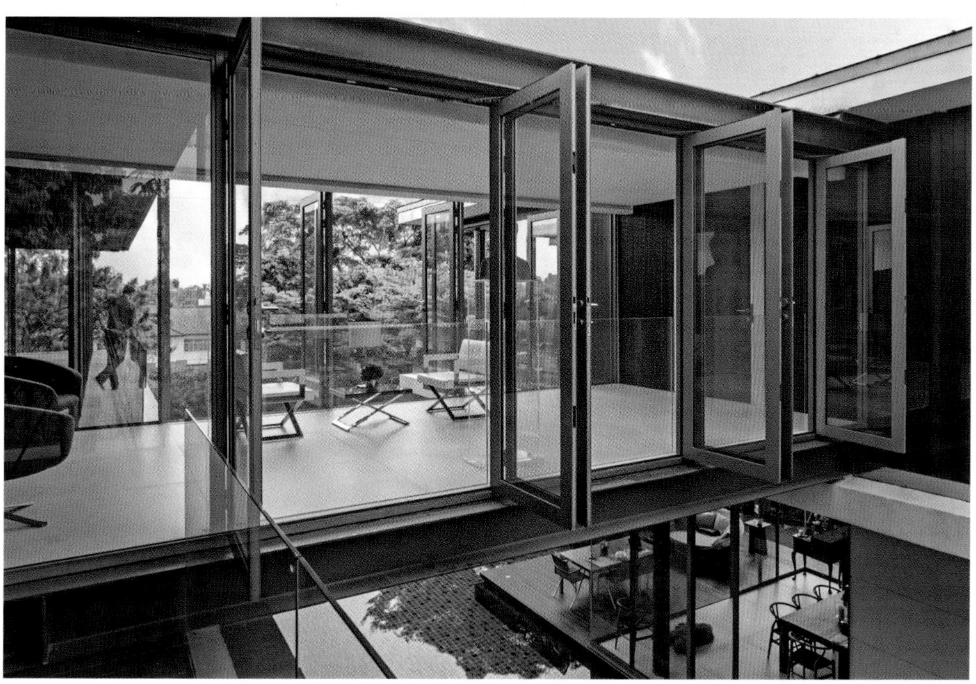

Above and below The glazed footbridge doubles as a small sitting area with views down to the pool and garden.

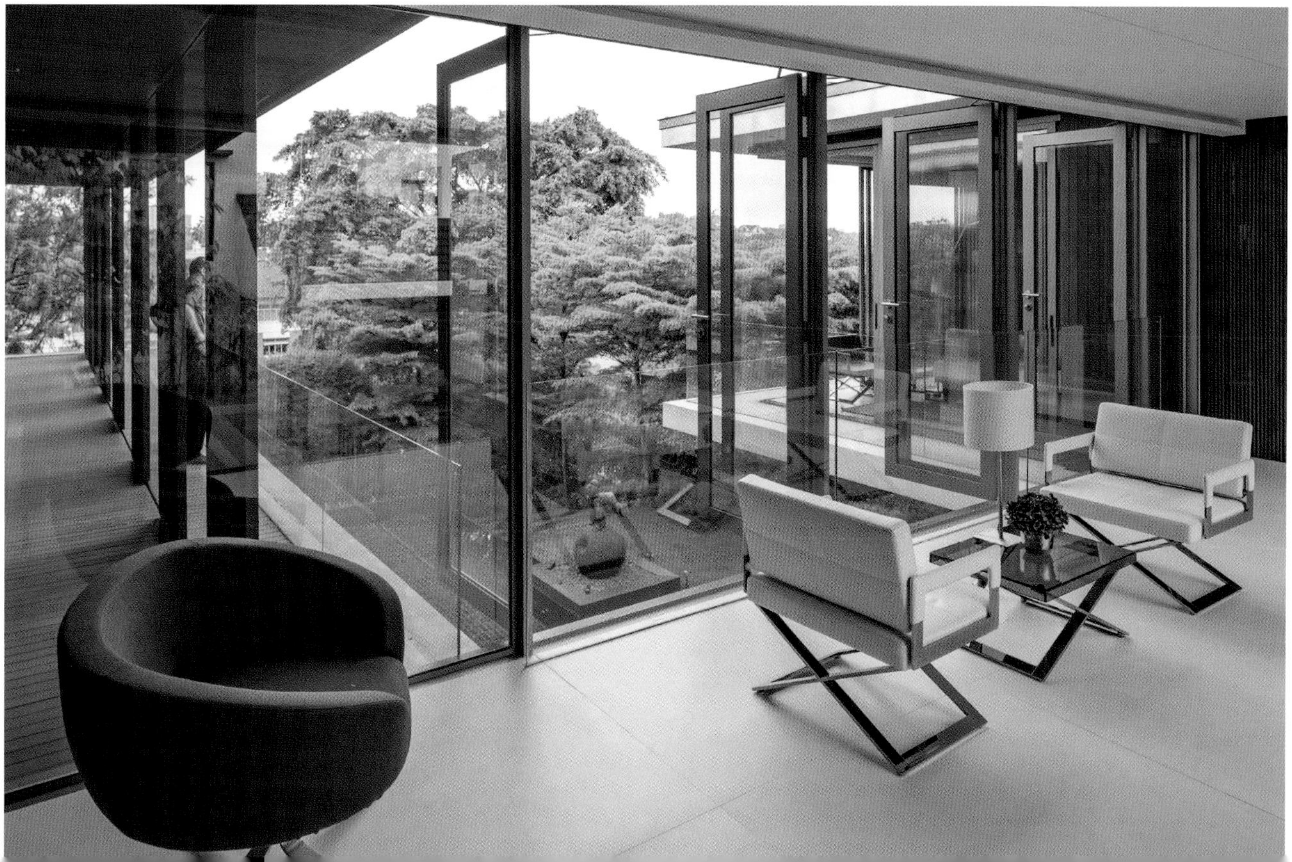

is the public domain containing the large living area, broad terraces, the garden areas and the dining pavilion that appears to float out over the pool.

While the planning provides for separation, there is always a sense of connection because of the cross-views and high levels of transparency. The parents' wing is connected to the children's wing by a glass bridge, its floor finished in homogeneous tiles and wide enough to provide a sitting area. The children's bedrooms are connected by sliding panels to encourage the children to interact, and they share a bathroom.

Similarly, the large living room opens up to the deck and pool, while at the end is a delightful powder room, like a floating pod, open to the outside with a breezeway and timber screens that cast delicate shadows over the pond.

Wide overhangs and deep setbacks make this a fine example of contemporary tropical living. While

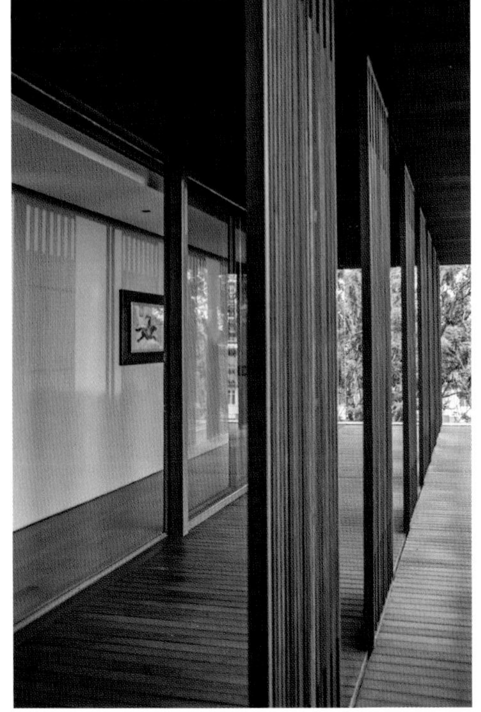

the upper level seems quite solid compared to the seeming transparency of the first storey, in fact the second storey is also very transparent. It is just that the rooms along this upper wing are set well back. Linked by a corridor running down the side, there is a secondary, external corridor only partly enclosed by the elegant timber batten screens that provide privacy, protection from the sun and a dark-toned decorative element to offset the white concrete of the building—together with the softening aesthetic of the shadows cast back into the house.

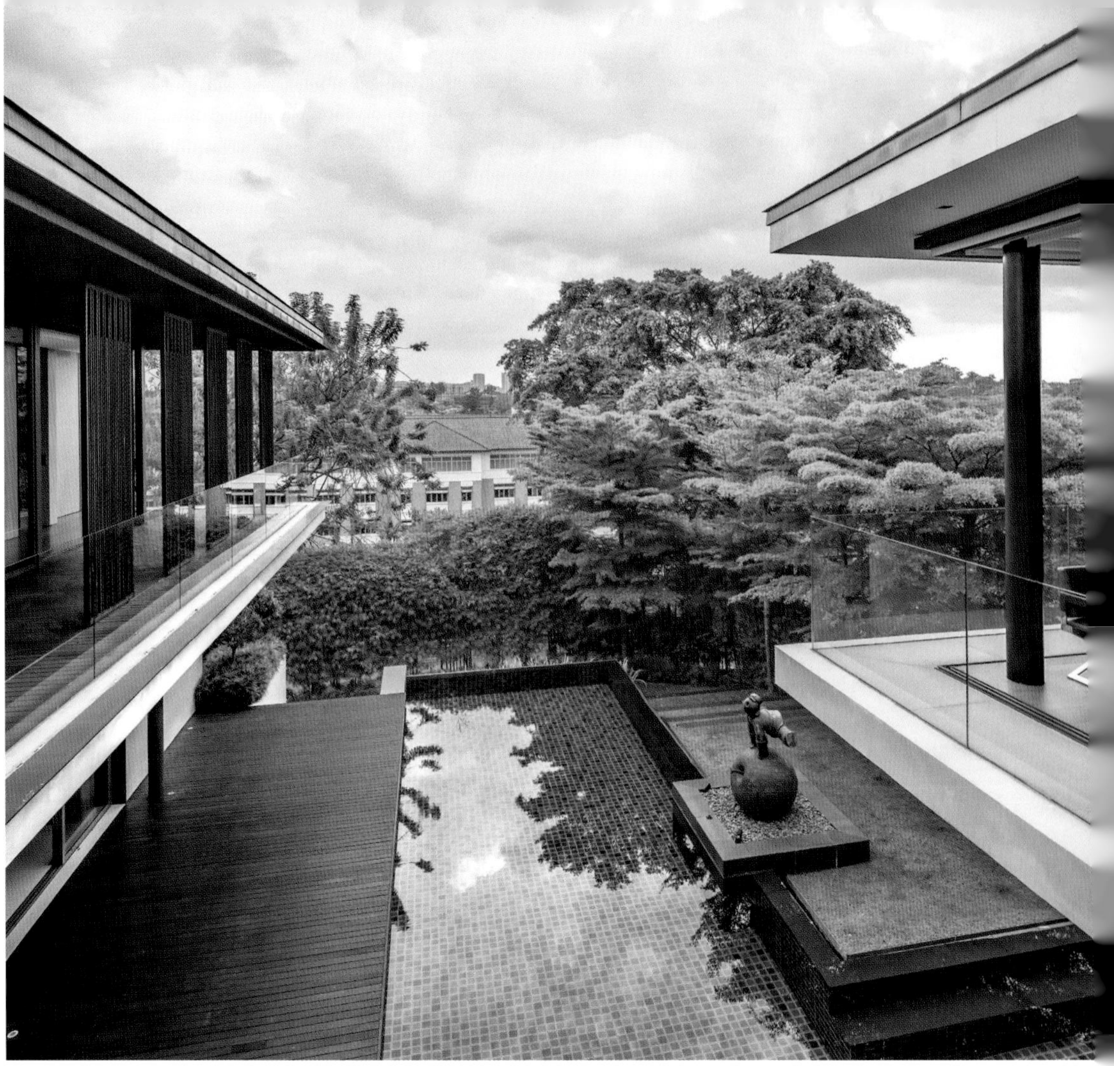

This is simultaneously a subtle house and one with some grand gestures. Its clear, almost classical planning makes it an exemplary multi-generational house, sustaining a family that is separate and yet together.

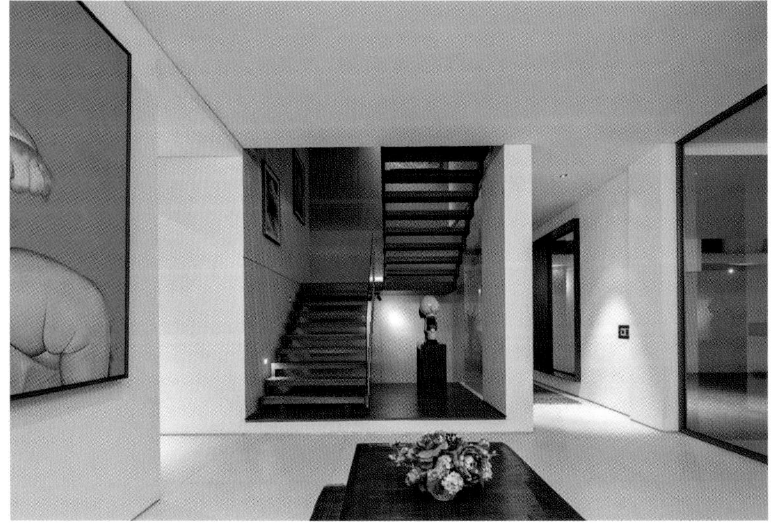

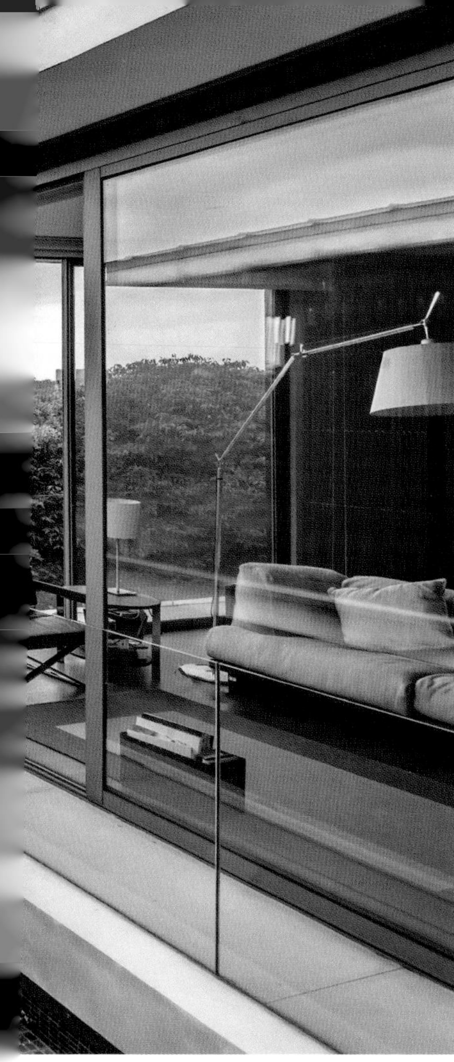

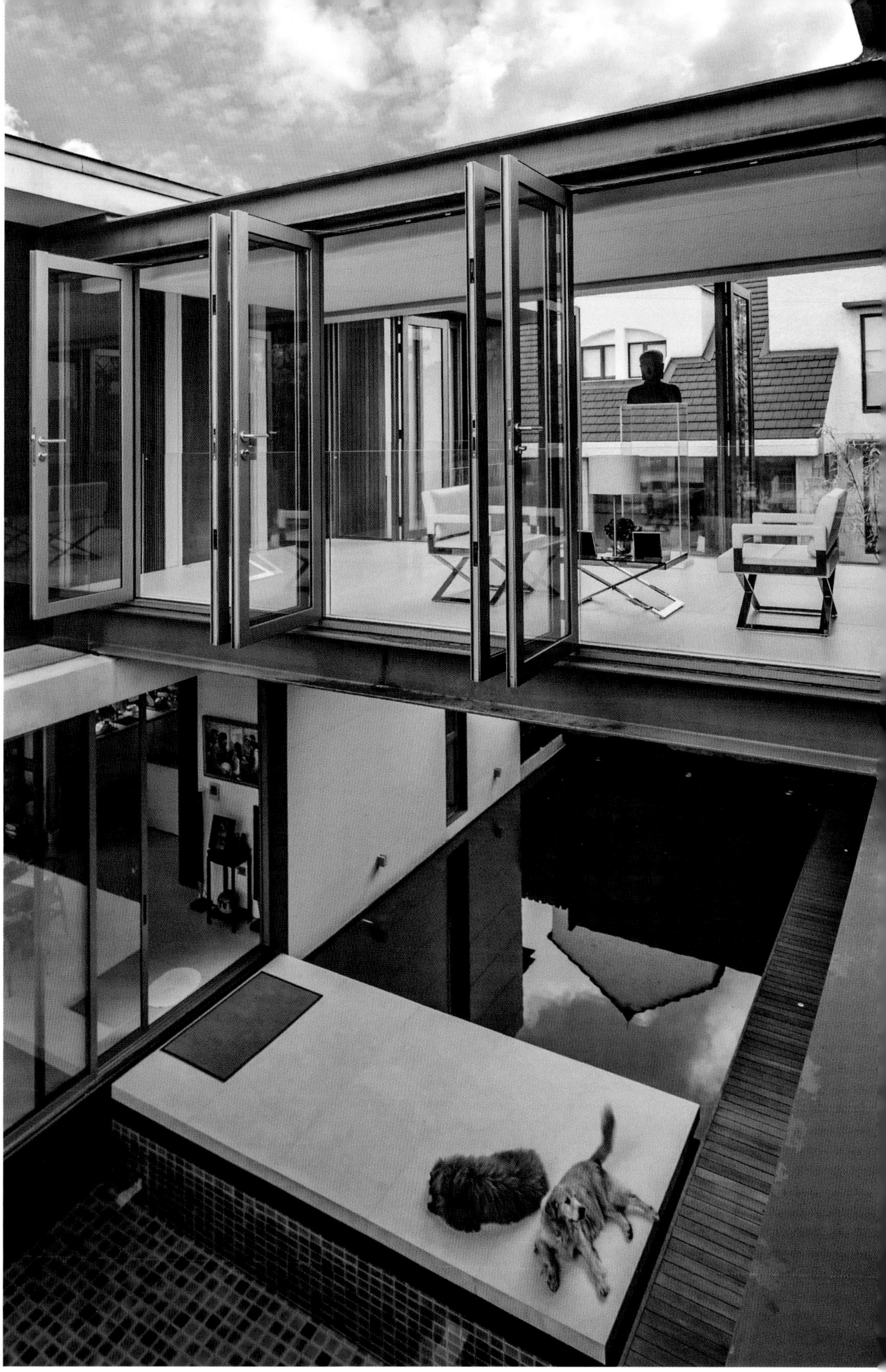

Above left The screened timber gallery linking the bedrooms.

Above The second storey takes advantage of the house's elevated site to capture panoramic views.

Left The entry lobby off the basement car park.

Right Even the glazed footbridge can be opened up to generate cross-ventilation.

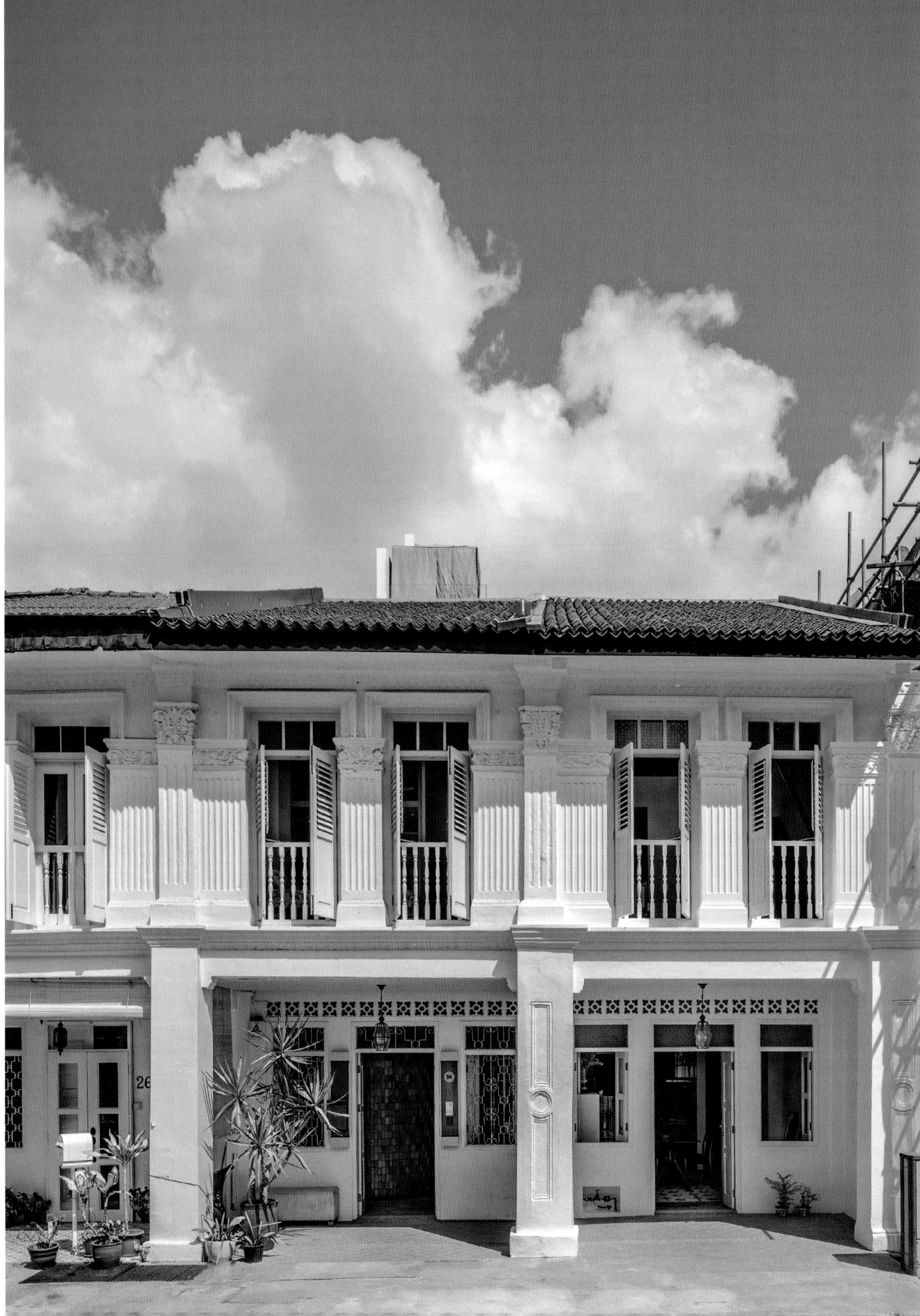
26

THE CRANES
EXPERIENCE DESIGN STUDIO, ONG&ONG

'The idea was to create something that was akin to a neighbourhood within a house. We did not just want to build rooms and pretty spaces for people; we also wanted to create chances for people to interact.'—CLIENT

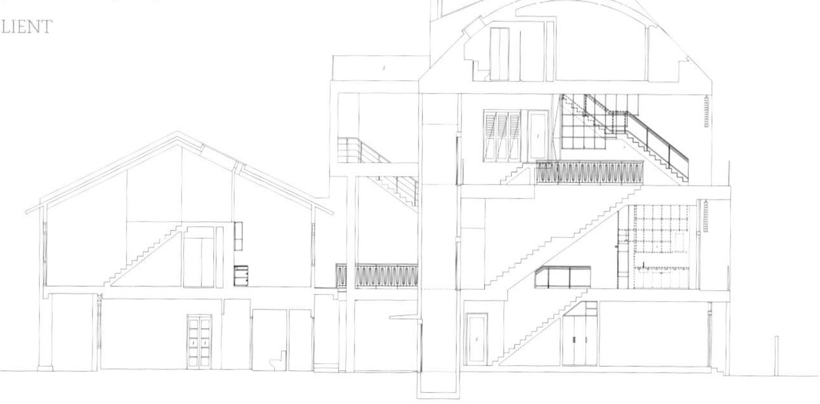

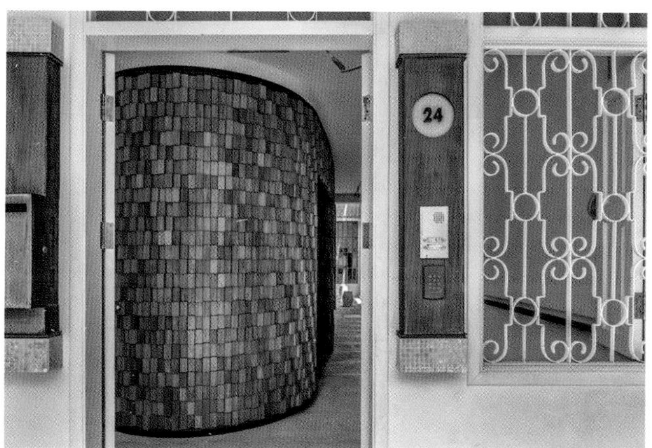

Opposite The restored street façades of the two, now connected, shophouses.

Above Section.

Left The curved textured timber wall, which contains a ground floor apartment in No. 24 Crane Road.

Below The curved timber wall has frosted glass windows that create an atmospheric space at night.

This project began as the restoration and redevelopment of a shophouse at No. 24 Crane Road, Joo Chiat, in eastern Singapore, but was subsequently extended to include the neighbouring shophouse (No. 22). The driving force was to create a new kind of multi-generational home that provided the necessary privacy but also offered a sense of belonging to a small community. Each house comprises three largely self-contained units. Each has a strongly interconnected character and this interconnectedness is extended to the relationship between the houses. They are connected to one another by a common central courtyard, which in the original shophouse was the airwell, and extends up through the four levels of the houses.

In addition to the courtyard, there are also four other communal spaces: a laundry, a public dining room on the ground floor at the front of No. 22, a smaller 'private' dining space on the second storey

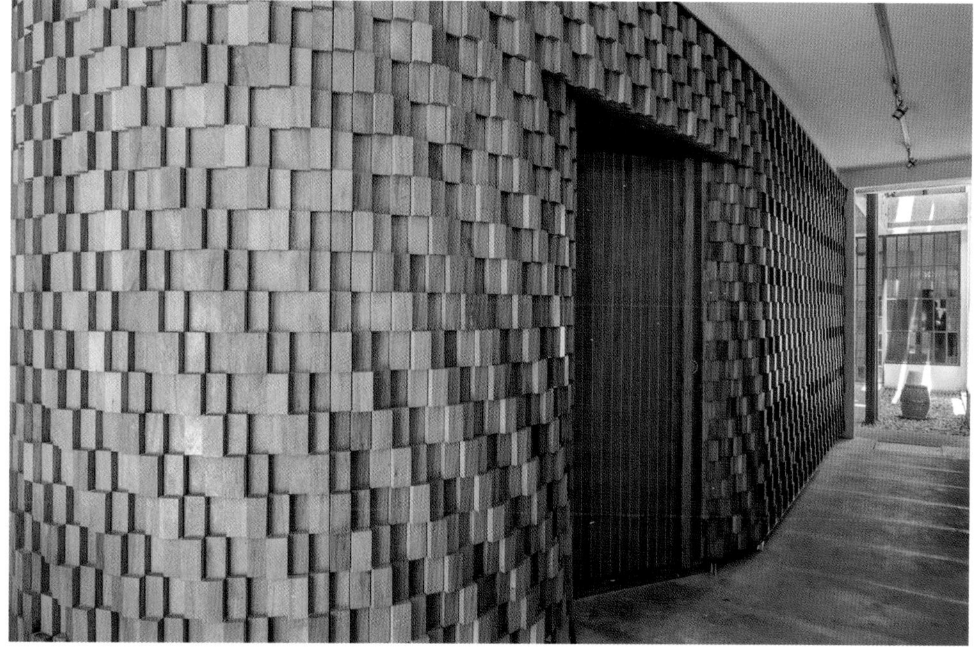

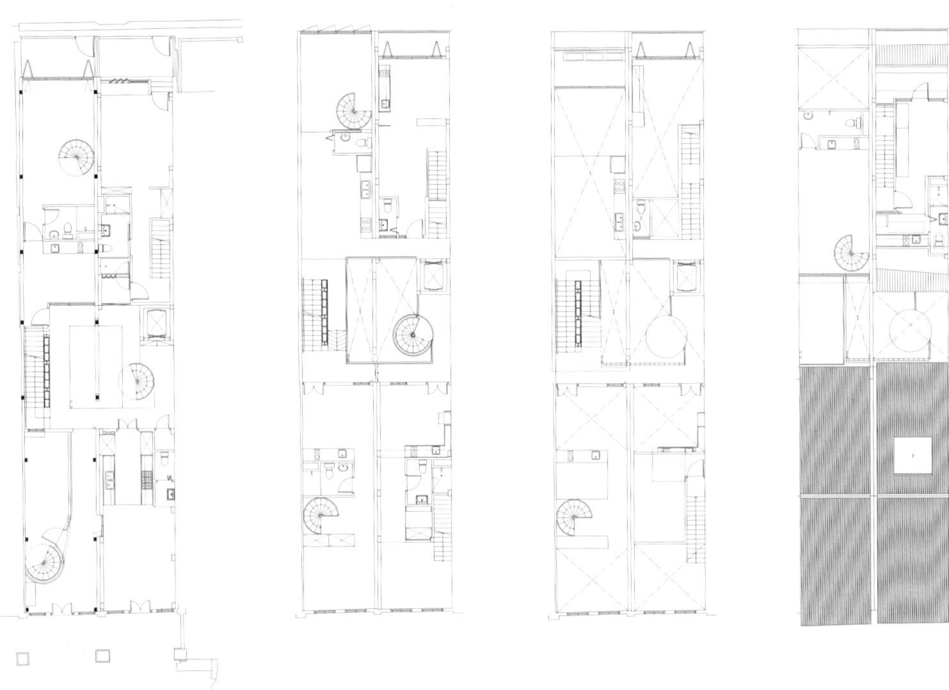

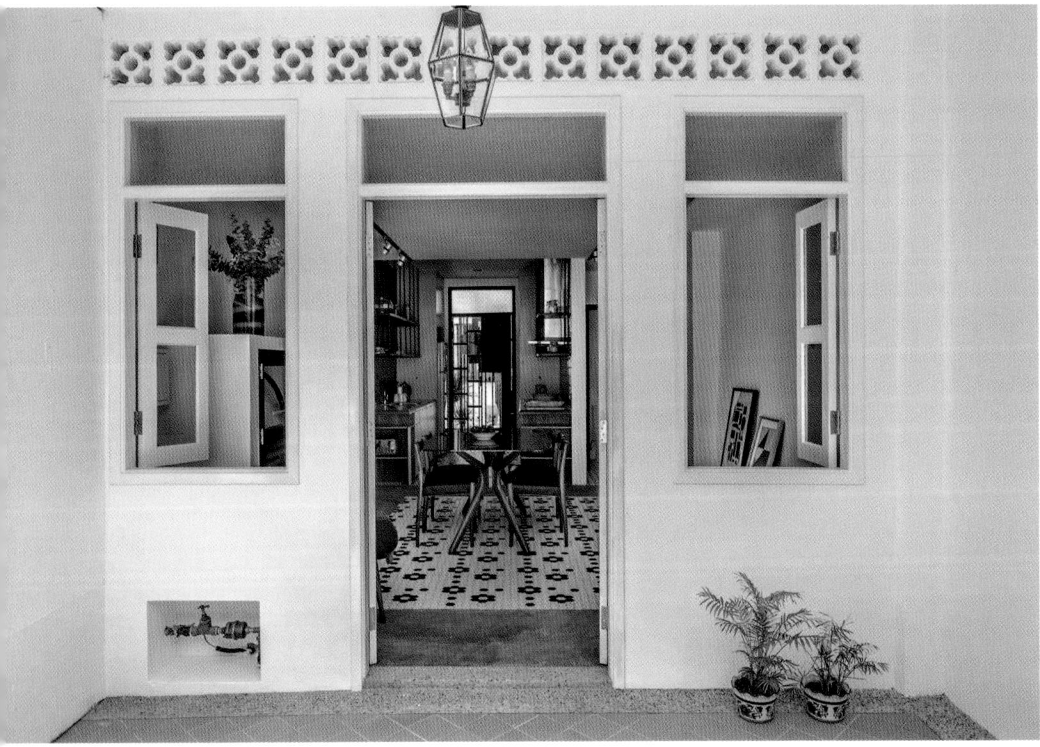

of No. 24 and a private 'reading corner' on the second storey of No. 24

The Joo Chiat neighbourhood in the east of Singapore is known for its rich Peranakan (Straits Chinese) heritage, and for this reason is one of the districts which Singaporeans now look to for authenticity and a sense of history and continuity. The area is now very diverse, boasting a huge variety of food outlets and a strong sense of community, especially among the long-term residents.

The client is a boutique developer who bought the dilapidated property with a view to living there with his extended family. Although this particular row of shophouses was not listed for conservation, the client chose to restore the buildings rather than demolish them and rebuild. The row of shophouses has since been classified conservation. While the client wanted as many self-contained spaces as possible in the two shophouses, a parallel agenda was to have the buildings draw inspiration from the area and also to make a contribution to sustaining the vibrant culture of Joo Chiat. The public dining room on the ground floor of No. 22 is an illustration of this strategy. It was inspired by the clan association houses, many of which still exist, that have a dining room at the entry to the house on the ground floor, invariably open to the street outside. With the clan houses, as with The Cranes, this enables guests to come and go without entering the rest of the building.

The architects took a cue from the kampong, seeing Joo Chiat as a kind of village where people knew one another, left their doors open and felt a strong local bond, with interactions taking place on doorsteps, through windows and in 'third' spaces around the village. They saw the first house (No. 24) as having a porosity to the street through its shuttered windows and double timber entry doors. However, they also took the village model as the basis for their internal planning, in the process creating 'a microcosm of the Joo Chiat neighbourhood within the site through three different housing and spatial types'.

The architects identified three types of house: the Street House (colonial two-storey conservation

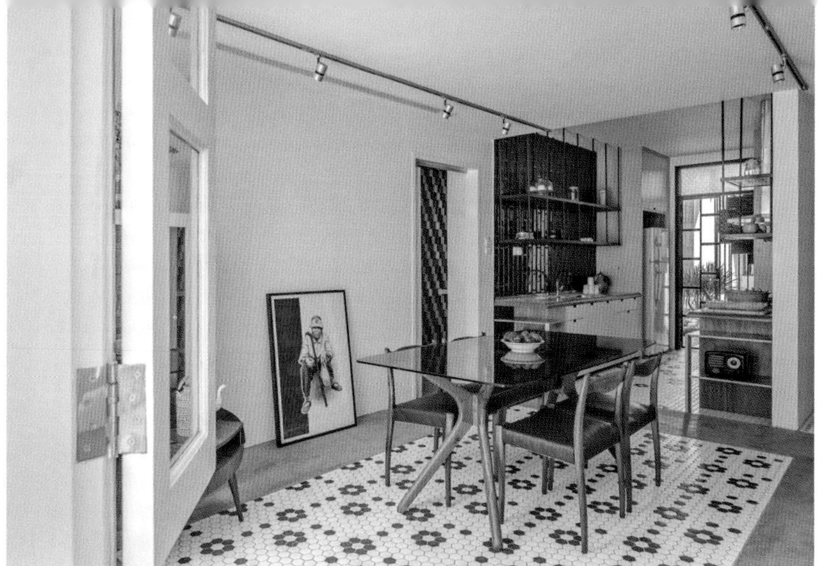

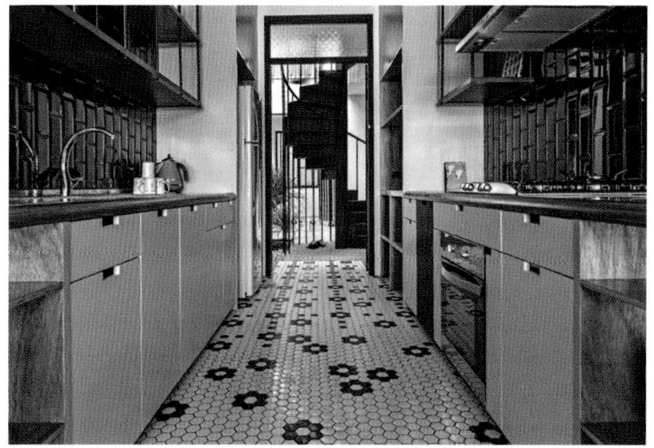

Opposite above First storey, second storey, mezzanine and third storey plans.

Opposite below The entry to No. 22 Crane Road and the main dining/kitchen space.

Above left The main communal dining area takes its cue from clan association buildings, which open to the street.

Above The communal kitchen is high quality and fully equipped.

Below The communal kitchen connects through the courtyard.

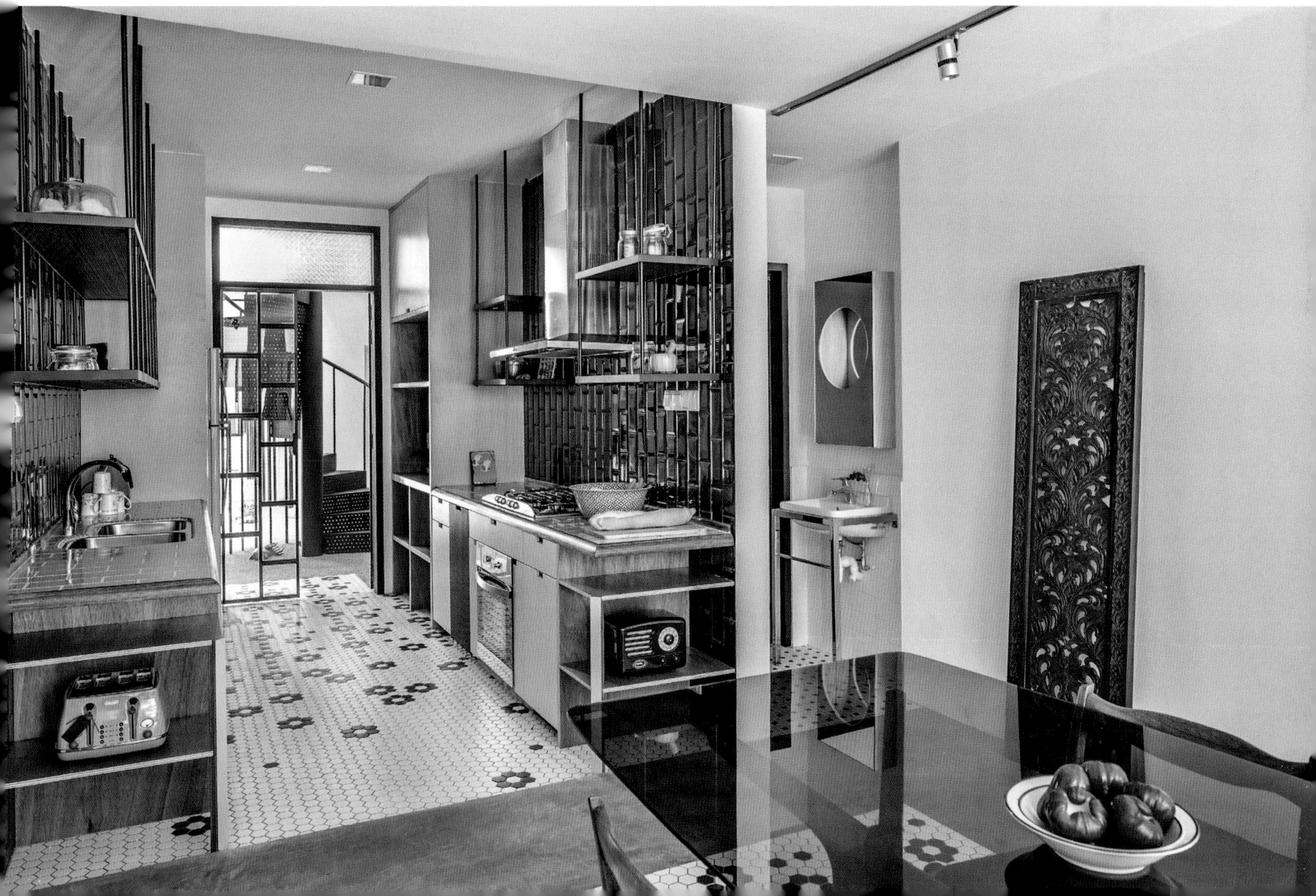

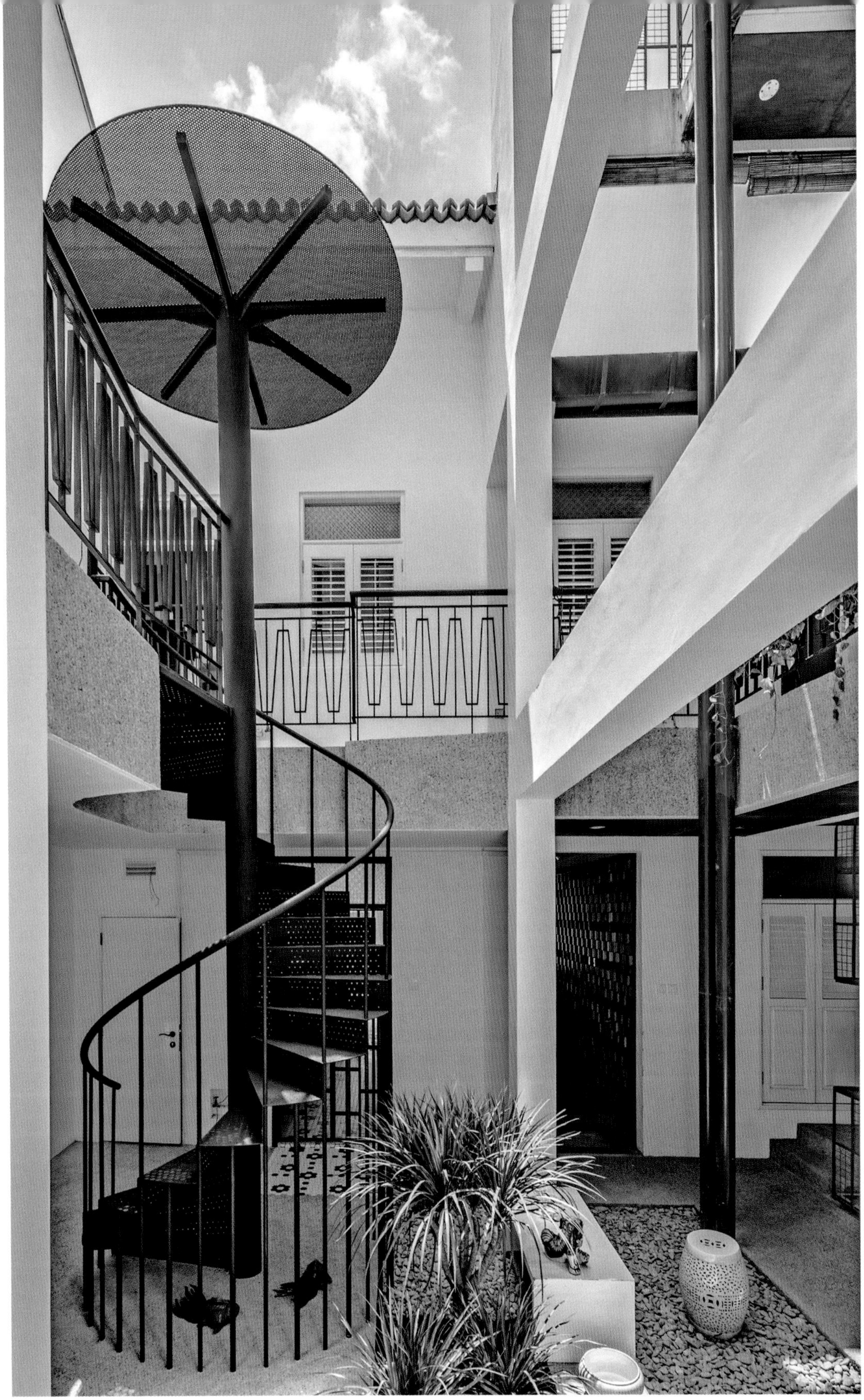

Left The two courtyards are now connected, drawing ample natural light into the centre of the complex.

Below The communal dining/ kitchen area on the second storey of No. 24.

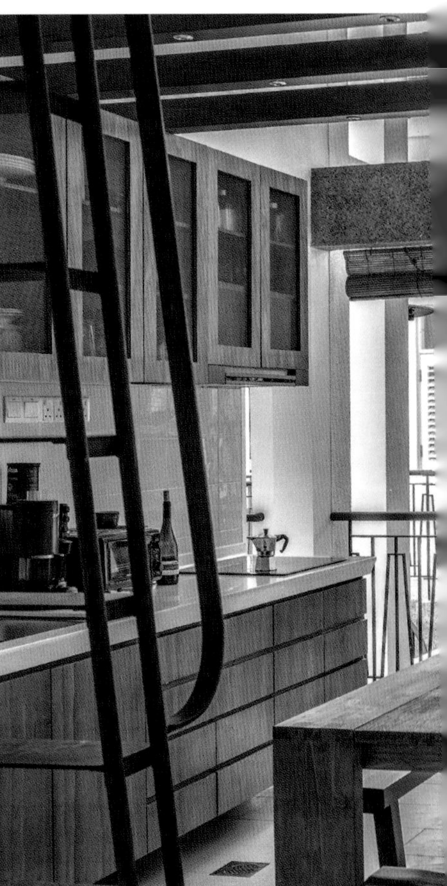

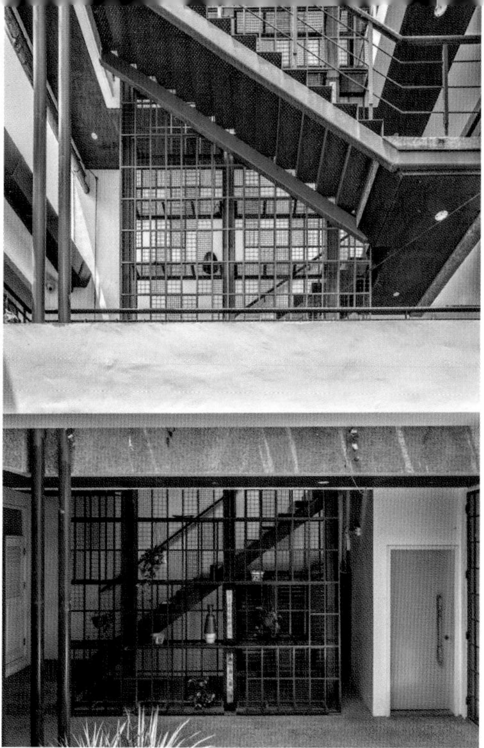

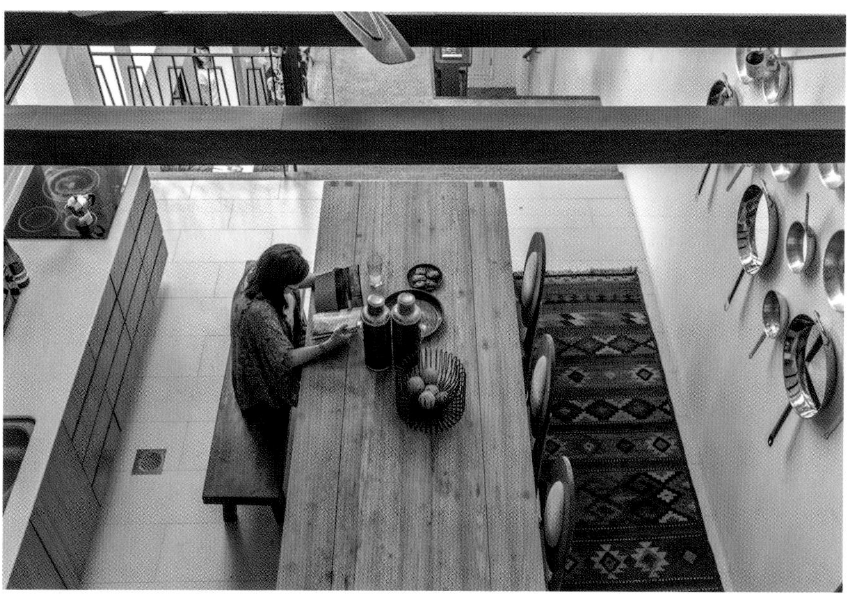

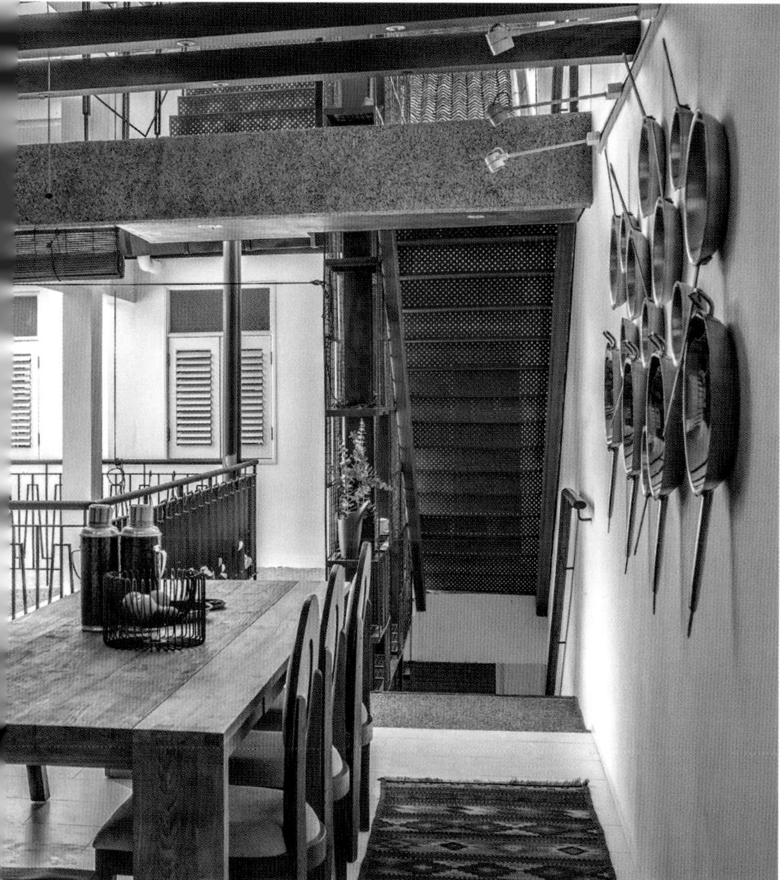

Above left The brilliant blue diaphragm wall, which acts as an 'internal street' linking all levels.

Above Looking down to the communal dining/kitchen space in No. 24.

shophouse), the Garden House (two-storey unit with garden and private side entrance) and the Sky House (modern two-storey, high-rise, walk-up apartment). Applied to No. 24, the result was the restored two-storey original shophouse and a three-storey addition with attic at the rear, all together providing three units modelled on the three types identified. However, the units form a community with an internal 'street', a vibrant blue steel diaphragm wall with attached stairway that connects them. The wall incorporates plants, objects and Peranakan tiles that conceal LED lights. It sits in the courtyard, forming a vertical internal connection for the whole complex, drawing in light, and providing shade and home to a herb garden and other green elements.

This is one of a number of 'third spaces' designed to create a sense of community. The first is on the entry level where a curved, textured timber wall with frosted glass insert windows forms part of a gallery space with works of art on the opposite wall. The timber wall contains the sitting room of the Street House and, if someone is in here at night, the light shows through the frosted windows like an illuminated work of art and, according to the architects, a simulation of the night lights of Joo

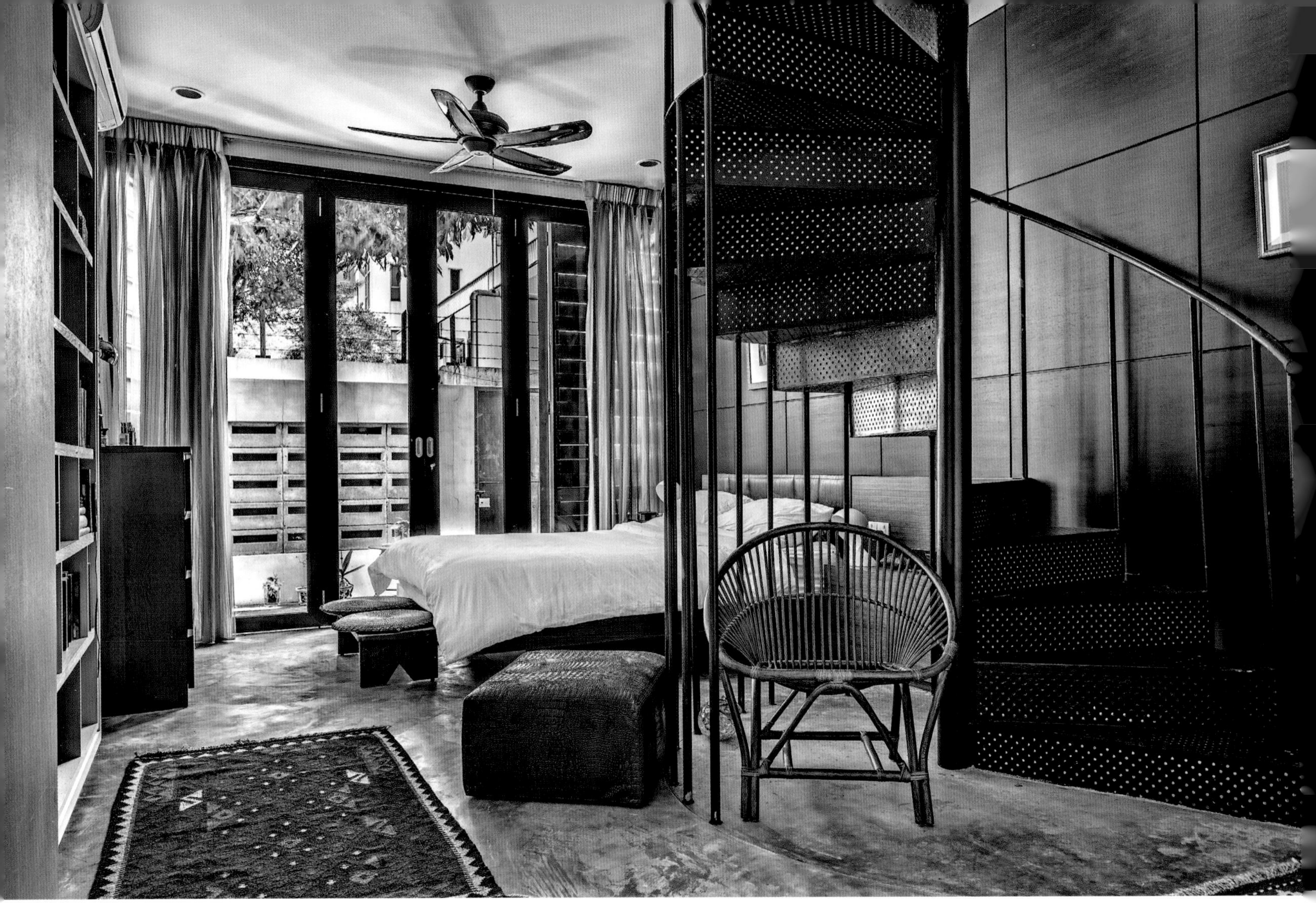

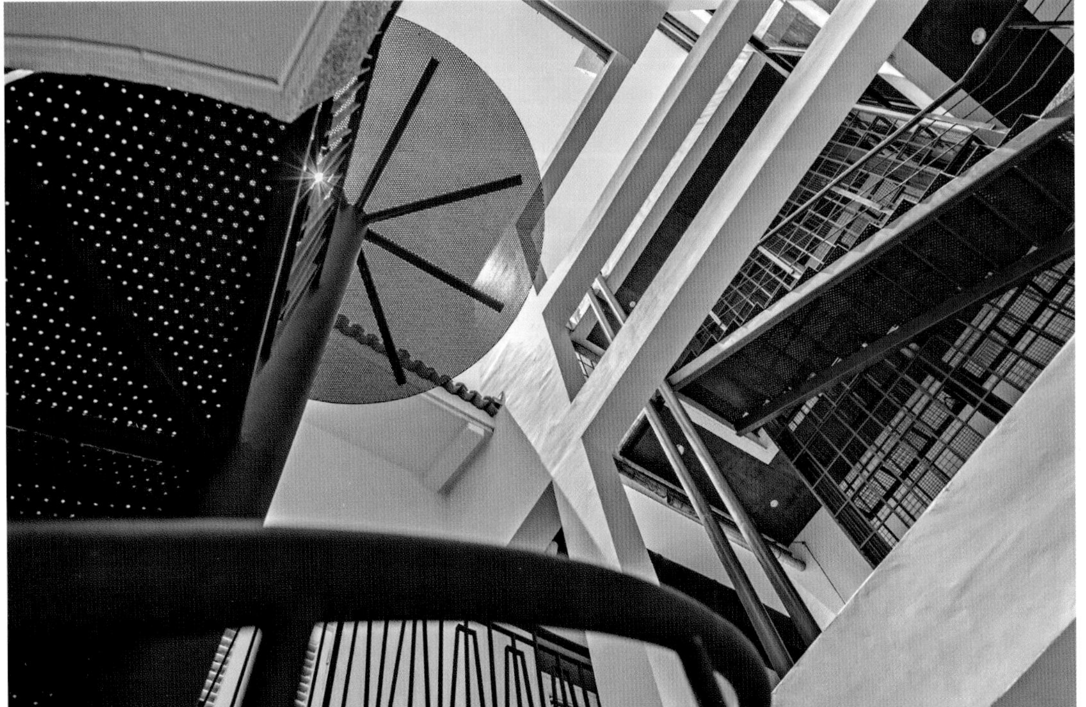

Above All the units have two levels.

Left Looking up through the central courtyard.

Chiat. The Street House includes the upper level of the original house as its bedroom. At the heart of the house, on Level 2, is the communal kitchen and 'private' dining space. Although each unit has its own kitchenette, the communal dining spaces bring the residents together and enable them to entertain guests. The private dining space on the second storey in No. 24 is also the entry level for the Garden House which has its bedroom at the bottom of a spiral staircase on the ground floor at the rear of the addition. Finally, the Sky House at the top has access to an outside deck. The configuration allows for a three-generational home: kids on top, parents in the middle and grandparents on the ground floor, all coming together in the communal kitchen/dining space.

Designed to facilitate chance encounters and an ongoing sense of community balanced by privacy, The Cranes offers multiple spatial and aesthetic experiences as well. In No. 24, for example, the journey through the house, beginning at the front door, is constantly stimulating. At the same, the vertical experience is just as enthralling, both as a public and as a private experience. There is the public progression up through the central courtyard stairway, but there is also the private experience, since each of the apartments is over two levels with its own internal connecting spiral stairway. This engagement in plan and section is then matched by a rich palette of materials and colours, including the art works and the plants.

While the complex is seen primarily as a new kind of multi-generational house, the architects feel that it is also a model for a different style of multi-residential living in Singapore for a new generation with a new lifestyle, or for a growing demographic of mobile expatriates. It is equally interesting, however, for its cultural sustainability, providing a contemporary way of life, but one that is engaged with and responding to the cultural continuum of its neighbourhood.

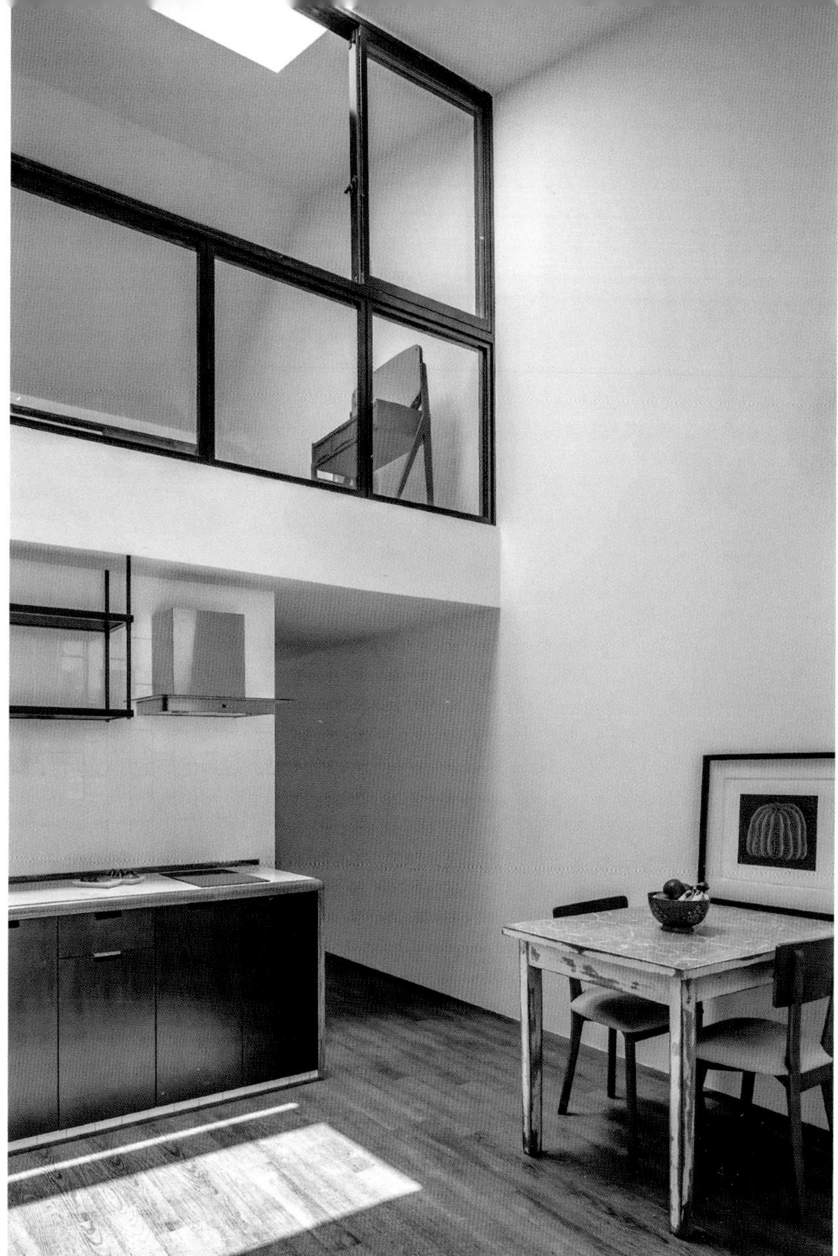

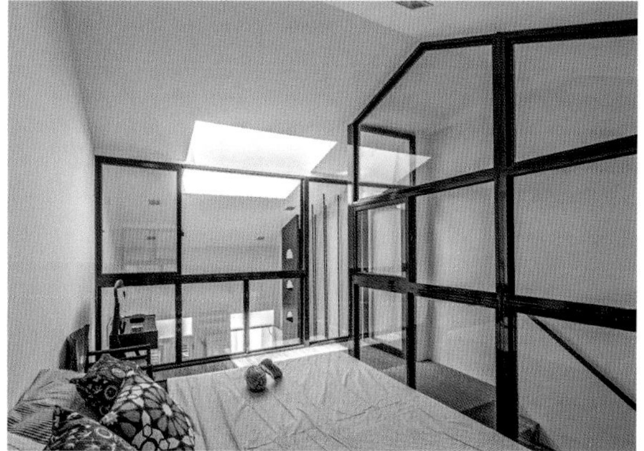

Above One of the rear apartments with its mezzanine bedroom space.

Left The bedroom mezzanine in the same rear apartment.

Below The upper level of one of the front apartments.

Bottom left A rear apartment.

Bottom right The communal laundry area in No. 22 looking towards the rear of the building.

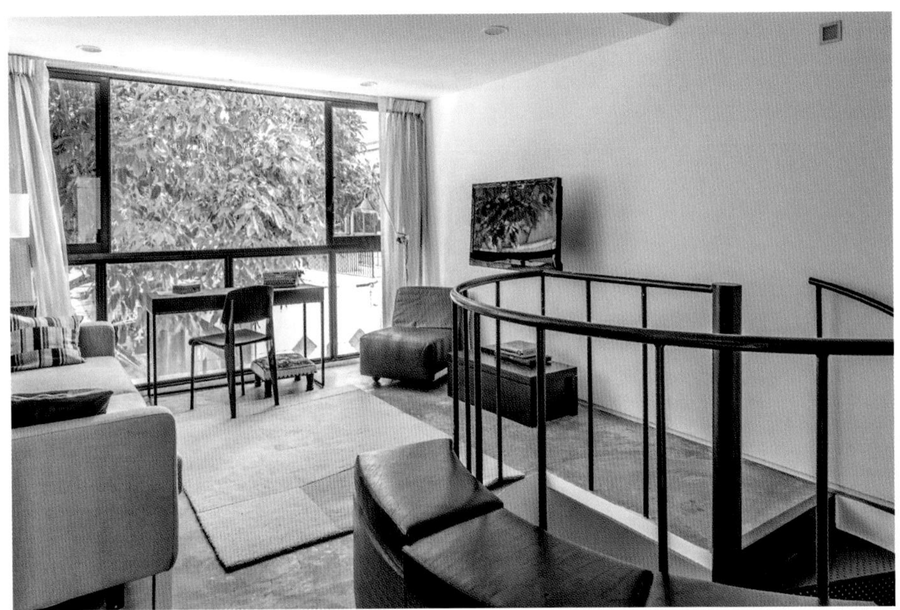

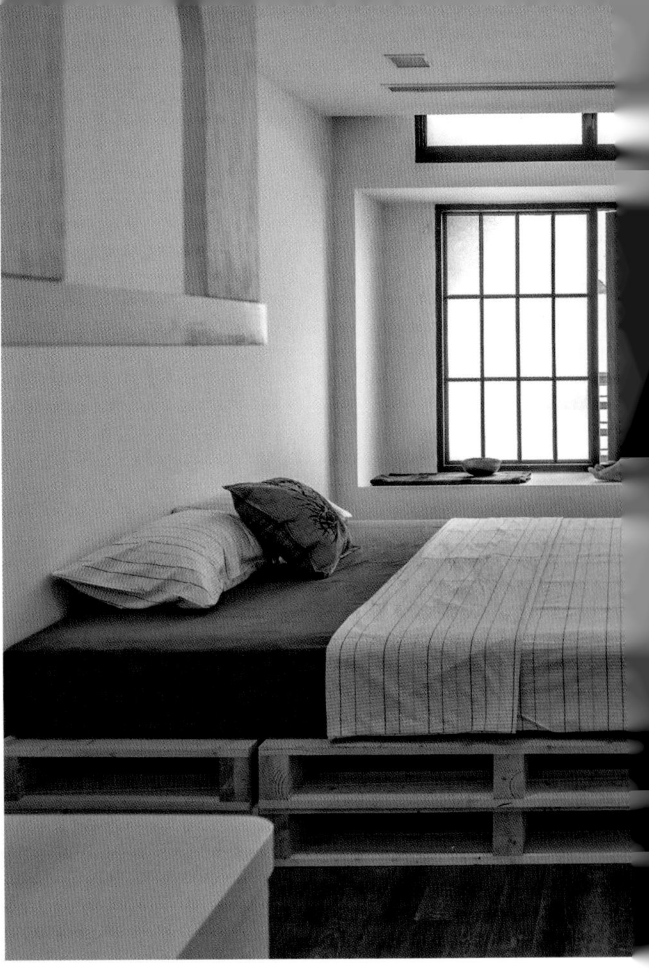

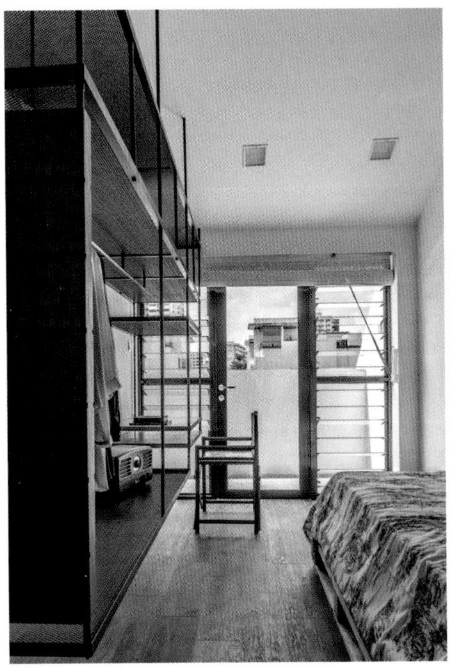

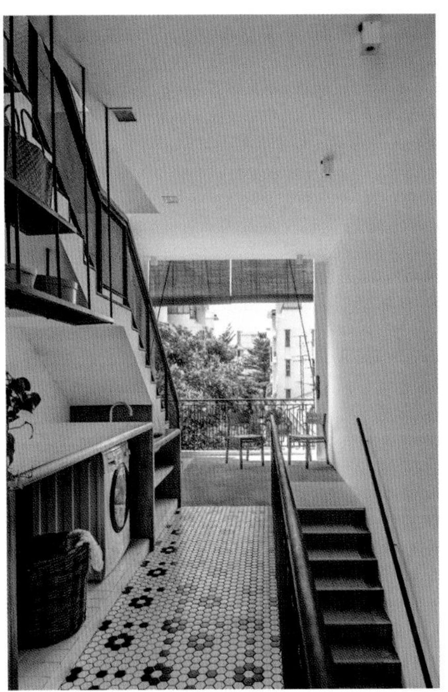

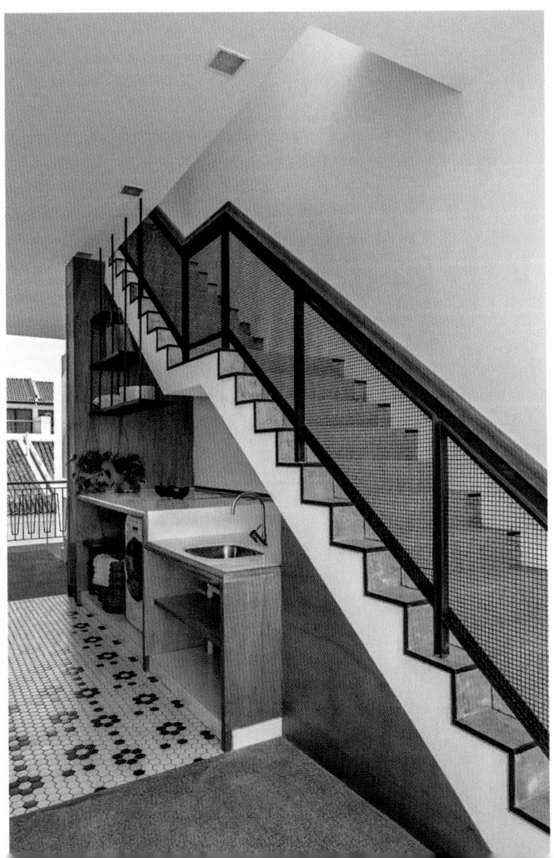

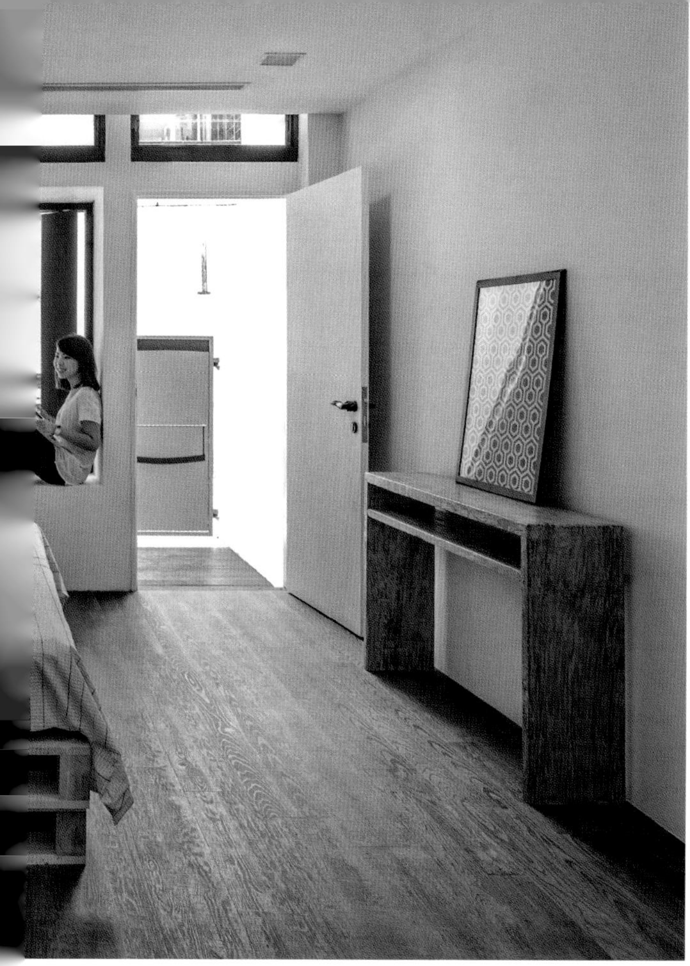

Right The bathrooms are compact but playful in their finishes.

Below Skylights draw in additional light throughout the complex.

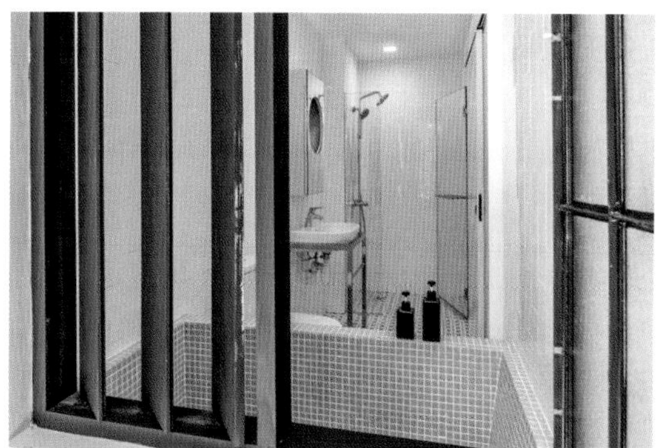

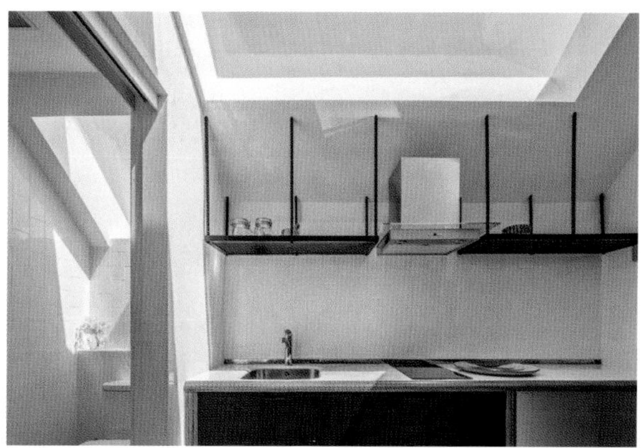

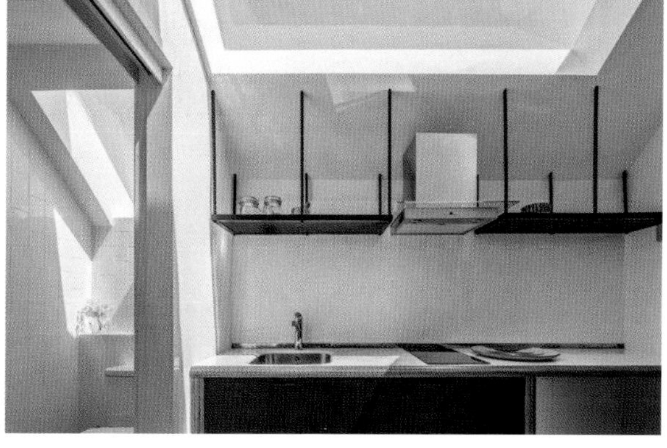

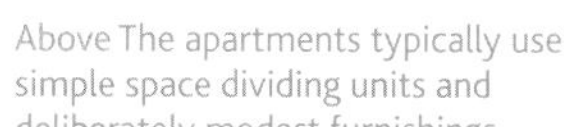

Above The apartments typically use simple space dividing units and deliberately modest furnishings.

Left The communal laundry area, with stairs to the mezzanine.

Right At the top of the complex, the courtyard organization supports the mood of communal living.

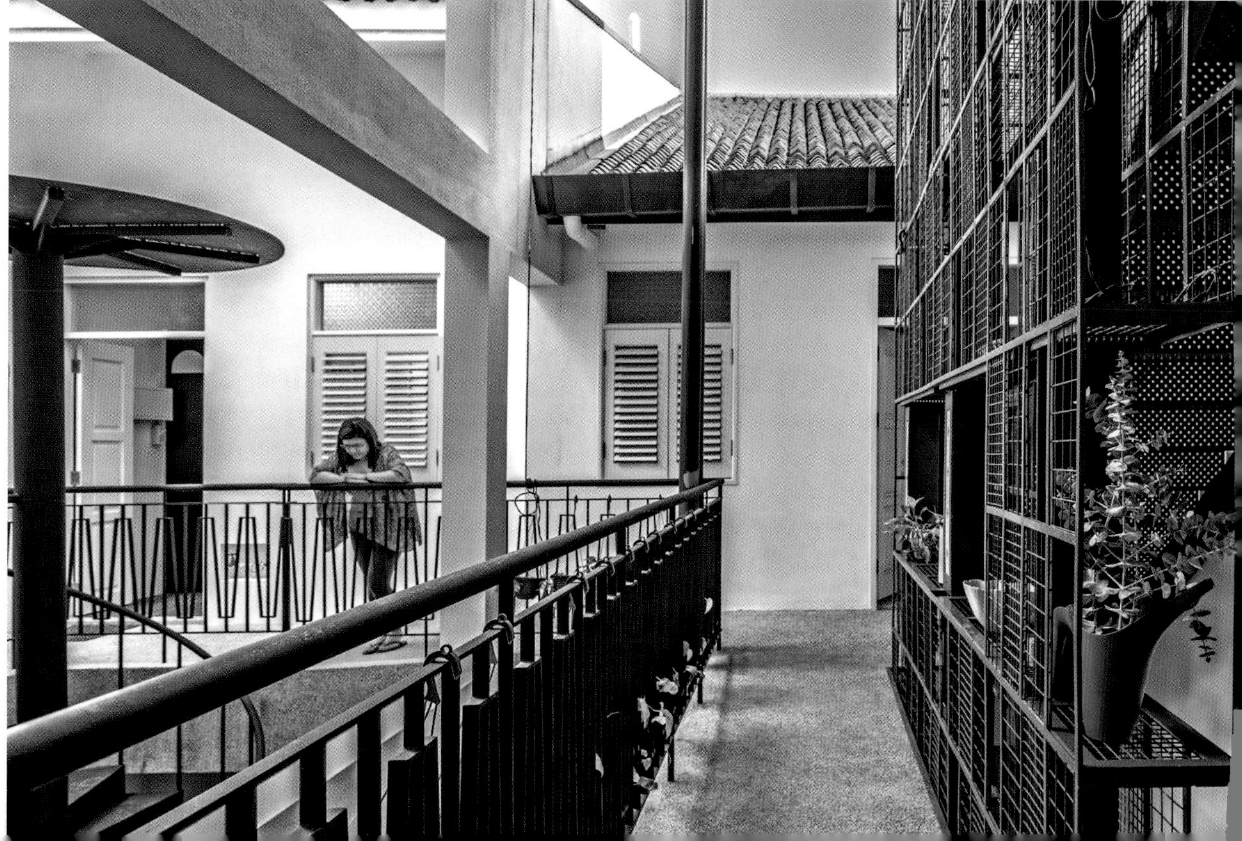

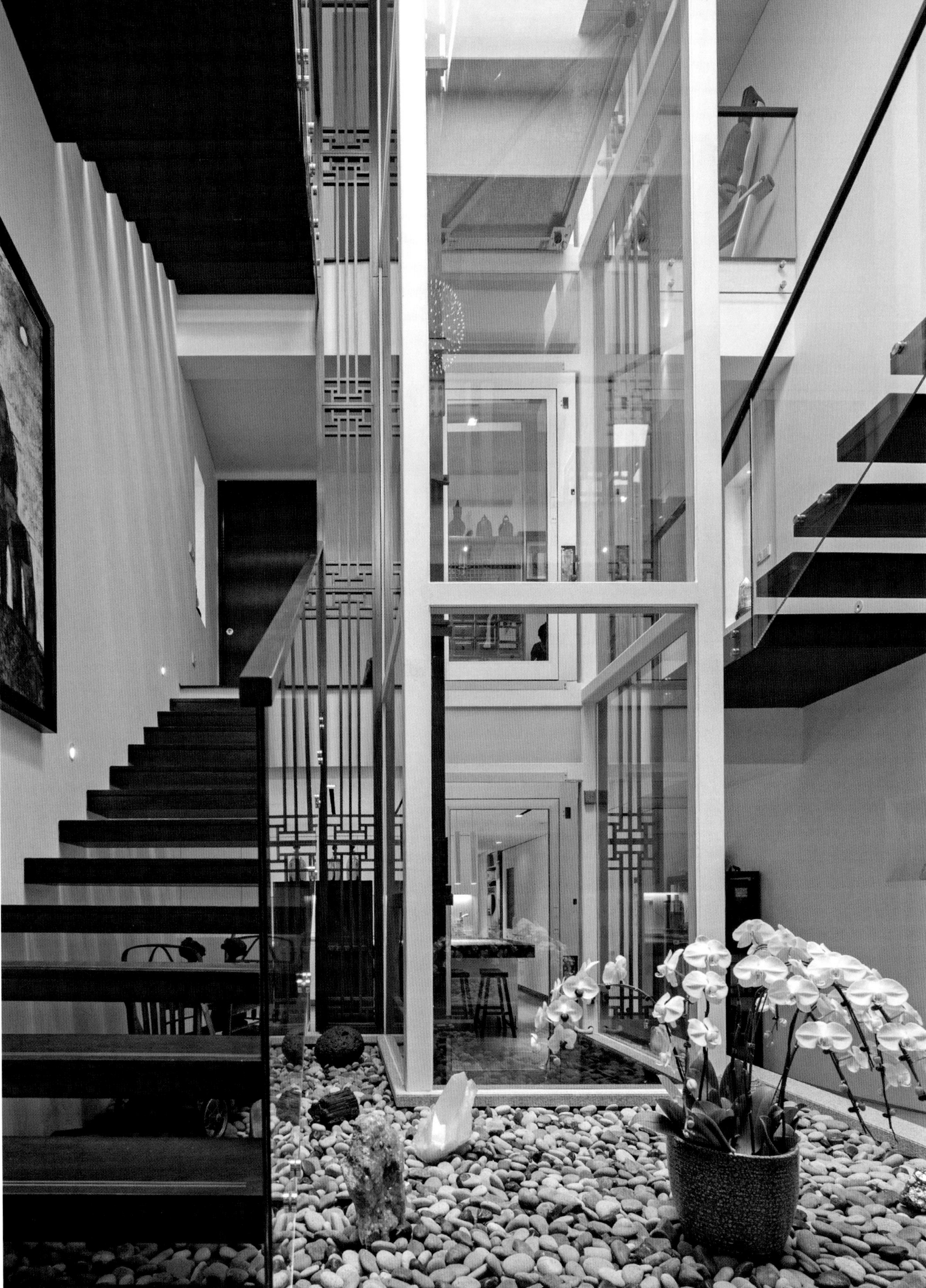

CAIRNHILL ROAD SHOPHOUSE RICHARDHO ARCHITECTS

Opposite The space is centrally divided by the glazed liftwell.

Below Section.

Bottom The shophouse benefits from its corner position, enabling new windows down the side.

'As usual with all my shophouses, I wanted to show the construction. This means you really have to think ahead.'—RICHARD HO, ARCHITECT

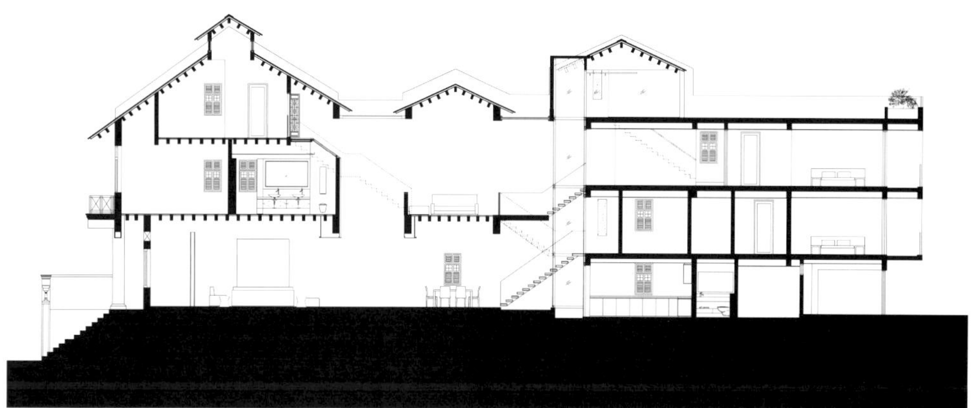

Richard Ho's practice is diverse, but he is particularly known for his sensitive restoration and adaptation of heritage buildings. His reputation gained new heights when he was named Designer of the Year in the 2013 President's Design Awards. In its citation, the jury commented: 'Richard Ho is one of the most respected and recognized architects in Singapore for his body of work. Displaying great sensitivity to the history, culture and climate of sites and places, he has an innate talent to create architecture that has resonance with those who use the spaces, and to rekindle memories of the past.'

Ho is the epitome of the sustainable architect, typically working to give buildings that already have a history a new life, adding another chapter to their story. This involves giving those buildings a fresh purpose for an owner with contemporary needs, but always with a sense of connection to what has gone before. The house becomes a repository of intangible memories, not in any backward-looking sense but in the way those memories subtly sustain a richer present.

This house is just a few doors down from another shophouse reinvented by Ho and featured in my previous book, *The Sustainable Asian House* (2013). Similar strategies have been used here but to very different effect. Essentially, Ho draws attention to the original structure of the house, for example, the exposed original timber beams in the living area in the front part of the house. At the same time, various things such as the air-conditioning, the pipes to the master bedroom directly above this space, the lighting and the hi-fi are all hidden. This not only lends an elegant sleekness to the long rectangular plan of the space but also draws attention to the original structure without overstating the case. It is through strategies such as these that Ho is able to design a fully contemporary home which, nonetheless, resonates with its past. It is a new home but one that comes with a ready-made past, with the material and emotional layering that typically enables any home to sustain the people who live there.

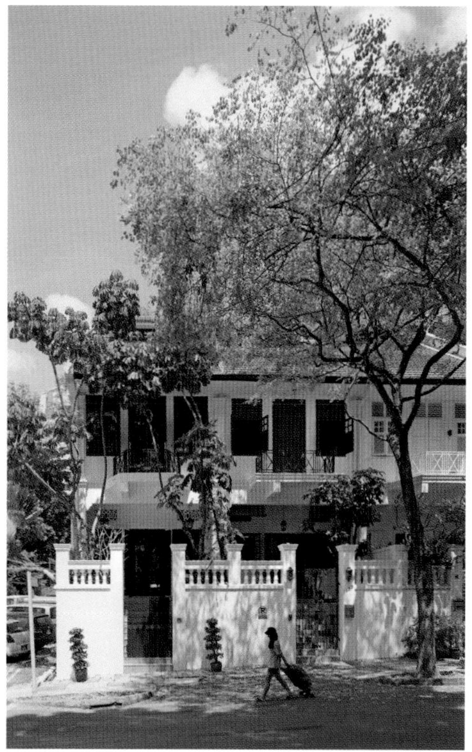

At the end of the living/dining space and separating it from a well-equipped Western-style dry kitchen, is the original lightwell, now occupied by a lift. This is where the old house ended. The new addition consists of three storeys and a rooftop pavilion and garden, with the lift going all the way up to the roof garden. Instead of Ho's usual water feature at the foot of the lightwell, here there is a pebble garden with the stairs to the left, partially obscured by the liftwell. The stairs, as always with a Ho shophouse, define and animate the central void of the lightwell.

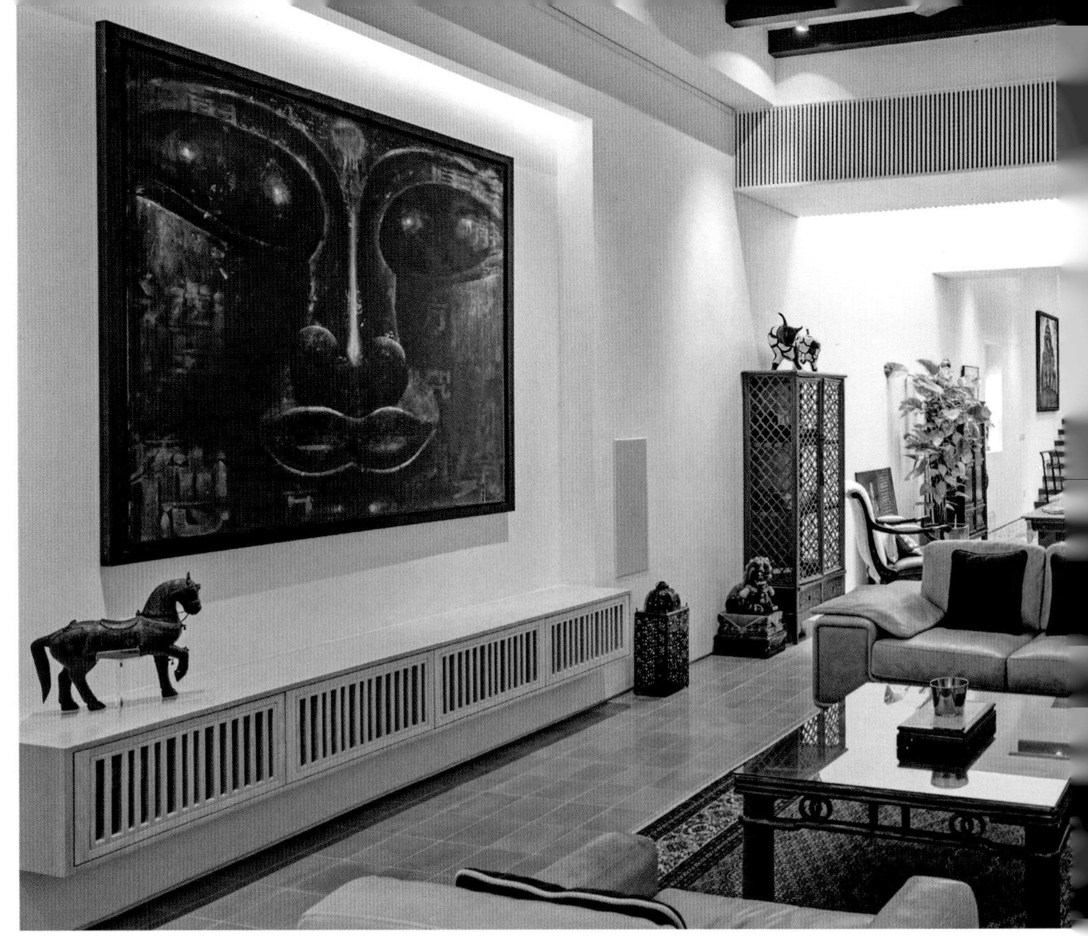

Also typical of Ho's strategy of cultural connection are various aesthetic touches. At the entry, for example, he uses traditional Vietnamese cement tiles that were once used extensively in Singapore. The same tiles are used again, artfully lit, in the entry corridor to the master bedroom on the second storey. Just inside the entry where traditionally a screen would temporarily obstruct the visitor's view to the interior of the house, Ho has also placed a timber screen made by local craftsmen. This becomes part of a sequence of arrival, which begins with the steep steps up from the street. From the street, shophouses generally appear modest in scale but inside Ho likes to celebrate the space. Here, the screen delays the moment when the visitor has the full height (14 feet) and extent of the entry level interior revealed.

The house is for a family of four and the family bedrooms are on the second storey. The master bedroom at the front of the original house is lent privacy and a sense of mystery by being enclosed in a timber 'box' formed by a timber screen. It is

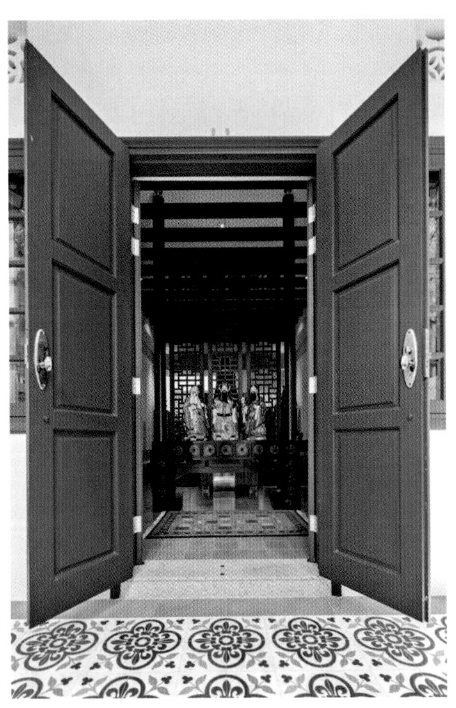

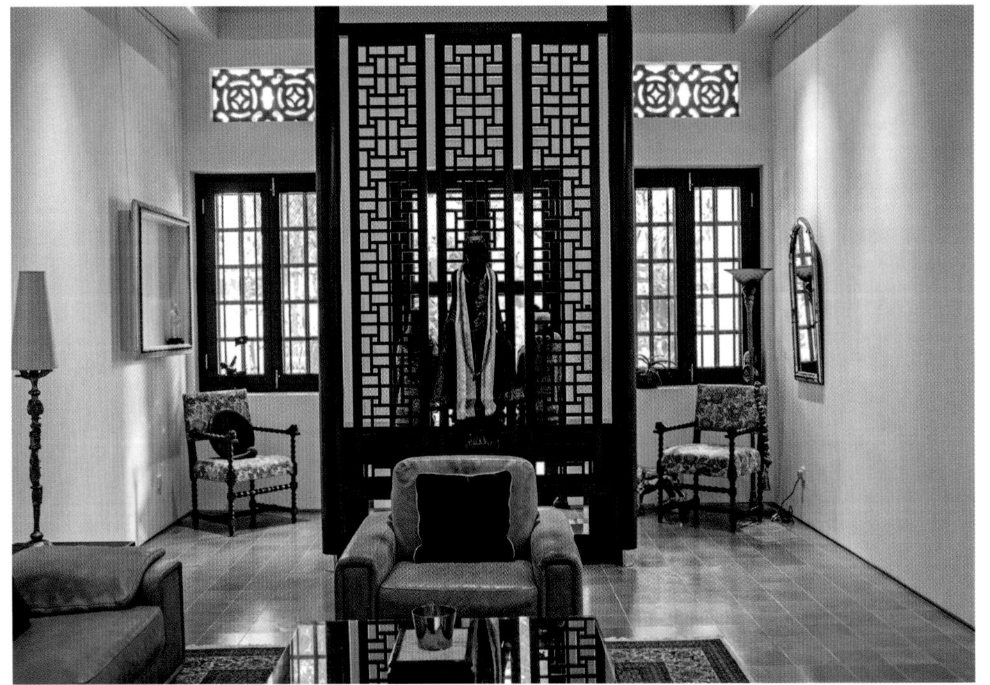

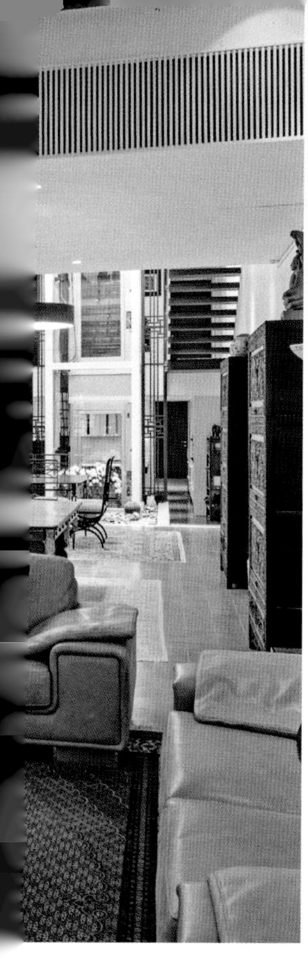

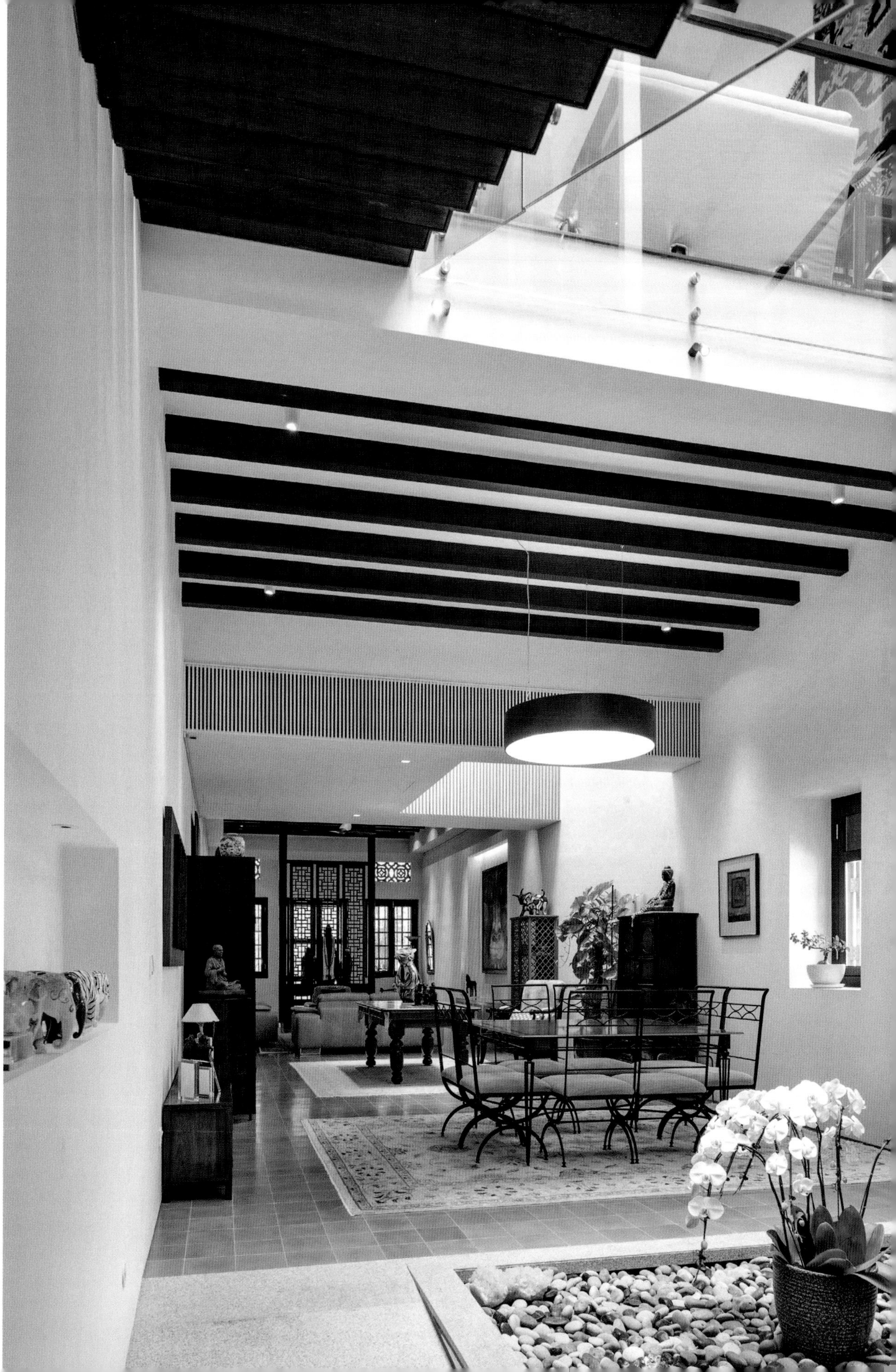

Above Entry is directly into the living area, with its elegantly subdued palette, the walls softly washed by hidden lighting.

Far left The restored entry features Vietnamese cement tiles once commonly used in Singapore.

Left In keeping with the traditional shophouse, a carved screen masks the entry to the house.

Right Looking back down the dining/living space towards the entry.

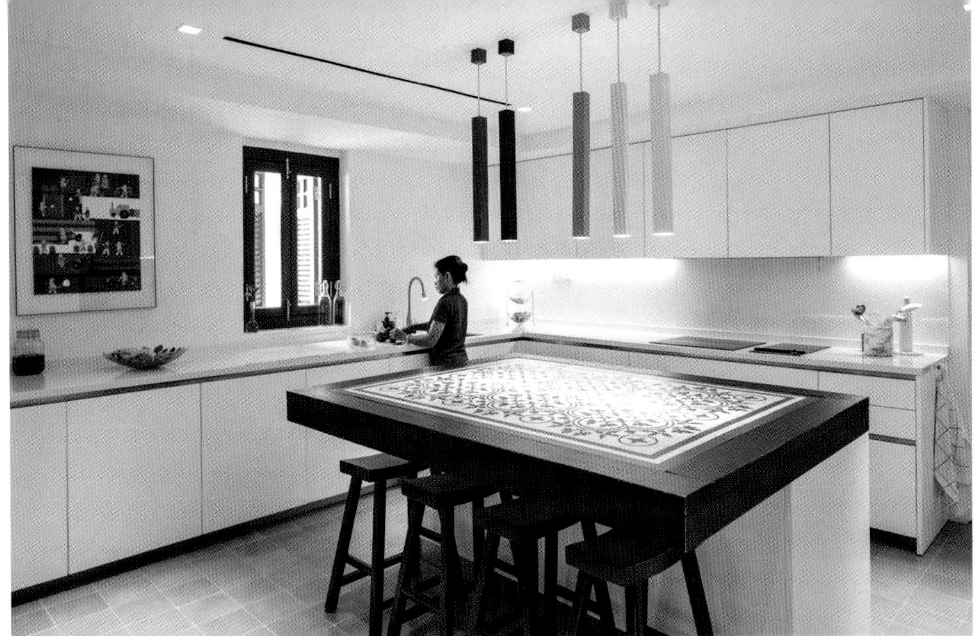

Left The contemporary kitchen on the ground floor is positioned behind the liftwell.

Below left Plans.

Below The powder room is located behind the kitchen.

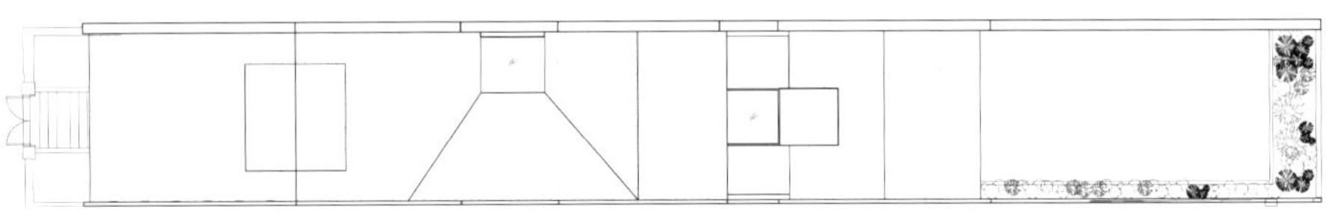

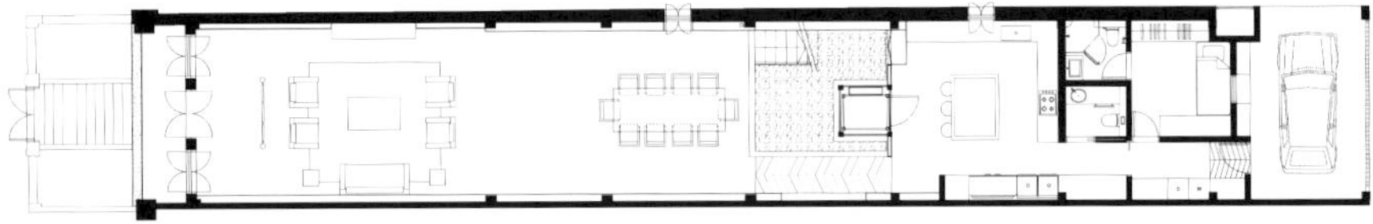

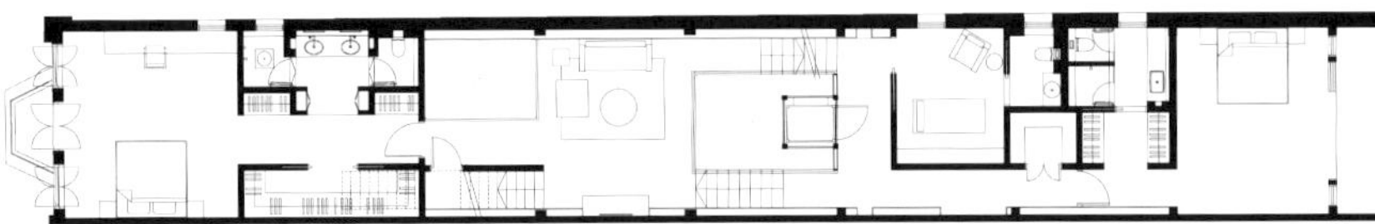

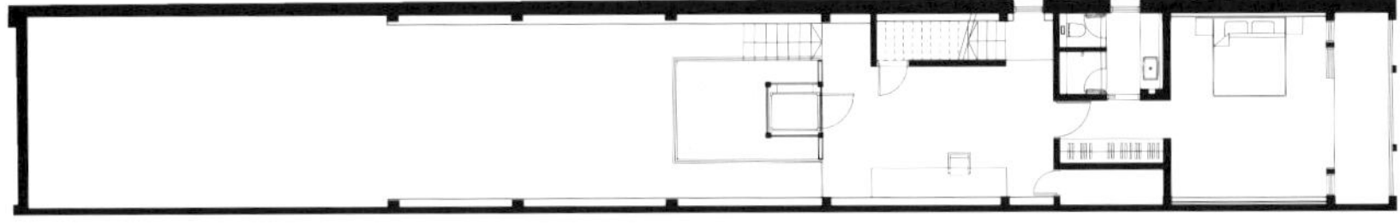

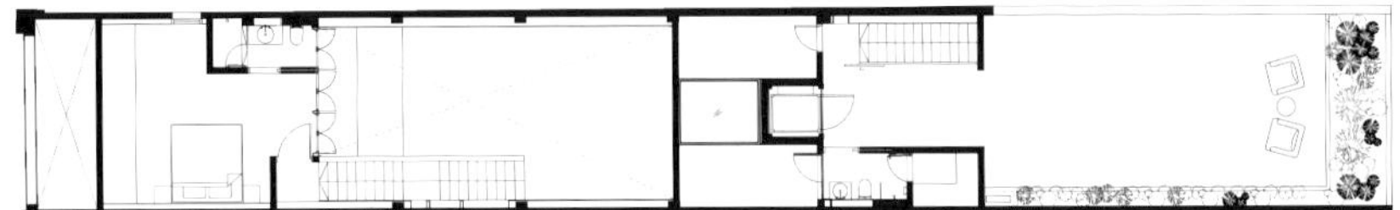

entered along a short corridor that extends off the connecting walkway across the void, dimly lit by wall lights and decorated by the Vietnamese tiles. Since the house is on a corner site, there was the opportunity to insert extra windows to gain more natural light. The new windows have the same proportions as the existing windows (a requirement of the URA) and the same louvres on top. But they are not exactly the same. 'When you are in here,' says Ho, 'you can see that they are of the same family, but not twins. They are siblings, one older than the other.'

The screen masking the master bedroom does not attempt to do anything other than hint at the history of the house. But on the third storey, masking a studio and the guest bedroom, genuine antique Chinese screens are integrated into windows that overlook the lightwell. When the lights are on at night in the studio or guest room, the lightwell

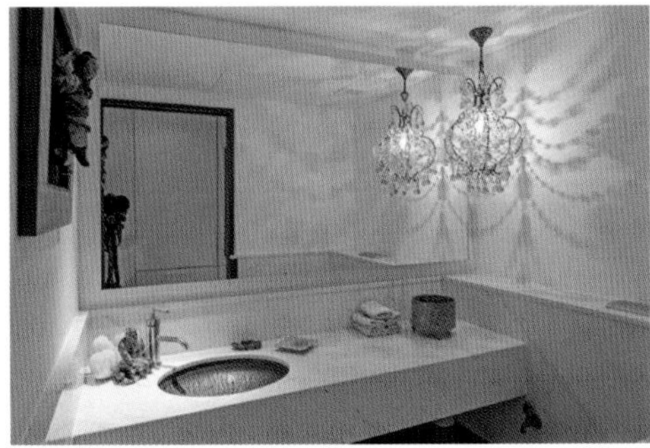

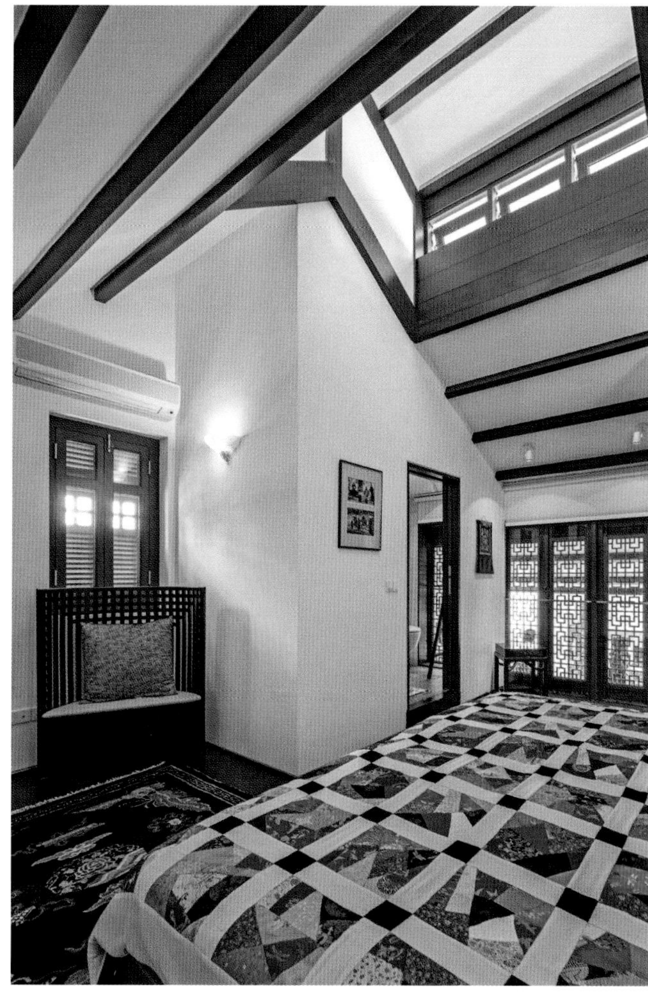

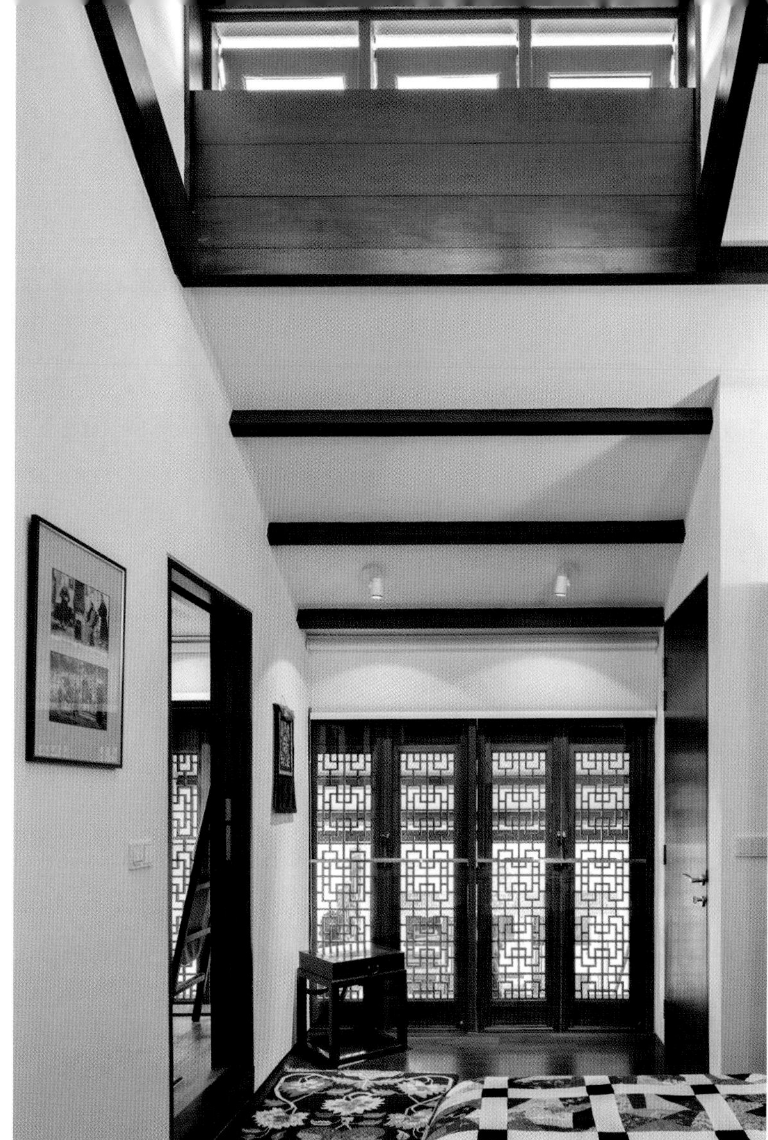

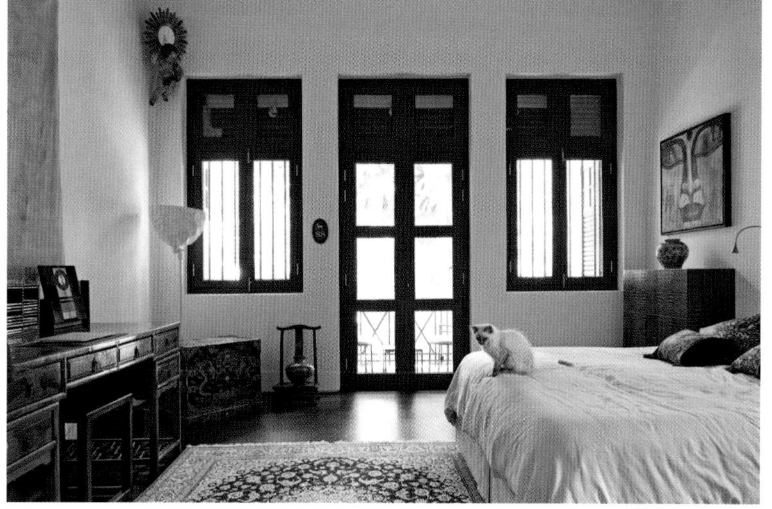

Above The master bedroom benefits from new windows along the laneway side of the house.

Above right The screen to the void seen from inside the master bedroom.

Right The window and door treatments add a subtle touch of modernity to the house.

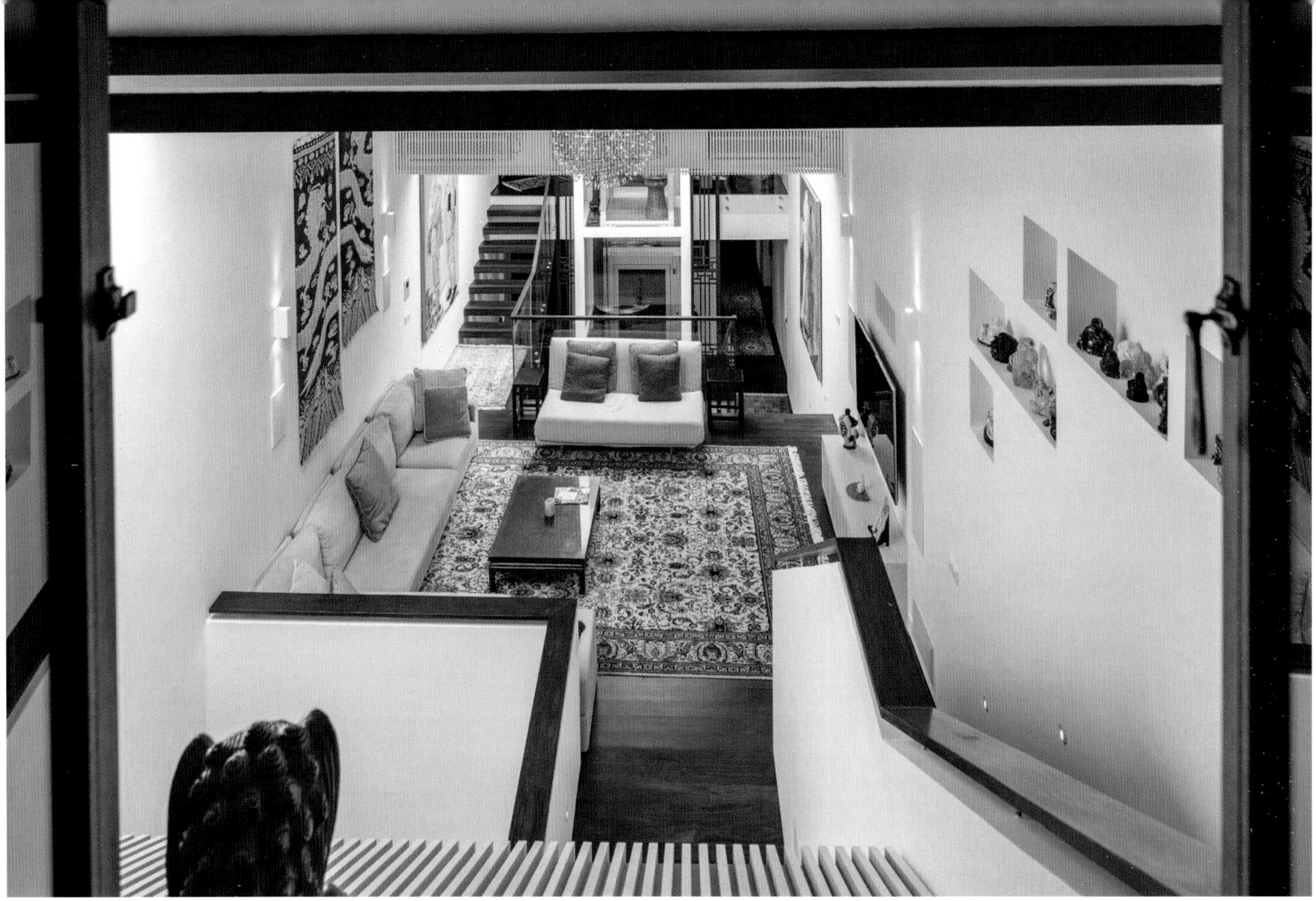

acts like a lantern and attracts attention upwards from downstairs. The guest bedroom features some fine detailing, especially the sliding custom joinery doors concealing the wardrobes. Overhead, operable highlight windows can let air out on a hot day.

Other amenities include a consulting room on the second storey, a home office on the third storey and a steam room on the roof where the garden borrows the lush landscape of the hill at the back of the house.

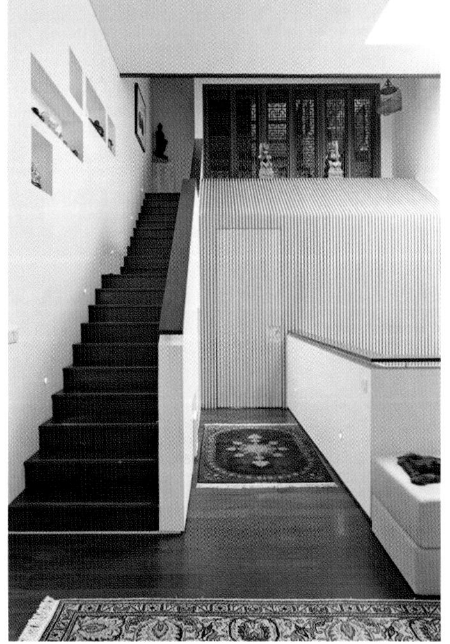

Above The view from the third level down to the living space.

Left Looking up to the third level, with its antique screen overlooking the void.

Below Detail of the antique screen.

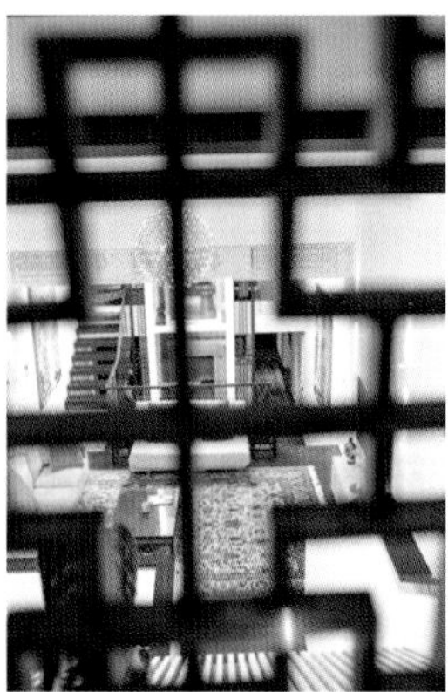

Right The roof terrace borrows the verdant hilly landscape at the rear of the house.

Below Looking back to the cabana and spa from the roof terrace.

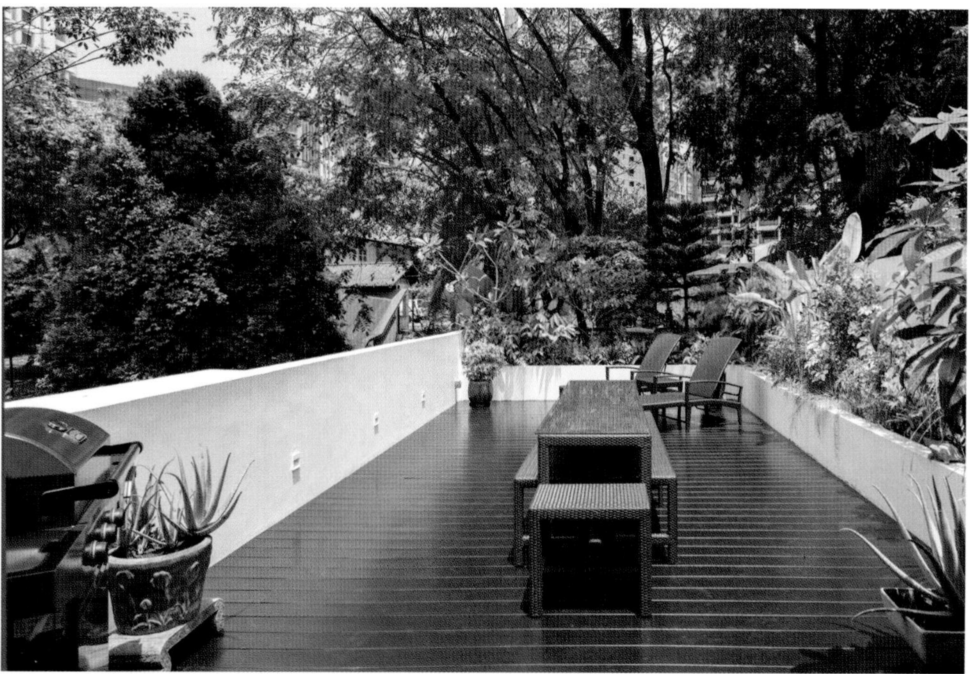

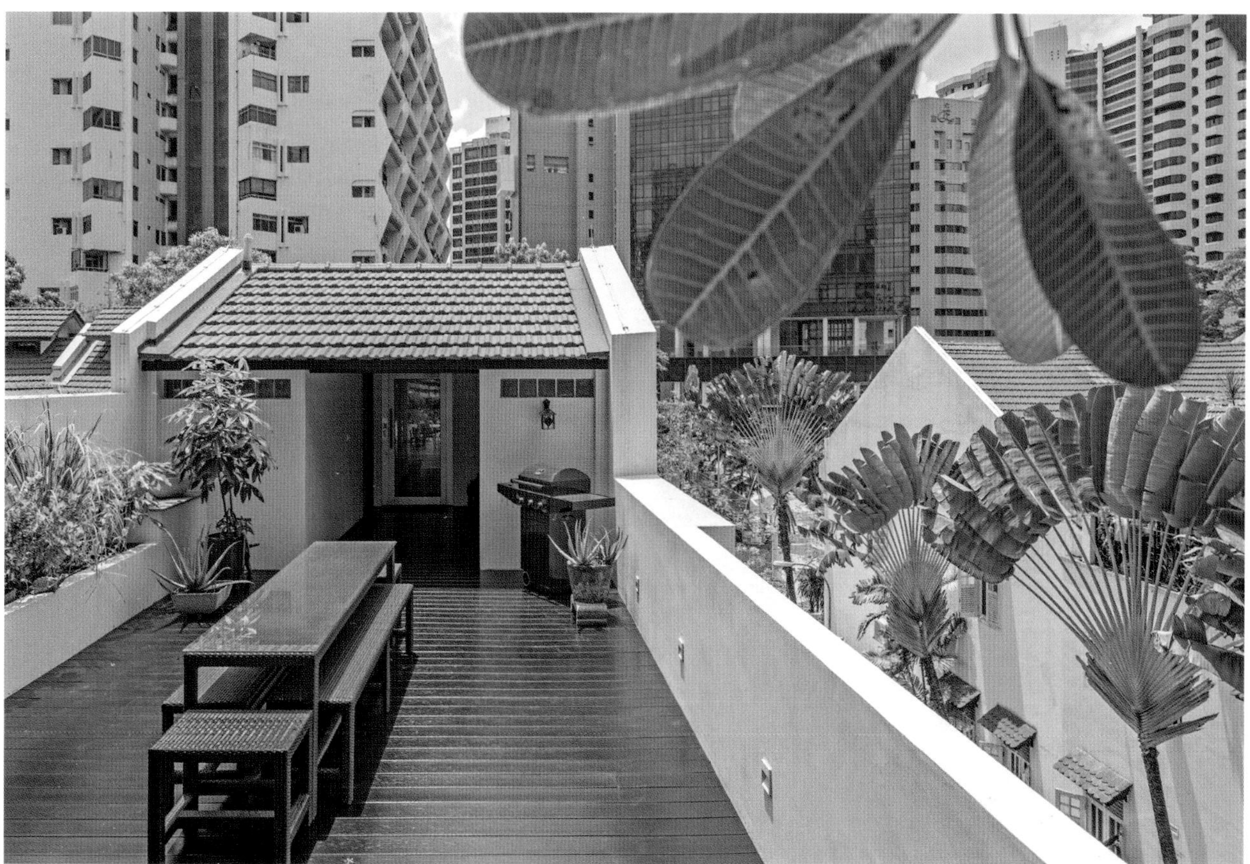

THE ARCHITECTS AND DESIGNERS

A D Lab Pte Ltd

The architectural firm A D Lab Pte Ltd was set up in Singapore by Warren Liu Yaw Lin and Darlene Smyth. In 2000, the pair incorporated Dlab 3, a small experimental design outfit that focused on cutting-edge residential projects. Now renamed A D Lab Pte Ltd, the research-based practice has grown in size and recognition and is centred on creating new or emergent experiences by addressing the site, economics and programme of every project. In all of A D Lab's work, there is an intensive search for a convergence to a simple and elegant solution that evokes a sense of complexity and, at the same time, solves all the issues and concerns of the design in an economical and poetic manner. The design solution synthesizes parallel design objectives of the context, cost, programme and environmental concerns while giving the buildings their identities and expressions. A D Lab's approach sees architecture as an extension of a place and a context that addresses specific technological, geographical, programmatic, social and economic conditions as an interconnected system. The polymorphic nature of individual architectural projects is fully embraced to allow their complexity, uniqueness and 'now-ness' to emerge from that process. This results in rich and unexpected experiences that resonate with the site and context.

Some of the specific issues considered within the projects are the adaptability of the space, the prolonging of the occupancy lifespan of buildings, the integration of systems and the relation of the spaces with the environment. Warren Liu Yaw Lin was shortlisted as the Singapore President's Award Designer of the Year and has won awards such as the Singapore Institute of Architects Awards and AUDE's 20 Under 45. A D Lab's works have been exhibited in the prestigious AEDES gallery in Berlin, Germany.

A D Lab Pte Ltd
229 Joo Chiat Road, #02-01,
Singapore 427489
Tel: 65 6346 0488
admin@a-dlab.com
www.a-dlab.com

Aamer Architects

Aamer Architects is a small architectural firm that views design as finding an ideal solution to a combination of factors, including site, culture and climate, structure and services, with an economy of means to arrive at an aesthetic whole. The firm's aim is to reconcile function and beauty in design, backed by strong service and management support to ensure the satisfaction of clients.

Each project, whether archi-sculpture, architecture, landscape design or interior installation, is seen as a work of art, conceived through a thorough appreciation of the site, context and brief, and carefully sculpted to congenially fit into the site while keeping to the client's brief.

Aamer Taher established his studio in 1994, two years after his return to Singapore from London, where he trained in the Architectural Association School of Architecture and practised with several firms, including the prestigious Michael Hopkins and Associates.

In Singapore, he worked with SAA Partnership where he spearheaded the design of large projects, ranging from institutions and condominiums to city master plans in China, as well as the area office for the Housing Development Board (HDB) and military academy in Singapore and the national aquarium in Pudong, Shanghai. SAA Partnership now has offices in Kuala Lumpur and Shenzhen in China.

Aamer Architects remains a cutting-edge boutique design firm providing a one-stop full range of architectural design and professional services, including master planning, interior design and landscape design, helmed by a dedicated team of professionals.

Aamer Architects has built many luxury bungalows, detached and semi-detached homes in Singapore. Its work has been widely published and it has produced its own book, *Sculpting Spaces in the Tropics: 13 Houses in Aamer Taher's Design Journey*, recording Aamer's most significant residential projects over a ten-year period.

Aamer Architects
5 Burn Road (Tee Yih Jia Food Building),
#06-02,
Singapore 369972
Tel: 65 6280 3776
Peter Eimer's Mobile: 9615 5699
info@aamertaher.com
www.aamertaher.com

Atelier M+A

Atelier M+A is an architecture design studio headed by Masaki Harimoto and Ng Ai Hwa, which was established to create inspiring designs with a constant mindfulness to explore possibilities and to challenge boundaries. It aims to create space, structure and environments that celebrate a timeless quality detached from any pursuit of specific design styles or trends. Harimoto and Ng set up Atelier M+A in 2009 after working for Kisho Kurokawa Architect & Associates (KKAA) in Tokyo on international projects, ranging from residential to commercial, offices, aviation and museums.

Harimoto and Ng are involved in all the firm's projects from the very outset, from drawing sketches to overseeing building design, controlling the overall integration of the exterior and interior design, providing structure services and supervising construction works to ensure a consistently high quality of the overall process.

They are also currently part-time lecturers in the Faculty of Interior Design at La Salle College of the Arts, Singapore.

Atelier M+A
89B Tanjong Pagar Road,
Singapore 088510
Tel: 65 6222 4405
ma@atelier-ma.com
www.atelier-ma.com

CHANG Architects

Born and raised in Singapore, Chang Yong Ter's passion for architecture was discovered during his university studies at the School of Architecture, National University of Singapore. Upon graduation, he worked under Tang Guan Bee for several years before starting his own practice, CHANG Architects, at the beginning of the new millennium.

In his early years of practice, he was one of 20 architects to be selected by the Urban Redevelopment Authority of Singapore to showcase the works of young and emerging architects in Singapore in *20 Under 45: A Selection of Works by Under-45 Singapore-registered Architects*.

In recent years, his practice has received several architectural awards, including the Singapore Institute of Architects Design Awards, Best Project Below $1Million Construction Cost, the President's Design Award, the Gold Medal for the Architects Regional Council of Asia (ARCASIA) Architecture Awards, the International Property Awards for the Best Architecture Single Residence, and the Green GOOD DESIGN Award.

Chang believes that architectural design is a work from the mind and the heart. While rationality and logic can fulfil functional briefs and achieve pragmatic efficiencies, an intuitive, poetic approach resonates with the soul and transcends limitations of rationalities. Part of the design process thus includes unlearning and forgetting and self-discoveries of the basics/origin.

CHANG Architects
16 Morse Road, Unit 216,
Singapore 099228
Tel: 65 62718016
Fax: 65 62718219
Mobile: 65 977 70216
cyt@changarch.com.sg
www.changarch.com

CSYA Pte Ltd

Chan Sau Yan (Sonny) was born in 1941 in Kuala Lumpur, Malaysia. He received his primary, secondary and tertiary education in Malaysia and the United Kingdom, graduating as an architect in 1963 from the Northern Polytechnic of London. After completing post-graduate Tropical Studies at the Architectural Association School of Architecture in 1964, he worked in London with Arup Associates. He moved to Singapore in 1965, where he first established Kumpulan Akitek and then his present practice, Chan Sau Yan Associates, in 1993. In 2011, Chan Sau Yan Associates was incorporated and is now known as CSYA Pte Ltd.

Chan's experience encompasses a wide range of residential, commercial, institutional, recreational and tourism-related projects across the region and elsewhere.

Chan was a founder member of the Singapore Planning and Urban Research Group and has been an external tutor, examiner and adjunct associate professor in the School of Architecture at the National University of Singapore and an external examiner with Universiti Malaya. He has also served in various capacities in professional institutes and government bodies in Singapore. He is the recipient of several architectural awards for design distinction, including the prestigious President's Design Award in 2011.

CSYA provides the full range of architectural services, including master planning, conceptualization and detailed design, documentation and supervision, in addition to an interior design service. The firm, which is active regionally and internationally, is committed to design innovation and the integration of appropriate technology. It firmly believes that design excellence requires the close and active collaboration of the client supported equally by the skills of specialist consultants.

CSYA Pte Ltd
5 Keong Saik Road,
Singapore 089113
Tel: 65 6324 3128
nor@csya.com
www.csya.com

eco:id Architecs

Eco:id Architects is a multi-disciplinary architectural practice established in Singapore in 1996 by founding principals Sim Boon Yang and Calvin Sim. The eco.id creative process continually strives to successfully interpret personal client requirements and to give form to designs that are both exciting and sensible. This intensive design approach is equally committed to achieving sophistication and endurance while keeping ahead in the varied projects.

The practice has won numerous accolades for its designs of hotels, such as The Metropolitan (Bangkok), W Retreat & Spa (Maldives) and Naumi Hotel (Singapore). Other noteworthy luxury developments on eco.id's list include the Ritz-Carlton Residences (Singapore), Hamilton Scotts (Singapore), Clearwater Residence (Kuala Lumpur), Ficus Lane (Bangkok) and Saladaeng Residences (Bangkok).

Eco.id's manifesto stresses the importance of executing good architecture and interior design resulting from clarity of progressive concepts that are managed rigorously from design to execution. The practice's approach marries the importance of market awareness with sensuality of experience to create functional environments that leave an impression.

Eco.id is headquartered in Singapore, with regional offices in Bangkok (Thailand) as well as Guangzhou (China), and has more than 100 staff. The firm was certified ISO 9001 in July 2001.

eco:id Architects
28 Maxwell Road, 04-01,
Singapore 069120
Tel: 65 6337 5119
ecoid@ecoid.com
www.ecoid.com

Experience Design Studio, ONG&ONG

Experience Design Studio, Ong&Ong, otherwise known as Studio OX:D, provides the service of experience design at the well-known architecture and design firm of Ong&Ong established in 1972, leveraging on the group's broad range of projects to expand their discipline. The studio was founded with the conviction that beautiful physical environments alone do not always equate with successful experiences. Great experiences result from an innovative combination of products, services and environment to make a compelling story. Central to the discipline is a human-centered focus that involves interviewing people and staff to find out their needs, as well as on-site observation. The studio thus works with clients to establish a story and a strategy for memorable experiences that emotionally engages its users and impact on culture. The studio has a collective expertise in architecture, interiors, branding, business, product and film, framed by a design thinking approach centred on understanding human motivation and behaviour.

This has led to the company designing innovative experiences for both the public and private sectors, such as OCBC's award winning Gen-Y bank Frank, HDB's Branch Office of the Future at Punggol, Sentosa's POLW family attraction and Singapore Airline's new Silverkris Lounges' 'Home Away From Home' concept worldwide.

Mark Wee, Co-Director of Experience Design Studio, is an award-winning architect whose achievements include the President's Design Award, the URA Heritage Award, the Singapore Institute of Architects Design Award and the Interior Design Confederation (Singapore) Colour Award. He is an SIA council member and was the chairman of the Architectural League from 2010 to 2012, a new initiative to serve the needs of the younger architectural community that is dedicated to identifying future leaders of the profession. Wee was the Chairman of Archifest 2012, where he led a change of festival format to one more community focused and a celebration of the city.

Ken Yuktasevi, Co-Director of Experience Design Studio, is a designer, artist and cultural entrepreneur. He specializes in the field of experiential design, working across the fields of architecture, interior design, branding and organizational transformation. He studied arts and design at Stowe College in the UK where he received the Roxburough Prize for Architecture. He then took a BA in film and cinematography at Bond University in Australia. His passion for telling human stories on celluloid compelled him to recreate that experience in 3D space. This began during his directorship in Leo International Design Group.

Yuktasevi's projects include Singapore Airlines, OCBC Bank, the Singapore Stock Exchange, The Coffee Bean & Tea Leaf and the Kempinski Hotel in Moscow.

Experience Design Studio, ONG&ONG
Mark Wee
510 Thomson Road,
Singapore 298 135
Tel: 65 6258 8666
wee.mark@ong-ong.com

Formwerkz Architects

Formwerkz, founded in Singapore in 1998, comprises a progressive, multi-disciplinary group of 25 like-minded professionals specializing in architecture, urban design, interior design and landscape design. It has a collaborative structure that encourages diverse and overlapping areas of expertise to achieve more comprehensive design solutions to transform seemingly ordinary narratives and context into objects of meaningful beauty. Formwerkz has no interest in architecture that is preoccupied with an obsessive pursuit of minimal refinement as an end. Instead, the practice's efforts are directed towards the recovery of mutual human relationships and the restoration of primordial relationships between man and nature.

Formwerkz's numerous projects have received critical acclaim both locally and internationally. Its works have been featured in numerous regional and international publications. In 2010, the three design partners were selected by AUDE's *20 Under 45: The Next Generation* exhibition, which aimed to promote a greater awareness and appreciation of design excellence. The Apartment House was listed in *Monocle*'s Singapore Survey as one of the Best of the Modern, alongside the likes of Paul Rudolph's Colonnade and I M Pei's OCBC Bank. In 2012, Formwerkz won the Punggol Mosque Design Competition, jointly organized by SIA and MUIS. The new mosque aims to demystify a traditionally closed religious institution, positioning it as an integral part of the larger community. In 2013, The Extended House by Formwerkz won both the Building of the Year Award and the Design Award in the 13th SIA Design Awards.

Formwerkz Architects
Alan Tay
12 Prince Edward Road, Bestway Building, Annex D 01-01/02,
Singapore 079212
Tel: 65 6440 0551
admin@formwerkz.com
www.formwerkz.com

Guz Architects

Guz Architects declares that its projects both derive inspiration from and relate closely to nature. Structure, materials and technology are used to express as seamless a transition as possible between inside and outside. The resulting designs are both responsive and responsible to the site and its occupants, with consideration being given to the integration and preservation of the surrounding natural environment.

The practice makes extensive use of sustainable design technologies, and both passive and active design principles inform all design decisions with the intention of creating long-lasting, timeless architecture.

Guz Architects believes that its role is to help neutralize the effects of global warming incurred by its projects by planting trees wherever possible, Guz Architects contributes a percentage of its profits to organizations such as Future Forests.

Guz Architects
3 Jalan Kelabu Asap,
Singapore 278 199
Tel: 65 6476 6110
guz@guzarchitects.com
www.guzarchitects.com

ip:li Architects

Yip Yuen Hong established ip:li Architects in 2002 in partnership with Lee Ee Lin. Since then, the practice has worked across a wide range of projects, including commercial interiors, but with an emphasis on residential design. Yip graduated from the National University of Singapore in 1984. He subsequently worked for William Lim & Associates, the Housing Development Board and Arkitek Tenggara. In 1993, he established HYLA Architects with Han Loke Kwang and Vincent Lee.

Ip:li Architects is particularly interested in designing for a tropical context and has explored the re-invention of the kampong house as a contemporary tropical home. One such project was the Sunset Place House (2006), which won an SIA Architectural Design Award. The practice is notable for the quality of its finishes and its sensitive selection of materials, which range from the industrial to the natural and recycled.

ip:li Architects
Yip Yuen Hong
315 Outram Road,
#02-06 Tan Boon Liat Building,
Singapore 169074
Tel: 65 6536 9881
info@ipliarchitects.com
www.ipliarchitects.com

LATO Design

LATO Design is an award-winning, boutique-sized architecture and interior design firm providing a full range of professional design services and project management for both residential and commercial projects. Established in 2001, it is a corporate member of the Singapore Institute of Architects and the Interior Design Confederation of Singapore. The company is headed by Lim Ai Tiong, who holds a BA in architecture with Honours from the University of Newcastle, Australia. LATO Design is currently deeply engaged with solving the problem of 'disintegrated spaces' by improving and amalgamating the intimacies between different areas and activities in a building.

LATO Design
27 Soch Road,
#03-10 Hoanam Building,
Singapore 209264
Tel: 65 6295 1847
Mobile: 93800 288
latodesign@yahoo.com

Jonathan Poh

Jonathan Poh is a freelance architectural and interior designer based in Singapore. He received his MA in architecture from the National University of Singapore. His thesis, 'Operative Landscape', was exhibited at the Annual City Exhibition organized by the Architectural Society of NUS and at the NParks Greenthumbs Exhibition in 2007.

He has worked on a wide variety of projects locally and overseas in offices such as K2LD, RichardHO Architects, Novotny Mahner Assoziierte (Shanghai), Teh Joo Heng Architects and Chan Sau Yan Associates (now CSYA). Notable projects include the Madrasa at Kampong Siglap Mosque, which won the PAM Silver Award in 2013, and Mont Timah, a cluster housing project shortlisted for the World Architectural Festival Award 2011 and winner of the PAM Gold Award and the 2012 SIA Architecture Design Award.

Poh's design approach stems from the notion of form serving function through understanding the needs of the client. He is mindful of not being relegated to a mere space planner, which is why he feels that strong concepts are pivotal in framing his works so that ideas will naturally fall into place and the design made richer, much like putting together the syncopated rhythms of a jazz piece.

Jonathan Poh
Block 58 Dakota Crescent #06-279,
Singapore 390058
Tel: 65 9118 2557
jonpoh@me.com

RichardHO Architects

Richard Ho graduated from the National University of Singapore in 1981 and thereafter worked with William Lim Associates and Kerry Hill Architects. He set up RichardHO Architects in 1991 upon his return to Singapore after working for six years in Austria and Italy, the last two years in Milan with Aldo Rossi, a world-renowned architect and Pritzker Prize recipient in 1990.

Ho was awarded the Designer of the Year in the President's Design Awards 2013, the highest award given by the state to a design professional. In 2000, he was awarded the Gold Medal in the ARCASIA (Architects Regional Council of Asia) Awards, the first Singaporean architect to be accorded this honour. The ARCASIA Architecture Award is an Asia-wide award programme held biennially to acknowledge architectural work of excellence in Asia.

In 2006, his practice was awarded the Singapore Institute of Architects (SIA) Design Award for a monastery complex, the highest accolade for excellence in architectural design in Singapore. He had previously received the SIA Design Award twice, in 1995 and 2001, besides also winning Honorable Mentions in 2001, 2010 and 2012. His practice has won four URA Architectural Heritage Awards in consecutive years 2009 to 2012.

Besides practising, Richard has been appointed as Adjunct Associate Professor and teaches architecture and urban design in the Department of Architecture, National University of Singapore.

His work has been exhibited in Austria, France, the USA, Denmark, the United Kingdom and Finland and published widely in many international and local architectural journals and books.

RichardHO Architects
Richard Ho
691 East Coast Road,
Singapore 459 057
Tel: 65 6446 4811
info@richardhoarchitects.com

RT+Q Architects

RT+Q is a deliberately small practice founded in 2003 by Tse Kwang Quek, a graduate of the National University of Singapore, and Rene Tan, a graduate of Yale and Princeton Universities in the US who subsequently worked for Ralph Lerner and Michael Graves before returning to Singapore to work with SCDA Architects from 1996 to 2003.

The practice is committed to an architecture based on clarity of form, transparency of spaces and articulation of structure, along with a respect for the client's aspirations. The practice aims to speak in its own design language, one that is grounded in a search for shapes and forms akin to plastic sculptural art. The practice has worked in Malaysia, Singapore and Indonesia on projects ranging from small homes to condominiums, resorts, offices and commercial buildings.

The work of the practice has been widely published and has received numerous SIA and PAM awards, including the Singapore President's Award in 2009. Both partners teach extensively at the National University of Singapore and La Salle College of the Arts in Singapore, the University of Hong Kong, and Berkeley and Syracuse Universities in the US.

RT+Q Architects
Rene Tan, Tse Kwang Quek
32A Mosque Street,
Singapore 059510
Tel: 65 6221 1366
Mobile: 9694 0851
admin@rtnq.com rtnq.com
www.rtnq.com

W Architects

Mok Wei Wei graduated with a Bachelor of Architecture (Hons.) from the National University of Singapore in 1982. After graduating, he worked in partnership with William Lim at William Lim and Associates. Following the retirement of William Lim, Mok recast the company as W Architects where he is Managing Director.

Mok's projects have received critical acclaim both locally and internationally. His work has been featured in numerous regional and international publications. In 2006, he was invited to exhibit at the prestigious AEDES gallery, Berlin. In 2012, he was invited to lecture and exhibit in Milan during the Milan Furniture Fair.

Mok is an active participant on the arts scene in Singapore. He was a board member of The Substation, an alternative arts group, from 1995 to 2004. In 1996, he was awarded the Japan Chamber of Commerce and Industry's Singapore Foundation Arts Award. In 2010, he was appointed by Singapore's Ministry of Information, Communications and the Arts (MICA) to be a member of the Arts & Culture Strategic Review Committee (ACSR). The committee was tasked with planning Singapore's next phase of cultural development until 2025.

Mok has been a part-time tutor at the Department of Architecture, National University of Singapore, since 1992 and a member of the Advisory Committee for the Temasek Polytechnic School of Design from 1999 to 2003. He is also a member of various scholarship committees.

Mok was a committee member of the Singapore Heritage Society from 1995 to 2001. Since 1996, he has been a Board Member of the Urban Redevelopment Authority, Singapore's national land-use planning agency. In 1999, he was appointed as a member of Singapore's Preservation of Monuments Board and is currently serving as its Deputy Chairman.

In recognition of his contributions to Singapore's architectural scene, including his understanding of local heritage, Mok was awarded the President's Design Award in 2007, the nation's highest honour for design.

W Architects
Mok Wei Wei
Block 205, Henderson Road #04-01,
Singapore 179033
Tel: 65 6235 3113
office@w-architects.com.sg

Wallflower Architecture + Design

Wallflower Architecture + Design was established in 1999 by Robin Tan Chai Chong and Cecil Chee. Both graduated with a Bachelor of Architecture (Hons.) degree from the National University of Singapore in 1995 and both subsequently worked for the Jurong Town Corporation and Bedmar & Shi.

Wallflower's philosophy is that each project has its unique needs and qualities which require innovative and fresh solutions. To ensure seamless integration, Wallflower offers total design solutions, fusing urban, architectural, landscape, interior, lighting and furniture needs. Wallflower believes that beauty and cleverness are inseparable in good design, the value of which enhances the environment in which people work and live and, ultimately, enriches the human experience and spirit.

Wallflower Architecture + Design has won many awards, including the 10th Singapore Institute of Architects Architectural Design Award 2010 (two Design Awards for the Individual House Category). It has also scored a number of successes in the Singapore Institute of Architects–ICI Colour Awards. Wallflower was selected as one of the case studies by Ministry of Information Communication and the Arts for DesignSingapore, an initiative aimed at developing Singapore as a leading design hub in Asia. Wallflower's work was exhibited at SingaporEdge in London in 2005 to showcase Singapore's design and creative industries to the international community.

Wallflower Architecture + Design
7500A Beach Road #15-303,
The Plaza,
Singapore 199591
Tel: 65 6297 6883
admin@wallflower.com.sg
www.wallflower.com.sg

Zarch Collaboratives

Randy Chan Keng Chong is Director and Principal of Zarch Collaboratives. One of Singapore's leading young architects, Chan was featured in *20 under 40* up-and-coming architects by the Urban Redevelopment Authority in 2004 and in the acclaimed international magazine *Monocle* by critic's choice as the local firm to look out for. Chan's architectural and design experience includes work on projects as diverse as stage design, private housing, cluster housing and master planning, all of which are guided by the simple philosophy that architecture and aesthetics are part of the same impulse.

Chan won the Gold Award in the 3rd SIA Façade Design Excellence Awards in 2006 for his work on the Singapore Pavilion at the World Exposition 2005 in Aichi, Japan, and has shown versatility in his portfolio as the principal set and stage designer for both national and international events like the Singapore National Day Parade 2005, 2008, 2009 and 2011, the Singapore Pavilion 'Supergarden' for the 2008 Venice Biennale, and the inaugural Youth Olympic Games hosted by Singapore in 2010. His flair in creating identity through stringing together story and design concepts has also been showcased through his work in various museums and galleries, most notably the Marina Barrage.

A Jury panel member with the Singapore Institute of Architects, Chan takes a multi-disciplinary architectural approach to his projects and specializes in the convergence of art and architecture. His work has been published in numerous books and local and international architecture magazines. His private art works, including *dark nights & white days*, *bodies* and *moves*, commissioned by the French Embassy, have been exhibited to much acclaim. A collaboration with a local fashion designer has given rise to *Building As a Body*, which was awarded the Design of the Year at the President's Design Award 2012.

Zarch Collaboratives
Randy Chan
6001 Beach Road,
#3-00 Golden Mile Tower,
Singapore 199589
Tel: 65 6226 0211
admin@zarch.com.sg
www.zarch.com.sg

BIBLIOGRAPHY

Bachelard, Gaston (trans. Maria Jolas), *The Poetics of Space*, Boston: Beacon Press, 1994; first published 1957.

Barrenche, Raul A., *The Tropical Modern House*, New York: Rizzoli, 2011.

Brook, Daniel, *A History of Future Cities*, New York: W. W. Norton and Company, 2013.

Davison, Julian, *Black and White: The Singapore House 1898–1941*, Singapore: Talisman, 2006.

_____, *Singapore Shophouses*, Singapore: Tuttle, 2010.

Knapp, Ronald G., *Chinese Houses of Southeast Asia: The Eclectic Architecture of Sojourners and Settlers*, Singapore: Tuttle, 2010.

Lim, William and Tan Hock Beng, *Contemporary Vernacular: Evoking Traditions in Asian Architecture*, Singapore: Select Books, 1998.

Locher, Mira, *The Complete Works of Shunmyo Masuno, Japan's Leading Garden Designer*, Singapore: Tuttle, 2012.

McGillick, Paul, *The Sustainable Asian House*, Singapore: Tuttle, 2013.

_____, *25 Tropical Houses in Singapore and Malaysia*, Singapore: Periplus Editions, 2006.

Malinowski, Bronislaw, *Coral Gardens and Their Magic*, London: Allen and Unwin, 1935.

_____, 'The Problem of Meaning in Primitive Languages', Supplement 1 in C. K. Ogden and I. A. Richards, *The Meaning of Meaning*, London: Kegan Paul, 1923.

Powell, Robert, *The New Singapore House*, Singapore: Select Publishing, 2001.

_____, *Singapore Architecture: A Short History*, Sydney: Pesaro, 2003.

_____, *Singapore Houses*, Singapore: Tuttle, 2009.

_____, *The Urban Asian House: Living in Tropical Cities*, London: Thames and Hudson, 1998.

Robson, David, *Beyond Bawa: Modern Masterworks of Monsoon Asia*, London: Thames and Hudson, 2014; first published 2007.

Waterson, Roxana, *The Living House: An Anthropology of Architecture in South-East Asia*, Singapore: Tuttle, 2009; first published Singapore: Oxford University Press, 1990.

Weng Ho Lin, Kar Kin Tan and Sau Yan Sonny Chan, *Green Ink on an Envelope: The Architectural Practice of Chan Sau Yan Sonny*, Singapore: Singapore Heritage Society, 2012.

Yabuka, Narelle, *24 Crane Road*, Singapore: 24 Crane Road, 2010.

ACKNOWLEDGEMENTS

In the field of architecture, it is easy to focus on the architect and forget that buildings, of whatever type or scale, come about as the result of a whole team of people, from the clients and all the people in the architect's office to the many contractors and consultants who each make their own contribution. The final result depends on the synergies of all of those involved.

Books are no different. My name appears on the dust jacket but I need to thank many people for their part in bringing the book to realization. First, to Eric Oey, my publisher, for having the faith in me to put it together. And then to all his staff who have worked so hard to produce and publish it.

A special thanks needs to go to all the clients who have so graciously allowed me and our photographic team into their homes and then agreed to share their beautiful homes with a broad public. Thank you to the architects and their staff for facilitating this whole process and for accommodating my relentless requests for information.

For this book I have worked long distance with my photographer Masano Kawana and his assistant Wong Teck Yen. Given that we had such fun on the road doing our last book, this was disappointing. What is not disappointing is the consistently wonderful photographs that Masano produces. I can't think of another photographer who captures the spirit of a house as well as Masano.

Lastly, my wife Charmaine (Xiaoming) Zheng has provided the essential support on the home front while still dealing with her own demanding professional life. Living with writers is not easy and her support has been invaluable and helped facilitate the work from start to finish.

THE TUTTLE STORY

BOOKS TO SPAN THE EAST AND WEST

Many people are surprised to learn that the world's largest publisher of books on Asia had its humble beginnings in the tiny American state of Vermont. The company's founder, Charles E. Tuttle, belonged to a New England family steeped in publishing.

Immediately after World War II, Tuttle served in Tokyo under General Douglas MacArthur and was tasked with reviving the Japanese publishing industry. He later founded the Charles E. Tuttle Publishing Company, which thrives today as one of the world's leading independent publishers.

Though a Westerner, Tuttle was hugely instrumental in bringing a knowledge of Japan and Asia to a world hungry for information about the East. By the time of his death in 1993, Tuttle had published over 6,000 books on Asian culture, history and art—a legacy honored by the Japanese emperor with the "Order of the Sacred Treasure," the highest tribute Japan can bestow upon a non-Japanese.

With a backlist of 1,500 titles, Tuttle Publishing is more active today than at any time in its past—inspired by Charles Tuttle's core mission to publish fine books to span the East and West and provide a greater understanding of each.

Published by Tuttle Publishing, an imprint of Periplus Editions (HK) Ltd

www.tuttlepublishing.com

ISBN 978-0-8048-4475-8

Distributed by
North America, Latin America & Europe
Tuttle Publishing
364 Innovation Drive
North Clarendon, VT 05759-9436 U.S.A.
Tel: 1 (802) 773-8930; Fax: 1 (802) 773-6993
info@tuttlepublishing.com
www.tuttlepublishing.com

Japan
Tuttle Publishing
Yaekari Building, 3rd Floor
5-4-12 Osaki, Shinagawa-ku
Tokyo 141-0032
Tel: (81) 3 5437-0171; Fax: (81) 3 5437-0755
sales@tuttle.co.jp
www.tuttle.co.jp

Asia Pacific
Berkeley Books Pte. Ltd.
61 Tai Seng Avenue, #02-12
Singapore 534167
Tel: (65) 6280-1330; Fax: (65) 6280-6290
inquiries@periplus.com.sg
www.periplus.com

16 15 14
10 9 8 7 6 5 4 3 2 1

Printed in Singapore 1411CP

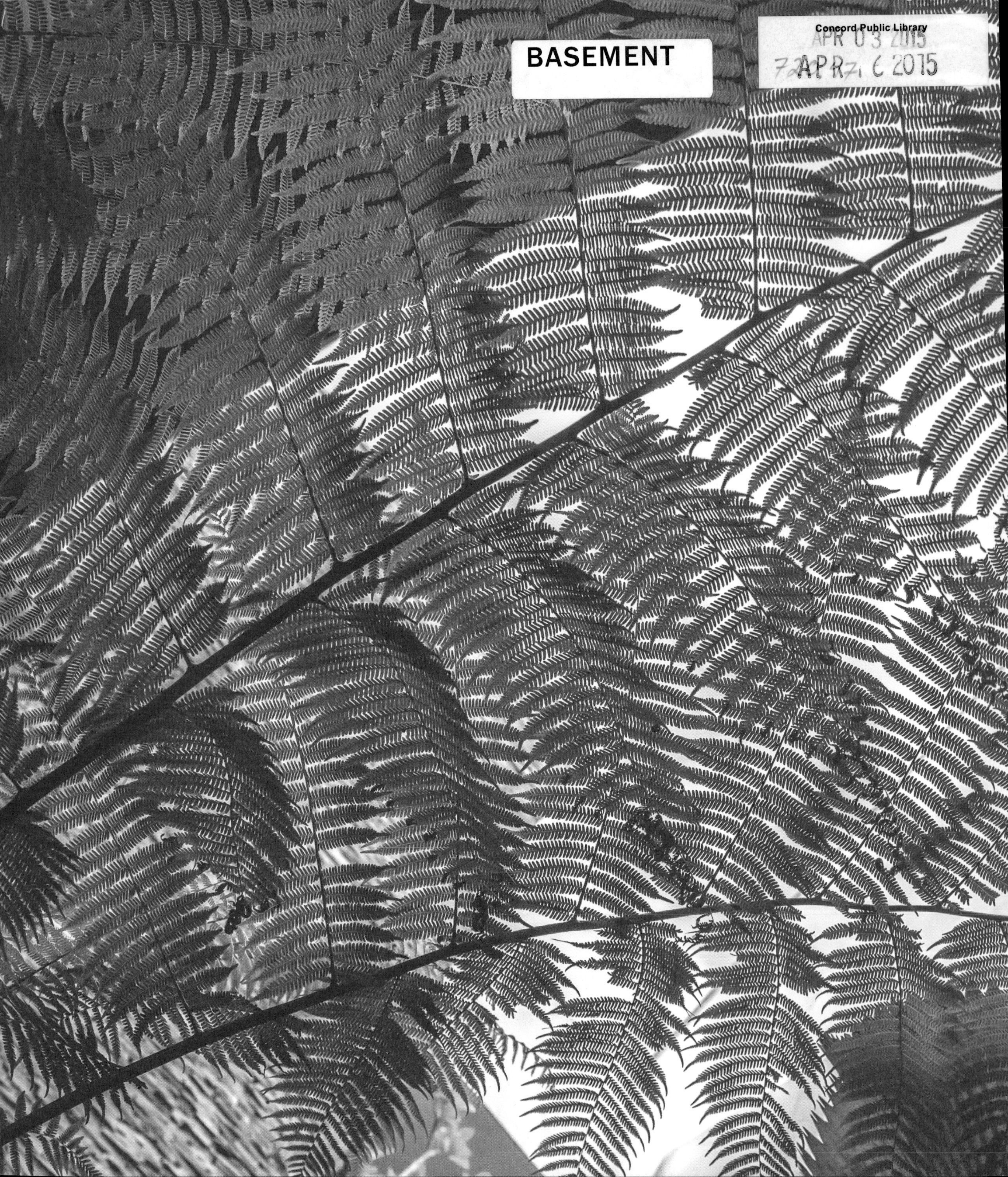